A RAGE TO LIVE

John O'Hara

A
Rage to Live

John O'Hara

THE MODERN LIBRARY

NEW YORK

1997 Modern Library Edition

Biographical note copyright © 1994 by Random House, Inc.
Copyright © 1949 by John O'Hara
Copyright renewed 1977 by Wylie O'Hara Doughty

This work was originally published in 1949 by Random House, Inc.

Jacket photograph by F. J. Higgins

LIBRARY OF CONGRESS CATALOGING-IN-PUBLICATION DATA
O'Hara, John, 1905–1970.
A rage to live/John O'Hara.—Modern Library ed.
p.   cm.
ISBN 0-679-60266-6 (acid-free paper)
I. Title.
PS3529.H29R35   1997
813'.52—dc21   97-2092

Modern Library website address:
http://www.randomhouse.com/modernlibrary/

Printed in the United States of America on acid-free paper

2   4   6   8   9   7   5   3   1

JOHN O'HARA

John O'Hara was born in Pottsville, Pennsylvania, on January 31, 1905, the eldest of eight children. Even though his father, Patrick Henry O'Hara, was a prominent and relatively wealthy surgeon, the town's elaborate caste system pegged him as "the Irish doctor." Indeed John O'Hara, an Irish-Catholic outsider in WASP-dominated Pottsville, was a rebellious adolescent: he was thrown out of several boarding schools, and a drunken spree prevented his graduation as valedictorian from Niagara Preparatory School in 1924. The following year, O'Hara's world changed completely when his father's death plunged the family into poverty. Gone forever were the young man's hopes of attending Yale; instead he continued working as a cub reporter for the *Pottsville Journal* until chronic lateness (and frequent debilitating hangovers) eventually cost him his job.

Determined to escape Pottsville, O'Hara shipped out as a steward on a liner to Europe in 1927. (At various times in his youth he had found employment working as a soda jerk, running an amusement park, and reading gas meters.) Upon his return he hitchhiked to Chicago; finally in 1928 O'Hara headed for New York City, where he covered everything from sports to religion on a succession of newspapers and magazines, including the *Her-*

ald *Tribune*, the *Morning Telegraph*, and *Time*. In addition, he worked briefly as a press agent in the publicity department of RKO-Radio Pictures. A lone distinction marked O'Hara's early hand-to-mouth years in New York: in May 1928 he placed his first piece with *The New Yorker*, beginning an association that would continue stormily for four decades. (O'Hara produced more than four hundred short stories in his lifetime and later took great pride in having published more fiction in *The New Yorker* than any other author.) An ill-fated, two-year marriage to Helen ("Pet") Petit, a young Wellesley-educated actress from a well-to-do Episcopalian family, ended in divorce in 1933. This, followed by a wretched stint as managing editor of a magazine in Pittsburgh, left him in near-suicidal despair.

Finally resolving to concentrate only on fiction, O'Hara sequestered himself in a Manhattan hotel to write a series of integrated short stories that became, instead, *Appointment in Samarra*. An instant success when it was published by Harcourt, Brace in 1934, O'Hara's first novel was praised by Ernest Hemingway, Scott Fitzgerald, and Dorothy Parker. As John Updike has observed: *"Appointment in Samarra* is, among other things, an Irishman's revenge on the Protestants who had snubbed him, a book in which O'Hara had taken his own advice to his fellow Pottsville scribe Walter Farquhar: 'If you're going to get out of that God awful town, for God's sake write something that will *make* you get out of it. Write something that automatically will sever your connection with the town, that will help you get rid of the bitterness you must have stored up against all those patronizing cheap bastards.' "

The success of *Appointment in Samarra* made O'Hara attractive to Paramount Studios as a screenwriter, and he began the first of a sequence of jobs with major Hollywood film companies that continued into the 1950s. *Butterfield 8*, another popular novel, followed quickly in 1935, along with *The Doctor's Son and Other Stories*, his first collection of short fiction. Yet the 1930s remained a restless time for O'Hara until in 1937 he married Belle Wylie, the daughter of a socially prominent Manhattan physician descended from an old Southern family; thus began the writer's lifelong connection with the Episcopalian enclave of Quogue, Long Island, where the Wylies maintained a summer residence. (The couple's only child, their daughter, Wylie, was born in 1945.) Although O'Hara's next novel, *Hope of Heaven* (1938), was a failure, he quickly rebounded with *Files on Parade* (1939), a volume of short fiction that solidified his reputation as a master of *The New Yorker* short story. *Pal Joey,* his 1940 collection of epistolary tales about a New York nightclub entertainer, served as the basis of the Rodgers and Hart hit Broadway musical, for which O'Hara supplied the libretto. Two more volumes of stories—*Pipe Night* (1945) and *Hellbox* (1947)—ensued before he returned to longer fiction.

A Rage to Live (1949), O'Hara's first "Pennsylvania novel" since *Appointment in Samarra,* was a bona-fide bestseller, yet its success carried a price. A devastating review of the book in *The New Yorker* by Brendan Gill caused O'Hara to sever ties with the magazine—and abandon writing stories—for more than a decade. During the 1950s he published two minor novellas—*The Farmers Hotel* (1951) and *A Family Party* (1956)—as well as two major novels: *Ten North Frederick* (1955) won the National Book Award, and *From the Terrace* (1958), which O'Hara regarded as his major achievement as a writer, was a blockbuster bestseller. Although devastated by his wife's death in 1954, O'Hara married Katharine ("Sister") Barnes Bryan the following year and soon moved to the countryside near Princeton, New Jersey.

In 1960 O'Hara returned to *The New Yorker* with the novella-length story "Imagine Kissing Pete," which became part of the trilogy *Sermons and Soda-Water* (1960). Over the next ten years, O'Hara's output of short fiction was prodigious and established him as one of the finest short-story writers of modern times. Six popular collections of his new stories appeared: *Assembly* (1961), *The Cape Cod Lighter* (1962), *The Hat on the Bed* (1963), *The Horse Knows the Way* (1964), *Waiting for Winter* (1966), and *And Other Sto-*

ries (1968). Many critics felt that the mainspring of O'Hara's genius was his unerring precision in capturing the speech and the milieux of his characters, whether the setting was Pennsylvania, Hollywood, or New York. "The work of no other writer," Lionel Trilling once wrote, "tells us so precisely, and with such a sense of the importance of communication, how people look and how they want to look, where they buy their clothes, how they speak and how they think they ought to speak." Less memorable, however, were O'Hara's novels written during the 1960s: *Ourselves to Know* (1960), *The Big Laugh* (1962), *Elizabeth Appleton* (1963), *The Lockwood Concern* (1965), *The Instrument* (1967), and *Lovey Childs: A Philadelphian's Story* (1969).

When John O'Hara died on April 11, 1970, he left behind some fifty unpublished stories that were brought out posthumously in two volumes: *The Time Element and Other Stories* (1972) and *Good Samaritan and Other Stories* (1974). Likewise, *The Ewings,* the novel O'Hara finished shortly before his death, came out in 1972.

To Belle

NOTE

The capital of Pennsylvania is, of course, Harrisburg, in Dauphin County, on the Susquehanna River. Harrisburg is one of my favorite cities; Dauphin County, where my mother was born, is the scene of some of the happiest hours of my childhood, and the Susquehanna is an important and pleasant river. But because this is a work of fiction I have had to obliterate Harrisburg and Dauphin and the Susquehanna and substitute Fort Penn and Nesquehela, county and river. I also have made a complete substitution of the population past and present of Harrisburg and Dauphin County, and anyone who thinks he sees himself or anyone else in this novel is wrong.

J. O'H.

New York City, 1949.

To Toast our wants and wishes, is her way;
Nor asks of God, but of her Stars, to give
The mighty blessing, "while we live, to live."
Then all for Death, that Opiate of the soul!
Lucretia's dagger, Rosamonda's bowl.
Say, what can cause such impotence of mind?
A Spark too fickle, or a Spouse too kind.
Wise wretch! with Pleasures too refin'd to please;
With too much Spirit to be e'er at ease;
With too much Quickness ever to be taught;
With too much thinking to have common Thought:
You purchase Pain with all that Joy can give,
And die of nothing but a Rage to live.

Epistle to a Lady
ALEXANDER POPE

BOOK ONE

CHAPTER 1

It rained lightly on the morning of Wednesday, July 4, 1917, and the Festival Committee met to decide whether to postpone the Festival until the following Saturday. It was argued that Saturday was a better day than Wednesday, even if Wednesday did happen to be the Fourth. It also was argued by some of the Fort Penn businessmen that if the Festival was postponed until Saturday the merchants would be losing two and a half days that week: Wednesday, the Fourth; the regular Thursday half holiday which the Merchants Association members had decreed upon themselves; and now Saturday.

"The question is," said one committee member, "are we running this thing for the merchants or for the Red Cross? If we're running it for the Red Cross we have to take the weather into consideration. I mean, if it keeps on raining, the Red Cross will benefit by the postponement, even though the merchants might lose some sales. On the other hand, if we're running this thing with the welfare of the merchants uppermost in mind, I say let's have the God-damn thing today, rain or no rain, and if nobody comes to the Festival, we can sell the prizes and food and beer and sandwiches and soft drinks to the merchants at a big discount and they can get drunk and make pigs of themselves all night long, and that way they'll have their Festival the way they seem to want it, and at the same time they'll be feeling all right by Saturday morning, able to open up their stores bright and early, and receive all the customers that turn up Saturday." The speaker, a man named Miles Brinkerhoff, sat down, and immediately a man named Fred Bauer got up.

"Brother Brinkerhoff has strange ideas about we merchants. Strange. Brother Brinkerhoff now constitutes himself a farmer which we all know him to be, and we merchants, selfish, greedy, pig-like merchants, only hope Brother Brinkerhoff will some day be able to make a success out of running a farm the way he did running a store that gave him sufficient of capital to retire and buy a farm and thereby cast aspersions on we merchants. When Brother Brinkerhoff was a merchant we all feared him as a competitor, those in business competition with him, and whereas I myself didn't compete with him in business, many's the time I did try and compete with him in who could put away the most beers. But if you take a good look at me, a merchant, weighing no more than a hundred and fifty pounds, and take a good look at Brother Brinkerhoff, weighing near twice that amount, you can make up your mind for yourselfs who is more able when it comes to making a pig of themselfs."

There was laughter and applause, including laughter and applause by Brother Brinkerhoff, and Bauer went on.

"The way I look at it," he said, "we do not postpone the Festival. We advertised rain or shine, though some may forget already, and people all over the county will be coming. Some started early this morning, they did their chores and hitched up and even as we sit here they are on their way. We have a band coming up from the south end of the county—I don't have to tell the committee what preparations have been made. Also I don't have to remind all of German extraction, which means most here, this Festival has to be a big success, put over with a bang, as the fellow says. I heard a speaker say the eyes of the world are on Fort Penn because of so many of German extraction. This I do not

believe. I don't believe the eyes of Reading even are on Fort
Penn. But the eyes of my son are on me, my son in the Army, and
the eyes of all of you are on you when you go to sleep at night,
and Brother Brinkerhoff don't know that any better than I do, but
Brother Brinkerhoff likes to make jokes. Representing the Fort
Penn merchants I here and now underwrite the Festival. We
hope to show a profit of twenty thousand dollars, so we merchants will make up the difference between that amount and
what the Festival takes in. I have no authority to do this, but I
guess I am on safe ground."

They took a vote and it was unanimously decided to hold the
Festival, rain or shine. One more member got up. "I don't know
about you merchants," he said, "but here's one lawyer that's
going downstairs and get a beer." The meeting, which was being
held in the card-room of the Fort Penn Athletic Club, then was
about to adjourn, when Brother Brinkerhoff rose.

"Here's a reformed merchant that wants a beer too, but
oughtn't somebody call Mrs. Tate and tell her the Festival isn't
postponed? After all, gentlemen, it's her farm."

"The proper thing would be to call Sidney Tate, not his wife,"
said Fred Bauer.

"Well, all right, Fred. You do it," said Brinkerhoff.

"He's your neighbor, Miles," said Bauer.

"That's exactly why I want you to do the telephoning," said
Brinkerhoff.

"Very well, I'll do it."

As the committeemen went downstairs the sun came out.

———

The social stationery and business letterheads said Riverside
Farm, but the place was not called by that name. To some it was
known as the Caldwell farm or Caldwell's farm; in more recent
years the designation the Tate farm had caught on, to the degree
that Grace Caldwell became known as Grace Tate. On the
posters and in all other advertising for the Red Cross Festival the
directions were given with that ambiguity in mind: "11 miles N.

of Fort Penn on Nesquehela Pike. Turn at entrance to Tate Farm (old Caldwell place)."

It would have been impossible for anyone on the Nesquehela Pike that day to miss the place, no matter what name he knew it by. The real farmers, of course, had not been deceived by the light rainfall of the morning, and they had begun arriving as early as ten o'clock, while the committeemen still were deciding about a postponement. The early ones came in spring wagons and hay wagons and truck wagons, some drawn by draft horses, some by teams of mules, some by mixed teams of horse-and-mule; and the next to arrive were farmers more prosperous than the earliest, and they came in buggies and buckboards and democrats and surreys and barouches and cut-unders. There was even a team of goats from a neighboring farm, a nice turn-out with real leather, not web, harness and a small-size truck wagon. Then a little later came the trucks and automobiles: Ford cars and Maxwells and Chevrolets and Partin-Palmers and Buicks and Hahn trucks and Maccars and Garfords and Autocars and Vims, and a few Cadillacs, Franklins and one Locomobile and one Winton. And all this time there would be farm boys on horseback—some with English saddles, some with stock saddles, some with Kentucky saddles, some with a blanket-and-surcingle, and some bareback—and among these were a few fine saddle horses, but mostly they were work horses and mules, with one-piece ear-loop bridles and work-harness bridles with laundry rope for reins. And all day long too there were the farm boys with their bicycles, singly and in pairs, but more often in groups as large as twenty in number, causing their own particular sound, which was the hum of the wire wheels, and the sound of one bell quickly followed by twenty other bells. They were the grim ones, these boys, not quite of draft age, breaking the silence in their ranks to call out words in Pennsylvania Dutch, but ironically resembling the Belgian army cyclists, whose cousins the farm boys' cousins had beaten in war. The boys on horseback laughed; the boys on the bicycles had no laughter. Everything was clean and shining:

the Dietz lamps on the wagons and trucks and buggies, and the nickel studding on the work harness, and the silver conchos on the stock saddles, and the automobile radiators, and the sprockets on the bicycles, and the snaffle bits and curb chains and the ferrules on the buggy-whips and the painted hooves of the horses and the yellow felloes on the wheels of the cut-unders and the black leather dashboards and the white painted canvas tops of the spring-wagons and the brass-bound hose of the bulb horns and the three-by-six-inch windows in the barouches and the Prest-o-lite tanks and hub-caps of the automobiles, and the scrubbed faces and foreheads of the men and the women and the boys and the girls.

In the beginning there was a single trooper of the State constabulary stationed where the Tate farm lane met the Nesquehela Pike. At intervals he would hold up a hand to halt the northbound traffic, allowing the southbound to enter the lane, and then he would stop the southbound people and let the northbound go in. It was not hard work, but it was a muggy, gummy day from the time he took his post, and his uniform and equipment were enough to keep him sweating without even the limited exertions of directing the traffic. He wore a gray felt hat with a chin-strap and with the brim turned up on the left side, his whipcord tunic had a high collar, and he wore whipcord breeches and black puttees and heavy shoes with spurs, and around his waist he had a wide leather belt with cartridges for the .45 revolver in the open holster. His horse was somewhat better off; when the sun came out the sorrel gelding stood in the shade of one of the walnut trees that lined the lane. The trooper's feet cooked in the Tarvia-B with which the Pike was paved, and the dust from the lane kept the black uniform the color of the hat. Every hour or so a sprinkler cart would come down the lane and go back again, but the dust never settled for long, and when the crowd from Fort Penn began coming it never settled at all.

The Fort Penn citizens came by private automobile, jitney, interurban trolley, special railroad train, bicycle, motorcycle and on foot, and at the river edge of the farm they also were arriving by naphtha launch, motorboat, outboard, flatbottom, and canoe, the only size craft the depth of the river would allow.

From the Pike and, in considerably less numbers, from the Nesquehela River, they came rather steadily from about ten in the morning to four in the afternoon, the high point being around twelve-thirty, when the picnic parties came and the families who would eat dinner in the church-sponsored tents (to the relief of those women who would not have to do any cooking on this one day). The program was an all-day affair, although the big doings were scheduled for afternoon and evening. In the forenoon it was possible to spend money on home-made fudge, home-made root beer, home-made sarsaparilla, pony rides, embroidery, lucky-number games for fancywork, beer, ale, porter, frankfurters, somersausage, Ferris wheel, merry-go-rounds, train rides, .22 rifle shooting, tests of muscle, and other simple pleasures. The afternoon program included band concerts by two bands, loop-the-loops and other stunt flying by two biplanes of the Pennsylvania National Guard, a trotting race for county horses under the three-heat plan, a baseball game between the Pennsylvania Railroad Car Shops team and the Fort Penn Fire Department team, and the simple pleasures of the forenoon. Also scheduled were speeches by the Hon. Walter B. Buchwalter, County Chairman of the Red Cross; the Hon. Fred J. Bauer, president of the Fort Penn Merchants Association; Captain T. M. W. Smollett, M. C., of the Royal Flying Corps; Sergeant-Major A. V. Gudge, V. C., of the Royal Engineers; Colonel Hamilton J. Schoffstal, U. S. R. (formerly of the National Guard of Pennsylvania); Dr. J. J. O'Brien, chief of staff of the Fort Penn Misericordia Hospital and Surgeon-General of the newly formed Pennsylvania Militia; Mrs. Sidney Tate, Vice-Chairman of the County Red Cross, and His Excellency the Hon. Karl F. Dunkelberger, Governor of the Commonwealth. Supper would be served in the church tents from five to eight and at nine o'clock there would be a giant pyrotechnical display lasting for a full hour, and from seven to eleven there would be dancing to the music of Prof. Louis Kleinhans' augmented orchestra, alternating with the Pennsylvania Railroad Car Shops Band. It was announced that there would be a refreshment tent for those over twenty-one. (An unannounced and unscheduled feature of the afternoon was the presence of two girls from Mae Brady's place in Terminal Street, Fort Penn, who, with the co-operation of Mrs. Tate's hostler, Higgins, set up business in a clean, vacant box-stall in the Tate stable until discovered by two county detectives.)

At ten minutes of five Captain Herman F. Ludwig, commanding officer of Troop A of the state police, cantered down the Tate farm lane to the Pike. Trooper Duffy, still on duty, saluted the officer on the gray, and Ludwig returned the salute. "One-way traffic for the next half hour, Duffy," said Ludwig. "Let in ten cars at a time and then stop the others. Don't let any more in till five come out. That way we'll keep the lane pretty clear. We just got word the Governor's on his way out, left about five minutes ago, so he'll be here in about fifteen minutes."

"Yes sir," said Duffy.

Ludwig dismounted and hitched the gray to a whitewashed fencepost. He smoothed down his tunic and slapped off the dust, and took out a bandanna handkerchief and wiped the dust off his black boots and shook the bandanna and wiped the chinstrap and sweatband of his hat. "Jesus Christ, it's hot," he said, standing beside Duffy.

"I'll tell the world," said Duffy. "It's a piss-cutter."

"Who's your relief?" said Ludwig.

"Bollinger."

"That's tough luck!"

"Why?"

"Some little bastard fell in the river and Bollinger had to go in after him."

"With his clothes on?" said Duffy.

"Everything. Everything but his hat, and some son of a bitch swiped that," said Ludwig.

"Son of a bitch. New breeches, new tunic, new hat. Bollinger lose his .45?"

"It's in the river somewhere around," said Ludwig.

"Well, bye-bye a hundred smackers for Bollinger. Can't you put in for it, Captain?"

"About the only way we get extra uniform allowance is if we can show a bullet-hole. You oughta know that by now. That's why we gotta kiss this Governor's ass. Maybe squeeze out a little extra appropriation if he's in favor of it."

"That won't do Bollinger any good this year," said Duffy. "They don't vote on those appropriations till the end of the session."

"Just between you and I and that hitching-post, Duffy, Bollinger's gonna be okay, or I think he is. If I get a chance to talk to Sidney Tate alone, he'll make it up to Bollinger. He likes us, a friend of ours, that Tate."

"He's all right," said Duffy. "Where's Bollinger now?"

Ludwig laughed. "Bollinger? In the First Aid Tent, waiting for dry clothes."

"Nurses in that tent?"

"Nurses in that tent? No. Not nurses. But they got some young society kids in nurses' uniforms. They better stick together. Bollinger with that thing of his, sitting around like a hero with nothing on but an army blanket."

"Bollinger, the original one that fell in the manure pile and come up covered with diamonds. He saved the kid, eh, Captain?"

"Sure," said Ludwig. "I know what I'll do to that lucky bastard. I'll get him a bathing suit or a pair of overalls and make him find that .45."

Duffy, for the first time, laughed. "Captain," he said, "I was thinking. I been here since ten o'clock this morning, not even a lemonade did they send me, and I was thinking of Bollinger, on post over at the River, in the shade and nice and cool, and supposed to relieve me at four o'clock. Then I hear he falls in the water, saves a kid's life, has to take his clothes off for all those society quiffs—I hope that .45 is six foot deep in silt."

"Regulations," said Ludwig. "No such thing as losing your revolver . . . I thought that would take the fig out of your ass, Duffy."

"Thanks, Captain." Duffy was still half grinning when the gubernatorial Pierce-Arrow touring car, license Number One, halted before entering the lane. Duffy and Ludwig saluted and Ludwig stood at the rear door of the car. "Captain Ludwig, A Troop, Your Excellency. Madam."

The bulky man in the crumpled white linen suit and black vicikid oxfords and black shoestring tie took the greeting with a wave of his panama. The woman beside him bowed. "Good afternoon, Captain Ludwig, happy to see you again, sir." He turned to his wife. "Captain is state police, Irma. I had the pleasure many times before."

"Thank you, sir," said Ludwig. "If the Governor's ready, we've arranged to proceed up the lane to the residence of Mr. and Mrs. Tate and after that we'll leave you in their hands, sir. After the Governor's visit and speech I'll be standing by to escort you back to this intersection again."

"Very good, Captain. Whatever you say. You get in with Percy there."

"Yes sir," said the captain. He sat in the left front seat beside the chauffeur, slightly disappointed at not being asked to occupy one of the strapontins, but made happy by hearing the Governor muttering to his wife: "Efficient, courageous, experienced officer. Stern disciplinarian, but loved by his men. Fair and square. Tracked down some great murderers. Mixed up in some historical cases," while Mrs. Dunkelberger softly said, "Yes, Karl, uh-huh," to everything the Governor was saying.

It was a clay road under the double line of walnut trees until the lane curved, just before coming to the Tates' house, and the surface became gravel and there was plenty of room for the big cars to turn around. The turning space was vacant now, and Percy, the chauffeur, made a wide swinging approach to the porte-cochere of the big, rambling, white pine-and-fieldstone house. At the crunching sound of the wheels on the gravel, the double screen-door was opened and a man and a woman waited for the Governor and his lady.

The man was almost completely bald, darkly tanned and with

large, strong teeth. He was slender, sparsely built, and he appeared to be shorter than he was. He was wearing a Norfolk jacket, white flannels, white buckskins (now grass-stained), a soft white shirt with a gold safety-pin in the collar and a striped necktie. A white linen handkerchief was tucked in the panel of his jacket, and as the car came to a stop he knocked his pipe empty and from habit rubbed the warm bowl on the side of his nose before dropping the pipe in his pocket. He was forty, a friendly, unsuspicious man, accustomed to being liked. He had a long history of regular meals, none ever missed except by choice, and of good digestion and fifteen thousand baths.

The woman beside him on the steps was in a blue-and-white muslin Red Cross canteen uniform. She was slightly taller than the fashion of the day and would have been still taller if she had not been wearing "sensible" heels. At first she seemed to be achieving chic without departing from strict uniform, and with no jewelry but a plain gold wedding band and a Tiffany-setting engagement ring, but on her wrist was a man's watch-chain, wrapped twice around and with a small collegiate charm dangling from it, and under the band of her nurse cap her widow's peak was showing, and it directed attention down to her black-brown eyes and her mouth, her mouth and her black-brown eyes. She was thirty-four years old, and they were Mr. and Mrs. Sidney Tate.

Captain Ludwig got out of the car before it stopped, and opened the left rear door, which was nearer the steps. Thus Mrs. Dunkelberger descended before the Governor, and the Governor took a look at the awkward roominess of the tonneau and said, "I'll get out this side, it's easier." He then walked around the back of the car and protocol was further ignored: Mrs. Dunkelberger shook hands with the Tates, making her husband wait in the gravel. He then shook hands with Sidney Tate and reserved the last handclasp for Grace Tate, who put her hand in his arm and led the foursome into the dark, cool house. All her life she had known governors of Pennsylvania, more of them than she

could remember had come and gone in this house. Mrs. Dunkelberger did not take Sidney Tate's arm.

"Let's go to the sitting-room first, shall we? And then go out
and face the angry mob," said Grace Tate. "Or would you gentlemen rather inspect the den?"

"I'd rather stay here but I guess maybe I'll inspect the den,"
said the Governor.

"I'd like Mrs. Dunkelberger to see the upstairs, too," said
Grace.

"Very well, we'll see what's in the den and when the Governor's ready—your speech isn't scheduled till about ten or fifteen
minutes, Governor." Sidney led the way to the small room which
he used as bar, trophy room, and office of the farm. "Nothing
much new since the last time you were here, Governor, but I got
a half of Reading beer, just for the occasion. On draft."

"Reading, yet. Can't you make like it was from Allentown, Sidney?" said the Governor.

"All right, we'll call it Allentown beer. But Reading people
vote, too, don't they?"

"Democrat and Socialist they have in Reading, but first I have
to make water," said the Governor.

"Right," said Sidney, opening the lavatory door.

"I like the toilet downstairs," said the Governor. "It saves
climbing upstairs for just taking a little pea. At home—in Allentown, not Governor's Mansion—we don't have a toilet down.
Only up. In Governor's Mansion I got one down. Often-times at
home my bladder says, 'Dunkelberger, run up and take a little
pea.' But I know better. Too many times was I fooled by that. I got
up to take a little pea, I stand there five minutes, ten minutes, the
water in the spigot I turn on, I make in my mind pictures of the
Niagara Falls, Atlantic City, but no pea. I give up and come
down, and my bladder says, '*Now* Dunkelberger, *now!*' So what I
do, I go out in the flower garden, and if the neighbors have objections, turn their faces the other way. That's all this is good for
any more. Ah, a pea is good."

He sat in a leather club chair and took the seidel of beer, sipped it and smacked his lips and wiped his mouth. "Sidney, as the fella says, it's a great life you don't weaken, but most of us weaken."

"Too true," said Sidney, sitting on the edge of the desk with a seidel and pipe in hand.

"Talk some, Sidney, I like to hear you talk."

Sidney laughed. "Thanks, Governor."

"Bollix on the Governor, Sidney. I like to hear you say my name. You pronounce it Dunkel rhymes with uncle, and the -berger, I can't imitate you. You say Bigger, Donkelbigger, but that's not exactly how you say it. I noticed one night last week, for dinner I inwited Clarkston, the new fellow that's president of the Fort Penn University, he talks like you, pronounces my name the same way. Oh, well, I just said inwite, instead of invite. Irma tells me to stop being so Dutchy, it costs me wotes! But I guess if a man is natured that way he can't do anything about it so late. You talk your way, I talk mine. Just as long as we understand one another, eh, Sidney?"

"Right."

"I have good news for you, Sidney."

"By George! Did you get it for me?"

"I think so," said the Governor. "It aint official, but it's a promise. Lieutenant, or lieutenant-commodore, or whatever you call it."

"Lieutenant-Commander. By George, that's great, Karl. You're a peach!"

"Oh, well, nice people you like to do something for if you can."

"You're the best. And Grace'll be delighted too. I know you're awfully fond of her and she's been putting up with a hell of a lot, my slouching around, hang-dog, since April. And the children, the boys especially. Karl, you really are a kind, generous man. Is it okay if I tell Grace right away?"

"Well, those red-tape problems, maybe wait till next week,

Sidney. I'm pretty certain, but just between you and I for the present."

"Right, Karl, whatever you suggest, but Grace'll know. She always does. When it comes to keeping a secret from her I'm a dud."

"Yes, the women are better for secrets," said Dunkelberger. He chuckled. "A good thing. Maybe I couldn't stay in politics if Irma had a big mouth."

"Whatever you say, Karl. When we hear positive word I hope we can have a little celebration, you and Mrs. Dunkelberger and Grace and I. I know how busy you are, but—well, we'll see."

"Yes, Sidney, now if the ladies are through looking at the upstairs I guess it's time I went out and put the audience to sleep."

They left the house by way of the south porch and began a frequently interrupted walk to the speakers' stand. Dunkelberger was big of frame as well as portly, a figure to attract attention without benefit of recognition. He returned greetings in English and in Pennsylvania Dutch, and when he took his place on the platform a cheer went up that smothered the voice of the speaker, Doctor O'Brien, who was reading a prepared address on the Red Cross at Home. The doctor mumbled a few words and the Governor shook hands with him and bowed in apology. Colonel Schoffstal, who was in charge of introducing the speakers, came forward as the Dunkelbergers and the Tates took their places, and at that moment a man called out, "Who's the baby doll, Karl?" There was some embarrassed laughter and some shushing, but the man repeated, "Hey, Karl? Who's the baby doll?" Probably not fifteen grown persons in the crowd of three thousand who were attending the Festival did not know the Tates by name, and probably two thousand knew Grace by sight. (It was, of course, distressingly apparent that the drunk was not referring to Irma Dunkelberger, who was bravely ignoring the questioning.) Grace kept her attention on Hamilton Schoffstal's khaki shirt, pretending not to hear the drunk, but she was blushing.

"Ladies and gentlemen, His Excellency, Governor Karl F. Dunkelberger," said Schoffstal.

The Governor looked first to the right, then to the left. "Did you ever notice the ugly things come out of the ground when the rain is over?" He pronounced did, dit; ever with a w instead of a v; ugly, uckly. He made himself deliberately Dutchy so that he would have the predominantly Dutch crowd with him. The heckler lost his temper when the crowd laughed scornfully, and one of Captain Ludwig's men tapped him on the shoulder and thumbed him out.

The Governor spoke: "Ladies and gentlemen—no! Fellow Americans! (Applause.) We all know what the Red Cross is, because of what it has done in the past and must do in the future, both at home and abroad, civilian and military. This magnificent turnout today is emblematic of how we all know and feel about the Red Cross. Here on this platform as far as the eye can see, little booths and games and good things to eat and drink and athletics, and I suppose if the Governor is old and near-sighted, why he can't see as far as games of chance like paddle-wheel and bird-cage (laughter). No matter, it is a good cause, a worth-while cause, the best cause, the cause of pity and mercy. (Applause.)

"The good people residents of Nesquehela County, of which I happen to be one, uh, *temporarily* (laughter), can be proud of their record so far, helping the Red Cross, and especially should we Nesquehela residents be proud to number among our midst two such patriotic citizens as they who turned over the facilities of their beautiful farm today, I mean Mr. and Mrs. Sidney Tate who you see sitting modestly on this platform. (Applause.) I happen to know that when it first came up the idea to have a big Fourth July celebration, proceeds donated to the Red Cross, the first place that came in mind was the Fort Penn Baseball Park, but as most of you know, the Park is being made into an ammunition factory. The same thing for the Fair Grounds, a camp for the Army Ordnance soldiers. But never was any doubt when Sidney Tate heard of the plan. No sooner said than done, with Sidney.

He offered this beautiful farm, one of the most famous in our beautiful Commonwealth, and work began immediately.

"I am delighted to be here on this occasion and now I do not wish to keep you from the purpose you came here. I have three dollars in my own pocket, so I am going down now and spend it for the Red Cross, and if anybody sees me holding a lucky-number paddle in my hand, why, don't tell the Democrats. I thank you."

The Car Shops Band struck up The Star-Spangled Banner and the flag was lowered, although it was not time for that ceremony. Then the Governor held an impromptu reception on the platform and the band played "Shine Little Glow-Worm, Glimmer," which was a known favorite of the Dunkelbergers. The Governor and his wife shook hands with the leader of the band, then proceeded with the Tates to the midway to spend some money and a little time. The party of four moved step by step, more and less.

The Governor was a rich man in private life and was getting richer with his cement mill, silk mill, shirt factory and a nitrate plant. He had become Governor to please his wife. They were childless; on their deaths the money would go to a Lutheran college, Protestant and Catholic hospitals, a Lutheran orphanage and a Catholic orphanage, and a vast fish and game preserve in the Blue Mountains which Dunkelberger was leaving to the State. His wife had no society ambitions; in Allentown and in Fort Penn she taught Sunday School, she held a license to teach grade schools, she played the piano and organ and she was fond of painting china. She was a good cook and housekeeper, and she had the best of everything she wanted: a suite when she went to an Atlantic City hotel, a Pierce-Arrow limousine with cut flowers in the vase, a sable coat and hat, and the best doctors in Philadelphia for her eyes and abdominal tract. When she decided it was time some honor and recognition was coming to her Karl she went to the right people and the right people went to Karl, and he bought his election. After the war they planned to go to California and possibly to the Hawaiian Islands, and no matter where they went it would always be nice to be able to mention that Karl had once been Governor. It was a nice thing to be able to say.

For Irma it took something away from the dignity of the office when people like the Tates were able to be so casual—respectful, but casual—with Karl. Irma did not like it, although she never would show her not liking it. Pennsylvania was the second largest State in the Union, in population; one of the thirteen original colonies; bigger and richer than some European kingdoms. You could shoot bear and deer and wildcat from the porch of the place in the Blue Mountains, and less than a hundred miles away, without leaving the State, you could listen to grand opera, surrounded by men in full-dress suits, and women wearing diamond tiaras. Tobacco grew in Lancaster County, and next door here in Nesquehela County they dug thousands of tons of coal every day. People who had voted for Karl wrote him letters in Russian and in high German. A man in Karl's position was entitled to more respect.

It was not respect, as Irma understood it, for the Tates to be so friendly with Karl. Granted they liked Karl, but so did everybody, and everybody didn't take him right to the toilet without waiting to get acquainted. Karl's bladder trouble was no secret; everybody in the Senate and the Assembly knew about it and all the politicians and business acquaintances and family friends, but they didn't treat him like a little baby that was going to wet its pants if he didn't do Number One the minute he got out of the car after an eleven-mile ride. Irma herself didn't have to go, but Mrs. Tate had rushed her right off upstairs where she had to pretend to admire the plain old-ivory furniture and the chaise-lounge and a dressing-room for Tate and another for Mrs. Tate, and finally when she did go to the bathroom, that picture of a little French boy doing Number One right at you, and the picture of the French girl, no clothing on at all, and not even her body turned so that you didn't have to see lower down. Pictures in the bathroom anyhow!

Irma did not believe that the pictures in the bathroom constituted disrespect to her husband the Governor, but when Grace Tate took Karl's arm she was shocked by a fancy that Mrs. Tate might have posed for the drawing. Grace Tate and the model could have been the same height and weight. Model or not, Grace Tate apparently saw nothing wrong in hanging up a picture in her house that showed a woman lower down. Not even Art; Art didn't even show lower down. And if she was the kind of a woman that saw nothing wrong in that kind of a drawing, she was not the kind of a woman Irma Dunkelberger wanted taking her husband by the arm. It was only natural that the Tates would be having people for supper this evening, and when the women went to the bathroom they would see that drawing and they would all think right away of Grace and the next person they would think of was Karl, walking around with Grace holding his arm.

The Governor's secretary had a list of Fort Penn people that every Governor made sure of having at his house at least once a year. The list was headed Prominent Local Society, and the names Mr. and Mrs. Tate were among the underscored, or most important; people who could keep Karl—Governor or no Governor—out of the Fort Penn Club and keep Irma and Karl out of the Nesquehela Country Club. Clubs themselves meant nothing to Karl and Irma, but the most important men in the State went to the Fort Penn Club—half the membership were non-residents from Philadelphia, Pittsburgh, Scranton and other distant cities—and the country club was the nicest place to take politicians' wives to lunch. Irma accordingly would make a nice face, but she didn't want Grace Tate holding Karl by the arm. And when the Dunkelbergers were safely in the Fort Penn and Nesquehela Country clubs Irma didn't see herself entertaining the Tates any once a year or any once two years. For the present she had to make a nice face.

It was not easy. Grace Tate and the Governor had stopped at the Ferris wheel, and Irma and Sidney Tate halted too.

"Would anybody like to go for a ride on the Ferris wheel?" said Grace.

"Oh, no, Grace," said Sidney. It was the first remark he had made that made any sense to Irma; the rest of the time he had been trying to make conversation, acting as a guide, as though Irma never had been to a Fair in her life. She had long since decided that there wasn't much *to* Sidney Tate. He had no job, his wife had the money, he didn't seem to have anything to do but be polite.

"Why not?" said Grace.

"Because Governor Dunkelberger has to get back," said Sidney.

"I think maybe a ride will be fun," said the Governor.

"Well, of course I'm for it if the Governor wants to. How about you, Mrs. Dunkelberger?" said Sidney.

"Not me, or *Karl*, you either," said Irma. She saw quickly that there was a line of people waiting for the wheel to turn and empty one of the carriages. "We can't wait in line, and those people are waiting a long time so we don't want to go ahead of them."

"That's true," said Sidney.

"Oh, they won't mind," said Grace. She addressed a boy and girl who were at the head of the line. "Would you mind very much if the Governor and I went first?"

"No ma'am," said the boy.

"No ma'am," said the girl.

"Thank you ever so much," said Grace. "You see? Come on, Governor."

"You think it'll hold me, what I weigh?" said the Governor, smiling his thanks to the young couple.

"Of course it will," said Grace.

"Karl!" said Irma. She did not raise her voice.

"Well, maybe stay on the ground is best," said the Governor. "Some other time, Mrs. Tate. We go back now to the house?" He was ashamed of himself, not so much because he had yielded so readily to Irma, for that was habit, but because he had yielded to habit in front of Grace Tate. He thought she smiled at him contemptuously, but he could not be sure. She had been defeated as well and maybe she thought nothing of it, for she immediately took his arm and matched her stride with his, like lovers, he thought. No one here today would have thought of them as lovers; even a total stranger would only have thought them uncle and niece, father and daughter, maybe. Karl preferred to pretend they were lovers. This is how we would walk in the woods together, going to a secret place, and she would help and like me and want more as girls had wanted more in remembered days. Once in a great while he had a woman—not a whore; she charged too much for a whore— who came from New York City and stayed at the little red brick house on Fourth Street which was rented by his best friend, Ed Wachtel, who also had a hideaway apartment in Allentown. The whore always called Karl either Mr. Dunkelberger or sweetheart. She was safe in every way; she was clean and she was not a talker. She would get on the train for Allentown or Fort Penn whenever Ed telephoned her. Karl would say to Ed, "Ed, you look tired. Maybe you ought to see Doctor Frank," and Ed would say he thought so too. Later in the day Ed would telephone and say to Karl, "I just saw Doctor Frank about a half an hour ago. He just left." That meant that the woman had just arrived and she would remain in the apartment or the red brick house until Karl found a time to go there himself. If Percy, Karl's chauffeur, suspected that the visits to Mr. Wachtel were for more than a game of hassenpfeffer and a stein or two of beer, he kept his suspicions to himself, and Karl helped to divert suspicion by going to Ed's house four or five times a week, when "Doctor Frank" was not there. Some day, maybe, the day would come when Mrs. Tate would go to Ed's. Only once, even, with *her*.

They stopped five times for greetings and introductions on the way from the Ferris wheel to the Tates' house, and what Mrs. Tate and Governor Dunkelberger talked about was of the greatest impersonal unimportance: how long it had taken to build the stands for the midway, how many carpenters had been employed, how many more people had come to the Festival than they had hoped for. "And here we are," said Grace, as they entered the house. "Are you sure you wouldn't like some iced tea and sandwiches, Mrs. Dunkelberger?"

"We got to get back, thanks," said Irma.

"Well, if you must . . . I'm sorry the children missed seeing you. They'll be disappointed too," said Grace.

"What ages are they?" said Irma. "You have three, yes?"

"Two boys, thirteen and nine, and a girl in between, she is just eleven," said Grace. "The boys I imagine are down at the boat landing, at the river, and Anna's with her governess. She's been busy all day selling pony rides. I think principally seeing to it that her own pony was the most popular."

"So nice for them to grow up on the farm. Healthy," said Irma.

"Yes," said Grace. "All our own vegetables, or nearly all, and we have some Jerseys, six, I think, so we have our own milk, too, besides what we market."

"Five," said Sidney. "One's dry at the moment."

"You keep track of them, eh, Sidney?" said the Governor.

"You bet your life I do. We use a milker on the Holsteins, but the Jerseys I milk myself. We have forty-five head of Holsteins—"

"You milk a cow?" said Irma.

"Five cows, Mrs. Dunkelberger, twice a day. I won't this evening, but tomorrow morning, as usual."

"Well, they'll have to get used to somebody else when you're in the Navy," said the Governor.

"In the Navy?" said Grace.

"Oh, I put my foot in it, my big mouth."

Sidney laughed. "Well, I told you she'd find out. I'll tell you all about it, dear."

"Now we got to go, now I left the cat out of the bag," said the Governor. He put out his hand to Grace.

"Thank you for coming, Governor, and I'm sorry you can't stay for supper. Mrs. Dunkelberger, please come for lunch some day soon. We're not very far by automobile."

They went to the door and the Dunkelbergers got in their car, and the Tates waved until the car made the turn at the lane, then went inside.

"Are you in the Navy, Sidney? Is it final?"

"He thinks so. He has a promise that he said is better than official, so shiver me timbers and all that sort of hornpipe."

She kissed him on both cheeks. "Oh, I'm glad for you, Sidney."

They heard a screendoor slam. "Mrs. Barker with Anna," said Grace.

"Hello, Mummy. Hello, Father. I made three dollars and sixty cents," said the child.

"How wonderful!" said Grace. "Congratulations."

"Splendid, Anna. Three sixty."

"Three dollars and sixty cents exactly," said the child.

"And tell your mother and father how you did it," said Mrs. Barker. "I'm very proud of her. The practical side."

"Three dollars and sixty cents was the most anybody made," said the child. "The next most was one dollar and seventy-five cents. But *they* weren't *clever*. When *I* saw so many little boys and girls waiting for rides I had a bright idea so I took Ginger back to the stable and Joe and I took off her saddle and bridle and harnessed her and put her in the trap and drove back to the ring and that way I had three customers instead of one at a time and I charged five cents extra for any boy or girl that wanted to take the reins and the trap holds four but naturally I was free because I was working. That made fifteen cents a ride or twenty cents if somebody wanted to take the reins."

"The trap? Why did you use the trap? Why not the governess cart, it holds the same number," said Grace.

"The governess has just been painted and new cushions and those boys and girls wouldn't *appreciate* the governess," said the child.

"Well, you're right about the wear and tear, Anna, but don't you think you might have given them the best for their money?" said Sidney.

"They didn't know they weren't getting the best, Father. They thought the trap was the best. *You're* talking like *Joe*. That's what Joe said, why not give them the governess? It's none of Joe's business, and I told him so."

"It was Joe's business. It meant extra work for him because it's Joe's job to paint the carts and keep them clean. And I don't like you to *tell* Joe something was none of his business. I don't like you to speak that way to older people, no matter who they are," said Sidney.

"But Father, Joe didn't know what was going on, he wasn't selling pony rides. He was smoking in the stable and you told him never to and he was drinking whiskey out of a bottle and I don't see where I did anything wrong except talk fresh to Joe." The child was vehement but not yet crying.

"Well, we won't argue about it on the Fourth of July," said Sidney. "You were a good patriotic girl to make so much money for the Red Cross. Will you kiss me good night? *I* want to kiss *you.*"

"Yes, Father." He bent over and she kissed his cheek, and then when he put his arm around her waist she put hers around his neck and kissed him again and they smiled.

"I'll go upstairs with you, darling," said Grace. "Are you going to change, Sidney?"

"Are you?"

"I'm going to take a bath and I guess I'll put on my other uniform."

"I'll wait till you come down and then have a shower," he said. "Will you be wanting a cocktail?"

"Yes."

"Good night, Father."

"Good night, darling. Good night, Mrs. Barker." He waited for the three to reach the first landing, Anna holding her mother's hand and Mrs. Barker following, and his wife and his daughter waved to him and he went back to the den. He took out his pipe and looked at it and rubbed the bowl in the palms of his hands and for a little while that was the way he sat, as though he were listening attentively to a long speech or a long confession, and listening sympathetically, with a set smile. Then it was as though the speech or confession were abruptly ended and had affected him at the end in a way that the preceding words had not. The trace of a smile went away and in its place was more recognizably pain, and he raised his head and looked toward the ceiling, like trying to listen to what they were doing upstairs, but the only sounds were water running in a tub and the noises from outside, the bands and calliope and voices of people. Whatever they were doing, whatever any one individual was doing, inside the house or outside, it was being done without Sidney Tate. They would all go on doing what they wanted to do and what they didn't want to do, without him, for the next few minutes and for as long as the war would last, and after the war when he came back he would try to fit himself into the place he had occupied before the war, but that would be easy and impossible. It would be easy because there had been no place for him and because there had been no place for him it would be impossible to reinstate himself in the place he had occupied before the war. Through the French windows of the den he saw a man. He was carrying his hat and coat and collar and tie. The man was rather short of breath but not because he was running. Very likely some heart condition. The man was in no hurry, but as plainly as though he were carrying a sign the man said he was going to rejoin his family, and that meant he had a family to join, and they would be waiting for him now as they depended on him always and would be missing him now and missing him later when that heart trouble got him for good. Sidney opened the door wider and called out, "Say, there." The man who was outside the whitewashed fence that ordinarily kept animals and now kept people off the lawn, turned to Sidney. "You want me?" he said.

"I'm sorry," said Sidney, "I thought you were someone else."

"That's all right," said the man. "Somebody looks like me here today. That's twicet it happened. What's the name of the fellow you thought I was?"

Sidney hesitated until he could think of a name. "Uh, Hadley. A. T. Hadley."

"No," said the man. "A. T. Hadley. No, I don't even know anybody by that name. But he must be here somewhere, because like I said before a minute ago, people was mistaking me for somebody. Well, hope you find him. So long."

"So long," said Sidney. He drew back into the den to cut off any further conversation with the family man.

He pushed a wall button and then remembered that there would be no one in the kitchen to answer. He went out to the kitchen and pushed another button in the annunciator box, which action made the little sign that said DEN disappear. He chopped a quantity of ice sufficient for a few cocktails and brought it back in a silver bowl to the den. He mixed Martinis in the silver shaker, drank one, replaced the top tightly, and went up to his dressing-room.

Grace was putting on her silk knickers in the bedroom, dressing all over the place as she always did; from bathroom to her own dressing-room to bedroom to his dressing-room. She never walked about naked except as part of making love, but sometimes her walking about in her lingerie had made him want her without much lovemaking, artlessly and ferociously, and while they never mentioned it any more, they both believed that that was how they had started their second son, their third child, when they previously had agreed to have no more children or at least to wait a few more years. After that long, cold pregnancy he had learned to stay away from her at times like this, unless she touched him or invited him by saying, "Sidney?" But at such times he knew she was ready for him, and probably had been all day. Now he finished his shower and rubbed his scalp with his most recent tonic and combed back the thin growth of hair that was all that kept him from actual baldness. He put on one-piece BVD's and sat on the hassock in his dressing-room while he put on black silk socks, garters, and dull kid evening pumps. By this time she was in her fresh uniform.

"I was just out in the kitchen," he said. "Julie wasn't there yet, and neither was Louise."

"They're there now," said Grace. "I heard them come in while you were taking your shower bath."

"Well, it's about time. How many are we having for supper?"

"Eight or ten. It doesn't make any difference. It's cold things, and we're eating on the porch."

"I don't like that," said Sidney.

"Well," she said.

"Well what, Grace?"

"Well what? Well, that's the way supper's been planned and we can't change it now."

"I don't like the idea of—it's all right to have a cold supper. I don't object to that in this weather, God knows. But to have us sitting there on the porch, under the porch lights, it looks as though we were being exclusive. I know if I were just here to spend my money at the Festival and I went by this house and saw eight or ten people on the porch I'd be inclined to say, 'Who the hell do they think they are?' "

"I suppose you would. Well, if you did say it I'd answer, 'We're Mr. and Mrs. Sidney Tate, entertaining some people on their own porch in their own home and what are you going to do about it?' "

He tucked his shirt in his pants. "Who's coming for supper?"

"The following," she said, holding up her hand. "Captain Smollett. I'm having Jenny Keefer for him. Ham and Marie Schoffstal, Doctor and Mrs. O'Brien, Fred Bauer and his wife, Walter Buchwalter and his wife, and I told Miles Brinkerhoff he could come and bring his sister from the coal regions. Gibbsville. She's about my age. Her husband's away at camp in Georgia and she's getting here today and bringing her two children to spend the summer with Miles."

"She sounds very capable."

"In that case I hope she's capable of occupying her children between now and Labor Day."

He interrupted the tying of his tie. "That's only fair."

"What is?"

"That she should occupy her children till Labor Day."

"Why?"

"Well, *they* occupied *her* till *her* Labor Day. Get it?"

"Come again and don't stay so long," she said.

"Here I am, how do I look?" he said, coming out of the dressing-room.

She smiled. "You look like Mr. J. P. Morgan on his yacht."

He put his hand over his nose. "I *beg* your pardon. You never saw Mr. Morgan or you wouldn't say that."

"I mean you look spic and span, shipshape, jaunty. Blue coat, white flannels. You look very nice, Sidney."

"Thank you, so do you. There's something very enticing about a nurse's uniform. Nuns and nurses. Did I ever tell you about the place in Paris where the girls wear nuns' uniforms?"

"Habits, nuns' habits," she said.

"Anything *but* nuns' habits at the place I mean. Doctor O'Brien wouldn't—"

"You're in very good spirits," she said. They started down the hall.

"Is that so unusual? . . . Yes, I guess it is, lately."

"I'm glad you're getting what you want, Sidney," she said.

They descended the stairs. "Where are the boys?"

"I gave them each two dollars and told them they could have their supper at one of the church tents, and stay out till nine."

"Two dollars is a lot—oh, well."

"What, Sidney?"

"In a few weeks—fingers crossed—I'll be missing all this so much. Running the farm, disciplining the children. Will you miss me?"

"Of course we will," she said. "That question didn't even need to be answered. Of course we'll miss you." She paused, in her speech and in her walk. "I can't get a mental picture of this place without you."

"That's really what I wanted to hear," he said. It was not quite what he wanted to hear, but it was all he could expect and more than he had hoped for.

They went to the den and he gave her a cocktail and poured one for himself. He sat on the edge of his desk, cigarette in hand, his feet crossed. "I wonder why I don't like Miles Brinkerhoff," he said. "Miles is one of those men—I met him, suspended judgment, and when I made a decision it was that I didn't like him. Some men you dislike at first and keep disliking. Others you dislike and later you change your mind about them. Ham Schoffstal, I like him, with reservations. At first he was no more than a rather handsome, stiff fellow, wouldn't dare move out of Fort Penn for fear people elsewhere wouldn't understand who he was—and they wouldn't! Around here he's a Schoffstal . . . Fred Bauer, a cold forbidding man, afraid to show the innate kindness that he has. Liked him from the beginning. Who else? Buchwalter. A bag of wind and a bag of gold. A work-horse, and Ham tells me—as much as one of these Dutchmen will ever tell me on another Dutchman—Buchwalter's slightly crooked, according to Ham. Did you know that?"

"Not exactly," she said. "I didn't know it, but Father always used to say you had to keep your eye open when you were dealing with the Buchwalters."

"If I were a crook I wouldn't have the crust to get up and make speeches at every opportunity. I should think you'd keep yourself out of the public eye. But I s'pose he has plenty of brass. I s'pose any crook has. He probably reasons that by playing the part of a community leader, the public's interests at heart, nobody'd ever suspect him. The houses he builds fall apart in less than a year. *Those* people must suspect him. On the other hand, the poor bastards probably don't associate him with the East Shore development."

"You like Doctor O'Brien."

"I suspended judgment on him, *then* liked him. A good surgeon is very hard to like, Grace. Admire them, I do that. But they're something like medicine-men in an Indian tribe. They know something the rest of us don't know, and if we don't respect them they won't cast out devils or cure our pains in the belly. We're afraid of them. I had to see O'Brien tired before I began to like him. And I liked him better when *he* asked *me* for advice. It showed that outside of his specialty, his profession, he was like anybody else. He didn't have any supernatural secrets."

"What did he ask your advice about?"

"Didn't I tell you? Financial advice. He asked me if I knew anything about some U. S. Rubber stock and I said I had some and was buying some for you. It's turned out nicely and I suppose he thinks I have some supernatural secrets. He usually takes Fred Bauer's advice on those things, but he said he thought Fred was too conservative and he wanted to know what I thought, unconsciously implying I guess, that I wasn't too conservative with your money *or* my own. Since then he's asked me other things, such as did I intend to send the boys to Lawrenceville, was there any prejudice against Irish Catholics in Southampton? And maybe you've noticed the last four or five years, Doctor O'Brien dressed better than he used to. I'm the one that hinted about those wing-collars he always used to wear."

Before dinner Sidney, with the children out of the way, often did this, holding forth about friends and acquaintances with some wit and at great length, with her as his only audience. He had done it in the beginning of their marriage, when he was new to Fort Penn, and there were no children; then there were the years when the children had to be put to bed early and these meetings before dinner were briefer, but in recent years they had resumed the custom, and in the last year the audience had been increased by one, the presence of their son Alfred, who usually ate dinner with Grace and Sidney, and who would slip into the den and take a seat without interrupting Sidney's monologue. The boy, now thirteen, would keep watching his mother's reactions, laughing when she laughed, and the next day or the next week or much later he would quote his father's descriptions and comments.

The door slammed and there was a fast footstep in the hall. "Alfredo, or our first guest?" said Sidney.

"I don't think either one," said Grace.

"Mrs. Tate?" a girl's voice called. "Mrs. Tate?"

Grace got up and went out to the hall. "Hello, Mary," she said. "It's Mary Packard. What is it, Mary?"

A girl of eighteen in a uniform like Grace's nodded to Sidney. "Mr. Tate, Mrs. Tate, Katty Grenville fainted and we wondered if it'd be all right to bring her in here."

"Yes, of course, Mary. Where is she?"

"She's in the First Aid tent. She can walk. She's come to. But Mrs. Taylor told me to ask you if you could let Katty lie down a while. She got too much sun, I guess, or ate something."

"Of course, bring her here, and Doctor O'Brien's coming here any minute and he can have a look at her," said Grace. The girl left and Grace called Louise, the chambermaid, and they went upstairs to prepare a room for the sick girl.

The sick girl, accompanied by Mrs. Taylor and the Packard girl, arrived at the driveway door at the same time that the Schoffstals and the English officer Smollett entered the screened porch. Sidney greeted the first guests while Grace took the dazed, embarrassed Grenville girl to the guest-room.

"We've had a casualty," said Sidney. "First one, and I'm surprised there haven't been more in this heat today. You know Katty Grenville, Ham? Judith? Apparently keeled over a few minutes ago and Grace is putting her to bed upstairs. Captain Smollett, I shouldn't think you've had any recent experience taking care of fainting girls. Come in here, won't you?"

"On the contrary, Mr. Tate," said Smollett, "the mere sight of a British uniform has them fainting all over the place. Ha ha ha. How I wish that were true. Not too permanent a faint, to be sure."

"Oh, they were eyeing you, Captain," said Judith Schoffstal. "I saw them, all right."

"No, my dear lady, I'm afraid it was your husband, the colonel here, that inspired the maidenly sighs."

"No, there's something about your Sam Browne belt, and your uniforms look better than ours, anyway," said Ham Schoffstal. "We're not supposed to wear Sam Brownes till we get overseas.

General March doesn't approve of them, and General Pershing does."

"What can I get you to drink? Judith, we've been having Martini cocktails, would you care for one?"

"I don't know, Sidney. Is Grace having one?"

"Yes," said Sidney.

"Then I'll try one too," said Judith.

"Captain?"

"Do you suppose I could have a Scotch whiskey and soda? Would that be too much trouble?"

"Not at all. Ham?"

"Whatever you're drinking, Sidney."

"No ice, Captain?" said Sidney.

"Ah, I see, you've been in England?"

"Yes, twice," said Sidney.

"Is that so?" said Smollett.

"You went there on your honeymoon, didn't you, Sidney?" said Judith.

"No, but I visited relatives there before we were married."

"Still take the good old U. S. A., however, what?" said Smollett.

"Well, I'm an American, Captain. This is home," said Sidney. "Here you are, Judith. Captain Smollett. Ham . . . To the confusion of our enemies?"

"Jolly well drink to that," said Smollett. "Now you fellows are coming over we'll soon put Mr. Hohenzollern in his place."

"Who? Oh, the *Kaiser,*" said Judith.

They were drinking when Grace joined them. She greeted her guests and said, "I think she'll be all right, poor Katty. She's more embarrassed than sick right now. She wants to be left alone." She addressed Smollett. "The girl is one of our junior committee and her mother's very strict. Mrs. Grenville didn't want Katty to have anything to do with the Festival, because she and all the rest of the family have gone away for the summer, but Katty begged for permission to stay over until tomorrow. I just hope this doesn't get back to Catherine Grenville. She'll blame the Red Cross, us, the Germans, and the British too, for that matter."

"You have my word, Mrs. Tate. If I run across a Mrs. Grenville-did-you-say? I sha'n't say a word about her daughter's mishap."

The O'Briens arrived, and after the amenities Grace spoke to the doctor. "We have a professional chore for you, Doctor O'Brien. It isn't anything serious, but when I tell you who it is you'll understand." The doctor immediately left with Grace and while they were gone the other guests arrived. The men were served drinks, the women declined, and presently Grace and Doctor O'Brien rejoined the party and they went out to the porch for supper. Supper went off very nicely and after that the guests drank cool beer until it was time for the pyrotechnical display. Captain Smollett was taking a sleeper train in order to make a speech next day in Columbus, Ohio, and he missed the fireworks; the others, except the Schoffstals, went home early. The Schoffstals stayed about an hour longer, and during that time the Tate boys came in to say good night. The Festival crowd lessened and lights began to go out on the midway until the dancing ended with the playing of Home, Sweet Home. There were a few shouts by men who had had too much beer, but soon even these died down and the farm was quiet. Sidney and Grace, sitting on the porch, saw two state troopers lighting cigarettes and tilting back their hats. "When they do that," said Sidney, "you can be sure the party's over. They're staying all night, acting as watchmen."

"They are? Then let's go to bed. I'll look in and see how Katty is." Sidney and Grace went upstairs and Grace stopped in the guestroom while Sidney prepared for bed. He was in bed, reading *Everybody's* when she came into their room. "What's the matter?" he said. "Is she worse?"

Grace stood in middle of the room. "She'll be *getting* worse every minute from now to December. She's pregnant."

"That kid? Pregnant?"

"Yes," said Grace. "I don't know whether Doctor O'Brien found out or not. I stayed out of the room while he was in there. Just now when I went in she was completely awake, lying there staring straight ahead. I asked her how she felt and she said 'I was hoping you'd come, I can trust you.' And then she told me."

"She tell you who the man was?"

"No, and I didn't ask her. She said he's in the Army and she'll probably never see him again. She's going to Cape Cod tomorrow and tell her mother and she said she doesn't care what happens." Grace sat on the chaise-longue. "What a mess!"

"Is she suicidal or anything like that?"

"No, she was quite calm. She'll go to her mother, and Mrs. Grenville will get President Wilson if necessary to find out who the father is. Probably send Katty out West somewhere."

"She *can* trust you, *can't* she, Grace?"

"Yes." She had not been looking at him, but now she turned.

"She *knows* she can trust you," he went on.

"Yes, she must *think* that," said Grace.

"The place won't be the same without me, will it? But when I'm gone will you still be wondering how much I know, how much I've guessed, Grace?" He turned his back and pulled the sheet over his shoulder. "Good night, old girl."

"Oh, God," she said.

She said no more and watched him for an hour, perhaps two, until she knew him to be sleeping. Then she realized that if he could sleep, it followed that what he knew he must have known a long time, without saying anything, doing anything.

CHAPTER 2

Grace Brock Caldwell was born, the only daughter of William Penn Caldwell and Emily Brock Caldwell, on the twenty-ninth of April, 1883, at the Caldwell farm, which was and is in Brock Township near the borough of Becksville, Nesquehela County (not to be confused with Beckville, in Schuylkill County). She was therefore twenty years old when, on the second of June, 1903, she married Sidney Tate, of New York City, at the Caldwell farm.

Sidney Tate, who was born in New York on the sixteenth of March, 1877, was the son of Alfred Tate and Anna Harmon Tate, and their only child. At the time of his marriage to Grace they had been engaged for ten months, and had been acquainted for about two and a half years.

Alfred Tate, Sidney's father, was born in London, but came to America at an early age. He was distantly related to Sir Henry Tate, founder of the National Gallery of British Art, but as Alfred Tate was the first to remark, the kinship was so remote that he had not bothered to investigate it until he began hearing about Sir Henry's philanthropies, which of course were extensive and large, and by that time, Alfred Tate often said, it was rather late in the day to claim Sir Henry as a long-lost cousin. It is also true that Alfred Tate was in no need of financial help from Sir Henry; Alfred's father had made a comfortable fortune in the textile trades, and to this was added Alfred's own contribution, considerably more than his father's fortune, and a result of Alfred's banking activities. Consequently upon the death of Sidney's mother in 1908, which occurred two years after the death of Alfred Tate, Sidney inherited about $800,000, or the entire estate, which had been left in trust to Sidney's mother. That sum included a house in East Thirty-seventh Street, New York City, which had an assessed valuation of $22,000, and a country home at Good Ground, Long Island. Both properties were put on the market and sold at a good profit over the assessed valuations.

The news of Sidney's inheriting a million dollars was given wide publicity in and about Fort Penn and it had, without his being aware of it, a happy effect upon his standing in the community. Outside the small group who were Sidney's and Grace's intimate friends it was generally believed that Grace had married a poor man, or a fortunehunter, or both. But the $800,000, or the million, was cash in hand, so to speak, and Sidney's social and financial standing changed overnight. The Caldwells were acknowledged to be among the richest people in Nesquehela County and among the richest in the Commonwealth outside Pittsburgh and Philadelphia, but it had been a long time since an accurate estimate had been put on their wealth, with the result that some people said the Caldwells were worth five million, some said they were worth fifty million, and some said they couldn't pay their bills. But the good Nesquehelans *knew* Sidney had a million.

The few men in a position to speak with authority on the comparative fortunes of Grace and Sidney spoke only among themselves. No more than a dozen bankers and lawyers and their confidential employees could provide anything better than a good guess at the Caldwell fortune to the nearest million. The rumor that the Tates *could* not pay their bills had some slight basis in fact: the Tates *did* not pay their bills; not every month.

The Tate bills were paid quarterly, which was standard practice among many wealthy families here and abroad. Bills were met with income, and only the poor and pinched needed cash. The custom also suited the Tates because it provided time for their somewhat complex system of book-keeping: Sidney's money paid for household bills, the education and care of the children, and his personal expenses. Grace paid for the upkeep of the farm, improvements, purchases of livestock, etc., and her own clothes and luxuries. Under Sidney, as a kind of overseer, the farm had begun to show a slight profit after the fifth year of their marriage and his management, and for this he accepted ceremoniously a salary of one dollar a year, which he said made him a professional. The farmers and farmhands and farm equipment salesmen with whom he had business dealings needed no token one-dollar cheque for proof that he was a professional. They laughed at his accent and his riding breeches, but nobody stole from him twice. He caught one man who had been stealing from Grace and her brother and their father for years. He was the superintendent, a man named Faust, whose brother's farm in the southern part of Nesquehela County had been supplied with everything from a manure spreader to a Delco lighting plant with Caldwell money. Sidney had Faust arrested, but Grace persuaded him not to press the charge (specifically the theft of a De Laval cream separator), not so much because she hated a fuss but because the long record of thievery made her older brother Brock Caldwell seem stupid. Faust accordingly gave Sidney a long-term note and was allowed to work it out on his brother's farm instead of in the penitentiary. In two weeks' time the story was known to all of the farmers in northern Nesquehela County, and Sidney was credited by them with a shrewdness that he actually possessed and a compassion that he did not feel.

He needed all the help he could get, whether from an exaggerated statement of his wealth or a confused story of his kindness and alertness. Two facts were against him: he had been born outside of Nesquehela County, and he had married the Caldwell girl. "I didn't expect them to elect me Sheriff," he told Brock Caldwell in the second year he and Grace were married. "But for Christ's sake, have I grown horns?"

"You're an Episcopalian," Brock said, "maybe some of them think you didn't have to grow them."

But even then Sidney had no temptation to leave the farm. He was happy with Grace, he always had wanted to live in the country, he had no fondness for the banking business, and Grace loved the farm.

When he married Grace he was not unaware of her worldly goods or of her being a Caldwell (and a Brock for good measure). But he never had heard of Mr. Nettleton, a young historian at one of the New England colleges, whose research led him oftener and oftener and deeper and deeper into the past of Pennsylvania until he found himself writing a book, tentative title: *The Counties of Pennsylvania.* After he had spent four months in Fort Penn he remarked to a local classmate that it had been "damn decent of the Caldwell family to name the county after those newcomers, the Nesquehela Indians." The remark was repeated many times and in due course it was told to Brock Caldwell.

" 'Damn decent,' he said? Well, he's right," said Brock Caldwell. "It *was* a Caldwell that named it Nesquehela County."

Nobody challenged Brock on that statement; Brock was the current unofficial custodian of the Caldwell family history and, by extension, or ex officio, at least one of the qualified experts on the subject of Nesquehela County. A letter to the Fort Penn *Sentinel,* published in 1902 during one of many recurring controversies over the Nesquehela tribe, was signed A Reader, but it was generally believed by those who knew him best to have been written by Brock Caldwell, as it was partly informative and the style was typical of Brock's "snotty" manner.

Nesquehela, the river, is said to mean "the nose which sheds light," so called after the point in the river's confluence with

Black Creek where the "Nesquie" and the creek meet and, because of the widening of the stream, more light appears. Another school believes that there is some phonetic connection between Nesquehela and Swahili, the tongue of the Nairobi folk in Africa. Leading philologists at Fort Penn University, Bucknell, the University of Pennsylvania and the Harvard Graduate School accept neither of these theories but await the results of certain research being carried on under governmental auspices by unprejudiced scholars at Columbia University.

There is no such tribe as the Nesquehelas. The Nez Perces did exist as a more or less bellicose group, but they have been dismissed by anthropologists as not being homogeneous and at no time has a claim been seriously advanced or at any rate seriously considered which would establish the Nesquehelas for historic evaluation with the Iroquois, Sioux, Sac and Fox and other famous tribes. Standard works so far have not embraced to any discernible degree any data which have appeared during the present discussion in this newspaper. The writer strongly urges the exercise of caution by future scholars and researchers in quoting from these letters for substantial corroboration of lines of scientific thought pursuable in the already confused labyrinth of American Indian studies. Within the boundaries of the Commonwealth it is impossible to proceed by water from the Great Lakes to the Atlantic. Unconfined, the aborigines moved about with neither knowledge of nor regard for the still imaginary Pennsylvania–New York border line and the evidences are that the "Indians" made their compromise with the seasons, the luck of hunting and such other considerations as may have been propitious at the time. The Indian, not made effete by the tangible or intangible inventions of the white man, moved about as he pleased and in so doing he inter-bred, to the amusing confusion of the plodding latecomers who must rely upon clay-covered weapons of warfare and skeletons of man and beast for acceptable "milestones" and directions of the Indians' browsings. The copper-colored native, wrestling with a death wafted over an unimaginable distance, may well have been indulging an earthly sense of humor when he bequeathed an arrow-stuffed hillock to the learned Jesuit as a challenge to the vested one's patience for inquiry. Not a costly revenge did the bearded cleric take when he attached his French nomenclature upon a race of men and women he knew but by portents and eloquent little signs. The redskin dead was the soul unredeemed. Said who? Said the discoverer of the already enjoyed! Employ your birch-bark as you will or as you have done, declares the patronizing padre, but you shall be remembered in French! And so it is, and so be it, that confusion still obtains. The ugly gutturals of the men to the north of France are considered more likely to have been the speech-way of the Indian than the dining-room aspirates of the race of cooks and holy men by whom the Indians are chronicled. As to the Nesquehelas, no such tribe exists, partly owing to the wheezing Frenchman with his prayerbook; partly because of man's lack of foresight for the problem of keeping himself warm. He has only to be just warm enough. Otherwise he need not have existed, like the Nesquehela.

The letter appeared in full, another fact that convinced readers that it was the work of Brock Caldwell, or at any rate, no less a person. It was agreed that no-less-a-person's letter would have been handled so carefully, and it was also said by Brock's few close friends that he very likely had written the letter while he was royally lit up. When he was asked about the letter his reply was: "If the person who wrote it wanted to be identified he'd have signed his name. I'm always in favor of respecting a man's wishes on that score." The then managing editor of the *Sentinel* saw that there was trouble ahead and he printed a paragraph underneath: "With the publication of the above communication the *Sentinel* closes its columns to the Nesquehela controversy and respectfully suggests that further discussion be carried on in the classrooms and at meetings of the various historical societies." The editor was thus able to retire to a previously prepared position when the inevitable letters arrived from the *Sentinel*'s Roman Catholic readers, who were not disposed to take the insults to the Jesuits lying down. A very intemperate letter from the Right Reverend Matthew M. Brophy, Bishop of Fort Penn, himself, was answered—or an attempt was made to answer it—by a personal call on his Grace by Arthur James Hollister, editor-in-chief of the *Sentinel*, but Bishop Brophy sent down word that he was not at home. Nothing was said from the pulpits of the churches in the Fort Penn diocese, but within a week the *Sentinel* had lost four thousand in circulation and O'Brien's Boston Store (father of Dr. O'Brien); Schultz & McMullen, undertakers and embalmers; the Family Hotel (Mrs. Terence P. Ahearn, owner and proprietor); Lannagan & Doyle (real estate, insurance); Fitzgerald & Sons ("Everything for the Home"); Dougherty's Mule Yard; Dean & McCloskey (Gents' Wear); the Fort Penn Wagon Works (P. F. Sullivan, owner)—all had broken advertising relations with the *Sentinel*, and there were more. The *Sentinel* was compared, not favorably, with *The Menace*, a popular anti-Catholic paper with national circulation; it was said to be backed by the Patriotic Order Sons of America, the Masons, the Junior Order United American Mechanics, the Odd Fellows, and the White Ribboners, all organizations which did not welcome Catholics to membership with any more warmth than the Ancient Order of Hibernians and Knights of Columbus reserved for Protestants. The majority of advertisers who broke with the *Sentinel* were not big accounts; most of them took "cards" in the paper which ran year in, year out, until their very names were illegible. But accounts like the Boston Store and Dean & McCloskey could mean the difference between a profitable and an unprofitable newspaper, and even more ominous was the loss of the Catholic readers, who were almost entirely town, as distinguished from country, people, and therefore steadier and quicker customers of the Fort Penn stores.

Peace was made by maneuvers which involved confidential

talks between Arthur James Hollister and Andrew O'Brien, owner of the Boston Store, who had the ear of the bishop. Hollister said he was not free to name the author of the offending letter, but presumed that O'Brien had heard rumors and could make his own probably accurate guess. Hollister promised that there would be no repetition of the offense, which he personally agreed was gratuitously insulting; the *Sentinel* would undertake to cover diocesan activities as thoroughly and as favorably as any non-sectarian paper in the country; the directors and management agreed to a letter of apology to the bishop over Hollister's signature in lieu of publication of the bishop's own letter, which O'Brien conceded for the bishop had been too strongly worded.

The effect of the *Sentinel* v. Brophy trouble was, in most respects, good. The *Sentinel* from that time forward exercised tact in its editorial and news handling of religious groups, and thereby became a better-written paper and a quasi-liberal paper. In the second place, during the five weeks of the informal boycott (as O'Brien pointed out, an Irish custom to begin with), the *Sentinel's* competition was given a chance to catch on: the *News*, the other afternoon paper, which existed mostly on due-bills, the advertising of clap-doctors, and legal notices, got a new start and cracked, without quite breaking, the local monopoly.

For years the *Sentinel* did penance by being ready to print, uncut, any communication the bishop sent over. Brophy, however, never sent sermons or speeches, and his extemporaneous utterances for public consumption were worth quoting. They were often witty and they said something, and they were spoken by a man who did not seem to feel that God was forever spying on him. But nobody knew better than Brophy that he had thrown a scare into the *Sentinel*, and his successors at the cathedral were not above using their awareness of his experience.

Brophy was the first bishop of Fort Penn and the first Catholic priest to be invited to the Caldwell farm for a meal. Without clearly realizing it, William P. Caldwell, the father of Grace and Brock, had done his small share to get Brophy his mitre and

crozier. Long before Brophy was consecrated bishop, William
Caldwell had been asked questions about him, not startlingly direct questions and not always in the question form, but apparently casual mentions of Brophy's name that would evoke the
right kind of comments by Caldwell. Thousands of this sort of
question were asked, and Brophy was installed as bishop. In those
days the golfing priest was unknown, the society priest not heard
of, and the interdenominational priest a freak. And yet Protestant Caldwell knew and liked Catholic Brophy. If Caldwell had
been asked where he had met Brophy he would have said he had
met him in the Fort Penn Trust Company, and if he had been
asked how frequently he had seen him he would have said dozens
of times, and he would have added "at the bank, and come to
think of it, on the train." Caldwell went to Philadelphia at least
once a month on the eight o'clock morning train, and there he
had often seen Brophy, a powerfully built man with a deep voice,
who sat reading his breviary in his Pullman chair, taking his eyes
off the book to whisper prayers that he knew by heart, and when
the train was coming into Broad Street Station Caldwell and
Brophy would say, "Good morning, Father," and "Good morning, Mr. Caldwell," and pay their respects to the weather, and
when there was rain or snow Caldwell often had given Brophy a
lift in his hansom cab. In such close quarters Brophy smelled of
cigars and of wine, which of course he had drunk at the early
service before taking the train, and Caldwell would wonder how
so manly a man could do without women. In the United States it
was surprising how seldom you heard of a priest's getting into
trouble over women and he wondered how much real truth there
was to the nun stories. He had a vague recollection of a scan-
dalous report he had heard about a priest in Shoptown, the
railroad-yard district of Fort Penn, who had been stoned by his
parishioners; but they were foreigners; Italians or Russians, people who did not speak English. Well, it was none of his business,
really. If Brophy had women, more power to him. His own pleasure in that way, in the only woman he had ever spent the night

with, was a thing of the past, and if a man kept busy, that sort of thing didn't bother him too much; when it did you controlled it as best you could, which was probably what Brophy did.

The more William Caldwell thought of Brophy in that connection the closer he was drawn to him, and once he found himself wondering whether a man who did not believe in Brophy's church could ask him carefully phrased questions. But that idea was preposterous. Nevertheless Brophy's solution to the problem, or seeming not to have a problem to solve, was rather comforting to Caldwell, and by the time Brophy had become accustomed to the title bishop there was a fixed cordiality between the two men, with the older man, Caldwell, somewhat in the position of acting the younger, in that he would be the first to speak, the first to smile, the one who brought out the cigar case.

Once a year, then, Brophy would come out to the farm to dine with the Caldwells and a few friends. The Caldwells knew no practicing Catholics intimately and there were not many who belonged to the Caldwells' set. Desmond and Sheila O'Connell had a farm about the same distance south of Fort Penn as the Caldwell place was north and they were the Caldwells' only Catholic intimates. O'Connell was a lawyer, senior partner of O'Connell & Partridge, who were counsel for the Fort Penn Trust Company, the Nesquehela, Fort Penn & Lebanon Railroad, Schoffstal & Company, the Nesquehela Light, Heat & Power Company, Bauer Brothers, the Caldwell Estate and similar blue-chip clients. Desmond O'Connell belonged to the noble-Roman school; he had white hair and was clean-shaven in a day when not to grow a moustache was an eccentricity. He looked more like a bishop than Brophy did; Brophy looked more like a politician or a well-heeled saloonkeeper. O'Connell, a devout Catholic, was respectful to Brophy before as well as after he was given the See of Fort Penn, but Brophy was not O'Connell's choice for the holy office and Brophy knew that. The O'Connell & Partridge firm took care of the diocesan legal affairs and charged no fee, and that was as far as O'Connell felt he had to go. He was an embarrassed man when he was asked to dinner at the Caldwells' "to meet the Right Reverend Matthew Mark Brophy." His embarrassment passed quickly enough to permit him and his wife to accept promptly. William Caldwell and his wife never had the two men together again: "O'Connell is a snob, Emily. He was snubbing the bishop all evening long," said Caldwell. "I always thought I liked O'Connell, but now I'm not so sure I do."

"I don't like either one of them," said Emily. "I was never fond of Desmond, and I'm not at home with Roman priests."

"I shouldn't think you would be," said Caldwell. "Well, we needn't have them again. Having the bishop this time was the same kind of social obligation as having the Governor, but we don't have to have anybody that you don't like."

"No, we'll have the bishop again next year, but we won't ask Desmond at the same time. I don't like to see my guests rude to one another. Next year there'll be a new Governor, I suppose, and when we have him we'll have the bishop."

"But we always have Desmond when we have the Governor. The leading legal light," said Caldwell.

"We'll see. One or the other, but not both."

When Brock Caldwell's famous Indian letter appeared in the *Sentinel* he almost brought Brophy and O'Connell together. Brophy had no love for the Jesuit order, but he was a priest forever, and O'Connell was a Fordham man, a "Jebby boy." He was out of town the day the letter was printed, and as the *Sentinel*'s lawyer he was in an awkward position. Then when he was shown Brophy's off-the-handle protest he was able to justify his next position. "For the moment I'll keep my hands off," he told Hollister. "You talk to Andy O'Brien. Andy and the bishop are very close. I won't appear at all, but you tell me what comes out of your talks with Andy and I'll decide your next moves for you. We'll come out all right."

"Who's we, Desmond?" asked Hollister. He was trying to be funny.

"If a client of mine ever had any doubt about whose cause and case I'm advocating, I would hand him a roster of the County Bar Association. I say I would. It's never happened, Arthur. Does that answer your question?"

"I beg your pardon, Desmond. I was joking."

"And *I'm* trying to save your God-damn *necks* from the consequences of your own stupid inefficiency. If you think Bishop Brophy couldn't wreck your paper you have another think coming, my laddy-buck. None of you realized that the only thing you had to cool him off was that letter of his, and I'll tell you something else while we're about it: even if you had realized how valuable that letter was—Bishop Brophy's letter, I'm talking about—it wouldn't have done you any good, because I'm the only man in the State that would know exactly what to do with the letter, and *Brophy knows that.* That's why Bishop Brophy is going to back down. You'll have to yield some, but you'll come out all right . . . Hereafter, Arthur James, make your jokes at the corner saloon. The next time I might be on the opposing side." O'Connell had not raised his voice; he never did. He stood up, indicating that the interview was finished and that Hollister could leave. "Why say," said O'Connell, "here's something you fellows seem to need." He reached into the small loving cup on his desk and handed Hollister a thick blue pencil.

"Thank you, Desmond."

"Go with God," said O'Connell, imitating Brophy's brogue.

The Caldwells in those days had a sizable red brick house on Second Street. In later years, after William and Emily Caldwell died and Grace was married, Brock lived there all the time. During their lifetime William and Emily occupied the house from the first of November to the end of April; it was warmer than the house on the farm; the eleven-mile train ride from Fort Penn station to the Becksville station took nearly an hour on schedule and longer when the weather was bad. The distance by carriage or cutter was too long by half for a pleasant ride. L'Affaire Brophy occurred the winter before Grace's wedding and throughout the weeks between the printing of Brock's letter and the treaty of peace William Caldwell had maintained silence on the subject. The quiet house on Second Street was kept out of it. William had no wish to disturb Emily, who never read a newspaper unless to study in type an item which already had been related to her orally; Grace was visiting friends in New York; and Brock was acting as though no letter had been written and nothing had happened. The Caldwells did not own the *Sentinel,* but William Caldwell and almost any other stockholder could exercise control, and although the paper was by no means one of the Caldwells' major holdings, it was a satisfactory one. William Caldwell believed that it was the duty of himself and "men similarly situated" (a euphuism which he preferred to "the rich"), to support a newspaper, for information and guidance. He read the Philadelphia *North American* and the New York *Tribune* at the Fort Penn Club, and the *Sentinel* at home. He recognized the letter as some of Brock's handiwork and kept his own counsel, as he made a practice of doing where Brock was concerned. He had given up on Brock as a son who would "amount to something." Brock was in his middle twenties and William Caldwell was sixty-two, and William was no more settled in his ways than Brock was in his. Brock was not what was called a willy-boy; he had left Princeton in his third year principally because he spent too much time in Trenton with a woman, a young grass widow who later married a street-paving contractor, and William did not delude himself concerning the sporting activities at the gun club which Brock and nine contemporaries supported downriver. He admired Brock for announcing three years before that he was going to spend some time in Philadelphia; he did not know how long. "Would you like to know what for? You wouldn't, but I'll tell you," Brock had said.

"I can guess what for," William had said. "I'm ashamed of you, but at least you have the decency to get clean and not expose your family and friends. I'll pay for it, but don't come back till the doctor says it's all right. At the same time, son, I admire you for—

for protecting—protecting your reputation. And I hope the treatment doesn't hurt too much."

"Thanks. I'm telling Mother I'm doing some work at Penn," he said. "And it isn't *my* reputation I'm protecting. It's yours."

"Thank you for *that*, Brock. However, it's the same thing, you know. Mine, and yours. I've always tried to protect yours by protecting my own."

"Well," said Brock, "I guess you never had to go as far as Philadelphia for six months or a year maybe."

"No," said the father. "I was lucky in that respect."

When Brock returned from his sojourn in Philadelphia the activities at the gun club were resumed and so were the rest of the habits he had temporarily forsaken. He had arranged his daily schedule so that he saw his mother and father and sister no more than he had to. He had two rooms and bath, his own apartment, on the fourth floor of the Second Street house. In the morning at nine or thereafter, when he was certain his father had gone to the office and his mother was out doing the marketing, he would get out of bed and whistle into the speaking-tube (down which he had poured water when he was a boy) and tell whoever was in the kitchen that he was ready for breakfast. The food would be put on a tray and hoisted to his floor in the dumbwaiter out in the hall, and the chambermaid, already busy in one of the bedrooms, would bring the tray to Brock's room, set it on the marble-topped table and light the gas log in his bedroom. He would take his time over breakfast and dressing and reading his mail, and by the time he was ready for the street he had smoked half a dozen Sweet Caporals; they were not fashionable cigarettes but when you inhaled one you knew it. Eleven o'clock had always struck before Brock was ready for his walk, which took him north on Second Street and south on Front Street, along the river, and in-shore again to the Fort Penn Club, where Brock spent most of his days. Before he was twenty-five he was already a fixture there; the tiny white wooden peg beside a member's name, which indicated that the member was in the club, was in the hole beside Brock's name earliest and longest of all on the roster. He and Fairfax, the shining black servant who took hats and coats and checked in the members, would exchange only the most perfunctory greetings, as though they were saying, "I'm here, Fairfax," "I see you are, Mr. Caldwell."

Brock would read the letters from his box, answer them in the library, and it would be time to join the round table at lunch, and then all afternoon he would play pool or whist until the drinkers dropped in for their glasses of whiskey. The bar was small, hardly more than a service bar; most men had done a day's work and preferred to sit at tables. A head of cheese, crackers, salted peanuts, and hard pretzels were the free lunch, placed on lazy-susans on the larger tables. Brock always sat at the same table, always sat with the down-river gun-club group, who were younger members of the Fort Penn club and content not to mingle with the oldsters. They shook dice to see who would sign for the afternoon whiskeys, and every afternoon Brock would walk home accompanied by the same two men, Charlie Jay and Duncan Partridge, who lived near him, and who were his best friends.

When he dined at home Brock would sit with his mother and father, and sometimes Grace, for an hour before going back to the club to play pool or cards. His father would read the paper and smoke a cigar, and his mother somehow, somehow made conversation. She would have husband and son holding a tape measure for new curtains; she could stretch out a discussion of Brock's shirt supply to twenty minutes; she had a letter from a cousin; she lost an umbrella; the cook's brother was caught between cars in the railroad yards. The discussion—and she had the knack of making her listeners' participation easy—was rarely about anything that was not related to the two houses and the people who lived in them. (When she died Brock said to Grace, "Mother never seemed to talk about anything but spools of thread and where she left her glasses, but I always listened.") The hour would pass and Brock would say: "I'll be at the club if anything comes up." This was a family joke: it had begun as a childish mimicry of his father, which was taken in good part at the time. It was dropped even before Brock went away to boarding-school, and everybody forgot it until one evening shortly after Mr. Caldwell had admitted defeat in the campaign to make Brock a business man. Brock suddenly remembered the line, spoke it, and the laugh that followed made for a friendlier atmosphere, although both Brock and his father were conscious of the sad finality in the disinterred joke. He would not kiss his mother or say good night to her or to Grace or to his father; they all pretended that Brock was only going for a stroll to stretch his legs, the way older men of the period would talk about going down to the corner for a cigar. But they all knew that Brock was gone for the evening and they all knew that many nights he only got home because he had been carried.

In this period William Caldwell once said to his wife when they were alone: "To all intents and purposes Brock is as old as General Doerflinger."

"General Doerflinger was in the Civil War! He's eighty if he's a day."

"I know. But I still say . . . General Doerflinger married Mrs. What's-Her-Name only about ten years ago. He still takes an active interest in a great number of things, like the G. A. R., and the bank, rides a horse in parades. He tries to keep young, the old General. But Brock, Brock's a mystery to me. He has no ambition, Emily; you can't argue with me on that."

"He has the history."

"Well—yes. Yes, he has that."

The history of which Emily was speaking was a project which did not so much disrupt Brock's way of life as complement it. Only a man with the time to spare and no money worries could undertake to write a history of his family, and at irregular intervals Brock would spend three or four days among old letters, family Bibles, headstones, diaries, parish records, receipted bills and county papers. It began with William Caldwell's saying, at lunch on a Washington's Birthday: "George Washington . . . My grandfather, your children's great-grandfather, shook hands with George Washington. And *my* great-grandfather, *your* great-*great*-grandfather, probably saddled his horse, polished his boots, all sorts of things. I remember my grandfather's mentioning that Washington either spent the night or at any rate had a meal at *his* father's house, down-river at what used to be Uncle Ben's farm before he died. Washington was on his way home from that time he was with Braddock, General Braddock. Now of course those old people, I s'pose they had a way of remembering things that didn't happen sometimes, but Grandfather was usually reliable. Isn't that interesting, though? Us sitting here, and we had two ancestors that at least they had some connection with the father of our country? Touched him. I think it's interesting, and I've always meant to look into it more thoroughly. And of course it was my grandfather, Elias Caldwell, he was in the Continental Army. He was only a boy in his teens, but he got in, carried a musket."

"I never heard you talk about this, Father," said Grace.

"Oh, I have," said Brock. "You know, I have a notion to read up on some of those things. It might be interesting to write a kind of a history."

"Yes. Of course the only way to do it is do it honestly. Don't cut corners, or leave out the bad parts. For instance, Brock, I know for a fact, both your mother's side of the family and mine had Tories. You have to be prepared for some unpleasant surprises. And the religious aspect. Both sides used to be staunch Quakers, and the Caldwells haven't been for—well, our branch, not in my lifetime. I guess it was my grandfather that changed, if he went to war. The Quakers, naturally, they were opposed to war, and of course still are."

"Have you any objection to my working on a history?"

"Notta tall. Far from it. I'll be glad to help, any way I can, so will your mother, won't you dear?"

"I'll write to the Norrstown branch tomorrow," said Mrs. Caldwell.

That was the start of Brock's project, which he carried on for the remainder of his life. It was a genteel occupation, that of writing a family history. To family friends Brock became known as a writer. That covered up his not going into business or the law or medicine; kindly members of the older generation persuaded themselves that Brock worked every morning from sunrise to noon, and it was not easy for anyone not in the Caldwell household to prove that such was not the case. The task he had set himself also excused him from social chores: "I'm awfully sorry, Mrs. Zumbach," he would say, "but a week from Thursday I'll be in Philadelphia, the only chance I'll have to meet with Professor Schmidt. You know—my scribbling." Mrs. Zumbach would be understanding about Brock's scribbling. Moreover, it would have been impolitic *not* to be understanding with a young man who was writing a book that involved so much digging into the past; in 1902 too many Fort Penn families became uneasy with the knowledge that a rich, secure, and rather cold young man was believed to be thumbing over birth certificates, marriage records, and documents of that sort. A single generation was as far back as many of them hoped he would go, and they were quite correct in their alarm. When he did create time to delve into the records Brock came up with some amusing, unpleasant facts to be enjoyed with Charlie Jay and Duncan Partridge. Nor was he above inventing details concerning the ancestry of Partridge and Jay themselves. He told each separately and privately that he, Partridge or Jay, had Negro blood. He enjoyed their dismay for a day or two before confessing to the fiction.

The joke almost cost him the companionship of Duncan Partridge, the oldest of the three. (They were known as the Three Musketeers without further specific identification, although Brock might have been called the Athos, Duncan the Porthos, and Charlie the Aramis.) When Brock admitted that he had been joshing Duncan about his Caucasianism, Duncan said, "You're a thorough son of a bitch."

"You have to take that back, or we're quits."

Duncan thought a moment. "I take it back. I admire your

mother. But you, you're a—well, no use calling names. Childish. But imagine going to all that trouble to make somebody believe he was part coon. I don't see anything funny in it."

"I did the same thing to Charlie, and he thought it was funny when I told him. He got the joke."

"Well, Charlie's more like you anyway," said Duncan.

"Is that supposed to be an insult to Charlie?"

"No, you know I don't insult people behind their backs. If I have something to say to a man I'll tell it to his face. If I can't take care of myself I'll keep my mouth shut or take my beating, one or the other."

"Oh, balls, Duncan, you have no sense of humor."

"If it takes a sense of humor to treat it as a joke when one of your best friends tells you you're part nigger and then admits he made it up, that's not my idea of a sense of humor."

"Balls. You're not above practical jokes yourself. Don't be so high and mighty. You go in for more horseplay than anybody else in the gun club."

"Nobody minds a little rough-housing," said Duncan. "That's fun."

"A broken arm's no fun." This was a reference to Brock's going through the boatlanding at the club when he stepped on a two-by-four that Duncan had sawn.

"Well, I was always sorry about that, Brock."

"All right, then I'm sorry you couldn't take a joke when I played one."

"I can take a joke . . . Oh, balls," said Duncan. His father's forensic ability had not been handed down to *him*.

Charlie Jay, as Brock pointed out, had taken the joke more gracefully. Charlie, as Duncan pointed out, was more like Brock anyway. Charlie was the youngest of the three, nearly two years younger than Brock. Duncan was a big man, who had been a rusher on the Yale team; Brock was between tall and short; Charlie was the same height as Brock, but slender and strong and fast. He could keep his hands to his sides and challenge Duncan to land a blow on his face. He loved violence and one of his favorite jokes was to dress like a dude—not too radical a change from his customary style—and go to a Shoptown saloon and pretend to be an effeminate. He would simulate a lisp and say, "Dear me, thith plathe nautheateth me," until someone from the railroad took exception to his existence, whereupon Charlie would cut the man's eye and cheekbones with his fists, which were armored with a heavy signet ring on each hand, hidden by the fawn-colored gloves that were part of his get-up. He also knew the technique of the knee in the groin followed by butting the work-man's chin. He also knew discretion; he never stacked the odds too high against himself. Before he pretended to be a sissy he would have studied the saloon's customers and the distance to the door, and on these excursions he carried a shot-and-leather truncheon, which he knew how to use.

Brock never went along on these visits to Shoptown. He kept away from fist fights; he had neither the inclination to get into them or the ability to get out of them. But he liked to hear about them. It is possible that if Brock had not given his implied approval by listening to Charlie's stories, Charlie, with his awe of Brock, might have given up his brawlings. He at least would have kept silent about them. He worshipped Brock. Charlie's father had been struck by lightning at a picnic when Charlie was four years old, and Mrs. Jay, though not poverty-stricken, was not rich. It was a great help to have the two boys play together, to know that Charlie would be brought home from Second Street every afternoon in the Caldwell carriage, and to have him spend his summers on the Caldwell farm. On the farm Charlie made the same pretense of work that Mr. Caldwell required of Brock—killing potato bugs, holding the reins during the haying, whitewashing fences, skimming milk, pumping water, picking berries, tending the cows. Their companionship had a setback when Brock became thirteen and kept secret the developments in himself that Charlie, who had talked about girls and women and men incessantly, had been anticipating. Charlie bored Brock.

But Charlie underwent the same changes within a year and after that the difference in their ages was never important again. Brock went to boarding school at fifteen and Charlie stayed at Fort Penn Academy until he was ready to go to college, so that the difference in their school classes was not continually reminding them of the difference in age. It turned out that Charlie entered Lehigh the same year Brock entered Princeton.

By that time they had their secret, which was so secret that neither boy ever spoke of it so long as they lived.

One day during a Christmas vacation, when Brock was home from his last year at Lawrenceville, the two were in Brock's room in the Second Street house. Brock was then eighteen, Charlie was sixteen. The snow had turned to rain, the streets were slush and mud, the river was not safe for skating, and there was no party for boys their age. Brock was smoking his first pipe, which was sanctioned by his father, to destroy the smell of the cigarettes he and Charlie had been smoking. Charlie had admired the new suit and shoes and neckties that Brock had brought home, they had had root beer and a plate of sand tarts in Brock's room, and they were momentarily out of conversational topics. They heard the front door close. They looked out the window and saw the Caldwell brougham driving away.

"That's Grace," said Brock.

"Is it?" said Charlie.

"Uh-huh."

"What's she doing?" said Charlie.

"I don't know, and care less."

"Tell her to come on up."

"What for?" said Brock.

"Go on, tell her to come up."

"I don't want her up here. I distinctly forbid her to ever come in this room."

"Go on, we can have some fun."

"You're crazy in the head," said Brock. "You oughta see her. She thinks she's the belle of the ball."

"That's what I mean, we can have some fun."

"No, I told her to keep out of my way and she told me to keep out of hers. 'Go away, small change, or I'll spend you,' I said."

"Where is she now?"

"I guess she's in her room."

"Let's go down there and have some fun."

"What kind of fun can you have with a snotty fourteen-year-old nincompoop?"

"Let's sneak down. Everybody's out except the maids down in the kitchen. Are you game?"

"What do you want to sneak down for?"

"Did you ever see her undressed?"

"Sure."

"Since you came home?"

"No."

"Do you know what? I'll bet she's just like that girl I told you about. You know. L. W. She's fourteen."

"You're crazy in the head."

"You don't have to go in her room. You can stay outside and listen if somebody comes."

"While you do what?"

"L. W.'s coming to my house again. Soon. Very soon. I won't tell you when if you don't come with me now. I didn't tell you *all* about L. W. either."

"What do you want to do?"

"Just have some fun. I won't hurt her or anything." Charlie got up and left the room and Brock followed. They made no sound and Charlie did not look back or hesitate. He quietly opened the door of Grace's room and closed it behind him. Brock listened, and he could hear them.

"Charlie Jay? What are you doing? Get out of my room."

"Do you want me to help you, Grace?"

"Stay away, now, Charlie."

"I'll go if you give me a kiss."

"I will not, give you a kiss. Give me my bathrobe. I'll call Julie."

"I don't care. I can be out of here before she gets here."

"I'll call Brock."

"Brock's outside the door, guarding."

"Brock is?"

"Yes. Come on, give me a kiss, Grace."

"Will you go if I give you a kiss?"

"Word of honor."

"All right. Just one kiss and then you have to go, but first give me back my bathrobe."

"Here you are."

"Charlie!"

"Please, Grace! I love you! Grace!"

Brock knocked on the door but there was no answer, and he found when he turned the knob that Charlie had slid the bolt. He knocked again and this time Charlie opened the door.

"What did you do?" said Brock. Charlie did not answer him, but ran downstairs and Brock heard him slam the door. Grace was on the bed.

"Were you there all the time?"

"I swear, Grace—"

"Go away, you coward. I'll never speak to you again."

During the remainder of the Christmas vacation Brock made no effort to see Charlie. They spoke when they met at parties, but only in greeting. Then while Brock was back at Lawrenceville he had a letter from his mother in which she commented that she thought it was nice that Grace had invited Charlie as her guest at the Washington's Birthday tea party of Miss Holbrook's School, which was held in the Parish House of St. Paul's Church. That, Brock tried to tell himself, proved that Charlie had not been nasty. It did not prove that he had not seen Grace lying naked on her bed. And whatever it did or did not prove, he never got another of Grace's silly weekly letters.

Mrs. Caldwell observed to her husband that Charlie Jay was a little old for Grace, belonged to an older crowd, but that it was all right to have him bring her home from dancing school and the few parties to which both were invited. She also gave her permission when Charlie asked Grace to be his guest at the Mercersburg–Fort Penn Academy baseball game, and Spring Day at the Academy. "I don't want her to be cooped up the way I was when I was a girl," said Emily Caldwell.

"Yes, I s'pose times are changing all the time," said William Caldwell. "And Charlie's a good boy. He's industrious, a good worker on the farm. Not a shirker."

"Brock isn't a shirker, Will, if that's what you're trying to say but won't say. Brock's just a different type than boys nowadays. I think Brock may have the artistic temperament."

"He may have, he may very well have, but not the art to go with it. Oh, Brock'll be all right. I'm not complaining. But speaking of the artistic temperament, Brock doesn't even play the piano, and Charlie does! And Charlie's very clever with the pencil, you know. He does all the drawings for the Academy paper."

"Well, this discussion's wandering all over the lot, helter-skelter. I started out worried you might disapprove of Charlie and Grace seeing so much of each other at their age. Now I see I needn't have worried. Well, that's one thing less to worry about."

"Yes, dear."

"And these, I don't know what to call them—crushes? I can't say for certain that it's gone as far as a crush, or puppy-love, or whatever you want to call it. But these uh, friendships! Friendships! Unless there's something solid they soon evaporate and young people forget all about one another."

"You're the one that sounds worried, Emily."

"Oh, I'm not. I'm just thinking out loud, as it were."

The friendship was terminated by a shrewd woman who understood her own son because she had had to understand his father. Jessie Jay was not a religious woman, but the bolt of lightning that killed her husband and the father of her little boy made her wonder. She did not hold with the theory of the outraged, vengeful God, and yet there was that lightning, so appropriately striking the one man at the picnic who had it coming to him—for Charlie's father was a great womanizer. Jessie Jay had had anonymous letters to that effect, and not that she needed them.

By the time Charlie entered his teens most people who knew seemed to have forgotten that his father had been a ne'r-do-well. The spectacular fact of his death had become the thing he was remembered by. But no child, rich or poor, in Fort Penn, had been brought up under such vigilance as Charlie, and the relationship between the Jay and the Caldwell family was so precious that Jessie would become ill at the thought that something might occur to endanger it.

The morning after Spring Day Jessie gave Charlie his breakfast.

"Don't leave the house till I've had a talk with you," she said. "I'm going upstairs to make the beds. You stay here."

"Isn't Willomena coming today?" said Charlie.

"She isn't coming today," said Jessie.

She returned to the kitchen, where her son was drawing pictures of track and field athletes. She sat across the table from him and folded her hands. "You can stop that now. I want your full attention."

"What's the matter, Mud?"

"I want no lies. I want the truth, the whole truth, and nothing but the truth, so help you God."

"I didn't do anything. Why're you taking on this way, like a judge or something?"

"What have you been doing with Grace Caldwell? . . . Oh, doesn't that bring the color to our cheeks!"

"I don't know what you mean, Ma. I swear I don't."

She slapped his face hard, and he jumped up. "I said don't lie to me, you contemptible, ungrateful thing. What have you been doing with Grace Caldwell?"

"I said I don't know what you're talking about."

"Sit down, I say. If you leave this house I'll consider you dead, 'cause mark my words, you'll never enter again. Now I want the truth, and I'll tell you right now: No, Willomena isn't coming today or any other day. I *know* about you and that little slut. She's left town and she's never coming back. *I* paid her fare and gave her twenty dollars, and her parents, they're *decent* colored people, they gave her a good beating and you'll never see her again, not in this town."

"She started it."

"I don't care who started it or anything else about it. I finished it. Now I want to know about what you did with Grace Caldwell, and no lies. Did you ever have relations with her?"

"What do you mean, relations?"

"You *did* then!"

"You didn't say what you mean!"

"Did you ever put yourself inside her? Answer me! You terrible creature!"

"Yes. Once."

"Once? When? What happened?"

He now was terrified and began to cry. "You ask so many questions, I can't answer everything at once."

"Very well. One question at a time. You did go inside of her."

"I don't know . . . Yes."

"What do you mean you don't know? When was this?"

"Christmas vacation."

"Where'd it happen?"

"At their house."

"In their house? I don't believe you."

"I'm not lying to you. I went into her room—"

"Where were Mr. and Mrs. Caldwell? Where were the servants? Where was Brock?"

"I can't answer everything at once. Mr. and Mrs. were out and the servants were downstairs, I guess. Brock was there."

"In the same room with you?"

"Standing outside."

"He knew what was going on?"

"I don't know. He was guarding, in case anybody came."

"Oh-ugh. Ugh. Had he done it to her before? Did he tell you that?"

"No. He didn't tell me anything. At least if he did he didn't tell me."

"Go on, tell me what you did. You went in the room while Brock stood guard outside. Where was she?"

"She was sitting on the bed, cutting her toenails."

"She had a scissors in her hand? Why didn't she threaten to stab you? Was she dressed?"

"She was wearing her bathrobe. She was getting ready to take a bath. The water was running in the tub."

"What did you do?"

"I told her I wanted a kiss and she said she'd give me a kiss if I went out right away."

"Did she take off her bathrobe to give you a kiss or did you tear it off?"

"I pulled it off and wrestled with her on the bed."

"She was naked on the bed?"

"Yes."

"What about you? Did you have everything on?"

"Yes. Then I got inside her, or I think I did."

"Did she faint or scream or anything? What did she do, or say?"

"I don't remember. It happened so fast and then I ran out, out of the house."

"Didn't Brock stop you or anything?"

"No, he just stood there, or he was when I ran out."

She stopped and drew a long breath. "Then when did you see her again?"

"See her?"

"Alone. Just the two of you."

"When she invited me to the Washington's Birthday party, at the Parish House."

"You weren't alone at the Parish House. Where were you alone?"

"Here."

"Here? In this house?"

"Down in the cellar. Willomena wasn't here and you were out shopping."

"In the morning?"

"No, in the afternoon. The day of the Washington's Birthday party. You said you were going shopping or playing cards."

"Did she want to come here? Who suggested it?"

"I don't know if she did or I did. She said she wanted to see me where we could talk. I guess I suggested it, coming here."

"What did she want to talk about?"

"She said she wanted to tell me—she forgave me for Christmas. But I must never do that again."

"But you did, right in this house!"

"Not the same."

"What did you do?"

"Kiss."

"What else?"

"Hold each other."

"There?"

"Yes."

"And that's what you've been doing ever since? Every time you've been alone."

"Not every time."

"But every time you had the chance. You say you never went inside her again. Did you ever have her naked again?"

"Yes."

"Where?"

"I won't tell you. It'd get somebody into trouble."

"Trouble! You're in enough trouble to be sent to the reformatory! Do you know that? Do you know that if Grace ever breathed a word of this, or anyone else, you'd be sent to the reformatory till you're twenty-one? Did you ever stop to think of that?"

"I don't know."

"Where did you go when you undressed her again?"

"I won't tell you. I *can't* tell you."

"Oh, yes you will. Oh, yes you will. You've told me enough to hang you already. In the South they'd shoot you. Where did you go, and why won't you tell?"

"Fraternity brother."

"Where was it? Now don't try my patience any further. You're going to be punished, but you're going to be punished a great deal more severely if you don't tell me everything."

"Ham Schoffstal's. The room over the Schoffstals' carriage house, when Walter was in the hospital, Walter their coachman."

"Did Ham do anything to her?"

"He wasn't there. I told him it was a fraternity secret. He doesn't know who it was."

"Is that why you have fraternities?"

"No, but if you ask somebody a favor in the name of Alpha Omega he has to do it, and then if he asks you something you have to do it. And you're not supposed to tell what it was, you *or* him."

"Ham's a lot older than you."

"That doesn't make any difference. Once an Alpha you're an Alpha forever. Alpha, Omega, from the beginning to the end, from the beginning of when you're initiated till the day you die. If they ever knew I told you this I might as well leave town. I could never get a job from another Alpha, or be invited anywhere, or they wouldn't speak to me and they'd ruin my reputation every chance they got."

"Where else did you meet her alone?"

"You mean where we did anything?"

"Yes."

"At her house. One afternoon when I walked her home from dancing school Mr. and Mrs. Caldwell were away and we stayed in the vestibule. Nobody knew we were there. That's all."

"Did she know you were carrying on with Willomena?"

"No."

"Did she ever carry on with any other boy? Grace?"

"No. I was the only one she ever saw except when she was little."

"And I s'pose you have plans for the summer on the farm, places picked out to be alone."

He did not answer.

"You were going to have things simply scrumptious, and I s'pose you were going to go inside her again, and then the first thing you knew, she'd be with child."

Again he was silent.

She rested her head on her hand and looked out the kitchen window. "Oh, Lord. Men," she said. She stood up and went to the kitchen door, her gaze fixed on the garden.

"I have my plans, too," she said. "You can forget yours. I'm not going to ask you to do any of these things. I'm ordering you to do them. You have no choice . . . Naturally, first, you're never to see her alone again. As long as you live in this house or as long as I'm supporting you, you are never, never to be alone with her again, not even to tell her what I'm telling you now. In the second place, you are not going to their farm. I'm sending you to your Uncle Dave's farm in Ohio. In the third place, if I catch you messing around with girls in any way, I'm going to send you to a military school in Virginia, a school that stays open all year round, summers included, and they're stricter than any reformatory. They beat the boys and feed them slop, and keep them busy from six in the morning to nine at night. It's the strictest school I know of, and if you run away from it I'm not going to have them look for you.

"Now Mister Big Man, you may think you're getting off easy . . . You're not. I'm saying this to you quietly, calmly, but I mean every word as I never meant anything in my life before. You're old enough now to—you're old enough to be the father of a child, that's how old you are. And you're old enough to take into consideration what I've sacrificed to give you a good upbringing, send you to private school. Buy you good clothing. See that you get enough to eat and live in the best neighborhood. You've paid me back by letting a yellow slut befoul your body in my own house. And you abuse friendship and hospitality and everything a gentleman stands for, treating the most important, kindest, generous family with no more consideration than if they were Willomena's family. It's up to you, now, son. Your future. No more threats from me. No more. I'm finished. I've said my say. If you disgrace me any more I'll consider you dead, and gather up what few pennies I can and go away from here. I don't even own this house. The bank owns it, and even the roof over your head is because Mr. Caldwell knows what a struggle I've had . . . Here's fifty, here's sixty cents. Go on out now, and don't come back till supper-time. I have to do my housework." She laid the money on the table and left the kitchen.

A few weeks later Charlie was packed off to his uncle's farm in Ohio. He wrote a letter to Grace before he left but he did not give it to her or send it as he might have done, through Connie Schoffstal, Grace's best friend. With his fear of his mother in those remaining weeks in Fort Penn it was an act of courage for Charlie to write the letter, but he did not trust Connie Schoffstal or anyone else, and the letter lasted only one day before he tore it into small scraps and flushed it down the toilet. In Ohio, so far away from Fort Penn and Grace, he first hated his mother before he began to realize that no matter what her reasons, she had got him out of two difficult situations. Willomena had become a threat and a nuisance; twice she had come to his room wearing one of his mother's rings and it probably would have been only a question of days before she stole it. And in their intimacy she had grown demanding. "I make you feel good, next time you gonna make me feel good or no more, Mistah Charles Jay, no more." He knew that all he had to do was to brush against her in the hall and she would come to him the first chance she got; on the other hand, every minute she was in the house he was trying to get near her to start her feeling that way, and sooner or later they would do what she wanted and then there would be hell to pay, a knocked-up servant girl, which was not the rarest event in Fort Penn history, but boys were supposed to keep their hands off colored girls, and seldom confided in each other when they violated the rule. Charlie, in his tales of experiences with "L. W.," had pretended she was a white girl and Brock had gone through the Blue Book and the telephone directory, in his eagerness to identify "L. W." Sooner or later, Charlie reminded himself in Ohio, Brock would have figured out that L. W. was Willomena, and then Brock would have had the goods on him for fair. The two boys came out about even on the afternoon Charlie attacked Grace: Brock could have been the injured brother, but he had stood guard.

In his meetings with Grace it was he who always wanted what Willomena wanted from him and it was Grace who was terrified of the consequences. In Ohio, going back in detailed recollection of each of their most recent meetings, he could see how Grace had been weakening little by little, and Charlie was sure that if he had gone to the Caldwell farm and kept the trysts they had planned he probably would have become a father at sixteen, and if that had ever happened in Fort Penn, at least among the people he knew, he never had heard of it.

Charlie came back from Ohio stronger, tanned, and handsomer, and with an excellent mental attitude: he had saved thirty dollars out of the pay his uncle gave him; he had had a summer free of woman worries, and that was a debt he owed his mother, which he repaid by according her a new respect. The fear of his mother had been the beginning of the first and almost the last wisdom of Charlie's life.

———

Grace had some pimples on her chin and forehead for the last month of school that term; her appetite was bad and she seemed to prefer solitude to the company of her family and friends. Her mother guessed that a change had occurred in Grace's life and she went to her daughter with the intention of confiding the briefest possible explanation of that change. Grace was leaning on the window-sill in the upstairs sitting-room.

"Aren't you feeling well, dear?"

"I'm all right," said Grace.

"Is it something you ate?"

"No, Mother. It couldn't be. I didn't eat anything to speak of."

"I noticed that. Your appetite hasn't been good lately. I wish we could have gone to the farm sooner but the plumbers won't be finished till next week. It was so cold this spring, wasn't it? Colder than we usually get in April and May."

"Yes."

"Well, another week and we'll move and then you'll get more fresh air. Fresh air's really good for you. And Brock'll be home and you two can ride, get exercise. Father's talking about taking up riding again. Won't that be nice?"

"Mother, couldn't we go some place else this summer?"

"Why you love the farm, Grace. You've always loved it. You and Father've always been the ones can hardly wait."

"I do love it, Mud. But I wish we could go some place else this summer. Were you ever at Cape May? New Jersey?"

"No, although it's said to be nice. But I don't think you could ride there."

"I wasn't thinking of riding."

"Have you lost interest in riding, Grace?"

"Not exactly. I was thinking of some place different. I haven't seen the Atlantic Ocean since I was little. It isn't anything against riding."

"I see . . . Grace, this—your not feeling well. Sometimes you're not going to be able to ride. Did you know that? I don't mean that you'll be forbidden. But for health reasons. Girls—every girl, every girl in the world, mind you—there's a change in you, sometimes it happens when you're fourteen, thirteen, fifteen, sixteen. Sometimes earlier. You'll notice that when you go to the *bathroom*—"

"Don't talk about it, Mother. I know. The period."

"Yes, but how did you know?" said Mrs. Caldwell. "Who told you? Connie?"

"No. Julie."

"How did *Julie* happen to tell you?"

"Don't be cross with Julie, Mud. Last summer I didn't feel well and when she brought me my tea and toast she—told me. She said sometimes mothers *forget* to tell their daughters and she thought I ought to know. So I know."

"What else did Julie tell you? Anything about men? Boys?"

"Oh, heavens, no, Mother. What does she know about boys? A face that would stop a clock. Julie's nice, but she couldn't know anything about boys."

"I beg to differ with you. Julie does know about boys. She's a widow, that means she was married once—but never mind about Julie."

"All right, I'll never mind about Julie. I don't want to talk about her. You asked me, you know, Mother. You were the one that asked."

"Well, I don't *want* her to talk about boys, and if she ever does, you stop her. When you announce your engagement—"

"*Announce* my *engagement!* Mother, please leave me alone, will you please? May I be excused? I want to take a nap." Grace did not wait for permission; she hurried out of the room.

Mrs. Caldwell took Grace to Cape May for a month that summer. They stayed with cousins and met more cousins and non-cousinly Pennsylvanians. Grace learned to swim in the surf for the first time and to play tennis on clay courts. The cold fresh-water dam on the farm and the grass tennis court and the Fort Penn friends and the house on the farm were different enough from Cape May to make Cape May seem more different than it was, and thus a desirable place for a vacation. It was decided that the next summer the Caldwells would rent a cottage of their own, and so it turned out that each summer until she was engaged to be married Grace visited Cape May with her mother and father, thereby slightly widening her circle of acquaintances, and providing her with a geographical topic when her Fort Penn companions talked about Eagles Mere, Martha's Vineyard, Watkins Glen, and Asbury Park.

After that first visit to Cape May Grace became closer friends than ever with Connie Schoffstal, the younger sister of Ham Schoffstal. The Schoffstal family branch of which Ham and Connie were members was the richest of many Schoffstals. A candidate for county office who carried the entire Schoffstal vote would have had a head start on almost any other candidate. There were Schoffstals in townships where there were no Schmidts or Hoffmans or Steins or Millers, and when a Miller or a Stein or a Hoffman or a Schmidt married a Schoffstal, he too became a Schoffstal. The Miller or Schmidt did not change his name; he didn't have to. It was known that he had married a Schoffstal, and a man's standing in his township or borough sometimes was determined by the closeness or remoteness of his kinship with the Fort Penn Schoffstals, and particularly the Isaac Schoffstals, who were the parents of Connie and Ham. In the city of Fort Penn no Schoffstal was out of work. Isaac Schoffstal saw to that. Isaac could not help it that there was a Schoffstal from down-river way who was in Nesquehela County Prison, Fort Penn, on a manslaughter conviction, the outcome of his having severed his wife's head with a sickle. That is what some people said: Isaac couldn't help that. But those people were inaccurate. A few, more accurate, pointed out that Isaac could help it, did help it. If the man hadn't been a Schoffstal, with his plight called to Isaac's attention, and Isaac's reaching into his pocket for a lawyer, the man would be in the graveyard, not the stoney-lonesome. Isaac never had seen the uxoricide, but to his knowledge and belief no Schoffstal ever had been hanged and none would be if he could help it. Any Schoffstal who came to Fort Penn, who was clean and neat and had a letter, preferably from the Lutheran pastor, was helped. He did not always get to meet Isaac, but after investigation Isaac's head bookkeeper or someone else in Isaac's office arranged for the newcomer to meet someone who would provide a job. In Fort Penn alone there was a Schoffstal at every little step, all the way up. There was a Schoffstal a crossing watchman for the Nesquehela, Fort Penn &

Lebanon. Crossing watchman jobs usually were reserved for men who had lost a leg on the railroad, but an exception was made for this Schoffstal, and he had the nicest arrangement of flowers and oyster shells around his watch-box on the whole N. F. P. & L. (sometimes called the Nesquie Falter, Pause and Linger). The Schoffstal family were represented in the Lutheran Churches of Fort Penn by a sexton and a pastor. There was no Schoffstal on the staff of the Schoffstal House, an Isaac Schoffstal holding, but it would not have been appropriate to have a close relation in the hotel business, at least in a hotel which was being carried at a loss against the day when it would be torn down to make way for a first-class hotel or office building. There was no Schoffstal in the Police Department. There was, however, a Schoffstal who was a tipstaff at the Court House; a Schoffstal was deputy sheriff in the same building; a Schoffstal was assistant county superintendent of schools and there were two Schoffstals on the teaching roster. Herman Schoffstal gave piano and violin lessons at his home in South Sixth Street and organ lessons in the Catholic Cathedral, where he was head occupant of the console (although not a member of the Roman church). Herman was an active figure at the Bach festivals in Bethlehem, Pa., and one of his daughters was on the faculty of the New England Conservatory. Another Schoffstal was watch inspector for the Altoona division of the Pennsy, and one of his sons taught higher mathematics at Fort Penn University while another was engaged in painting and paperhanging. A Schoffstal was boss of the open hearth at the Fort Penn Central Iron & Steel Company mills.

These and many more Schoffstals always went out of their way to speak to Isaac, and no matter what their ages, they all would say, "Good morning, Uncle Isaac," and he would return the greeting, often without a very good idea of which Schoffstal he was speaking to, but comfortably aware from the other's form of address that it was one of the family.

Isaac, they used to say, was all business. The firm name, Schoffstal & Company, went back to the fourth decade of the nineteenth century. In its day it had dealt in gunpowder, muskets, clothing, horses, tallow, seeds, paint, farm equipment, lumber, building materials, farm land, produce, letters of credit, real estate, steamship tickets, stocks, bonds, and insurance. In 1902 no one came in to the Schoffstal & Company office to buy a flintlock or a toe-jabber, but Schoffstal & Company would have found the rifle or the knife for a steady customer. The offices were on the street floor of the Schoffstal Building, at the corner of State and Second Streets. The lettering on the two large windows said Schoffstal & Company and no more. The offices were divided by the lobby of the building: on the east side, where the light was better, were the cashier and his assistants and bookkeepers and typists. On the other side were the members of the firm, consisting of Isaac Schoffstal and his brother-in-law, Philip S. Hamilton, and his brother William Schoffstal, in that order. Isaac had the front office behind the large window. A green silk curtain hung across the window at a height that made it awkward for passers-by to see what was going on at Isaac's fenced-off desk, but Isaac could stand near the window and look out on the street. The arrangement was in no sense accidental. Isaac, arranging for the lay-out of the offices, said of his own: "I do business out in the open. The whole world can look in if they want to and see who comes to talk with me." That was not strictly true. In order to obtain a good look at whoever was doing business with Isaac, a representative of the whole world would have had to stop at the window, stand on tip-toe, and stretch his neck for a view of the occupant of the chair beside Isaac's desk, which was in the corner of Second and State.

Isaac was a capitalist, a private banker. He took calculated risks that commercial banks were prevented from taking by law. He was licensed to sell insurance and to deal in stocks and bonds, and he had exactly the same right to sell steamship tickets and letters of credit as G. Locatelli, who sold fruit and vegetables and olive oil, and held the savings of his Tenth Street neighbors until they had enough to send to the Old Country for the Old Woman. Locatelli had a small safe, Schoffstal had a large vault.

William Caldwell and Isaac Schoffstal were the first Fort Penn residents to break the custom of going home for "lunch"—the first, that is, of the men who did not carry their lunch to work. Both men had houses within walking distance of their places of business, but the Fort Penn Club was beginning to catch on; men from Pittsburgh and Philadelphia and Scranton and Wilkes-Barre and Reading and Allentown were at the club every day while the Legislature was in session, and William and Isaac agreed that it seemed a pity not to meet those fellows and exchange views. There were views to be exchanged on doings in the locomotive industry, for instance, which Philadelphia fellows knew all about. The Pittsburgh fellows had their fingers on the bituminous and iron pulse, and the Scranton–Wilkes-Barre fellows had their fingers on the anthracite pulse. The Reading and Allentown men had views on textiles and cement and railroad equipment. It was Isaac who had the idea of lunching at the club, and Will who did the agreeing. They made many valuable friendships by establishing the new lunch custom, and without intending to do so, they effected a revolutionary change in the social life of Fort Penn: when other men saw Isaac and Will lunching downtown, they too took up the custom, and their wives, who had been hoping for an excuse for evening dinner, enthusiastically approved. Isaac's wife told Emily Caldwell that "We're getting just like Philadelphia." Ahead of its time, compared with other cities of equal size, Fort Penn went in for a metropolitan social life, with consequent prosperity for dressmakers, tailors, shoemakers, and jewelers at home and away. The proven plays of William Shakespeare, and the Philadelphia Opera Company enjoyed unprecedented patronage, and Sousa's Band was sold out a week earlier than on any previous winter appearance.

The luncheon innovation was one of the few in its category not to have originated with a member of the Caldwells, and the only one attributable to Isaac Schoffstal or a member of his family. The Caldwells were money-conservative and more progressive in their social habits and the clothes they wore. In actual fact the Caldwells often had entertained at evening dinner; but they generally observed Fort Penn custom. Isaac Schoffstal would have been incredulous if it had been suggested that his occasionally unorthodox business philosophy had been matched by his becoming a social innovator. It was not the Schoffstals' way. Isaac was a kind and kindly man outside of business. He had inherited money, name, and connections, which were useful and compatible with his acquisitive instinct, and deals were his fun. He had pride of family, as evidenced by his taking care of obscure relatives, but better demonstrated by his attitude toward his wife and children. They had, in the words of the old exaggeration, everything they wanted, everything that money could buy. But the new thing had to be carried or worn or otherwise enjoyed, and thus approved, by others before he would buy it. In most cases it was sufficient for wife or child to point out that the Caldwells had given their approval of the carriage or the cloak or the porch or the journey. Isaac probably was merely protecting himself and his own against the ridicule that the innovator risks. This attitude and practice did not protect him and his own against the lifelong charge that the Schoffstals imitated the Caldwells in all things. It was said by the unkind that the Schoffstals didn't dare to take a leak unless the Caldwells took one first. The charge was made that the Schoffstals didn't think any butter was good unless it had been churned at the Caldwell farm. (It was true that Riverside Farm butter, eggs, and milk were delivered daily to the Schoffstal home.) A casual overheard question—"Do you still buy your clothes in Philadelphia?"—had people saying that Ham Schoffstal copied Brock Caldwell, who was much younger than Ham. And when Fort Penn gossips declared that Connie Schoffstal was trying to be like Grace Caldwell, they had something to go on.

The girls were only months apart in age. Grace was born in April, Connie in February. Grace had not selected Connie to be her companion. It was only that Connie was always there, and always had been. Afternoons, after school, Connie would not go home to her own house; she went to Grace's. Even when Connie had a new toy or a new hair ribbon she would bring it to the Caldwells' house rather than risk Grace's refusal to go to the Schoffstals'. Connie would sit on the floor while Grace, a non-gregarious child anyway, worked a puzzle. Connie would sit in the parlor while Grace practised her scales. Connie would hear Grace's lessons, but Grace would not hear Connie's. "I'll get it, I'll get it," Connie was always saying. "I'll do it, I'll lift it, I'll close it, I'll turn it, I'll kill it, I'll tie it, I'll get it." Connie anticipated when she could, gave when she could, and was always there.

She had been there if Grace had wanted to tell her anything or everything about what happened between her and Charlie Jay, but Grace told her nothing, not then, not ever. Connie knew something was wrong, then right, then wrong again, and she knew she was being kept out of a secret which engaged Grace and Charlie, but there again Connie was fearful of a lasting rebuff, and she never asked Grace about Charlie. Connie's common sense and her affection for Grace told her that the sudden visit to Cape May had something to do with Charlie, and she was determined to be helpful when Grace got back. She risked one question: "Were any of those cousins boys?" Yes, boys, and men. A dandy swimmer who went to Episcopal Academy, a ducky tennis player who went to Haverford College, an older man who played football at Penn. They had all been nice to her and in four years when she had her ball—Fort Penn girls and their parents did not employ the term "coming-out party"—she hoped they would all come. And she had seen others besides cousins; the cousins had friends, naturally. Practically all of the boys smoked cigarettes; some of them even smoked cigarettes at home. She herself had taken a few puffs every time the tennis player dropped in at the house where she was staying.

Grace's smoking was almost enough of a confession to satisfy Connie's need for something secret to share with Grace. Almost. She wanted to ask Grace if she had been given any presents by cousins or cousins' friends, or if she had promised to write, but those secrets had to be free-will offerings. The smoking was a wonderful secret, properly appreciated by Connie, and Grace would tell what she had to tell when she was good and ready. Until then Connie was delighted to be paying a long visit at the farm. They swam in the dam, played tennis, made a pretense of learning to cook, climbed trees, sat in the hammocks, waded in the creek, drove the new cob in the buckboard to Becksville, two miles away, for milk chocolate; attended the Lutheran church in Becksville, watched the threshers for a little while every day for a week, tried on old dresses of Emily Caldwell's, helped put up preserves, smoked cigarettes, hunted chicken eggs, polished silver, rode the hay-wagon and the drag sled, killed a copperhead, went to bed soon after supper and had breakfast at eight, and spoke of the future.

Neither of the girls knew much about boarding schools but Grace was firmly convinced that she would not go to one. "It'd be the same as Miss Holy's, only at boarding school I always heard they feed you pig slops, and open your letters. Did you ever know that, Connie? At boarding school they open your letters that you send and the ones you get. Fancy that! At least Holy Holbrook can't lay her hands on a person's private correspondence."

"But I think I'd like to go to one for a year."

"What for, may I ask?"

"To see what it's like."

"Mon Dieu! I've *told* you what it's like. Pig slops and opening your letters. A person is entitled to their privacy."

"But Grace, don't you ever want to leave Fort Penn? Dear me."

"No. Except the Grand Tour. When I'm twenty-five I'll take the Grand Tour. And I'd like to open my own charge account in New York for clothes, but I wouldn't think of living in Europe. Just Cape May every summer. I remember when I went to New York that time. Mon Dieu! The fishy smell on the ferryboat, and we were up on the top! And where you get off and take the carriage to go to the hotel. You can't cross the street on account of the drays and beating the horses. Father was going to have a man arrested but he couldn't find a policeman. In Fort Penn nobody ever beat a horse in front of father. I learned my lesson. When we had to go across the Hudson River again I held my sachet to my nose."

In the weeks of Connie's visit they had only one quarrel. The threshers went from farm to farm, each farmer helping out his neighbors. The first two days of the week were spent at the Caldwell farm because there was more grain to be threshed there. Most of the men did not remember Grace from other summers, but they remembered her every time she appeared after that. On the last day, Saturday, one of them called out to another over the noise of the threshing machine:

"Wie daitscht gleicha fer in iera tzwivvela bet ruum grawva?"

The second man replied: *"Oll recht, fer vas frogha mier sie net?"*

All who heard laughed and stared at Grace. They had stared before, but one at a time; now they all stared, and she left the barnyard. When she picked up the reins she asked Connie what the men had said. "You understand Dutch."

"I couldn't quite hear them."

"You're a liar. You know what they said. Tell me."

"I couldn't—"

"Do you swear on your honor? They were talking about me and I want to know what they said. I *insist!*"

"Well, the man with the handkerchief over his face—"

"Do you know him?"

"Of course not, how would I know these farmers? You ought to."

"I couldn't tell for sure with the handkerchief over his face. What did he say?"

"Please, Grace, you'll hate me worse if I do tell you than if I don't."

"I *said* I *insist.* If you don't tell me I'll ask you to pack up and go home, and never come to our farm again or our house. Do you hear?"

"Well—the handkerchief man, he said he would like to get in bed with you."

"Is that what he said? What did the other say?"

"The other said why didn't he ask you, maybe you'd like to."

Grace was silent a moment. "What made them say that? What else did they say?"

"I didn't listen, I was so disgusted."

"Were you?"

"Yes, don't you know what they mean, Grace?"

She considered her answer. "Yes, I know what they mean."

She said no more during the rest of the ride and Connie was left to consider the inferences to be taken from Grace's tone. She wanted to think that Grace did not know what the farmers meant, and she wanted to think that Grace knew only too well what they meant. Connie wondered about the episode until Charlie Jay came home from Ohio.

Vacation ended, the girls went back to school, Charlie Jay came home from Ohio. His name was not brought up, and when Grace gave a dinner party before the Christmas Hop at dancing school Charlie was not invited. At her right she put Desmond O'Connell Junior, a pale, curly-haired boy who died practically unnoticed a few months later. A sweet boy, who everyone said went straight to heaven, he meant nothing to Grace, but his father and mother never forgot that she had been kind to him that last Christmas. It was the only sub-surface knowledge they had of Grace Caldwell, knowledge which happened to be in her favor. If they had asked someone close to Grace—specifically, Connie Schoffstal—they would have learned that the reason Junior O'Connell had been honored by Grace was that he was a harmless, uninteresting boy, who made no demands on a hostess or anyone else, and would do as he was told. But of course Mr. and Mrs. O'Connell did *not* ask Connie what she thought, and so they never knew, and so they never had anything but a good word to say for Grace Caldwell.

Grace's decision not to go away to boarding school, which had not been a decision before she thought aloud to Connie, was upheld by her father and mother. She was fifteen in 1897.

"Father and I," said her mother one day in the Spring of that year, "have been wondering where to send you to school next year. Have you any preferences?"

"Yes," said Grace. "Miss Holbrook's."

"No, I meant boarding school. Mrs. Martindale likes Westover. She's very pleased with Agnes and Jean."

"Maybe Mrs. Martindale is, but I'm not."

"Do you mean not pleased with Agnes and Jean? You like Jean Martindale."

"Who said I did? I'm sure I never said I liked Jean Martindale, and 'specially since she's been to Westover. Mon Dieu! One might think Jean Martindale—"

"I've spoken to you before about this, Grace. I won't have you saying Mon Dieu. It means my God, and it's just as sinful in French as it is in English. I've finally made Julie stop saying it in English, and now you say it every other word. That's just the kind of thing a good boarding school puts a stop to."

"I'm sorry, I'll try not to say it."

"You'll have to do better than try. You'll have to make up your mind."

"But when I make up my mind, then I'll have to try, won't I? And I've made up my mind, so all I can do from now on is try."

"That's still another thing that has to be corrected. You used to be an obedient, respectful girl, especially where older people were concerned, but lately I've noticed, I don't know, you pick people up on what they say. You seem to be losing your manners."

"I shouldn't call it losing one's manners to take one's own part. One has to take one's part."

"Oh, stop, stop, stop, stop. We're getting away from the subject. Now then, you have your mind made up against Westover. Well, Father and I'll consider that, but don't think if we decide that's the best place for you, that's where you're not going, if you see what I mean. We'll be the ones to decide. How about St. Timothy's?"

"Mother! If you want me to die, in a prison dungeon, put me

in the county jail. Alice McKelvie can tell you about St. Timo-thy's."

"It's done Alice a world of good. She was loud and a tomboy and Mrs. McKelvie was upset about Alice before she went to St. Timothy's, but she's outgrown all that and she's growing up to be a dignified, ladylike girl."

"Mother, I don't want to be disrespectful or anything, but why don't you ask the girls what they think of the schools, not their mothers. If you care to know what I think, I think the mothers sometimes send their daughters away to get rid of them. Alice McKelvie hates St. Timothy's, because she told me so herself."

"I've asked the mothers because they're in a better position to judge whether the school's good or not. Another place we thought of was Eden Hall, near Philadelphia. A cousin of ours went there and it's an excellent school. It's Catholic, the Sacred Heart runs it, but it'll help your French, and not Mon Dieu, either."

Grace sighed. "Oh, Mother. I s'pose you'd like it if I came home and said I was going to the Mass with Julie every Sunday. Julie and Higgins. 'Get up, Grace, it's time to go to the early Mass with Julie and Higgins. The Pope will send you to hell if you don't get up for the Mass.' "

"Now look here, young lady, that's quite enough of that."

"Help my French. What do I want to speak French for? I'm taking French now, and it's a waste. I'm never going to live in France. I'm going to stay right here in Fort Penn, not even in Fort Penn. I'm going to live on the farm."

"You may fall in love and have a husband, and—"

"He'll have to live on the farm or I won't marry him. I don't want to go to any boarding school with a lot of strangers."

"Do you mean to say you'd like to stay here in Fort Penn the rest of your life?"

"Yes, what's the matter with Fort Penn?"

"But I should think—well, you like boys and eventually you'll marry. You're not going to meet many boys here."

"Well, I'm not going chasing after them in New York and France either."

"No, I wouldn't want you to do that."

"Well, why do I have to go away then? Unless you want to get rid of me."

"Grace, you know *that* isn't true."

"And anyhow, you don't meet boys at boarding school. That's where you'll *never* meet them."

Emily Caldwell reported to her husband and they agreed to reopen the subject the next year. When it was reopened it was done so more casually, a passing question: did Grace still not want to go to boarding school? The answer was as they expected. William and Emily Caldwell were happy to have Grace at home with them, and her progress in body and mind made them not want to disturb well-enough. And they were secretly delighted that Fort Penn suited her, that she was not the restless kind that wanted to get away from home.

Grace's decision was the first of many whimsical ideas throughout her life that disproportionately influenced the life of Fort Penn. Girls who wanted to rush off to boarding school the moment they put their hair up were checked by reluctant fathers and mothers who would point to Grace and say, "Miss Holbrook's is good enough for Grace Caldwell." Likewise girls who did not want to go away reminded their pushing parents that Grace was staying in Fort Penn. Not the least pleased was Miss Holbrook herself, who had no notion that the original decision had been Grace's own, but who was wise enough to realize that Grace had had something to say about it. Miss Holbrook became almost insufferably confident, was able to conduct a campaign for funds, and thus effected improvements at the school which made it approximately as good as she thought it was. This fact, in turn, spread the school's reputation and Miss Holbrook (in 1901) proudly announced that owing to numerous requests, the school, after due consideration was open to a few, carefully selected boarders.

Grace was sixteen, and rapidly overtaking seventeen, on the

last night of the Old Century. William Caldwell had been nominated the summer before to be head usher at the Turn of the
Century Ball, which was to be held at the Schoffstal House on
the thirty-first of December, One Thousand Eight Hundred
Ninety-nine, subscription twenty dollars. "Gentlemen, thank
you, and you must know how grateful, how honored I am, but I
must ask you to withdraw my name. Naturally I expect to be
there, to be present that evening, but as a youngster in my twenties, may even have been in my teens, I hoped to live to see that
night—still am hoping, for that matter. A lot can happen between now and December. Anyway, when I was younger, even
before I was married, I made plans to be with my family at the
stroke of midnight that night. Well, the good Lord has let me live
this far, I have my family, and for just a few minutes at midnight
my wife and I are going to slip away from the Ball, go home,
drink a toast to one another, and to all of you and all of our
friends, and then return to the party. I hope you will understand
this little sentimental, uh, quirk, and I know you will when I tell
you that I happen to know that the night this present century was
born, my grandfather was with his family that night, all together,
with his father and mother and brothers and sisters, on a hard-
scrabble farm they had right in this county about fifteen miles
down-river." William Caldwell's name was thereupon withdrawn
and he nominated his good friend Isaac Schoffstal, who was
elected head usher. Edgar Martindale, who was not a Fort Penn
native but had married a Bordener, whispered to his brother-in-
law: "Can you beat it? Will Caldwell's family have a tradition that
they all get together every new century! People like you and me
are satisfied to get together every Thanksgiving, but not Will
Caldwell. Every *century*, that's the way traditions run in the Caldwell family. Jesus H. Christ!"

"Now, Edgar," said Scotty Bordener.

"Yes, I know. I'm being naughty. Furthermore, I understood
we were to have the Ball in the 1st Regiment Armory, but just
you watch the sentiment change in favor of the Schoffstal House.
I hope nobody drops a match on New Year's Eve. The Governor

and his staff and all the highbrows in Fort Penn'll go up in smoke in that fire-trap."

Will and Emily Caldwell slipped away from the Ball and arrived home at eleven-thirty. Grace was there, with Connie, one of the Martindale girls, Winfield Scott Bordener, Frederick William Klein, and Samuel Brock, a cousin of Grace's from Williamsport, visiting Fort Penn to show there were no hard feelings. The more or less homogeneous young people had sat down to a big and late dinner at half-past eight. From a little before ten until a little before eleven they had sung all the songs they knew that Grace and Scotty Bordener could play on the piano, and when the repertoires were exhausted they played kissing games. Grace and Fritz Klein had stayed out of the room the longest. Fritz, who was able to report on the way home that Grace Caldwell opened her mouth as soon as you kissed her, was having the time of his life when Connie knocked on the door of the hall closet and announced that Mr. and Mrs. Caldwell's carriage had just drawn up out front.

"Have you been having a nice time, everybody?" said Emily Caldwell.

"Yes, Mrs. Caldwell. Oh, yes. Fine time."

"Didn't seem to drink much punch, and the cookies," said Mrs. Caldwell.

"Well, if you'll all excuse me for just a minute—that's grape-juice, that punch? Emily?" said William Caldwell.

"Yes, dear."

"Well, I'll be back in just a moment."

"Are we going to have champagne, Mud?"

"I don't really know, but it wouldn't surprise me."

William Caldwell brought the champagne from the kitchen. "Here we are," he said. "I spoke to all your fathers and mothers and you have their permission to toast the new century. Sam, you're in the family, so I'll assume the responsibility for you."

"Oh, Father, you opened it out in the kitchen," said Grace. "I wanted to hear it."

"Well, I was thinking—might be a splash, get it all over some-body's dress. But I know. I can give this bottle to Julie and the others out in the kitchen, and we can open another bottle in here." He took the opened bottle back to the kitchen and re-turned with the unopened. He removed the cork with a satisfac-tory *pop!* and filled the glasses.

"This is a really great occasion," he said. He continued to talk while filling the glasses.

Off with the old, on with the new, but not, uh, not like any other New Year's any of us have ever seen before, from the oldest to the youngest. A lot of good things, the good things we enjoy, came out of the old century, but think of what we have to look forward to. There's war in the world, but thank God we're not in it. England has the greatest number of men under arms in the history of the Empire. I read that today at the Sentinel *office. They have to work Sundays, you know, to get out the Monday paper, to-morrow. Too bad the New Century couldn't have started on the first day of the week, isn't it? But we're at peace, and what's more, we're going to stay that way. Our wheat crop was over a half a billion bushels, and both the English and the Boers, the South Africans, both are trying to buy our wheat, and I think President McKinley will probably say, "Now you fellows, you stop this bloodshed or you can't have any of our wheat," and believe me, they need it.*

I don't think Bryan can cause any serious trouble in our country. I hope not. And you young people have no idea how much it's going to mean to the United States, this, uh, new Open Door policy in the Far East. Untold wealth. Untold. Wealth beyond the dreams of avarice. And here at home. Think of what they'll be able to do with electricity. In a few years I don't think we'll use gas for anything but cooking, and I must say I'll welcome that. The X-ray, they're working on that all the time, so that it won't be long before the doctors won't have to cut you open to see what's the matter with you.

There we are.

"Well, I make it—oh, yes, there go the whistles. Five minutes left of good old nineteenth century. Five minutes, the old cen-tury ticking away. Just a few minutes before Nineteen Hundred.

Come here, my dear, and hold my hand, the last few minutes of the century that brought us together, and all your fathers and mothers together. Boys and girls, I drink to you, the hope of the 1900's, and to our friends, your fathers and mothers."

"I have two minutes of, Sir," said Scotty Bordener.

"Not quite two," said William Caldwell. "Now! Now it's less than two."

"I have less than a minute!" said Samuel Brock.

"I think I'm right, Sam. You're a little fast. At midnight, the stroke of midnight, they're going to start ringing the chimes at our church."

"But what if their watches are fast or slow?" said Grace.

"Oh, no, Grace. I'm sure they'll be right on the dot," said William. *"There!"* He raised his glass high. "Happy New Century to you all." They all raised their glasses, and before he drank he bent forward and kissed his wife. "My girl," he whispered. He drank, and then he kissed Grace. "Our daughter Grace," he said. They all became teary-eyed at this unprecedented exhibition of William Caldwell's. "Now, I want to kiss you, Connie, the daughter of my best friend, and you too, Betty Martindale." He shook hands with the boys. "Auld Lang Syne," he said. "Grace will you officiate for us?"

Grace opened the songbook.

"Wait a second," said William Caldwell. He went out to the kitchen and called in the servants to join in the singing. "Happy New Century, Julie. Agnes. Mrs. Higgins. Neal. Hope the team don't run away in all this noise."

"They're standing nicely, Sir," said Higgins. "I'd a look at them."

"Well, then," said William Caldwell. "To you all."

"Thank you sir, ma'am," they said, and raised their glasses. "God bless you."

"About five minutes, Neal," said William. The servants left.

"Couldn't we have another bottle of champagne, Father?" said Grace. "I don't feel anything."

"I hope you don't feel anything, one glass," said William. "You don't take one glass of champagne to feel gay, it's the ceremony. The occasion, Grace."

"But I'd like to feel something. I'm nearly seventeen, after all."

"Emily?"

"Well, all right," said Emily Caldwell.

He opened another bottle and put it in the bucket. "Now we have to go back to *our* party," he said. "Good night to you all."

"And, girls, I don't like to remind you, but one o'clock I promised your mothers, no later. So Grace, your job is to send them home at one. And it's terribly cold out. I mean that now, Grace. Good night everybody."

"Good night, Mrs. Caldwell, Aunt Emily. Mr. Caldwell, Sir, Uncle Will."

For a few minutes after the Caldwells' departure no one said anything.

"I wouldn't be surprised if they had the sleighs out again to-morrow," said Sam Brock.

"I don't feel anything about the New Century," said Grace.

"Oh, I do," said Betty Bordener.

"What?" said Grace.

"I don't know, but something like a huge gate opening into an enormous valley."

"Pish and tush," said Grace. "That's not the way I feel. The noise and champagne, that's different, and people all dressed up. But otherwise it's just like any other Sunday."

"I never saw your father so—romantic," said Connie.

"Neither have I, but once in a hundred years." She suddenly got up and kissed each of the boys, saying "Happy New Century," as she did so. She watched the other girls as they imitated her impulse, and when they had done so she said, "Connie, you take Fritz, Betty, you take Sam, and I'll take Scotty."

"I don't think we ought to play any more kissing games," said Betty Martindale.

"Would you rather go home? You'll have to go soon anyway."

"No, but what if Julie walked in all of a sudden?"

"Somebody ought to be playing the piano," said Fritz.

"No, it's too late to play the piano," said Grace.

"Maybe I *better* go home," said Betty.

"Very well, suit yourself about that if you're afraid," said Grace.

"I am *not* afraid," said Betty. She took a step and put her arms around Sam and kissed him. "See?" she said.

"Connie, you and Fritz can go in the front room and we'll go in the library," said Grace.

She turned out the library lights and sat on the sofa and Scotty kissed her, and almost immediately she stretched out and made room for him to do likewise. "Do you want to do anything?" she said.

"What?"

"Besides kiss. If you do, go ahead."

He put his hand on her breasts and pressed them gently. "Like that," she said. She kissed him and put her hand at the back of his head and drew him down to her bosom. "I wish I could open it, but I can't."

"I can," he said. "The hooks and eyes?"

"Yes, but you couldn't hook them fast enough if anybody came."

"Well, all right."

"Don't get cross, Scotty. You can do other things."

"This?"

"That, yes, that. Oh, heaven. Oh, heaven, Scotty. Do you like to do that?"

"Love to, love to."

"Do you want me to do something to you?"

"Yes."

"The same thing? Like this?"

"Oh, Grace! Grace!"

"Do you want me to stop now?" she said.

"If you want to."

"All right, Scotty dear."

"Grace dear."

"If there's enough snow on the ground would you like to go for a sleigh-ride tomorrow?"

"Sure."

"I'll get the cutter. I'll tell Mother I'm going to take Connie but I won't, I'll take you. Third and Montgomery at ha' past three."

"What about Connie?"

"She won't mind. She doesn't like sleigh-riding anyway. I think you better go in the lavatory and see if your clothes are all right."

"They're all right."

"Then I guess it's time to go home."

"And then you'll do what we did, with Sam."

"No I won't."

"Did you with Fritz?"

"No. I only kissed him but I didn't like him."

"Why?"

"I didn't ask you what you did with Betty."

"Why didn't you like Fritz? You stayed out long enough."

"He wanted to, what we did, but I wouldn't let him. Not even my bosom. While he was trying to that was when I wanted you. Remember, I picked you. I didn't pick Fritz again. And I didn't ask Fritz to go sleigh-riding tomorrow. Will you be there?"

"I just hope you don't do this with every fellow."

"That's a nice thing to say to a person that likes you. You never heard of me even kissing a boy before. Did you?"

"No. But that's what makes it hard to understand."

"It just happened to me."

"Somebody else must have. Did they? Who? I'm not the first that ever did anything to you, you can't tell me that."

"Just because I know what happened to you? I've seen it happen to stallions. People are almost the same."

"I'll bet Charlie Jay did."

"He tried to kiss me when I was only fourteen and he was almost eighteen."

"He has a bad reputation."

"Then he deserves it. He thinks he's such a beautiful dancer but I won't ask him to my ball unless I have to. I don't care if I never saw him again in all my whole life. It must be one o'clock, Scotty. Will you be there tomorrow? Third and Montgomery?"

"All right."

"Kiss me again, Scotty."

"All right."

They joined Connie and Fritz, who were sitting in the bay window, with the window slightly raised while they shared a cigarette. Betty was sitting on Sam's lap in a hall chair. Grace and Scotty were the ones with the most convincingly innocent look.

Chapter 3

S idney and Grace, as has been noted, had been acquainted two and a half years before they became man and wife. In their later life together they often were given the opportunity to assert that they almost didn't get together at all. "I couldn't stand Sidney," Grace would say.

"Couldn't stand me, dear? Why, she didn't even know I was alive."

"Oh, I knew you were alive," she would say. "But I thought you thought me just a babe in arms, and I *pretended* I didn't know you were alive."

"When it came to pretending she was a corker," Sidney would say. "I beg your pardon, dear. One word Grace always objects to is corker."

"I don't know why, either, but I do."

"You must admit I hardly ever use the word any more."

This conversation, first spoken within six months of their marriage, was repeated at least annually all their life together— including the animadversion and contrition upon Sidney's use of the word corker.

Grace and Sidney followed not one but two of the standard plots which end at the altar. They almost never saw each other again after their first meeting, which is part of one of the standard plots; they almost did not meet at all, which is part of another standard arrangement. And as in all altar-bound plots, not excluding the one wherein the two principals grew up together from babyhood, the hand of fate could be seen, especially when attention was called to it as Grace and Sidney would do when it came *their* turn to tell how *they* happened to get together.

It is impossible to say where the hand of Fate began to intervene in any getting together of man and woman, but Sidney and Grace were in agreement that in their case it most likely was the day Sidney and Brock Caldwell arrived at Lawrenceville. That was as far back as Sidney and Grace cared to go. Sidney already had been at Lawrenceville for two years and was able to identify Brock as a new boy. Hazing was not a practice that came easily to Sidney, and the Form below his had been treated more kindly by Sidney than the Form above had treated him. However, he invoked the *droit de seigneur,* so to speak, when he saw that this new boy was carrying only one valise while he, Sidney, an old boy, was lugging two. "Say, you with the straw hat, give us a hand here."

"Go to hell," said Brock.

"Oh, is that so? Who *are* you, you unspeakable pisspot? What's your name and who do you think you're looking at in that tone of voice?"

"My name, if it's any your business, is Brock Caldwell, from Fort Penn, P-A, and you're the piss in the pisspot. Do you wanna fight?"

They fought, and though the actual fighting was ended in less than ten minutes, with Sidney unmistakably the winner, for two years at Lawrenceville Brock went out of his way to avoid speaking to Sidney. Sidney, who was the singles champion of the school, captain and shortstop of his House team, and a high-stand boy in his Form, joined with the rest of the school in giving Caldwell up as a bad job, and after Lawrenceville Sidney went to Yale, Brock to Princeton, and they had no further encounter until Christmas 1900.

Sidney had had a series of conversations with his father in the summer of that year, following his graduation from Yale. The final colloquy was as follows:

"Well, Father, I've turned it all over again in my mind."

" 'It' being your future plans."

"Yes, sir."

"And?"

"Well, first let me say, I did what you told me to do the last time we talked. I looked at it in the light of being fair to you, fair to Mama, and fair to myself."

"Please go on. I see you've prepared a stump-speech, or whatever you wish to call it, but go on, I'm game."

The father and the son laughed. "Yes, I did do a little work on this," said Sidney. "Without any false modesty, I'll put fairness to myself first. Because, as you said, or implied, if I weren't fair to myself, how could I be honestly fair to you and Mama."

"I didn't say quite that, dear boy. I never 've said anything like 'honestly fair.' Fair implies honestly. Go on."

"You're right. As usual. But, uh, well—I don't like business and I don't consider that I'm cut out to be a business man. Therefore, since that's my honest, well-considered opinion, I couldn't do an honest, *that is to say fair* job in business. I've done as you suggested. Looked about in other businesses and of course at New Haven I had ample opportunity to consider the various professions, and in this country of course we don't classify what a gentleman can do, such as Holy Orders, the Law, or Politics, the Army. Nobody'd ever think of making the Army a career unless he happened to be born into it."

"And you were not."

"And I was not," said Sidney. "No, the more I looked about, the more I was convinced of one thing about myself and my future, and that was, that I couldn't live cooped up in an office. Business office, doctor's office, lawyer's office or any other job that largely kept me indoors ... Now please don't say anything quite yet, Father. I know what you're thinking, and I've anticipated you. Perhaps you were going to say engineering. Well, it's true I know some fellows that are going in for engineering careers, building dams and blasting mountains and digging canals. Out of doors. Adventure. But there again, I like excitement, but the life of adventure doesn't appeal to me. At the proper time, the proper girl, I'd like to settle down and raise a family, have my own home, and so forth and so on. Just as you have. *And*—note the emphasis on the and—and I've decided I'd like to buy a farm."

The older man examined the long ash of his cigar. "I rather thought you'd come to that. It isn't so strange, you know. You're not far removed from the land. Your mother's father was a farmer and a prosperous one, and on our side of the family, why dear me, we've got sod on our boots down to this minute. My, yes. Textiles connote life in the country, if that's the word I mean. Connote. Yes, I'm sure it's a suitable word. And so what do you purpose doing next?"

"I'm going to start looking at farms, investigating. I have in mind some fellows that'd put me on to a good farm if they knew about one. Fellows I knew at New Haven."

"Yes. Of course you understand that a good farm is usually kept in the family, that's the reason it's a good farm, and you'll rarely find a good farmer letting go his farm if he can possibly avoid it. Your grandfather, Mr. Harmon, had no sons to come after him. That's why he sold."

"I've thought about that."

"And I hope my son, regardless of his reluctance to fit himself into the business world, I'm sure a son of mine—errrr-uh-hhh—well, you've heard of the warning, '*Caveat emptor.*' "

"Yes. But this may please you, Father. I don't plan to buy a big moneymaker, well established. I know you'll be generous, but I'm rather counting on finding a farm that *isn't* too successful, and therefore *isn't* too expensive, but has possibilities that *I* can develop."

"So far, so good. You have my blessing, and I have every confidence in you."

"Thank you, Father."

"Take as long as you like, and when you've found what you want we'll have another talk. The only advice I can offer: I believe land that's hilly can be bought more cheaply than flat lands, but without having been a farmer, it seems to me man and beast have enough to put up with without borrowing more trouble on land that's up and down, up and down. And my guess is hilly land is liable to be rocky land, and there's no profit in rocks."

"Have you ever wanted to be a farmer, Father?"

The older man chuckled. "Ho-ho! Me a farmer? . . . Yes, my son. All my life."

One of the fellows Sidney had in mind as likely to put him on to a good farm was Paul Reichelderfer, who lived in Lebanon, a town about twenty miles east of Fort Penn. Paul had been in Sidney's class at Yale. He was an amiable fat boy with a remarkable capacity for beer. He was so big that he had to go to a tailor for his clothes, but he did more than go to a tailor; he went to a good one. Like all fat men, he had to have money to eat, but he had more than enough for that; he was rich. Buried in the fat face was a thin handsome face, with a neat, rather sharp nose and small, alert blue eyes. He ate big, drank big, smoked big, and his frolics with women were prodigious, but at Yale he had not exceeded his capacity for activities of the table and the bed, and he was a social success. He was Phi Beta Kappa and Kappa Beta Phi, and the Phi Beta Kappa key confused strangers who belonged to Kappa Beta Phi as much as the Kappa Beta Phi key annoyed Phi Betes. In a gathering that was likely to be predominantly scholarly he would wear the drinking club's key, and he would wear the other key in a group of high-life men, and after enjoying their furtive examinations of the key he was wearing he would display the second. This was good for a laugh, and the loudest laugh always was Paul's.

He also had been tapped for Death's Head, the Yale senior society to which Sidney belonged. As part of his initiation into Death's Head a neophyte was required under oath to reveal any and all facts concerning his L. H., or Life History, and C. B., or Connubial Bliss. The life history part was not so embarrassing as details of connubial bliss. "C. B." was so called because in spite of the fact that most of the members of Death's Head were bachelors, now and then it would turn out that a neophyte was secretly married and it became necessary to hold a ceremony in which his wife was made a Death's Head wife. But married or not, the neophyte was compelled to tell the members of the society all they wanted to hear about his relations with women, and more than once it had happened that a man had had to admit to maximum intimacies with a girl whose brother or fiancé was present. The theory was that one Death's Head man could have no secret from another, and that the brotherhood existing among the members transcended all outside considerations. One Death's Head man was supposed to be able to rise above the fact that the girl he was going to marry had been sleeping with another Death's Head man.

Sidney Tate and Paul Reichelderfer had had to make no awkward confessions regarding sisters or fiancée. Sidney had neither sister nor fiancée at the time, and Paul's three sisters were older than he and inclined to be as corpulent. Sidney thus had no hesitation about writing to his friend for the kind of farm information he sought. Paul was delighted to hear from his brother in Death's Head. "You have come to the right man," he wrote Sidney. "I don't recall your ever asking me what business my father was in. Had you asked me, you would not now be hesitant concerning my knowledge of farm prices in this vicinity. My father is an attorney-at-law in the firm of Reichelderfer & Reichelderfer (my father is the one on the right, i.e., senior partner). He is also principal owner of the Lebanon Bank & Trust Company. Therefore, he makes it his business to be conversant with the values of farms in the county. He can tell you at the drop of a hat how much any farm is worth. If he does not hold the mortgage, he knows who does. He also makes it his business to have a speaking acquaintance with the individual farmers. He is the man to see . . . I suggest you visit us. Kill two birds with one stone. If you would honor us with your august presence during Christmas holidays you will be able to talk more to the farmers individually, as their work is done until Spring. They have more time on their hands. Also we can take in the dances, etc. Reading is closer, but Fort Penn is larger. The latter has prettier girls on all social strata."

Sidney considered the invitation and accepted it. A town in Pennsylvania offered a different kind of Christmas holiday from the New York kind. He told Paul Reichelderfer that he would arrive in Lebanon two days after Christmas.

The visit was unsuccessful in its principal purpose. Sidney learned the truth of his father's warning that a good farm usually stayed in the family. Paul's father drove him out to look at a few farms that would be on the market in five or ten years, when the owners could be expected to retire or die, but he too warned Sidney that he could not recommend purchase of any farm then up for sale. "The land is sour," said Mr. Reichelderfer, pronouncing it sahr. "You would lose too much making it good land. Sit still is best, young fellow, a year yet, two years yet, five years yet. One of those days I write you a letter, 'Dear Sidney, come quick, I have your farm for you.' "

The secondary purpose of the visit was fulfilled. Paul Reichelderfer was a host in any group or at anybody's party, and Sidney was made to feel that he was the visitor Pennsylvania had been discovered for. On the fifth of the six nights Sidney was the Reichelderfers' guest Paul gave him a chicken-and-waffle supper. Paul booked the dining-room of a farmers' hotel about ten miles north of Lebanon. Sixty young men and their ladies were invited. Some came in hay-wagons from which the wheels had been removed and four runners substituted. Some came in cutters, and sleighs with room for six. The men had a drink or two—no more—of straight rye whiskey while the ladies were getting their furs off. At dinner wine and beer were served, but this was an eating, not a drinking occasion. They began with oysters on the half shell, followed by thick chicken noodle soup, stewed chicken, mashed potatoes, candied sweet potatoes, string beans, lima beans, pickled beets, creamed carrots, squash, endive salad, apple pie, cream pie, shoofly pie, hot or cold mince pie, rhubarb pie, cocoanut cake, chocolate cake with vanilla icing, and angel food with chocolate icing. Also on the table were seven sweet and seven sour relishes, somersausage, bologna, liverwurst, and quill toothpicks, after-dinner mints, macaroons and spun-sugar kisses. The waffles were served with the chicken and it was not considered good form for a man to eat fewer than ten waffles, with chicken gravy or maple syrup. Sidney ate fourteen waffles, and Paul ate twenty. The ladies averaged five waffles. The party sat down at eight-thirty and got up from the table at eleven-fifteen. The ladies retired to the upper story and the men went to the bar for cigars and peach or cherry brandy. The men who were going to drive home took coffee; the others declined. Paul delighted the gentlemen with the longest and loudest breaking of wind, more or less a local tradition, and when the ladies rejoined the gentlemen in the dining-room, which had been cleared, the party listened to the piano, violin, and cello, and conversed politely, chiefly about what they had just eaten, until one young lady looked at her little watch on its fleur-de-lis pin and exclaimed, "Heavens! Ten to twelve! Mother'll lock me out, and then what'll I do?" It was suggested that someone—not the gentleman who had escorted her to the party—would have to marry her. On this high and risqué note the young people started for their conveyances and the cool, snuggly ride under the buffalo robes.

The other nights of Sidney's visit had been arranged for. The first night he dined with the Reichelderfer family ("We'll take care of that first," Paul had said). The second night he attended the Masonic Ball. The afternoon of the third day Paul and Sidney took a train to Reading and changed there for Gibbsville, a town to the north of Reading, where they put up at the Gibbsville Club and went to the Gibbsville Club ball. They slept until noon the next day, and having declined invitations of several Yale friends to stay on, they returned to Reading. "We got to have

one stag night in Reading. They're not expecting us home till tomorrow." They had dinner at a rathskeller and went to the bur-
lesque show, drank whiskey at a saloon near the theater, and
proceeded to a whore-house on South Fifth Street. "You ought
to get your wick dipped once while you're here, Sidney, and the
place I'm taking you to—safe as a nunnery. Only the biggest
business men, professional men, no small change goes to this
place. But anything you want. You want to be frenched. Two at a
time. A little dark meat. I come here regularly so I know them,
but they always have new talent too. This is as good as any place
in New York or Philadelphia. First person ever took me here was
my uncle, my freshman year."

"Do we spend the night?"

"Can, but I wouldn't like to be seen leaving here in the daylight. As a rule I get in about this time of the night and either I
leave before morning or stay till the next night. Tomorrow night
we're supposed to go to a hop at the Wiedemyers' so maybe we
ought to leave before daylight. Once I stayed here three days and
three nights at a stretch, but that was last summer when the parents were away."

For the fourth time in his life Sidney hired a woman. She was
young and pretty, the first girl brought in to him for inspection.
They had a large room containing an outsize double bed with a
canopy, a gas-lit crystal chandelier, gilt chairs and marble-
topped table, and mirrors in the wardrobe and hall doors. They
had champagne and cigarettes while she told her story, which he
believed: her father was a coal miner, who beat her, and her
mother sold her to the boarders. She ran away when she was fifteen, she was now eighteen. She stood up and unhooked her
evening gown and then drew it shut again, watching to see the
effect on him. She hung up his clothes in the wardrobe and lowered the gaslight burners and suddenly dropped her gown and
stood straight, with her legs close together, and hardly breathing
until he spoke to her. "Come here, Sonya," he said.

He had her quickly. "Now the next time will be better," she
said.

"There isn't going to be any next time," he said.

"Oh, don't say that."

"You'll get your money."

"I know, but I'm not thinking of money. Paul is paying, and I get the same if you have me once or all night. No, the next time we both enjoy it."

"No, let's have some champagne," he said.

"Your mouth is dry? All right. But not too much to drink. Don't go to sleep, don't get too drunk."

"Sonya, I'm through for the night."

"You want to bet me? I'll bet you a kiss."

"No betting."

"No, no betting. It's foolish to bet on things like that. But you will want me in a little while, Sidney, because I like you. Unless you put me out."

"No, stay right here."

"You'll let me stay here?"

"Sure."

"And talk to me?"

"Why not?"

"I'll get you a glass of champagne. Do you wish a cigarette?"

"Please," he said.

She pulled a sheet off the bed and wrapped herself in it. She poured champagne into two glasses and lit two cigarettes and put them in her mouth and carried the champagne to his side of the bed, holding her elbows close to her body so that the sheet would not fall.

"The only drink I like, champagne," she said.

"You have expensive tastes."

"Oh, yes. That's why I'm here. Here I will meet some elderly man or in his forties or like that, and what he will say, he will say, 'Sonya, I am taking you out of here and put you up in your own house, here, Philadelphia, New York City. Somewhere.' And he will do it, too. Why? Because I am young and pretty, not worn out. And because he likes me to beat him with a whip."

"You mean there is such a man?"

"Hundreds, thousands. You don't believe this. Sometimes in this place I have gone a whole week without—a young fellow. Young and strong, like you. I would go to bed with you for nothing. For pleasure."

"Really?"

"When I get this old man you can come to see me. I'll tell Paul where I am. Are you married?"

"No."

"I know you aren't in love with anybody, so you can come and see me and I won't charge you, because the old man will be giving me money."

"Well, thank you, Sonya."

"Maybe sooner than you think, too. I'll let Paul know where I am, see? And you can come all the time till you fall in love with a rich girl from your own class, and then I'll have to get another young man. With what you got, Sidney. Sweetheart. Honey."

It was daylight when Sidney and Paul reached the street again, better friends at least for the time being than the mumbo-jumbo of Death's Head had made them. They returned to Lebanon on an afternoon train and resumed their places in the polite society of Eastern Pennsylvania.

All week Paul had been telling Sidney that the sixth night of his visit to Pennsylvania would be the climax of the seasonal gaiety. Sidney had been given to understand that the Fort Penn affair was the big affair. The Gibbsville people had told him he was a fool not to stay over for their Assembly, and the Reading people swore by the Reading Assembly, but Sidney had noticed that in Gibbsville and in Reading the supporters of local festivity offered little resistance when he said he was booked up for the Fort Penn Assembly. In Gibbsville they said, "You're not going to give us the go-by in favor of Reading, are you?" In Reading they said, "You're surely not going to the Gibbsville Assembly." They had nothing to say against Fort Penn, but they most certainly had nothing to say in favor of it. He looked forward to Fort Penn.

At the last minute he almost did not go. "Our invitations fi-nally came," said Paul. "I'm on their list, but when I wrote in and asked for a card for my guest they wanted to know all about who you were and what et cetera."

"What did you tell them?"

"I told them you were a high muckamuck in New York soci-ety, and I guess probably they wondered what the devil you were doing visiting me in Lebanon. But I told them you were here on business, in case they were wondering, and I mentioned a couple of the fellows at New Haven that live in Fort Penn."

"Who? Do I know them?"

"Oh, sure. Les Poffenberger. Joe Cunningham. Jack Stephens. Emlen Deatrick. George Wall. They were all in our class."

"Yes, I know them all. I didn't realize they were all from Fort Penn."

"Uh-huh. Radcliff Dickinson too, but I didn't mention his name."

"Glad you didn't. Was he from Fort Penn?"

"He's from Fort Penn all right. They know about him there, too. La de da. But anyway, everything's fine and dandy. I got the cards today from Brock Caldwell."

"Who did you say?"

"Brock Caldwell. Do you know him, Sidney?"

"It must be the same chap. Did he go to Lawrenceville?"

"Yes he did."

"It's the same fellow. No wonder there was a delay. Mr. Cald-well and I don't see eye to eye. On anything. I gave him a thrash-ing the first day he arrived at Lawrenceville and he never forgave me. We never spoke again, for two years. And I haven't seen him since."

"Holy smoke! I wish I'd known that, Sidney. You're going to see a lot of him the next twenty-four hours. We're spending the night at his house."

"Oh, we couldn't do that, Paul. The trip's off, as far as I'm con-cerned," said Sidney. "But you go, of course."

Paul's face had become all fat, none of the sharpness was there. He seemed about to puff or pout. Then suddenly he was alive again. "No, by George. Brock's supposed to be a gentleman, and he wrote this note. Here, take a look."

Dear Paul—

I trust you will pardon the delay in sending the enclosed cards. I was responsible for the delay, owing to my being out of town when the Committee forwarded your application for a guest card. I believe I attended Lawrenceville with Mr. Tate. You will both be our guests overnight as it is impossible to secure suitable hotel accommodations. My mother said she will be delighted to have you. You are also welcome to remain longer if convenient. Please let me know by Postal Telegraph whether you can stay with us, but I assure you that you and your guest are more than welcome. Thanking you in advance for your overlooking the delay, I remain,

Sincerely yours,
Brock Caldwell

"Well, I'll be damned," said Sidney.

"Why?"

"Well, you don't realize. He was an insufferable horse-cock at school. I told him so. 'You're a horse-cock yourself,' he said, and away we went. He was game, but I was in training and I suppose he wasn't. For two years we never spoke. And then, out of the blue sky comes this. I'd say he came off very well. I didn't consider him such-a-much, but you never know from where you sit where the man in the gallery's going to spit."

"He's probably changed an awful lot since you knew him. I know him to say hello to. My father knows his father. The Caldwells are the Stuyvesant Fishes or Astors, the Fort Penn *crème de la crème*. I don't know whether they're the wealthiest, but when it comes to exclusive and all that—one family. The Caldwells. The Schoffstals they generally consider the wealthiest, but the Schoffstals ape the Caldwells in every way, shape, and form.

They say the Schoffstals won't take a leak unless they get permission from the Caldwells."

"Come to think of it, I called him a piss-pot, not a horse-cock. But all this puts another light on the situation, Paul. You see what he's doing? Apparently he's the crown prince, heir apparent, in Fort Penn. Splendid opportunity to put me in my place. Have you sent the telegraph message?"

"Yes."

"Good. I'd like to see how Mr. Brock Caldwell handles the situation, meaning me."

"They'll treat you like a prince. They're fine people," said Paul. "Mr. and Mrs. Caldwell are the genuine article, a real dyed-in-the-wool couple. Lady and gentleman."

A colored man was carrying their valises down the steps of the Nesquehela, Fort Penn & Lebanon depot when they saw Brock, who was getting out of a sleigh. Brock directed the colored man and hurried to Paul and Sidney. "Our railroad's getting punctual for a change," said Brock. "How are you, Paul? How are you, Tate? I haven't seen you in years. Very glad you could come. Did you know each other at Yale? I guess that's a question with an obvious answer."

"You're very kind, Caldwell, putting us up and so forth and so on."

"A pleasure to do so, Tate. I have a sleigh here. I'll sit up front with our man, and point out the places of interest, ha ha. Not many, are there, Paul? I take it this is your first visit to Fort Penn, Tate."

"First time in Pennsylvania, outside of Philadelphia."

"Everybody says Fort Penn's got a great future, but I just hope it isn't going to be another Pittsburgh. Now then, you two in the back. Paul takes up a little room. Boy, put two of the valises in the back and we can accommodate two up here, can't we Neal? This looks as though you fellows were going to stay a while."

"No, three of the valises belong to Sidney. He's going back to New York from here, tomorrow. How're Mr. and Mrs. Caldwell?"

"Both in excellent health, thanks."

"And your sister?"

"Grace? Growing up too fast, if you ask me. Sixteen, and disappointed she wasn't allowed to go to the ball tonight. Sixteen, mind you. Next Christmas she's going to have her own shindig and I'm against it, but Mother and Father weakened. She'll be eighteen a few months after next Christmas, and she's persuaded them. She's tall but she's only a child. Just a kid. A kid."

The three young men had separate rooms and shared Brock's bathroom. They freshened up and by the time they went downstairs to meet Mrs. Caldwell a maid was drawing the shades on the library windows.

"It gets dark so quickly," said Mrs. Caldwell. "When Brock left for the station it was still daylight. Gloomy day, but it wasn't dark."

"Fire feels good, Mrs. Caldwell."

"Yes, I like a fire. I suppose it's the older you get, but I light a fire sometimes in July, at the farm. Any excuse. Dampness. A cool turn in the weather. I'm very fond of a nice fire in the fireplace."

"So am I," said Paul.

"I'd rather have it in the fireplace than in the bookshelf," said Brock.

"Oh, Brock, now you stop treating your mother like an idiot," said Mrs. Caldwell. "He's been teasing me all day. The most awful things, I'm afraid to look at you, Mr. Tate. Paul's an old friend but Brock's been accusing me of wanting to flirt with you, all day, before you got here. Flirting, at my age! Or any age!"

"I hope you do flirt a little, Mrs. Caldwell. I'll flirt right back."

"Oh, now. And poor Grace. I'll be surprised if she shows her face in this room or at meals or anything, Brock's been teasing her so. If *she* dares look at you Brock's *bound* to accuse her of flirting."

"Nonsense," said Brock. "Would you like to smoke a cigarette, Tate? Paul? I have Richmond Straight Cuts, if you like them."

"It's all right," said Mrs. Caldwell. "I like the smell of cigarettes and cigars. I like pipes too, while they're going, but ugh. Lying on a table or mantel. Ugh."

"I'll be sure to keep mine in my valise," said Sidney.

"By the way, your dress suits are being pressed. Paul, I told the maid to lay yours out on the bed where there'd be more room, but yours'll be hanging in the wardrobe, Tate."

"Oh, now, Brock, Paul isn't as big as all that and I think it's rude to tease a guest, and I wish you wouldn't call Mr. Tate by his last name. If he isn't Sidney, he's Mister Tate. While he's with us I'm going to call him Sidney."

"I thank you, and I feel welcome, Mrs. Caldwell," said Sidney.

"Now that's a graceful speech. Sidney," she said. "We're going to have tea and sandwiches in a few minutes when Mr. Caldwell gets home, because you're dining quite late. Unless you'd rather have something now, Sidney? Paul?"

"Oh, no thanks, Mrs. Caldwell. You know me, I can always raise havoc with food, but I think I can stave off the pangs of hunger till Mr. Caldwell gets here."

They heard the front door and vestibule door close.

"There," said Mrs. Caldwell. "There he is now. You see you get your reward for being polite . . . Oh, no. It isn't Mr. Caldwell. Come in, Grace."

"I'll be right down," said Grace, from the hall. She did not look in and they saw her only briefly, darting past the library door.

"She'll be right down," said Mrs. Caldwell. "Ring for Ella, Brock, please. We'll reward Paul and Sidney anyway."

Tea was served, and water-cress sandwiches and little cakes. The three young men had had second cups of tea and had lighted cigarettes before Grace Caldwell made her first proper appearance. She did not curtsey when she was introduced. She knew Paul slightly. She stood behind her mother's chair. "Why don't you sit down, dear?" said her mother.

"I'm comfortable standing."

The young men sat down.

The chairs and the people in them were grouped in the center of the library, a room that nearly always needed artificial light from lamps or fireplace. As Grace stood behind her mother's chair she was out of the light of the single lamp and the blazing fire, but what Sidney saw he admired. Her skin was healthy and clear. Without previous information it would have been difficult to guess her age accurately; the length of her dress was a length that was being worn by girls in their twenties. Her bosom and hips were as mature as Sonya's, whom he suddenly thought of and as suddenly tried to banish from his mind. He watched her while the conversation went on. She hardly looked at anyone; she gazed into the fire. She would breathe regularly through her nose, then every few minutes she would part her lips and moisten them with the tip of her tongue. He was convinced that she was trying to act bored, and being helped along in her act by the fact that the same reticence which in an older, sophisticated girl meant boredom, could also mean, in a girl of sixteen, no more than good upbringing; respect for her elders, not speaking until spoken to. But Sidney knew that she wanted him to think she was bored.

"I'm sorry *Miss* Caldwell isn't going to be with us this evening," he said. He was indeed sorry, but he felt certain the remark would deflate her.

"Well, time enough for Grace next year," said her mother.

"Time enough the year after next, if you ask me," said Brock.

"*Did* anyone ask you?" said Grace.

"Children—"

"*Children?*" said Brock. "Now really, Mother."

"Children if you behave like children. When you tease Grace, especially in front of company, you put yourself on the same basis as Grace, I don't care how old you are."

"Rats," said Brock.

"Have you any brothers or sisters, Sidney?"

"No, ma'am, I'm the only child."

"Lucky you," said Brock.

"Well, I don't know, uh, Brock. I often wish I'd had a brother or a sister."

"A younger sister'd be all right I guess," said Paul.

"Oh, now, Paul," said Mrs. Caldwell. "You're spoiled. I happen to know, your nice sisters spoil you."

Paul laughed. "No, ma'am, I never noticed it."

"Oh, now, you know they do," said Mrs. Caldwell.

The conversation was getting away from Sidney's intent, which was to talk across the others to Grace. He lost interest, and so did she. She frowned at the fire and said no more until her father came in. The tea things had been removed before he arrived; apparently it was not his custom to take tea. He was jovial and affectionate, kissed his wife and daughter; but after acknowledging the introductions he looked at his hunting-case watch long enough to have read all the numerals and then looked at his wife.

"Yes, dear," she said.

"I'm very sorry, Paul, Mr. Tate, but Mrs. Caldwell and I have to be changing. In fact, if we left now, as we are, we'd be no more than punctual. As it is—you'll excuse us, Mr. Tate? Paul? And of course we'll see you at lunch tomorrow. I'd ask you to have lunch with me at the Fort Penn Club, but they don't serve breakfast after nine-thirty, and, uh, well, this past week I expect we've served breakfast here, at the Caldwell Club, as late as four o'clock in the afternoon, isn't that so, Brock?"

"One afternoon it was half past five, if anybody doesn't get the point. Yes, I had breakfast at half past five the other day."

"Well, gentlemen, you're invited to lunch with me, but only if—no, that's foolish. I withdraw my invitation. If you felt like getting up in time for lunch that could only mean you'd had an uninteresting time at your party. Hope I'll see you all tomorrow afternoon."

"Not me, I'm afraid, sir," said Sidney. "I'm taking an afternoon train back to New York."

"Oh, no. Why—in and out like that? Not giving us a chance to see something of you? Well, now, that's a pity. Brock, you see if you can't persuade your old schoolmate to—Grace, you try."

"I think you're very kind to have me at all, sir. You and Mrs. Caldwell. And Brock."

"Well, I'll have to leave it up to my son and daughter, because my wife and I have to scurry, but I hope you change your mind. Good night."

Mr. and Mrs. Caldwell left and Grace said, "I'll say good night, too. Good night, Paul. Good night, Mr. Tate. Good night, Brother dear."

Back in New York the next night Sidney removed the gloves from the tail-pocket of his dress suit and the white tasseled dance programme from his waistcoat pocket. He examined the gloves and decided they needed to be cleaned; he examined the programme, and tossed it in his waste-basket. None of the names meant anything to him, not even Caldwell, since it signified only the easily forgettable young lady whom Brock Caldwell had escorted to the ball.

He wrote and rewrote his bread-and-butter letter to Paul's mother and another thank-you letter to Paul's father and another to Paul. He wanted to be sure that he left a good impression because through them he might be able to see the Caldwells again. He was even more careful with his letter to Mrs. Caldwell:

Dear Mrs. Caldwell:—

    Despite my groping for the proper words, I find I cannot tell you how much I appreciate your kindness to me, the stranger whom you took into your home for the (to me) all too brief tenure of my visit. Suffice it to say I look back upon my stay at your home as the high point of my visit to Fort Penn and thanks to the warmth of your hospitality I hope I may count myself on your approved list of friends should you contemplate a visit to New York in, let us hope, the near future.

                               Very sincerely yours,

He had stopped at a florist's on the way to the train in Fort Penn and sent a basket of whatever the florist selected for Mrs. Caldwell, five dollars' worth, but he wanted the letter to be eloquent, and he was rather proud of it. The whole point of it was to suggest with emphasis that he would like to be on the list when the Caldwells were issuing invitations to Grace's ball, and he considered he had done that rather well. He also had not been above failing to pack his silver-backed military hair brushes, which were unmistakably engraved S. T.

His bread-and-butter letter was opened at breakfast, in the presence of the addressee, her husband, her son, and her daughter.

MRS. CALDWELL: "A charming note from Sidney. Sidney Tate."

WILLIAM CALDWELL: "Is that so? Read it."

BROCK CALDWELL: "I could tell you what's in it without even reading it. He enjoyed Fort Penn, but most of all he enjoyed staying here with the charming Caldwell family."

MRS. CALDWELL: "He does say it was the high point of his visit."

BROCK: "Naturally, naturally. Lord knows he was rude enough at the ball."

EMILY CALDWELL: "Rude, Brock? How rude? I don't think it's in him to be rude."

WILLIAM CALDWELL: "I don't either. I didn't see much of him, but he impressed me as a young man of impeccable manners, impeccable."

BROCK: "Oh, he's too smart to spit on the floor—"

MRS. CALDWELL: "Please, you're at the table."

WILLIAM CALDWELL: "Yes, you could profit by his manners."

BROCK: "Exactly what he hopes to do. Profit by them. His manners are as insincere as they come, as insincere as the man himself."

MRS. CALDWELL: "You haven't said how he was rude."

BROCK: "His manner. Not his manners. His manner. There's a way of doing all the proper things that's just as bad as if you picked your teeth with the oyster fork. Haughty. He made no effort to be cordial or considerate. He bored the deuce out of all the girls. Made no effort at conversation. He was a New York boor, that's what he was. Trying to put on the dog for the benefit of the country yokels."

WILLIAM CALDWELL: "I got no such impression of the young man. He had good manners, and he seemed to me sincerely, genuinely respectful."

MRS. CALDWELL: "He tried to bring Grace into the conversation that afternoon. What did you think, Grace?"

BROCK: "Oh, why ask Grace?"

WILLIAM CALDWELL: "Because your mother might like to know what Grace thought."

MRS. CALDWELL: "Exactly."

GRACE: "If he bored the girls at the ball, maybe they bored him."

WILLIAM CALDWELL: "A very good answer."

MRS. CALDWELL: "Yes, it is."

BROCK: "What you'd expect from Grace. Grace, next year's *femme fatale*. Oh, Grace's going to show Fort Penn, all right all right."

GRACE: "I think you're just jealous because I'm having a ball and boys can't have balls."

BROCK: "What!"

WILLIAM CALDWELL: *"Brock!"*

MRS. CALDWELL: "Grace, you'll be late for school. Hurry on, dear. Oh, that's right. No school today."

WILLIAM CALDWELL: "I have to get along, too. I'll speak to you later, young man."

BROCK: "If you like, but I'd like to get this straight once and for all, who is this Tate? I never knew anything about him. I think he was a climber at Lawrenceville, sticking his nose into everything, busy as a bee all over the place. And may I ask who brought him here? We all know Paul Reichelderfer's father and mother can hardly speak English and I could tell you things about Paul that wouldn't make him welcome in this house. And may I ask, if he's anybody—I mean Tate—why would he want to spend Christmas in Lebanon? If you ask me, he wasn't invited anywhere in New York. I'm very suspicious of New York people that show up here at Christmas-time, and Lebanon!"

MRS. CALDWELL: "He wants to buy a farm. Paul told me. He's been looking at farms near Lebanon."

BROCK: "But did he buy one?"

MRS. CALDWELL: "I'm sure I don't know, but George Wall and Leslie Poffenberger spoke very highly of Sidney."

BROCK: "What did you expect them to do? Dear old Yale boys."

WILLIAM CALDWELL: "Yes, and they all *finished* Yale, too."

Breakfast adjourned at that point, without Mrs. Caldwell's having read Sidney's letter to her family. Later in the day, however, Grace reminded her mother of that fact. "I'd like to read Mr. Tate's letter," said Grace.

"Very well. It's on my desk." Emily Caldwell did not look up from her sewing.

"He has a nice handwriting," said Grace.

"Yes, I thought so too. Strong, I'd say. I don't know whether that means anything, but sometimes I s'pose it does."

"I didn't like *him* very much."

"Didn't you, Grace? Why?"

"I couldn't say, but it's a nice letter. Did *you* talk to him about buying a farm?"

"No. Paul told me."

"He didn't look like anybody that'd want to own a farm."

"Why? You only saw him in city clothes. Dress suit."

"That's true."

"Don't judge a book by its cover, Grace."

"No."

"You know, nobody looking at you would say there's a girl that loves the farm."

"Why wouldn't they, Mother?"

"You're too pretty."

"Am I?"

"Oh, yes, you know it. No fishing."

"No, but that's the first time you ever told me in so many words I was pretty," said Grace.

"The next letter from Sidney I won't mention at the breakfast table."

"The next letter?"

"Naturally he'll write again to thank us for sending him his hair brushes. He forgot his hair brushes. Forgot? No, he left them, but he didn't forget them ... Have you done any more about your invitation list for next year?"

"Why?"

"We could easily find out Sidney's address, just by looking at his stationery. How convenient!"

"Oh, Mother, *you're* teasing me."

"Well, I'll copy it down and put it in my book so we'll have it."

"But I said I didn't like him."

"All right, if you feel the same way next Christmas we won't invite him."

At her mother's direction Grace wrote a note to Sidney:

Dear Mr. Tate:—

Mother has asked me to tell you that we found your hair brushes in the room you occupied. We have packed them and they have been sent to you by Adams Express. They should reach you in a few days. If not, please notify us and a "tracer" will be put on them as they are insured. If they are not found after a reasonable length of time Mother will try to duplicate them at the local jewelry store and send the new brushes to you. With best wishes from Mother and myself, I remain,

Yours sincerely,
Grace Caldwell

The next item in this correspondence was dated January 31, 1901, and was written on the stationery of Almond's Hotel, Clifford Street, London.

Dear Mrs. Caldwell:

I have just received a letter from my Mother in which she mentioned that a parcel containing my hair brushes had been forwarded by Adams Express. Please forgive me the delay in answering but as you see I am in England and Mother's letter only just reached me.

I must apologize for my forgetfulness and the inconvenience it must have caused you; but I confess that I was also secretly delighted to have a note from the charming Miss Grace Caldwell, in which she, as your amanuensis, told me of your thoughtfulness in forwarding the hair brushes. Selfishly, I am delighted that while the hair brushes may have been a nuisance to you, they afford me the opportunity to keep alive our acquaintance by letter.

I have been in England for slightly over two weeks. My trip was a sudden one. I don't think I told you that I am English on my father's side. In fact, he has never become an American citizen, although I, of course, am a citizen by birth. My mother, I hasten to add, is American to the core, having descended from a long line of New York and "York State" people. My father invariably replies, when asked why he has not become an American citizen, "Who could be more American than I?" But he will not give in on the subject of citizenship. It has always been in the back of his mind to have me go to Oxford. Therefore, when I finished at Yale he dropped hints here and there about my going to Oxford, but I was interested in farming (the reason I visited Paul Reichelderfer was to look at some Pennsylvania properties, and thus I became acquainted with the delightful Caldwell family). When I discovered that there was nothing suitable available at the moment I returned to New York and acceded to my father's suggestion that I might at least have a look at Oxford. I therefore have been "having a look," but I very much fear that I am too American for that institution, or, perhaps, to be truthful, smugly satisfied with the amount of education I have had. At any rate, I do not intend to matriculate at Oxford. On the contrary, after a visit to cousins whom I am seeing for the first time, I intend to visit France and Italy, after which I shall return home in order to resume my quest for a farm. I expect to be home shortly before Easter, whenever that is this year; and at this time I should like to repeat my invitation to you and any and all members of your family to stop with us when next you visit New York. Our house is too large for so small a family, and there is more than ample room for our guests. You would be free to come and go as you pleased.

Thanking you again for your kindnesses in the past, I beg to remain,

Yours sincerely,

Sidney Tate.

In her wisdom Emily Caldwell deemed it inexpedient to encourage further correspondence at that time. She saw, or thought she saw Sidney as an inevitable and desirable suitor of Grace's, but she was beginning to look at every young man with Grace's future in her mind, and Sidney was merely the pick of the lot at the moment, and he was the pick chiefly because of Emily's accidental discovery that he wanted to live on a farm. Grace was going to be a beauty and she would attract young men, inspire love, and would unquestionably love in return. If, indeed, she did not love first. When love came to Grace the object of her affection might be a young man who cared nothing for the country life, and Grace might easily abandon a way of life for life itself. Sidney was a good-looking young man with exquisite manners who made an effort to get along well with people, which implied patience and tolerance and active consideration for the rights of others and some intuitive—intuitive because he was so young—knowledge of human frailty. Emily knew her daughter to be a girl who would make demands on these attributes of Sidney's. Grace was difficult now, inclined to be lacking in respect where respect was indicated if not due; she was introspective, and she was often imperious. Emily Caldwell gave thought to the imperiousness, which she blamed partly on the obsequiousness of Connie Schoffstal, but if it hadn't been Connie Schoffstal it would be someone else, and so Emily Caldwell did nothing to supplant Connie with a girl of sturdier, more independent character. Moreover, Emily believed in imperiousness-within-limits for her daughter, the girl in that position. It was the exercise of a right which Emily believed in. There was no girl better in Fort Penn; there was no girl quite so good. The facts, as Emily saw them, were that Grace was a Caldwell and a Brock, the best blood in Fort Penn, families who by custom got things without even asking for them, because the people of Fort Penn acknowledged some kind of superiority. The Schoffstals had more money, it was true; the Walls and the Martindales had Newport connections; but the subtle difference in business and in the social life of Fort Penn was that people came to the Caldwells, while the Caldwells went to nobody. They did just about as they pleased.

It was painfully plain to Emily Caldwell that her son was not going to continue that kind of domination. He had a special strength of his own, which was not going to take the form of rebellion, as it might have done if he had possessed a solid talent for one of the arts or even for dissipation; but he already seemed to have determined to lead his own useless life in the way he chose, and in Fort Penn that took a perverse courage. Grace, on the other hand, had announced *her* position, and that was to live in Fort Penn, particularly to live on the farm, and without being aware of any implication, to dominate Fort Penn from there. A husband would be needed to complete that plan, and he would have to be selected (if the plan were to be followed, and it seemed increasingly desirable as Emily reconsidered it) for his qualifications as consort and stallion; a man who would have sense enough to know that he was the gainer in this world's goods, but not so much the gainer that he would gradually lose his self-respect.

As of that Spring of 1901 Emily Caldwell was content with the status quo, having accepted the compromise that placed her daughter rather than her son in succession as eventual ruler of Fort Penn. The girl had outgrown two typical "crushes"; one on Charlie Jay, whom Emily recognized as a boy who might have been difficult to deal with in a more serious love affair; the other on Scotty Bordener, who Emily foresaw would grow into too dull a man to keep Grace out of the divorce courts after the dullnesses of marriage set in. With Charlie and Scotty, two innocuous experiences, gone and forgotten, the girl could be expected to have another fairly soon, and Emily Caldwell was prepared to have to deal with a more romantic experience next time, but all well and good. If the young man filled the bill, Grace could announce her engagement and marry him in a year. If he was not eligible, there were ways to delay an announcement, then to delay the marriage, and if the undesirable romance persisted, Europe was a long way off. Emily had no objection to a comparatively early marriage for Grace. It was not then the Fort Penn custom to marry at eighteen or nineteen, but Emily believed in setting Fort Penn customs, not in being bound by them.

Meanwhile the pick of the lot was behaving in a manner that Emily could not have improved upon if she had given the orders. He was in Europe, presumably testing his infatuation for the young Caldwell girl, and, Emily hoped, sowing some wild oats. Emily was satisfied that Sidney had had experiences with women, and she was not going to hold it against him if in France and Italy he had some more. Her own first nights with her husband had been trying, to say the least, and as a candidate for marriage with Grace it behooved Sidney to know all there was to know. In her own case Emily's total ignorance and William's lack of experience had not turned out badly. They learned together, and they had love on their side. Emily was dubious about the extent of her daughter's patience. She had no doubt that Grace would go to the marriage bed as ignorant as she herself had been, but having learned the pleasures of passion, and suspecting the depth of it in Grace, Emily was fearful of the effects on Grace's marriage of unsatisfactory intimate relations. Emily hated to admit it (and she discussed it with no one, not even her husband), but she could easily imagine Grace in bed and naked and duplicating her own discoveries and inventions, but only if the young man were helpful. One never talked about these things, but somehow one heard of the disasters in the lives of one's friends: the pregnant virgins, the young wives who did only what their husbands told them to do, the girls who married men who did not like woman at all, and the wives of rapists. None of these things must happen to Grace. Grace must be perfectly married, to a man who would be a companion, a source of entertainment, and a true partner right up to their climaxes in bed, right up to the delivery of their children. Emily, who was not without humor, wryly admitted that she had no positive way of examining the candidates without going to bed with them herself, and putting aside the fact that no hand but William's ever had been under her dress, it was too late in the day for any of that sort of thing. But it amused her—and she knew it was wicked—to hand a young man a cup of tea and, as he took it, to search his countenance for indications of the directions he would go if passionately aroused by her pretty young daughter. The only conclusions she came to were that if she were a girl again she would not welcome the advances of young men with cherubic faces (she suspected they were cruel); men with remarkably small noses (she invented a theory that they were remarkably small elsewhere); men whose fingernails were too long (they would scratch); and men who laughed at everything and anything (they probably were hiding something). Sidney Tate's nose was not large but it was not remarkably small, and he had a high-cheek-boned English look about him that was anything but cherubic. She believed that if he were to hold up his hand, palm facing the viewer, his nails would not extend higher than the tips of his fingers. And when he laughed it was the minutest fraction of a second slow in coming and the joke or the situation had earned the laughter. And then finally, although the two men looked not a bit alike, she conceded that Will Caldwell matched Sidney's score on these items. "Well," she thought, "if Grace gets as good a man as Will, she'll be fortunate. And that, after all, is what I want for her."

All she wanted for herself out of this concern for Grace was to know that her daughter (and, ex officio, her daughter's husband) would occupy the undefined but understood position in Fort Penn that William and Emily Caldwell had held just for her. . . .

Shortly after Easter a parcel addressed to Emily arrived. It contained two identical small ivory fans in their original boxes from Charpentier et Cie., Paris. One box contained Sidney's calling card, with nothing written on it; in the other box the card was written on, in Sidney's neat, strong hand: "Please do not think me forward. Saw these at Charpentier's. Tho't of Madame & Mademoiselle and bought them instantly. S. T."

Now this, Emily told herself, was a worthy young man. He wanted to keep their memory of him alive, so he bought an irresistible, expensive, but simple present, one for the mother, one for the daughter. The present was just right; to send it back would be ceremoniously ingracious; to keep it was to contract to write thank-you notes. The notes would have to express the polite hope that Emily and Grace would see him at some indefinite date; whereupon it was up to this tactful young man to present himself, if only accidentally, where he could be seen and more important, where he could see. He could see Grace again; that was what he wanted; if she was as lovely, as attractive as he remembered her, he would conspire with Paul Reichelderfer and Fort Penn friends in order that he might see her again. If—and Emily well in advance had her doubts about this—Grace no longer appealed to him, he could go his way, to South Africa to fight for the Boers, for all Emily cared, and all he would have lost would be the price of two irresistible ivory fans.

"*Dear Sidney:*—

The exquisite fans, as you must have known, defied my better judgment which urged me to return them with thanks. It was kind of you to remember us when you were so many miles away. My impulse to return the fans was weakened by my realization that my daughter Grace is no longer the child we have been thinking her, as after all she is "coming out" next winter, and I trust that you will still be in quest of a farm so that the holidays once again will find you in our midst and that you can be present on that occasion. But pray do not hold off visiting us until then. The "latch string" is always out for you at our house . . .

Emily Brock Caldwell

Dear Mr. Tate:

I wish to express my sincere thanks for the beautiful ivory fan which you so kindly purchased in Paris. It is an excellent specimen of the fine workmanship one expects of the French artisans and I am already the envy of the few close friends whom I have permitted to see it.

To say that I was pleased would be to put it mildly and words fail me in my efforts to convey my appreciation. Hoping that we will have the pleasure of another visit from you soon, I remain,

Sincerely yours,
Grace Caldwell

A conversation between Grace and Connie Schoffstal, which took place in the summerhouse at the farm, late in June 1901:

CONNIE: "Where did you get that?"

GRACE: "Get what? *Oh*, this *fan?*"

CONNIE: "Yes."

GRACE: "Didn't I ever show this to you before?"

CONNIE: "Of course you didn't. You know you didn't."

GRACE: "I don't any such thing, know I didn't. You know, Connie, I don't show you everything."

CONNIE: "Nearly."

GRACE: "I beg to differ with you. I have presents I *never* showed you. I'm sure I have lots of things you never saw."

CONNIE: "Aw, what, for instance?"

GRACE: "Well, dear me, you can't expect me to rattle off a list of presents that I got last Christmas or when I was in Cape May."

CONNIE: "I don't remember you getting any presents in Cape May."

GRACE: "Well, I did though, whether you remember it or not. Maybe I didn't happen to show them to you."

CONNIE: "What, for instance?"

GRACE: "There you go again, what for instance. I can't remember almost a year ago what presents I got."

CONNIE: "Well, what *one* present did you get then?"

GRACE: "Well, for instance, did you notice on my straw hat, a striped hatband? Blue and white?"

CONNIE: "No, or maybe I did. What's a hatband? Anybody can have a hatband."

GRACE: "Oh, is that so? Well, if you're so smart, then perhaps you know all about what the hatband stood for."

CONNIE: "What?"

GRACE: "If you think you know everything, Connie, what's the use of my telling you?"

CONNIE: "I don't say I know everything."

GRACE: "But you act as if you do."

CONNIE: "What's special about the hatband?"

GRACE: "Did you ever hear of Delta Phi?"

CONNIE: "What is it, some fraternity?"

GRACE: "It's the best fraternity at the University of Pennsylvania. Everybody says it's the best."

CONNIE: "I never heard anybody say it. I never even heard the name mentioned before."

GRACE: "I'm not talking about you."

CONNIE: "Well, I'm somebody, and I never heard of it."

GRACE: "Oh, well, let's not talk about it then. I wouldn't *think* of *boring* Lady Vere de Vere. But personally if I never heard of Delta Phi I'd never display my ignorance."

CONNIE: "How could you if you never heard of it? If you never heard of it you wouldn't bring it up. And if somebody else brought it up how could you talk about it if you never heard of it? If I don't know anything about Phi Delta—"

GRACE: "Delta Phi."

CONNIE: "I don't care if it's Alpha Ipsa I Eta Pi, I never heard of it, so why should I let on I did?"

GRACE: "Oh, dear."

Grace languidly fanned herself and in so doing re-aroused Connie's curiosity.

CONNIE: "You never did tell me where you got the fan."

GRACE: "I beg your pardon?"

CONNIE: "Oh, you heard what I said."

GRACE: "But truly I didn't, Connie. I was a thousand miles away."

CONNIE: "I asked you where you got the fan."

GRACE: "It was a present, I think I told you."

CONNIE: "I know but who from?"

GRACE: "Who from? *Not* the same person that gave me the *Delta Phi hatband.*"

CONNIE: "Oh, is *that* what the hatband was? Fraternity colors. I thought you had to be engaged."

GRACE: "Did you?"

CONNIE: "But you're not engaged, because you got the hat-band last summer and you got the fan . . ."

GRACE: "See? You don't know *when* I got the fan."

CONNIE: "When did you?"

GRACE: "You're right. I got the fan after I got the hatband."

CONNIE: "Who gave you the hatband?"

GRACE: "Who gave me the hatband?"

CONNIE: "One of your cousins?"

GRACE: "That's for me to know and you to find out."

CONNIE: "I don't think you're being a bit nice, that's what I think. I'm not going to ask you any more questions. I'm supposed to be your best friend, and for almost a year you've been getting presents and never told me a single thing about them. I only wish I could go home. I never kept any secrets from you."

GRACE: "You talk as if I'd been mean to you."

CONNIE: "That's what you have been, mean. Cruel."

GRACE: "Cruel? Was I cruel? When was I cruel?"

CONNIE: "Just now. Out of the blue sky you suddenly started telling me about presents you got and you never said anything to me about them before this. Nobody likes being left out in the cold by their best friend."

GRACE: "Oh, I'm sorry, Connie. Maybe I have been cruel, but it wasn't intentional. If I was cruel and mean it was pure thought-less. Thoughtlessness, on my part. I've had things on my mind that I couldn't tell anybody, not even you."

CONNIE: "What things?"

GRACE: "Oh, at Cape May, the one that gave me the hatband. He always wanted me for a partner when we played tennis."

CONNIE: "Yes, I wish I could play better."

GRACE: "Oh, but that was only an excuse, Connie. He was al-ways trying to be alone with me."

CONNIE: "What was his name?"

GRACE: "His name? Oh, I'd never tell anyone his name, not even you. He's engaged to be married."

CONNIE: "But you could tell *me*. I don't know any of the peo-ple down at Cape May, and besides, I never broke any of your se-crets."

GRACE: "I know, but I'd—I could never say his name out loud."

CONNIE: "Whisper it."

GRACE: "No, not even whispering. Well—Jack."

CONNIE: "Jack? I don't remember you saying anything about anybody named Jack."

GRACE: "No, naturally. That's the first time I ever said his name."

CONNIE: "Did you let him kiss you?"

GRACE: "Oh, no, Connie."

CONNIE: "But you let other boys kiss you."

GRACE: "But I never wanted them to. They were always the ones that wanted to."

CONNIE: "Oh, that isn't what you told me."

GRACE: "What *did* I tell you? I never said I wanted them to kiss me."

CONNIE: "Scotty Bordener and Charlie Jay."

GRACE: "I don't remember saying any such thing, Connie. If they wanted to kiss me so much that I couldn't stop them. But I never wanted them to."

CONNIE: "But I remember one time last winter and I was spending the night at your house and you *said* to me, 'Wouldn't it be nice to have two boys to kiss?' "

GRACE: "Connie, you must have dreamt that, or I was joking. Either one."

CONNIE: "Maybe you were joking, but I didn't dream it, because I was awake and you made me scratch your back."

GRACE: "Oh, well then I was joking."

CONNIE: "Well, I misunderstood you then, but I'm glad you were joking. I don't think you ought to kiss so many boys."

GRACE: "I don't kiss so many boys. You sound as if I kissed boys and kissed boys . . ."

CONNIE: "Well, not so many boys, but quite a few times the ones you do."

GRACE: "How can you say such a thing, Connie? Do you think I just kiss them and kiss them or let them kiss me when I'm alone with them? Scotty, for instance?"

CONNIE: "That's what you said, that's what you told me."

GRACE: "That's where you misunderstood. Just because I was alone with Scotty—he was lucky to get one kiss. If he told you anything else he was a damn liar."

CONNIE: "Scotty? He never told me anything."

GRACE: "Well, or Charlie Jay."

CONNIE: "He didn't either. It was just you always made me think you enjoyed kissing."

GRACE: "Oh. Well, I did that on purpose. I wanted *you* to—if you felt like kissing a boy, or letting him kiss you, I didn't want you to think I'd tell on you or think you weren't nice if you let them."

CONNIE: "Oh."

GRACE: "You see what I mean, Connie?"

CONNIE: "Uh-huh."

GRACE: "That must have been why I let you think I enjoyed it."

CONNIE: "Uh-huh."

GRACE: "Because I don't like boys. Young boys. The person that gave me the fan, do you know how old he is?"

CONNIE: "How old?"

GRACE: "Twenty-two years old."

CONNIE: "Twenty-*two?* Isn't that how old Brock is?"

GRACE: "That's how I know how old Sidney is. They went to Lawrenceville together."

CONNIE: "Sidney What's-His-Name? That visited you last Christmas? He's the one gave you the fan? He was only at your house one night."

GRACE: "That's why I didn't tell you. I hardly said three words to him and he went abroad. To Europe. And when he came back he brought me this fan."

CONNIE: "How did he get it to you? Does your mother know?"

GRACE: "He brought her one, but he had to do that, to cover up."

CONNIE: "She let you keep it? It looks expensive."

GRACE: "It's from Paris, hand-made. Of course she let me keep it."

CONNIE: "My mother wouldn't of let me keep it."

GRACE: "I know, but your mother's different. My mother's letting me come out next winter."

CONNIE: "I know that."

GRACE: "I know you know it, but your mother won't let you. Your mother's different than mine. We live one way, and you live another."

CONNIE: "Yes, I know. But what about Sidney?"

GRACE: "Sidney Tate? I wouldn't say this to another soul. You must say may God strike you dead if you ever say this to anyone. Even me. You must never repeat this even to me, unless I bring it up first."

CONNIE: "I won't."

GRACE: "You didn't say God can strike you dead."

CONNIE: "May God strike me dead if I ever repeat this."

GRACE: "I think Sidney Tate's in love with me."

CONNIE: "In love with you? Grace, how could he be if you only saw him that one time?"

GRACE: "I believe you can tell."

CONNIE: "How?"

GRACE: "The fan. Hinting to be invited to my ball. Wanting to see me again."

CONNIE: "Grace!"

GRACE: "Yes."

They were silent a moment.

CONNIE: "Did you get a letter from him?"

GRACE: "No. But Mother did. He makes excuses to write to her, and I'm sure, it's plain, he wants to see me again. I wrote to him twice. Once when he left his hair brushes at our house. I wrote to him because Mother had a felon on her finger and told him we were sending the brushes. But that was an excuse. He didn't forget his brushes. He left them, but he didn't forget them, if you know what I mean. And the other time, I wrote and thanked him for the fan."

CONNIE: "Goodness!"

GRACE: "Uh-huh."

CONNIE: "Are you in love with *him?*"

GRACE: "Time will be the judge of that."

CONNIE: "You sounded just like your father."

GRACE: "Well, why shouldn't I?"

Part of a colloquy between William Caldwell and his wife Emily, which took place in the sitting room of the house at the farm, July, 1901:

WILLIAM CALDWELL: "You know, the house seems deserted without Grace. Not deserted, but . . ."

EMILY: "Yes, I know what you mean."

WILLIAM: "The first time she was ever away so long alone. I hope she doesn't get homesick."

EMILY: "I hope not, but I don't think she will."

WILLIAM: "I s'pose not. Plenty of young people there, Cape May."

EMILY: "Yes, and a great many of them she'll know from last summer."

WILLIAM: "That's true."

EMILY: "Mm-hmm."

WILLIAM: "And even if she does get a little homesick, I'm not against that."

EMILY: "Oh, it might be a good thing."

WILLIAM: "Yes, and getting to know outsiders."

EMILY: "Exactly."

WILLIAM: "*And,* especially young men. That's the only objection I have to her staying home instead of going to boarding-school. I wish Brock could have stayed at Princeton till he finished. So she could meet more young men."

EMILY: "Why, Will, it's usually the mother that worries about those things."

WILLIAM: "Aheh-ahem. A certain mother I know never seems to give the matter a thought, so it's up to a certain father to—"

EMILY: "Oh, I think about it, Will, but I don't worry about it. You watch. Grace's going to be a real beauty, and if a town like Fort Penn gets the reputation of having one beauty, just one, the young men come from miles around."

WILL: "Yes, that's very true. I used to hear the fellows talk about a girl in Lancaster, or maybe it was York. York or Lancaster. They used to get up coaching parties and drive all the way to Lancaster, and the real reason they went was because there was supposed to be a great beauty there."

EMILY: "Jessica Shambaugh."

WILL: "That's *exactly* who it was! Lancaster. By George, you remembered that. Jessica Shambaugh. Married—let me think. Married I believe a man from Baltimore. How did you remember her name?"

EMILY: "Oh, all of us girls knew about her. You came very close to going on one of those coaching parties."

WILL: "So I did . . . But you saw to it that I didn't?"

EMILY: "I saw to it that you didn't."

WILL: "Hmm. Thirty years later I find that out. How did you stop me from going?"

EMILY: "It wasn't so hard. I said to you, 'What do you think of those silly boys driving all the way to Lancaster to look at a pretty face.' I said, 'What Fort Penn girl could ever again have the least respect for a young man that'd drive that far just to look at a face he'd never seen.' "

WILL: "Hmm. Well, well. I hope for Grace's sake the young men nowadays aren't so easily dissuaded."

EMILY: "They won't be. Nowadays you can drive from Lancaster to Fort Penn by machine. And our daughter is handsomer than Jessica Shambaugh ever thought of being."

WILL: "You *have* given the matter some thought."

EMILY: "Naturally, I'll think about it, but I refuse to worry about it."

A snatch of dialogue which was spoken in the dining room of a cottage in Cape May, New Jersey, July, 1901:

GRACE CALDWELL: "Good morning, Cousin Clarence."

CLARENCE BROCK: "Good morning, Grace. You had *your* breakfast."

GRACE: "Yes, thank you. I'm going for a walk."

CLARENCE BROCK: "Going for a walk. I wish I could be going for a walk. This damned gout. When you reach my age, Grace, don't get gout."

GRACE: "I'll try not to."

CLARENCE BROCK: "You do that. Say, you're pretty as a picture this morning. And of course! Of course! You're still wearing the Delta Phi colors. That's the ticket!"

GRACE: "I kept it all winter, Cousin Clarence."

CLARENCE BROCK: "Good girl. If I were thirty years younger you'd be wearing my badge too, we're not that close cousins."

GRACE: "Thank you, Cousin Clarence."

A letter to Paul Reichelderfer from Sidney Tate, November, 1901:

Dear Paul:—

. . . By the way, I am going to hold you to your invitation of last summer. In case it may have slipped your mind I hereby take the liberty of reminding you that when you were visiting us at Good Ground, you patiently lent an ear to my "girlish confidence" on the subject of a certain Miss G. C. Remember I confessed how smitten I was by the diamond in the diadem of Fort Penn? Well, old chap, you gave me a carte-blanche invitation to the Reichelderfer manor house any time I felt that I could no longer live without feasting my eye on the young lady in question. Candidly, my thoughts returned to her many times, and more than once I all but yielded to the temptation to go "farm-hunting" in the vicinity of Lebanon as an excuse to visit the neighboring metropolis of Fort Penn and accidentally on

purpose drop in on my old schoolmate Brock Caldwell in the hope of seeing his sister. I kept a firm pressure on the curb bit, however, and did not avail myself of this slim opportunity of catching a glimpse of Miss C. Now the time has come and I have a legitimate reason to see her. I have, in point of fact, been invited to see her. Joy is me! for I have been invited to her coming-out party.

Perhaps the wish is father to the thought, but knowing the Caldwells for the gentle-folk they are, I should hazard a guess that not many days will pass ere I receive an invitation to visit Stan Ross, George Wall, or Les Poffenberger, as I have sent my acceptance to the Caldwells and they will in all likelihood see to my being put up at the home of some mutual friend. I prefer, however, to be able to say that I shall be visiting you, and then if you can arrange to get me invited to a mutual friend's house, all well & good. I should not like to have the Caldwells think me their responsibility as they undoubtedly will now that I have said I intend to be present at the Ball. You understand how I feel and why.

Of course if your mother has made other arrangements I will understand, but inasmuch as it was through you that I met Miss C., I prefer to renew acquaintance under your auspices. If you have no special preference among the Fort Penn fellows I always considered George Wall a closer friend in college than the others listed above . . .

Earlier in this chronicle mention was made of the fact that Grace and Sidney followed several plots on their way to the altar, and it was stated that they always believed that they almost did not get together at all. So far as they themselves were aware, they were telling no more than the truth, but it was not the whole truth. Moreover, Emily Caldwell, astute though she was, had to have some outside help in bringing about the marriage of her daughter and the young man who, after the Christmas holidays of 1901–1902, not only remained the pick of the lot, but became in Emily's eyes the only suitable candidate for the position of husband to Grace. In the weeks succeeding the holidays, Emily's maneuverings lost all tentativeness; they were planned without thought of an alternate candidate, with Emily allowing only tactically for a change of heart by either Grace or Sidney. They were attracted mutually, affection would increase, love would ensue, and a marriage would take place. Nothing less than death itself could now disrupt Emily's plans for Grace and Sidney. She felt altogether capable of handling anything and everything less than death. She would space out their absences from each other and keep alert for the signs that one or the other was in danger of being attracted to a third party. Of Sidney's love for Grace she was certain; of Grace's feeling for Sidney she was less confident. Grace was not in love with Sidney; that Emily knew. And Grace was a girl who just possibly might become dangerously infatuated with a more dashing, possibly unscrupulous young man. Emily therefore made a show of devoted supervision of Grace's social life, such as it was in Fort Penn, and in so doing allowed Grace to see no young man whose charm and appearance compared favorably with Sidney's. Sidney was personable enough in his own right, but to be on the safe side Emily protected him against the *possibility* of invidious comparisons.

Death itself, the only factor which Emily conceded to be a potential disruptive, was instead an expediter. Death—numerically, two deaths—actually hastened the marriage of Sidney and Grace . . .

It was known as the Baum Case. On a murky afternoon in February, 1902, one Louis F. Baum entered the outer office of Dr. Angelo Terranova, and found it empty. He thereupon broke open the door of the inner office. There, on the leather-cushioned operating table, was Baum's wife Christine, naked, as frequently happens in physicians' offices, but with her was the doctor, also naked. Baum fired five shots from a .32 caliber nickel-plated Hopkins & Allen revolver. Two of the bullets struck Terranova, one below the left eye and the other above the heart. A third and fourth bullet struck Christine Baum in the right ear and in the right side of the neck below the ear. The fifth bullet creased the doctor's shoulder and passed on to the glass-fronted medicine chest. The office occupied two rooms on the first floor of a frame house, one of a row in Shoptown across the street from the Pennsylvania Railroad freight yards on the South Side of Fort Penn. The sound of the shots was heard in a grocery store two doors north of Doctor Terranova's office and in the corner saloon two doors to the south. Men and women rushed to the street from the grocery store and the saloon in time to see Baum running to the Pennsy yards. The shots also brought Mrs. Terranova downstairs to her husband's office and her screams attracted several women shoppers to the office. One of these women had presence of mind enough to return to the street and call out, pointing to the escaping Baum, "Stop the murderer!" The cry was taken up by the other men and women, and Baum was caught by Special Officers Donovan and Malarkey, of the Pennsy police, as he was about to board a departing freight train.

Feeling, according to the Fort Penn *Sentinel,* ran high in the Italian colony, where Doctor Terranova was a leader in social and fraternal circles. Notwithstanding the inferences which were drawn from the position and condition of the bodies, Doctor Terranova (and, by implication, Christine Baum) was believed innocent of wrongdoing, the victim of a jealous husband who had murdered the doctor and his patient, and stripped and rearranged the corpses. Despite the fact that few members of the Italian colony were qualified voters, other prominent Italo-Americans were able to enlist the aid of a far-seeing politician in an effort to see that justice was done. Little came of this movement, however, as Baum told reporters that he intended to plead the unwritten law and throw himself on the mercy of the court, by which he apparently meant that he was going to plead guilty.

Baum, who earned his living as a clerk in the Fort Penn Water Company office, was a slight, bewildered man of thirty-seven who at first refused to hire a lawyer. His wife had been a stylish stout blonde, six years younger than he, and they had been married twelve years. They had two children, the younger of whom was said, after the homicides, to bear an unmistakable resemblance to the late Doctor Terranova. The Baums lived a fair distance from the doctor's office, but Baum explained that he doctored with Terranova because Terranova was cheap. All the other doctors in town, he said, were too dear. If Baum had shot any other Italian he would have been allowed to take the least possible punishment, such as two years for manslaughter. But Baum had shot one of the three most important Italians in Fort Penn, and he also had shot his own wife, who was not Italian at all but good, German stock, for which reason there was some reaction against Baum among his own people.

The grand jury found a true bill against Baum and the case was put on the calendar for the March term of the Nesquehela County Criminal Court. Among the reporters and lawyers at Fort Penn it was not difficult to find several men who were willing to bet that Baum's goose was cooked, and that the best he could hope for was life imprisonment.

The Baum Case, with its adulterous aspect, and an Italian principal at that, was hardly a subject for discussion in mixed company; polite society contented itself with other topics. In the Caldwell household the case was not mentioned except by Emily to William, the backstairs people among themselves, Brock to the members of the Fort Penn Club, and Grace to Connie Schoffstal.

"Will," said Emily, one evening, "I came home before dinner and found Grace reading the *Sentinel* account of that Italian-doctor murder."

"Oh, dear," said Will Caldwell.

"Well, aren't you going to say something at the paper?"

"No, Emily. I never like to interfere there."

"But you must. Not only Grace, but other young girls the same age, reading that scandal."

"I agree, the details are explicit, to say the least. Judging from the bullet wounds he must have been on top of her, and I heard some more about it, too."

"Of course he was, but we can't have thoughts like that in

Grace's mind. She sees enough at the farm without reading about human beings in the paper."

"I agree with you, I agree with you, but then it's your duty to keep the paper out of her hands. I'm not going to interfere at the *Sentinel* office. They know their business, and that's final. Sorry, Emily."

Two weeks after the preceding conversation Emily was sitting in her sewing-room, second floor back, working on a throw and nursing a cold. She heard the doorbell and presently May, the upstairs girl, appeared: "It's Mrs. Jay, ma'am, wishes to speak with you."

"Mrs. Jay? What does *she* want? She's never been here in the morning before. All right, ask her to come up please."

Emily pulled the comforter over her legs and tucked it under to appear more invalid-like.

"Good morning, Jessie. I'm sorry to make you climb the stairs, but doctor's orders."

"I hope it's nothing serious, Emily."

"A touch of quinsy, he says. Nothing dreadful, but you know."

"Oh," said Jessie. "Yes." She was ill at ease, but obviously determined to speak her piece.

"Take off your coat. Sit over there, Jessie. I can tell you have something on your mind."

"Thank you, Emily. Yes, I have something on my mind. Something terrible, or I wouldn't bother you, sick and all."

"If I can help you, you can always count on me, you know that."

"Well, I won't take any longer than necessary," said Jessie.

"Take as long as you like. That's what old friends are for. When someone's in trouble."

"It's not me personally, Emily. It's a cousin of mine. My first cousin. You've read about or heard about that murder, the Italian doctor and the white—I mean, American woman?"

"Yes."

"Louis Baum, the man that did it, is my first cousin."

"He *is?* How?"

"Do you remember your German? Baum?"

"Baum? Baum means tree. *Tree!* Jessie Tree. I never think of you as Jessie Tree any more. Oh, dear. Nobody else knows it, do they? I mean to say, have people bothered you, Jessie?"

"No, I don't guess anybody's thought of it, Emily. My father changed his name from Baum to Tree, but Louis' father kept the Baum."

"Jessie, excuse me, but I think you'd better sit in this chair, here. I see they've opened the top windows in the bay window and you'll be in a draught. May catch cold."

"Thank you, Emily." Jessie moved to the chair Emily indicated.

"But I'm sorry, I didn't want to interrupt, but you've been worrying, I can see that, and worry lowers your resistance."

"You're very kind, Emily."

"Notta tall. Now go on about your cousin. I don't know who *he is,* exactly. I remember your father very well. Frederick Tree. Frederick L. Tree."

"Yes, Frederick Louis Tree. My uncle's name was Louis Frederick Baum, and this man in all this trouble is Louis Frederick Baum, Junior, although he never uses the Junior because his father died, oh, thirty years ago or more. He was raised by his mother, my Aunt Esther. I don't think you ever knew her. I'm sure you didn't. She was from Lancaster County, father was a farmer. Louis' mother, this woman I'm speaking about, she was very poor, but she kept a roof over her head and had food to live on by doing sewing and fancywork, housework by the day, and managed somehow. Whenever I think I have a hard time I think of Aunt Esther. Well, she raised him, Louis, and when he was sixteen he got a steady job with the Water Company and he's been there ever since."

"And never any trouble before this?"

"Never. An upright, decent man. Handled money for the Water Company for many years. Didn't drink or smoke. Reliable, trustworthy. Wasn't what you'd call a Beau Brummel by any manner or means, and *she* was all right, *too.* Her children, one girl and one boy—the boy's still a baby—they were neat and clean, and her house was neat and clean. No *sign* of anything out of the way. But I guess she must have been carrying on with this doctor, the Italian, and some way Louis found out about it or got his suspicions aroused. You know—or *you* don't know, but *I* do. Sooner or later the wife or the husband finds out, hears something."

"Yes, I suppose so," said Emily. She was wondering whether Jessie had come to her only for conversational release, but her common sense told her that she could not expect to get off that easily.

"It must have been a dreadful time for him," said Jessie. "Never known anything but work and poverty all his life. His mother working herself to death, and she did, she did. And then he works like a slave for a miserable salary, and having to look neat and clean with an office job, keeping up appearances. And then I suppose he thought it was worth it all to have a nice home, with a good wife and two nice children. Then to find out that the woman he'd been doing all this for was carrying on with this Italian. A pleasure woman for a man with a wife and children of his own, and doing it while his own wife was upstairs! She used to go to his office, you know. She pretended she had something wrong with her, but what was wrong with her was . . ." She stopped to take a deep breath.

"Yes, I don't like to pass judgment, or say she got what she deserved," said Emily. "But a woman as reckless as that, maybe she never even thought of the consequences. I suppose with a doctor he could see to it that she didn't become pregnant."

"He could see to it? He *didn't* see to it. I understand the younger child belongs to him. Poor Louis thinks so."

"Have you been to see him?"

"No, Emily, I haven't. I'm ashamed of myself to lack the courage, but what little position I have in Fort Penn, I've been afraid to jeopardize it."

"No one would think the less of you, Jessie."

"That's not true, Emily. For myself I don't care, but I have a son and I want to see him established. That's what *I've* worked for."

"I think you've been very successful with Charlie. I don't doubt for a minute he'll make his mark in the world."

"Do you think so, Emily? I'm glad you do."

"But on thinking it over, I don't s'pose Fort Penn is any different from any other place when it comes to gossip, and I'm inclined to agree with you. It's better for you and Charlie's future to keep out of this. Is that why you came to see me, Jessie? You wanted my advice? And of course, I'll say right away, I'm honored by your confiding in me."

Jessie looked away from her before continuing. "No, Emily, I didn't only come to you for advice. I came to you for more practical help."

"And I think you knew in your heart that to ask it is to receive it, if it's in my power."

"Thank you, but this is—"

"Is it money, Jessie? I have my own, and Will wouldn't have to know if that's what worries you."

"No, it isn't money. It's something else. It's power! I'd never borrow money that I couldn't some day pay back, but you have power, and I want to borrow some without any hope of ever paying it back."

"Well, tell me, Jessie."

"All right. I want you to get Mr. O'Connell to be Louis' lawyer."

"Desmond O'Connell?"

"Yes."

"You want me to ask him to take your cousin's case, defend him."

"You don't have to ask him. Will Caldwell can ask him. I know you'll tell Will everything I've told you this morning. I'm prepared for that and it's only right. But that's what I plead with you to do: ask Will to ask Desmond O'Connell to take the case. If he doesn't, my cousin will hang. I haven't seen Louis, but I'm in touch with somebody that has seen him, and this person told me that it would take Desmond O'Connell to save Louis. Louis doesn't care what happens to him. He wants to plead guilty and throw himself on the mercy of the court, not even hire a lawyer. But he can't do that. Mr. Eisenhuth, the district attorney, isn't going to let him plead guilty. Eisenhuth—you know, that politician—he wants to hang Louis, and the person I've been talking to says Louis as good as has the rope around his neck right this minute. He didn't say O'Connell could save him. What he said was it would take *a* Desmond O'Connell to save him and even so he had his doubts."

"Oh." Emily lay back in her chair.

"That's what I mean by your power, Emily. You have the power. If Will goes to Desmond O'Connell and tells him to take the case, Louis has a chance. Desmond O'Connell won't say no to Will. Nobody says no to Will in this town."

"That isn't quite true, Jessie."

"Just about."

"Perhaps. Will usually gets what he wants, but he doesn't abuse that privilege, if that's what you'd call it. He gets what he *asks* for, as a rule, but that's partly because he doesn't get to the point of asking things that he knows are useless to ask for. You see what I mean?"

"Yes."

"So, assuming I went to Will, and Will went to Desmond, why should Desmond undertake to defend your cousin?"

"Because Will Caldwell asked him to."

"But Desmond would want to know why on earth Will was interesting himself in the worst murder case we've had in years. What could Will say to that?"

"He could say—he could tell Mr. O'Connell that—well, just what I've told you this morning."

"That's another person you'd be confiding in, Jessie."

"I'm not afraid to confide in a lawyer. They're told secrets all the time."

"Then I think you should have gone to Desmond direct, instead of coming to us."

"I thought of that. He'd turn me down. I don't know him very well, but I know him well enough to know he'd never be Louis' lawyer to please me. I'm nobody."

"You mustn't underestimate yourself that way, Jessie. You're somebody. You're a brave, conscientious woman. Possibly you are right about Desmond, though. It's not so much that you're nobody, but he thinks he's somebody. And I guess he is, if he can save a man from the gallows. But that's not the point you and I are discussing. In fact it isn't a discussion any more. It's a matter for me to decide: whether to go to Will and have him go to Desmond O'Connell . . . Jessie, I don't see how I can do it."

"Why not?"

"Because something tells me it'd be wrong to interfere. I'll tell you something. I asked Will when this thing first happened, I asked him to speak to the people down at the *Sentinel* to stop the articles about the murders. I came home one afternoon and found Grace reading one, and I was shocked and worried. But when I spoke to Will he refused to interfere at the paper. He said he never interfered. I know how you must feel, that I haven't given you any very good reason for not getting Will to speak to Desmond O'Connell, but I honestly believe we ought to stay out of it. On the other hand, if you yourself can persuade Desmond, I give you permission to say we'll foot the bill, but as to our going to Desmond—sorry as I am, the answer is no."

" 'Sorry as I am, the answer is no,' " said Jessie. "Louis Baum, I Emily Caldwell, sentence you to hang by the neck until you are dead."

"Well, I don't think I quite deserve that, Jessie. I've made you an offer."

"Knowing that Desmond O'Connell probably wouldn't even see me."

"I don't know that. If you sent in your card, he'd see you. He's a gentleman. He'd see you."

"And put me out like a gentleman, too, I daresay. Or maybe not even that after I told him what I came for."

"Well, you can try, and my offer holds good any time."

"How gracious of you, Emily."

"Now, Jessie, I think you'd better go. I know you're disappointed in me, and maybe rightly so, but there's no use having recriminations and saying things we'll regret later. If you talk to Desmond and he wants some assurance that we'll pay his fee, tell him to get in touch with me."

"Desmond O'Connell is out of the question and you know it, Emily Caldwell."

"No, I don't know it," said Emily, straightening her shawl.

"But I have something else to say, and it has nothing to do with Desmond O'Connell."

"Now, Jessie, please. I'm tired and not feeling well, and certainly not up to any unpleasant words."

"Be a good girl, Jessie, and go your way. You've had your audience with the queen. But I'm not a good girl. I'm the cousin of a murderer, the worst murder case we've had in years."

"Oh, I'm sorry I said that."

"I don't care whether you said it or not, because it's true. It was so bad that you wanted to have Will interfere and keep it away from the innocent eyes of that pure little daughter of yours."

"Now I do insist on your going. You have no right to speak that way of Grace."

"Yes I have. I can speak of Grace in any way I please. I know what she is."

"Oh, go away. You don't see Grace from one year's end to another."

"No, I don't see Grace from one year's end to another. She's careful to come to my house when I'm out. That's why I don't see her. She's not interested in me. She's interested in my boy. How long since I've been invited to this house? A long time. But my son *had* your daughter in this house, in her own room. And she liked it enough to come to my house time after time, and time after time he had his pleasure with her."

"You crazy-woman, get out."

"I discharged a yellow girl for doing the same things your high-and-mighty princess did in my house. I had to send my boy away, out of the State, before she ruined him."

"You're a raving maniac."

"Then have me locked up, if I'm a raving maniac. But before you do—don't ask your innocent little daughter if I'm telling the truth, if I'm a raving maniac. Ask your son. Ask *Brock* Caldwell if he didn't stand outside the bedroom while my boy was taking his pleasure with the little princess."

Emily looked at her for a moment, the pitying look of a fighter who has been struck down but knows he can get up and win, is going to get up and win, and is going to be unmerciful in winning. "Even you couldn't invent this story, so I suppose it's true. But do you think you can blackmail us with it? Do you think *you* can do anything at *all* with it?"

"Yes," said Jessie, whispering. "I just did, Emily. I did do something with it. I couldn't blackmail you with the story, but I hurt you. I really hurt you, didn't I? That's all I wanted to do. I was never going to tell anybody that story, but I made up my mind if you refused to help Louis, I'd hurt you in a way you'd never forget. And you'll never forget this. Isn't that true, Emily?"

"It's true, Jessie. It's true. But I'm still me, and you're still you. I imagine that hurts you almost as much."

Jessie Jay left then, and Emily was alone with her misery, her tears. After a while she took to her bed and left word that she did not want to be disturbed by anyone except Mr. Will Caldwell. She usually spoke of her husband and her son as Mr. Caldwell and Mr. Brock, but she wanted no mistake about this order.

She heard the comings and goings of the household at luncheon, when Grace came home from school. She slept a little in the afternoon, so that by the time Will came home she was ready to speak to him, and ready to handle him.

He kissed her, asked her how she was, and sat on the edge of her bed. "Do you think you'll live?" he said.

"I'll live forever," she said. "After today."

"Oh. Did you have a bad time today?"

"Not with my illness. I had a caller," she said. "See if those doors are closed tight, will you please?"

He tried the doors and they were snugly closed. "Who was your visitor, to occasion door-closing and low tones?"

"Jessie Jay," she said. "She came to me with some information that I didn't know and I'm sure you don't. This man Baum, that murdered his wife and the doctor?"

"Yes."

"Jessie's first cousin. Do you remember that Jessie's father changed his name from Baum to Tree?"

"Well, I do remember it now, but I hadn't thought of it," said Will. "Go on."

"She wants us to get Desmond O'Connell to be his lawyer. She said she's heard that it will take Desmond to save Baum from the gallows."

"I wouldn't be a bit surprised if she's right, and I'm not at all sure Desmond could get him off. But why are we involved?"

"She said Desmond wouldn't take the case if she asked him, but if we asked him he would."

"But why *should* we ask him?" said Will. "We don't know Baum, and besides, Desmond hardly ever takes criminal cases."

"Well, I think we ought to ask him, Will."

"Why?"

"I think we owe it to ourselves. Jessie's always been a friend of ours, not close, but in our circle of friends, and her son Charlie's a friend of Brock's, and they do represent something."

"In other words, members of our clahss."

"Yes," she said.

"Well, if we're going to start looking after the unknown cousins of members of our clahss, I hope the Schoffstal clan stays out of trouble. We'd need a thousand Desmond O'Connells. But I suppose you're right. If we belong to a clahss, or a class, it's not worth much if we don't come to the rescue when one of us gets in trouble."

"Thank you, Will."

"However, as I see it," he said, rubbing his brow, "people will wonder why Desmond suddenly takes up the defense of someone he obviously never heard of. They'll ask questions about that."

"Desmond can cope with that situation, but I have an answer all ready for him. He can say that Baum's home was violated and he took the law into his own hands."

"Probably exactly what Desmond *will* say," said Will. "And what if they ask who's paying Desmond—and who *is* paying Desmond?"

"Nobody. If necessary we will, or I will, but you must convince him that he's doing this for the good of the home and the clahss. If Desmond wants to be a member of the clahss, let him pay his dues."

"Don't worry about that, if there's a clahss Desmond's a member of it."

The next morning Emily wrote a note and sent it by her maid: "Will is speaking to Desmond today. You are not to reveal your connection with L. F. B. unless called upon to do so, nor are you to attempt to see Desmond." She did not sign the note. Later in the day a dozen hothouse roses arrived for Emily. The card read: "I cannot forgive myself. Some day I hope you will forgive me.— Jessie."

May, the maid, was waiting to see what Emily wanted done with the flowers.

"Take those things down to the furnace and burn them," said Emily.

"Yes ma'am," said May.

Emily was extremely careful not to indicate, after Jessie Jay's disclosures, that Grace or Brock had incurred her displeasure. She managed not to be alone with either of them (an easy task in Brock's case) during the next week; she was sure of herself, as sure of herself as any woman that ever lived, but wanted to guard against the temptation, the impulse to ask questions of Grace and of Brock. She was certain that if she ever asked Brock questions which would indicate the extent of her information, Brock would blow his brains out, or leave home, and she wanted neither. If she were to ask Grace an informative question, Grace would lie and might change into a tiresome liar, and so far as she knew, except for the episode (as Emily called it) with Charlie Jay, Grace never had been a liar. Technically, she had not lied even then; or perhaps it was more accurate to say, she had lied then only technically. It was technically a lie to say that you had been with Connie Schoffstal when the whole truth would have included a mention of a visit to Charlie Jay's house. It was technically not telling a lie to keep a secret if no one asked you a question that related to the secret. Technicalities to one side, Emily found herself believing that Grace had not lied to her, and as she examined that belief she commenced to have a new respect for Grace's handling of the whole Jay business. For a woman who spent virtually no time in the worldly society of Philadelphia and New York, Emily Caldwell had an extraordinarily worldly point of view. Her speech included "No girl ever did such-and-such," but she knew better. She could say, "No girl goes skating alone with a young man until she's engaged," but she knew about juggled dates on birth certificates and long, long trips away from home that were not the result of proper behavior. In Fort Penn she knew of at least one child who must have been born at the age of seven or eight months, and not merely seven or eight months in utero. She knew of another case in Fort Penn where a young man and his wife adopted a four-year-old child which had the mother's nose and the father's red hair. Emily admitted that she had been at fault somewhere in not keeping an eye on Grace and in not conveying to her, without breaking the custom of saying nothing, the knowledge that a boy's pecker (as Emily called it and as Will called it) could make a girl have a baby, and that no girl had a baby before she was married. Emily was rather grateful to Grace for keeping her secret, whatever it was. If the girl no longer was a virgin, she at least had not become a moody or hysterical non-virgin. To all outward appearances, there had been no change in her, and therefore except for the nincompoop Brock, and the now terrified Jessie Jay, no one in the world could say anything about Grace. There was Charlie Jay, to be sure, but Charlie was in all probability the most terrified of all. There was an excellent chance, Emily told herself, that Charlie and Grace had done nothing more than let their spooning go too far; touchings, fondlings, kissings. No matter what Jessie Jay believed, Emily remembered that with Will, in the beginning, he had had to ask her if he was inside her, and in the very beginning there had not been time to ask. Very secretly, the most secret thought she ever had had, Emily was pleased that Grace had used a man when she wanted him.

But that thought was not to be an element in Emily's plans for Grace. It occurred to Emily that whatever Grace had done with Charlie Jay, she was likely to have done with Scotty Bordener, and there might even be someone else. Say three. Three who had touched her, three whom she had touched. That had to stop, and the way to stop it was to know where Grace was at all times, to keep Grace from devoting her time to one young man, to keep changing her scenery. It was going to be difficult to know where Grace was at all times without arousing her suspicions, but it was now a duty and it would be done. The second part of her new plan was only a different version of her earlier strategy of discouraging young men who might compare too favorably with Sidney Tate, whom she trusted. The third part of her plan was another variant of the earlier scheme of devoted supervision of Grace's social life.

Emily Caldwell, an Episcopalian by membership, held the private opinion that churches got between the individual and God, and she was not at all sure that she did not regard Christ as part of the Church and therefore in the way. Her religion was between herself and God the Father, with whom she felt on good terms. She believed that God understood that what she did was for the best and that He understood and approved, even on those rare occasions when lesser ones might be critical. She also believed that when she lost her temper or acted untrue to form—the form which she and God understood—she was punished. In the present instance she believed that she had been punished for neglecting Grace by God's allowing Jessie Jay to learn what she had learned. In future she would look out for her daughter's welfare more diligently, and for the present she thanked God for Sidney Tate.

———

Now that Grace was "out"—Fort Penn acknowledged the fact while continuing to reject the term—she was often in the company of older young ladies and gentlemen, including the younger married set. She was the first girl in the history of Fort Penn to have a ball while still attending Miss Holbrook's; she was not yet eighteen and would not be until the twenty-ninth of April; but it was no more than right that a Caldwell should be the one to establish the precedent. Everybody said it was no more than right. Everybody welcomed her, and not only as a Caldwell, but as a handsome, friendly girl, who was the picture of grace—one of a thousand puns on her name—on the ballroom floor, on the ice-covered river, at the piano, and everywhere she went. In Fort Penn there were skating parties on the Nesquehela, followed by tea or supper at someone's house or the newly built country club; there were Fort Penn balls, the Governor's receptions, the Military Ball, sleigh-riding parties to Becksville, near the Caldwell farm; small dinner parties, and trips to Philadelphia and New York. Numerous trips to Philadelphia, where the cousins had done their family duty by sponsoring Grace, a not disagreeable task when a girl is handsome and rich.

"You don't think she's overdoing it, do you?" said Will to Emily.

"No, I don't. I want her to have a year she'll always remember," said Emily.

There was one trip to White Sulphur Springs, which fitted into Emily's plan for changing Grace's scenery. The weather at

The White was something short of heavenly, but Emily said she was just as well satisfied to have Grace take a rest. The rest worked out very well. By the time Emily was ready to return to Fort Penn the Baum Case had been disposed of: Louis Baum had been allowed to plead guilty to second degree murder and was sentenced to twenty years to life. A few Italians muttered and complained, but their protests were heard only by other Italians and Roger Bannon, the politician, who shrugged his shoulders and said, "Well, you know what I been telling you good people. You can't fight them Dutch bastards if you don't all take out your papers. Live right and vote right, that's what I'm all the time telling you to do. But you can't vote till you get your citizenship. Not here, not in this Dutch-infested ass-hole of the nation. They watch me like the devil watches an underpaid bank clerk."

"It was not a Dutchman that got him off," said one of the Italians.

"Of course it wasn't! Do you think I don't know that? It was an Irishman! That's what I'm all the time telling you. Desmond O'Connell, an Irishman, not one of their own thick-headed kind."

"But you blame them."

"I do indeed. But I don't blame them for being so aware of their own shortcomings that they have sense enough to get an Irishman, a smart, brilliant, clever counselor. Do you see what I'm leading to, Bongiorno?"

"Not quite."

"Then pardon me if I wax immodest, dear boy. I can do the same for the Italian that our friend O'Connell does for the beer-bellies. When they want something they have to go to an Irishman. Why shouldn't you avail yourself of the same opportunity? Your friend Roger Bannon is no lawyer, but an enormous lot gets accomplished outside of the courts of law. I repeat, for the ten thousandth time, get your papers, become voters, and I'll see to it that no Italian travels steerage. We'll all ride first class and maybe even be waited on by the present owners of the boat, if you see what I mean."

"Yes."

"The trouble with too many of your people, they sweat and slave from morn till night on the navvy gang, workin' on the borough, doing this for the Pennsy and that for the Nesquie, getting no higher than engine-wiper—and satisfied! Satisfied to take the guff of the big lads and abuse your bodies till you're wracked by consumption and spitting blood on your pillows at night. For what? For the little money, the eight hundred dollars, the two thousand that will enable you to go back to the old country and buy a farm, and bring up your children to slave again on your few acres in Italy. Well, I was born in the old country too, but if one of my kids said he wished he could go back to Ireland and live, I'd half-drown him. When the time comes, my eldest goes to college, if I have to steal the money. You know him. Roger Bannon, Junior. A boy of fourteen now, but already as big as his father. I let him have a paper route, but nothing harder than that till he's reached his growth. I'll do without the pennies he could earn now and wait till he's educated and strong and bringing in the dollars. The same with his brothers. They don't entertain any thoughts of a little farm in Wexford, where I come from. I'd like to see more of that kind of thinking from you people. Then we'd get somewhere."

The Italians nodded dreamily, never questioning the reference to beer-bellies by the owner of Bannon's Café; never protesting that Roger Junior had acquired a paper route by using his fists on an Italian boy. They accepted these facts because Roger Bannon was the only non-Italian who ever showed the slightest interest in them.

———

An eighteenth-birthday party in Fort Penn would have been an anti-climax, Emily Caldwell felt, after Grace's large and successful ball; and it better suited her immediate and long-term plans to take Grace to New York in April. A week was the longest period Grace ever had passed in New York, but in her new life the young lady surely would discover that the big city, with its shops and theaters and people, offered forms of entertainment that had not commanded her attention on previous visits, and Emily got up a schedule for a two-week visit that Grace would enjoy. In New York the Caldwell and Brock families had no relatives who could be depended upon for dutiful sponsorship of a country cousin, but money like the Caldwell money—clean money and in quantity—has connections of its own. The Nesquehela, Fort Penn & Lebanon railroad was on friendly terms with the Reading, and the Reading was on even friendlier terms with the House of Morgan, and while it was whispered that the Morgan name alone was not enough to guarantee a man's admission to a club, it was socially helpful to appear under Morgan auspices. George Langways, although not a Morgan partner, was close enough to the House and close enough to Will Caldwell to be influential and considerate when Will Caldwell, in a postscript to a business letter, asked George to look in on Emily and Grace when they were in New York. George, of course, did not wait to look in. George's wife immediately offered the comforts of her home, and insisted that all her life she had been eager to give a dinner party for Emily and now Emily and Grace. The invitation to stay at the Langways' house was delicately declined, but Emily responded graciously to the idea of the dinner party, knowing that Maysie Langways would have her party early in the fortnight and that it would lead to other invitations. Maysie would have the Beaumonts and the Otises, acquaintances of the Caldwells, who could be depended upon, and for Grace there would be some young gentlemen.

Maysie called on Emily the day she and Grace arrived at the Knickerbocker.

"Yes, I did think of someone," said Emily. "Do you happen to know Sidney Tate?"

"Why, of course. We've been to their house dozens of times, Alfred and Anna Tate. Sidney and Alan—our youngest son, I think he's always been at school when you've been here—they ride together twice a week. Does Grace ride?"

"Yes, that's one of her accomplishments."

"I almost asked Sidney before you said anything. Is he a—is he a beau?"

"Oh, no, but he *has* been to our house, when he was visiting Yale friends."

"I *could* put him *next* to Grace."

"Oh, don't do that. Just so there's one familiar face about her own age. That is, not our age."

"I think you're right. And if Sidney can't come for dinner he can always come in later. That's how we'll leave it."

"Yes, you know how it is, Maysie, this is all new to Grace."

At that point Grace returned from the first shopping expedition she ever had gone on alone. "Oh, I don't think we'll have to worry about this young lady," said Maysie. "She'll have New York at her feet."

Sidney came for dinner; his acceptance of a prior invitation for that night had to be withdrawn, but he withdrew it. He was not able to get Grace alone for a minute, but he had less difficulty monopolizing the company of Emily, possibly because Emily placed herself at his disposal at least long enough to tell him what hotel they were stopping at, and how long they were going to be in New York, and how nice it would be if he could have tea with them while they were in New York. He in turn reminded Emily that since he had been a guest in the Caldwell home, it was quite in order for Emily and her daughter to come to dinner chez Tate. An evening was decided upon, and Mr. and Mrs. Alfred Tate had their first look at the girl who they hoped was to be the one to make their boy happy. There were no other young people at the Tates' dinner; Mrs. Tate had wangled an invitation to a dance at someone's house nearby. An impressive number of young gentlemen demanded introductions to Grace, and Sidney was pleased and happy to be that much in control of the pleasure of the girl whom he admittedly loved.

He went in to see his mother, who was having breakfast in bed the morning after her dinner party. "Hmm, smells good, that coffee," he said. "You get fresh coffee, and I only get Father's warmed up."

"Pray help yourself to a cup of fresh coffee. The only reason you came to call on me this morning. Pray do have a cup of fresh coffee, Sidney. Dear me. Poor boy."

"Not poor boy. I merely commented that—"

"This coffee is no better than the coffee you had. You had Father's warmed-over coffee, but I have your warmed-over coffee. You came in to ask me what I thought of Grace. Exquisite. Not only in face and form, but the way she handles herself. Such dignity for a girl her age. She is quite young."

"She'll be eighteen in a week or two."

"I suppose I could have the exact date if I pressed the point," said Anna Tate. "She looks like her mother. Does she look anything like her father?"

"Yes, the forehead and the softening around the mouth. But she does look more like her mother than her father."

"I'm glad she doesn't look entirely like her mother. Oh, Mrs. Caldwell's a handsome woman, but I wouldn't like to think you were marrying her exact replica."

"Who said anything about marriage?"

"Oh, you didn't come in here to practice deception on your old mother surely. . . . Apparently they're people of considerable means and position in Pennsylvania. Well, I'll be frank and open with you. If you want to marry her, I have no objection. I think it's almost time you married and I don't suppose I'll ever really know any more about Grace than I do this minute. As to your father, I'll even relieve your mind on that score. We talked before going to sleep last night, and he's—well, he's pleased. He even liked Mrs. Caldwell, and I didn't, of course."

"Why 'of course'?"

"Sidney, you were always a very level-headed boy, with sound judgment about other people and about yourself, but since you've met this girl you've assumed a modesty, a self- is the word depreciation?"

"Deprecation."

"Whatever. I haven't liked it one bit. It's an insincere pose, that's what it is, and I want you to stop it."

"What's this got to do with Mrs. Caldwell?"

"Hold your horses," said his mother. "Let me just tell you that you're a very, very eligible young man, and nobody knows that better than Mrs. William Caldwell of Pennsylvania. I know it isn't she you love, but Grace. But keep your wits about you and your self-respect, and don't go into this marriage thinking you're getting everything and offering nothing. Oho-no. You have good blood, you're hardly a poor boy, and you have a nice way with people, kindness and consideration, and you're intelligent. You'll make a good husband and father. Oh, no. You're not all getting and none giving. And down deep you know it."

"I suppose I do, or I wouldn't be putting my name up—"

"Uh-uh. This isn't a horse race, Sidney. This is a marriage. This is the woman you live with and die with."

"I hope it is."

"I hope it is too."

The conversation thus ended without Anna Tate's having to expatiate upon her opinion of Emily Caldwell. The discussion was not reopened, ever. In their social intercourse the mothers acquitted themselves in ladylike fashion, with mutual respect and tacit antagonism, each understanding the other, knowing that she was understood. They seemed to agree, almost as if they had conferred, that the marriage would be a good thing; and this had the effect of a truce. Emily conceded that Sidney's mother had gained a momentary advantage by her acute realization of what Emily was up to, and Emily knew that Anna still had time—the big past and the immediate present—on her side and could have prevented the marriage in the two weeks of the Caldwells' New York stay. On the other side, Anna realized that Emily would gain an advantage the moment she took Grace home. Once Grace was out of New York, with the courtship continuing, Sidney was, so to speak, lost, and Emily would assume the power to influence

Grace against Sidney, which would make for Sidney's unhappiness, possibly for the rest of his life. Mother Tate wanted her son to be happy, and Mother Caldwell wanted her daughter securely married. The ladies to all purposes achieved a rapprochement by keeping their distance.

Emily Caldwell cheated a little bit, but she had a reason: Jessie Jay's outburst, that not even Grace knew she knew. She refused Grace permission to go with Sidney to the Yale-Harvard boat race and the Yale-Princeton baseball game, on the strictly conventional ground that Sidney and Grace were not engaged to be married, but her real reason was that it was up to Sidney to make the trip to Fort Penn and thereby publicly confess that Grace meant that much to him; and while he was in Fort Penn he would be placing himself under the supervision of Emily.

On Grace's birthday Emily had given a dinner party in a private dining-room of the Knickerbocker in return for those who had given parties in compliment to her and Grace. The birthday was not mentioned in the invitations, and Sidney was the only guest who had brought a present. He had guessed correctly that Mr. and Mrs. Caldwell would give Grace something in the diamond line. He gave her a set of three gold pins: a miniature hunting crop for her stock, an oar to be worn on the river, and a tennis racquet with a pearl for a ball. In contrast with her parents' diamond pendant his gifts appeared suitably inexpensive, but the pearl tennis ball took the gifts out of the trinket class and was a bold gesture on his part. It meant, and it was inferred to mean, that he was taking himself out of the casual admirer class. When they returned to Fort Penn Emily noticed that Grace was never without one of the pins. At first she thought Grace wore the pins only on the appropriate occasions, but she discovered that even when Grace was in an evening gown one of the pins was hidden somewhere about her person, usually under a flounce, but at least once pinned to her stocking garter.

"You never know when a pin will come in handy," said Emily, when she saw the oar on the garter.

"Oh, you noticed it. Well, I wear it because Sidney gave it to me."

"You like him the best?"

"I like him the *only.*"

"Yes, he's very nice. I think so too."

"If I were older I'd marry him, if he'd ask me."

"Well, you know, dear. Marriage is a very serious thing at any age."

"I never thought it wasn't, Mother," she said. "I want to ask you something."

"Yes?"

"Please don't you and Father make me graduate from Holbrook's. It's bad enough to keep going there, even the way I've been staying out this year, but don't you think it's carrying it too far to make me put on a cap and gown and sit with those children? I consider them children."

"What do you consider yourself?"

"I'm eighteen. I can own property in some states. I consider myself a woman."

"All right. I'll speak to Miss Holbrook."

"Oh, thank you. You can't realize how I hated the thought of sitting there—"

"I think I can. What about your diploma?"

"Diploma? What for? What good's a diploma? I never expect to prove I'm educated. I'm not, anyway. Or at least I am, as much as I have to be for the life I want to lead."

"What's that?"

"I've told you. Live on the farm. If a horse ever asks me a question in Latin I won't be able to answer him, will I?"

"Grace!" Emily smiled. "A horse—Latin."

"But do you know what I'll do if he does, Mother?"

"What?"

"I'll give him a good kick in the ass."

"Grace! Why I—what—"

"See, Mother? I belong on the farm, not in polite society." She kissed her mother and, laughing, left her mother laughing. But when Grace was gone a minute Emily's laughing stopped, as she remembered that such language was not innocent vulgarity, not in Grace's case. In July, when she went to Cape May, she was vigilant as ever over Grace, but now she watched for another reason; she was on the lookout for a sign or signs that Grace was missing Sidney. The sign came. "This year I'll be glad to leave Cape May," said Grace. "We couldn't ask Sidney down here, but we can ask him to the farm."

He came to the farm for a week's visit early in August. They were up at seven every morning, saddling their own horses, and covering the fields and timber before the heat of the day. In the afternoon they played tennis and swam in the dam, and in the evening they sat on the porch with Will and Emily until Will would announce that it was time to turn in, leaving Sidney and Grace alone for half an hour but no more, as Grace had been instructed. The Caldwells had no other guests during Sidney's visit, not even for meals; Fort Penn was not taken into the family's confidence concerning Sidney's presence at the farm, which is not to say that Fort Penn was unaware of his presence. Fort Penn knew what train brought him to Fort Penn, and what train took him away. The Schoffstal family, who were the most likely casual callers, were at Eagles Mere, in Sullivan County, and not due to return before the end of the month, a fact which both Emily and Grace bore in mind when they invited Sidney to the farm. All other Fort Penn friends respected the figuratively closed gate at the end of the lane.

"The week's gone so fast, the happiest I've ever had. You know I love you, Grace, don't you?"

"It was my happiest week, too."

"And you know I love you."

"Yes, I think so, Sidney."

"When I go to Fort Penn tomorrow, on my way to the train I'm going to stop and speak to your father," he said. "Shall I? I should have asked you that first, but I have your permission, haven't I?"

"Yes."

"What do you think he'll say?"

"I don't know, Sidney. What are you going to say to *him?*"

"I'm going to tell him that I'm going to ask you to marry me."

"I think he'll say it's all right. He's stopped making remarks about how young I am, so I guess he thinks I'm old enough to be engaged."

"I've never loved anyone but you, so I can't say I love you more than anyone else. Do you love me?"

"Yes."

"What?"

"I love you, Sidney." They had been conversing quietly, as though their speeches showed the calmness of their relationship, but suddenly, when she said she loved him, Grace kissed Sidney on the mouth and opened her mouth and put her arms around him at the waist. If he had not been so surprised Sidney could have had her then, that minute, but when she felt him against her she stopped kissing him.

"Don't let me kiss you like that, Sidney! Don't! Get away from me, don't let me touch you. I mustn't feel this way."

He moved away from her and she turned her back until she was in control of herself. "Isn't it awful?" she said. She smiled faintly. "I don't know what happened to me."

"It's all right, darling. It's all right. You're supposed to feel that way."

"Is that the way I'm supposed to feel?"

"Of course."

"I thought not till you were married."

"You can't control how you feel."

"But we must. *I* must, rather," she said. "Oh, I don't know what came over me."

"I do. We're in love."

"And that's what happens?"

"Yes."

Sidney had his talk with Will Caldwell the next morning.

"This is no surprise to me, Sidney, and surprise or no surprise, I can't say I'm displeased. You go ahead, and I hope she says yes—if she hasn't already, eh there, boy?"

"No, sir. I haven't actually asked her, but I'll be candid. It won't entirely surprise me if she says yes. We've talked about it."

"Of course you have. Well, when you do ask her, and when she says yes, then you can tell her that she has my permission to marry you. That'll save you another visit with me. Oh, we like you. You know that. I'm just thinking of when I became engaged to Grace's mother. These, uh, conferences with the prospective father-in-law, they can make a young fellow damned uncomfortable."

"Thank you, sir."

"But there is one thing we have to have a meeting about. You and I. I know your family are well fixed, so you may not like this, but I know it's extremely important to Grace."

"Anything Grace wants."

"Now, now, now. Don't, don't. Let me state it first. It has to do with your pride." Will looked out the window. "If and when you and Grace are married, I want you to live on the farm. Now hear me out, please. I've thought this over. I've considered giving her the farm as a wedding present, but whether she gets it as a wedding present or through inheritance, the farm's going to be hers. The house in town is going to be Brock's. Now then, it may hurt your pride a little, not to be allowed to provide a home of your own, but I tell you this is very important to Grace's happiness. I think she'd go anywhere with you, anywhere in the world, but all her life that's been her home, the farm. I think it's good to have this out now, Sidney, instead of later when you want to announce your engagement. For all practical purposes, the farm belongs to Grace, and when I die she'll have a considerable income, and when her mother dies there'll be more. Now this is what I would suggest as a way you could handle the problem. If you can carry it, I suggest that you pay your joint living expenses, and the general support of your wife, precisely as you would if you went to live in New York or anywhere else, and when you have children, they're also your financial responsibility. You're an only child, and I presume the sole heir, so later on—oh, and I almost didn't mention that you've always wanted a farm, so later on you can work out something with Grace to buy the farm from her, if you care to. But for the immediate future, Sidney, I think I'd almost make it a condition of my, uh, approval of the marriage that you give us your word, or assurance, that for the first two years you'll live on the farm."

"I give you my word right now."

"Well, think it over. It'll mean you'll have your mother-in-law and father-in-law for company a great deal oftener than if you lived elsewhere, but we're not going to last forever, and the truth is, now that I no longer ride horseback and the dam is too cold for me to swim in, the farm isn't the treat it used to be. I'm retiring in a year or two and Mrs. Caldwell and I expect to spend more time away from Fort Penn. For instance I've always had a hankering, I s'pose you'd call it, to see China, and now that we're more welcome there, or at least safer, I might take a trip and see the place. And South Africa. Be safe to visit there in a year or two, I should think. Well, meanwhile, speaking of travel, you have your train to catch. Good luck, my boy, and tentatively, at any rate, I welcome you into the fold."

Sidney again visited the farm for the Labor Day week-end, or what was called the Labor Day week-end in most states. In Pennsylvania it was then the first Saturday in September, and owing to a great strike of anthracite miners there was some sympathetic unrest among the working people of Fort Penn. On the Monday the Caldwells had a few friends for dinner. Will Caldwell made a little speech: "Dear friends, I have an announcement to make that may or may not come as a surprise to you, but surprise or otherwise, I think you'll all be as pleased as Emily and I are that this afternoon Sidney Tate asked for the hand of our daughter Grace, and, quite obviously, if you'll glance at them both, we have given our consent. I therefore propose a toast . . ." Will acquitted himself very well, quite as though he had not been informed within the hour that some labor rowdies had thrown a brick through a curved glass in the house on Second Street.

The announcement was not made official until October, which gave Connie Schoffstal time to arrange the large luncheon at which the announcement was made, and Grace by that time had her ring. Between October and June Sidney made the trip from New York to Fort Penn at least once every two weeks, and the respective parents paid official calls at the respective homes. So long as they remained unmarried they were the outstanding engaged couple in Fort Penn, at least, and they put on weight from the rich food that was served by hostesses trying to outdo one another. Sidney and Grace after the first few months of their engagement arrived at a method of mutual satisfaction of their passion, but they postponed ultimate consummation until their wedding night.

The wedding was conceded to be the biggest thing of its kind ever held in Fort Penn. Everybody agreed on that, from the very small group who actually witnessed the ceremony to the thousands who knew all about it. Like everything the Caldwells did, it had to be unique. Grace's wedding started being unique with the invitations: the important weddings in Fort Penn always had followed the system of taking care of the sheep and the goats by inviting the persons of goat status to the church but not to the reception. Grace adamantly refused to be married in Fort Penn. She told her mother that she had decided to be married at the little church in Becksville and that the reception would take place at the farm. The church could seat only eighty persons, and consequently cards to the church were the more highly prized tokens of Caldwell esteem. Not even the Governor of the state was invited to the church, although he was invited to, and attended, the reception. A compromise had to be effected so that an Episcopal clergyman could officiate in the Becksville church, which was Lutheran. The compromise was effected and the church thereby acquired its first pipe organ. It had been rumored that

Fort Penn was to witness its first "motorized" wedding; that Grace was importing automobiles as transportation for the bridal party between the church and the farm. Nothing could have been further from the truth. "If I see one automobile I'll tell them to go away," said Grace. A special train, of locomotive and five coaches, shuttled back and forth between the Fort Penn station of the N. F. P. & L. and the farm, which was not a regularly scheduled stop on the line, but which had a small shed at which trains stopped on signal from the conductor. The old Becksville–Fort Penn two-horse stage, idle a dozen years, was found to be in fair condition in the trolley-car barn. It was repainted and greased, and put into service to take infirm guests from the train to the Caldwell lawn, where the reception was held. In ignorance of Grace's threat a score of motor cars reached the farm, and a ferry service was instituted for the convenience of guests who lived on the eastern shore of the river, who might otherwise have had to travel a considerable distance to cross by bridge. Five mess tents were obtained at the National Guard armory. One of the tents was for the use of the bridal party and immediate family (the other guests ate under the sky, but as someone said, it was Caldwell weather). A second tent was for the hot plate and other foods, a third tent was for the champagne, whiskey and punch bars, a fourth tent served ice cream, other desserts and coffee, and the fifth tent was pitched to the east of the house, a good distance from the lawn and out of sight of the guests. It was reserved for ladies and small children. The gentlemen were directed to the stable. Professor Herman Schoffstal, who played the pipe organ at the church (it had been installed in time for the ceremony), also conducted the orchestra on the lawn. He had eight violins, two violas, two cellos, one bass viol, two harps, two flutes (one flautist and one harpist were ladies), and piano.

After they were made as one the bride and groom stepped into their victoria under a shower of rice, confetti, and serpentines. In honor of the occasion Higgins, the coachman, and his son had been fitted out in silk hats with cockades, black whipcord tail-coats, white doeskin breeches, and hunting-style boots, and they wore starched stocks. Prince and Duke, Emily Caldwell's chestnut cobs, were used, and they were in the silver-mounted harness, the set which was erroneously believed to have solid silver hames. The happy couple, followed by the bridal party in equally smart turnouts, proceeded to the Caldwell house. There Grace was taken by her husband to Will Caldwell's den, and in the presence of those ushers who were members of the Yale secret society called Death's Head, she was initiated with the brief ceremony reserved for all brides of Death's Head men. This solemn ritual concluded according to the rubrics, the bride and groom were permitted to continue with the schedule, which allowed fifteen minutes for bride, maid of honor, bridesmaids, bridegroom, best man, and ushers to empty their bladders, then to stand in line under one of the militia's tents until Sally Wall, a bridesmaid, keeled over in a faint, and two more bridesmaids appeared to be about to follow suit. At that point some six hundred men, women, and children had observed the amenities, but at least two hundred more were deprived of the pleasure of shaking hands with the ladies and gentlemen on the receiving line. For the first time in four strenuous hours (except for her rides in the victoria and her visit to the bathroom) Grace sat down, at the U-shaped table. The primary toasts were drunk and then Sidney and Grace took to the tennis court, now boarded over for dancing, and Professor Schoffstal, who had been providing subdued renditions of Mendelssohn and the like, struck up some Strauss, beginning with *An der Schönen Blauen.* The sterner Methodists turned their backs while the Episcopalians, Presbyterians, Lutherans, Reformeds, Baptists and Catholics partook of the dancing mood. Emily Caldwell danced the first dance with Alfred Tate, the second with Sidney, the third with Will Caldwell, and the fourth with his Excellency the Governor. The Governor, a handsome figure in his frock coat, but not the mould of form on the ballroom floor, thought he heard Emily muttering words that sounded like "damn you." "Mrs. Caldwell," he said, "my

dancing isn't all it should be, but did I hear you say, 'damn you'?"
They laughed together as she made a convincing denial, which
was somewhat the more difficult because she *had* said "Damn
you," but not as a criticism of the Governor's dancing. She had
seen Charlie Jay on his way to the bridal party's tent, and her
complete thought had been: "We're safe from you now, damn
you." Jessie Jay had regretted the invitation to the reception, but
she had sent some wedding present or other.

The presents were on view in the hall, the dining-room, the
sitting-room, and the library of the big house. They were being
guarded by three Pinkerton men disguised as waiters and Chief
Lengel of the Fort Penn police, who, although not intended to be
disguised as Admiral Dewey, had evoked recollections of the
hero of the recent war because of a resemblance one to the other,
or possibly because the chief's cap and moustache looked like
the admiral's. In his uniform Chief Lengel was a reminder to the
guests that they were looking upon articles of great value, in case
there was a single person more than ten years old who was so stupid as to need a reminder. Upstairs, in the wall safe in her
mother's bedroom Grace had stashed the pearl necklace Emily
had given her, the diamond bracelet from Mr. and Mrs. Tate, the
diamond-and-ruby ring from her father, and the diamond-and-
sapphire brooch from the Schoffstal family. But on the linen-
covered tables along the walls downstairs—"A man could easily
retire on what's here," said Chief Lengel to one of the Pinks. In
the sterling and Sheffield line there was enough to furnish a
small, expensive hotel, what with the chests of flat silver, roast
platters, butter dishes, tea services, tea-service trays, smaller tea-
service trays, bread trays, coffee services, samovars (in the event
Grace decided to have a Russian-type cozy corner), cigar boxes,
cigarette boxes (of which one was engraved with the signatures
of Sidney's best man and ushers), candelabra, pairs of candle
holders, candle snuffers, salvers, salt-and-pepper shakers, pepper mills, cup-holder and saucer sets, decanters, demi-tasse
spoons, cake knives, spatulas, ash receivers, matchboxes, punch

bowls, tureens, bon-bon dishes, tea canisters and infusers, matching and unmatching sugar bowls and cream pitchers, coasters, water pitchers, chafing dishes, statuettes, inkstands, complete desk sets, flasks (for the saddle), bells, and the Death's Head loving cup (one to every Death's Head bride). "I can't help thinking of that William J. Bryan," said Chief Lengel to the Pink.

The golden articles were easier to keep an eye on; they occupied a smaller space. There was a gold inkstand, a gold pen. A cigarette box, a bell, clock, paper-knife, stamp box, powder box, candlestick for sealing-wax, paperweight in the form of a cannon, demi-tasse spoons, snuff box, napkin rings, miniature picture frames, and a nugget from the Klondike mounted on a wooden base.

The guards paid little attention to the treasures in one of the rooms. The names Spode, Stiegel, Sevres, Lowestoft, Wedgwood, and Chi'en Lun signified nothing to Chief Lengel and the Pinks, and the only reason they went in that room at all was that they didn't want anything broken while they were on duty. Nobody would *steal* that stuff. In this room there were numerous bon-bon dishes which had been hand-painted. Women and girls all over the country spoke of their "painting," their "taking up painting," and their "giving up painting." By painting they meant decorating dishes and pitchers with gilt bands and, in this case, the script initials G. C. T. These art works had been the cause of great concern on the part of Miss Holbrook, whom Emily had engaged as social secretary a couple of months before the wedding invitations were to be sent out. Miss Holbrook earned every cent of the five-hundred-dollar honorarium which was paid her. The invitation list was her first task, involving not only Grace's relatives, friends, and acquaintances, but Sidney's as well, which in turn required two trips to New York for consultation with Sidney's mother. Miss Holbrook got the most help from Nicholas Bonniwell, of Kemp & Bonniwell, the Tiffany & Company of Fort Penn. A delicate situation had been created by the Caldwells' decision to have the invitations engraved by the actual

Tiffany, the New York Tiffany, but Miss Holbrook reminded Mr. Bonniwell that Kemp & Bonniwell had been selected to do the invitations for Grace's ball, and they couldn't expect everything, and moreover, most of the wedding presents would be bought at Kemp & Bonniwell's, Fort Penn's fashionable jewelers. Nicholas Bonniwell saw the light and turned over his mailing list to Miss Holbrook, and did not even mention the fact that Miss Holbrook's School had been patronizing the newer firm of Schmidt & Burke. The Bonniwell list, the roster of members of the Fort Penn Club, a judicious study of the telephone directory, and scraps of paper which Emily Caldwell handed Miss Holbrook from time to time made up the Fort Penn part of the list. When it came to making a list of the wedding presents and their donors Miss Holbrook had more trouble; a tree-of-life roast platter had been sent by the President of the United States and Mrs. Roosevelt (they were friends of the Tate family) and duplicates had been sent by five other parties, but the hand-painted bon-bon dishes were the challenge to Miss Holbrook. There was nothing to do but measure each one and write a full description of it so that Grace could identify it when she wrote her thank-you notes. "Just think," said Grace to Sidney, a day or so before the wedding. "I'll have to write a letter for each and every one of these things. But some day I'll be able to tell our children who sent every spoon, every dish."

In the linen and fancywork line the place of honor was given to the doilies which had been crocheted by the women backstairs, the bedspread embroidered by Julie, the cook, and the hemstitched napkins by Amelia Reifsnyder, wife of the farmer. The bride and groom received individual gifts from Higgins. Grace's was a set of hand-plaited reins: "It's years since I put me hand to this kind of work, and they look rather Western, but they'll do for hacking on the farm," said Higgins. His gift to Sidney was a thin little whip: "I carried this the last race I ever rode at the Fair Grounds, Mr. Tate, and I hope it'll bring you the same luck. I won."

At a few minutes before seven the bride and groom disappeared from the party. The cry went up, "Where they going? Where they going? Does anybody know where they're going on their honeymoon?" Connie Schoffstal caught the bride's bouquet, and put on a wise look when she was asked the happy couple's destination, although in truth she knew no better than anyone else. The dance floor and the tables were deserted at the cry of "Here they come—there they go," and Grace and Sidney were driven away in a brougham, with Higgins on the box and one of the cobs in the shafts. They were taken only to the end of the lane, and there they changed to a dog-cart and Beauty, Brock Caldwell's fast trotter, which was being held by young Neal Higgins. They drove to Fort Penn station, where their luggage was waiting, and took the evening train to Sunbury, about forty miles away. They had agreed not to spend their wedding night on a Pullman, but to go to the Sunbury hotel for the night and the next day board the Buffalo express, which would enable them to spend their second night in Niagara Falls.

"I've hardly seen you, all afternoon, and yet I know you're the loveliest thing that ever drew breath," said Sidney on the train.

"The only one I wanted to look nice for, and he didn't see me."

"I saw you. I'd have seen you if I'd been blind. This is the way I'll always remember you."

The proprietor of the hotel was expecting them. He and a boy carried their bags to the parlor, bedroom and bath on the second floor. "Mr. Reichelderfer said we shouldn't wait supper but we did. There's the pork chops if you want them, on the regular dinner, but maybe you'll like better the roast chicken we roasted special. You can have it up here. You don't have to go down the dining-room."

The man and the boy, his son, brought the meal and some ice for the bottle of champagne in Sidney's Gladstone. "When you're done just put the dirty dishes outside in the hall and somebody'll get them. Good night, all."

"I'm hungry, are you?" said Sidney, when they were alone.

"I'm starved."

"I like our quarters, very much."

"I do too," she said.

"And I like that man. He didn't treat us like—what we are. Honeymooners."

"The little boy stared."

"Well, little boys do stare at pretty girls. He isn't much younger than you are. Only about four years younger, I should judge."

"Still, I suppose he's better than the usual hotel bellboy. I've always hated hotel bellboys, I don't know why. I know why!"

"Why?"

"I can tell you. I never told anyone else. I hate them because when they carry your bags upstairs they go right into your bedroom with you. See what I mean? I've known you over two years and you've never been in my bedroom, but these nasty bellboys have been walking right into my bedroom every time I've ever stayed at a hotel. It's very fresh. The hotel owners ought to change that."

"You may have a big problem on your hands, getting them to. Isn't this good chicken?"

"*Isn't* it?"

"I never expected to eat such good chicken in Sunbury, Pennsylvania."

"Well, I don't see why not. I've always told you the Pennsylvania Dutch are very good cooks."

"Oh, are we still in Pennsylvania Dutch-land?"

"Not like Fort Penn, but this man's Pennsylvania Dutch. Didn't you hear him talk? I'm glad you brought this champagne. It's my favorite drink. Here's to you, my husband."

"And to you, my wife."

They drank and then she stood up. "I'm not hungry any more, Sidney."

"I'm not either, really."

"While I'm taking a bath you can put the dishes out."

"All right. I'm going to take a bath, too."

In about ten minutes she called from the bedroom and he went in. She was in bed, and the only light was coming from the bathroom. "Oh," he said.

"What?"

"I guess I'll undress in the parlor."

He undressed and put on his pajamas and dressing-gown and walked through the bedroom to the bath. He came out again wearing the pajamas and gown. "What do you think about the light?"

"I don't know," she said.

"Just the bathroom light? Could we have that?"

"Yes. Whatever you want."

"I've never seen you."

"I've never seen you, either."

She suddenly threw off the bedclothing. "Here *I* am," she said. He had been thinking she had on a nightgown, but he was wrong.

"Just let me look, a little while."

In a very little while she began to squirm under his gaze. "I'm looking at your face, Sidney. It excites me as much as if you were touching me. Now close the door." He did so and got into the bed, and the moment he touched her the rage began. "Do everything! Kiss me? Kiss me here? Let me—no. No! Go in me. Quickly, Sidney, please. I'm going, I'm going. Don't do anything else, go in me. Oh, you're in me and I'm all around you, just in time, time, time. Oh, such wonderful, exquisite."

"Yes, yes. Dear Grace. Did it hurt?"

"No."

"Not at all?"

"No."

"That's good. I never want to hurt you."

"Sidney."

"Yes, darling."

"Are you happier now?"

"Oh, Grace, I've never been so happy."

"I don't mean just happy."

"Yes."

"I am too. You know, sometimes, girls that ride a lot—"

"I know."

"Don't look, Sidney. I have to get up and go to the bathroom."

He obeyed her; he did not look. He heard the water running in the tub.

"To think of lying with you all night," she said, when she came back.

"Yes."

"If you want to touch me, all you have to do is touch me."

"Yes."

"Oh, what people don't know that have only kissing, and playing with each other. Think of being able to lie here together."

"Yes."

"And from now on, every night," she said.

The pace of her speeches was slowing down, as though she were talking herself to sleep. He had his right arm under her neck, his left hand holding her right hand. Her breathing became deep and regular and she fell sound asleep. For a few minutes he thought protective thoughts and grateful thoughts. He was rich and free, strong and mated, lucky and happy and wide awake. He slid his hand away from hers and caressed her breasts until the nipples hardened and—though the rhythm of her breathing was not disturbed—she reached for him and found him, caressed him, and this time it was as though years had passed since their first time, or as though she had learned and grown in her sleep. The second time made the first time forgotten; like a mistake to be disremembered. It was dark now; no light from the bathroom; and she was not the untried bride in the veil and lace, no more than he was the bowing, properly self-effacing bridegroom of the church and the reception. He was not shocked by the words she knew or her directions, because he was not sure that the words she was speaking were not words he was uttering himself. At the approach of the climax she began calling to him, and after they reached it together he could have no doubt of the fact. Her words were gently spoken: "Don't move." He stayed that way until he was sure she wanted him to move, and then he lay beside her without her protesting. "Do you know how I feel?" he said.

"Tell me," she said.

"I feel as though we'd built something great."

"I hope it wasn't a baby," she laughed.

He laughed. "Grace, you know you shock me."

"I suppose I do," she said. "Do you know why I'm sure I do?"

"Why?"

"Because nothing *you* do shocks *me*, and nothing *I* do shocks me. But you! Ah, Sidney, poor Sidney. Nobody'll ever know you married a bad woman. But you're bad, too. I don't consider you a little choirboy with rosy cheeks. Oh, I'm glad you married me."

In other years he often would think of what they had said that night, and of what they had not said.

—

All the guests got home safely from the reception, aside from six or seven cindered eyes on the special train; Isaac Schoffstal's attack of acute indigestion, which was relieved with some Arm & Hammer baking soda; a McKelvie girl's finger, which was pinched in the Caldwells' kitchen screendoor when she went looking for salt to take out a stain on her dress; the back of Mrs. Fred Bauer's neck, slightly burned when grazed by a cigar in the hand of Walter Buchwalter; Agnes Martindale's left little toe, bruised, and a day later discovered to be broken, by Paul Reichelderfer's walking on it; Philip S. Hamilton's right ear, stung by a wasp in the Caldwell barn.

Two days after the wedding the last of the out-of-town guests had gone home and the citizens of Fort Penn began looking forward to the Fourth of July, but in their hearts they knew that the Fourth, while it offered firecrackers and baseball games and the annual big doings on the river, was not going to be in it with the Tate-Caldwell wedding, with all its excitement of private cars from New York, the fashionable strangers in the hotels, the lines of carriages at the pre-wedding parties, the last-minute hustle and bustle in the stores, the savage curses of the people who had not been invited, the unbearable hauteur of those who had been invited to the church, the spending, the tips, the curiosity and conjecture over Sidney Tate, Shoptown's speculation on Grace's chastity, the angry disappointment when Grace chose to be married in the remoteness of the country. Said *Sentinel* Editor Arthur James Hollister: "It all comes down to this: if the telegraph wire said a thousand people had been killed in an earthquake in Chile, the important news in Fort Penn would still be that a rich and beautiful young girl was going to go to bed with a handsome, more or less unknown city slicker. It's regrettable, out of proportion, but it's true. Or, God damn it, *is* it regrettable? Come to think of it, if the people of Fort Penn were more interested, morbidly interested in the earthquake and a thousand people killed, I'd quite the newspaper business, or at any rate I'd get out of Fort Penn."

———

At an indeterminate point in their lives Sidney and Grace became the Tates. Someone said to someone else, "The Tates were there," or "I stopped by the Tates'," or "I haven't seen the Tates." Someone made some such statement, and the fact that the speaker made the statement was not nearly so significant as the fact of its acceptance by the person or persons who heard him. It was an indeterminate, undeterminable point, but it was the right moment for the remark to be made and heard. At the moment the statement, in that form, was accepted, the marriage was established. People would go on saying, "Sidney and Grace were there," and "I stopped by Grace's," and "I haven't seen Sidney and Grace"; but the other form—"The Tates"—had been given circulation and was even more permanent than "Sidney and Grace" had been. After a while the new form was more acceptable, had more of an intimacy about it, than "Sidney and Grace." The climbers, the not-yet-arrived, the remote-but-acquainted might speak of "Sidney and Grace" and snobbishly feel in so doing that they had proclaimed a close relationship. They were wrong. Once the Tates had been called the Tates, and the form had been adopted, "Sidney and Grace" lost its value as a sign of constant and relaxed friendship with the persons named. There was a simple reason that this was so: a genuine intimate of Sidney's and Grace's called them the Tates because there was something rough-and-ready about calling them the Tates that did not obtain otherwise. In calling them the Tates a woman or a man was proving that he was their equal. A man might say, "Katharine and I are playing tennis with Sidney and Grace," and reveal nothing more than that he and his wife were about to receive a beating by the best mixed-doubles team in Fort Penn. If, however, his wife said, "We're getting up a picnic: the Walls, the Poffenbergers, the Tates, and the Cunninghams," she not only announced that she was placing herself in a position to be stung by a bee from the same hive as the bee that might sting Grace, but that she regarded Grace and her husband as welcome and desirable companions, but no more so than the Poffenbergers, the Walls, or the Cunninghams.

The difference in snobbism between those who said "the Tates" and those who said "Sidney and Grace" was slight and incalculable because there would have had to exist different standards of measurement. The "Sidney and Grace" people were strivers, and could not be gauged by the same rules that would be used on the secure, or "the Tates" people.

Then there was the absence of a difference, the thing in common: it was the admission as made with many a direct deed and obliquely by many a word that the Tates were unique.

"Now tell me why," said a mythical stranger to a mythical but observant citizen of Fort Penn, "are Mr. and Mrs. Sidney Tate unique? Go on, tell me."

"Well, first of all, their appearance," replied the citizen. "You've got to grant me that, right off the bat, they're as goodlooking a couple as you'll find in a month of Sundays or, if you're pressed for time, a day's journey. She's a handsome woman. We all knew she would be, even from a little girl. She had those eyes, you'd say they were big eyes, big brown eyes. But they weren't big at all, you know. They were only average size eyes, and as a matter of fact, I'll bet if you measured them and you found a deviation from average size, I wouldn't be one bit surprised if the deviation was on the small side, rather than the large size. And another what you might call contradiction: You'd think to look at her—not only when she was a child, but when she was pretty grown up, and even today, as far as that goes—you'd always think she was the kind of pensive, deep-thinking, brooding girl that was working out algebra problems in her head, or hearing music that she was getting ready to put down on paper, such as the Berceuse from Jocelyn. But I happen to know she was never very good in school, in her lessons. She always got promoted, and I suppose she deserved to be as much as most of the girls that went to that Miss Holbrook's, but she never stood out as a student. Never took any prizes of any kind. And as to music, she can sit down and play a tune on the piano and if she has the music in front of her she won't hold you in suspense while she's trying to find a chord. She could also play some pieces by heart. Chopin pieces she learned. Some Beethoven. Some Bach. Schumann. But as to composing anything, that was the farthest thing from her mind, if results mean anything. No, she mostly depended on having the music right there in front of her. You know, the piano she learned on, it was an upright and it had places to hold candles, candleholders, on either side of the piano."

"Never mind about the candleholders, please. I'd rather learn some more about Grace."

"Very well, but you'll pardon me if it's my opinion that environment is just as important as heredity, and a piano with candleholders was part of Grace's environment. Don't worry, I'll say no more on the subject, but that's my honest opinion."

"All right, you've put that across," said the stranger. "Now are you all finished with her eyes, how she appeared to be a brooding sort but didn't shine in her studies or music?"

"Well, kind of," said the citizen. "Except that with those brooding eyes she naturally was thought of as a Latin type, and the Latin type in this country we always associate with—well, Carmen. Emotional, tempestuous. But I never heard any of that sort of talk about Grace. For a while there she wasn't even *popular* with the opposite sex."

"Perhaps they were afraid of her."

"That's a possibility, but here in Fort Penn—I'm just telling you what I know—never any talk about anything out of the way. And here's a funny thing I just happened to think of: I've known one or two cases where a young fellow'd bet Grace had blue eyes."

"Well, of course that doesn't necessarily mean anything. You've heard of husbands that didn't know the color of their wives' eyes."

"Yes, I've heard of that, and I can believe it. I just put that in because I thought you might be interested."

"I am. It's worthy of some consideration," said the stranger. "But go on, please."

"Well, that's all on the question of her appearance, bearing in mind that she got better-looking all the time. And she married a handsome young fellow, so they make a handsome couple."

"That's true, but it doesn't make them unique."

"You're right. That alone doesn't make them unique. That alone wouldn't make *any* couple unique, unless you happened to run across them in a very ugly-looking crowd. And here let me say once and for all, our Pennsylvania Dutch couples can be mighty easy on the eye, at least when they're young. You take some of our young husbands and wives. They don't usually run very tall, but the girls are a nice little handful. As a friend of mine said one time, everything's right there where you can get at it. The boys—the third generation ones are getting taller and a good many of them are losing that straight line in the back of the head that makes them look like the Prussian Guard. Of course weight they still have to contend with, the boys and the girls both. After they start making babies the girls get dumpy and the boys too. Sometimes a fellow wonders how they get near enough to have another baby, but they find a way, they find a way. And they're good eaters."

"I've heard that, but aren't we getting away from Mr. and Mrs. Tate?"

"Excuse me, we are. I just got started on the Pennsylvania Dutch compared with Mr. and Mrs. Tate."

"That's all right," said the stranger. "We have to do some comparing if we're going to find out why the Tates are unique. Let's take a firm grip on ourselves and forget about their appearance. Let's talk about money, for instance, or family background."

"Money is always interesting to talk about," said the citizen. "Grace Caldwell comes of a moneyed family, so we can combine these two subjects, money and family background. If you went back over the history of Fort Penn I'd hazard a conjecture that the Caldwells and the Brocks—remembering that Grace's mother was a Brock—they were always among the richest people in this part of the country. As near as I can make out, the Caldwell money came from the land. They used to own thousands of acres here in Nesquehela County alone. First they had a trading-post and that became a store, and the country storekeeper you know was always a banker in some respects. Hardly any cash business between him and the farmer, and not a hell of a lot more between the storekeeper and the fellow he bought his goods from in Philadelphia and Lancaster, but at least more cash than the farmer ever saw. Well, it goes without saying, farmers'd have a bad year or two or three, and in that way the Caldwells'd get to own farmland, because the farmers'd be on the Caldwell books for every penny the farm was worth, and if a farmer had too many bad years and got sick or tired and discouraged and went out to the barn one morning and hanged himself, the way a lot of them did, the storekeeper would *have* to take over the farm. Back say fifty or a hundred years I have no idea what those individual Caldwells were like, crooks or skinflints or nice and easygoing, but I do know this much: the storekeeper's credit with

Lancaster and Philadelphia was better than the farmer's credit with the storekeeper. The storekeeper had the job of marketing the farmer's goods and in that way he got his hands on a little cash, and the fellow in Philadelphia thought more of the man that was handing him a little cash than he did of the farmer's wagonload of turnips."

"A more or less familiar story. What about the Brock family?"

"The Brock family? They're more recent than the Caldwells, in this neighborhood. They were Philadelphia people and their branch turned up in the northern part of the county, looking for coal. They found it. Plenty of coal being dug out of the ground right today, only not much of it means money in Emily Caldwell's pocket, because you see the problem then was to get the coal to market, just as it is today, but before the railroad had time to be built those Brocks ran out of money and certain Ohio people are making the money today. But the Brocks stayed in these parts and went into the lumber business. There your transportation was solved for you by the Nesquie, the river. But Grace Tate's father and mother weren't lumber people or farming people. Grace's grandfathers were bankers. They put up the money, when they were so inclined, then let the other fellow worry about the weather. And Will Caldwell, he and Emily own all the choice parcels of real estate in Fort Penn. Land that Will's grandfather took over as farm land is now all residential. North Fort Penn belongs to the family, and I have no idea how much footage on the river front and building sites in our business district. Bauer's store, for instance. Will owns the land it's built on. Won't sell a square inch. Soldiers Park? Where you see the statues and the Civil War cannon? That's on Caldwell land, not public property at all. Once a year it's closed off to the public so you and I can't walk across it and establish eminent domain. I don't say Will Caldwell'd ever do such a thing, but he has the legal right to tell the Park Commission to take their cannon and statues some place else. It wouldn't be hard, either, inasmuch as Will's chairman of the Park Commission . . . Now don't get impatient—"

"No, this is interesting," said the stranger.

"Thank you," said the citizen. "Well, what I was aiming at is, the Will Caldwells are probably not the richest people in Fort Penn, and I've heard it said they never were the richest, but you can safely say that Grace's family have been among the richest longer than any other family in Fort Penn."

"But they're not the richest?"

"No. I could name two or three families today I think have more money. The Isaac Schoffstals, and some say coony old Andrew O'Brien, that owns the Boston Store. And Fred Bauer's often mentioned, and I've heard it said Miles Brinkerhoff has more than you think. Miles has the bakery, but he's also in with a powder mill that cleaned up in '98, and I understand he got his hands on a big block of Power & Light through one of the country banks when the local light company was, uh, amalgamated, if you know what I mean."

"Aheh-ahem. I think I do," said the discreet stranger. "Getting back to Mrs. Tate's genealogy—"

"Ah, yes. I see what you mean. I say amalgamate, and you get my meaning. You say genealogy, and I get your meaning," said the citizen. "If you're inquiring about Mayflower passengers, colonial governors—no. I'm under the impression that there was a Caldwell connection in the House of Burgesses, but the connection isn't very close. Collateral, I guess. I think Grace's parents are pretty level-headed about that kind of bragging. They'll be the first to admit they had Tories in the closet, and Will's the kind of man that wouldn't claim George Washington and leave out Benedict Arnold if he was related to both. No, if you want the Pilgrim Fathers and that kind of thing Fort Penn has plenty of them before you get around to Grace's people."

"What about Tate?"

"Tate? Rich, but not as rich as Grace's family. Father was born in England and he wasn't any bloody nobility or we'd have heard about it by this time. Mother was Hudson Valley stock, Harmon by name. We have some Harmons in the next county, very fine family, so maybe Sidney's no stranger after all."

"I beg your pardon?" said the stranger.

"Oh, excuse *me*," said the citizen. "No offense intended, none taken I trust."

"None taken, surely," said the stranger. "Then, to recapitulate, we have Sidney and Grace, a pair of individuals who are pleasing to the eye, but are not the local apple-winners. They represent a lot of money, but if they started throwing dollars at any of three or four other families, Sidney and Grace would run out of dollars first. And as to their family history, their papers are in order as far back as a reasonable man would care to go, but other Fort Penn folk presumably were wearing shoes several generations before Sidney and Grace's ancestors were. And yet, and yet—they're unique."

"No question about it," said the citizen. "But while you were speaking just now I caught a figure of speech you used, and therein may lie some hint as to why Sidney and Grace are unique, or outstanding."

"What was that?"

"Well, the metaphor about how if Sidney and Grace got into a battle and used dollars for ammunition," said the citizen. "You know, friend, it's true, if the Ham Schoffstals started pegging cartwheels at the Sidney Tates, and the Tates threw one every time the Schoffstals threw one, it's true the Tates would run out of ammunition before the Schoffstals did. But I think I'd bet on the Tates. I don't think they'd throw a dollar every time the Schoffstals threw one. I think the Tates would make every dollar count. They'd get more out of their money. By God, they do in actual practice."

"Thank you for a pleasant conversation, and good day to you," said the stranger.

———

It took about as long for their life together and their individual lives to follow a seasonal pattern as it did for Sidney and Grace to adopt a daily one. They thought of the farm as home and they were governed by the daily weather and the seasonal, which governed the changes inside the ground and inside a cow's belly. It would be time to plant and it would be time to plow, to nourish, and to harvest, and to begin preparations for next year's timothy and next year's calves. Sidney would come in from an afternoon in the saddle and say, "Jack's started shedding." Jack was a sorrel gelding that Sidney had picked up for a miserly three hundred.

"Spring is here," Grace would say.

"Seems like only yesterday he was getting his winter coat."

"That's what I was just thinking."

"But I'm afraid Spring's not here yet. What did you do while I was out working so hard?"

"Out getting nice rosy cheeks and getting to feel wonderful, you mean. Give me a kiss."

"Do you think I ought to? A kiss got you the way you are today."

"Oh, no it didn't. Not a kiss. And I never believed it did. Oh, baby, hurry up and get out of there so your Daddy can get in."

"If this child could understand what we were saying . . . You know sometimes when I think it might be a girl I get embarrassed talking this way in her presence. Very sorry, young lady."

"It's no young lady, and it's no gentleman either, kicking his mother this way."

"More kicking?"

"Moving around, I guess, the way you do in your sleep. I'll tell you what I did this afternoon. I wrote the last thank-you letters for our Christmas presents—"

"It's always good to get them off before the following Christmas."

"—and Connie came out on the trolley and stayed for about an hour. *Ham* is buying an *automobile,* a foreign Mercedes."

"The Schoffstals' horses'll be glad to hear that. Give their mouths a chance to heal."

"I thought that too, but I didn't say it. And let me see what else is new. Scotty Bordener's moving to Philadelphia to work for some new company down there. He's either leaving any day now or is already gone."

"Mm-hmm."

"Darling, smoke a cigarette, will you please? Not your pipe. I'm sorry, but I can't help it."

"I'm sorry, sweetheart."

"It's just now, you know."

"Sure, I forgot. What else is new?"

"Well, let me see. You care to hear what all the ladies wore to Mary Wall's bridge whist?"

"Be in tonight's paper, won't it? Just saving you the exertion."

"Thank you, dear man. You're so considerate. But the most important thing I did all afternoon, would you like to hear what that was?"

"Yes."

"I prayed that my dear husband would come home early—and pour me a whiskey and water. You haven't even taken one yourself."

"Well I will now."

"Doctor O'Brien is coming out to see me tomorrow instead of next day. He's going away for a few days. Wouldn't it be nice if I could have the baby on our wedding anniversary?"

"It would, wouldn't it?"

"On the other hand that would make it late, and we don't want that."

"No. My guess is you don't have much to say about when it's born. When it's ready it'll let you know."

"Well, I hope he appreciates what I'm doing for him."

"We do, sweetheart, speaking for him and myself."

"You're a dear, Sidney."

She had the baby on May 10, 1904, a few weeks before their anniversary. The child weighed nine pounds and was delivered with a minimum of damage to himself and his mother. The rejoicing was great. He was the first-born of his parents, the first grandchild on either side of the family, the first child born in the big house on the farm (the Sam Reifsnyders had had three in their house), the first child born to a member of Grace's class at Miss Holbrook's. The infant by being born was the cause of a curious rearrangement in the Fort Penn attitude toward himself and his father: while Grace was carrying the child it was known as Grace's child, like Grace's hair, Grace's smile, with little attention to the fact of the child or of its paternity. But when the baby was born the people of Fort Penn immediately thought of the child as the child of *both* parents, and Sidney as the husband and father. The child established the father as a Fort Penn figure. He remained an alien, but with the difference that he was not just any alien, but one of Fort Penn's own aliens. He could never not be an alien, but at least he was the father of a Fort Penn native.

In the evening of the day the baby was born Sidney sat with his father-in-law in the den. "Well, it's been quite a day, Sidney. Have you had anything to eat?"

"No, I haven't. Have you?"

"I had some lunch at the club," said Will Caldwell. "You haven't even had a drink, have you?"

"No, and I don't suppose you have either. We're not behaving true to form. We ought to be getting royally drunk."

"All right, let's," said Caldwell. "I haven't been drunk in years. I don't even know when the last time was. I can't remember."

"How'd you like some cold roast beef and champagne, sir?"

"I think that'd fill the bill."

Sidney went to the kitchen and returned with a bottle of champagne. "We're not going to have anything as simple as cold roast beef. They wouldn't hear of it out there. They're getting supper ready for Mrs. Caldwell, to take up on a tray, so our picnic is called off but at least we can have our champagne." He poured the wine and the older man stood up.

"Well, Sidney, to your son and my grandson, I hope he's as good a man as his father."

"And then he can try harder and be as good a man as his grandfather," said Sidney. They drank. "Do we smash the glasses in the fireplace?"

"I don't know if it's the custom, but here goes mine!" said Caldwell.

They smashed the glasses, thus breaking a set which had been a wedding present. They expended the champagne in toasts and Sidney fetched another bottle, which they drank while their supper was served them at one end of the dining-room table. They went back to the den for cigars and coffee and more champagne.

"Well, I've lived to see it," said Caldwell. "A grandson. What a man looks forward to, I guess from the birth of his first child. I know I did when Brock was born. You looking forward to a grandson, Sidney?"

"I don't know, sir. I don't know whether I have or not. I lived a whole lifetime in my thoughts today. I woke up about ha' past five this morning, pretty sure this would be the day. Doctor O'Brien—now there's a nice Irishman. You know, Mr. Caldwell, that's a fine man. You know that, of course, better than I do, but I want you to know I appreciate Doctor O'Brien. He saved my wife's life."

"How, Sidney?"

"By—what he did today."

"Oh, delivering the baby."

"Right. In a time of need I'll never forget Doctor O'Brien. You know I'm not a very religious man, Mr. Caldwell, but in a time of need I'll always appreciate Doctor O'Brien. Won't you?"

"I certainly will."

"Anybody that didn't appreciate Doctor O'Brien is no friend of mine, I can tell you that, but I knew you'd appreciate him, Mr. Caldwell. I appreciate you too, Mr. Caldwell."

"Thank you, Sidney."

"I think my own father is as fine a man as I ever knew, Mr. Caldwell, but that isn't taking anything away from you. You're Grace's father and I appreciate you. You believe that, don't you, Mr. Caldwell?"

"Yes, I do, Sidney."

"We don't often talk like this, but I just want you to know that. I'm a father myself now, you know, and I can understand how you feel. You want the best for your daughter and I'm not the best, but I don't think I have to tell you this much. The luckiest day in my life happened at your house. Do you know when that was? That was the day I first saw Grace, I saw her for the first time. I feel the same way you do, Mr. Caldwell. Her happiness is all that matters."

"You've made her happy, Sidney."

"Have I? Have I, Mr. Caldwell? I hope so. I'm going to tell that little fellow upstairs, when he gets old enough, I'm going to tell him that he was put on this earth to make his mother happy, and everything he does he has to ask himself first, 'Is this going to make my mother happy or unhappy?' That's what I ask myself, and if the answer is yes, I do it. If the answer is in the negative, I don't. What do you think, Mr. Caldwell? Do you think we ought to go out in society more than we do?"

"I don't know, Sidney. You and Grace've only been married a year and considering she was pregnant most of the time—why do you ask?"

"A friend of mine. I saw him about a month ago, and he said— this is a fellow I knew before I came here. He said the Fort Penn people would like to see more of us, or Grace, anyway. He wasn't offensive or anything of the sort, but he made it clear all right. As though I were a snob."

"But you're not a snob, Sidney, so what do you care what people say, or think?"

"Not a damn, at least about me, about myself. But what they say about Grace is another matter."

"Why should it be? Why should either one of you care what they say or think? Sidney, they've been saying that about us as long as I can remember. They said it about Mrs. Caldwell and me when we didn't go to every party we were invited to, and natu- rally they say it about you and Grace. They even said it about Brock."

"Hmm."

"Why 'hmm'? I don't mind if you and Brock aren't bosom friends . . . Oh, I see the light. It was Brock that said you were act- ing snobbish."

"Well, he wasn't the only fellow that brought it up. If it'd been Brock and nobody else I wouldn't have given the matter another thought, but another fellow mentioned it too. You know, Mr. Caldwell, if Grace liked going out, I'd like it. What she wants to do, I want to do. But she likes it here on the farm and always has, and I always wanted to live on a farm. I'd never bother to discuss this with anyone else, but I just want *you* to know, you and Mrs. Caldwell. We're living the way we want to live, it suits Grace, it suits me."

"We know that, Sidney, Mrs. Caldwell and I. And it's only fair to tell you, we appreciate you. You've made Grace happy and that's all a father or mother can hope for. I'd like to see Brock happier than he is, but I don't know what we can do to bring that about. If you have any suggestions on that score, I'd like to hear them."

"The only thing I can suggest is for Brock to look the whole world over and find a wife like Grace."

"You think Brock ought to marry."

"A girl like Grace."

"A girl like Grace," repeated Will Caldwell.

"Exactly like Grace. But he won't find her. There is no girl like Grace."

"Oh. I was afraid you were suggesting that Brock was so fond of his sister that other girls didn't measure up."

"I'm not the man to talk about Brock, Mr. Caldwell. He doesn't see things the way I do, and I don't see things the way he does."

"No, of course not."

They had a little more champagne and talked a little while longer, until Sidney dozed off in his chair. Will Caldwell got an ulster out of the hall closet and covered him with it, and quietly went up to bed.

———

The christening took place at the baptismal font of the Cathedral, which did not entirely make up for Grace's decision to be married in the Becksville church, but at least showed the suffragan bishop that Sidney and Grace intended to bring up their child in the Episcopal faith. The boy was named Alfred William, after his grandfathers. In his honor each of his grandfathers gave a thousand dollars to the children's ward of the Misericordia Hospital, and at the direction of Doctor O'Brien a small brass plate was screwed into the swinging door of the ward. It bore the appropriate wording: "In Appreciation of a Gift in Honor of Alfred William Tate."

The point at which Sidney and Grace became the Tates was not indeterminate in Sidney's mind. It occurred after the birth of his first son, after Grace was up and well again and the Ham Schoffstals had a motor car, then someone else had a motor car, then someone else; and the service on the trolley line was improved to the extent that a friend could take the car at one of the downtown corners in Fort Penn and alight at the farm three-quarters of an hour later. The automobile and the interurban made for more frequent dropping in at the farm during the day. The change in accessibility did not make the farm a more popular meeting-ground in the sense that more people felt free to drop in uninvited, but those who were welcome, and knew it, came to call more frequently, and Grace discovered that she liked being a hostess. "I still don't like going to other girls' houses, but it's nice when they come out here," she told Sidney. They came in all seasons, listened politely to Sidney's and Grace's reports on farm activity, and went away with the memory of Sidney and Grace bidding them au revoir, an enviable picture of domestic felicity that was an inducement to change from town life to country life. But the fashionable non-agricultural suburb came later to Fort Penn, and, inevitably, grew up around the first country club. As George Wall said to Mary Wall: "*Sure* it'd be nice to live on a farm like the Tates', but Sidney's a gentleman farmer and I have to go to work every day. A big difference. If Sidney wants to take a couple days off and go to Philadelphia, his farm keeps going just the same. Between you and me, maybe it goes better. But if I take a few days off, I lose money. We can think of a farm when we're rich and retired."

George's statement did not reach Sidney's ears, but he found out that what George had said was typical of the thinking of most of their friends. For more than a year Sidney had been saddling a horse almost every day and riding over the countryside until he knew all of the roads and most of the paths west of the river to a distance of three or four miles and half way to Fort Penn to the south and six or seven miles to the north. It was all farm land except for the tiny villages like Becksville, an occasional stone quarry. Becksville had a farmers' hotel, a church, a flour mill, a general store, a blacksmith shop, and a couple of dozen homes, and it was larger than most of the villages. It seemed to Sidney that he was living in a part of the county that would be ideal for fox-hunting. He had begun his daily rides with no purpose other than to get to know the land and the men who farmed it, but after he had taken his first fence the fox-hunting idea was born. He had not been a fox-hunting man any more than he had been a polo man, but when he spoke to Grace about founding a hunt she agreed that it was a good idea. She was pregnant but she would be ready to ride by the time the fall came around and a small hunt club could be formed. Accordingly they had ten couples and some extras for dinner and after dinner Sidney made a little speech. All the men and most of the women present knew how to ride and some of them were keen horsemen.

"I don't want you to blame Grace for this, but the fact of the matter is, I may have gotten you all here under false pretenses. I'm sure you all thought you were coming out to have a nice dinner and then after dinner we'd have a game of cards. But I had a secret ulterior motive. Grace knows about it, but no one else does. My motive is to broach the subject and have a discussion about forming a hunt club."

"A hunt club? You mean a fox-hunting club?" someone asked.

"Yes. All of us here like to ride—when we're able—and those who are able, do ride, some of you ride several times a week. But as far as I've been able to learn, there's never been a hunt club in Fort Penn."

He knew from their expressions that there never would be a hunt club in Fort Penn. He went on describing the countryside that they knew better than he, and stating advantages to body and soul that are gained in the pursuit on horseback of M. Reynard. He conceded there were obstacles, like fences, to be overcome, but since this was only the first meeting, and not even a meeting, really, he thought that if in this particular group he could stir up some enthusiasm, it would be at least a beginning. "George Wall, you've been a horseman all your life. Let's have a few words on how you feel about the idea."

George Wall reluctantly stood up: "Well, I think it might be fun, good exercise, and as you say, there are a lot of obstacles, and I don't want to be a wet blanket, but I just wonder when I'd be able to find the time. I'm at my office at eight-thirty every morning and I think quite a few of the other fellows present are too, and when we'd get a morning off'd be hard to say. I don't think we have enough or would have enough members to make it worthwhile to buy a pack of hounds, and where would we stable our horses. I don't know, Sidney. I ride every time I get the chance, but that isn't once a week any more. Why don't you call on Ham?"

"All right. Ham Schoffstal?"

"Well, I ride oftener than George does, because I drill with the Troop at the Armory in the winter, once a week, and Saturdays and Sundays at the farm, but I'm afraid George is right about we fellows riding on work-days."

A few others were called upon but they spoke only the same words and fewer, and Sidney then took over and closed the subject: "Well, it doesn't seem to be feasible now, but I do wish you'd all give it a thought once in a while and perhaps in a few years we could get together again. We could start out with paper chases and if there were enough interest it might develop into a real hunt. But now let's play some cards."

After a few minutes of awkwardness the people at the card tables brought up the subject again. Sidney, at one table, heard someone, one of the women, saying, "I'd like to hunt, but who'd there be but the Tates and some of we girls."

When the guests had gone Brock remained. He and Connie were spending the night at the farm. Connie said her piece: "I wish my brother Hamilton had a mind of his own. He's always wanted to have a hunt club here in Fort Penn, but when he heard George Wall he had to pretend to be a businessman too." She and Grace retired and Sidney was left with Brock.

"What do you think, Brock?"

"About the hunt club?"

"Yes."

"I'd join one if we had one. Probably do me a world of good."

"I'm sorry I picked George Wall. I like George, but he's too busy carving out a career for himself."

"That isn't where you made your mistake. You handled the whole thing wrong," said Brock.

"How did I?"

"Well, do you want to have it straight from the shoulder?"

"Sure."

"Well, here it is, then. In the first place, old man, you weren't the fellow to handle it at all. Allow me to give you a piece of advice. Any time you want something done in Fort Penn, get someone else interested and you stay out of it."

"Not the man, eh?"

"No, not if it's a new idea. It isn't that they hold anything against you personally. It'd happen to anyone from out of town. If you'd spoken to me, I wouldn't have brought it up either, but I could have given you the right advice so that now instead of having a funeral over the hunt-club idea, they'd be sitting around this minute, figuring out ways and means. What you should have done was tell me what you had in mind, then I'd have talked to Ham Schoffstal, and Ham'd begin to think it was all his idea and the first thing you knew, Ham'd come to you and ask you if you wanted to start a hunt club. I know this town if I don't know anything else, old man."

"You're right," said Sidney. "Well, at least I learned something. The Tates aren't the ones to initiate something."

"The Tates?"

"Oh, yes, Brock. The Tates. I overheard us being referred to as the Tates. That's something, I guess."

"Yes, I guess you are known as the Tates now. I suppose that is a big step forward."

"Yes, it is, *old man,*" said Sidney. "We never will get along, will we, Brock?"

"I don't know. Don't we get along? What do you mean 'get along'? I'm not supposed to think you're Jesus Christ because you married my sister, am I? You didn't change your opinion of me when you married Grace. You think I'm a prick, and I think you're one, so what the hell, Sidney, let's leave it at that. We keep out of each other's way, as much as possible. Remember our manners when company's present, and that's about all there is to it. . . . I'm for bed. Good night, old man."

"Good night, old man."

Brock halted at the door and smiled at Sidney. "Oh, by the way, I just said I didn't have to think you were Christ because you married my sister?"

"So you did."

"Well, I don't. I ran into a friend of yours recently. Not exactly *ran* into her, either. Sonya."

"Sonya? I don't know any Sonya. What's her last name?"

"Oh, I think she changes that from time to time. But she knew your last name. When I was introduced to her she said, 'Oh, are you related to Sidney Tate?' I guess your friend Paul Reichelderfer told her all about your getting married."

"Oh, I know. *That* Sonya. Well, I hope you had a very pleasant evening. That gives us something in common, doesn't it, old man?"

"Undoubtedly," said Brock. "She's in Fort Penn at present, and she seemed anxious to see you. You must have known her quite well."

"Quite well, one night."

"Oh, the way she talks about you I'm sure it must have been longer than that, old man."

"No, just one night, old man. And before you create a three-act play out of it, get this straight. It was before I met Grace."

"Oh, hell, old man, I don't care when it was."

"Good night."

"Four-eleven South Third Street. It's a new place."

Sidney did not reply. He got up and opened windows. "Beginning to stink in here," he said aloud, as though to himself. Brock was still standing at the door.

"It never used to, just the last year or so. Good night, old man," said Brock.

This time he left, and Sidney smoked his pipe until he was ready to go upstairs. Grace was scrubbing her teeth and their bathroom door was open.

"Well, I made a botch of that," he said.

"The hunt club?"

"Yes," he said. "Brother Brock's been telling me where I made my mistakes."

"How does he know? He makes nothing but mistakes himself."

"Thank you, Grace."

"Oh, I knew you two'd act like children the minute you were left alone. Why do you pay any attention to him? He's only out to annoy you."

"I realize that, but I have to come back at him. I can hold my temper with nearly everyone, but he's like a gadfly."

"Well, you didn't marry him or anyone else in the family but me. We don't have to see him very much."

"No," said Sidney. She finished with the bathroom and got into bed, and he hung up his clothes. "I learned something through him that I should have known myself. From now on—from now on it's going to be just the way it's always been, tonight being the exception."

"What's that?" she said.

"Well, we've always lived our own lives, not interfering with other people and generally keeping other people out of our lives. Tonight I made the mistake of trying to introduce a scheme of mine, and if these people tonight, the people we know best and see the most of, if they can't be more responsive to an idea, just because it happened to be mine—then what the hell is the good of my thinking of those people at all?"

"I agree with you."

"You know how from time to time I've thought of one thing or another that might be good for Fort Penn, or might make life a little pleasanter for our friends. I even thought of going into politics in a small way—"

"Oh, you never told me that. I'm glad you didn't."

"In a small way. Everybody'd know I was honest and didn't have to take graft—"

"Sidney, the men who take graft don't like to see men who don't take graft in politics. Father told me that. I'm sorry it isn't original."

"Very sound, whoever said it. This is a good thing, my getting rebuffed tonight, in an unimportant thing. The experience is valuable, and hasn't cost me anything. Slight blow to my pride. No more. So—from now on I'm a farmer."

"We'll live our own lives. It's best that way," she said.

He got into bed with her and what they had been talking about was forgotten in their pleasure in each other.

———

On the tenth of June, 1913, Sidney and Grace celebrated their tenth wedding anniversary. Sidney was thirty-five years old; Grace was twenty-nine. They had three children: Alfred, who was nine years old; Anna, seven, whom her father sometimes called Annotate, a second-generation joke in the Tate family; and William Brock, known as Billy, who was five.

The new life, the children, had not quite made up for the death toll: Will Caldwell died in 1907; Emily Caldwell died in 1908. Sidney's mother died in 1908, and his father had died two years earlier.

In this world's goods the Tates' gains had been considerable, without being spectacular. Sidney disclaimed any aptitude for finance, but he was conservative with his own money and preached caution when it came to handling Grace's. George Langways was Sidney's adviser in New York, and in Fort Penn his affairs and Grace's were administered by Percy Hostetter at the Bank. The uniform conservatism of Sidney, George, and Percy had kept Sidney and Grace from being wealthier than they were, during a period in the nation's history when it was almost impossible to gamble because there were so many "sure things." In Fort Penn Sidney and Grace jointly and Brock no longer were in the richest five families but belonged in the richest ten.

Their position with regard to Fort Penn society was the same as it had been in 1903; it could not have been bettered in 1903, but in the succeeding ten years it had not worsened. They still were able to go anywhere they pleased and to regret any invitation that did not interest them; and, as had been true of Will and Emily Caldwell's invitations, to be summoned to break bread with Sidney and Grace was to go. From 1909, when they bought their first Pierce-Arrow, Sidney and Grace appeared oftener on the streets of Fort Penn, winter and summer, and by 1913, when they had a second Pierce, and Sidney had a Mercer phaeton, and the farm had an International Harvester two-cylinder truck, one of the Tates was almost sure to drive to Fort Penn every day, if only to take the children to school or bring them home.

They now could call their marriage established, according to the commercial custom of waiting ten years before putting Est. and the year on the firm's letterhead. They could also quote witnesses: "I don't know a happier couple in Fort Penn." Sidney lunched alone at the Fort Penn Club on the day of the anniversary. He and Grace were having their bridesmaids and ushers and closest friends for dinner that night, and he had gone to Fort Penn for a haircut, which was hardly more than a trim around the edges. He drank a glass of sherry, contrary to his custom of not drinking while the sun was up, and ate the Irish stew. He sat in the dining-room instead of the grill, to take advantage of the unwritten rule that in the dining-room you chose your company, while in the grill anyone theoretically could sit at your table. He wanted to think about Grace and their marriage, because he believed that on a tenth anniversary that was the right thing to do. To cast accounts, to recapitulate.

This is a good marriage. I love my wife and I am confident she loves me. I think if she loves anybody, the children excepted, she loves me. She loves me in bed, and she never shows the slightest interest in any other man, and that's remarkable when I think how many men try to make themselves appear at their best with her. Yes, she loves me. I can truthfully say I think my wife loves me. And God knows there's never been any doubt about my loving her. I am hardly conscious of other women, even now, after ten years. I like a pretty face, and I have wondered about a lot of our friends, what they would be like without any clothes on, what they would do, what they would not do. I have caught them looking at me and wondering too. But when I've caught them, when I realize that if I accidentally met them in Philadelphia or New York, I have discouraged them with politeness, and I never have held one of their hands, and I don't think I ever will, and I hope, I expect, I pray to God that Grace never will let anyone hold hers . . . This is bad, this is bad luck, to deliberately think along these lines! I must stop! This is bad! Nothing has happened. Nothing's going to happen. It's warm out today, it's pleasant. The calendar has nothing to do with me, or Grace. Very well, we've been married ten years and it's customary to observe an anniversary, but come on, let's stop this dangerous, unlucky tinkering with how I feel and how I think Grace feels. . . .

"Hello, Sidney." *Ah, a welcome interruption, notwithstanding it's my unwelcome brother-in-law.*

"Oh, hello, Brock. Have a seat."

"Sure you don't mind?" said Brock.

You know the rules, God damn you. You wouldn't let anyone sit at your table. "Not at all, sit down," said Sidney.

"Thanks," said Brock.

"Have you had your lunch?" said Sidney.

"I had a sandwich in the grill."

"Have a drink?"

"I don't believe I will, thanks," said Brock. "Well, this is the big anniversary, eh?"

"The big tenth, yes," said Sidney. *That's why you're not having a drink; so you won't have to drink to the anniversary.*

"God damn it, sometimes I look around at you fellows, you old reprobates, and I think maybe I could have swung it too," said Brock.

Oh, it's the old-reprobate line today? "Well, it's a thing you can't do alone. Make a good marriage, I mean."

"It's not the only thing you can't do alone, if you know what I mean," said Brock. "Takes two for a piece of tail too, you know." He had acquired a slow, puffy laugh that made him sound twenty years older than he was and ten years older than he looked.

"Always did, uh-huh," said Sidney.

"Yes, I look around. My old crowd's all married now. I'm the last one, but I look for one or two to be back on the night shift again before long. Permanently, I mean, unless they get tangled up again. Permanently. Oh, there's hardly a one that doesn't take an occasional—well, you know what I mean, Sidney. I don't know about you. Often wonder."

I'm going to fool you: if you think I'm going to enter a denial, listen to this: "That's the way I want it to be. And of course if I *should* go on the night shift, as you put it, I'd make sure you'd never hear about it."

Brock was about to take offense, but instead he puffed out a chuckle. "You're a pretty clever geezer, Sidney. I have to take my hat off to you."

"Anything else, sir?" said the waiter.

"No, thanks," said Sidney. He signed the check.

"You off?" said Brock.

"Going over to get a haircut."

"Yes, you can stand one. Hun-huh-huh. But don't let him take too much off the top, hun-huh-huh. See you this evening."

"Oh, are you coming?"

"Sure, you had to invite me to this one, hun-huh-huh."

"But you didn't have to accept, huh-huh-huh. So long, Brock."

"Good old Sidney, hun-huh-huh."

"Good day, Mr. Tate," said Fairfax.

"Good day, Fairfax," said Sidney.

He went to the barbershop in the Schoffstal House, the largest and easily the most distinguished tonsorial parlor in Fort Penn. It was patronized regularly by all members of the Fort Penn Club, by the men on the Club waiting-list, by members of the Fort Penn Athletic Club, by men who could have joined the Fort Penn Club, by men who could have joined the Athletic Club, by senators and assemblymen who had served more than one or two terms, and by total strangers. The patrons were served in that order and in that order they were treated, from deference down to common politeness. An affluent stranger, with a diamond stickpin in his cravat and a gold watch-chain across his belly, was not Next if a member of the Fort Penn Club was waiting, even though the stranger had been there ahead of the clubman. Likewise, a state senator who was not a member of the Fort Penn Club and was only on his second term, had to keep his seat while a member of the Athletic Club took the first vacancy. Peter Ringwalt, the proprietor of the shop, made the rule and personally supervised the order of service. "Dem politicians," he said. "Say dey don't get reelected? Vy shoot I botter mit dem? My Fort Penn customers, dem I look after. Politicians don't like how I run my business, it's plenty odder boppa shops mit my permission dey patronize." His attitude drove most of the legislators to their own barbershop, but the career men among them got their shaves and haircuts at Peter's rather than admit that they had to use the Senate shop.

"Yes *sir*, Mr. Tate, good afternoon," said Carter Birdsong, Junior, son of Fairfax of the Fort Penn Club.

"Afternoon, Carter."

"Yes sir, just rest your hat, please, sir. Be with you in two shakes of a ram's tail. A nice high gloss on the uh, on our *brown* shoes we're wearing today. Brown oxfords. Now I think you're the very next one if I'm not mistaken, and—yes, you are. There's Mr. Herman Miller, smiling and bowing and getting his chair ready to receive you, Mr. Tate."

"Good afternoon, Peter," said Sidney.

"Hoddy do, Mr. Tate. Herman waiting," said Peter.

Sidney seated himself in the Koken chair. He looked in the mirror and Herman Miller, also looking in the mirror, smiled as he drew the sheet over Sidney. Herman always waited for Sidney to say the first word, always smiled at him in the mirror. In ten years here, at least, nothing had changed; from Carter's prolix greeting to Herman's quiet beaming. "Well, Herman, think you'll get enough for a mattress today?"

Herman chuckled at Sidney's old joke. "A small mattress," he said. "So big." He held out his thumb and forefinger, separating them by about an inch. That was his part of the joke.

"Getting smaller, isn't it?" said Sidney.

"Vell, you know vot's the saying. Grass don't grow on a traffled street."

Then an amiable silence between the two friends. Ten times fifty is five hundred. Half of five hundred. Two-fifty. "Herman, do you know how many times you've cut my hair?"

"Oh—I couldn't give a good guess."

"About two hundred and fifty times."

"So? Two hundret fifty. Ay, yi-yi."

"I've been coming here about ten years, just about every two weeks, and in that time I've never had anyone else cut my hair. Comes to about two hundred and fifty."

"Vot made you think it?"

"Today's my tenth wedding anniversary."

"So-oh? Congradulations, and Mrs. Tate congradulations, too. Ten years, dot's nice. Ven I go home I tell my vife and she bake you a little cake. I leave it Fort Penn Clup tomorrow so your drifer call for it."

"Oh—well, thank you very much, Herman. I wasn't hinting,

but I can always put away one of Mrs. Miller's cakes, without any help. You know that."

"Yes. The boys too. No trouble to make them shy still once I promised little cakes."

"Yes, they'd have their hair cut every week to get some of Mrs. Miller's cookies."

Another silence between them while Carter polished Sidney's shoes. The usual fifteen-cent tip for Herman Miller, the nickel tip for Carter, and Sidney was on his way.

His next stop was Kemp & Bonniwell's jewelry store. Nicholas Bonniwell, with his hands on the counter, smiled and bowed. "Good *afternoon,* Mr. Tate. I have it *ready* for you," he sang. He went to the vault and returned with Sidney's present for Grace, a gold mesh bag with a ten-dollar gold piece inside. Nicholas laid it on a blue velvet pad. "Now that is what I call a handsome gift, handsome. And there won't be any other like it in Fort Penn, that I can guarantee you, Mr. Tate."

"Well now you're sure of that, Mr. Bonniwell? You know how the ladies—"

"Oh, I can guarantee you, Mr. Tate. This particular item you won't even run across it in the larger cities, for instance Philadelphia and New York. New York don't have anything on this order *or* Philadelphia. This was made up special for you, and the wholesaler we deal with, they always keep their word, Mr. Tate." He put his thumb under his chin and his elbow on the counter and studied the bag as though he were waiting for it to do something, like say a few words. He raised his eyes to see whether Sidney was waiting too, but Sidney was only nodding in approval.

"If Mrs. Tate isn't entirely pleased, anything the least way unsatisfactory, we'll be only too glad—but I know, Mr. Tate. I been in this business too long. This'll make the biggest hit you ever saw." He began to wrap the bag. "Ten years," he shook his head. "Can't hardly believe it. I can remember your wedding so well. That was the busiest we ever were in the history of the store, outside of Christmas. We were swamped. We had to send any number of people to our competitors. Our regular clientele, we tried to take care of them as best we could, but those that waited till the last minute, if we didn't have what we considered nice enough for Miss Grace *Caldwell*, we threw up our hands and said *try* Schmidt & Burke and see if they have anything. In gold this here snap, you know how soft gold is, the snap is apt to wear, but Mrs. Tate can always bring it back when it shows signs and we can repair it right here in the store overnight." He had to take the bag out of the tissue paper to show how the snap would wear. "Take another look inside. Yes, gold piece. Very original sentiment. Ten dollars for ten years. Tissue paper. Velvet box. More tissue. Sealing wax. K and B seal, and there we are. There, Mr. Tate. Our very best congratulations and many, many more."

"Thank you very much," said Sidney. "Good day, Mr. Bonniwell."

"I'll walk to the door with you. Come in any time, any time. Good day, sir."

Sidney's next stop took him out of the shopping district to an address on South Fourth Street near the stockyards, about ten squares away from Kemp & Bonniwell. While still in the shopping area he raised his panama eight times to bid the time of day to eight ladies, and he said "How are you," "Hello," or "Hyuh" to twelve men of his acquaintance. When it was "hyuh" or "hello" it was also a first name; when it was "How are you" it was with a last name, a Mister and last name, or no name at all. South of the shopping district, when he was spoken to by workmen whose names he did not know, he said "Hello." The workmen included two men who had done carpentry at the farm, two plumbers, two painters, a farmhand, an electrician, and a young fellow named Maurer, whose father was Jake Maurer, the R. F. D. man from Becksville. Every man who had done some work for Sidney spoke to him, but in the business district not every man who had been introduced to him had spoken. The difference was that the workmen had no doubt about their being greeted in return; the business-district men would have been greeted in return, but they were not sure of themselves. They stared down at the bricks in the sidewalk or looked in the store-windows rather than risk a snub.

There was a wooden statue of a badly proportioned white horse, mounted on wheels, in carriage harness, and with real mane and tail, standing on the roofed sidewalk in front of the address on South Fourth Street. It was the establishment of Victor Smith. The faded sign that hung from the roof bore the legend: Victor Smith—Saddlery—Harness—Leather Goods—Findings—Est. 1866. There was a wooden bench on the four-step porch and a wire mat, with aggies embedded in it, for scraping the shoes before entering. The door was open.

"Anybody here?" Sidney called.

There was no answer and he went out again and sat on the bench and lit his pipe. He waited five minutes before Mr. Smith turned up. He was a short man with an informal goatee, wearing a shirt without a collar but with a gold collar button, and a pair of overalls and hard black boots.

"Hello, Mr. Smith. How're you?"

"I'm all right I guess."

"I see you have a fly net on the horse. Why not a straw hat too?"

"Aah, them things," he spat out some tobacco juice, only as an expression of contempt; as a confirmed user of Red Man he neither swallowed nor spat very much. "They make the animal look ridiculous and they don't do good, they do harm. A dirty blood-sucking son of a bitch of a horsefly gets under one of them God damn dirty son of a bitchin' *straw*-hats and he's there till he falls off with a shotglass full of blood in him. That's what I think of them God damn *straw*-hats. I don't carry them. I don't carry nothin' I wouldn't use on a horse of my own." He pointed at Sidney. "I wouldn't sell *you* a curb *bit* if I thought you didn't know how to use it. Go on in there and look high and low, see if you can find a pair of spurs with them two-inch rowels. Sure, sure. I got these God damn clodhopper son of a bitchin' bastards off the farms coming here. 'I wanna buy a pair of spurs. I wanna buy a pair of cowboy spurs.' 'All right,' I say to them, 'go on back to your farm and tear the picture out of the catalog and *send away* for your God damn cowboy spurs,' that's what I tell them. I been here close to fifty years, young fella. I don't take any guff from anybody. They want cowboy spurs, Sears and Roebuck'll sell them cowboy spurs. What was it you wanted me to put an order in for now?"

"Stirrups. Safety stirrups, or kick stirrups, some people call them."

"Oh, yes. When was that?"

"About two weeks ago."

"Oh, yes. Well, I don't think they're here yet. I gave my clerk the day off to go somewhere. I think he went to a funeral. Hell's bells, I don't care if he wants to go to a funeral or go out and get drunk. He doesn't have to tell me about it just so long's I know a day ahead of time so I can make preparations. I don't say a man has to be here eight o'clock in the morning till six in the evening, like the banks. Did you ask Willie? My harnessmaker?"

"I didn't see him. I called out, but nobody heard me."

"In the back? Did you go all the way back to the shop?"

"No, just inside," said Sidney.

"What's the trouble? You bashful? Afraid we'd think you'd swipe something? You should of taken a walk back in the shop. Well, I will."

He went inside and Sidney heard him calling Willie. He came back shaking his head. "Went for a shit and the birds got him, I guess. No Willie. Well, I guess I know what happened to Willie. We got a big order from one of the coal companies, repairing nine or ten sets of harness for them mules that they got down in the mines. Canaries, they call 'em. I guess Willie got so sick and tired of looking at mule harness he couldn't stand it any longer and quit. Well, he'll be drunk tonight, all day tomorrow, tomorrow night and the next day, then he'll remember he has pay coming and he'll come back here and want to beat me up because I won't give him his pay, but I'll give him a pint and he'll think I'm a good fella and he'll sleep it off back in the shop and the next day he'll be as good as new. Willie's one of the greatest harnessmakers in the United States of America, but he wants change. Variety. Put him on a set of mule harness and he's all right for one set, but after that you gotta put him on a different job altogether, a nice little set of fancy goat harness, or let's say a McClellan from the Troop, a nice change. I saw this one coming. I should of let the coal company wait and gave Willie a rest away from them mules. Hard work, that mule harness. Built to last, but my God. If the mule wasn't so close to the horse family I'd tell the coal companies to use all-chain harness and be done with it. Let's go inside and take a look. Maybe your stirrups come while I was around the corner."

They went inside, Mr. Smith allowing Sidney to pass, and when he had done so Mr. Smith closed the door behind them and took a pint bottle of whiskey out of his desk, uncorked it and handed it to Sidney. "I know we aint gonna find no stirrups, but here's just so you don't consider it a wasted trip."

"Thanks. Happy days."

"Drink hearty," said Mr. Smith.

Sidney took a good-sized swallow and returned the bottle.

"That's a man's drink. This aint gonna last us very long." Mr. Smith took a swallow and handed the bottle to Sidney.

"Another?" said Sidney.

"Sure, you go ahead."

Sidney raised the bottle but before he put it to his lips Victor interrupted him. "Excuse me," said Victor. "But I think your nose is bleedin'."

"It is?" Sidney put his handkerchief to his nose and it became liberally soaked with blood.

"You got a regular nosebleed. You been pickin' it?"

"No," said Sidney.

"Then what you got's a plain old-fashioned nosebleed. Let 'er bleed. Best thing in the world for you. Just sit down there and hold your head back and when she's ready she'll stop. Wuddy you been doing? Workin' too hard?"

"Wouldn't say that," said Sidney.

"How old a man are you?"

"How old am I? Thirty-five."

"Not old enough to shoot," laughed Victor. "Just let 'er bleed. I'll put a little cold water on your handkerchief, and you can hold it there."

"Thanks, here's my other handkerchief," said Sidney, handing it to him.

"Don't put that handkerchief up your nostrils."

"Why not? I'm not a horse. I can breathe through my mouth," said Sidney, irritably. "Anyway, it's stopping."

"That's the ticket."

"Sorry I barked at you," said Sidney.

"That's all right."

"I haven't had a nosebleed since I was a kid."

"Then you needed this one," said Victor.

"Can I wash this out somewhere?"

"Sure. Out in the shop."

Sidney rinsed out the handkerchief while Victor stood beside him.

"You feel all right?" said Victor.

"I feel fine, thanks."

"You want to know what the trouble is, the way I size it up?"

"What?"

"Thinkin'," said Victor. "Thinkin' on a warm day. You realize this is the warmest day we had this Spring? Thinkin' and frettin' on a warm day—ah, no. You're an outdoor man, not a desk and chair man. You come in from the farm today and you wanted them stirrups for your wife, so you come down to see me and nobody here, so you sat there thinkin' and thinkin' till I came, then when I did come I even forgot to order them stirrups. How's that?"

"Afraid you're wrong, Mr. Smith. I wouldn't think myself into a nosebleed over a pair of stirrups."

"We often worry more over little things than big things," said

Victor. "Sometimes we worry without knowin' we're worryin'. You come with me and we'll make sure this order gets sent out first thing tomorrow . . . Here's a piece of paper. Watch me write. 'Don't—forget—order—stirrups—for—S.—Tate.' Now I'll hang this up here, where my clerk can't miss it. There."

"Right."

Victor laughed. "There's one I never noticed before. You know what if you died what it'd be?"

"No."

"The estate of estate. Get the drift? The *estate* of S. Tate. Did you ever think of that before?"

"Not exactly in that way," said Sidney. "While I'm here will you give me a box of snaps, assorted sizes? And some rivets? My older boy's starting to become a harnessmaker, making tie-straps."

"Waste of good leather, unless he's using old reins."

"That's what he *is* using, Mr. Smith."

"Well, then it's a harmless pastime, but tell him there aint any money in harness these days. The rate they been going lately there won't be a horse on the street inside of three years. Fire department putting in auto trucks, coal mines putting in electric dinkeys, hospital put in a Winton-Six ambulance, month ago. No money in it. Tell your boy to start playing with a gazzoline engine. Well, what the hell, I don't have to worry about him with the money he'll come into. The estate of estate. That's pretty good . . . Let's take a look at the price on that box. Mm-hmmm. All right, good day, young fella. Come in again."

"Good day, Mr. Smith," said Sidney. "Thanks for the drink."

"Don't mention it," said Victor.

Sidney's Mercer was parked at the Fort Penn Club. The top was down and the leather seat, lacking the summer cover, was uncomfortably warm from the sun. He got in and opened the windshield and took off his hat and in a few minutes of driving he felt all right. He wished that he and Grace could stay away from their own party and drive out to a country hotel for supper but when he reached the farm his feeling about the party had changed, and he was glad that they would be spending the evening with friends who would be in a festive mood. Spurious or spontaneous, the mood would be catching, the hours would pass, and the anniversary would be over, and the next one that demanded recognition was fifteen years off. *At which time I'll be fifty, Grace'll be almost forty-five, Alfred'll be twenty-four, Anna'll be twenty-two, Billy'll be twenty. We'll be quietly middle-aged, and they'll be grown. We might even be a grandfather and grandmother, if Anna marries young.*

———

They were having a cigarette before going upstairs. All their guests had gone home. Sidney was stretched out in his chair, with his feet on a footstool, his hands at the back of his neck. Grace was sitting on the sofa, leaning against the arm.

"I thought it went off very nicely, didn't you?" she said.

"Very nicely, yes," said Sidney.

"Paul looked well. He told me he's lost twenty-six pounds."

"Twenty-six more won't do him any harm. But Paul's all right."

"I wonder if he'll ever marry Connie."

"Why should he?" said Sidney.

"Do you think he's sleeping with her? I don't."

"I don't either. I don't think Connie's ever slept with anybody."

"I guess she hasn't or I'd have known about it. Would you have married me if we'd slept together beforehand?"

"Uh-huh."

"What do you mean uh-huh?"

"I wouldn't have wanted *that* running around free for the other fellows."

"Sidney!"

"Well, you asked me a question and I gave you an answer. I also married you for your money."

"No you didn't. You could have married richer girls than I was."

"They didn't have a farm, then," said Sidney.

"They could have bought *ten* farms, some of those I met."

"I know, but I wanted a farm that'd been lived on, so I married you. I really married the farm. You went with it. Your father gave me his word that you were getting the farm, so we shook hands on it and I said under the circumstances I'd be glad to take over, lock, stock, barrel, and you."

"I wish Father and Mother could have been here tonight."

"We'd have to put another leaf in the table."

"He never saw Anna or Billy," said Grace.

"Yes, he did. He saw Anna."

"That's right. He did see Anna, but not Billy. Did Mother ever see Billy?"

"No. She died—"

"I remember. She died just before Billy was born."

"Grace, sometimes you astonish me."

"Why?"

"Your memory. You can remember what somebody wore to a children's party when you were six years old, but a thing like remembering whether your mother saw this child or that child, and they happen to be your children. And your mother."

"They were all dying at the same time I was having children. Both our fathers died the same year and both our mothers died the same year. If I'd stopped to think I could have remembered it that way, but at this hour of the morning it's too much trouble."

"Next year I think I'll put in an elevator. I wonder how much an elevator would cost."

"The Schoffstals have an elevator for old Mrs. Schoffstal."

"I've seen it, and I don't approve of it. They ought to make her walk up the stairs so she'd be good and tired and go to sleep. But I need an elevator. Tonight, for instance, I can't be tired when I get upstairs. I have work to do."

"Is that so? If you consider it work . . ."

"Oh, there's pleasure connected with it too."

"Thank you."

"Notta tall. Thank *you*, Mrs. Tate. Would you care to carry me upstairs?"

"I *would* not."

"Fireman's hold?"

"Stop talking silly and let's go to bed. You just go, and I'll put out the rest of the lights."

"I may be sound asleep by the time you get upstairs."

"Not for long, darling. *I'm* only twenty-nine."

"And smart as a whip," said Sidney.

———

Within the octave of their anniversary Sidney was thinking again about his relationship with Grace. He was mindful of his intention to abandon that line of thinking, but it kept cropping up when he was thinking about something else. He would try, for instance, to divert his thoughts by concentrating on the children: we've been married ten years, and we have three lovely children. But he could not think of one child or all three without rediscovering Grace in each child's face, and speech, walk, personality. Each was his own human being, but they did derive from their mother. Which was all right in itself, but not when some characteristic of one reminded him of Grace, whom he was trying not to think of in terms of ten-year wife. Wife and mother, mother and wife, he finally admitted that it made no difference which came first; she was both; and the firm jaw-line of his oldest child made him think of the woman he loved, and the arrogant nostrils of Grace-asleep made him think of the children, because it was the one feature common to Grace and her daughter and sons.

He decided it was going to be all right to think of Grace and their marriage, on condition he would deny himself the right to questions that concerned the fact of love, the degree of love, the quality of love. Take it for granted, he told himself. *She* hasn't questioned it; why should I? If it doesn't seem to be all there— but it is all there. To say "If it doesn't seem to be all there" is to start a question in another form, and that I have relinquished my right to do. It was going to be all right to use the anniversary as a proper time for a long paternal look at the children.

They have been growing up—getting born and growing up—with so much attendant fuss and feathers, pleasure and pain, and simple, ordinary doing for them that I haven't taken the time to judge them. I've done it for horses in the last ten years. I've bought Holsteins and Jerseys and watched them get better or worse. I've hired men and watched them turn out good and bad, rewarding them and firing them. I've been conscious of change in my dealings with our friends. Our friends are in most cases, but not all, the men and women we chose to be with when our marriage was just beginning, but we see less or nothing of *some* of the early ones, more and more of *some* of the later ones. If I can give my time and the exercise of my judgment to men and animals that mean little enough to me, certainly, as the good father I try to be, I can give my time and judgment to an appraisal of the three young creatures that make me believe in God . . .

THOUGHTS WHILE SMOKING A PIPE AND BONING A BOOT: ALFRED

Alfred is quite big for nine years old. He isn't as tall as I'd like him to be, for the weight he carries around. There doesn't seem to be much hope of his ever being over six feet, judging by what I know of his mother's family and mine. Mr. Caldwell was very deceiving, and so was my father. And I guess I am too. An older man—a man over thirty—who is slender and carries himself well, is apt to look taller than he actually is. Alfred walks with his head 'way back. Sometimes the way he holds his head makes me think the little son of a bitch is too snotty for words, and one of these days he's going to get it. Other times he seems to be wearing an overhead checkrein. That may be my fault. I want to be fair with him, but if he doesn't get discipline at home he'll get it outside, and the discipline he'll get outside will be only discipline, without any element of fairness or consideration of extenuating circumstances or making the punishment fit the crime. He is a snotty kid, but only since he's been going to school in Fort Penn. The other kids probably go from one extreme to the other; kissing his ass because he's part Caldwell, and other times making his life miserable for the same reason. I think he does rather well, all things considered. I don't think he has more conceit than he's entitled to, and the self-assurance is something I want him to hold on to the rest of his life. If he thinks he's a little bit better than anyone else, and can prove it in any way at all, I want him to go on thinking he is. Just a little. He likes team sports and he's not the kind of kid that has to pitch because he owns the ball. He is good enough at his lessons. He moves along with the others. He gets promoted when he should get promoted, and when he first started out he skipped two grades, or at least one grade, and was younger than his classmates. It probably wasn't too easy for him to see his father's and mother's friends and relations waxing enthusiastic over the little sister and little brother, but he seems to have come out of that all right. He is very nice to Billy, and he seems to have stopped hitting his sister except when the provocation is irresistible. I have had to give him about five whippings in his life, and the first time I did it I got drunk and swore I'd never take the strap to him again, but he is strong and wilful and when he has been defiantly disobedient or disrespectful or destructive he has always known that we have to use the strap. I have never struck him with my hand, although his mother has slapped him, but not in a long while. He asks intelligent questions and has an active curiosity about many subjects, but when an explanation requires too much concentration he loses interest. That is partly my fault too, because I try to tell him all I know on a subject, and if a boy of nine asks you about the gasoline engine you ought not to go into a lecture on internal combustion but tell it simply and leave the harder part till another day. We have taught him good manners and they have stayed with him, but I have seen him acting with the greatest politeness toward men and women whom he couldn't stand. They have been charmed by his manners and made favorable comment. I do not believe that is hypocritical on his part. He may not see the reason for it now, and therefore he may feel that he is being hypocritical and that we are hypocrites to bring him up that way, but this is the only world he has to live in and some day he will understand that you make it easier for *yourself* by being polite when your instincts are to be rude. I don't think he will change much in appearance, or at any rate I think I know what he will look like when he is a grown man, and when that time arrives I hope he can be as proud of me as I am going to be of him. Not a prodigy, not a shark at anything much, very likely, but a clean, decent gentleman, with the best characteristics of my father and of his Grandfather Caldwell, plus whatever I can protect him from that is unworthy of him, and whatever I can give him out of love.

THOUGHTS WHILE SMOKING A PIPE AND SHARPENING SOME SICKLES ON A RAINY DAY: ANNA

Anna is quite a different cup of tea from Alfred. If I could understand Anna I could easily understand what it is about her mother that I don't understand. I promised myself I wouldn't go off on this line again, but I have to admit that since she was three or four Anna has been a puzzle to me. She used to like to sit with me and look at a picture book and sometimes she would go to sleep leaning against me. But Anna and her mother let you in on just so much and no more. They let you know them just so well and not one bit better. I don't think this indicates any lack in me. I have no false modesty. I pride myself in my ability to get to know anyone who interests me and I think I have been very successful in getting to know and understand those few people I love. Therefore I do not bother to accuse myself of the inability to understand my wife and daughter. It's just that they hold on to something in themselves that no one can ever get to. I suppose I may have some of that myself. I have no chicanery about me. I have nothing to hide and have no inclination to hide anything but I plead guilty to possessing a certain amount of reserve, as it is called. That is natural in an only child, as I am, and it also comes down to me from my father. Mr. Caldwell had it too, but my father more so. Mr. Caldwell almost seemed to put his on, whereas my father seemed to lapse into it as a natural part of him or phase of him. Outwardly Mr. Caldwell was a friendlier man than my father, not that he was insincere, but he did seem to be able to put on a smile where my father's smile was different. It came, when it came, from inside spontaneously, just as his retreat into himself always seemed perfectly natural and unassumed. Mr. Caldwell had great dignity, but just a touch of practice about it, assumed, and not the reposed dignity my own father had. Well, I have been accused once or twice, at Yale and here in Fort Penn, of the habit of the turtle, going back into my shell. If it is true, and I suppose appearances make it true, it is only because I never have felt that life was so long that I wanted to waste more than simple politeness on people who didn't interest me. I am seldom rude to anyone and when I am it is usually deliberate, to put a stop to a boor. I think I am considerate and I will go so far as to admit that I am a kind man. I have avoided brawling all my life but I have never lost a fight, the few I have had. When the occasion demanded I have wasted no words but simply used an upper-cut and as I have always been fast and strong, the majority of my few fights have ended there. One that lasted longer, with a New Haven townie or rather two New Haven townies, ended in a victory for me because I have always exercised and have consequently been in better condition than most boys and men. With the exception of one winter when I was a child and had a bout of rheumatic fever I have been out of doors, if only for a stroll, every day of my life. I seem to be getting off the subject, thinking about myself instead of Anna. Where was I? Let me think. My so-called reserve, and that goes back to how Anna and her mother have something like my reserve, but something that goes deeper. It isn't that they won't tell you something. They may have nothing to tell. They don't lie. I have never known Grace to tell me an untruth. But I have seen her look away, staring off into space, and when I have said, "What are you thinking of?" or "A penny for your thoughts?" she has answered that she wasn't thinking of anything, or was just day-dreaming. I have seen Grace do that so often that it is practically habit with her. Anna's way is different. She also lapses into silences, but when you ask her, she says, "Oh—nothing," which is a polite way of telling you to mind your own business. And she is most likely saying the proper thing, because we are all entitled to our thoughts. Sam Reifsnyder, over yonder, is thinking his thoughts while he greases the axles of that wagon, and I respect his right to his reverie, just as he respects mine. Why then must I intrude on Grace's reveries, and Anna's? Well, one answer is that I don't love Sam Reifsnyder and in fact I don't give a damn about him. He is a good farmer, a hard, honest worker, but I think Mr. Charles Darwin would find Sam more interesting than I do. Anna, at seven, has more real intelligence than Sam in his early forties. She can play ten pieces on the piano. At seven she plays a good game of Hearts, not only Lotto and Parcheesi, and she is beginning to understand Bridge. We have had to discourage her being advanced too rapidly in school in order not to let her become the youngest child in the grade where she belongs. She can carry on a conversation in French and another thing we have had to discourage is her habit of correcting her mother. She does it politely enough, but we believe she should not do it at all. She is also good at group games, like Alfred, but unlike him she takes command and instead of being the one who accepts congratulations with becoming modesty, as Alfred does, she is the one who offers the congratulations. She also can be sharply critical of her playmates, if so youthful a word can be used in connection with Anna. The Reifsnyder children are afraid of her, and I suppose I am too. I have given all this thought to her, but I must admit I don't understand her. She seems to approve of me, with some unspecified reservations, but there is never the slightest doubt about her love for her mother. Even when she has corrected Grace it is easy to see that the child thinks she is doing it for Grace's own good. Sometimes this seven-year-old child looks at me as though she were about to give me a good talking-to, but then she seems to think better of it, as though it would be a waste of time. At such times I confess I am secretly in sympathy with Alfred's yielding to the urge to violence, but I love her just the same. I suppose I'm afraid to discipline her because I want her to love me.

THOUGHTS WHILE CLEANING AND CUTTING THE CAKE OUT OF SOME PIPES: BILLY

Whenever I see Billy he smiles and I smile, and now, when I start to think of him, I smile. Now there's a child who's *all* reserve. "Hello, Billy. What you been doing?" you say to him, and he smiles before answering, "Nothing." You may have been watching him climb the easy oxheart cherry tree or sitting peacefully on one of the lower limbs of the apple tree in front of the farmer's house or he may have been playing by himself in his sandbox, not building any great elaborate castle, but only up-ending pail after pail of sand. But he always says, "Nothing." He'll keep his hand on the knob of the door, looking up at you as if you were God Almighty, or Santa Claus—no. No. Looking at you and smiling that way because you are Sidney Tate, his father. It is almost more than you can bear, to look at such free, happy love for you. "Don't do it, boy," you want to say to him. "Please don't look at me like that. I'm only me. I am *only* Sidney Tate, father of you." You turn away, to get that sun out of your eyes, and you want to be rough, to reject his offering because you know you cannot match it with something of your own. But he doesn't want anything. To think I can give such pleasure by no more than being. I never did anything to deserve this, but more than that, I never set out to earn it, to purchase it, to inspire it. I didn't know it was there, I hardly knew he was there, except as a baby. But then one day it *was* there, has been there—but of course it won't always be there. It will pass as he begins to leave the heaven he seems to be in. And the strange, unbelievable thing is that I can keep that heaven existing for him by no more than saying, "Hello, Billy. What you been doing?" and ruffling his hair a little, asking him to do me a favor by getting me something I could easily get myself. "Will you reach me those matches, please?" I say to him, and someone of an alien tongue might think, looking at Billy, that I had said, "You can stay home from school tomorrow," or "Here's a five-pound box of Huyler's for you and you alone." I am familiar with admiration-and-love and respect-and-love, if for no other reason than that I have felt them and sent them out. But Billy loves me freely, happily, wholly, trustingly, without my having to sing for him, bat a ball for him, jump a fence for him, do a trick for him, carry him, feed him, or even touch him. He will rub the back of my hand when it is resting on the arm of a chair, and he will kiss my cheek in front of the ear while I am eating my breakfast. But the gestures of affection must originate with him and he does not expect them to be reciprocated. It amuses Grace. She smiles at Billy and me. She is a good girl, Grace. She has had the good sense and kindness not to deprive Billy and me of our love as she could easily do if she were to tease him or embarrass me. Grace knows that Alfred is a conventional boy and that I am a conventional father to him; she knows that Anna has no illusions about me; so surely she knows, knowing me so well, that what I get from Billy is so rare that I could never get it from anyone else, and most men never get it at all. I think Grace understands Billy's love because for a long time she got something very like it from me.

———

On another rainy day—this one was in the early part of August, 1916—the Tate family were finishing lunch.

"Anybody get the mail today?" said Sidney.

It was Alfred's job to walk or ride to the end of the lane every day and get the mail out of the R. F. D. box.

"I didn't forget," said Alfred.

"I told him not to get it today, it was raining so hard," said Grace.

"I wanted to go," said Alfred.

"He wanted to go, but I don't think they ought to go out when it's like it's been all morning. This infantile paralysis. I don't want them to catch colds."

"I agree with you. Children, hear your mother? You have to be extra careful not to catch colds when this infantile paralysis is around," said Sidney.

"Yes, Father," said Anna.

"What the dickens, I'm no infant. Even Billy isn't an infant. He's eight," said Alfred.

Billy smiled his thanks at being taken out of the infant class.

"It doesn't only affect infants," said Grace.

"Then why do they call it infantile paralysis?" said Anna. "That's silly, calling it infantile if infants don't get it."

"Well, they do get it," said Grace. "In New York City they've had thousands of cases of it."

"I'm glad *I* don't live in New York," said Billy.

"So am I," said Sidney.

"Thousands of children in New York City, or adults?" said Anna.

"Both," said Grace. "Sidney, you know more about it than I do."

"Well, unfortunately nobody seems to know very much about it, not even the doctors," said Sidney.

"Not even the *doctors?*" said Anna. "It wonders me that they go to sick people if they don't know much about it."

"Anna, don't say 'It wonders me,' " said Grace. "That's very P. D."

"What's P. D.?" said Sidney.

"Pennsylvania Dutch," said Grace. "We decided to use just initials so that if we were overheard it wouldn't hurt anyone's feelings."

"It makes do'n ukly," said Alfred.

Sidney laughed and so did the others.

"That's all right," said Grace. "You can say P. D. things when you don't mean them, but the young man that just said it makes down ugly happens to talk very P. D. without realizing it."

"I can't help it. If you sent me away to Lawrenceville or Andover then I'd stop talking like Sam. When are you going to send me away to boarding school, Father?" said Alfred.

"We haven't decided, but it won't be this year, and maybe not next, and maybe it won't be Lawrenceville or Andover. You're only twelve, so there's plenty of time."

"In England they go to boarding school before they're twelve. You told me that yourself," said Alfred.

"They do a lot of things in England we don't do here. A lot of things you wouldn't like, too. Would you like to go to Eton? Well, at Eton they give you a caning for the least infraction of the rules. Not just a strap, old boy. But a caning with a wooden stick or a riding crop. You be satisfied with where you are for the present."

"I didn't say I wanted to go to school in England," said Alfred.

"Well, that's good, because I assure you you're not *going* to school in England," said Sidney.

"Father?" said Billy.

"What is it, Bill?"

"Tell Anna about infantry paralysis."

"Oh, of course. Thank you for reminding me," said Sidney.

"Thank you, Billy," said Anna.

"Yes, when Father's talking about one thing we all ought to pay attention. It's rude to interrupt. We all know that," said Grace.

"Well, nobody really interrupted," said Sidney. "We just got sidetracked. As I was saying, the doctors know very little about infantile paralysis, because they haven't known about it very long. For years and years they thought it was something else. In fact they thought it was several things. But lately they've come to the conclusion that there is a sickness that for a while they called infantile paralysis, but now they have another name. It's uh, let me think . . . Polio-my-el-itis. Poliomyelitis."

"Oh, yes," said Grace.

"That's the sign they put on the door when they quarantine people. Poliomyelitis. The quarantine sign doesn't say infantile paralysis. They use the new medical name."

"What about children?" said Anna. "Why do they call it infantile?"

"I believe because they get it more easily than grown-ups. More cases of it among children than grown-ups. But anybody can get it, so please be careful about not getting colds, will you all three promise your mother and me?"

They promised.

"Good," said Sidney, rising. "Well, I think I'll go down and get the mail."

"Father!" Billy screamed. "Don't go!"

"It's all right, Billy," said Grace, putting her hand on the boy's arm. "Father'll wrap up carefully. He can put on his rubber boots and raincoat, won't you, Father?"

"Yes," said Sidney. "Don't worry, Billy. I'll be very careful. You come with me and watch me put on my boots and things."

"Sister dear, do you wish to engage me in twenty-five points of pocket billiards, Mademoiselle?" said Alfred.

"All right," said Anna. "After I go to the bathroom."

"I won't catch cold, Billy," said Sidney, taking the boy's hand. "You come with me to the kitchen porch and I'll get my boots and stuff out of the porch closet. My, this rain is really a corker, isn't it?"

"Yes," said Billy.

They had not noticed it, but they had left Grace sitting alone in the dining-room.

Sidney returned with the contents of the mailbox, took off his boots, raincoat, and checked cap in the kitchen and hung them in the porch closet, put on his sneakers again and went to the den, where Grace was having a cigarette by the fire.

"This is the coldest day all summer," said Sidney. "The fire's a good idea."

"Anything for me?"

"Yes. A couple of letters and some postcards. Franklin Simon catalogue," said Sidney. "Had a chat with Miles Brinkerhoff."

"Where?"

"At the mailbox. He was in his car with another fellow while I was getting the mail. He stopped. Neighborly."

"Neighborly?" said Grace.

"Well, he's going to be a neighbor, very soon. That house he's building's almost finished. He expects to be in it by the end of September."

"Do you mean to say that house is as far along as that?"

"Oh, yes. He had the contractor with him. A fellow named Bannon. Roger Bannon. Roger Bannon, Junior, whoever Roger Bannon, Senior was. I've seen this fellow in town. He played football for Fort Penn U about ten years ago."

"His father was a politician," said Grace.

"That's the fellow. His father must have died soon after we were married, but now I do remember the name being connected with politics."

"What about Miles's house? Have you ever had a good look at it?"

"It's off the Pike, not as far back as this house, but there's a grove of trees in front of it. I haven't had a good look since they began building in earnest. Miles asked us to inspect it any time we wanted to."

"Any house that Miles would build, you can be sure it won't add anything to the landscape."

"Well, maybe not, but maybe he let Bannon do it, and Bannon's built some pretty nice medium-priced houses in the North End."

"I expect to see a big streamer, Brinkerhoff Bakery, across the front of the house. Or painted on the fences."

"Well, let's ride out and take a look, tomorrow or the next day. It's only about two miles," said Sidney. He lit his pipe and began reading his mail.

"Letter from Clarence Bogart," he said.

"Where's he this summer?" said Grace.

"Plattsburg, where I ought to be. God, it makes me so mad I didn't enroll."

"Well, I'm glad you didn't. It's all right for college boys and a few years older, but you have a wife and a family."

"Clarence Bogart's my age and has a wife and two children," said Sidney. "This latest thing, the Black Tom explosion, it's a damn outrage."

"Yes, but let the soldiers take care of it. Clarence Bogart and Ham Schoffstal, people like that. Ham's belonged to the Troop all his life, and Clarence belongs to something in New York."

"He used to belong to Squadron A," said Sidney. "Do you want to hear what he has to say? He writes an amusing letter. 'I am now officially a sharpshooter' (Clarence is one of the best shots in the country) 'having scored 190 the other day, so when your daughter grows up I will see to it that she gets a full-dress wedding complete to Springfield rifle. However it will be mostly threat if I have to depend on the weapons we are using . . . I am glad to say that the Sec'y of War, Mr. Baker, has at last heard about Plattsburg, the first line of defense. He paid us a visit the other day but I wish he had picked another time. For his benefit we hiked eight miles with a 47 lb. pack under a broiling sun and I trust it gave him more pleasure than it gave us. I thought I was in pretty good shape but believe me I was all in at the end and you know which end I mean. I almost wish I had stayed in the Cavalry but at least we know when we are going home and I hear the boys in the Squadron believe they are going to stay in Texas until the threat of war is over . . .' "

"Ham thinks the same thing about the Troop. Connie says

they heard rumors they were going to stay in Texas and Mexico until war was declared."

"Speaking of Ham, I have a letter from him too," said Sidney.

"Be sure and save his letter for Connie."

Sidney read the letter to himself. "Well, Ham came close to some fighting. Some friends of his in the 8th Massachusetts Infantry killed five bandits near Fort Hancock. Two of our soldiers were killed and one was wounded. Hot there, too. Food terrible, morale not very good. Bugs. If we declare war I think I'll try to get in the Navy."

"All right, but please wait till we do. Wait till they attack us."

"They've already attacked us, Grace. They sank the *Lusitania*. They blew up Black Tom, right on our own soil, and this *Deutschland*, their submarine. You have to admire them for their courage, but I hope the British sink the damn *Deutschland* as soon as it gets out of American waters. I think Wilson must be out of his mind, letting them take rubber and gold and nickel back to Germany, to use against us."

"It's not against us, it's against the British and the French, isn't it?"

"It'll be against us. First they want to rule Europe, then us. If we don't go to the rescue of Europe soon it may be too late. Sometimes I think Wilson's a little off, but for the most part he's been right about the Germans. I'm going to vote for him. He's a Democrat, but I'm against the idea of swapping horses in midstream."

"Whatever you say, but while we're on the subject, will you bear in mind that practically everyone we know in Fort Penn is all or part German, German descent?"

"I'll bear it in mind. I'll also bear it in mind that you're not, I'm not, our children aren't, and if some of our friends want to secretly send money to Germany, as they're doing, I'll at least come out in the open and say I'm pro-Ally, and if they don't like it they can go to hell for all I care. The amount of money that goes out of Fort Penn every month to help Germany is disgraceful. Ten men, each giving a thousand a month, is over a million a year, just in Fort Penn."

"Are there ten men giving a thousand a month?"

"Maybe not ten, but there are easily five, and that isn't taking into consideration the smaller amounts. The large cash with-drawals the banks know about, but the hundreds and five-hundreds aren't so noticeable. All cash. No cheques. No wonder the *Deutschland* can take forty-million dollars' worth of gold back to dear old Kaiser Bill."

"Can't the banks stop it?"

"No, they can't, but a couple of the banks wouldn't if they could."

"Well, shall we give some money to England?"

"No," said Sidney. "Not till we're in it. I want to keep my con-science clear. So long as we're neutral, let's stay neutral. If we gave money to England the pro-Germans could say, 'Vell, if der Tates giff moneys to King Georch vy can't ve giff moneys to der Kaiser?' "

"But Sidney, you're not neutral."

"You bet I'm not. I guess you're the only neutral person I know."

"That's because I don't think there'll be a war."

"But there *is* a war, Grace."

"Not ours."

"No, not yet, but you'd have a hard time convincing my cousin Joyce there isn't a war. Two sons, and one husband, for King and country. By the same token you'd have a hard time convincing a lot of people around here, but on the other side."

"I just have a feeling we'll stay out of it."

"That's not a feeling, that's a wish," said Sidney.

———

The Miles Brinkerhoff house, as Sidney had said, was not visible from the Pike. The entrance to the lane was unmarked and might have been little more than an old loggers' road, cut through the stand of trees that Sidney had called a grove. The road was red shale, half covered with pine and spruce branches and it was wide enough for only one truck. The house was being built in an abrupt clearing, far enough away from the woodland to be clear of the tallest tree that would be struck by lightning. "I don't want to spend a barrel of money building a house and the first thunderstorm I get a tree falling on it," Miles had told the builder. "And I don't care for lightning anyhow."

There was the big house for Miles, a small cabin for a caretaker, and a shed for wagons and automobiles. The smaller structures were at the edge of the clearing, not out of range of a falling tree. "Now here's what I want," Miles had told the architect. "I got here about thirty acres and I don't intend to cultivate a foot of it. I want what you call a country home, a gentleman's country home. You won't see a plow on the place. It's no farm. In the fall I hope to be able to stand on my upstairs porch and shoot quail for my breakfast. I want it warm in the winter and cool in the summer. I want plenty of bedrooms and bathrooms, the latest in kitchens and one big room downstairs I'll use for a dining room when I entertain my friends and maybe one little room for eating in when I'm alone, or almost alone. I'll want plenty of water to take a bath in, and by the way I'll want hot water every time I turn on the hot-water spigot. My room I want a big bathroom on the one side for myself, and the other side you can put a lady's bathroom. That's the only place where I want it to look like there was ever a woman within a mile. Lots of times I expect to bring the fellows out here for the single purpose of getting away from their wives and getting drunk, so I want it to look like a man built it for a bunch of good fellows. But there'll be plenty of times when I want to entertain a lady friend and I want her to have nothing to complain about. I'm not a married man and you know that and I get sick and tired of smuggling women into my house just because I happen to live in town. Now I can bring 'em out here at high noon if I want to. I want a lot of big fireplaces and—well, you got the general idea. No fancy wallpaper. This place is for me to entertain my friends, play poker, drink ourselves deaf, dumb and blind, give a young lady a hosing, and if there's a half a dozen of the delightful creatures running around here bare-assed, why that's because they feel at home and no-body's gonna have to worry if the shades aren't down. I'll spend twenty thousand dollars plus your fee. So go ahead."

Lee Bader, the architect, had been recommended by Roger Bannon, Junior, who, although many years younger than Miles Brinkerhoff, was a crony of Miles. Miles and Roger were in the same kelly-pool crowd at the Fort Penn Athletic Club, they often took steam baths together, they made trips together to persuade promising high-school football players to matriculate at alma mater Fort Penn U, and they made other trips together in Miles's Packard touring car to see what the farm girls would do for a dol-lar. That was one of their approaches. They would see a girl on a country road, they would slow down to see if they got a little smile, and if they did they would stop and wait for her to come to the car. "Hello, kiddo. What'll you do for a dollar?" About half the time she would get in the back of the car with one, then the other, and later they would tell her to be at the same place a week from that day. Sometimes, when she was memorable, they would keep the appointment. Sometimes, when they did, the girl would bring a friend.

In the wintertime Miles and Roger were somewhat restricted to Miles's house. Roger had no place to offer; he lived at home with his mother, whom he took to late Mass every Sunday, cup-ping his big hand under her fragile elbow and almost seeming to dare the world to think a naughty thought while she breathed the breath of life. After the Sunday roast Roger would announce that he was going to walk off that dandy dinner, and his steps would lead him to Miles's house.

"What'll we do this aft', Miles?" he said one day.

"What do you feel like doing?"

"Go for a drive?"

"The weather's mean."

"Yah."

"Maybe the poker game hasn't broke up," said Miles.

"Nah. Doesn't appeal to me, bleary-eyed bunch of fellows needing shaves. Cigar butts and sandwich crusts. Nah. If Myrtle wasn't so stubborn."

"She swears up and down, she'll never come near this place in the daylight."

"It's too central a location. You oughta buy a farm, Miles."

"Farming I don't care for, without working even I don't care for it. Being around horses makes me sneeze and get all blotchy. They affect me like sherry wine. You know how hivey I get when I drink sherry wine? That's how horses have an effect on me."

"Well, we could find out if there was a cock-fight going on."

"They're having one down-river, but the weather's too mean to drive. If you'd like to take the car, Roger, it's out in the garage."

"Nah, I wouldn't want to go alone. I wish I was a drinker. This is the kind of an afternoon I'd get drunk on."

"Be thankful you don't have the taste for it, Roger," said Miles. "You're better off without it."

"Yah, I guess I am at that." Roger's fingers sought imperfections in his perfect shave. "New York City we could go to a show. We're a couple of twelve-o'clock fellers in a nine-o'clock town."

"I got a little jag on last night, so I'm contented to sit here and get rid of it, little by little."

"Yah, you were wound up like an eight-day clock," said Roger. He leaned forward and grunted, and rubbed his hands together. "You oughta have a pool table here, Miles."

"Not on a day like this. I'd be lucky to see the God-damn rack, let alone make a ball."

"Yah. I wish it'd get dark."

"Maybe we can think of somebody that don't have Myrt's scruples."

"Screw Myrt's scruples," said Roger. "Who, for instance?"

"I don't know. Let's call up Billy Harris, he'll be at the Orpheum about now. Maybe a couple came in for the new show."

Roger went out to the hall and telephoned the Orpheum.

"The son of a bitch don't answer," said Roger, returning to his chair. "Fort Penn, the City Beautiful, but as dead as a doornail on Sunday afternoon. Can't get your ashes hauled, can't play a game of pool, can't even take a steam bath and get pure. What a pimple on the ass of progress this burg is."

"Um-hmm."

"You sound like the Governor himself. Oh, that reminds me, that reminds me. You remember that one we got in the car, we had her believing you were old Dunkelberger? Where was that, Miles?"

"Down-river," said Miles, thinking. "Near Small's Ferry, I think. You mean the one that didn't want to take the money?"

"She said—what was it she said?"

"She said a dollar's too much. Chust getting inside the nice big auto mit the nice fat Governor. Old Dunkelberger knew that he'd be down-river like a cat shot in the ass."

"He won't have to go down-river," said Roger. "She's here in town. I was getting in my tin lizzie over at Fourth and Brock and I said to myself I thought I knew her from somewhere, this baby-doll getting on the trolley. So I was all done for the day anyhow so I stayed behind the trolley till she got off. She got off at Twentieth and Spangler. It was the same one, but with high-heeled shoes and city clothes I couldn't hardly believe my eyes, but it was the one. I watched where she went, and she went in the kitchen door of Twenty-twelve Spangler. A servant girl, she must be. We oughta get her for old Dunkelberger."

"Dunkelberger has somebody and I guess one's all he can take care of."

"Well, I can easily find out who owns Twenty-twelve Spangler and see if they have a phone. Only we don't know her first name."

"I do. Her first name. That's all we need. She said her name was Beulah."

They never did anything about Beulah. They sat there in Miles's warm sitting-room, dozed off in their chairs, and when they woke up it was dark enough for Myrtle and a friend to come over and cook the sauerkraut. In the happy confusion that followed they forgot all about Beulah and the Governor, but a few days later Miles said to Roger: "Between you and I and the gatepost, I bought a piece of property today."

"You did? Whereabouts?"

"I didn't buy it, but I forked over the downer money. It's the farm we were talking about Sunday."

"Miles! You bought a farm?"

"Not for growing potatoes on. All I'm gonna grow on this land is my whiskers." He described the land, and the kind of establishment he wanted. "You and I go out and take a look at the property and then you start building."

"You wanta have an architect work on this, Miles. I can get together with a first-class carpenter and between the two of us we can put up a two- or three-story frame house, but there I'm watching pennies. Here you want the best and you'll have to watch dollars, Miles. Take my advice. It'll cost you a little more now, but an architect'll save you money in the long run. Lee Bader."

"Lee Bader?"

"You know Lee Bader. Old Levi Bader the painter and paperhanger's son."

"Yah, I know the fellow you mean, but I don't want old Levi spoiling my idea with gold-leaf wallpaper."

"You don't have to worry about that. Young Lee's been waiting for a chance like this, so you can depend on him to do a good job for you. I'll get the lumber and so forth wholesale for you—"

"Now wait a minute, Roger, I want you to make a profit on this."

"Nah. I'll be using the place, won't I?"

"You bet your boots you will, or I won't build it."

"Well, it's only right to save you some money on it. I'll save you on the lumber and so forth *and* I'll save you on Lee Bader's fee. See, we'll figure the cost at wholesale and pay him fifteen percent of that instead of if we figure fifteen percent of what you'd have to pay another builder. See what I mean Miles?"

"Sure, but I don't wanta be a cheap skate."

"A cheap skate? It is to loff, old chap. Man wants to spend twenty thousand dollars on a palace of pleasure and worries if I'm gonna think he's a cheap skate. Go way back and sit down, you old reprobate." Roger made a fist and tapped Miles lovingly on the jaw, and Miles grinned happily.

Bader went ahead with the plans, and he was so little trouble to Miles and Roger that he was no trouble at all. Alone with Roger he did say, "Roger, these estimates on these cost sheets, they're way low. Lumber's up, cement's up, and the closer we get to war the higher everything's going."

"I'm in the building business. I know all that."

"Oh. You're in this with Brinkerhoff," said Bader.

"I didn't say I was in it. It's his, and I don't own a single two-by-four, so don't go around saying I'm in it."

"I wasn't going to, but you sure are saving him a lot of money."

"Listen, Lee, I threw this your way because you told me yourself you want to get some of the upper-crust country-home business. Well, you do this right and it'll be a show-place."

"The way Brinkerhoff talks about it a show-place is the last thing he wants."

"In one way, yes," said Roger, laughing. "But Miles has a lot of rich friends that'll be coming out here."

"Granted, but how many of his rich friends are going to admit they know all about *this* whore-house?"

"You don't understand the latest thing. Psychology. You can't keep a secret in this burg. Sooner or later every son of a bitch in town's gonna know about Miles's place and then pretty soon they'll all be sucking around trying to get invited there, like the way some want to get invited to the Caldwell farm. Catch on? Then the poor boob that wasn't invited, he'll ask the fellow that was, what's it like? And the ones that'd been there'll describe it like it was—what's some famous dwelling? Buckingham Palace. E. T. Stotesbury's house in Philly. See what I mean, Lee? The ones that'd been there'll exaggerate. Then pretty soon those that are thinking of building country homes, they'll say,

Lee Bader was the architect for the classiest country home around here,' and the wives won't take any architect but Lee Bader. Catch on?"

"Yes."

"And me. Do you think I expect to spend the rest of my life with the stuff I'm doing now? Not on your life. I got my eye on the future. First-class suburban homes, all different. No two alike in an entire development. Lee, you know there's a fortune in it for both of us."

"Not if we do business this way. By these figures you don't stand to make any money, I don't either."

"The future! The future! You lunkhead. This is our sample house. Chris' sake. Yes or no?"

"Yes, but don't forget yours truly."

"Listen, kiddo, you said yes and I know you don't break your word, so I'll tell you this. My opinion, you're the only architect in Fort Penn. Just between you and I and the lamp-post, Miles puts up the money, you and I build a sample house, and all *we* lose is our time. Miles gets his house cheap. Everybody's content. How's Esther these days?"

"Getting another baby."

"Makes three?"

"Makes four."

"And me with none."

"It takes two to make a baby."

"Yah."

"How's your mother lately?"

"Poorly, Lee, poorly. Mom was healthier and livelier when she was raising us and the old man was always starting revolutions."

"She was twenty years younger then, too."

"Yes, I suppose so. I think the world and all of Mom, but she don't take an interest in anything but me. No girl's good enough for me, she thinks. Two dates with the same girl and Mom starts in criticizing. If it isn't this, it's that. Oh, well, if she didn't think the sun rose and set on me I wouldn't like that either. Plenty of

spunk in her, you know. Sharp as a tack. Takes off everybody
from the bishop to the woman does the housework. She imitates
colored, Dutch, Irish, Guinnies, I don't know who-all. Size you
up quick as a trigger. I said to her many's the time, I said with her
brains and my physique I could go in the ring with Jess Willard
and cut him to ribbons."

"You have your own brains, they're all right."

"They wouldn't give me a degree out at the U. I make a living
and have a little fun on the side, but—aah, I don't know what the
hell I want, even."

"Well, let's get rich and see what happens," said Bader, and
went ahead with the plans and the execution thereof. Roger visited the place every day, and he and Miles were comically like a
middle-aged couple of a type that was institutional in that period
of the national history; the husband and wife who every Sunday
"took a ride out to look at the property." For a while they called
it The Rock Farm and made jokes about sending away for rock
seed so they could grow rocks. A joke lasted a long time in Fort
Penn in the crowd of fellows Miles and Roger belonged to. Both
Roger and Miles received packages of pebbles labeled "Rock
Seed" from their cronies at the seashore. Another well-loved joke
was to paste the calendar-size insurance-company picture of
Gibraltar over the cabbage on the railroad gondola in the Hen-
derson Seed advertisement. The place also acquired inevitably
the name Miles's Erection, with inevitable, appropriate, sure-fire
jokes about that. But the profusion of jokes did not imply any
lackadaisicalness by Miles or Roger. To the contrary, the jokes
were successful because of the seriousness and intensity with
which they followed every detail of the construction. Roger kept
an outfit of work clothes in the shanty so that he could crawl and
climb of a Sunday afternoon. On weekdays he would pull up
buckets of pitch and kegs of slag for the roofers when the pull-
up laborer took a few minutes off. He poured cement and
wheeled a barrow and cursed the rain. He hurried through his
other jobs so that he could drive the Ford truck out to the Rock

Farm at the end of the day and return the workmen to their homes in Fort Penn, thus giving himself the opportunity to inspire the men—or at least to try—as he had done with football teams he had coached and played on. The fact that he was able to communicate any enthusiasm at an hour of the day when the men wanted nothing more than a glass of cool beer and a dunk in the wash-tub was an indication of how hard he tried. "To be fair, Roger, I ought to pay you wages. You ought to put yourself on the payroll," said Miles.

The obliquely expressed appreciation pleased Roger. "We wanta be in by fall, don't we?" he said.

"Sure, but *you* don't have to kill *your*self."

"Hell, Miles old sock, I never felt better in my life. You stand around by the pitch under the sun and it boils it out of you like no steam bath. Take a look at this." He thumped his belly, hard. "I'm up and down those ladders, carrying a hod, Toncan, conduit, keg of nails. Christ knows what all. I was all right before, pretty good condition, but now I could last a full game. Lafayette had an end, he used to make a horse's ass out of me, but I'd give him his roony-croots now. Look at my hands."

"They're like sandpaper. Put that inside a delightful creature's leg and she'd yell bloody murder."

"Wrong, Miles. They like it. Tickles 'em, if you know enough to take it easy. The only trouble, I can't hardly feel very much myself."

"Well, you don't want to overdo it."

"Right, and I'm getting pretty stemmy. Shall I tell you something? I'm in training. Another week, we'll start and put the flooring in and then's when I get my wick dipped. First time in a month, that'll be."

"You're crazy, Roger," said Miles.

"Aw, well, we'll have plenty of good times in this place, and I'll say to myself, 'Roger, you son of a bitch you, you're entitled to it in this house. You helped built it.' "

The hardwood floor men arrived a week later. They were imported from Philadelphia, were not to be hurried, they encouraged no criticism or comment, were fine craftsmen and were well aware of it. When a suggestion had seemed foolish or impertinent they had been known to pick up their tools, walk off the job and go back to Philadelphia. In ignorance of their proud independence Roger, whose building experience had been limited to cheap and medium-priced houses, committed a faux pas when they arrived. "How long do you men figure on?"

"Why?" said the man in charge of the three-man crew.

"*Why?* Jesus Christ! Who do you think you're talking to?"

"Who do you think *you're* talking to?" said the foreman. He turned to the others. "Don't unpack. We're going home." He was a thin, short man with a Chester Conklin moustache and gold-rimmed spectacles. "The wood belongs to you," he said to Roger. "The firm'll send you a bill for our time and expenses. Will you give us a ride back to town or will we take the trolley?"

"You really quitting?"

"What does it look like? Mister, you aint dealing with no ditch-diggers. Do you know what we get an hour?"

"Sure I know, that's why I asked you how long you figured on."

"The firm told you when you made the deal, but the way you asked us, you sounded as if you was gonna take it into your head to foreman the job, the hurry-up. But we don't work that way. Well, which is it, you giving us a ride or the trolley?"

"Who's your boss?"

"The way *you* think of a boss, I don't have none. And I might as well tell you since this is your first experience with the firm, I'm part of the firm. So are these two men here. And if you wanta make any trouble, you signed a contract. Maybe you didn't read it carefully. Each man entitled to his wages, room in first-class hotel, no interference by contractor or sub-contractor, et setter. Truck or trolley, which is it?"

Roger smiled, but the smile was not returned by the foreman, who began to whistle something like Jingle Bells, while he looked about the room as though he never had spoken to Roger, never had seen him. He took out his hunting-case watch. "Mister, in a situation now like we got here, our time ends when we got off the train at Philadelphia, Broad Street Station, so if you want to save yourself some money, I recommend you make up your mind."

"I made up my mind. If I said something wrong, I apologize," said Roger.

"Well, that's polite."

"So will you unpack? Go to work?" said Roger.

The foreman turned to his associates. "What say?" One shrugged his shoulders and the other spoke. "Up to you, Henry," he said.

"Well, I tell you," said Henry to Roger. "They just as soon go home and sleep in their own bed and eat home cooking, and so would I. But you apologized. He apologized, boys. So that being the case, I think we'll do the job. Now you understand, Mr. Bannon, if we want you we'll leave you know, but otherwise we don't need no help, no help what-so-ever. When the job's finished we'll be on our way. We always got plenty to do, Mr. Bannon. We got more than we can take care of. Well, let's get started. Sooner finished, sooner home."

Roger sauntered out of the room, the large living room on the first floor, and sat on a sawbuck in front of the house. It was now about eleven o'clock of a fine mid-September morning, with the sun warm but away from the sun a warning hint of the nippy weather to come. He was chastened and amused by his encounter with the hardwood men. He had no idea what the two associates looked like but had some sense that they were duplicates of Henry, and it amused him to think of taking guff from the likes of the three of them, especially now, when he could lift, carry, pull, push and bend as much and as well as at any time in his life. For a few seconds he contemplated the future satisfaction of getting the three of them in the same room, locking the door, and giving them a beating they never would forget and might not survive, but that undoubtedly would cost him money and his freedom, if not his own life, and he counted either sacrifice too great. "But God help the next one that crosses my path."

As it happened, the next one to cross his path was Grace Tate.

From his position on the crosspiece of the sawbuck he could look down the narrow lane to the Pike, and he was astonished to see, about half way down the lane, a horse and rider emerge from the woodland and turn toward the house. The horse was at a walk and for a moment Roger wondered who the man was, and then as details became clear in the dark lane he saw that it was a woman, riding 'stride. She had on a black tricorn and a habit which consisted of a gray or black sleeveless jacket and breeches and a white shirtwaist and black hunting boots with patent leather tops. Even before he could quite make out her features he knew it was Grace Caldwell Tate. He rose to meet her.

"Good morning," she said. She laughed. "Oh, I thought you were colored, you're so sunburned."

"Good morning, Mrs. Tate," he said. "No, I don't think I have any touch of the tar. My name is Bannon. Irish."

"Oh," she said. "Is Mr. Brinkerhoff about?"

"No, this is too early for him. He hardly ever comes till late in the afternoon."

"Oh, you're Mr. *Bannon,*" she said. "You're the builder. Mr. Brinkerhoff told my husband we could drop by for a look around, but I'll come some other time."

"No, don't go. I was there when Miles invited your husband. You're free to come any time you like and I'd be pleased to show you around."

"Thanks very much, but I'll come some other time."

"No, please. You'll be the first person, man or lady, I showed the place to. Workmen excepted."

"Oh, really?"

"Positively," said Roger. "I can take your horse down to the shed. It isn't a stable, but it's covering."

"Well—all right. Are you sure you're not busy?"

"Positively. I have some men working on the hardwood floors

inside, but they don't need any help from me, and a couple of laborers grading the path back there, but otherwise I'm just out on an inspection trip myself."

"This horse won't stand at a tree. Could you ask one of the workmen to hold him while we just quickly look around?"

"Well—I could hold him."

"The wrong side, Mr. Bannon," said Grace. "No, thanks, one of the workmen will be all right, as long as he isn't afraid of horses. This fellow won't bite, but I don't want him to have any grass."

"Hey, you! Pasquale!" Roger yelled at the workmen and the horse shied and backed away.

"Jesus Christ," said Grace. "I'm sorry, but the sudden noise. Good boy, good boy. Boy, boy. We're all right, boy." She patted the horse's neck. "I'm sorry, Mr. Bannon, but I think I'll come some other time. We'll *drive* over. Thank you very much. Goodbye."

She turned the horse and circled Bannon, talking to the animal while making the circle, and then she rode off, down the lane. Roger stood in the ring of hoofprints and watched her as half way down the lane the horse broke into a trot.

"I wouldn't mind being where that saddle is, you bitch," he said.

———

While they were having their cocktail that evening Grace told Sidney that she had visited the Brinkerhoff place. "I wanted to see if a path we used to take was still all right to ride on. You know on our northern boundary, the field you had in oats this year?"

"Where there's an opening in the stone fence?" said Sidney.

"That's the one. When I was a girl that was a road."

"I know. I used to ride over it. When we were first married, remember when I used to ride every day? When I was going to start a hunt club?"

"Sure," said Grace. "I still have the boots I bought then."

"And they still fit you. You'll always have good legs."

"The breeches I had then wouldn't fit me now, I regret to say."

"I don't regret that. A little matronly expansion here and there."

"Well, anyway, I thought I'd kill two birds with one stone and take that path, and if it still came out where I remembered it did, I'd have a look at Miles Brinkerhoff's Versailles."

"And?"

"And it did. And I rode up to the house and there was a man there sitting on a sawbuck. I think he thought at first I was a man, and when I saw him I thought he was a coon. But he turned out to be Bannon, the architect. A big sunburned slob, pleasant enough at first and offered to show me around, but then I asked him to get—I was riding sorrel Charlie, and you know how he won't stand, and this Bannon bellowed out for somebody to hold Charlie, and naturally Charlie reared and I was almost thrown, and I guess I swore at Bannon and anyway I said I'd be around some other time, by automobile. I think he got the point."

"What point?"

"That he wasn't fit to be around horses. Then I came home by the Pike. All I saw of the house was what I could see riding up the path and two minutes while I talked to Bannon."

"That's too bad, because that's probably all we'll ever see of it."

"Why so?"

"Because from hints I've heard dropped I don't think your kind of female's going to be welcome when Brinkerhoff opens the house, and I don't think I'll be invited either."

"Nonsense, you could go there any time you pleased. Miles Brinkerhoff'd give his eye teeth to have you come to a party of his."

"I suppose so, but I don't want his eye teeth. You know the big idea of the whole establishment, don't you? A kind of harem for the tired business man. The place is notorious before Brinkerhoff's had a chance to open a bottle of beer. God knows what kind of reputation it'll have a year from now."

"In that case I'd like to see it. All sorts of filthy pictures and bidets and things of that sort? Do you think?"

"Search me," said Sidney. "No, I don't think he'd have that kind of stuff in now, and after he does you won't get in. That is, I *hope* you won't get in. You know, if it weren't for this damn war I'd take you to Paris and show you some of those places and satisfy your curiosity."

"That's what you've been saying for years, but you never did it."

"Well, there was always some reason. The children," said Sidney.

"I guess you always will have some reason, so let's drive out to-morrow and look at Brinkerhoff's. If there's nothing interesting now, at least if I hear stories about the place I'll know where to imagine they happened."

"Let's see. Tomorrow's bank meeting."

"You're always home at four o'clock from bank meeting. Joe can bring the children home from school."

Grace was waiting for Sidney when he stopped the Mercer at the porte-cochere. She was wearing a cashmere suit and matching tam o'shanter. "We have a date, remember?"

"I'd been hoping you'd forget about it," Sidney said. "All right, get in."

They drove over to the Brinkerhoff place and were greeted by Roger Bannon. "Good afternoon, Mr. and Mrs. Tate," he said. "This is neighborly of you."

"Good afternoon, Mr. Bannon," said Sidney. "You met my wife yesterday."

"Yes, and owe her an apology for scaring her horse. I'm not much around horses. They don't like me and I don't like them, so that makes us even."

"Oh, I'm sure they'd like you, Mr. Bannon," said Grace. She muttered to Sidney: "He's such a horse's ass," and hummed something to cover her muttering.

"Let me show you around," said Roger.

They got out of the car and went with him on the tour of the property. Roger's recital confined itself to the simple details. "Up here we have Miles's bedroom and rooms for the guests. . . . All the latest in kitchen equipment. . . . You notice these men, they're laying the hardwood floors. . . . Down there's the path to the river. Next Spring Miles wants to put up a boat-house but we won't need it this winter, so March or April'll be plenty of time to get started on that. And, I guess that's about all there is till the furniture starts coming in."

"I think it's a very interesting place, and you've done a fine job, don't you think so Grace?" said Sidney.

"Yes, I do indeed. You can be very proud of it."

"Well, I did the best I could—excuse me. What is it, Henry?"

Henry, the hardwood craftsman, joined them. "We're done for the day, Mr. Bannon. We're ready when you're ready."

"Oh," said Roger. "Well, I don't have my truck. I'm waiting here for him to come back with it. He oughta be here now."

"Anything we can do?" said Sidney.

"No, thanks. The hardwood-floor men are through for the day and I have to take them back to Fort Penn, but my fellow with the truck had to go some place else."

"How many are there? Maybe we can help you out."

"Three of them, but I wouldn't hear of that, but thank you very much for the offer."

"Notta tall," said Sidney. "We'll be glad to."

"I can do it," said Grace. "I can drive Mr. Bannon and the three men into town and then stop at school for the children. It'll work out perfectly. Joe hasn't left the farm, and if we see Mr. Bannon's truck we can save him a trip."

"There you are," said Sidney.

"Well, if you're sure I wouldn't be putting you out," said Roger.

"Not a bit," said Sidney.

One of the men sat on Roger's lap until they got to the Farm, and when Sidney got out Roger joined Grace in the front seat.

"What hotel are they stopping at?" said Grace, taking the wheel.

"Schoffstal," said Roger.

They did not speak again until five miles later. "Here comes my truck," said Roger. "I'll send him home." He got out and instructed the driver and then resumed his place beside Grace. "Well, this sure is some car. Those fellows back there travel first-class all the way, but I'd be glad to bet they don't get in Mercers every day of the week." He lowered his voice. "Hardwood-floor men, you know. They aren't any ditch-diggers. They're the aristocracy in the building game."

"Oh, is that so?" said Grace.

"Oh, my yes. You have to handle them with kid gloves," he went on. "If you don't handle them gently they walk right off the job."

"I see," said Grace.

"I think next year I'll buy one of these. I was gonna put my money in a Hudson, but this rides better and puts up a much better appearance."

"I'm crazy about it. It's my husband's car, but I drive it every chance I get."

"The way I feel now I'd give you one for one night in bed with you, you snotty bitch with your skirt blowing up over your spats and you can feel me looking at those legs." She looked away from the road and at him, and for a fraction of a second he was afraid he had unconsciously spoken aloud.

"Would you like to take the wheel?" she said.

"I sure would, but we're coming into the outskirts of town and people would think it was funny, me driving your car. Your husband mightn't like it." He spoke quietly.

"Are you worried about my husband or *other* people?"

"Both," he said.

"Well, I'm not worried about my husband, and most assuredly I'm not worried about anybody else." She slowed down.

"I might strip the gears of something like that, but thanks anyway," he said.

"Whatever you say," said Grace. They were silent again until she swung the car into the space in front of the Schoffstal House.

"Here we are," she said.

Henry and friends thanked her and left them.

"I can get out here," said Roger.

"Don't you want me to drop you somewhere?" she said.

"I think I better get out here," he said. "It'll be all over town tomorrow that you had me and three other men with you in your care. But nothing toward what it'd be if it was me alone."

"Thank you for being so discreet. I mean that. I'm not being sarcastic." She put out her hand and he took it. She looked at him and then looked down at their hands. "Don't do that," she said.

"What?"

"Pawing my hand with your hand. Let go, please."

"It's little enough considering what I'd—"

"I'm *not* considering what you'd like," she said, and suddenly pulled her hand out of his grip. "Get out."

"I apologize."

"Get out, I said."

"I apologized, didn't I?"

"When I offered to do you a favor I didn't realize I was letting myself in for a pest. A bore, maybe. But not a pest. Now if you don't get out of this car this instant I'm going to drive over to the Fort Penn Club and there'll be somebody there to throw you in the gutter. Where you belong."

"There's nobody in the Fort Penn Club could do that, Mrs. Tate. But if anybody there ever bothers you, you can always count on me. Do they bother you, Grace?"

"It'd take a lifetime to explain the difference between you and the men in the Fort Penn Club."

"I'll do anything they'll do. Try me out some time." He got out of the car, closed the door, but rested his fingers along the top of the door, and one foot on the running-board. He was about to resume talking but she suddenly took her foot off the clutch and tramped on the foot-throttle and the Mercer jumped away, and his thigh was slapped sharply by the rear fender, and he sprawled in the gutter. He first turned around to see if anyone had noticed

what had been done to him, but the passers-by seemed to be unaware of the cause of his predicament. He was on his feet in a
second, brushing off his clothes, and then he saw, in the second-
floor-lobby window, Henry, the hardwood man. Roger forced a
grin, but Henry merely took his pipe out of his mouth and spat
into the tall brass cuspidor.

Henry, of course, wore those thick glasses and may not have
seen anything, but Roger knew better than that. He became a
pedestrian and remained one as far as the Fort Penn A. C. He
went up to the locker-room and got into his gym suit and played
volleyball for an hour. His service that afternoon was hard and
fast, but inaccurate; his smashes were terrific. After a swim he
joined Miles Brinkerhoff in the bar. He was glad to see that Miles
was sitting alone.

"What's that you're drinking?" said Roger.

"That? That's just a shot of rye whiskey. My only consolation
when things go wrong, my friend in adversity, also my companion when I got some reason to celebrate."

"Which is it today?"

"Today? Today it's just a shot of whiskey before I make up my
mind what I wanta eat. Why? You probably seen me put away a
thousand gallons of this stuff and you never asked me about it before. You thinking of trying it?"

"Harry, give me the same as Mr. Brinkerhoff has here."

The waiter blinked but nodded.

"Got a toothache?"

"I got something worse than that."

"Got an African toothache? If you have, liquor's the worst
thing for it."

"How would I get an African toothache when the closest I
been to a quiff in over a month is *sitting* next to one?" said Roger.

"You must of been sitting next to a warm one that said no,
then."

"Have a cigar, you hit the bull's-eye," said Roger.

"Before you drink that, are your intentions to get drunk?"

"The first time since we beat Lehigh and I made the winning touchdown."

"Well, if you want a word of advice from old Uncle Miles, I aint saying don't get drunk if your mind's made up, but as an old hand at consuming the booze, let me suggest you mix it with half water or you'll be on your ass before you know what hit you. This is Mount Vernon, good whiskey, and it won't take many. I'm not a man goes around diluting good whiskey, but take my advice, Roger. I get my exercise raising the glass. You get yours the right way, but you'll no more get any pleasure out of a pint of this nectar than I would out of a game of volleyball. I have sense enough to stay away from the volleyball. You take that whiskey with half water."

"I'll think it over," said Roger. He tossed the whiskey down his throat, squirmed a little, chased it with water, and whispered "Another one," to the waiter. "The next one is half water," he said to Miles.

"God help the poor sailors on a night like this," said Miles. "Do you have any plans, getting drunk to one side?"

"Nope," said Roger. "Yes, one thing I'd like to do is go over to the Fort Penn Club and offer them out."

"All of them?"

"Any two of them. Any three of them," said Roger.

"Well, I've often had the inclination, but that's as far as it ever got. No particular one? Just any two or three?"

"Yah."

"I don't know," said Miles. "It'd be better if you narrowed it down to one that you had a grudge against. They'd forgive that. But just going in and challenging any two or three—and I think you could get some of them to mix it with you—that don't sound like a good idea for a young fellow just beginning to make his mark in the business world. Not in this particular town. In the first place, it wouldn't be long before you'd starve to death. Those aristocrats, you know they have the say who gets loans at the banks. They could screw you up something fierce on building permits. And of course there you got that idea of branching out in the country home business, and if I'm not mistaken, they're the ones gonna be building them country homes. Who the hell do you hate over there, anyway?"

"All of the bastards."

"Oh, you're just a Socialist. Wasn't your old man—didn't he have Socialist tendencies?"

"He was crazy, he was all foam and no beer. Talk, talk, talk. Like to drive you crazy listening to him. I don't inherit any of his half-assed ideas. No, it's something happened to me this afternoon." He told a more or less straightforward story of the afternoon.

"Uh-*huhhh*," said Miles. "Grace Caldwell. Well, I don't blame you for wanting to give her a little frig. Delightful creature. Ever since she was a little kid with a pony-cart I can remember prophesying to myself how I'd like to offer her a lollipop. When she couldn't of been more than fifteen *years* old. This the first time you ever got the itch for her?"

"Aw, see her in a car or walking on the street, I'd notice her, but nothing special. This is the first time I was ever that close to her, today and yesterday. *You* wanted it from a *distance,* but when you get close to, and she's a woman now, and you can't convince me she's getting all she wants at home. That Tate, he's too much of a *gentleman.*"

"I don't know, Roger. I been on parties with those *gentlemen,* and they used to have a boat-house down-river, her brother was one. They take to it just the same as boilermakers or blacksmiths. The arm muscle aint what counts. It's what you do with what Nature gave you . . . I think you're doing the sensible thing."

"What's that?"

"Get drunk, we'll get a couple whores, and forget about it. Tomorrow you'll feel so awful all you'll think of is your head and you'll get her out of your system."

"That's easy for you to say."

"I take the responsibility, too," said Miles. "You not getting any nooky the last month while you were working on my place, that's why you fell for Caldwell. You want a surprise? I was talking to Bert Botley and he's got two new ones over at the Commercial House, from Chicago working their way east in easy stages. They must be good because they won't listen to anything under ten simoleons. I half way made a date with them for eight o'clock. We can take them over to the Rathskeller and fatten them up a little, get a few drinks in them, and take them back to my house. That appeal to you?"

"Sure."

In accordance with custom, Cora and Mildred, the passing fancies from Chicago, met Miles and Roger in Miles's Packard, which was waiting at the darker entrance to Soldiers Park. Miles and Roger were standing on the sidewalk beside the car. Cora, who was closer to thirty-five than to thirty, said "Hello, boys. I'm Cora. Let me make you acquainted with Mildred."

"It's a pleasure, I'm sure," said Mildred, who was ten years younger than Cora.

"Greetings, Cora, Mildred," said Miles. "This is Roger."

"Roger, I like the name Roger," said Cora. "And what was your name again?"

"It's still Miles, huh huh huh," said Brinkerhoff.

" 'The Courtship of Miles Standish,' " said Mildred. "I consider that romantic. Will I sit with you, Miles, and they can go together?"

"That suits me right down to the ground," said Miles.

"Say, wait a minute," said Cora. "Is he drunk? He looks drunk to me."

"Nah, nah," said Miles. "He had a couple but he's not used to them."

"Let him say it," said Cora. "Roger, are you drunk, sweetheart?"

"Nah," said Roger. He was leaning with one hand against the car and grinning at Mildred.

"He's all right, girls," said Miles. "We'll all get a steak inside us and feel better all around."

"What Roger wants first is a cuppa coffee, don't you, Roger?" said Cora.

"He'll be all right, girls. Cora, you and I get in back."

"Is Roger gonna take the wheel?" said Cora.

"I drive better than when I'm drunk than when I'm sober," said Roger.

"I thought you said he wasn't drunk," said Cora.

"I thought he said he didn't drink," said Mildred.

"Come on, Roger," said Miles. "The girls are hungry."

"Whatever your wish is my desire," said Roger. He opened the door for Mildred and bowed low, and as soon as he took the wheel and started to drive he was more articulate and coherent; he was at that stage where something to do with his hands helped him to conquer his dizziness. He talked to Mildred, asked her where she was from and other such questions, and did not wait for the answers.

The Rathskeller was one of the three good restaurants in Fort Penn, and of its type as good as any in the country. It was popular with the legislators who could afford it, the members of the A. C. and their wives, and commercial travelers, but Grace Tate, to name one, never had been inside the place and was barely aware that it existed, and it was not patronized by the upper or the lower-upper families. It had a "funny" reputation, based on the fact that it had private dining-rooms, the fact that the lighting was dim, and the fact that men like Miles automatically took women like Cora and Mildred to dinner there. It was run by Fritz Gottlieb, a Bavarian who was not a Pennsylvania Dutchman, a stout, unsmiling man, who parted his hair in the middle and wore a black waistcoat with lapels, black trousers, black bow tie tucked under his collar, and sleeve garters. He had one joke, with which he dealt with the young and the new who asked him if the house ever bought a drink: "The house buys a drink on Christmas, but Christmas we're closed." Whenever he produced the joke he did not have to finish the second part; the regulars would sing in chorus: "But Christmas we're closed." He was otherwise unco-operative with the customers in that he pretended he did not understand Pennsylvania Dutch, with which most of them were familiar.

Fritz bowed and said good evening to Miles and Roger, without mentioning their names. He looked sharply at Roger but made no comment. "Upstairs or down, gentlemen?"

"Down, if you have a wall table, Fritz," said Miles.

"The back booth, yes?"

"Fine and dandy," said Miles. They were seated in the booth and Miles quickly ordered their food, conveying with a wink and a nod to the waiter his eagerness to get the soup on the table.

"Is this town local option? Fort Penn isn't dry, is it?" said Cora.

"Oh, you'd like a little snifter, girls?" said Miles. "When he comes back I'll tell him. We had ours. Say, I heard a little story I gotta tell you. This is a new one for you too, Roger. It seems this fellow went into a bar and a girlie was sitting there by herself and the fellow liked her looks, the way we like your looks. So one thing led to another and he bought her a cocktail. She drank it down in one gulp, and so did he. Then he asked her did she care for another and she said sure. I forgot to tell you, this fellow wasn't used to drinking. So anyway, she had the second and gulped it down, and so did he gulp it down. And she had a third, and he had a third, and when he got finished the third, he said to her, 'Say, if I have another one of these, I'm gonna feel it,' and *she* said, 'Say, if I have another, I'm gonna *let* you.' "

Cora laughed. "Oh, my. 'I'm gonna let you.' "

" 'I'm gonna let you,' " said Miles.

"If you ask me, I think Roger musta had *his four,*" said Mildred.

Roger laughed. "Yah," he said. "I'm gonna get Mildred a pussy café."

"Oh, that's old, but I like the other one. I never heard that one before. 'If I have another I'm gonna *let* you.' " Mildred laughed.

The soup came and they started to eat, but Roger had only

one spoonful. He laid the spoon down. "What was it you said a while ago, you? You? I forget your name."

"Cora," she said.

"Local option. We don't have local option here, Miles. Let's have a drink, all around."

Miles kicked Cora under the table, but too late. "I'll take a shot of gin with a little Worcestershire in it," she said.

"That's what I'll have," said Mildred.

Miles and Roger had straight rye. They stuck to their choices throughout the meal. The others were not seriously affected, but Roger finished the latter half of his steak in his fingers, and spilled a cup of coffee down his shirt-front. As soon as it was spilled Miles asked for the bill, paid it, and suggested going to his house.

"Do you think this fella's all right?" Cora whispered to Miles. "We don't want trouble."

Miles patted her leg. "Everything hunky-dory," he said.

They went out, Roger with his arm around Mildred's shoulder. They drove to Miles's house without accident, but left the Packard in the driveway. "Well, here we are home," said Miles, genuinely relaxed. "Girls wanta go pee-pee?"

"I do," said Cora. "How about you, Mildred?"

"Uh-huh."

"Want us to come up with you or will you call us or you feel like a snort? I got everything you can name," said Miles.

"I'll bet you don't have champagne."

"I'll just bet you I do. You want champagne?" said Miles. "We'll bring up four bottles and ice and glasses."

"Meet you upstairs in about ten minutes," said Cora.

Roger carried the small tub with the iced bottles, and Miles carried the glasses. They had a few drinks and then Roger said, "You carry the bottle, and I'll carry you." They left Miles's room.

"He's a handsome specimen, but I think the world and all of Mildred, and I'm afraid of these ones that get a jag on once in ten years," said Cora.

"They'll be all right, Cora dear, so how about you and me having a little fun," said Miles.

They had their fun, and when it was over Cora said: "Not a sound out of them. Not even laughing."

"Maybe we didn't hear them," said Miles. "Thick doors in this house. Here smoke a cig—" The first scream cut his words.

"God damn it, I knew it!" said Cora. She pulled a counterpane around her and started for the door, just as the door was opened and Mildred ran to her.

"Get me outa here, get me outa here, for God's sake, get me outa here."

Her mouth and nose were bleeding and the blood streamed down on her body. Her eyes were discolored and beginning to close. She put her arms around Cora and Cora held her close.

"Have you got a gun?" said Cora.

"Good God," said Miles, looking at Mildred. "What happened?"

"Have you got a gun, damn you. That bastard's crazy. He'll kill you, he tried to kill her, he'll kill all of us," said Cora.

"I got a gun, but—"

"Get it, then. I don't wanta be killed. You saw what he did to this poor kid. Come on in, we'll go to the toilet and lock the door, poor kid." They closed the bathroom door and Miles heard the bolt. He took a .25 automatic out of the bedside table and quietly moved down the hall to Roger's room.

"Roger," he whispered.

There was no answer. Miles entered the room, and he could see Roger's legs on the bathroom floor, and then he moved closer and saw that the younger man had vomited all over himself and was asleep with his chin and one arm resting on the toilet bowl. Miles put the pistol back in his bathrobe pocket and draped a couple of Turkish towels over the younger man and went back to his own room.

He knocked on the bathroom door. "It's me, Miles," he said.

"You gotta get a doctor for this kid," said Cora, through the door. "Get a doctor and get her clothes outa that room. Where's *he?*"

"Out like a light, asleep. He won't bother anybody."

"You bet he won't. You got seven razors in here, and I'll cut his head off, the dirty bastard. Get that doctor. Maybe she's bleeding to death."

Miles went to the phone extension in his upstairs sitting-room. He gave the number. "Mrs. Littauer? This is Miles Brinkerhoff. Is the doctor there?"

"One minute, Mr. Brinkerhoff," she said.

"Hello," said Littauer.

"Doc, this is Miles Brinkerhoff. Can you come over to my house right away? I cut my finger and it's bleeding like a stuck pig."

"Which finger is it?" said Littauer.

"Uh, two of them. Just bring something to stop the blood and some bandages."

"Well, I was in bed, but I'll be over's soon as I can."

"Yah, but hurry as much as you can, please. I'm losing blood."

Miles went back to the bathroom door and told Cora the doctor would be over in a minute. He returned to Roger's room and sat with the pistol in his hand until the doorbell rang. He opened the door for Dr. Littauer.

"What the hell's going on here?" said Littauer.

"I didn't cut myself—"

"Oh, hell, I knew that. If you cut your finger you'd faint. What is it?"

"A hell of a God-damn mess. Roger Bannon beat up a little hooker. He was drunk, the first time in ten years, and he beat the hell out of the poor kid. I hope that's all it is. Now you know, Doc. I've always been right with you, so do the best you can here. Come on upstairs, she's in the toilet with the other hooker."

Miles told Cora and Mildred to come out.

"Holy smokes, look at that face," said Littauer.

"Shall I put her in bed?" said Cora. She and Mildred had bloodstained towels around them.

"Put her in the chair first till I get a look at her."

Mildred was weeping, but as though from a distance, uncomprehendingly.

"Good God, Miles," said Littauer, as he went on with the examination. "Where's Bannon now, did you say?"

"Asleep on the floor in the other bathroom."

"He doesn't give you a slap on the wrist when he wants to play," said Littauer. "This girl's nose is broken. Have to stitch both eyes and both lips." He stood erect and looked at Miles. "She oughta be in the hospital. She's got a concussion, probably when she hit the floor, and she's lost a lot of blood, but you can see that for yourself. She oughta be in the hospital, Miles."

"Well then take her," said Cora.

"Are you gonna pay for it, Sister?" said Littauer. He went on with his patient.

"Like hell we are, they're gonna pay, they're gonna pay good."

"Yeah, but I mean the hospital," said Littauer.

"Can we get her in under an assumed name?" said Miles.

"Her name isn't what's gonna make the difference. Any hospital in the state sees this woman and it's a police case. They won't admit her on my say-so. They'll *know* there was something funny going on."

"Take her down to your place, eh Doc?"

"Hey, what is his place? A clap joint?" said Cora.

"Clap and syph and abortions," said Littauer. "You've heard of them."

"Take her to a regular hospital," said Cora. "I don't care what the cops do," said Cora.

"I didn't ask your preference," said Littauer, "so shut up till I do. You open your trap in this town and you'll get ninety days in the House of Refuge so quick you won't even know what the judge looked like. Now be quiet." He spoke again to Miles. "I don't see where you have any choice but my place, but I just want you to know, it's gonna come high. A hundred dollars a day, and she'll have to be there at least two weeks. Maybe longer, depending on the concussion."

"Is that on the level? The concussion?" said Miles.

"Positively. That's why I'm charging you so much. I admit I'm holding you up a little, but I'm taking a hell of a chance if she dies at my place. But no worse than you are if she dies here, or in the hospital."

"Dies! Dies!" cried Cora.

"Oh, shut up, will you?" said Littauer.

"All right, Doc, take her to your place," said Miles.

"What about you, Sister? You care to accept my hospitality, ten dollars a day? You can sleep in the same room with your little friend."

"Let him pay for it," said Cora.

"All right, only get them outa here," said Miles.

"What about Bannon?" said Littauer. "Shall we go take a look at him? Sister, you can start putting some clothes on, and get some on your friend."

Littauer and Brinkerhoff went out. Before they re-entered Roger's room Littauer halted Miles. "I didn't want to tell you this in front of her, Miles, but that kid's right breast—I don't like the looks of it. That's a no-good son of a bitch, that fellow, drunk or sober. I'm gonna put him to sleep now, and when he wakes up tomorrow you better get rid of him. Me, I can just about hold on to my license and I'm lucky I kept it this long, but this bum makes me feel like John B. Deaver. You pay this whole bill yourself. It's worth it to get rid of him."

"I don't know, Doc. He was never like this before."

"Maybe not, but this was coming a long time. I could see it coming."

"Maybe you're right. I like a good time, but maybe you're right. He could turn on me and smash my face just as quick as he did that little hooker. Well, I'm ready for him." Miles showed Littauer the automatic.

"You won't need that. I'm gonna give him a hypodermic that'll keep him asleep, and then when he wakes up he'll have such a headache he won't know what hit him."

"That's what I told him earlier." Miles smiled.

Roger got awake when the needle pricked him, but in a few seconds he was asleep again.

"Cover him up if you want to," said Littauer. "If it was me I'd let him get pneumonia."

The doctor and Cora supported Mildred to the car, and Miles went to his bedroom and locked the door. He slept badly with the light on and with the .25 under his pillow.

Elmira Spotswood, Miles's housekeeper, lived out, and a rule of the household required Elmira to knock on his door, and ask Miles what he wanted for breakfast before prowling about with dustcloth and Bissell. Elmira thus was able to wake him up, take his order, and give him the chance to bring some serenity into the chaotic picture that was often the Brinkerhoff second-story at eight o'clock in the morning. This morning Miles switched off the light, put the pistol in the drawer, and unlocked the door.

"Come in, Elmira," he said.

"Yessuh." She always brought coffee first. She now poured it, sugared it, and handed the cup to Miles. He drank it.

"Mr. Bannon spent the night. He was very sick. Not seriously, but indigestion. I had to have the doctor."

"Well, I'm glad he's over it. He din say nothin'."

"How do you mean? Have you seen him?"

"Give him his breakfast. He din eat as big a breakfast as usual, but two eggs and bacon, two cupsa coffee."

"Oh," said Miles. "Oh. Is he still downstairs?"

"He still down, yessuh. Want me to call him for you?"

"Yes. I'll have the usual. Oatmeal or Cream of Wheat. You got any scrapple, I'll have that. And tell Mr. Bannon to come up."

They ignored the bottles, the glasses, and the bloodstains. Elmira, although a religious woman, was hotel-trained, not home-trained, and tracks and traces of debauchery were not new to her.

"I didn't expect you to be up," said Miles, when Roger entered the room.

"Woke up about an hour ago. I felt kind of dizzy, but I got dressed. What the hell happened?"

"Well, Roger," said Miles. "I better not start beating about the bush."

"No, don't."

"You may be in serious trouble."

"I was afraid of that. How serious? What happened to the women?"

Miles nodded. "What happened to one of them, the prettier one, is, she aint gonna be pretty any more, Roger."

"Me?"

"You. You beat the hell out of her. Do you remember any of it?"

"I saw the blood. Tell me the rest of it."

"Sure, I'll tell you," said Miles. "The booze hit you and you went crazy, I guess. I was here in bed with the other one, Cora, and we heard these screams and then your one came in looking like she was hit by a Mack truck."

"Mother! Where was I?"

"You, you were in the toilet, out like a light, puke all over you. I got Doc Littauer and he took the women to his place." Miles paused judicially.

"Tell me the worst of it," said Roger.

Miles continued his pause before going on. "I don't know the worst," he said.

"Well, for Christ's sake, Miles, I didn't kill her. Did I?"

"Doc Littauer says she has a concussion."

"Concussions, you can get them playing football and get over them."

"Sure, I know. But on the other hand you can like get over them for a few days and then keel over. But even without any concussion, that kid—you broke her nose, opened up her eyes so they had to be stitched, knocked some teeth out and her mouth looks like hamburger."

"Gee." Roger put his hand to his brow. "What started it, do you have any idea?"

"Nope. You must of just went crazy. And what she don't know, or Cora, but the doc told me. You hit her up here, the right breast. That's a trouble-maker, Roger."

"How's that?"

"That's how they get cancer."

"What can they do to me if she gets cancer?"

"Roger, you aren't taking this thing seriously enough."

"I'm taking it seriously, for Christ's sake. I'm only asking you."

"Yes, but you're asking me in a way that's like you didn't think it was serious. You're putting up an argument. I'm giving you the straight goods, not exaggerating."

"I know, Miles, but you can't blame me if I'm trying to consider the whatever they can do to me. I've heard of hookers getting beaten up, and a hundred-dollar note squared it."

"Wait a minute," said Miles. "Come in, Elmira."

She laid the tray on a small marble-topped table and left the room. Miles tucked the napkin under his chin, and ate as he talked, gesturing with knife and fork when his mouth was full.

"A hundred-dollar note," said Miles. "That's ten dollars under what Littauer's charging me a day, for two weeks at least. A hundred for the one you beat up, and ten for her friend to stay with her. That's fourteen hundred plus a hundred and forty. Fifteen-forty at least. That's medical expense, without taking into consideration what they'll want for blackmail."

"You won't have to pay it, Miles. Why should you pay it? I'm the one that did it."

"It happened in my house and to some extent I consider myself liable for letting you get drunk. And I know enough about your bankroll to know how long you can peel off a hundred and ten a day. I'm not worrying about the money, but I am worried about you putting up an argument when I try to tell you, this kid might croak. And if she croaks it'll take every nickel I can lay my hands on to keep the both of us out of jail. I'd like to see you get a little scared, here. What if she *doesn't* die? What if she wants to press charges? Assault and battery, intent to kill, mayhem. What if she has connections we don't know anything about? I didn't get much sleep last night, revolving it over in my mind. Bert Botley. He'll have to have a present, a nice fat present. I can make trouble for Bert in the ordinary course of events, and he knows it. But here the shoe's on the other foot. He knows we had those women and were bringing them here. He'd be a witness for them if we didn't give him a nice present. Fritz Gottlieb. That pig-eyed bastard'd testify you were drunk and noisy. He never liked it for sour apples when you spilt coffee and hollered all over the place. I saw him looking over at our table. And I got some neighbors here, if they heard those screams—they'd have to be in the next county if they didn't. And Elmira. She never says anything, but I'll bet she wouldn't tell a lie on the Bible."

"Where are you, Miles? Are you on my side?"

Miles carefully poured a thin trickle of molasses on his scrapple, up and down, like an exercise in handwriting. "Do I have any choice which side I'm on? Where'd it happen? This house. I guaranteed the expenses already. I don't know why you want to ask me a question like that for."

"I wanted to know if you were on my side. I don't consider that an answer."

"What do you want? I should give you congratulations yet? It's possible you beat a woman to death, maybe while we're chewing the rag here she croaked, and you want me to pin a medal on you yet. If this costs me under five thousand dollars I consider myself lucky. But forget about the money. What about the good times? They're passed and gone. This story'll be all over. The two-dollar hookers down on Railroad won't let us come within ten feet of them. If I want a little party I'll have to go away somewhere out of town. You're a young fellow, but I gotta buy mine. There isn't a woman in this town'd marry me, that I'd marry anyway." He put the napkin to his lips and poured some water from the tumbler on his fingers. "It seems a shame. It's too damn bad you didn't drag Grace Caldwell off in the bushes and get it out of your system. If you were so sure she wanted it you didn't have to go and beat up a hooker."

"Don't talk to me like that, Miles."

"Are you giving orders around here?" said Miles. He moved quickly to the bedside table and took out the automatic. "I was ready to use this last night."

"On me? You'd shoot me?" Roger had not risen.

"Any crazy man I'd shoot if he came after me."

"I'd never gone after you. What do you take me for?"

"The fellow that made hamburger out of that kid's face, that's all I take you for."

"Put the gun away." Roger got up and poured some coffee and drank it, and Miles put the gun back in the drawer. "I never thought I'd live to see the day Miles Brinkerhoff pulled a gun on Roger Bannon. A gun. Miles Brinkerhoff. Pulled a gun. I guess I oughta leave a nickel for the cup of coffee, but I guess if I started paying you back for all the coffee I drank in this house I wouldn't have much left."

"Where are you going now?"

"Now? First I wanta go down Doc Littauer's and see how she is, if she's alive or dead."

"Stay away from there. Don't show your face near there. I'll be the one to get in touch with him."

"I guess that's a good idea. Then I was going to the office and see how much money I owed and how much I could borrow. You can have the business. I don't owe much."

"I don't want the business. Anyway it wouldn't be any good without you running it."

Roger bowed. "Thanks for the compliment. I'll be all done at your place in about another week or ten days. I'll have to send you a bill for that because I got other people to pay, but my intention is I'm gonna pay back all this trouble costs you."

"All I want is you to stay in town and don't leave. The hell with the money consideration."

"Aw, hell, if I killed her I couldn't go far anyway. Well, so long—William S. Hart."

In the weeks that immediately followed Roger would call

Miles on the telephone, in the evening at Miles's residence. Miles's reports, summarized, provided the information that Mildred's concussion was not dangerous; the nose was damaged beyond restoration but not repair; the stitches in the lips and cheeks would leave scars; the injury to the breast was not treated by Littauer. Cora left the Littauer house after two weeks and was busy with gentlemen every evening until Mildred's month under Littauer's care was up. Miles gave Cora five hundred and Mildred a thousand dollars in cash, in the presence of his good friend Russ Kelland, the Fort Penn captain of detectives, who impressed upon them the desirability of their permanent absence from the county. Bert Botley was not very grateful for the hundred dollars he received, but Russ Kelland reminded him that the accident would never have happened if Bert had not made a profitable practice of housing such guests as Mildred and Cora. Bert did not in his turn point out that the practice was more or less indirectly profitable for Russ.

The telephone conversations were informational and in no sense social. At the Fort Penn A. C. it was immediately apparent that Miles and Roger had had a "falling out" over something or other, and after Bert Botley had spent his hundred dollars the "falling out" was attributed to a wild party at Miles's house, and then by degrees an approximation of the actual story was circulated. As gossip it was not too successful. Because the women were prostitutes and but briefly present and active in Fort Penn and therefore not recognizable local figures, they did not lend themselves to scandal as they might have if they had been non-professional or resident professional. It also was true that the gossip could not be kept alive by jokes at the expense of Miles and Roger. Although the friendship obviously had been rearranged by the circumstances, the two men still spoke cordially enough when they met on the street or in the Fort Penn A. C., and it was a fact that Roger had continued to work on Miles's country house after the wild party. The friendship, however affected, did exist, and no jolly member of the A. C. was willing to risk the consequences of teasing Roger or Miles, especially since violence on Roger's part was the outstanding detail of the story. There probably were not ten men in the Fort Penn Athletic Club who felt they could stay three rounds with Roger, and no man who could lick him.

Moreover, since the women involved were not known to the matrons and maidens of Fort Penn, an element of successful scandal was missing: the good women were left without a villainess. And again, neither Roger nor Miles was married or spoken for, which left the irreproachable women without a heroine. Two bachelors and two strumpets had got into a mess.

Wilson got re-elected and Fort Penn U. tied Penn State and beat Bucknell and railroad bridges were being patrolled by the National Guard against destruction by agents of the Central Powers. The war was not yet, but in Fort Penn the National Guard was being expanded and an Irish infantry company was formed. Roger enlisted, "more for the exercise than liking the idea of getting ready to fight on the same side as the English." The Irish company drilled once a week, then oftener, in the 114th Infantry Armory, wearing campaign hats and civilian trousers; khaki army blouses and laced canvas leggins; khaki breeches and striped silk shirts; uniforms complete, and civilian outfits with cartridge belts. As the logical man to lead his platoon, Roger was picked for a second lieutenancy and upon being commissioned he became more frequently a visitor to the Armory than to the A. C. He went to Philadelphia and bought a uniform at Jacob Reed's, and his coolness toward the Sassenach abated to the extent that he campaigned for a British-type tunic, with the open collar and flared skirt, against the regulation throat-cutter and short coat. ("If our Roger don't shoot the enemy, it's blind them he will with them boots, and tickle them with them spurs.") He made a provisional deal with his cousin Joe Mullaly, a master carpenter, to take over the contracting and building business in case war actually came. Cousin Joe was an older man, a man in his late forties, who knew how to read a blueprint or to build a house without one. Roger picked him for his experience and honesty and because Mrs. Bannon, Roger's mother, suggested him. The deal was simple enough: Joe would be the construction boss, Roger's mother would emerge from retirement as front-office executive, and Lawyer O'Connell or someone in the O'Connell & Partridge office would read the contracts. Roger Bannon Junior Incorporated changed its policy from residential to industrial construction; Fort Penn was getting its share of war industries, and Roger was seeing to it that Roger Bannon Junior Incorporated got its share of Fort Penn's share. In Roger's words, a boy scout that knew how to put up a lean-to could build the kind of plants they were building, and it would be a sin and a shame to pass up those cost-plus government contracts. A drunken man with a level, a claw hammer and a contract could make money; an established contractor like Roger Bannon Junior Incorporated could get rich.

Proud of his uniform, fit to fight, with the cold, hard ground broken for the gun-stock factory at South Fort Penn, his first government contract, Roger hummed and whistled all the day, those early months in 1917. There were only two persons capable of marring his joy: Miles Brinkerhoff and Grace Tate.

It was true that Roger had stayed on as contractor until Miles's Rock Farm was ready for occupancy, but he never had been inside the house as a guest. He upbraided himself for even momentarily expecting to be invited, but the truth was he considered himself entitled to an invitation. He had more than fulfilled his part of the bargain, saving Miles a lot of money and finishing the house when he promised he would; the least Miles could have done was to offer the use of the place. Roger would have politely turned him down, but Roger did feel entitled to the opportunity to decline.

The house was ready for occupancy while Mildred was still under the care of the happily available Dr. Littauer, but in the circumstances Miles pigeonholed his plans for a housewarming of the kind that he had been anticipating even before he had chosen the color of the roof. There was something anticlimactic but at the same time suitable in his selecting Myrtle, the Fort Penn girl who would not enter his town house before dark, as the first lady friend to pass the night on the farm. In contrast with the great week-end Miles and Roger had mapped out, the inaugural party was hardly a party in anything but name: whenever Miles telephoned Mildred she would ask him, "Do you want to party?" and consequently the first night at the farm was, strictly speaking, a party. On the way out in the Packard, driven by Teddy Spotswood, Elmira's nephew and Miles's new manservant, Miles found himself reflecting as they drove past the old Caldwell farm that the Scottish bard had it right when he said what he said about the best laid plans. The house was warm as to Fahrenheit, but it was so quiet, empty-sounding that Miles resolved never again to be host to a woman alone. In future he would always arrange to entertain at least another couple. Once a week thereafter he had guests at the farm and in a few months the housewarming had been indefinitely or forever postponed.

Roger, however, heard only that this man and that man, this woman and that woman, had been to the farm, and they added up to a goodly crowd, since Miles favored variety. Roger was rather hurt by every man's name. He also was distressed and embarrassed by the lack of a place to take his own lady friends; if a lady had no apartment of her own—and those with apartments were few—he had to drive her to one of the country hotels, unless she was willing to rough it in his office, which had a leather couch, but also was likely to have a surveyor's transit, rod and bob, axes, and steel chain, as well as raincoats, rubber boots, and the strictly utilitarian office furniture. The Commercial House was out of the question so long as Bert Botley continued as manager, and Roger was worried that the minute he got a little flat of his own, his mother would find it out and it would be the death of her. In one respect at least he had an easier time keeping fit to fight than if he had remained chummy with Miles.

But then one day, whilst he was considering the good things

that were happening to him—his commission in the Guard, his government contract—he realized that his status in relation to Miles had been changed, by history, as it were. He thereupon acted as promptly as it took him to pick up the receiver and telephone Miles. He asked Miles to meet him at the A. C., in the library, where they could be alone.

Roger was there first. He was cordiality itself. "Miles, me boy, have a chair."

"You're in a good humor today, I was afraid you might be in trouble."

"Far from it, Miles," said Roger. "Far from it. But it was kind of you to come, thinking I was in trouble. Kind of you. But that doesn't happen to be the case, Miles. In fact, I'm anything but in trouble. However, the unfortunate experience we had during the fall, I've been brooding over it, Miles."

"Uh-huh?"

"Oh, yes. Yes, never a day passed since without a guilty feeling for what trouble I almost caused you."

"You almost caused me, Roger?"

"Aside from money, Miles, you didn't suffer."

"Well, that may be one way to look at it, I suppose."

"Therefore," said Roger, "and being's we hear rumors every day how we're going to be mustered in and made a part of the Regular Army, I have to be prepared to go at a moment's notice. My uniform and equipment are there, ready to put on any hour of the day or night in case the hostilities break out, and being an officer I'll be one of the first they call. I'll have to be there ahead of time when the men in my platoon report for duty."

"Naturally, mm-hmm."

"All my affairs are in good order. I guess you heard all about how the business is branching out."

"Yes, I was glad to hear it."

"Thank you. But one little matter was hanging over me, Miles. That money, that expense you went to when we had that last, what-you-might-call ill-fated party."

"Uh-huh."

"Give me a figure, Miles, and I'll write you a cheque for the whole amount, here and now."

"What?"

"That's what I said. If we get into hostilities, it's only natural some of us are going West. Killed, in other words. I don't expect to have any trouble with the enemy when it comes to hand-to-hand fighting, but artillery fire, mustard gas, mines, submarines going over there. A man has to be ready and not leave—"

"By this you mean you're leaving, Roger?"

"I'm leaving if we're ordered to, and anyhow, if I did have my orders it'd be a military secret and I couldn't tell anybody. Not even a parent, or a close friend. Nobody."

"Mm-hmm."

"So, as they say, if my name is on a piece of artillery shrapnel over there, I don't want Miles Brinkerhoff thinking I was a man that didn't pay my just debts, Miles. Give me a figure, old man."

"Zero," said Miles.

"Zero? Now come on, Miles. You told me you'd be lucky to get out for five thousand iron men. Is it five I owe you?"

"If you remember that then you remember I said I was going to pay it myself. No, Roger, thanks very kindly for the offer, but that, uh, accident—that party's all paid for. Water over the dam."

"Why, I won't have it."

"Now, now, Roger, forget it. Closed book," said Miles.

"Well, I'm *willing*. You know that. I made you the offer. Never let it be said I didn't make you the offer."

"Now let's talk about something else. I think if you're so close to going away to war, I think I oughta give a party for you."

"I wasn't hinting for that, Miles."

"Nobody said anything about hinting, Roger. I'd just like to give a party for you. What kind of a party would you like?"

"Well, this is the first I thought of it. How do you mean, what kind of a party?"

"Well, a big party or a small party? And one of our regular

258 · John O'Hara

kind of parties or more on the order of married couples, your
mother. That kind of a party."

"What married couples?" said Roger.

"The ones we know, the fellows at the club and their wives."

"Oh," said Roger. "Well, I don't know, Miles. That grand little
lady, she's in bed every night by nine. She was never much of a
one for parties."

"Your mother, you mean," said Miles. "What made you say
'Oh,' like that, just now. You asked me what married couples, and
when I said the fellows at the club and their women, you said
'Oh' as if you were disappointed. Who else *would* I mean?"

Roger chuckled. "Well, I'll be honest with you, Miles. The
other day I was driving by in front of the Caldwell Estate—"

"Oh, Tuesday, in front of the office there, when I was standing
talking to Grace Tate and her husband."

"Uh-huh," said Roger. "You seemed to be laughing and talking there like real buddies."

"Well, I tell you how that was. Some of the farmers out where
we are are trying to get more phone lines in and we had a couple talks about it. The way it is now they got as many as eight parties on one party-line and everybody can listen to everybody
else and we're trying to see if we can't get some privacy. Separate
lines."

"Uh-huh. Real neighbors, huh? What do you do, Miles, go in
for a cup of five-o'clock tea every afternoon? The next thing
you'll be in the Fort Penn Club."

"No, I always had sense enough to keep my nose out of places
it didn't belong," said Miles.

"If the shoes fits, wear it, eh Miles?"

"Yes, I guess if the shoes fits, wear it. I catch on now why you
wanted to know what married couples to have at a party. Roger,
that mess last fall, you remember what was the start of the whole
thing. You got fresh with Grace Tate and she put you in your
place, so you got crazy drunk and took it out on a poor little
hooker. You *God* damn near killed her, and maybe you *did.* You

don't know if you gave her cancer. Now listen, boy, there's some people—"

"Ah, now Miles, I know what you're gonna say. And all I can say is, does she have three kids or don't she? She musta got a hosing just like everybody else. She knows what it is, and believe you me, she likes it. She likes it as much as I like it, or you like it. I know the look. I know when they like it when you're doing it to them, and I know if they're gonna like it before you do it to them. I played my cards wrong before, but I'll never make the same mistake twice. Instead of a party, I know what you can do for me. Let me stay at your farm four or five days."

Miles laughed. "You're a son of a bitch all right. Sure, you can stay at the farm. Stay as long as you like. But you won't see her."

"Oh, I can go for walks."

"All right. But be sure and walk back to Fort Penn every day. They're living in Fort Penn for the winter."

"Where? The Caldwell house?"

"That's where they are."

"I was wondering. I see they got a new limousine and she rides around in it. I was wondering why she was around town so much."

"How do you think you're going to talk turkey to the delightful creature this time? I'll bet you you land in the gutter again."

"Patience. This time butter wouldn't melt in me mouth."

"I never knew another son of a bitch like you in my life."

"It's worth the try, isn't it?" said Roger.

"It's worth the try, all right," said Miles.

Roger stood up. "Miles, we're almost back to the same buddies we used to be," he said. "How do I look?"

"Like a wedding prick," said Miles.

"That's your boy," said Roger.

He left the club and got into his car and drove the few blocks to the immediate vicinity of the Caldwell house. He parked in the next block, shut off his engine, and waited. In a little while he was pleased to see the Tates' new limousine drive up. The chauffeur held the door open for Grace and a little boy, who went inside the house. Roger took out his watch. Five-twenty.

The next morning he again parked near the house, but this time in the block to the north of the house. At ten minutes of nine three children carrying schoolbooks and schoolbags came out and stood waiting for the limousine, which appeared a minute later. They were taken away and about fifteen minutes later the limousine returned and Grace got in. Roger followed the limousine, which stopped at the Isaac Schoffstal house long enough for Miss Schoffstal to join Grace Tate. It was a cold, rainy day and the carriage-starter at Bauer's store—one of the few in Fort Penn—held his large umbrella over the ladies. Roger parked his Dodge in the alley and had a cup of coffee and an order of flapjacks in the Childs across the street from Bauer's. He excused the second breakfast as providing a place from which to watch Bauer's entrance without himself becoming conspicuous and being accosted by noisy friends. He had a long wait at the Childs and he was afraid Grace and the Schoffstal woman might have slipped away, but the limousine stayed at Bauer's. Then he was startled to see them march past the Childs, on the same side of the street, and cross and get in the Pierce and drive away. Apparently they had come out of the store, with an umbrella hiding their faces, and had continued their shopping elsewhere. He hurried to the Dodge, but he lost the limousine.

He decided to abandon the shadowing tactics. All he wanted to gain was a knowledge of Grace's day, what time she did this, what time she did that. But a woman like Grace didn't have a typical day. Three children had gone to school that morning, but the day before only one of them had come home with Grace. Tomorrow she probably would not call for the Schoffstal woman. This afternoon she was apt to be going to a bridge party or one of those affairs, and not call for the little boy at school. Tomorrow there might be good weather and she would drive to the farm, or she might catch a cold and stay in bed. The next day she might be on the committee for a church supper . . .

Church supper? The Fort Penn papers were always having

something about church suppers, and he was always buying tickets for them. He couldn't count on her asking him to buy tickets for a charity, but somewhere in that direction, that was how you got into the good graces of those people. Charity. He had bought books of tickets and chances from Catholic, Protestant, Jew, Italian, African Methodist—the whole shebang. They all had the same smile for you when you gave something to their charity, rich or poor, high or low.

After drill that night Roger waited on Andy O'Brien, captain of the Irish company, and son of the late Andrew O'Brien, founder of the Boston Store. "Andy, can I have a word with you when you're not busy?"

"Sure," said Andy. "Now?"

"If you're not busy." Roger knew that Andy, a Georgetown graduate and a son-in-law of Desmond O'Connell's, regarded him as the scum of the earth, but he in turn regarded Andy as a putter-on of delicate airs who was captain of the company only because he had been to the Mexican Border the year before and was worth plenty of money.

"What's on your mind, Roger?"

"I was thinking how our company, we're the Irish company, but the thought struck me, wouldn't it be a good idea if say we had a ladies' auxiliary but instead of only our own kind, Irish wives and Irish mothers and sisters and sweethearts, wouldn't it be a good thing all around if the Protestant element would take an interest? You remember when we started the company the papers were full of it, then it all died down. For morale wouldn't it be a good idea if all the denominations and every strata of society took an interest? Like if say Mrs. Hamilton Schoffstal promised to write newsy letters to Corporal Patrick Francis Xavier Kane in my platoon. Not that she'd have much news for Pat Kane, but that's the general idea."

"Not that she'd have much time to write to anyone but her husband, either, but it's a good idea. At least it listens well now. How would you go about it?"

"How would I go about it? Well, I don't know. I can think of a couple ways. Your wife, Mrs. O'Brien, moves in the upper strata and she could stir up interest among this Junior League society. Let her form a committee and chairman it herself or get somebody like, oh, Mrs. Schoffstal or one of those. Mrs. Tate. Have all the denominations represented."

"I don't think it'd be the best idea to do it through the Junior League. There are only two Catholics in it and they wouldn't want to impose on the other denominations. But I think it is a good idea, the more I think of it. Mrs. Tate, Mrs. Schoffstal, Mrs. Wall, Mrs. Cunningham—and of course some of the older women. The younger ones are going to be called on for a lot if we enter the war, and the older women would be just the ones to write letters—"

"Well, I wasn't only thinking of writing letters. I just used that as an example. I was thinking more like drill nights a few of them or maybe a lot of them could come down here and serve coffee and sandwiches, and if we got away they could do charity work with the wives and children."

"Oh, you mean business, eh Roger? Then why don't you get the thing rolling?"

"Hell, Andy, the women in my family—my mother's one of the grandest sweetest women ever walked God's earth, but she doesn't say two words a year to a Protestant if she can help it. She has no acquaintance with those people. Mrs. O'Brien's the one, but if you want me to make any suggestions I'll write them out on a piece of paper."

"All right. You do that now. You created a job for yourself."

Roger wrote out his suggestions, embracing a rough table of organization and helpful hints that if carried out would have made the Irish company socially as active as the Coldstream Guards, free of financial responsibilities, as well fed as the members of the Chicago Stockyards Club, and as protected from petty worries as the justices of the United States Supreme Court.

"You don't want much," said Andy, when he read the suggestions.

"That's exaggerated, but if a bum asks me for a nickel for a cup of coffee, like as not I tell him to go to hell. But if he asks me for a half a dollar I want to know what it's for, and sometimes I end up giving him a dollar."

"If his story's good enough."

"If his story's good enough. But, Andy, if you'll pardon me for saying so, but any daughter of Desmond O'Connell that can't tell a good story—you know what I mean?"

"Yes, I guess so. I'll talk to Marguerite tonight," said Andy.

The moment was right for the organization of an auxiliary for the Irish Company. In the predominantly non-Irish community the popular impression obtained that a laughing, joking, singing group of grown-up children had come together for the purpose, if necessary, of laughing, joking, and singing their way to Berlin, where they would gaily place the Hohenzollern clowns on an infamous gibbet, and all come laughing, joking, and singing back to their shanties in Shantytown. It was true that in the beginning some of the Company believed all this of themselves, but they changed their minds after rifles had been issued and practice was held on the range in the armory cellar, where a man could hear the noise and feel the kick of a Springfield, and, with a minimum of inventiveness imagine himself receiving from a Mauser as good as he sent with the Springfield. However, the racket in the armory cellar caused the citizen soldiers to cover up by acting like the New York *Tribune*'s idea of an Irishman, and at the auxiliary's first serving of coffee and sandwiches Corporal Patrick Francis Xavier Kane *did* have a lovely conversation with Mrs. Hamilton Schoffstal. Marie Schoffstal (one of the Presbyterian representatives) luckily was a woman whose zeal for the worthy cause was not exhausted by Ham's reasonable demands.

Grace Tate did not appear at the first klatsch, but Roger had seen her name on the auxiliary ladies' list, and he respectfully doubted that she would have permitted the use of her name if she had not intended to do some work. His faith was justified; on the second appearance of the auxiliary, Grace was there, in the same tam o'shanter she had worn once before, handing out white enameled tin cups of coffee from her position behind the planks on wooden horses. As a lieutenant Roger did not queue up for coffee; the morale operation was intended for the enlisted men and non-commissioned officers. He kept out of Grace's sight until the men had been served seconds on the coffee and home-made crullers, and as they left Roger joined Andy O'Brien and with him went to Marguerite. She had a smile for him because the auxiliary already seemed assured of success and he had given her the idea. "Andy," she said, "if you're going to thank the ladies you'd better do it now before they go home."

"I did it last week," said Andy. "Roger, you do it."

"Me? . . . All right. You introduce me, though."

Andy rapped a spoon on a tincup. "Ladies, some of you who were here last week I know thought you'd never get home, I took so long thanking you. Tonight I've asked Lieutenant Bannon to do the honors, and make it short and snappy."

Grace was piling saucers when Andy rapped for order. Without seeming to recognize her, Roger watched to see what she would reveal when she saw him. She revealed that she had had no idea he was present or going to be present, and that what she saw was pleasing to her, whether she knew it or not. Roger removed his campaign hat and tucked it under his arm. He smiled the smile that had made more than one farm-girl forget to ask for her dollar.

"Captain O'Brien, and Ladies of our Auxiliary, it'll be short and snappy, you can count on that." He looked from one end of the group of fifteen women to the other, deliberately avoiding Grace's eyes in the hope that she would think he was unaware of her presence. "We Irish are supposed to have what's called the gift of gab. If that can mean, to be able to say, what one feels, easily, and gracefully, and freely, to express one's thoughts, with conviction and sincerity, to convey, one's thanks, in a manner, that will be acceptable, to one's listeners—then, this evening, for the first time, in my life, I wish, I had, the gift of gab. For truly, ladies, I would call it, a gift indeed, if I could tell you, for Captain O'Brien, my brother officers, and myself, how deeply, we appreciate, what your coming here, has meant, to our men." He took a deep breath, and so did many of the ladies.

"By your coming here, your kindness, your gracious presence, you have taken, this training, this training for war, out of the realm, of drudgery, and made, these evenings, a joy. We know, all of us, down deep, that, perhaps, only, a matter of weeks, will pass, before, these evenings, will end, and we, must—leave you. But I hope, I pray, that, all of you, will realize, what, your coming here, does, for our men, and that, your realization, will keep you, showing, the kindness, and enthusiasm, by attending, our drill nights, whenever, you can.

"You have my word, you will never, regret it. Thank you."

The applause was hard and sharp and long, and some handkerchiefs were brought out. Andy O'Brien shook hands with Roger, and under the applause muttered: "Splendid. Where did you ever learn to make such a good speech?"

"You never heard my *father* make a speech," said Roger.

"No, but I'll bet he was good," said Andy.

"And I used to coach football, don't you remember?"

One by one the ladies shook his hand and made promises of attendance and punctuality. Roger was delighted with Grace's predicament; she could not stay out of the line without being rude and calling attention to herself. But apparently she was going to risk it. She went to Marguerite O'Brien, obviously intending to say good night and pass around the line, but Marguerite took her arm and brought her to Roger.

"Excuse me," said Marguerite to the auxiliary lady who was swearing never to desert the Irish Company. "Roger, just a minute please? Mrs. Tate, this is Mr. Bannon. Lieutenant Bannon."

"Good evening, Mrs. Tate."

"I have met Mr. Bannon," said Grace.

"Oh, you have?" said Marguerite. "Oh, I didn't realize that. Must you go? Couldn't you come back to our house for some ice cream, or a night-cap?"

"Thanks very much, Margie, but I really have to get home. It's quite late."

"Is it? What time *is* it?" said Marguerite. "I have no idea."

Roger looked up at the large clock on the wall. "It's ten of eleven."

"Who'd you come with?" said Marguerite.

"I drove myself, that's why I'd like to get home."

"Oh, heavens. Roger, why don't you ride home with Mrs. Tate. It is late to be driving alone."

"I wouldn't think of it," said Grace. "It's only a few squares."

"I know, through some of the darkest streets in Fort Penn. Roger, you get your coat."

There was no doubt that the well-intentioned Marguerite was not going to be responsible for Grace's murder in the darkened streets of Fort Penn, and Roger in a few minutes found himself in the Mercer, which had the top up and the side curtains in place.

"There wasn't anything I could say," he said.

"Oh, well."

"If anything happens to Andy, Marguerite'd make a good officer."

"Yes," said Grace.

"Mrs. Tate?"

"Yes?"

"I may never see you again. Will you give me five minutes of your time?"

"It'll take us that long to get home, just about."

"I didn't mean five minutes that way. I meant like this." He grabbed the steering wheel with his left hand and spun it so that the car made for the curb, and simultaneously he switched off the ignition.

"Now look here, Mr. Bannon. I'm not going to have any nonsense from you. Give me back that key or I'll call the police."

"What would they arrest me for? If you get out of the car I'll just sit here till you come back with the police, the key'll be in the switch, and I'll be just sitting here waiting for you. No violation of the law there. And as for you, yourself, I don't intend to lay a hand on your person. And don't you think I'd be more likely to know the cop than you would?"

"That I do believe. Yes, from what I understand about you, you've had dealings with the police. Or you'd be in jail this minute."

"That's what I want to talk about. Who told you about me? Your husband?"

"No, not my husband. It doesn't make any difference who told me. I know that you beat up some woman and got arrested for it."

"I've only been arrested once in my life, and it wasn't for beating up a woman. I was arrested for stealing a crate of oranges when I was thirteen years old."

"Huh."

"Whoever told you the other story about me couldn't have known much about it. Will you let me set you straight on it?"

"I'm not at all interested. All I'm interested in is to have you return that key so that I can go home to my husband and children."

"The day you dumped me in the gutter—"

"Please don't get started on a story, Mr. Bannon. I have to get home. This minute."

"Every interruption from you keeps you away from home that much longer. Let me tell it and you can go home."

"I'm not making any *bargains* with you. Give me that key, you insolent pup."

He laughed. "Insolent, but by Christ, you can't call me a pup."

"I could call you a lot worse, you can bet your boots."

"Yes, and you will after you hear my story. Will you listen, please?"

"Oh, for God's sake, go ahead. Get it over with. Is this supposed to be Catholic confession? Tell your sins and go out and do them all over again, the way you people do?"

"A lady doesn't make insulting remarks about a man's religion."

"A lady? What do you know about a lady? Where would you

ever learn about a lady? Have you ever *seen* one? You contemptible son of a bitch, you wouldn't know a lady if you saw one."

"Yes I would. You're a lady, and probably you're acting like one."

"Oh, balls. Give me the key, Tiresome."

"In a minute. You said for me to tell the story and get it over with, so here it is." He paused. "That afternoon, you drove away and left me in the gutter. I picked myself up, and for the first time since I was a kid at Fort Penn U I had a drink. I had a lot of drinks. I realized since then, I didn't need any drinks, because I was crazy from what you did to me, knocking me in the gutter like that. What happened later probably would have happened so, as the Dutch say. But I made sure of it, I guess. I drank I don't know how many drinks and then I went to this friend of mine's house and had more, and all I know is the woman in bed with me got beaten up, and I must of been the one that did it. That's all."

"Well, what in heaven's name does that have to do with me, may I ask?"

"Everything. You were the cause of it."

"I was the—oh, Mister Man. Even your small brain. You got fresh and you got what you deserved, or partially what you deserved."

"Yes, I did, but I only said you were the cause of it. I didn't say you were to blame."

"I'm terribly sorry, but I'm afraid we haven't time for you to explain *that* piece of logic, if that's what you'd call it. Come on, now, Mr. Bannon. I listened to your story, now keep your part of the bargain."

"If you just let me explain the difference. I said you were the cause of my trouble, but not to blame. Well, you're not to blame, but you were the cause. I was crazy about you, crazy for you. I was then, and I am now. Here's the key."

"Thanks," she said, putting the key in the switch. She started the car and they drove north. He did not take his eyes off her face, studying her in the dim light that came from the dashboard, and the unrevealing flashes from street lamps. The only sign of anything she gave was that she seemed to be chewing her lip, which he did not know to be a sign at all. But he grew aware, without having looked at the landmarks, that they must have gone beyond her house. When he became convinced of that he hardly breathed, did not blink an eye, for fear of risking a false move. She stopped the car and he had only the vaguest idea that they were in a side road in the North End. She turned off the engine and the lights, put her head back and held out her arms. "Kiss me," she said. He kissed her, more gently than he had kissed anyone in his life before. "Kissing isn't going to be enough for us," she said. "Not even tonight."

"It never will be, Grace. We're not kissing people."

"We can't go on the ground," she said. "I've never been with anybody but my husband. Is the back of the car any better than the front?"

"Yes."

"But let's stay here a little while, feeling and loving and kissing, like children."

"Like children?"

"Weren't you bad with girls? I was with boys, or they were with me, or no, I was with them as much as they were with me."

"You were? I should have been one of those boys."

"Yes, you should have been the grocery boy and I could have taken you into the closet, or on my bed upstairs. I wish we were on my bed upstairs now. Shall we get in the back now?"

Once she called out to him, but they were not together long and they were both shaking a little when it was over. She kissed the back of his hand after she got behind the wheel again, and she did not immediately start the motor.

"Are we going to see one another again?" she said.

"If I can help it we are."

"Then we have to think. This is like children tonight, but we're not children. You can tell that about me as much as I can about you. Tonight was sweet and tender, but it won't always be that way with us. I'm sorry I insulted your religion, Roger. I think that was the only time I hurt you, but I won't do it again. Have you a place where we can go?"

"No, not a good place."

"What about your friend Brinkerhoff's place?"

"Would you go there?"

"If we could go there without anyone knowing. Would he have to know? I suppose he would. You'd tell him, wouldn't you?"

"No."

"I think you would. But now you will anyway, so if he has our secret we might as well have his bed."

"Wouldn't you mind if I told him?"

"Roger, you're going to tell him, so what difference does it make whether I mind or I don't mind. I'd rather you didn't, but I don't think you can help it. And there's nothing I can do now. You've had me. But I don't want my husband to find out. Other people don't matter, but he does."

"Do you love him?"

"Yes. I love him, he loves me. He and I'll be together when you're raising little Irishers. If you're discreet. We have to go now."

"Yes. How will we meet?"

"Well, not through this armory business. That's where we have to be most discreet, all those women. I'll have to always call you. You must never call me. I'll say I'm somebody's secretary. Who shall I say?"

"Mr. Duke."

"Who's Mr. Duke?"

"Nobody."

"Good. I'll say 'This is Mr. Duke's secretary on the wire,' and you'll know it's me, and then I'll tell you where I can meet you and what time, and all you'll have to say is yes or no, in case anybody's in your office."

"Fine."

She started the car and drove homeward. "When we get to my house we'll put the car away, and you walk through the house with me, talking just the way you would. About the Guard. And then I'll ask you if you wouldn't like a night-cap or a glass of milk, and you'll say no-thanks, and I'll thank you for seeing me home and then you go out the front door. My husband will be upstairs, but probably won't be asleep. I don't know how I'm going to get used to this, but I don't know how I'll get used to being away from you, either. I've started wanting you for tomorrow!"

He had left her and was half way home before the steady unfamiliar sound of his boots and spur chains reminded him not only that this lovely affair was not going to last forever, but that a total stranger, the President of the United States, could end it with a scratch of his pen. For the first time Roger hated the war. Nevertheless, he slept a peaceful sleep.

———

Tuesday, Wednesday. Saturday, Sunday, Monday. Wednesday, Thursday. They came slowly and went quickly, with no word from her and only one glimpse of her, and in that she was so much in her own life that he wanted to call out to her and tell her that she was his. She was in her limousine, talking her silly head off with two women. He was walking on Second Street, just before noon, and he not only was full of wanting *her*, but almost as great as that was his wanting to *talk* to her and ask her to tell him why she had changed from a contemptuous enemy to an eager piece. And there she was, leaning forward to look at the faces of the women on the seat beside her, absorbed in her own speech and its effect on them; and somehow the flowers in the two cut-glass vases in the automobile made him angriest of all. They made a difference that was enormous, those flowers. He did not know why, but they did. The limousine itself was bad. The chauffeur in the bearskin coat was bad. The coach lamps were bad. Her easy friendship with the two women was bad. But the flowers in the vases, he later came to realize (after the realization that it *was* the flowers), symbolized her life: most of the limousines in Fort Penn came equipped with cut-glass vases, but only rarely did you see flowers in them. In Grace's car there always were a couple of roses, probably from the hothouse in her back yard. The driver would put them in fresh every day, throw away the old ones, pour out the stale water, pour in fresh. And the driver would do it without being told to do it. Told once—or maybe not told ever—and he'd replace the flowers as a regular thing, exactly as he would pump gasoline into the tank, fold the robes a certain way, and raise his cap when he said "Good morning, Ma'am." The flower touch was in the same class as the way a street had been named after her family: some Fort Penn people asked the Council to name streets after them; but the Council had asked the Caldwells for permission to honor a street with their name. Visit the hospital, and the children's ward had been named after one of her kids; look in the prospectus of Fort Penn U, and there was a pre-med scholarship named after her old lady; win the big cup for the best all-around saddle horse at the State Fair, and your name and your horse's name would be engraved on the cup, but the cup was called the Caldwell Cup; and the Governor of the Commonwealth tried to speak to her, she didn't try to speak to the Governor; and her name began with T, but it led the society page lists; and Roger recalled that his mother once had told him that just on the Caldwells' say-so a man had got away with two murders, just because the man had been a distant cousin of some friend of theirs; and he remembered fifteen years earlier, his father saying, "It's the Will Caldwells is the workingman's worst enemy. It's no trick at all to foment indignation against the George Baers and the J. Pierpont Morgans, but try convincing the man in Fort Penn that Will Caldwell's cut from the same bolt of cloth and he'll laugh in your face. 'Will Caldwell? That decent, kind-hearted man?' they'll say to you. 'That friend of Bishop Brophy's?' they'll say. And by God if you don't watch your step you'll find yourself giving ground to J. Pierpont himself because Will Caldwell writes an annual cheque for the deserving poor, and never gave the order to fire muskets at the advocates of union labor, met in peaceable assembly at the mouth of the pit to voice protest against the usurpation of their bread and butter by the traitorous scab."

"Well, Dad, I did it to his daughter, if that's any consolation," Roger would have said, but he knew it would have been no consolation, and he directed his thoughts quickly away from his father, a man whom he regarded as a fool, when he thought of him at all.

———

Half-past six in the evening, and almost a fortnight gone, with only a torturing glimpse of Grace in her automobile, and not a sign of her at drill. "The secretary of a lad named Duke called you up on the telephone," said Roger's mother.

"When?" said Roger. "What time was that?"

"If it's important to you, rest assured it didn't sound like it was to her. In fact, she said in so many words, it wasn't important and she'd reach you tomorrow morning at your office. Who is Duke?"

"A government man."

"Oh, another government man. From Washington?"

"Yah."

"Have the officials of the government taken to gallivanting about with female clerks, or secretaries, whatever they call themselves?"

"Don't act so suspicious. Duke is a fine man, J. W. Duke, powerful and influential. The woman I guess was more than likely the public stenographer at the Schoffstal House, or a clerk in the Federal building?"

"I see. Ought I to be meeting this Duke man, and your cousin Joe Mullaly?"

"Not till I've had a few more talks with him."

"Don't you be getting mixed up in any graft. Your poor father never touched a penny, and neither will you so long as I have breath in my body."

"Well, he had the name if not the game. I'd take it if I had to, only I don't have to. What time did she say she'd telephone tomorrow, Duke's secretary?"

"The morning's all she said."

The macaroni and cheese that was his favorite Friday supper took him longer to eat than ever before, and he almost told his mother that she would have to go to the Stations of the Cross by herself, but she was suspicious already, and he yielded a delay of an hour and a half before he would be able to talk to Miles Brinkerhoff.

After he brought his mother home from church he telephoned Miles and they met at the A. C.

"Well, stranger," said Miles.

"Yah, I guess I am lately. If I work as hard in the Army I'll be a colonel before I get out."

"I hear they're gonna call you any day now, so maybe you oughta quit work and pay some attention to the fair sex. Hey? Or have you?"

"Well, if I did could I have the use of the farm?"

"Sure, when do you want it?"

"Maybe tomorrow."

"Saturday and Sunday? Sure. Is it all right if I'm there too with a delightful creature?"

Roger shook his head. "Not at the same time. I have to be frank with you, Miles. This is married."

"Oh. Oho. Not who I think it is?"

"I don't know who you think it is."

"Oh, yes you do. I'll bet a broken dirty old truss, that's who it is. And little Roger's protecting the fair lady's name. Hell, you can have the place. I only have Myrt. When shall I tell Edgar you're coming out?"

"I don't know for sure, but I'll only be there in the afternoon."

"Uh-huh. Now I'm sure it's who I thought it was. I'm not asking you any more questions, Roger. I'll tell Edgar you're coming out some time after noon hour and if you don't want him around, send him out looking for trout. It's too early for trout, but

Edgar'll go fishing when the ice is so thick you can drive a Mack truck across the river. Well, well, well. Roger Bannon, I'm proud of you. You don't have to say anything or admit anything. I know it's her. But some day I wanta know all about it. Oh-h-h-h. Dee-lightful creature."

"I got another favor to ask you."

"Why sure," said Miles. "I know what it is. You wanta go there any time she can make up a pretty story."

"Yah."

"Why, sure. Sure thing. Something like this, you gotta take it when you can get it. And if old Uncle Miles is any guesser, you've had it already. Huh? You can say that much."

"Uh-huh."

"I'm proud of you, proud of you, proud of you. Next to me you're the one I'd rather have it. Well, well, well, well. This caps the climax of many's the jolly old times."

———

"Was it because I gave you the key? The key of the car?" said Roger.

"Yes, I guess so," said Grace. "I guess that had something to do with it, at least."

"Do you know what I thought? I thought my speech had a lot to do with it. I aimed it at you."

"I know you did. The speech was buncombe. I thought it was—would you like to know what I thought?"

"Sure."

"I thought, the next thing, this creature's going to open his fly. I knew the talk was aimed at me. I was the only woman you carefully avoided looking at. Please, when I go to the armory again, don't think you're acting subtle by not paying any attention to me. Those women aren't all fools. Flirt a little, be attentive, and let me snub you. Goodness, Roger, there are only about three of us you'd give a second glance to, so if you ignore me they'll get suspicious."

"All right."

"I think I can sneak off the day after tomorrow, if that's convenient for you. You still maintain you didn't tell Miles Brinkerhoff."

"I never mentioned your name. All he knows is I'm meeting a married woman."

"*You* never mentioned my name, but did *he*, and you said yes?"

"No."

"Nevertheless, you may be telling the truth, but he knows. He knows. He stopped my husband on the street two or three days ago and asked all about my health and happiness. He never did that before, and my husband thought it strange."

"Sidney."

"No names, please. I repeat, let's keep this entirely separate from anybody else. You and I, and nobody else. It has to be that way or it has to stop."

"You can't stop now."

"Yes, I can, Roger. Yes, I can. I know it's got to stop some time, we've always known that. If there's a war, or the first sign that my husband's suspicious."

"He'll be suspicious if you keep on staying away from him."

"Well—I don't know. Very likely."

"You mean you're gonna let him."

"I don't know," she said.

"The day after you do I'll know it."

"No you won't."

"You mean you have already?"

"Yes, I have."

"God damn you, I'm through."

"Oh, stop. Calm down. I haven't, but I'm going to have to. It's a week now, over a week, and he has his rights. If I deny him his rights he's entitled to go elsewhere or get a divorce."

"Then let him go elsewhere."

"He loves me."

"And you love him."

"Yes, I do. Do you want me to say I don't? Well, I won't, because I do. For heaven's sake, let's stop this bickering. What do you care if I sleep with him, as long as I give you pleasure?"

"Well, I do care."

"No. You think you ought to, but you don't. Let's be satisfied with what we have. Something I never thought I'd do, and I'm doing it. Maybe it means I'm no good. Maybe I'm not. I've often thought I'm not. You're not the first man I wanted to go the limit with since I've been married. I could name dozens but for the opportunity."

"Then why did you pick me?"

"I didn't pick you, any more than you picked me. I saw you here that day, and I thought you were awful, and I kept thinking you were awful—but I kept thinking. You know, Roger, you could have had me that very first day. If I'd got off that horse, and you had touched me, I'd have swum into you just the way I did in the car. Oh, my. Are you ready to kiss me and make up, and make love to me? My, you are, aren't you?"

They went together then, and it was for the last time. The war did come, and the 14th was one of the first regiments to be mustered in, but even before the sixth of April the other reason Grace had anticipated became real.

They had moved to the farm, and Sidney came in the house one afternoon to find Grace reading the *Delineator*, and Ann tossing her sewing-rings at an andiron, as in quoits. "That's about enough of that now, Miss Annabell Lee," said Grace. "Pick them up and use them as they're supposed to be."

"But I'm not doing anything wrong, or hurting anybody."

"You may be hurting yourself," said Sidney. "And you may be doing something wrong."

"But, father, they're too light to hurt anybody. Even if I threw them full force," said Ann.

"That isn't what I meant. It may seem far-fetched, but you can hurt yourself by doing what you're not supposed to do. It can hurt your character. See what I mean? Your mother sees what I mean, I'm almost sure."

"Yes," said Grace, looking up.

"You understand, when I talk to you like this, Ann, it's a part of trying to bring you up the way your mother was brought up. To be a good girl, and then a nice wife and mother."

"Thank you," said Grace.

"What your mother's mother had in mind. What her mother and father hoped she'd be when she grew up, and got married, and had children."

"It's time for your bath anyway, Ann. Get along," said Grace. She turned to Sidney. "Thanks for the compliments."

"You taking what I said as compliments?"

"Well, that's what they sounded like."

"If you think over exactly what I said you may discover I didn't commit myself," said Sidney. "I, uh, I've decided to go to New York for a few days."

"All of a sudden like this? What for?"

"I've just decided to go to New York for a few days."

"Aren't I invited?"

"No." He stood in the doorway, looking at her and waiting for what she would say next.

"When are you going?"

"I'm going tonight."

"On the sleeper?"

"No," he said. "I'm going upstairs now and change my clothes and pack, and I'll have time to catch the eight o'clock and eat on the train."

"How long are you going to stay?"

"I don't know. I haven't thought that far ahead. Maybe you ought to telephone me. I'll stay at the University Club."

"What's the matter, Sidney?"

"I don't know that, either."

"Is it business?"

"No, it isn't business," he said. "Well, yes. It may be. Of the simian variety. Will you tell Joe I want him to drive me to the station?"

"Goodness, I can drive you."

"Never mind, thanks."

"Which car do you want?"

"Well, the Mercer, if you're not planning to use it."

"I'm not planning to use it," she said.

"All right, then, the Mercer."

For the first time since the day they became engaged he left her overnight without kissing her.

He was gone a week, and neither telephoned the other. She met him at the train, although his telegram had said, "Please have Joe meet Broadway Limited—Sidney." He did not kiss her in the station.

"Thanks for coming in to meet me," he said, in the car.

"That's all right," she said.

"How are the children?"

"It's kind of you to ask."

"I knew if there'd been anything wrong you'd have telephoned or sent a telegram."

"Did you have a nice time in New York?"

"All right."

"Who'd you see?"

"Oh, I looked up some fellows I hadn't seen in years. Just went through the telephone directory and if they were there, I called them. If not, I'd call someone else. Saw a couple of shows, had a great deal of alcoholic refreshment, bought some shirts, had a nose-bleed, played some bridge."

"Are you having the shirts sent to the farm?"

"Yes, why?"

"Well, I just wanted to know if you were planning to stay."

"Yes, I am," he said.

They drove for a while without saying anything.

"I don't exactly know why I'm staying, but on the other hand I don't know why I shouldn't. Can you help me out? Think of a very good reason why I shouldn't?"

"No."

"Can't eh?"

"No. I can think of four reasons why you should."

"The children."

"Yes, and the fact that I love you."

"You do?"

"Yes. I've never loved anyone else," she said.

"I see. That may be true, Grace. That may be the cold fact. Did you see Mr. Bannon while I was gone?"

"No."

"You see I had a right to ask that question, because you already asked me who *I* saw."

"I see."

"I, uh, asked you how the children were but we got off on a tangent."

"They're all well. I'm letting them stay up to say hello to you."

"Thank you, Grace."

"Well, they're half yours." Suddenly she gasped and sobbed. It lasted no longer than a few words would last, or a simple declarative sentence, but it was distinct and audible through the stroke of the motor.

———

A conversation which took place in the summer-house in June, 1917:

CONNIE: I wish I had more to do to occupy my energy.

GRACE: I don't see how anybody could do much more than you are.

CONNIE: What am I doing?

GRACE: You're at the Red Cross nearly every afternoon.

CONNIE: I don't call that doing anything. I hate to think how unoccupied I'd be without it, but it's not *doing* anything.

GRACE: And your theater.

CONNIE: My theater! Huh. I can't get anybody interested in that any more. I'm thinking of closing it up till after the war.

GRACE: You are? Why?

CONNIE: For lack of interest. The men don't want to come out any more and the same way with the girls. The married girls think their husbands are going to be called any minute and they ought to spend as much time with them as possible. If I could think of some war charity I'd turn the theater over to it.

GRACE: There'll be something. I'm sorry, though. You were just getting the people's interest aroused.

CONNIE: Well, I'd hardly say that. A lot of our friends bought tickets, and the ones that acted or helped around, but I don't expect all Fort Penn to sit on uncomfortable chairs and watch plays that they don't understand. It was a selfish thing all along, Grace. You must have secretly suspected that. I didn't spend over eleven thousand dollars of my own money to educate the hoi polloi. I'm after the experience for myself, so when I go to New York I'll know exactly what I want to do and what I'm capable of doing. If I had your looks I'd be an actress, a star. But with in-between looks like mine, you've noticed I never even put myself in anything but a maid part or equally inconspicuous. Well, I have no intention of going to New York and act a maid part just because I love the theater.

GRACE: It's queer, you falling in love with the theater. Nobody else in your family ever showed the slightest interest in it. I can't understand it either. This always makes you hit the ceiling, but I think the theater's childish. I like to go, be entertained, to listen to the new numbers, see what they're wearing, all that. But I never had the slightest desire to act, and directing, and all that other business. Settings? I never notice whether one's good or one's bad. If it's supposed to be a drawing-room and it looks like a drawing-room, that's good enough to suit me. This directing—honestly, Connie, what difference does it make if Mary Wall doesn't stand a certain place while Raddie Dickinson is crossing the room or whatever?

CONNIE: It makes a hell of a lot of difference, but I don't expect you to understand it.

GRACE: That's good, because I'm not even going to try. I wish you'd have taken up painting or something.

CONNIE: I know. But every time we have a performance of a play it's as satisfactory to me as if I'd painted a picture. That is, if the actors and actresses do what I tell them to do. When they disobey me I want to take a knife and cut them to pieces, the way an artist does when a painting doesn't come out right.

GRACE: I'll never act for you again.

CONNIE: I'll never ask you. Your beauty doesn't add to a play, it detracts.

GRACE: You never used to say I was beautiful.

CONNIE: Because you weren't. You were—stunning—but not beautiful. You had no real beauty before you were thirty. Very few women have. You began to be beautiful when you fell out of love with Sidney.

GRACE: What a ridiculous thing to say! I've never been out of love with Sidney.

CONNIE: About four or five years ago. I s'pose he began to bore you. You had the children and you were sure of his love. That's when you began to be an interesting-looking beautiful woman.

GRACE: You're crazy. Have you been thinking like this all the time or is this just something to make conversation. If it is, I find it distasteful.

CONNIE: Oh, stop talking like a play, Grace. I know you too well for that.

GRACE: It seems to me you don't know me at all. I won't have you talk like this about Sidney and me.

CONNIE: Very well, let's talk about the war.

GRACE: All right, anything to get away from your crazy ideas.

CONNIE: They're not crazy, and you know it. You're so touchy now because you're afraid I'm going to get on the subject of

Roger Bannon. Your affair with Roger Bannon is—your affair. I was only talking about what happened to you four or five years ago. Your affair with Roger Bannon was a natural consequence of it, and in my opinion not very important. In fact, the only surprising thing about it is it didn't happen before.

GRACE: Connie Schoffstal!

CONNIE: Now don't bother to look around. There's nobody near us.

GRACE: But what are you saying about Roger Bannon and me? I hardly know him.

CONNIE: I don't think a woman has to necessarily know a man very well to use him. That's what I think you're doing with Roger Bannon.

GRACE: My God!

CONNIE: Did you think you could keep that secret in Fort Penn?

GRACE: Yes, I thought so . . . So he talked.

CONNIE: Somebody did, and I guess he was the one. With a person like that half the fun is bragging about it.

GRACE: Then Sidney *knows*. I thought he was guessing, without being sure. I wonder who told him. I wonder who'd do that to him.

CONNIE: Brock would.

GRACE: No. Brock hates Sidney, but he's my brother and he wouldn't want to endanger my happiness.

CONNIE: Unless he thought you'd be happier without Sidney.

GRACE: No. Because I wouldn't be. I wouldn't be anything without Sidney.

CONNIE: That's foolishness, that kind of talk.

GRACE: No it isn't.

CONNIE: It most certainly is. If you got a divorce from Sidney you'd be married again inside of two years. The children'd remind you of Sidney, but that's all.

GRACE: Oh, no it isn't. I'm not bright and quick the way you are, Connie, but I know what's best for me, and the best thing that ever happened to me was meeting Sidney. I've never seen another man I'd want to marry.

CONNIE: You haven't seen them all, and they haven't seen you.

GRACE: Oh, I wish I knew exactly what Sidney knows or has heard.

CONNIE: If you'll take some advice from an old maid, don't try to find out how much he knows. If he's guessing, or you think he's guessing, you'll do well to wait till *he* tells you what he knows. Don't go to him as a guilty, unfaithful wife, beseeching his forgiveness. You have to have dignity or you'll lose him. You must fight, Grace. If you go to him and say yes, you did have an affair with Bannon, the battle's lost. You surrender on his terms. And another thing, if you go to him, he has his pride, you know, and he has to take a stand. Unless you're absolutely sure he knows all about it, you wait till he speaks first. Find out how much he knows, and if he knows a great deal, you may have to admit your error, but don't be humble. Say it happened and you're sorry if it hurt him, that you love him and only him, and—*I know!* You tell Sidney that if he wants to get a divorce, you'll agree to one, but to wait a year so that it won't look as if he were divorcing you on account of a nincompoop nobody like Roger Bannon.

GRACE: He's not a nincompoop nobody to cause all this trouble.

CONNIE: Don't defend him to me. He was the only stallion around when you came in season, if that's blunt enough for you.

GRACE: Then do you think Sidney would wait a year and by that time he'd—he wouldn't want a divorce?

CONNIE: I think Sidney'll be in your bed long before a year is up. But I warn you, Grace, don't you go to him. You make him be the first to bring the subject up. Now the next thing is what we can do to chastise Mr. Bannon.

GRACE: What do you mean, chastise him? Do you know him?

CONNIE: I've met him. He isn't hard for us to meet. He's a climber . . . I infer you've broken off with him entirely.

GRACE: Yes. I haven't seen him for a while.

CONNIE: Have you wanted to see him?

GRACE: Have I wanted to see him?

CONNIE: Yes.

GRACE: I'm ashamed to say it, but I guess in a certain way I have.

CONNIE: I understand. But are you going to see him?

GRACE: No. No, I don't think so.

CONNIE: Grace, you have to be sure. You can't see him any more. You can't have a lover. You're Grace Caldwell. Other girls can slip and nobody pays any attention, but the only reason why this got around is because you're you.

GRACE: How much has it got around?

CONNIE: As gossip it's got around a lot. I mean, a lot of people ask each other if it's true. As far as facts go, what I heard was that you'd spent the night with Bannon at Miles Brinkerhoff's farm and were seen leaving by a caretaker or carpenter.

GRACE: Why didn't you tell me?

CONNIE: Oh, hell, you'd have denied it.

GRACE: I guess so. Anyway, it wasn't true. I never did spend the night with him. I wonder if that's the story Sidney heard. If it was I could deny it.

CONNIE: There's another story, that you were together with him in one of the rooms at the Armory and a watchman surprised you both in a compromising position. Naked.

GRACE: That's not true, either. I'll tell you the truth. The first time was in my car. After that we met at Miles Brinkerhoff's.

CONNIE: Often?

GRACE: Six or seven times. Oh, it was a full-fledged affair. He's had me. If he's gone around telling people he has, he's only telling the truth, God damn him.

CONNIE: Well, the thing for us to do is formulate a plan to stop his going around bragging. What would you think of my going to Ham?

GRACE: Ham Schoffstal? He'd never speak to me again.

CONNIE: Don't be so sure. Ham isn't the way you always picture him. Cold and starchy. He can be very kind and warm.

GRACE: Oh, I know that, but I wouldn't want him to—I don't know.

CONNIE: I won't say anything till after you've had a chance to think more about it, but Ham is Bannon's superior officer in the Guard, so he has him under his thumb there. And in a business way, Ham could make things difficult for Bannon.

GRACE: Bannon's making money hand over fist.

CONNIE: As a war profiteer. But those people don't know what to do with money when they get it, and really, Grace, when it comes to financial matters you wouldn't really put Bannon up against my brother Ham. Ham knows who every dollar in this town belongs to . . . I'll just say to Ham, 'I think that Roger Bannon person's getting too big for his breeches,' and that's all I'll have to say. Ham'll know what I have in mind.

GRACE: What'll Ham do?

CONNIE: I don't know, but it'll be the right thing.

GRACE: Oh, Connie, I wish I'd been able to tell you everything.

CONNIE: I'm glad you didn't, dear. You had to get this out of your system. It was a long time coming, but be a good girl hereafter, will you?

GRACE: I'll try to be.

CONNIE: Don't kiss me, Grace. I don't like you to.

GRACE: Yes I will. You're my best friend, and I haven't kissed you for years.

CONNIE: Don't, I said. I don't want you to.

GRACE: You don't think I'm nice any more. Is that why?

CONNIE: No, that's not why. I just don't like it. It's childish.

GRACE: I guess so, but at least it doesn't get you into trouble.

CONNIE: No? Well, I've been here long enough.

The conversation was resumed the next day at Connie's house.

CONNIE: How's your big shindig coming?

GRACE: The biggest thing in the history of the county. I talked to the Governor today and he's going to honor us with his presence.

CONNIE: That slob.

GRACE: Mm-hmm, and his charming wife, she's coming. That must mean my bad reputation hasn't reached the politicians.

CONNIE: Not necessarily. I don't think Mrs. Dunkelberger knows two people in Fort Penn, and I don't think two people know her.

GRACE: True. How was rolling bandages?

CONNIE: The same as usual. In a way, Grace, I wish you were still doing it instead of running this thing at the farm.

GRACE: Why?

CONNIE: Well, I'd like you to be there every day and that way they wouldn't get as much chance to gossip about you. They don't do as much of it while I'm around, naturally, but I hear things. I go out of my way to. But if you were there you could, uh, stare them down.

GRACE: Well, I began working on the Festival around the same time they began talking about me, I guess. I guess it is too bad. Too bad I'm not there, but it couldn't be helped. Was there any talk today?

CONNIE: Yes. I don't know what it was, but one table stopped talking when I got there, so they were either talking about me or you.

GRACE: Who are the talkers?

CONNIE: All of them.

GRACE: My friends?

CONNIE: Of course, Grace. They only gossip among themselves, but you can't expect a girl just because you've known her all your life, she's not going to keep quiet when something like this comes along.

GRACE: I suppose not. If I heard that someone like Mary Wall was diddling with Emlen Deatrick I'd gossip about it.

CONNIE: What a terrible word.

GRACE: If you'd rather hear me use some of the others I know them all.

CONNIE: I know you do, and so do I, but I haven't heard you say any of them for years, since we found out what they meant.

GRACE: I've said them, though, and I could let go with a nice long stream of them when I think of those dried-up neglected friends of mine.

CONNIE: Do you include me among your dried-up neglected friends?

GRACE: No. If I did I wouldn't have said that. I know you're not a virgin—

CONNIE: You don't know any such thing.

GRACE: Somewhere along the line you went the limit with some boy, even if you didn't tell me about it. I think you have your fun when you go away on these trips to New York and Philadelphia. And I wouldn't be a bit surprised if all these years you've been having a whirl with Paul Reichelderfer.

CONNIE: Paul Reichelderfer! He'd crush me to death.

GRACE: Now, Connie, don't be so innocent. He wouldn't *have* to crush you.

CONNIE: Oh.

GRACE: Oh, indeed. What I dropped in for, I've been thinking about your suggestion, about having Ham speak to my partner in sin.

CONNIE: I wish you wouldn't be facetious about this. It's serious.

GRACE: I know it's serious, but you've heard of people joking before they went in the operating-room. Anyway, what I was going to say was, I don't want Ham to say anything to Roger Bannon. At least not for the present.

CONNIE: All right.

GRACE: I think I know that man pretty well, and if Ham did say something, Roger would talk even more than he has. He'd do it in a way that Ham wouldn't catch on, and the gossip would go on and on instead of running its course.

CONNIE: I think you're right.

GRACE: But—a great big *but*. You have my permission to tell Ham the truth. Tell him as much as you feel like. In other words, I could never tell him myself, vis-à-vis, but through you I'm taking Ham into my confidence. You can tell him that. And I know Ham well enough to know he'll never repeat it to another soul, or show in any way that he knows. Except—*except* in his manner to Roger. He'll never say a word to Roger, but that Irish bastard will be able to tell from Ham's manner. And it'll put the fear of God into Roger. It'll confuse him. It'll frighten him, where he wouldn't be frightened if Ham actually threatened him. You see what I mean?

CONNIE: I certainly do. I didn't know you were so intelligent, frankly. When did you think this out?

GRACE: Connie, dear, I have all the time in the world to do nothing but think, these nights. Sidney's the soul of politeness in front of the children and other people, and you'd think we were only married a few months. But not when we're alone, not at night. We sleep in the same room, because if we didn't the servants would notice it. I don't mean that we discussed that, but I know that's the only reason he still sleeps there.

CONNIE: It must be—how can you stand it?

GRACE: I have to. I know it can't last forever. I think Sidney is making up his mind what he wants to do. He's such a gentleman, you know. I think what's in his mind is he's trying to get a commission in the Navy and when he does he'll say good-bye and never come back. Not as my husband, anyway. He's using political influence to get a commission. The Governor's one of the people he's spoken to, and he's even written a letter to Teddy Roosevelt. His father knew Teddy Roosevelt, and Roosevelt has a nephew one of the high officials in the Navy. So Sidney's dead set on it, and I imagine he'll get what he wants, and then he'll go away just like anyone else going to the war. That's what I mean about his being so gentlemanly. No fuss, no scandal, none of that what-we-were-talking-about-yesterday. Before he leaves I suppose we'll have one big talk, and he'll tell me then what he knows about Roger and me, and announce whatever his plans are. But you were wrong yesterday, Connie. He'll never be in my bed again. I've done what he would never do. He believes all those things you're brought up to believe. Honor. Vows. Promises. The Golden Rule.

CONNIE: He never wanted anybody but you. Therefore he can't take credit for what he didn't do.

GRACE: Yes he can. He's a passionate man and he's been tempted. I know of two or three friends of ours who'd have gone to bed with Sidney the first chance they got.

CONNIE: All these things you're telling me, Grace. They're so sad. And suddenly you're so sad, but at the same time you could be talking about another person. You were never a cry-baby, but—I don't know.

GRACE: If I cried, that would be feeling sorry for myself, and I don't feel at all sorry for myself. When I went into that thing with Mr. Bannon I was taking my chances, and you were right yesterday. I used him to give me pleasure and excitement. Oh, God, he did. He was so awful and I was so awful. I'd save up wanting him till I couldn't stand it another minute, and I'd telephone him—we had a kind of a code. And I'd meet him and throw myself at him and squeeze him and eat him—

CONNIE: Grace! Stop this! Grace, darling.

GRACE: Well, I couldn't help it, I couldn't help it. I—I—I—I don't hate anybody, I don't want to hurt anybody, I love Sidney, I love my children. Connie, please?

CONNIE (going to her): I know, Grace. You cry, Grace. Put your head on my shoulder.

GRACE: I feel sorry for myself, I pity myself.

CONNIE: Yes, girl.

The war was not catching on very quickly in Fort Penn or anywhere else, but on forty-eight hours' notice the officers and men of the 114th Infantry met at the Armory, passed a night sleeping on the Armory floors, and the next morning marched to the station.

Connie telephoned Grace on the morning the regiment was to entrain. "They're leaving on an eleven o'clock special," she said. "We can watch them from Ham's private office if you want to."

"Yes, but will there be anybody else in the office?"

"Not if we get there ahead of time. I can close the door and nobody'd think of intruding."

"What about Marie and the children?"

"Marie'll be at the station. Officers' wives will be allowed to go to one of the waiting rooms."

"I'll pick you up," said Grace.

They went to Ham's office, a corner room with windows in the west and south walls, which had been preempted by several office employes who promptly and silently filed out when they saw Connie.

"They hate us for that," said Grace.

"Well, they're probably not hating us for the first time, so to hell with them," said Connie. "They have no right to be in this office anyway, and they know it. They can go to the other windows."

"Yes, to hell with them," said Grace. "I'm excited, Connie. Are you sad?"

"No, I don't think so. You know how Ham and I've always been."

"Yes, I know," said Grace. "But even so, you've always been closer than Brock and I."

"I cried a little last night when he came to say good-bye. I didn't even have a present for him. Of course they're not going straight to France. They'll be in camp for months."

"They're starting to clear the street," said Grace. "My, I never realized Fort Penn had so many motorcycle policemen. We must be growing up. Look at them."

"Uh-huh."

"I'm glad we're over the heads of the crowd. Look, Connie. A moving-picture camera taking pictures, on that truck. I think that's the first one I ever saw in Fort Penn. Oh, no. Inaugurations they have them. What're they taking pictures of? I don't see anything coming."

"The people, I guess."

"Oh, now they're stopping. I guess they're going to wait there and take pictures when the regiment comes."

"Well, here they come. At least I hear the band."

People along the curb stepped out and looked when they heard the music, and in a few minutes the marchers came into view.

"Look, Connie, Troop A, the State Police. My, look at them. That's Captain Ludwig on the gray. I know him. Look at their tack, Connie. Every one of those troopers takes care of his own, that's why they're so proud of it. No rust on those bits, you can be sure. You know what they do? When they have inspection Captain Ludwig wears white cotton gloves and runs a finger over a saddle and if there's any dust, the man that owns that saddle, he can't leave the barracks for a week."

"They're only going as far as the station, Grace."

"Well—why there's Dunky."

"Who?"

"The Governor. Governor Dunkelberger. Marching with— looks like Fred Bauer. Yes. Fred Bauer. And who's that other man? It's, I know who it is. It's the mayor. Mayor Walthour. Wouldn't you hate to be his daughter and grow up with people calling you Walthour the Wallflower?"

"Dreadful. I'd change my name," said Connie. "What I'm looking for is the regiment. Who are all those men with the mayor and the Governor? I recognize a lot of them, but do they belong to some organization?"

"I don't know. They're all carrying little flags."

"Yes, it's a good thing they don't have to carry anything heavier. Oh, I know who they are. They're the Patriotic League."

"Oh, yes. I should have known that. Walter Buchwalter and Doctor O'Brien and Fred Bauer. They're all helping with the Festival on the Fourth, at the farm. Do you recognize those flags, the Boy Scouts are carrying? Do you know what they are? They're the flags of all the Allies."

"Well, I didn't expect to see the German flag."

"Who are those women? Oh, the Red Cross motor corps. Mustn't say anything against them, you know. They're so awfully chic, don't you know. Those uniforms. Aren't those belts just too ducky for words? Half of those women can't even turn a car around."

"Who are these men?"

"Let's see if I can read what's on that flag Spanish—American. Oh, yes. Spanish-American War. Blue shirts? I thought blue was for the Navy. Do you remember the Spanish-American war, Connie?"

"I was old enough to, so were you. One of my uncles was in it."

"I don't remember anything about it except that the Spaniards sank the Maine. We used to say, 'Do you remember that tree that used to stand in front of So and So's house?' and the other person would say yes, and then you'd say, 'Well, forget that and remember the Maine.' "

"Oh, yes. Very clever."

Connie suddenly clutched Grace's arm. "I see them, Grace! Here they come."

They saw the colors and the color guard, and Ham marching alone at the head of the regiment, and their first view was of solid olive drab, with lines drawn regularly through it, indicating the rifles and campaign hats, rising and falling rhythmically to the tune of the Old Gray Mare. The two women went silent as the regiment came nearer. Under the cheers they could hear the incessant steady growling of the marching feet. As Ham came abreast of the Schoffstal Building a personal cheer went up for him from the people at the other windows, and he held his head back a little more and raised his eyebrows, but he stared straight ahead and did not, by smile or salute, acknowledge the greetings.

"He's wonderful," said Grace.

"Yes he is, and he's a German," said Connie. "So am I a German, don't forget."

"You are not. You're Americans and nothing else," said Grace. She put her arm around Connie's shoulder, but Connie moved out of the slight embrace.

"I'll smoke a cigarette," she said. "The parade isn't over for you, yet."

"He's in Company J. They wanted to be Company I for Irish, but there is no Company I." Grace ticked off the companies as the letters on the guidons became visible. "I see him," she said.

"Yes, I do too," said Connie.

"See him?"

"Yes," said Connie.

"There he is," said Grace. "He's awfully big."

"Mm-hmm."

"He looks younger today. I should have seen him one more time," said Grace.

"No."

"He telephoned," said Grace. "Well, there he goes." She withdrew from the window and sat in one of Ham's chairs. "He was carrying a pistol," she said. "On account of me he almost killed a girl one time."

"Don't think of him any more, Grace."

"Oh, no. Of course not," said Grace. "Where are they going from here, do you know?"

"Yes. Mount Gretna."

"Mount Gretna? Only about twenty miles?"

"They won't be there long. Then they're going South."

"But I could start for Mount Gretna and be there before the train."

"Yes, if you wanted to ruin him and yourself and Sidney and your children. Besides, I'm not sure it is Mount Gretna. They may be going some place else. Grace, this is the time for the things Sidney believes in. You have to think of Sidney. He's going away soon, and there's just as much chance he'll get killed as Bannon. You have to be a wife to Sidney till he goes away."

Grace laughed. "What does *that* mean? Would you like to hear something interesting? When Sidney came back from New York, do you know one of the things he did? Without saying anything to me about it he started giving Julie his socks to darn. That's how much his wife I am. We're just dead, Connie. That's the way we're living now. Just dead. He wants to be away from me, so I might as well be alive with that awful creature that just marched by."

"I don't understand you, Grace."

"Well, then don't try."

"Don't cry?"

"I didn't say don't *cry*. I said don't *try*. Don't t, r, y, to understand me. I don't understand myself. Oh, Christ, Connie, I'm not going to do anything. I'm only talking to hear myself talk."

"Then you'd better t, e, l, l yourself to try to make Sidney as happy as you can between now and when he goes away."

"Why are you suddenly taking Sidney's part?"

"Because I just saw my brother go to war, and I think what we have to do is do whatever we can for them. With them it can be life and death. With us, minor inconveniences."

"Bannon telephoned me. According to your way of looking at it I should have had another fling with him."

"No. You don't belong to Bannon, and Bannon doesn't belong to you. The truth is, Grace, I think it's time somebody told you you're damned selfish, and if you weren't you wouldn't be in this state you're in now."

"A few days ago I was beautiful and interesting. Now that you've seen your brother go off to war I'm a selfish no-good bitch."

"I didn't say that, but the selfish part still goes."

"Well, if it still goes I'm going too. I don't think I care to have you as a friend any more, Connie. I don't like to think of you disapproving of me or my conduct or the way I feel."

"I'm sorry, Grace. We've had these spats before, but you'll cool off."

"Cool off? I've never been so *cool* in my *life!* Good—morning!"

Grace left the room, closing the door behind her, and as she marched across the carpeted outer office her steps were to the beat of a band in the parade outside. It was like that all her way to her car.

CHAPTER 4

And now the night and the quiet were upon them and they were alone.

They lay there, both of them awake, kept awake with their wakeful awareness of each other, kept alive by the shallow breathing that each knew meant no sleep for the other. It was their farm again and no longer the scene of the Festival; it had been an hour and more since the last of the Festival crowd had gone singing his drunken way toward the Pike, and he could be heard until an automobile stopped and gave him a lift. Then quiet again for a little while; the insects, and the cold gurgle of the water spilling over the breast of the dam. Then the voices of two men in the stable yard, the brief clangor of iron-shod hooves on the cobblestones in the yard and almost immediately the daintiness of foot of the fast-walking horses in the lane and the creaking stirrup leathers and the pleasant voices of the riders, the state troopers, beginning their long ride in the moonlight to their barracks.

There was a child's cough.

They listened. It stopped for only a minute or two before starting again.

"It's Billy," said Grace, getting quickly out of her bed. "I'll give him some cough medicine." She put on her dressing-gown as she hurried out of the room.

She was back in a few minutes, walking slowly now in the unlit room. "He wanted you, but I told him you were asleep."

"What did he want?"

"Nothing in particular. He said if you were awake he'd like to see you, but I said you had to get up early. Don't go up, Sidney. That cough medicine has something in it that puts him to sleep, and he needs his rest too."

"I didn't like the sound of that cough."

"He's all right. I took his temperature and it's only 99. Just let him sleep."

"Well—I like to be there when they want me," said Sidney.

She lay down in her bed. "They're going to have to get used to your not being here."

"Why? Oh, you mean the Navy."

"Yes. What else could I mean?"

"Several things. I've been waiting for you to ask me for a divorce."

"You have? I've been waiting for you to tell me *you* were going to divorce *me,*" she said.

"No. I thought of it, but why make a mess? Now I'm pretty certain of going away, I think the best thing is if I don't come back after the war. Not to live, at least. I'll always want to see the children, but you'd never stand in the way there. You see? I've been thinking of you as decent for so many years, I still think you would be, on some things."

She turned on the lamp on her night table and lit a cigarette before speaking again. "Do you want to have our talk now, Sidney?"

"Our talk? . . . If you wish." He lit a cigarette.

"Do you want to start?"

"Not particularly. I think you ought to," he said. He looked across at her and she looked away from him.

"I'd rather you started," she said.

"Very well. There isn't a hell of a lot *to* talk about. By that I mean—no accusation, and denial, and then more accusation and denial till finally I guess you'd break down and say yes, you had an affair with this son of a bitch. Or do you mind if I call him a son of a bitch?"

"Not at all, in fact I wish you'd call him a son of a bitch to his face."

"You do? Why? Would you like to see him give me a beating? Probably could, although it wouldn't be over in a few seconds, you can bet on that. Is that what you'd like? To see your husband and lover brawling for you?"

"No."

"Because I don't look at it that way. If your wife suddenly falls in love with another man, naturally you want to kill the bastard—the man, I mean. Not the wife. But every time I started for Mr. Bannon's office I'd think over my little speech, how I'd say, 'Bannon, you're having an affair with my wife.' Smacko! Or if one didn't start hitting the other, he might say, 'Yes, I am.' Well if he said that, I couldn't tell him he'd better stop that kind of conduct, it was naughty. Because he'd have a perfect right to say, 'Look here, Tate, you take this up with your wife. She's the one going out of her way to meet me.' And of course he'd have me there on a point of fact. My wife *was* going out of her way to have rendezvous with him, and if I wasn't man enough to keep her home, curb those tendencies, I had no real right to go to a man's office and try to beat him up and get a beating myself in the process.

"In other words, the one that deserved the beating was me. And, in one sense, I was getting it. I was getting what I deserved. It didn't make *you* any the less disgusting, but as they say in horse-racing, I had no excuses. I don't think the weight was too much. Maybe the food was too rich. I don't know. Forty years old, wasted my time, my youth. Never did a God-damn thing worth a day's pay. This war's a very lucky thing for me. I've seen this kind of thing happen to fellows I've known, and one or two of them blew their brains out, and some of them became souses. At least this Navy proposition gives me a new start, and just the right moment. . . . Well, I've talked myself blue in the face. What about you?"

She shook her head. "I have nothing to say."

"Come on, you didn't start this to hear me talk. You have the floor."

"I have nothing you want to hear."

"Well, for Christ's sake, tell me what I don't want to hear. Don't start sparing my feelings at this late date."

"I only had one thing to say before you began talking, but it would be a waste of breath, after hearing you."

"Let's hear it, let's hear it."

"All right. I was going to ask you to forgive me."

He lit a fresh cigarette from the end of the first. "Yes, and I could have, but for one thing."

"What was that?"

"You. Yourself. I've always admired you as well as loved you. You always had courage and independence. Real guts. Not only physical. You have as much of that as any man. But courage of the spirit. Well, when you took up with this Bannon, you knew what you were doing. You knew I loved you. You must have thought of the children and the possible chance that I might take them away from you. And your reputation. You can be as independent as you please, but no girl like you, uh, wants to lose her reputation. So you had all those things to lose. Beautiful children, devoted husband, reputation. Nevertheless, you went out of your way to carry on with this fellow. Every time you met him you had to think of the risk, and take it. And you took it. Therefore every time you met him you said to hell with me, and the children, and your friends' opinion of you. You weren't just caught up by some physical thing. Infatuation. Intoxication. You were going into this deliberately and continually."

"You're wrong in one place."

"I doubt it. Where?"

"That's all it was, physical."

"Well, maybe. It's enough. As far as I'm concerned it's enough. What do you think I am? Do you think I have no balls for anybody but you, all these years? Do you think I never saw anybody I wanted to screw? You must think you had the big secret or some such thing, if that's your thinking. I wanted to, and I could have. And I wouldn't have had to go to Irishtown for it. But the difference is, you see in this world you learn a set of rules, *or* you *don't* learn them. But assuming you learn them, you stick by them. They may be no damn good, but you're who you are and what you are because they're your rules and you stick by them. And of course when it's easy to stick by them, that's no test. It's when it's hard to obey the rules, that's when they mean something. That's what I believe, and I always thought you did too. I'm the first, God knows, to grant that you, with your beauty, you had opportunities or invitations. But you obeyed the rules, the same rules I obeyed. But then you said the hell with them. What it amounts to is you said the hell with my rules, and the hell with me. So, Grace—the hell with you. I love you, but if I have any luck, that'll pass, in my new life."

"I love you, and it'll never pass, in any life."

"I'll never believe you again, anything you say."

"I know you won't, Sidney. But if you could, you'd have more love than ever before. Do you want to try to?"

"No. Not with you. And probably not with anyone else."

"I'm sorry," she said. "Will you tell me one thing?"

"I know what you have to know. You want to know how I found out about your affair."

"Yes."

"Friendly advice for your next time out. Don't choose an Irishman with a little old Irish mother."

"His mother told you? How?"

"How the hell do you think? First she telephoned, without saying who she was. Then an anonymous letter. Then she wrote and asked me to come and see her. Signed that one, of course. So I went and she filled me up with a great deal of information. She said you pretended to be somebody's secretary, and met her son at Brinkerhoff's farm. So forth and so on."

"How did she know?"

"I asked her that, too. She wouldn't tell me. But I knew she wasn't making it up. Quite a woman, but I don't think you'd like her as a mother-in-law. She doesn't like you at all." He snapped off the light. "Neither do I. Good night."

"Sidney, can't I come over? Please?"

He laughed. "Nope. Good night."

BOOK TWO

BOOK TWO

The letter from the Bureau of Navigation authorized Sidney to appear before the medical board at League Island Navy Yard. He read the letter to Grace at lunch.

"What was the date?" she said.

"First of August, eight o'clock in the morning. That's a week from tomorrow," he said.

"Does that mean you're leaving a week from tomorrow, Sidney?"

"Not for good," he said. "I go to Philadelphia and take the examination, and then I come back and wait for what they have to say. If I pass the physical examination then the next step is I go before another Board, and I think after that they swear me in. Soon after that. Why? I *could* arrange to leave here a week from today and not come back, if you want me to."

"I don't want you to. I don't want you to leave at all."

"I want to wait here till they tell me I've passed the physical examination. Then I can leave and not come back. Be anticlimactic if I went away next week and then didn't measure up physically."

"You will. You're as strong as anybody half your age."

"Half my age is twenty," he said. "When you're forty they can find things wrong with you you didn't know you had."

"Last year you had that examination for insurance."

"Well, it's not the same kind of a test. I know I'm okay, but now your bringing up the insurance one—sometimes I think if you're paying a big enough premium they're likely to overlook a thing or two here and there. Doctor Ziegman, the one that gave me the insurance exam, he knows I'm not a heavy drinker, lead an out-doors life. Healthy kind of existence. So naturally he'd be likely to think of me as a good risk . . . I don't know why I'm talking this way, knocking my own condition, except I don't want to count on anything till I have it." He looked at the ceiling. "Recent experience has shown me that it's foolish to count on anything, even when I think I do have it."

"Hoping you weren't going to say that."

"I had to, nevertheless." He stood up, taking out his pipe. He studied the pipe. "I think I'll quit smoking between now and the examination. Get plenty of sleep. No drinks. Enough exercise to get up a sweat every day. And of course I have one advantage over most married men. At least it could be called an advantage. You know when a prize-fighter's training for a big bout, the first thing they do is tell his wife to go hide. No women."

"You must be getting used to that, Sidney."

"Pardon me, but you don't ever get used to it."

"Well, any time you want one . . ."

"Thanks, but I'm not taking wet decks," he said.

"What does that mean?"

"If you give it a minute's thought it'll come to you. It's proba-bly the nastiest thing I ever said to you. I'm sorry."

"I am too. I get what it means, but that's not why I'm sorry. I'm sorry because it shows how foolish I am to keep hoping every day and every night."

"It's foolish, all right."

"What are you going to do this afternoon? Are you going back up to the field?"

"For a little while. We have an extra hand coming this after-noon and they're short a pitchfork. I'll take it up and use that as an excuse to see they get started. He's getting forty-five cents an hour and supper. Then I'm coming down and work on the diving-board. It's still too floppy for the children."

"You're a strange man, Sidney."

"Why so?"

"Oh—in a little while you'll be leaving here forever, but that doesn't stop you from doing little things around the place, the kind of things that a man does that's planning to stay all his life. What was it you did yesterday?"

"You mean while it was raining?"

"Yes. In the barn."

"I was fixing stanchions. There were a couple of stanchions that didn't close properly. That's the kind of thing you do on rainy days. Nothing strange about that, Grace. I love this place, and I owe a lot to it. I've been happy here. I wouldn't stop doing those little things, not and stay here. I expect to keep busy until I do leave, and I have a list of things to be done after I've gone I'll give you later on. There's always something to do on a farm. The farmer looks forward to a rainy day and a little rest, take it easy. But then it rains and there's more to do than he could finish if he had all summer. And you think you know all about your farm, but for instance yesterday I found a dozen crocks I didn't know we had. They were in the spring-house. Not a chip on them. I wouldn't be surprised if they'd never been used. I don't know how I happened to miss them all these years, except it's dark in there. Well, have to deliver a pitchfork . . . You see, Grace, I realize I've never been much more than a de-luxe handyman around here. Worth about, not quite forty-five cents an hour, and supper. But when I leave you're never going to be able to replace me. You should have thought of *that*, too."

"Just a minute, Sidney. Before you go. Now, I mean. I think I ought to sell this: when you leave—for good, that is—I'm going to sell this place."

He laughed. "You forget one little detail. You can't sell it, because you don't own it. I own it, and I've left it to you and the children."

"Oh, well, I can buy it back from you and then sell it."

"Like hell you can. It's not for sale. You were awake and sober when you signed the papers, and I've gone without a lot of things so I could pay you out of my income. The only way you can sell this farm is for me to die while the children are under age. That's what it says in my will, and I'm not going to change it."

"Why not?"

"Because I wanted you and the children to have it."

"But you and I are getting a divorce."

"Well, I'll rent it to you for a dollar a year till Billy's twenty-one. If they don't want it, I'll come back and live on it till I die."

"You realize that's another reason for our staying married."

"It could be, possibly, but I don't see it that way. When I leave you can start paying me rent, dollar a year . . . We can discuss it later. I won't be leaving for another two or three weeks."

"All this talk about leaving. I hate it. You're leaving now to take a pitchfork up to the field. Then you're leaving a week from tomorrow, next Wednesday. Then a couple of weeks after that and you'll be leaving for good."

"Yes, the air is full of talk of leaving. Leaving, without leave-taking. That's rather poetic. I wonder if I'm quoting Browning or one of those fellows."

"For all I know you are. You know me and poetry."

"You know *me* and poetry."

"I know you and everything," she said.

"I guess you do," he said. "Well—"

"Better than anyone ever will again, Sidney. I know I've been wrong. I know I've been bad, disgusting. And Sidney, dear, I knew what the consequences would be. But even knowing that, I did what I did. So it was something where I lost control. I wasn't my-self. I'm not that much of a fool, that I'd lose you, and probably the children. They'll know you've left because of something I did, and sooner or later they'll know exactly what it was. For God's sake, Sidney, I'm not that much of a fool."

"But you were."

"But I was. Exactly. I knew what the consequences were, and I went ahead anyway. Doesn't that mean anything to you? Think of me. Just think of me. I've always been careful and selfish, and never risked anything, but then I did. *I* did. *Grace.* Doesn't that prove I must have been—well, crazy. Out of my mind."

"Wait a minute. Don't let yourself go now. You just said you've always been careful and selfish. Well, in this instance you were selfish all right, but just not careful enough. Here's something you don't understand, Grace: I don't *want* you any more. You broke the vase, or cut the rope. Whatever way you want to put it. I can stand here and talk to you for an hour, but as far as your effect on me, I might as well be talking to Mrs. Dunkelberger. I can stand her, God damn it, talking about the worst thing that ever happened to me, but you, the cause of it, and the reason for its being the worst thing that ever happened to me—you could be a harness peg."

"That's not true. You're trying to make yourself believe that, and you will. But we stayed together while I was having the affair with Bannon and you were satisfied and pleased with me. Until you found out about me. That means it's your pride that was injured. I don't think our marriage was."

"Well, God damn it to hell if you aren't the—I don't know what to say to you. Coming right out with it, that you were sleeping with that son of a bitch same time you were me."

"You know it."

"Sure I know it, but you don't have to talk about it. I don't bring it up. I don't think of it. If I let myself think of it I'd beat the hell out of you and probably kill him. You're what the stable-boys call a two-timer, and by God I think you're proud of it."

"All I wanted was to make you see that something came over me that I couldn't control. It wasn't anything against you. And I wanted to show you that it's your pride that was hurt. I'll do anything I can to save our marriage. You can sleep with other women, and it'll kill me. I don't even like to see you being nice to Connie Schoffstal. But I'll agree to anything that'll keep us together."

"I don't think you pay much attention to what I say. You miss the whole point. I wouldn't need your permission to go philandering. I'd go. I'd have gone years ago. But if you do that you haven't got a marriage. Even if the one that's philandering keeps it a secret from the other poor simp. I hope the principles I've been trying to teach the children—I hope the children listen better than you do."

"Sidney, it's the children I'm thinking of, at least partly. That's why I want to stay married to you. Other people have this problem. Adultery. But they make a compromise. You know yourself a lot of the men you know have other women besides their wives. Usually it's the men, but sometimes it's the wives. And they stay married on account of their children."

"From what I've seen of them they're pigs, and they raise pigs. The children know. They're wise. They see what's going on and they say to themselves, what the hell's the use of trying to be decent, so they end up in the gutter."

In their discussion they had moved from the dining-room to the den. Grace had seated herself on Sidney's swivel chair. He paced back and forth except when he halted to emphasize a point, and through it all he seldom looked at her. She turned the chair and in so doing she caught a glance at the communication from the Navy, which lay on the desk. She touched it, pushed it an inch away from her.

"All right. I give up," she said. "We'll get a divorce and I'll try to keep the children out of the pig-sty. While you're at the war I'm not going to tell them anything. When it's over you can come back and tell them you're divorcing me, and you can tell them why. If they haven't guessed, or heard from their friends at school."

"Very well."

———

On the next Tuesday, the last day of July, Sidney boarded a parlor car in a Chicago–New York train. He wanted to be sure of a night's sleep before the examination in the morning. The train was hardly past the yard-limits sign, beginning to pick up speed, before he found that he was feeling better than he had felt in months, indeed better than he had expected ever to feel again. He was slightly ashamed until he realized that the present near-euphoria came from his sense of relief that he was free, and that bad as it was, it was as good as it could be. And he actually felt a kind of friendliness for Grace, because he could trust her to continue to bring up the children as he thought they ought to be brought up; and he could trust her to present at all times a fair picture of him. But most of all he looked forward to a new freedom, different, and larger than any he ever had known. He was strong in physical fact and in his principles and in his will (it would have been easy enough to yield to Grace's humiliated attractiveness), and he had become—overnight, you might say—a mature individual, equipped with a mature unhappiness and fortified by whatever wisdom had come with the good and the bad of the years with Grace.

Looking back now, in the reasonably comfortable Pullman chair, he realized that he had everything he wanted, had been the happiest of men. Looking out on the Dutch country, the toy-store farm houses and the straining draft teams in the fields—he had had that life, which was what he had wanted. He had had it with the only woman he had loved, and with her he had bred three sound, handsome children. There had been no trouble about money. And he had kept his self-respect and had gained the respect of the men whom he wanted to respect him, the men whom he did business with, especially the farmers. He could lift anything they could lift, such as a bag of cement; bend anything they could bend, such as a mule shoe; eat as many waffles, drink as much beer, do it to his wife as often, work as many hours, and make as much money. He could, if he chose, get off the train at Lancaster, assume another name, and hire out as a hand on one of those toy-store farms that whizzed by his train-window. He allowed himself the pleasure of this kind of thinking before going on to the next phase. He had, yes, been the happiest of men—

and after all those happy years he qualified as a farm hand, capable of earning forty-five cents an hour in war times. For that his mother and father had spent large sums of money on his education, to teach him manners, to clothe and feed him, to train his body for games. And they had handed him the fortune that permitted him to marry the woman he wanted to marry. And during those happy, happy years he had been preparing himself to qualify as an itinerant farm hand. And like many farm hands he had hired, he had behind him a disappointment in a woman. He could get himself a job as a farm manager, but how many such jobs were open in the entire world? No, in the man market he was worth forty-five cents an hour, and come to think of it, he couldn't get a job on each and every toy-store farm in the Pullman window; he hadn't learned to speak enough Pennsylvania Dutch.

If that's all he was worth in the man market, of what use would he be to the Navy? This alarming thought took away some of the joy of his new freedom. But then he reassured himself: they needed officers, and he had a college degree, he had handled men, he was a good physical specimen, and he had important connections.

He usually walked from the station to the Bellevue-Stratford or the Union League Club, but this day he took one of the huge Packard taxicabs. He was being as careful of his body as a track athlete or a bride-to-be. He had heard of men getting a hernia from lifting a suitcase while their muscles were in a wrong position. And when he got to the hotel he soaked and scrubbed as though he were going to meet a noble lady that night rather than a Navy doctor the next morning. After dinner he loafed in the lobby, which was unusually alive for August, what with men in the uniforms of the leading Allies and their women. He saw no one he recognized. In spite of the heat he slept well and did not get awake until the telephone rang at seven in the morning.

He took one of the taxicabs to League Island, and the next few hours were a not unpleasant confusion. He was mildly and agreeably surprised not to find himself one of dozens of candidates for examination. He had not yet learned to distinguish rank by the stripes on the officers' shoulder boards, but a Commander Williams seemed to be in charge, and Sidney was not long in suspecting that Williams was conscious of Sidney's connections. Williams was the first and again the last of many doctors he saw that day, and all of them were affable, polite, respectful, or even obsequious. When the young orderly finally brought him back to Williams' office the commander said he hoped it had not been too much of a bore or ordeal, shook hands with Sidney, and told him he would hear from the Navy in a couple of weeks.

"You couldn't give me a hint now, could you?"

Williams smiled. "*I* couldn't, because I haven't seen your papers, Mr. Tate. But you'll hear, and I must say you don't have the appearance of a decrepit old man. Good luck."

On his way uptown he caught himself wanting to telephone Grace. A few minutes later he caught himself wanting to go to Schoenhut's to buy some presents for the children, but the children were in Cape May with their cousins and would be away for another week or two. He stopped for a drink at the bar of the Union League.

His Tom Collins was on the way when a British officer came in. It was the middle of the afternoon and Sidney was the only member in the grill. The officer came straight to him.

"Aren't you Sidney Tate?" he said.

"Yes."

"I'm not surprised you don't recognize me in this get-up, but I'm Joe Bartholomew. I was a year behind you at Lawrenceville."

"Well, by God. How are you? It sure is nice to see you again," said Sidney.

"Thanks. Good to see you. You haven't changed."

"Well, I don't have much trouble keeping the hair out of my eyes."

Bartholomew laughed. "I noticed that, but otherwise you're the same. Do you live in Philadelphia now?"

"No, just in town for the day. I live in Fort Penn."

"Of course. You married a sister of Brock Caldwell."

"Yes. You a Philadelphian, Joe?"

"Well, I am and I'm not. I was born here, but after I finished Lawrenceville my people moved to London, so I don't know what I call myself. I'm a British subject, back here now making speeches. I guess it's because I never acquired an English accent and they think it'd be good propaganda to hear a Philadelphia twang coming out of this uniform. You going in this thing?"

"That's what I'm in town for. I just came from an examination at the Navy Yard."

"Stay out of it if you can. War's for fellows half our age. Believe you me, I know it is. I don't carry this stick for swank." He rapped his thonged malacca stick on his left foot. "Stay out of it, Sidney."

"Let's sit down. I want to hear all about you, Joe."

They went to a table and ordered drinks; another Tom Collins, a double whiskey and soda. "I'm serious, you know. The Navy isn't so bad, I imagine. I was in the London and Middlesex regiment, and we were given a good thrashing, but it doesn't make much difference, if you're going to be in a war it's no damn good wherever you are. War's like any sport. The minute you get too old to play it well you ought to stay out of it, or perhaps coach it. *You're* too old to play it well, but not old enough to coach it. I'm much too old to play it well, in spite of being a year or two younger than you. But I'm damn near old enough to coach it! It's a bloody mess, war is. Have you gotten in too deep? Can you still get out of it?"

"I'm pretty well connected, I guess."

"Well, get yourself the cushiest job you can find, and from then on keep your mouth shut, your bowels open, and never volunteer. That's what our fellows say."

"We had a fellow named Smollett at our house about a month ago."

"I know Smollett. He's all right. I know his brother in England,

and I've run across your Smollett here and there in my tours. But how old would you say he is, your Smollett?"

"It's hard to tell about an Englishman, but I'd say he was about thirty-five."

Bartholomew nodded slowly. "Tommy is twenty-six or -seven. You see? An Englishman usually looks a great deal younger than he is, but that's what war can do to you. And he was only twenty-three or -four when he went in. Stay out of it, Sidney."

Sidney laughed. "I hope you don't mind my saying so, but you're a hell of a propagandist."

"Oh, on the contrary, I'm very good. But the minute I spotted you the first thing I remembered was your all-around kindness to the fellows in our form. Whenever one of your fellows got too nasty with us you always put a stop to it. Say—that's funny, you marrying Brock Caldwell's sister. Didn't you and he have some feud?"

"We did indeed."

"It must have turned out all right."

"Between us, it didn't, but the world's a big place. Brock and I see each other as little as the law allows."

"He in the Army or anything?"

"Not yet, but I suppose he will be."

"He ought to be. What we call a brass hat. High rank. Gloves and swagger stick. Staff car. A mistress in St. John's Wood. I can see him with all that because I know a fellow actually looks like Brock and that's what he is. Brock ever marry? I'll bet he didn't."

"No. What about you, Joe?"

"Oh, yes. I married an English girl. We have two peaches-and-cream daughters, just getting old enough to know that Daddy isn't nice to Mummy. Another woman. There's a fairy hangs around our garden gate, waiting to kiss the hem of Rose's garment. I don't think he's done any more, so I guess he's a fairy. He's in his forties, a clergyman, and has a wife of his own and a couple of kids, but he's around our house two or three times a week, telling Rose how noble and long-suffering she is. Which she may well be. We're sticking it out till the girls get married off—if there's any young men left in England by that time. How often have you been blessed, Sidney?"

"Two boys and a girl."

"I imagine they keep you busy. What, uh, what's your line?"

"I'm a farmer."

"Well, a farmer's home most of the time. Keep an eye on each other. Before the war I was with a Philadelphia firm, Baldwin Locomotive, and I traveled all over the place, and being a somewhat less admirable man than I imagine you are, I sometimes would check my marriage vows at customs whenever I went to France or Russia, one of those bloody countries. In due course I was found out and that was when the fairy took over. You, Sidney? You pleased with the holy state of matrimony?"

"Oh, yes," said Sidney.

"You say it rather quickly, but I suppose you haven't given the matter a great deal of thought. Still, that may be the best sign of all. If you haven't had to think about it, it must be all right."

The two men suddenly lost interest in each other, and after a couple of polite efforts to break the silences Sidney remembered that he had a train to catch. The warmth of their parting was genuine enough, but they both knew that they never would meet again, unless by serious accident which they would take care to avoid.

Sidney sent Grace a telegram from the hotel and she met him at the station. She was standing at the platform gate, where she always stood. She waved her hand when she saw him, and he waved his hat. They said hello. All for the benefit of Fort Penn. But they did not embrace. The porter took Sidney's bag to the place on the driveway where he knew the Caldwells and the Tates always parked their cars, and Sidney got behind the steering wheel of the Mercer.

"What's the news?" said Grace.

"I won't know anything for a week or more. The head doctor

seemed to think I looked healthy enough, but he didn't know any more than that . . . I ran into an old classmate of Brock's."

"Who?"

"A fellow named Joe Bartholomew. He lost a leg or a foot in the British Army."

"I don't remember him," she said. "Should I?"

"No. He was a classmate, but no particular friend of Brock's."

"Then he must have been quite nice. Or one that *you'd* think quite nice."

"I liked him passably well . . . Now listen to me, Grace. I hope you're going to remember all the excellent advice I'm going to be giving you the next week or so."

"Are you joking?"

"A little. But seriously, don't feel you have to start admiring Brock just because you and I are breaking up. You were always very sound about Brock, and I wouldn't like to think you were beginning to like him just because I don't. Brock is a horse's ass. He always was, always will be, and you've known it all along. So just don't change your opinion of him on account of me."

"It's all right for you to tell me things about the farm, and business matters, but I'm not going to appreciate your advice about who I should like or not like. You're leaving me, so I'll like whoever I damn please. You're not just going away on a trip. You're leaving for good, so please don't try to influence my likes and dislikes."

"All right, if that's the way you want it." He was angered.

"That's the way it is."

"But don't get to liking too many men as much as you liked Mr. Bannon, or I'll come back to my farm and take my children and kick you the hell out. . . . I can be nasty, too, you know. Don't get snotty with me. I was trying to be agreeable just now, but when you start pulling this hoity-toity attitude, you haven't got a leg to stand on."

"Is that so? How interesting." She was about to hold forth when their progress was halted by the traffic semaphore.

The traffic officer stood on a small platform under an umbrella. He touched his stiff-brim Stetson. "You think it'll ever get cool again?" he said, speaking to Grace.

"I hope so, Oscar, for your sake," said Grace.

"How're you enjoying this weather, Mr. Tate?"

"Oh, not very much."

"This ain't the worst it was all summer, but hot weather don't ever agree with us fat men. Well, here you go," he said, smiling at Grace. He pushed the handle which gave them the Go-sign and turned the umbrella. Sidney shifted the gears, and when the car was in third speed Grace resumed her speech.

"I was about to say—"

"Yes, you were," said Sidney. "What were you about to say?"

"I was about to say, when we were stopped by the signal, how interesting, these threats about taking the children and kicking me the hell off the farm. Then Oscar Tillinghast stopped us. Very appropriate. You noticed he really spoke to me, not you. He was polite to you, but he was really talking to me."

"Well, you're a handsome woman. Nobody ever said you weren't."

"That had nothing to do with it. He speaks to me because he always *has* spoken to me. Just that way, too, Mr. Tate. It's the kind of thing you'd find out about if you ever went to law against me in this county. I don't care how bad *I've* been, if *you* went against me they'd laugh you out of court."

"Well, let's hope we're spared that embarrassment."

"It wouldn't embarrass me, not if you went into court and tried to ruin my reputation. In the first place, I don't think you could get a lawyer to take the case."

Sidney stepped on the gas before responding to her. They went weaving through the early evening traffic at a foolish speed until she protested: "Kill yourself, but I don't want to die," she said. "Let me out."

He slowed down to a moderate speed. He took off his hat and dropped it behind his legs. "I wanted to cool off," he said. "Miss

Caldwell, you're living in the Dark Ages." He held up a finger. "What you've been saying would have been true any time since we've been married—any time, up until about two months ago. But not any more. If I wanted to, I could take the children right now. And, what's more, O'Connell & Partridge, attorneys-at-law, they'd advise you not to appear in court."

"Oh-ho-ho. How little you know."

"How little *you* know. Listen to me, old girl, all the years we've been married I kept out of trouble for one reason, I loved you. That was reward enough for me. You were my wife, and everybody in this town knows I never as they say looked at another woman. I didn't want any reward, just your love. But I lost that. But—" He waved the finger slowly. "—But I gained something I never asked for, never counted on. The respect of the kind of people you draw your friends from. I know. I can tell by the way they look at me. I know it, and so would O'Connell & Partridge, and so would your brother Brock, Ham Schoffstal, Connie Schoffstal—maybe not Connie, she doesn't like me, but almost everyone else. Don't ever fight me in court. You won't win."

"Is that so," she said.

"Yes, it's so. You know damn well I never *would* go to court unless you became a real whore, but you watch your step or I'll have my own definition of what a whore is. We'll get our quiet divorce and it's right for the mother to bring up the children, but don't sit around here thinking you can behave like some female Miles Brinkerhoff. You can't."

"No? Well, don't you for one minute think you can talk to me like the Pope of Rome. We'd beat you in the courts if it took every cent we had."

"Who's we? You and Brock?"

"Brock, and the Williamsport branch, and Philadelphia. Dozens of people you haven't even seen. Some *I* haven't seen, but don't you forget this: my father once lent the Philadelphia branch a *million dollars* when they were in trouble, and he didn't know them very well. We didn't even used to send them Christmas cards, but when they were in trouble, Father didn't wait for them to ask him. He volunteered it."

"He got some nice stocks for that, too."

"He may have, but he took a chance on losing the whole million. Oh, you've been having a beautiful time taking this holier-than-thou attitude, telling me I was a slut and disgusting. Very well, give a dog a bad name."

"You gave yourself the name."

"But if you give a dog a name, he'll live by it. Now just you try, just try to make trouble for me, Sidney, and I'll fight you just as dirty as what you say I am. I'll have all the Penroses and Vares and everybody else on my side, you see if I don't. You imagine the Governor'd be on your side?"

"No."

"He certainly would not. And even if he did, we could have *him* thrown out."

"Say, there. I must have married the Czarina, or a Hapsburg."

"You'd find out there's nothing funny about it. You make your threats, but I say, never point a gun unless you're going to shoot."

"All right, I'll say it too. Don't point all this artillery at me unless you're going to shoot," said Sidney.

"You'll learn who has the cannon and who has the BB gun."

"Little David, that's me," said Sidney. They did not again speak until he turned the car into the lane at the farm, where they always slowed down to walking speed.

"A hateful mess, isn't it?" he said.

"Yes."

"A hateful, sorry mess," he said again, in the gloom of the walnut trees. She replied to him only when he stopped to let her out. She opened the door of the car but looked away from him and stayed in the seat until she spoke:

"Yes, and I wish you'd been the one that caused it. *I'd* have been *kinder* to *you*." Then she got out and went inside.

He backed the car into the garage, precisely and neatly straddling the drip-pan. Joe, the groom, watched the operation. "You're home sooner'n I thought," said Joe.

"No, I only planned to stay overnight," said Sidney.

"I don't know, I thought you'd be two-three days. Are you in the Navy?"

"I won't know for another week or so, Joe."

"How can they conduct a war then, if they lack the intelligence to know is a man fit to fight or isn't he? One single human being, and their shilly-shally, dilly-dally red tape takes them a week. It seems to me they oughta be able to tell by looking at you, you're sound in wind and limb, your teeth are excellent."

"I suppose so. I'll talk to you in the morning, Joe."

"I don't see you taking orders from the likes of them."

"Well, I'll have to learn," said Sidney. "See you after breakfast."

"I'll be wanting to talk to you in the morning about giving notice."

"Why? I want you to stay."

"No thank you. I'll stay till the Missus finds someone else, but not if it's going to take up in the months. Weeks only. To be candid and forthright, there's not enough work to keep me busy and we've nothing in the way of a show to prepare for. Therefore I've come to the conclusion that I'd better be leaving when you do."

"What about the children?" said Sidney. "They're counting on you."

"No they're not. They're more interested in motor cars and games and sports. Not horses. They either have it or they don't have it, b' the time they reach the use of reason. If you want my advice you'll sell all but the gray for Mrs. Tate and the sorrel for yourself. The sorrel goes well in harness or I'd say sell him too and when you come back from the war buy another like him. In the meantime you won't be needing me. Let that Pennsylvania Dutchman take care of the sorrel and the gray. It won't hurt him to be around a good horse or two. It won't hurt him at all."

"What's the matter with you, Joe? I gave you a raise two months ago. You got a woman on your mind?"

"I didn't bring up the subject of women, and nor should you.

I'm leaving, maybe I'm joining the Army. I could be a farrier. I know the work, God knows."

"Mrs. Tate depends on you."

"That's very flattering I'm sure, but I may get away from horses entirely. They pay very high wages in them shipyards."

"Oh, hell, you in a shipyard?"

"No? What about you a naval officer? There's changes going on all about us all the time. So, you'll want to see me after break-fast, then?"

"Yes," said Sidney. He studied Joe's flat blue eyes and thin lips, the mouth ever making a chewing motion whilst his upper and lower plates rested comfortably in a mug in the tack-room. If Joe had anything more to tell him he was not going to tell it except in so many well-chosen words. Sidney turned away and went to the house.

On the landing outside the bedroom he remembered that he had left his overnight bag in the Mercer and he waited a moment to see whether Joe would bring it to the house. He stood there some minutes and then decided there was nothing in the bag he needed and he opened the bedroom door. Grace was in a pongee dressing gown hanging up the linen suit she had worn to the sta-tion. Her back was turned.

"Why did you listen outside my door?" she said. "What did you expect to hear? Sobbing? Did you think what I just said in the car was me beseeching you to be kind to me? Did you think I'd be on my knees?"

"Oh, cut it out."

"Well, what did you expect? Why did you try to listen through the door? I knew you were there all the time."

"I was waiting for Joe to bring my bag," said Sidney.

"Well, here he comes now. He gave you plenty of time to eavesdrop. Is that the way you arranged it? 'Joe, in five minutes bring my bag up to my room.' That gave you plenty of time." She was looking out the window.

He took off his coat and tossed it on his bed and sat on the chaise-lounge. "You know, *this* is the low point of our marriage. This minute, Grace. We've never been as far apart as we are this minute. If the last minute hadn't happened, the things you just said, and what you accused me of—there might have been one chance in a thousand of our getting together again."

"I stopped asking for that chance," she said. "I told you you could go where you pleased, I was through."

"I know, but let me say this, will you? I did leave my bag in the car. I forgot it, because I had other things on my mind. To tell you the God's honest truth, what I had in mind was what you said in the car. That you'd have been kinder than I've been. That was the one thing you could have said, the only thing, that's had any effect on me. You got out of the car and I drove to the garage, took a minute or so backing in, but it was long enough for me to suddenly realize that you were right. If the circumstances had been reversed, I honestly think you'd have been kinder than I've been.

"So, while I was putting the car away, I was thinking how to say it to you, that maybe we ought to make another try at it. Our marriage. Not because of how long we'd been together, or the children, or anything else. But because simply on a basis of fairness. If the circumstances'd been reversed, you'd have been more tolerant. Kinder.

"Then I had a chat with Joe. I tried to break away from him but then he told me he was going to give notice and I tried to convince him he ought to stay. That took a few minutes. And by the way, he's not going to stay."

"Oh, he's your pet, not mine. I'd have fired him long ago, and I was going to fire him the minute you left."

"No matter. So I came in and up the stairs and then on the landing outside there I remembered my bag, and I thought Joe'd very likely see my bag in the back of the car and bring it up here, as he's done before many times. The delay outside on the landing gave me a chance to re-collect my thoughts, and also, which was more important, I could wait for Joe to bring the bag and give it to me out in the hall, and that would prevent his interrupting us when I started talking to you. In here."

"You should have been Omar Khayyam. This story'd save your head for one night at least."

"I insist on telling it, however, whether you believe it or not. Anyway, there's nothing left to tell. I waited, Joe didn't come, so I walked in here and immediately am accused of doing something that's so against my principles that it's as though you never knew me. As though we'd never had any intimacy of body or mind, Grace. I don't know how many million words we've spoken to each other, but apparently not one word, or not ten million words had the effect of showing you what I believe in. All this time you haven't been listening! Nothing I said, or did! for that matter, has taught you what kind of person I am. I would never read another person's letter without his consent, if my life depended on it. Or listen in on a telephone conversation, or stand outside your door or anyone else's door and eavesdrop. This is the low point of our marriage. I said that because I was so angry. Now I say it again, not because I'm angry, but because our marriage has been going steadily downhill, and this is as low as it can get. You've forgotten me." He laughed. "I'm almost tempted to make love to you, to see what you'd be like with another man."

"I'd advise you not to try it. If you came near me I'd hit you with that poker."

He laughed again. "Don't worry, kiddo. It was just an idea up here—" he tapped his head—"not down here"—he pointed to his groin.

He stretched out on the chaise-lounge. "During this interesting conversation another up-here idea occurred to me. I'll only take a minute of your time and then you can have your bath."

"What?"

"Just a second," he said. There was a knock on the door and Sidney opened it and took the bag from Joe, thanked him, and closed the door. "I hope he wasn't listening. Anyway, this is my idea. You see we've been so careful about appearances, I guess we might as well keep up until I go away. But we can make it easier for ourselves. Tomorrow why don't you join the children at the seashore. I won't go with you, but I'll leave with you. You pack your bags and so will I mine and we can leave here together in the Mercer and I'll drive you as far as Philadelphia. To all intents and purposes we'll be going away together, but I won't go all the way to Cape May. I'll stay in Philadelphia for a few days and then come back here and wait for my instructions from the Navy. Then you can come back and bring the children with you so I can see them before I go away, and that will be that. What do you think?"

"I think it's a very good idea. I don't see how we can go on sleeping in the same room," said Grace.

"I don't either. You know, I've often cursed myself these recent weeks because I didn't do what I said I was going to do last year, namely, build a sleeping porch outside this room."

They later agreed upon one alteration in Sidney's plan: instead of his driving Grace to Philadelphia he would accompany her to the early train that left Fort Penn at 7:05 the next morning and made a connection for Cape May. If she saw anyone she knew she would say that Sidney was motoring down. Accordingly, he took her to the station, saw her to her seat in the Pullman, and left the city of Fort Penn almost as soon as she did. The difference was that he had no idea where he was going.

He headed eastward on the Reading Turnpike and one of the first signs he noticed gave the mileage to Lebanon. "Paul!" he said. "I'll pay a surprise call on my best man."

He had not seen Paul since before the Bannon trouble. Paul sometimes played golf at Fort Penn, and in the recent motorized years he often came to Fort Penn without letting Sidney know he was coming or was in town. Lebanon was only about the same distance from Fort Penn as the round trip between the Caldwell town house and the farm, and Paul had a handsome green Locomobile touring car that shuttled back and forth from Lebanon to Fort Penn and Lebanon to Reading, so that it was not discourteous of him to fail to telephone Sidney every time he was in the immediate neighborhood. Sidney and Grace, on the other hand, had visited Lebanon only four times since their wedding. Despite the relatively short distance, their visits were made big occasions by Paul's still living parents, and Paul, who understood people, understood that from the Tates' point of view father and mother offered friendliness but not informality, and that therefore Sidney and Grace considered the visits a social chore.

Less than an hour after Grace's departure Sidney was in Lebanon—too early to go to Paul's office. He had a second breakfast at the hotel and after eating he sat on the hotel porch and smoked his pipe. Shortly after nine o'clock he saw Paul in the Locomobile, being driven to his office. He chuckled when he saw Paul taking a second look at the Mercer, which was parked near the hotel but not in front of it. Knowing Paul, Sidney anticipated correctly the activities of the next few minutes: the Locomobile stopped in front of Paul's office; Paul got out and entered the office; the telephone rang inside the hotel; the clerk came out on the porch and asked Sidney if he happened to be Mr. Tate, and if he was would he please call Mr. Paul Reichelderfer. "I'll do better than that," Sidney told the clerk. "I'll go to his office."

Paul rose to greet his friend. "I *said* I knew that car, and no town man has a Mercer. You didn't sleep at the hotel, because they didn't have your name on the register, but—come on, now Sidney, explain yourself."

"I came to see *you.*"

"Well, I hope so. I'm glad you came today instead of yesterday, too. Yesterday I wouldn't have been here. I was down in Atlantic City with my parents. They're spending the summer in Chelsea. It's good for them. But hereafter let a fellow know you're coming so he'll be sure and be here, Sidney. You don't come often enough so's it is, and I wouldn't want you to waste a trip. How's Grace, and the children?"

"Oh, all well, thanks. Listen, fellow, you have a day's work to do. Suppose I kill time driving around and I'll meet you for lunch at your house."

"Well, I don't want to send you away, but I can find plenty to keep me busy this morning, first day back at my desk. Can you spend the night, Sidney?"

"Be delighted to. Grace went to the seashore this morning, so I'm a free man. Children are there, too, so—sure, I'd be glad to spend the night."

"I tell you, what if I don't eat lunch with you but knock off here about two-thirty or three and we can find something to do? I'd take you out to the farm, but I guess you get all the farming you want, and anyhow our home here is cooler than out on the farm. Mrs. Lichtenwalner, you remember our housekeeper, she keeps the shades down and it's real pleasant. If you want to go for a swim we can go out to the farm, but I recommend our home. I'll tell Mrs. Lichtenwalner to be ready for you any time."

Sidney made a mobile inspection of the nearby countryside until the sun was high overhead. When he had seen more Holsteins than he, a Jersey fancier, wanted to see again for a long while, and had been reminded too often that the Lebanon County farms got more out of their land than he did out of his, he doubled back to the town and the Reichelderfer home. Mrs. Lichtenwalner fed him bologna, somersausage, ham, cold chicken, baked sausage, tongue, lamb, potato salad, pickled beets, endive salad, cherry pie, beer, and coffee. After lunch he took off his shoes and lay down on the large double bed in his room, and when he got awake it was past four o'clock and vaguely he could hear Paul and the housekeeper softly sing-songing a conversation in Pennsylvania Dutch. He dampened his face at the marble-topped wooden washstand, with its swan-necked hot and cold water spigots, in his room. His suits had been pressed and were hanging in the closet, his shirts and B. V. D.'s and ties and socks and handkerchiefs were laid away. His shoes were polished and stuffed with newspapers to serve as trees. These attentions were remarkable enough in themselves, but in addition there was the fact that when he lay down on the bed he had not even unpacked his bag, but had set it on the floor at the foot of his bed. Most touching was their (whoever it was) covering him with a light quilt while he slept. He looked out the front window and it was no surprise to him that his car was no longer there. He went downstairs and out and under a grape arbor to the rear of the back yard, where Paul was lying in a hammock in the shade, reading the *Reading Eagle*.

"You're taking your life in your hands when you get into a hammock," said Sidney.

"Sail canvas," said Paul. "Special for me, this hammock."

"Trees have to be pretty strong, too."

"They are. These trees grew up with me. They wouldn't let me down, Sidney. That's a joke," said Paul. "Well, you can have beer or lemonade. At this time of the day I admit I take a pitcher of lemonade and a crock of cookies."

Through the open door of the carriage house Sidney could see his car, washed and polished, and inside, while the Locomobile stood out in the sun. He decided to make no comment on that.

"Maybe you'd rather iced tea or iced coffee. Iced coffee may wake you up. You must have been tired, old man."

"I guess I must have been," said Sidney. "I think I must have some Southern blood. The few times in my life I've taken a nap after lunch I've slept like a log."

"Southern? My father's taken a nap every day as long as I can remember, and there's no Southern blood in him. No, I tell you what it is. It's the climate. We have as hot in summer as most Southern states, and those that can, we ought to take a nap. I usually do. If I don't I fall asleep anyhow about three o'clock, so I might as well stretch out and be comfortable . . . You look rested, Sidney. You needed that nap."

"I suppose so. I haven't been sleeping well," he said. "You're right about the Pennsylvania climate, Paul. I don't know about farther north, but it certainly gets hot as hell in Nesquehela County, and here too, judging by today."

"Farther north you have another proposition. Farther north in Pennsylvania it gets as cold in winter as Canada. I'm surprised you never went after bear up-state. You like to shoot."

"Grace has some cousins that live up-state. They have asked me, but I consider myself a farmer, you know, and when winter comes I like to take it easy. As a matter of fact, when winter comes—well, you know what we do. We become town people. Children in school. We go out quite a bit. Trips to New York, Philadelphia. The fact of the matter is, the winters are too short for me."

"We're going to have rain. Hear that thunder?"

"Uh-huh."

"It's going to come over the mountains—I just got a drop."

"Uh—so did I."

"Let's go sit on the side porch. I like to watch the rain. I wax deeply philosophical when it rains. Descartes, Spinoza, Aquinas. I got them beat all hollow when I'm watching the rain."

"Do you know your car's out in the rain?"

"It won't be for long. Lamarr'll see to that."

"Who's Lamarr? Is he the mystery man that unpacked me and everything?"

"Lamarr Hoy. With that name he sounds like one of us Dutchmen. And maybe he is, half. He's a black man, but he talks Pennsylvania Dutch and has that name. He came around one day when we still had the horses. Just started helping out. Wasn't asked, and *he* didn't ask, but he made himself so useful that the man we had working for us let him sleep in the hay-loft, and I guess Mrs. Lichtenwalner saw he had enough to eat, and my father gave him a few dollars every Monday—not Saturday. Saturday my father figured Lamarr'd get drunk, so he paid him Monday. Then one day Earl, the regular man, died, and my father bought Lamarr a suit of clothes and a derby hat and we had the smartest, most loyal coachman, handyman, jack of all trades you ever saw. Only don't leave any money around. He'll steal it."

"Is he a drinker?"

"No. That's the funny thing about Lamarr. He has no bad habits except chewing. Doesn't smoke, doesn't drink, and he's getting a little old now for a wench. But he steals money. Mrs. Lichtenwalner carries her own money around in a pocket in her petticoat, so it's safe there. But the house money she has to change the hiding place every week or Lamarr'll catch on, and it'll disappear. If I left a pile of silver and some paper money on my bureau, in ten minutes it'd be gone. The way drunkards smell out booze, that's the way Lamarr smells out money."

"What does he do with it?"

A thunderclap caused Paul to wait before answering. He laughed. "He puts it in the bank."

"He what? In *your* bank?"

"Yes sir. Lamarr takes the money and puts it in our bank. The last time I looked Lamarr had a savings account of over two thousand simoleons. That's pretty good for a man that gets six hundred dollars a year pay. I said to him one day last year, I said, 'Lamarr, you're a thrifty man so I suppose when you pass on you'll have a sizable sum to leave somebody. Have you ever thought of making a will?' 'That I have,' he said. 'That's all taken care of. My estate goes to Mrs. Lichtenwalner that picked me out of the gutter.' Mrs. Lichtenwalner no more picked him out of the gutter than you did, and I had a sentimental idea Lamarr was stealing this money and then would leave it to us. It'd make a good story that way. But nobody knows Lamarr."

"Maybe Lamarr thinks Mrs. Lichtenwalner is the real boss around here, and that's his way of keeping in her good graces."

"The only thing wrong with that theory is that she doesn't know she's the potential heiress, and he asked me not to tell her. No, I guess it was the fact that she gave him *food* in the beginning, and my father only gave him impersonal things, like money. It stands to reason Lamarr can't repay Mrs. Lichtenwalner with food, but by naming her as his legatee he shows his gratitude in a dignified, practical way. That's as close as I can come to an explanation."

"It's a good analysis," said Sidney.

They watched the downpour for a few minutes, and rocked slowly in the white wicker chairs. Then there was a great flash of lightning, followed in a couple of seconds by the loudest thunder of the storm.

"Jesus, that was close!" said Sidney.

"Eight seconds to the mile, they say," said Paul.

"Then that wasn't more than an eighth of a mile away," said Sidney.

"There was a friend of mine killed playing golf over in Reading this Spring. Maybe you read it in the paper."

"What?"

"I said there was a friend of mine, Lou Weissinger, struck by lightning. He was playing golf at the Berkshire Club. About the latter part of May, early June."

"I'm sorry, Paul, I wasn't listening. I was wondering what it must be like to have that kind of noise for hours at a time."

"In battle, I guess you mean?"

"Yes," said Sidney. "I took an examination for the Navy the other day, and I ought to be hearing soon. About a week."

"What do you want, enlisting at your age, with a wife and three children? War's for the young fellows, not the middle-aged like us."

"I don't see it that way. I consider myself damn lucky to be able to go. I don't like the idea of killing, but at the same time I honestly believe every man ought to be in at least one war."

"That's a philosophy, but I don't care so much for it."

"You don't?" said Sidney in surprise. "You're a German. The Germans are a war-like race."

"So they seem, and my blood is all German, but I don't care for war, and neither does my father. I had two uncles in the Civil War, and 'way back we had ancestors in the Revolutionary War."

"Which side?"

"Both sides. My mother's people had one or two, and my father's had some."

"I meant which side of the war. Were they in the Continental Army or were they Hessians?"

"Oh, I see," said Paul. "Well, maybe I had some ancestors with the Hessians. I don't know. But I was speaking of the ones I do know a little about. They were on the colonists' side. If you'd like to inquire whether I'm pro-German, you don't have to do it that way, Sidney, by genealogical research. Just ask me point-blank."

"All right. Are you?"

"No. Not when the Germans, the Central Powers, are the enemy of the United States. If Germans were fighting, uh, Italians, I'd be for the Germans, maybe about as strongly as I am for Yale against Harvard. Maybe not quite so strongly ... Am I under suspicion, Sidney? I'm beginning to think I am."

"No, but you have to admit you're pretty matter-of-fact about the war."

"I don't see what else I can be. I couldn't get in the National Guard when they went to Mexico. It was a foregone conclusion, but I tried, just for the hell of it."

"Oh, I don't think you could have got in."

"No, and I didn't either, and I don't want to take any credit for trying. But, just for the hell of it, I made the effort," said Paul. There was a flash, and they waited out the thunder. Paul shifted his big body, recrossed his legs and rubbed an ankle. "I think you have this coming to you, Sidney: you know my people were settled here and had villages and towns named after them a hundred years before the Tates *thought of* leaving England. More than a hundred years. Closer to two hundred. My mother's name was Allbrecht. Tonight when you go to bed I'll give you a book, the Allbrecht family history. Read some before you go to sleep, it'll be instructive. I don't know how we compare with the Caldwells. We came later, I guess, but if you have time tomorrow I'd like to take you out and show you the dates on some Reichelderfer headstones."

Sidney smiled. "I had it coming to me. I'm sorry, Paul."

"Well, we both got that nonsense out of our systems. Good thing for the two of us, I hope. I got rid of my ancestor boasting in front of you, instead of getting my dander up in front of some son of a bitch I shouldn't condescend to answer ... What do you feel like doing this evening?"

"Oh, shooting the bull with you, I guess. I hadn't given the matter any thought," said Sidney. "It's peaceful here."

"Shooting the bull is always fine with me, but if you'd like to play cards I could arrange for a couple of tables of bridge, or there's a poker game . . . Oh, that's right, you never did join the Masons, did you?"

"No."

"There's a poker game at the Shrine tonight, but it's more or less limited to members."

"Rather warm for a poker game, don't you think?"

"Yes, it is, even with the electric fans . . . Well, I don't want to lead you astray, and it's warm for *it*, too, but we could drive to Reading and cool off on the way, and who knows? We might get our ashes hauled. It's never too warm for that."

"Let's see how we feel after dinner."

"It's over two weeks for me, staying with my parents, so I'm almost ready for some female consolation."

"Change the subject, here comes Mrs. What's-Her-Name," said Sidney. "This rain'll cool it off."

Mrs. Lichtenwalner spoke through the screen door: "Supper'll be ready in five minutes if you young men want to wash."

"No time to take a bath, Mrs. Lichtenwalner?" said Paul.

"There was time, but not now no more. You should of thought of that earlier instead of talking. I made a cheese soufflé and that's not going to wait on any splashing around the bathtub. I don't know about you, Mr. Tate, but Paul's good for an hour when he takes a bath. Poor little boy, he has so much skin to soap."

Paul, with a straight face, said, "We used to make better time when she'd lather me, but she has a new fellow."

"Oh, go on, you stop, Paul Reichelderfer, giving wrong impressions," said Mrs. Lichtenwalner. "I never gave him a bath since he was three at the most."

"You don't have to pretend in front of Sidney. He knows all my secrets."

"Absolutely," said Sidney.

"Oh, now you too, Mr. Tate. What if somebody overheard

you, Lamarr or somebody. Go on up and wash your face and hands now. Skedaddle."

The two men had no chance for private conversation during the meal; Mrs. Lichtenwalner, with her arms folded, stood near the kitchen door, relating how she had put in her time all day; what she had talked about with the hired girl (who was not being allowed to serve this meal), and an up-to-the-minute report on the house's state of repair.

"Will you be out late tonight, Paul? There's a prayer meeting and I'll be home around nine, if you want me to lock up."

"Yes, Mrs. Lichtenwalner, we'll probably be out late. We may be carousing around till daylight. We're thinking of going to Reading to a sporting house."

"You know he thinks he always fools me with that kind of talk, Mr. Tate. He says these terrible things and makes them so terrible I'm supposed to think they're so terrible he'd never do them. But if you ask me, he does do them. He goes and does them, and he thinks he has me hornswoggled. Oh, no. Not me. I've lived too long. And I know the men he does these things with. I could name them. The Shrine loafers, and the poolroom loafers."

"Tonight it's a Fort Penn loafer," said Paul.

"Oh, no. Not Mr. Tate. A man with a wife like Mrs. Tate has no time for those other kind. I know. I've lived too long."

"Come on, Sidney, we'd better get out of here or she'll spoil our evening." Paul tried to sound as though the kidding were still on, but the three of them knew that the conversation had gone beyond rough little jokes. Paul and Sidney got up from the table and the old woman bowed slightly and said good night to them, with a look half censorious, half pleading.

The men moved to the side porch, Paul carrying a bottle of crème-de-menthe from the sideboard. He poured it over the ice in two wine glasses, and they lighted cigars. The rain had stopped and the air was a little cooler.

"I've told you about her, haven't I?" said Paul.

"You mean her past life? I don't think so," said Sidney.

"Her husband was killed, oh, thirty years ago or more. More. I only know about it from stories I've heard. He was humping some woman here in town, a railroader's wife, and the husband came home and gave them both barrels, or maybe it was before they had double barrels. Anyway he killed them and killed himself. She I think was either going to have a baby or just did have one. Whichever it was, it never lived."

"Whose baby? The murdered woman's?"

"No, no. Mrs. Lichtenwalner. I never inquired very much into that side of the story, but either she was in the family way or had a small baby that died soon after this thing happened. I think she was in the lunatic asylum for a while, and then my mother got her out and gave her a job."

"Jesus."

"What?" said Paul.

"Well, I don't know, but it's not my affair, but it seems to me you're rather rough with her, considering her past history."

"I use psychology on her, Sidney. People like Mrs. Lichtenwalner, if you once start bottling them up, some day you'll have a real problem on your hands. Whenever I see this church-missionary business coming on I talk as down to earth as the law allows."

"Really? Did you always talk that way to her?"

"Well, I started when we were at Yale. That was when she began trying to keep an eye on me and naturally I resented her sticking her two cents in my business, but then I heard her story and I began talking that way to her. It was a kind of a treatment. You know if you take too much of some drugs they don't have any effect on you. A small dose of some drugs will kill you, but a big dose won't have any more effect than a glass of Benedictine."

"I've heard that, yes," said Sidney.

"I was always fond of her, and she was fond of me, too. Confidentially, she used to let me play with her tits when I was around twelve, thirteen."

"She did!"

"Sure, don't act surprised. Didn't you ever get fresh with the servants around your house?"

"No . . . Well, not in my own house. There was another fellow, we used to wrestle with a chambermaid at his house and I guess I got my pants wet with her."

"The same idea," said Paul. "But in Mrs. Lichtenwalner's case it wasn't wrestling."

"Is that all she'd do?"

"That's all. It was enough."

"How did it happen to stop there? I mean, if she was willing I'd have thought she'd have got all worked up and made you go through with the whole business."

"How did you stop with that chambermaid? You get scared or disgusted. I wasn't either one, I don't think, but what I did, I fell in love with a girl my own age. Young puppy love, and besides, I went away to boarding-school."

"Was Mrs. Lichtenwalner pretty? Didn't you want to play with her again when you came home for the holidays?"

"Maybe I wanted to, but I didn't. You see, I don't think she admitted to herself that she was getting any excitement out of it, and I grew up very fast, all of a sudden. I came home from school with my first long pants and Mrs. Lichtenwalner most likely thought to herself, this is a man. The person she used to let fondle her tits—that wasn't sinful. I was a child. But not with long pants. There I was a man. And as far as I was concerned, I was around the age when I could hardly wait to go to a whore house for the first time."

"I thought you said you were in love with somebody your own age then."

"I was, but you're trying to make things too neat, Sidney. You were raised in New York, and I guess the boys in the big cities get a different upbringing. In small towns you know all about whore houses and who the whores are from the time you're ten years old. Maybe you don't end up going to one, but you talk about it. I know some fellows that their own fathers took them to a whore house."

"I've heard of that," said Sidney.

"Well, and didn't you ever hear of a young fellow being in love with a decent girl, and going to a whore house? Sure you did."

"Yes, I did."

"Well, that's how I was. I was in love with a little girl, but I wanted to tell you about Mrs. Lichtenwalner. After I stopped fooling around with her I didn't stop being fond of her, and when I got to college and took psychology I used to think of her, particularly after I read in several books how a lot of young kids fool around with older women—*and,* a lot of older women fool around with young kids. So I used to think of her somewhat the same as if I were a doctor and she were my patient. And that's why I'm so outspoken with her. She thinks I use it as an excuse to cover up my, uh, peccadilloes, but she doesn't know what's behind it all. All I'm doing you might say is lancing the boil, seeing that too much pus doesn't gather."

"Didn't you ever want to be a doctor, Paul?" said Sidney.

"I did for a while, but not after I found out what it would have cost me."

"Why, your father has plenty of money. I'll bet he'd have been elated."

"The money's not the only cost. Time. Study. Hard work."

"Phi Beta Kappa," said Sidney.

"That wasn't hard for me. I did that because my parents sent me to Yale to get an education, and if you want to get an education you have to study, and at Yale if you study you'll most likely make Phi Bete. I owed that to my parents. But once I was educated, at least to their satisfaction, I decided I owed myself a good time, and you can't have a good time and be the kind of doctor I'd have wanted to be."

"What kind is that?"

"A mental doctor. Not a quack, or a phrenologist, and not a brain surgeon, either. A mental pathologist, you might call it. A psychologist, neurologist—oh, hell, there's no one title covers it. But I would like to, or would have liked to have been the kind of doctor that takes cases like Mrs. Lichtenwalner, only a lot worse, and does something for them. It's practically a whole new profession these days. You never hear much about it, and I only hear a little myself. Regular doctors don't have much time for it. It's psychology. Psychology literally means the study of the mind, the spirit, the soul. But this is more than that. Ah, hell, let's go to Reading. I made my decision years ago. My decision was to go to Reading whenever I felt like it. You feel like it?"

"I might as well," said Sidney.

Paul had half risen in his chair. "Wait a minute," he said. He sat down again. He puffed on his cigar and studied Sidney for a moment. "I would have been a poor doctor. I'm a poor host, and I'm a terrible friend."

"The hell you say," said Sidney.

"You're in town twelve hours," said Paul. "You came to me for help—I know you did. Some kind of help. Even if it was only decent friendship. And all I did was pay attention to my own business, and talk about myself, and worry about my own pleasure. Sidney, you ought to slap my face."

"No, no, no. You're an excellent host. The best."

"If you went out in the street and threw stones at me I'd deserve it."

Sidney laughed. "Well, I'm not planning to do that."

"The reason I'm so ashamed of myself is I know why you came here, and I've known it all along in the back of my mind. It's Grace, isn't it?"

"Yes, we're separating. How did you know?"

"I'll try to make up for my rudeness, my lack of consideration, by being an honest friend. I heard you and Grace weren't getting along."

"And I suppose you heard the reason."

Paul ran his hand across his forehead. "Yes, I heard *that.*"

"A fellow named Bannon?"

"Yes. Roger Bannon. I know him. I haven't seen him lately," said Paul.

"He's in the Army. Gone away."

"No, but before that, he avoided me. He knows I'm a friend of yours."

"It's too God damn bad the son of a bitch couldn't avoid my wife as well as my friends," said Sidney.

"Yes."

"It's no use beating about the bush. Not you. Me. I'll say it. She had an affair with him, slept with him God knows how many times, had secret codes over the telephone so they could meet. She cuckolded me, she disgraced the children, ruined her reputation, and what else she did to me I don't know. If you want to see a crazy man, take a look at one. You don't need to go to any lunatic asylum. If you were the kind of doctor you wanted to be, I'd be your patient all right. But I doubt if you could do anything for me. I'm through, licked. Jesus Christ Almighty! How she could do that to me, how one human being could do that to another. I lived for nothing but her, I made her life my life. I've been decent, honest, and faithful to her. I've kept from making mistakes, helped her bring up the children and kept her from making mistakes with them, without her even knowing. And love. Hell, I won't even mention love . . . Paul, if you don't mind, I'm going to drink whiskey."

"Help yourself, there's the bottle."

"Let's get started for Reading, and take the bottle with us. Is the priceless Lamarr going to drive us?"

"No, I'll drive."

"That's good. I won't have to watch my language."

They stepped down to the garden path, heading for the garage.

"You're neither a poor host nor a poor doctor," said Sidney. "This is the first time I've shot off and you're the only man I know of I could have done it with. I feel better already."

"Do you? That's good." Paul was skeptical.

"I *don't*, frankly, but I'm going to, so don't you worry about me."

The green Locomobile, polished, dry, was waiting out in front of the house.

"That's a one-man top," said Sidney. "Let's put it down."

"If it rained again we'd never get it up again," said Paul. "To tell the truth, we've never had it down."

Sidney examined the top. "I can see that now. It wasn't made to be put down. Well, I guess we'll get enough air."

"We can open the windshield, that lets in all the air you want."

"That's good, I may need it, because I plan to finish this bottle before we get to Reading. Not all alone, of course. I'll ask you to join me from time to time, when I remember my manners."

They drove out of the town and Sidney began taking small but frequent mouthfuls of the whiskey. After a few of them Sidney broke the silence. "You know, Paul, you're a very unusual fellow, especially for a best man."

"So?"

"So," said Sidney. "I think you'd have made a *good* doctor. You let me fly off the handle, and that helped me get rid of excess steam."

"Only temporarily, Sidney. You know that."

"Yes, but it was a good thing I did. But there was another thing you *didn't* do. You didn't try to defend Grace."

"What would be the good of my defending Grace?"

"None, probably, but you were our best man, and in this kind of situation one would expect the best man to try to patch things up."

"Between two headstrong people like Grace and you? I wouldn't try that. And anyhow, maybe it's a good thing, you two separating."

"Now that's interesting," said Sidney. "Why?"

"I shouldn't have said that, but I let it slip out, so it's too late to take it back," said Paul.

"You mean I made a mistake marrying Grace?"

"Not exactly made a mistake marrying her, but yes, maybe it was a mistake. Sidney, you should have had a job or a profession. You know, no matter how hard you worked on the farm, you never got credit for being a worker, and that made you angry inside."

"Something you don't know is that I own the farm. I bought it years ago."

"That I didn't know, but it proves my point. I didn't know it, your best friend, so how were the Fort Penn people to know it."

"I didn't give a damn whether they knew it or not."

"Yes you did. You bought it secretly so you could have the secret satisfaction of saying to yourself, 'The hell with the bastards that think I'm living off Grace. *I* know I'm not.' But that isn't much of a satisfaction, not for long. Sooner or later you want to tell the bastards, but being Sidney Tate, you never do. So consequently you bottle it up inside you."

"Oh, I don't think so. I got enough satisfaction out of knowing I was paying my way, and better than paying my way."

"You didn't, or you wouldn't have just said that, 'paying my way and better than paying my way.' You have to have somebody know it, even if it's only me, one person. Nobody is as self-sufficient as you like to think you are. You do it better than anyone I ever knew, but sooner or later, Sidney, you need other people. It doesn't have to be a lot of people. Just one, maybe. But there it is, the fact that you need one other person, just one, that shows that—well, I tell you what it does. It breaks the ice. It breaks the illusion of satisfactory solitude. You see what I mean?"

"In other words, if I need one I might as well need 'em all."

"Yes, as far as being able to go through life without anyone else is concerned."

"But I wasn't alone by any means. I had Grace, and I had the children."

"Well you have to take into consideration that a man and wife have a different kind of relationship, particularly if they were married as long as you and Grace. You were in the habit of living with this woman, so she wasn't either an insider or an outsider. She was part of you. The children don't count. I never had any of my own, but your children I think are still too young to be people. As long as they depend on you for the essentials of life, food and shelter, they aren't people. They're intelligent animals, plus that you love them."

"True enough, I suppose, I had as many friends as I ever

would have had anywhere, Fort Penn, New York, Boston, London. You know who our friends are, like the Schoffstals and the Walls and the rest, but also I have friends like Victor Smith, Percy Hofstetter at the bank, Oscar Tillinghast the policeman—well, not Oscar. He's more a friend of Grace's. But a lot of people I see in the course of everyday life."

"Who's Victor Smith?"

"Oh, a very interesting old codger, has a harness shop in Fort Penn."

"Then I'll count him out. He's part of Fort Penn, and you've never considered yourself part of Fort Penn. Stop deluding yourself, or me, Sidney. You don't pick your friends from interesting old codgers that run harness shops."

"Well, you."

"Me, sure. But you don't think of me as Fort Penn. When we first went to Fort Penn we went on the train together, so in your mind I'm almost as much of a stranger as you are."

"All right, what's all this got to do with my having a job?"

"Simple. A job in a store or a bank, or a profession, either one would have put you in everyday association with Fort Penn people, helping them, competing with them, but seeing them, getting to know them at the same time they were getting to know you, and taking you for granted, and you'd take them for granted. Inside of two or three or five years they'd have got used to your ways, your New York accent."

"If you'll pardon my saying so, you Dutchmen certainly set great store by accents. When I first came to this part of the country I had as much trouble understanding you as you have me."

"It would have been the same if you spoke high German. The important fact is that it was different. I'm not saying your accent would have changed after five years. It would have been new and different for every new person you met. But those you were seeing every day, they would have taken you for granted and you them. The people you were working with, living with. They'd have gotten used to you."

"Damn nice of them."

"Well, you were in the minority, so more of *them* had to get used to *you*. That's no more than fair. You were the stranger, so it wasn't up to them to change. It was up to you. Or not change, but get used to each other."

"You think I would have been finally absorbed? I'm going to have another small sip of this fine Pennsylvania whiskey. Have some?" He drank and handed the bottle to Paul, who put it to the corner of his mouth and drank.

"And you think Grace and I could have made a go of it if I'd had a job?" Sidney went on.

"Now, now, Sidney. Not so neat again. You like everything to be so neat, and life doesn't work out that way. What I do think, if you'd had a job that would have got you mixing more with people and letting them get to like you, then you mightn't have had this chip on your shoulder for the Fort Penn people."

"And where does Grace come in?"

"That I'm not sure of, because only two people could ever know the facts. But my analysis of the situation is this: you got to resenting Fort Penn and what Fort Penn thought about you, and without your knowing it, maybe you got to thinking Grace was as much Fort Penn as she was your wife. Then maybe you got to thinking she was more Fort Penn than she was your wife. That way you could easily fall into the habit of neglecting her."

"Oh, no, Paul," said Sidney. "I'm sorry, but it won't hold water."

"I say this goes on in the back of your mind. I don't say you quarreled with her about it."

"Sometimes we did have discussions about it. I often told her that most of the Fort Penn people gave me a pain in the ass, and she understood that but thought I could make an effort, and I'd simply say I'd married her and not Nesquehela County."

"Well, maybe she resented your attitude. Maybe inside her *she* was thinking that *you* were a *stranger*. And Grace, unless she's changed, she never gave a damn what went on outside the county line."

"She kept herself busy enough inside the county line, I must say. In fact, right in the township. I understand she usually met this son of a bitch Bannon at the farm next to ours. . . . Be that as it may, you think it's a good thing we're parting company?"

"A separation may be a good thing. Personally I could never live with one woman longer than a month. I like my privacy too much."

"What if you'd married the little girl you were in love with when you were thirteen?"

"Every day of my life I ought to get down on my knees and thank the Lord I didn't marry her. She lives in town. She runs Christian Endeavor, and church suppers and all that."

"Have a drink on that," said Sidney.

"I sure will," said Paul. "Say, this is just about going to last us till Reading."

"Yes, I've been quietly warding off snakebite. I must say I'm enjoying myself, too, Paul. All this unburdening my troubles, I feel as if I were talking about some fellows I used to know, not myself at all."

"That's good."

"I'm even beginning to have a mild curiosity about what kind of women we're going to screw tonight."

"You can always depend on Minnie Faust."

"Minnie Faust is our hostess? Is that the same place we went to years ago?"

"Oh, hell no."

"Too bad," said Sidney.

"Why?"

"Well, there'd be something propitious, if that's the right word, if we went to the same place. You know, rounding out a cycle. Appropriate, maybe. I went to a whore house with you just before I met Grace, and now I'm going to another, now that we're broken up."

"You might get together again, you never can tell. Maybe after you come back from the war."

"Possibly, possibly. Bannon's away. It may depend on who gets there first," said Sidney. "She doesn't love Bannon, for Christ's sake. Sunbury. That was the place. Have you ever been to Sunbury, Paul?"

"Passed through it on the train."

"Yes, and you know what I'm thinking, too. You were my best man, and you made the reservation at Sunbury. Did you think it would end this way?"

"I didn't think it would end at all—and maybe it hasn't."

"The hell it hasn't, old boy. The hell it hasn't."

"Here we are," said Paul, stopping the car.

"This place? This beautiful example of middle-class respectability? It can't be. I expect something garish and ornate, something a lot more like the Schoffstal town residence in Fort Penn. Would I be impertinent if I asked if you ever did it to Connie Schoffstal? Grace always thought you'd make a nice couple."

"You'd be impertinent, but the answer is no. I don't think anybody ever did it to Connie Schoffstal."

"I don't either. Well, what do we do now?"

"Follow me," said Paul. He opened the outside door of the three-story brick house and they waited in the vestibule. He did not ring, but a woman's face appeared behind the glass of the inside door and the door was opened.

"Hello, Paul," she said. "Brought a friend, I see."

"Sidney Tate, from Fort Penn. This is Minnie Faust."

"Charmed," said Sidney.

Minnie was a pale thin woman with obviously dyed black hair. She wore a shirtwaist and skirt and carried a palm fan with advertising printed on it. The house was quiet as a house of sorrow, with only some little sounds stirring distantly in an upper story. Minnie led them into the front parlor and they took chairs.

"How's business?" said Paul.

She fanned herself. "Oh, miserable, miserable. You were away, weren't you?"

She spoke to Paul, but she did not take her eyes off Sidney.

"Sizing me up?" said Sidney.

"I always do," she said, not at all abashed.

"Yes, I was down at Atlantic."

"How is it there?" said Minnie. "I can open up there if I want to."

"I don't know, I didn't go any place this time."

"That's it," said Minnie. "You know if business was good there I can't see the Philadelphia crowd letting *me* open up. They'd have first choice. I could go there and open up and inside of a month I could go broke."

"You? With all your money?" said Paul.

"Oh, all my money. Nobody gets rich in this business. If everything goes all right you make a living and that's all. And now I hear the Army's going to start some raids. What's the matter with those people? The boys have to have a girl. If they don't they'll start buggering each other and what kind of an army will you have then? Not that they'll bother me, the Army ... You aint in politics, are you, Mr. Tate?"

"No."

"I didn't think so, but being's you're from Fort Penn I had to ask. Are you acquainted with Ed Wachtel over there?"

"No," said Sidney.

"He's an Allentown man but a great personal friend of the Governor and he knows a lot of people."

"I know him," said Paul.

"Oh, sure, I knew that, but I wondered about Mr. Tate."

"What do you do? Do you send out for the girls?" said Sidney.

"What makes you ask that?" said Minnie.

"It's the quietest place I've ever been in," said Sidney.

"I take that as a compliment," said Minnie. "That's the kind of a place I run. Ask Paul."

"Uh-huh," said Paul.

"Is that the kind of a place she runs, Paul?" said Sidney.

"Uh-huh."

"What would you care for in the liquor line?" said Minnie.

"I'd care for some whiskey, but while we're here I'd like to have a look at some feminine pulchritude," said Sidney.

"Keep your shirt on, Sidney," said Paul. "You'll see."

"What kind of whiskey?" said Minnie.

"Old Overholt," said Sidney.

"Water chaser, or beer?" said Minnie.

"Water," said Sidney.

Minnie left the room, and in a couple of minutes a woman of thirty or slightly more appeared, carrying a tray on which was a fresh bottle of Old Overholt. Her black gown had deep decolletage and was slit in the skirt half way up her thigh. She placed the bottle on a table, smiled, and went out, carrying the empty tray. In like manner a girl in a blue gown and another girl in a red gown, both cut like the black one, brought in glasses and a pitcher of ice water, and went away.

"Catch on?" said Paul. "They don't solicit. You have to say which one you want."

At that point Minnie returned and started to open the bottle. "Did you like any of those girls?" she said.

"Well, of the three of them I preferred the one in red," said Sidney.

"She's a very sweet little girl. She's been with me near a year. But you can have a look at some more."

"How many more have you got?" said Sidney.

"Well, that I don't divulge, Mr. Tate," said Minnie. She handed them their drinks. "I'll bet you like Sarita."

"Sarita? That's an unusual name," said Sidney.

"It's a combination of the two names Sara and Rita. It makes Sarita," said Minnie.

"I get it," said Sidney. "Let's see Sarita."

Minnie left again and in a moment a tall, very young peroxide blonde in a white gown made an entrance. She carried a lacquered Chinese cigarette box and offered it to the men. She held a match to their cigarettes and went out without smiling.

"I guess that's Sarita, the prize heifer, but she looks like cold canned salmon to me."

Minnie reappeared. "I heard what you said, but you're wrong,

Mr. Tate. She'll do anything you prefer. Most of my other girls will but not all, but Sarita leaves it up to you what you want."

"I like Sarita," said Paul.

"Yes, you'd like her, Paul. I thought of you," said Minnie.

"Let's have another look at the one in red," said Sidney.

"She liked your appearance, I heard her tell one of the girls," said Minnie, with as close to a smile as she had come.

"That's nice," said Sidney. "Maybe *I'll* charge her."

"We don't have to get sarcastic, Mr. Tate."

"All right," said Sidney. He ignored her and poured two fingers of the rye. Minnie went out and Sarita and the girl in the red gown came in.

"My name is Consuelo," she said. She put her hand on the back of Sidney's neck. "Do you want to go up now or wait a little?"

"Let's go up now," said Sidney. "That is, if you two will excuse us."

Sarita was sitting on Paul's lap and he was lowering the panels of her gown. "Minnie doesn't like that downstairs," said Sarita.

"But I do," said Paul. "Do you have any objections?"

"Hell, no, I don't care, if you make it all right with Minnie," said Sarita.

"I guess we're excused," said Sidney.

Consuelo led the way upstairs to a surprisingly spacious room at the back of the house. It had to be a large room to accommodate the bed, which was the size of a single and double bed and had a dozen pillows of assorted sizes and shapes and colors scattered over the red silk bedspread. The bed itself was low.

"Nobody ever got hurt falling out of that one," said Sidney.

"Yes they did," said Consuelo. "I did. Look." She parted the skirt where it was slit.

"Looks more like teeth marks to me," said Sidney.

"Here, silly, the black and blue. Feel, there's still a little lump."

"Yes, I can feel a little lump. Do you mind if I feel a bigger one?"

"If you wish," she said.

"Mm-hmm."

"That's enough for now," said Consuelo. "Don't get too anxious all of a sudden, shall we?" She drew away from him, out of his reach, and put her hands to the back of her neck and deftly removed some pins and let her hair fall down over her shoulders. "How do you like my crowning glory?" she said.

"Glorious. I've never seen anything like it."

"I have a friend that likes to see me parade for him with my hair down. It puts him in mind of his childhood sweetheart."

"Did she walk around for him with her hair down?"

"I don't know. I guess so, if it puts him in mind of her."

"What happened to her? Did she die, or did she grow old, or just change the color of her hair?" said Sidney.

"How should I know, silly? I guess she died."

"Dyed her hair, or died dead?"

"Died dead, passed away. How should I know?" She stood still for a moment and studied Sidney. It could be seen that she was preparing herself for an unusual evening. She turned her back and inspected herself in the full-length mirror on the bedroom side of the bathroom door. She suddenly became animated. "Do you know what I'd like, Bud?"

"No, but you can have it if you call me Sidney and not Bud."

"Sidney? That isn't a name you hear every day in the week."

"You would if I stayed here a week."

"Oh, I have off tomorrow if you were thinking of that. I have to go to my sister's in Newark, New Jersey, tomorrow. We been writing one another letters about this visit and she'd kill me if I put her off one more time."

"Oh."

"You could get one of the other girls for tomorrow and I'd come back the day after though."

"It wouldn't be the same," said Sidney.

"How do you know? It might be better. I don't know what you're like. A little fancy, I'll bet. Not *too* fancy, I hope though. Some things I won't do."

"Such as."

"Well, let's wait and see if you try them. But Sarita, she's only here a short while but none of the customers thought up anything Sarita won't do."

"Does she kiss?"

"Does she kiss? Sure. I mean, how do you mean kiss?"

"Just kiss."

"I know, but how do you mean kiss. We'll all kiss. You can't work for Minnie if you don't kiss."

Sidney nodded. "Will this Sarita hold hands?"

"How do you mean?"

"Just hold hands. She takes your hand and you take hers. Will she do that?"

"But how? I mean, what else?"

"Nothing else. Come here and I'll show you."

She moved toward him, instantly at his command, but slowly, and frowning. He put out his hand and she took it and let herself be drawn to his side at the edge of the bed. "Sit down," he said.

She obeyed him, and for a few seconds he held her left hand in both of his, then he let go.

"Like that," he said.

"My God, you're a queer one," she said. "Is that all?"

"That's all I mean by holding hands," said Sidney.

She thought a moment, nodding until by degrees she had categorized him as of her wisdom and experience. "Do you take dope?" she said.

"No," he said. "Why?"

"You didn't look it, I didn't mean that. But I was acquainted with some that did—and I *used to,* till it started to get the better of me. What I started to say, what made me ask was because some kinds of dope a man'll get his satisfaction just touching you with the tip of his fingers. You know what I mean?"

"Well, I'm afraid I'm cruder than that. Look at my fingers."

"Yeah! You got hands like a coal miner or a day laborer. Say, I'm not supposed to ask you, but what do you do for a living? You don't look like a person that digs ditches, the rest of you. And you talk like an aristocrat. But these hands!"

"I'm a farmer."

"Oh, a gentleman *farmer*."

"All right, a gentleman farmer."

"Does your wife like it—pardon me."

"That's all right."

"No, if you do the talking we have to listen, but if Minnie got a suspicion I asked you about your personal life she'd fire me for good."

"What were you going to ask me? Does my wife like what?"

"Well, I wondered if your wife liked to have those hands traveling over her. Is that why you wanted to know if Sarita would hold hands? Maybe that's what you like. You like to rub your rough hands on women. I know you're queer. You don't have to make up any pretenses with me, Sidney. I'm used to all kinds when I'm working in a first-class house like Minnie's. No two the same."

"Why do you think I'm queer?"

"Because you are. Aren't you? Don't get mad. Everybody is. I don't mean you're a fairy queer. I can tell you like a woman. But you got certain little things that have to be just right for you, or you don't get any pleasure."

"This is very enlightening. Let's have a drink."

"That's what you promised me when I promised you I wouldn't call you Bud. Let's have a couple or three juleps. Did you ever have a mint julep?"

"Yes, but I'd like some more."

Consuelo got up and went to a speaking tube, blew the whistle and called down: "Miss Minnie, will you please send up four juleps please?"

Consuelo turned away from the speaking tube. "Why don't you get rid of some of those clothes? Take off your coat, and your collar and tie and be cool. You might as well enjoy the cool after that hot spell."

Sidney removed coat, tie, and shirt.

"Look at those muscles!" said Consuelo. "I'll bet nobody ever said you weren't built like a farmer. Looks are deceiving all right.

You know that saying, don't judge a book by its cover? I never would of took you for a man with a lot of muscles and rough hands. You got a sunburn like a farmer, but so do the gulf players, the ones that play gulf at the Berkshire gulf links . . . Say, I had one of them tell me a joke the other day. This farmer had his farm next door to one of these gulf links and this particular day he was plowing the field and he found two of these little white gulf balls. You know what they look like. So he brought them home and his wife took a look at them and said, 'What are those?' And the farmer said, 'Those? Those are gulf balls.' 'Gulf balls?' she said. 'Well the next time you shoot a gulf don't only bring his balls home.' She thought a gulf was some kind of an animal."

"That's a corker," said Sidney. "Tell me, now, Consuelo. Give me some more information on why you think I'm queer."

"I hoped you wouldn't remember that. I could see I did wrong in saying it."

"Not at all. Maybe just the opposite."

"Why, just the opposite? Are you having trouble with your Missus? You are, I can tell. You don't go to houses much, do you?"

"No."

"I could tell."

"How?"

"Because you don't feel at home, here."

Sidney laughed. "The funny thing is, I feel very much at home. This room reminds me of a room I know very well."

"What? Your room at home?"

"No, not at my house, but a room I know very well."

"Well, that's what we're for. If you're having a little de-fugle-tee at home, that's where we get near half of our customers, husbands having de-fugle-tees at home. The wife getting on in years or frigid. I don't say your wife is one of those, but there's a reason why you came here. Well, this is the right place. You can trust any of we girls. You won't take any African toothache home with you from this house. Minnie makes us get examined every Monday, every single Monday, no matter how many customers we had or didn't have, we go to the doctor every single Monday."

"That's very reassuring," said Sidney.

There was a knock on the door. "Drinks, ma'am," said Willomena.

"Oh, here we are, the juleps," said Consuelo.

Four juleps were on the tray that was brought in by a uniformed young café-au-lait-skinned girl. "Miss Minnie said if you want some more, call down, but she only sent four because she didn't want the ice meltin' and spoilin' the julep."

"Do I pay now?" said Sidney.

"No sir," said the colored girl.

"What about a tip for you?"

"If you want to," said the girl.

Sidney gave her two dollars and she departed.

"Thanks, Willomena," said Consuelo. She watched Sidney. "Isn't she beautiful for a colored girl?"

"Yes. What did you call her? Wilhelmina?"

"No, Willo-mena. It's the same name as her mother. Her mother has a house in the colored section but she put Willomena in here because she didn't want her to go to waste. Willomena has a couple regulars. She makes twenty or twenty-five a week clear. The two you tipped her, that's all she'd get for a piece in her mother's house. We all think the world of her because she knows her place and don't try to flirt with our customers. Notice she never smiled or took notice to you even to say thanks."

"Well, why should she?"

"Why should she? She shouldn't. But you take a certain class of white girls in this business, if you gave them a two-dollar tip for serving drinks you couldn't get rid of them. Of course if she aroused your interest I can easily get her back. I have no objections if you care to have her back. Would you like that, Sidney?"

"Well—we seem to be getting along all right."

"That's what I trust, but if you change your mind, I have no objections. Here's happy days," said Consuelo, raising her mint julep.

"The very best," said Sidney. They drank deeply. "Speaking of queer, you're a bit queer yourself, aren't you, Consuelo?"

She raised her eyebrows and pointed her thumb at the door, and Sidney nodded.

"Didn't I just get finished telling you everybody is?" said Consuelo.

For the first time Sidney liked her, and he put her back among the pillows and had her as a person and not merely as a bought body.

When she had attended to herself and returned to him he was lying with his hands at the back of his neck, staring at the ceiling.

"Don't get up, I'll take care of you," she said, and did so. "I'm safe, but it's better in your mind. You won't start worrying when you go home." She lit cigarettes and lay beside him.

"I just got a big surprise," she said.

"You did? Tell me about it."

"Tell you about it? You're it. You're the surprise."

"Why am I?"

"Well, all that palaver before, you had me sizing you up all wrong. All you were, you just needed a piece. Isn't that it?"

"I guess so. I feel fine now."

"That's good. I can't make out whether you're married or not. Which is it?"

"I'm married."

"Well, curiosity killed the cat, so here goes: is your wife in the family way or what? Sick or something?"

"Nope."

"You don't care to talk about her with a prostitute."

"I don't care to talk about her."

"I'm sorry," said Consuelo.

"You have nothing to be sorry for."

"Not me. You. I'm sorry for you. I'm sorry for her, too, but not as sorry."

"Why are you sorry for me?"

"What I mean is, I'm sorry she has another fellow. It don't take any mind-reader. The way you said you didn't care to talk about her, I didn't have to have any weejee board to guess what the matter was. Well, I hope if you come to Reading often you'll always come here and ask for me."

"Do you get any, uh, thrill out of this?"

"If I had a dollar for every time I was asked that question."

"All right, I'll give you a dollar if you'll answer it this time."

"Oh, it isn't the money. I get tired hearing the question. But I'll answer. I get a thrill sometimes, and sometimes I don't. Mostly it's because I give the man a thrill, and I get my thrill that way."

"Is that how it was with me?"

"Tonight it was. If we do it a few more times together, maybe it'll be because it's you, and I'll get one. But you can't let yourself get too many thrills, it wears you out, and you get thinking about one person too much and you can't be as nice to the others and it shows. And the first thing you know, one of your regulars says he wants to go up with somebody else, and the madam begins giving you the drunks and the strangers, and I hate strangers. That's how you get your teeth knocked out, those strangers. They get theirs knocked out, but that don't put yours back in again, that don't pay your dentist bill."

"Were you afraid of me because I was a stranger?"

"Uh-huh. You talked like some kind of a queer, and that holding-hands business, and when I saw your muscles. But I guess down deep I wasn't worried. And being a friend of Paul's. Everybody likes Paul. I never heard a word said against him, man or woman. It's always a mystery to me how some Dutch girl didn't get a hold of him . . . Say, are you gonna stay all night, you and Paul?"

"It's up to him. I'll ask him."

"You have to rest. I'll ask him."

She put on a wrapper and was gone so long that he finished the second watery julep and dozed off. When he awoke and saw her sitting on the edge of the bed the first thing he would have sworn to was that she had been in bed with Paul.

"You had a good nap," she said.

"What did Paul say?"

"He'd like to stay, he says, but he has to leave by eight o'clock at the latest, if you want to get up that early. Or if you want to sleep through, he'll come back in the afternoon after work. Whichever suits you."

"Well, I'll stay and go with him when he leaves at eight."

"You can have breakfast here. Paul usually does." She turned out the lights and got in bed with him. Some time during the blackest darkness he became aware of her competence and he had her again without ever becoming entirely sure who she was. He did not see her again, and after breakfast with Minnie, he and Paul set out for Lebanon with the sun behind them and the beginnings of another stifling hot day ahead of them.

For the first time in their long friendship Paul seemed to Sidney to look the part of the fat, rich rounder. They had shaved at Minnie's and they were as neat as possible in the circumstances of their linen. Paul, moreover, had the advantage of a black silk mohair suit that did not show the wrinkles if there were any, but Sidney noticed that he wetted his lips frequently with his tongue and was taking three or four deep breaths through his nostrils and one through his mouth, audibly exhaling. For the first time he saw Paul as a sybarite, but a sybarite who let nothing interfere with his business, and he realized that mornings just like this were customary in Paul's life.

"That God-damn rain did us not a bit of good. Today'll be another piss-cutter. I'll get out at the office and you can run this car home and finish out the rest of your sleep," said Paul. "You sleep all day if you like, if you *can,* but tell Lamarr to come to the office for me about quarter after twelve. How'd you like Consuelo?"

"All a man could ask," said Sidney. "I must owe you a hell of a lot of money, Paul."

"Not for last night. You're my guest." He leaned and smiled in Sidney's direction without taking his eyes off the road. "But if you feel like another excursion to the fleshpots, I could be persuaded."

"You mean tonight?"

"Tomorrow we die," said Paul.

"Then while we live let us eat and drink. Isn't that the Kappa Bete motto?"

"Dum vivamus, edimus et bibemus," said Paul. "But I'm not only thinking of my belly. A little below, too."

"You're a man of appetites, Paul."

"When they go, I go. I hope," said Paul.

"A Dutchman with a pagan Roman philosophy."

"I guess so," said Paul.

He spoke so softly that Sidney glanced over and saw that he had been displeased. "Do you object to the, uh, characterization?"

"Partly," said Paul. "Sidney, these days, don't remind your German friends of their German ancestry. Wait till you come home covered with medals and then lord it over us, but for Pete's sake, just now, a man with the name Reichelderfer doesn't need to be reminded where his people came from."

"Oh, hell, it means so little to me, I won't even say I'm sorry."

"I don't want you to say you're sorry," said Paul. "Hell's pups, if it comes to that I don't think you ever sincerely apologized for anything you ever did. That's how cocky I think you are."

"You mean I've never felt sorry for giving offense, or some stupid act? You're as wrong as you can be."

"I'm not wrong. You know, it's a good thing we got to be friends at Yale. We'd never made friends after you settled in Pennsylvania. You'd have looked down your nose at me, the same way you do fellows like Ham Schoffstal and most other Pennsylvania Germans. All other Pennsylvania Germans."

Sidney paused, and then said: "Paul, I'm going to let you in on a dark secret. You're right."

"I know I am. The war gives you an excuse to let it out of you, but it was always inside you," said Paul.

As he spoke they were passing a great farm, with a well-kept stone fence running along the highway, and up a lane, a quarter-mile from the highway, the farm buildings: the barns and sheds and pens and coops amply painted and whitewashed and free of advertising for whiskey, farm implements, nostrums; and in its own acreage was the owner's residence, bounded by a hedge, a three-story red brick house more suitable for a city situation, with its austerity relieved—if it was relieved—by the after-thought of enclosed porches at the east and west ends of the dwelling. In the pasture in front of the owner's acreage were an old swaybacked pony, about twelve hands high, and a gray jenny and a sorrel gelding. Neither animal had a halter on. Sidney watched for the mailbox and read the name on it: Peter Marburger.

"I guess you're right," said Sidney. "Peter Marburger. He's probably a fine man, but sight unseen I guess he wouldn't have a chance with me. And yet—sight unseen—I admire the man. I like everything I know about him from looking at his farm."

Paul smiled. "Say, if we had time I'd like to introduce you to Peter. Maybe we'll call on him later in the afternoon."

"You know him, of course."

"I know him, sure," said Paul. "Nobody around here with a farm like that I *don't* know. I know him a little better because he's one of my cousins. Maybe you met him when you visited us before you met Grace."

"The time we went to a hotel for my first chicken and waffle supper?"

"I guess you didn't meet Peter. He's a few years younger. That pony in pasture, I think Peter was still riding that pony when you came here that time."

"I don't remember the name, but of course that's so long ago."

"Long enough to make a pony grow old. And me. And you. I said it. And me, and you. We don't want to face the facts, but we're both around the coronary-thrombosis age."

"What the hell *is* a coronary thrombosis?"

"Well, a thrombus is a blood-clot—"

"What I'd call a stroke, in plain language."

"In plain language," said Paul. "You look all right. You're a thin fellow. It's us fat fellows have to watch out. But you thin fellows, sometimes you're so careful about everything you never relax. Get all tightened up. You're natured that way, as we say in the Dutch country. I think it's a good thing you went along with me last night."

"You're right again, Doctor," said Sidney. "I haven't felt so good physically in Christ knows how long."

"Since you found out about your domestic troubles."

"Yes."

Paul nodded. "Tied up. Full of things you want to say. Want to do. Have it out with Grace. Kill What's-His-Name. But all your life you've schooled yourself against showing your emotions so you most likely had a formal talk with Grace and let it go at that."

"I had several talks and they got pretty informal."

"Not informal enough, then," said Paul. "When you got here yesterday you were exhausted. You know at our age that kind of exhaustion can kill a man. That *kind* of exhaustion. You hadn't reached the *degree* of exhaustion, but you would have. You know, Sidney, we're almost home now or I wouldn't be talking so personally. You don't encourage that kind of talk and frankly I get bored by it too, but as a would-be half-assed doctor, I don't mind if we were on the verge of a fight several times in the last twenty-four hours. I don't say I provoked a fight, or did this deliberately, but I'm glad you let off steam. Why? Because when I took a look at you yesterday morning, when you went to our house and had your nap, I got to thinking I wasn't much of a man, much of a friend. When I heard about you and Grace, months ago, what I should have done by rights was to go to you and to hell with your reserve, that aloof manner, this man's in trouble and he has nobody to turn to. Take him out and get him drunk anyway. The only reason I didn't do it was because I didn't think of it. But somebody should have done it. Only there wasn't anybody."

"I tried to do it myself. When I found out about Grace and this fellow I went to New York for a few days. She didn't know I knew anything."

"Exactly. Exactly your way. You didn't want to make a fuss. That's where I think you made a mistake. I don't say it's in you to do it, but what you should have done was raise hell then instead of—well, you handed them those days on a silver platter. You have to admit that. Sidney, I'm fond of Grace, but a woman's a woman. The best thing would have been to say, 'Grace, pack a bag, we're leaving town in ten minutes,' and don't give her a chance to let Bannon know anything about where she was going or if she was going. Just make her pack a bag and go away that minute. Then have it out with her while you were away, and if she wanted to see the son of a bitch again, that was her hard luck. She could leave you and the children. The only thing wrong with all this—is you. It isn't in your character. It would have meant sacrificing—going against your principles, the way you think is the right way to behave. And maybe when all is said and done, maybe it is the right way for you to behave."

"I think it is. If I'd done what you think I should have done, it wouldn't have been like me at all, and maybe she'd have damn well refused to go. You know her that well. She'd be quite capable of refusing to go with me if I started ordering her about. I think she would have told me to go to hell. And if she'd done that, her next move would naturally be she'd have to walk out and go to Bannon. And if that'd happened I can tell you where my reserve would have gone. It would have gone up in smoke, literally. I'd have shot her and shot him. And I wouldn't have shot myself, either. I'd have killed both of the bloody bastards!"

They were now in the business section of Lebanon, slowly nearing Paul's office. Paul did not speak until he stopped the car, without turning off the motor. He rested his hands on the steering wheel and turned to Sidney: "Sidney, to all intents and purposes maybe that's what you have done."

"Done what?"

"Killed them. I may be wrong, and don't hold it against me if I turn out wrong, but do you know what I believe? I believe that as far as you're concerned, Grace is dead."

"Think so?"

"In your mind you've gone over it so often, thinking back over when you should have killed them and how you'd have done it— you've lived that scene so much that it's the same as if it actually happened."

Sidney cocked his head and considered what Paul had said, and then he smiled. "Grace'll never be dead," he said.

Paul opened the door on his side and put a leg out, but before taking the rest of his huge body away he reached over and squeezed Sidney's arm. "Good luck, good luck," he said.

"I'll see you this afternoon," said Sidney. "And thanks, old boy."

The folding doors were open at the Reichelderfer garage and Sidney carefully eased the big green Locomobile into a berth beside his Mercer. He was startled by Lamarr's voice coming from the semi-darkness.

"Mighty neat, Mr. Tate. Usually I seen some strangers they turn her in, then they ain't room for the hind end to pass the corner there, then they back up and take a wider swing, they then try her again and now it's too much on the other side. Back her up, bring her forward, back her up again, bring her forward again. Jesus-Christin', God-damin', son-of-a-bitchin', all the language in the Deuteronomy, but they's no closer to placing our Locomobile in her rightful position. Those men down at the garridge, I gave them strict orders long ago, I said 'Please, listen to my instructions if you know what's good for you, please,' I said, 'when you bring this automobile to this garage, kindly just leave her *out in the alley!* Don't *try*,' I said, 'just don't *try* easing her in. Leave her there in the alley. Nobody's gonna steal this large green Locomobile. Nobody's gonna commit a nuisance or mar the paint or blow the horn, so don't you go scratching and wrinkling our mud-guards,' I told them. You had your breakfast, sir?"

"Uh—"

"Don't be polite if you didn't. It's the rule of this household, you know, a man can't start the day without a good substantial breakfast, and even if you did have one breakfast and still feel a little hungry, eatin's a big speciality in this household. This kind of hot summer weather, people just pick at their dinners and suppers, but a healthy man eats a substantial breakfast every day of the year, and this weather, just picking at your dinner and supper, you gotta right to eat two big breakfasts to make up for not eatin' later in the day, y'understand. A nice piece of fried ham about so thick, no thicker'n that, and a thin gravy, just the juice of the meat but enough of it, so you can soak up about four pieces of home-made bread while you're eating the ham. And I like two cups of coffee with that, only one teaspoon of sugar to the first cup. If I imbibed the night before the best thing is a large cold glass of buttermilk. Yes sir."

"I thought you didn't drink, Lamarr."

"I *don't* drink. Who said I *did* drink? You misunderstood me. I said *if* I imbibed. But I don't. I'm just telling you what I know. Mr. Tate, if I told you baking soda was the anecdote for some kind of a poison you wouldn't go around telling people Lamarr Hoy tried to commit suicide. Good Lord. If I told you glasses was good for your eyesight, that don't mean *I* got bad eyesight."

"Well, you just told me what's good for a hungry stomach, and I have one, so I'll have some of that fried ham and home-made bread and coffee. Without the buttermilk, thanks."

"*Without* the buttermilk."

"No buttermilk. Ready in about fifteen minutes?"

"Yes sir, I'll deliver the message in the kitchen and fifteen minutes it'll be ready. You notice your little Mercer?"

"Not particularly, but yes. Looks nice."

"Went all over it with a chamois and took the floor rugs out and the seat-cushions. Filled the tank up with gasoline and it took some water. It's all ready to go wherever you say."

"Thank you. See you in fifteen minutes," said Sidney.

He went to the bedroom assigned to him. A complete change of clothing had been laid out for him. He took a shower and dressed and went down to the dining room. The maid, a stranger to him, bade him good morning and served the breakfast. He was having his second cup of coffee when Lamarr entered.

"Well, sir, I trust everything was satisfactory."

"Fine. That was a happy thought, that ham."

"I'm glad you enjoyed it, sir. You want me to bring your car around out front? I put your bags in already."

"Oh, you did? Well, take them out again and put them back in my room," said Sidney.

"You not leaving?"

"No, I'm not leaving."

"I thought for sure you was leaving," said Lamarr.

"Nope," said Sidney. "Before you get the bags, will you bring me a morning paper, please?"

"Morning paper? I don't know where there is one."

"Well, you shouldn't have any trouble finding one. Mr. Paul takes the New York *Times* and two Philadelphia papers, I happen to know. If they *have* been mislaid—and I don't think Mr. Paul will like that—but if they've been mislaid, suppose you run down to the railroad station and get me a New York *Times* and a Philadelphia *Record* and a Philadelphia *North American.* I'll write that down for you if you can't remember it."

"I'll take a look around first."

"That's the idea. Where's Mrs. Lichtenwalner?"

"I guess she's out doing the marketing. Why?"

"*Why?* Get those papers and be quick about it."

Lamarr turned and went to the kitchen and came back immediately with the three newspapers, which he laid on the table. "Now put the bags back in my room. I'll unpack them myself."

"I'll unpack them. That's my job."

"I don't want you to. You see, Lamarr, I know you're a thief. You were in my wallet while I was taking a shower, but you didn't find any money because I'd hidden it. As a matter of fact I'd taken it in to the bathroom with me, and I'd left my wallet in a certain position on the bureau and you didn't put it back in that position. It's a lucky thing for you there was no money to steal, because

I've already sent one man to jail for stealing. Is that why you were so eager to have me eat breakfast? Because you thought I'd leave my money upstairs and you'd have plenty of time. And what gave you the idea I was going away? Suggesting it to me because you couldn't steal from me?"

"That ain't why I wanted you to leave."

"No? Why did you?"

"I had my reasons."

"What were they?" said Sidney.

"Because Mr. Paul's a sick man and the doctor told him to stop this whorehousin' or he'd die, this drinkin' the minute he come home yesterday, drinkin' and drinkin' after supper, and whore-housin' over in Reading. Why'd he do that? Because you came. And I know *him*, he'll want to go cattin' again tonight. Who's to blame? You the one to blame."

"Are you under the impression that Mr. Paul only drinks when I'm around?"

"I know he's a drinker but he was told to stop and drink lemonade, not booze. But you come here and visit him and you want to drink booze. That's why we want you to leave."

"We? Who's we?"

"Mrs. Lichtenwalner and myself, that's who we is."

"I think you're a liar as well as a thief. Anyway the two always go together. This sounds like something you made up to cover up your stealing."

"What do you know about my stealing? What you know Mr. Paul told you, and he don't mind if I take five dollars now and again. He knows where it all went to. He never called me no thief."

"No? But he warned me not to leave any money around."

"Sure he did, and you took his warning and you didn't lose none of your wet money in the bathtub, but that's because Mr. Paul gave you the warning. He didn't tell you to call me no thief and order me around like the people I work for never ordered me around. I do my work and they treat me right and they don't go crazy about no five or ten dollars missing. They're good people, used to me. Mr. Tate you ain't feelin' good inside and I tell you to your face I wish you'd take your troubles some place else. Yours truly, Lamarr Hoy. That's me, yours truly." He wheeled and went out of the room, and Sidney heard the kitchen door slam. In a little while he heard the door slam again and heavy footsteps on the back stairs. He waited a few more minutes and went to his room; his bags had been unpacked.

Ethically and even aesthetically his position was unenviable. He had come out a bad second in every respect; he had lost dignity all around, beginning with his being led to eat a good meal that he had not particularly wanted. He had let himself go too far in his charge against the Negro and the Negro had turned it into a commentary on Sidney's inadequacy as a gentleman and a guest. Above all, Lamarr had counter-accused him of being an evil influence on a sick man (and there was no doubt in Sidney's mind that Lamarr spoke the truth about Paul; the lemonade the previous afternoon, the fact that Paul had not visited any of the Atlantic City whorehouses, were corroboration enough, without throwing in Paul's continuing preoccupation with sickness and health). Principles to one side, Sidney wished that for ten minutes they were all living in the Old South so that he could take a riding crop to Lamarr, but this was Pennsylvania and the year 1917, and a garrulous, impertinent Negro servant had accidentally shown him the truth, which was that he had selfishly used his best friend as a refuge without giving a second's thought to the friend's inclinations or abilities to provide the kind of refuge he sought. He would do the same for Paul, yes; but he had an embarrassing new conviction that Paul never would have gone to him. In fact, in fact, Sidney admitted, there was nobody in the world who *would* go to him in time of need. Oh—the children, yes; but that was different. It was a fact, all right, that he had so conducted himself that no one in trouble ever had come to him. He had voluntarily helped people in the past, but no one ever had come to him. Even Grace, notwithstanding her position in society, was more approachable than he. There was the pregnant girl at the Fourth-of-July festival, who confided in Grace, and that may have been a by-product of Grace's own behavior, but in justice to Grace, and in stern justice to himself, Sidney recalled other instances where men and women in trouble could just as easily have asked him for help—and they had asked Grace instead.

Well, there would be plenty of time to analyze himself, to probe his own soul, when he got in the Navy. He understood that standing long watches was conducive to that kind of recapitulation. For the immediate present his problem was to invent an acceptable lie to cover his departure from the Reichelderfer house. He dismissed as nothing the loss of face in the eyes of Lamarr. He would never visit Lebanon again and in a week's time he would have forgotten Lamarr and everything about him. He repacked his bag, went to the garage without seeing anyone, and drove the Mercer to Paul's office.

Paul was talking to two men and did not see Sidney, who waited until the men left.

Paul had a desk behind an oak railing and after he said goodbye to the men he saw Sidney. "Want to borrow some money? Money's pretty cheap now. Come in and sit down."

"I came to bid you au revoir," said Sidney. He tried to sound casual, and apparently succeeded.

"What's the matter? Aren't they treating you right at the house? Do you want a larger room?"

"Maybe that was the trouble," said Sidney. "Or maybe the light was wrong."

"Seriously, is there anything wrong, or do you just feel like moving on? I can understand that, if that's what it is. It probably gets pretty boring with nothing to do all day."

"To tell you the truth, Paul," said Sidney. "I want to be there when the letter from the Navy arrives."

"Well, I can understand that too. Yes, I can see why you would. Where is it going to?"

"The farm, and you know how deliveries are. I could lose a whole day without knowing the letter'd arrived. If I rang up now maybe there wouldn't be a letter, but it might arrive in the noon mail and lie there in the Becksville post office till tomorrow."

"Sure," said Paul. "Well, I'm going to see you before you take over Josephus Daniels' job, won't I?"

"Let's hope we don't have to wait that long," said Sidney. "Sure, we must have another big night out. I understand Daniels won't let us drink anything stronger than grape juice."

"Well, maybe we'd be better off if we all stuck to grape juice, but life wouldn't be as interesting. Let me hear from you when the letter arrives and we can make our preparations."

"Sure will, Paul. And—thanks again. You were a friend in need."

Sidney felt tired on the ride back to the farm. He offered the servants no explanation of his return and he sent Grace a telegram: "Have decided to wait here for navy letter love to all." It was over the ten-word limit but it said what he wanted to say. There were things to do on the farm the next few days, and preparations, and preparations for preparations, to be made against his departure. He drove in to Fort Penn every day, spent some time with Percy Hofstetter at the bank, making the preparations for preparations. On the third day he had lunch at the Fort Penn Club and there he saw Brock.

"Well, I thought you'd gone away somewhere," said Brock.

"Only for a day or two," said Sidney. He did not know how much Brock knew about what had occurred between him and Grace, but now he found himself not caring, how much, or how little. Indeed, he found himself regarding Brock as nothing more than a pest he soon would be rid of.

"How's your Navy business getting along? Have you had any news?"

"Not yet. Expect to in a day or so."

"Well, I hope you do, if that'll bring back Grace and the children. Uncle Brock leaves next week."

"You are? Where are you going?"

"Fort Riley, Kansas. Officers Training School."

"Well, I'll be damned."

"Yes, I suppose I'll have to salute you the next time I see you. I'll only be a lieutenant, they tell me, and I understand you're going to be a lot higher than that."

"I'll give you permission now not to salute me."

"Oh, no. Oh, no. Couldn't do that, you know. Bad for morale. And anyway, it's the uniform I'm saluting."

"I was about to say," said Sidney.

"Do you know what branch you're going in, to change the subject?" Sidney continued, after they smiled at each other.

"To change the subject, yes. At least I've applied for the cavalry."

"The cavalry? What the hell do you know about horses, Brock?"

"Well, you know, Sidney, when you're brought up with the damn things you absorb a certain amount of information about them. It just sticks to you without your realizing it. Of course I never cared anything about them, and God knows I'd never spend any money to keep one. And I certainly wouldn't try to start a hunt club."

"What a nasty memory you have," said Sidney. "I understand some of these remount horses are pretty bad actors. I've talked to friends of mine in the State Police, and they say Army remount horses often have very bad manners. Kick and bite. One state trooper got it right in the skull a few years ago. Split him right open the way you would an oyster. So you be careful, Brock. Naturally I'd be very distressed to hear of anything like that happening to you."

"Uh-huh," said Brock. "Well, I'll tell Grace that if anything does happen, anything like that, she's not to tell you till after the war. That is, of course, assuming you come back."

"Assuming I come back, eh? You mean, assuming I don't get killed?"

"No. No. Just assuming you come back. Not quite the same thing," said Brock, smiling.

Sidney smiled and said, "Well, is there anybody looking? We don't have to shake hands, do we?"

"No. We part just the way we met, our opinions of each other unchanged."

"You're wrong. When we first met I had absolutely no opinion of you at all. Now I have, of course." Sidney abruptly turned and left the club, with an extra cordial farewell to Fairfax.

Sidney had been so thorough in his preparations for preparations (and in any case he always had kept his affairs in good order) that on leaving the club he found he had nothing to do. He was, moreover, reluctant to drive out to the farm. If, he argued with himself, the reason he was reluctant to go to the farm was that there was no one there he loved, that was reason enough; if the reason was that by going to the farm he would take himself that much closer to the scene of Grace's misconduct, that was sufficient reason too. Then again, if the reason he felt like dawdling in Fort Penn was that he wanted to be in the midst of people, that was all right and nobody's business. He owed no explanation to anyone and it was rather late in the day to begin making explanations to anyone for anything he did. It was not a practice of his. He owed nothing to anyone, except his life to his father and mother. He owed no money; and to his wife he owed no love and no respect. The love he gave to his children was given and not owed, and the love and respect they gave him were given, he hoped, as cheerfully and wholly as he gave his to them. The unbargaining love that Billy diffused was secretly embarrassing to Sidney, and the cause of the beginnings of a worry: the world was not like that, he wanted to tell the child; harden yourself, he wanted to say to him; people don't want Christmas every day; your supply of love may be inexhaustible, but people think they have to respond in kind and to the same degree, and they are incapable of it, and because they are incapable of it they will not like you for having so much more love than they. Sidney, think-

ing of his boy, tried to keep the thoughts away from his own recent experience of having love rejected, but when he came close
to the thought of Grace he let himself go, and instead of re-
living misery he got little pain at all. In the place of pain he discovered a new hope for Billy: the boy would love Grace as he
always had, but Grace's way of accepting his love (and of giving
her own) was different from Sidney's, and in the difference the
boy would harden, he would show his love less recklessly, and in
time he probably would love like other people, most other people, who are equal to Santa Claus about once a year. Sidney knew
that this was as close as he would come to the romantic idea of
placing his own love among the world's great, and even this close
and even this far—using his son's love as a measure of his own—
was not comfortable or comforting. It was all the kind of thinking that was permissible, if ever, only when a man was alone,
tired, walking a tired horse home in the late afternoon.

———

The sidewalks of Fort Penn, state capital and county seat, always
were occupied by more visitors than the streets of a town of
equal size which had no governmental significance. The Fort
Penn natives, as a consequence, were accustomed to strange
faces, and this fact in turn affected the faces and the manners of
the natives, who became more citified than the population figures might seem to have warranted. In the downtown district
Fort Penn had a more or less calculable number of out-of-
towners who would be likely to transact business and do their
shopping in a city of 80,000; to this number were added the large
numbers of persons who had come to town on state or county
matters. The state and county buildings were tax-free and added
nothing to the public income of Fort Penn, but land in proxim-
ity to the governmental centers was more valuable, hence the
downtown district was assessed more highly than in other cities
of similar ranking in the national population figures, and consequently the buildings were taller in Fort Penn than they might
have been if the city had not been the capital and the county seat.

The larger and taller buildings were assessed at a different rate when they were erected, but it was a matter of sound business if not of pride for the owners to take care that the assessments were, in their view, reasonable. Property in that area thus became more valuable to the owners, and the rental income more than made up to these individuals for the lack of public income which resulted from the tax-free aspect of the governmental property. Routine complaints were made from time to time by the private property-holders, but such protests were raised automatically, in the manner of a housewife locking a kitchen window in a neighborhood that has a burglary about once in ten years. The standard complaint was that downtown municipal improvements were for the benefit of out-of-towners more than for the natives. Street paving especially was postponed or cancelled as often as possible on the outspoken theory that it was not fair to the people of Fort Penn to have to provide smooth surfacing for the people of Erie and Wilkes-Barre to wear out. Privately the property-owners, the more cynical of them, agreed that there was no need to spend a lot of money on paving and other such improvements when the bastards from Scranton and Pittsburgh had to come to Fort Penn anyway, if they had business in the capital. Actually the protests and complaints were made rather cheerfully by the larger property-holders, who admitted among themselves that they only kicked up a little fuss in order to keep the other fellow from kicking up a fuss of his own, the other fellow in this case being a remote possibility of the future, an overzealous mayor or, more fantastic than that, a city council that might take a jealous, more realistic view of the downtown assessments.

Sidney always had been aware of the real-estate situation in downtown Fort Penn, particularly as it concerned Grace's holdings, which were considerable. As adviser and in every sense but signature the executive for Grace's money he went along with the other fellows in their opposition to higher assessments and premature or unnecessary improvements. He was in no respect a reformer or anything but a conservative. On Election Day, which came at the pleasantest time of the year, weather-wise, he and Grace always had a few friends out to the farm for a turkey shoot and late-afternoon dinner. The male guests as well as their host did not vote on that day, but they were voted. Sidney was a Republican, and at the polling place in the Becksville school his vote was counted as though he had been on hand to mark the ballot. It was not even always necessary for him to appear in person at the primaries; he often gave his choices of nominees to a watcher, and this itself was not necessary except in strictly local contests, since the candidates who were favored by the *Sentinel* were always the candidates Sidney would support. Sidney regularly maintained his absenteeism to the extent of sending half a barrel of beer to the Becksville Hose Company for consumption after the polls closed.

But while he conformed as Grace's representative in real-estate tax policy, he was influenced in his personal affairs by the knowledge that some hardship was visited upon smaller business men by the extreme conservatism of the majority of his associates among property holders. At least that was one of the reasons why he patronized McSherry & McSherry. Sidney conceded that he probably would not have gone on patronizing them if they also had not been good tailors, but in the beginning, when he first had come to Fort Penn, Sidney had made the decision that whenever it was possible he would patronize Fort Penn merchants. His boots and shoes at that time were made by a firm in Oxford Street, London, and he knew they always would be; but he always remembered the pleasure it had seemed to give Grace's father when he asked Mr. William Caldwell for the name of the best Fort Penn tailor. The old gentleman had smiled and said, "That's a good sign, Sidney, a good omen. I wouldn't have suggested it in a hundred years, but you have no idea how that pleases me. And it's the kind of thing gets around, you know. New York man changes to a Fort Penn tailor. That's the real thing, you know. Means more than if you'd made a speech." The old gentleman had not turned out to be a major prophet, for in all the time Sidney had lived in Fort Penn no one ever had asked him the name of his tailor, and the Fort Penn men whom he encountered in McSherry & McSherry's shop had not seemed to consider his presence there remarkable, but Sidney had not been enormously disappointed by the failure of his good-will gesture. McSherry & McSherry were fine tailors, and Donald McSherry, the living brother, was a nice man to do business with. It was only in more recent years that he had spoken feelingly about the disgraceful condition of State Street, its effect on business generally, and the fact that if State Street were improved he might be able to charge less for his suits because he would sell more of them. "Mr. Tate," he once had said, "I cater to a class of men that don't have to lose any sleep nights over a fi-dollar, ten-dollar increase or decrease in what they pay me for a suit of clothes. Like yourself, for instance. You didn't pick up and go down to the Outlet when I raised my prices last year, fi-dollars. I don't make a suit of clothes under ninety dollars any more. I can't afford it and stay in business. Not and give you the cloth and the workmanship. I'll raise my prices any time to keep up the quality of my merchandise, and if my people start falling off, I'll go out of business before I cheapen the quality. But then if you want to look at it another way, Mr. Tate, I got room here for more business without sacrificing in the way of cloth and workmanship. I know where I can get a cutter that's as good as any in the United States today. He's as good as the one I have now, and there's no better than Sam. But I can't say to this fellow come on and I'll give you a job. He don't want to live in New York City any more and that's why I can get him. Only I can't. I can't ask a man to move his wife and family and furniture to Fort Penn and then at the end of three-four months have to let him go. So I lose him. And you know *why*, Mr. Tate. It's that street out there. State Street. The condition of it. My people don't walk on State Street any more'n they have to. I watch them, coming from the hotel or the Capitol afternoons. It used to be, years ago, they'd had a stroll, a constitutional, and that way I can tell you I used to sell more than one suit of clothes when a man'd be in my neighborhood, and a man that's taking a nice agreeable stroll with another man, maybe one man's an old customer and the other's not. Well, sir, you'd be surprised how, you know, an outgoing politician, he'd bring in an incoming one. Not any more. The profit in this business is the suit of clothes a man doesn't need, if it's a man buys a suit of clothes every two years or the man that buys two suits of clothes every year. That extra's where the profit is, but how you gonna sell a man a suit of clothes he doesn't need if he hates to walk on State Street? You just aint. They hurry past my window on their way home or to the Fort Penn Club or the hotel, and I don't blame them one bit. I don't know, Mr. Tate. Sooner or later, one by one the places like mine are gonna have to go out of business, and we've been here in this building since the Civil War, and I own the building. Maybe what I oughta do is take one of the offers I get for the building, every day somebody comes in. But what would I be then? I wouldn't want to open up again in some office building, not after fifty years in the same place, and if I retired I'd be dead and gone inside of two years. It wouldn't be too much to say that this State Street's shortening my lifetime. Sometimes that's the way I look at it."

Now, this August afternoon in 1917, Sidney remembered the past conversation with Donald McSherry. One thing about that conversation, here he was doing exactly what McSherry had said his customers did not do: he was *strolling* along State Street. He halted at McSherry & McSherry's shop, stood under the awning and looked in at the three or four bolts of cloth and the bronze nameplate which were the entire contents of the display window. On an impulse he entered the shop.

Donald McSherry appeared from the back of the shop, which was separated by a translucent glass partition from the forward part. It was surprisingly cool inside the shop and the oaken drawers and paneling were restful to the eye. McSherry as always was wearing a vest and around his neck as always was his tape measure, and on the vest were his decorations: a heavy gold watch charm, to proclaim his membership in the Knights Templar, and a badge containing a diamond, to indicate his continuing loyalty to Beta Theta Pi, Fort Penn University chapter. (He had once explained to Sidney that when he was a student at Fort Penn U he had belonged to a club, as there were no Greek-letter fraternities at the college then, but in later years the club had gone Beta and had initiated alumni into the national organization. He wore the pin, he said, because not many men in his business were college graduates and most of his customers *were.*)

"Why, hello there, Mr. Tate. A very good afternoon to you," said McSherry.

"The same to you, Mr. McSherry," said Sidney. "I was just strolling along State Street, taking a little constitutional."

"In this weather? This is a good day to be out on the farm in the shade, with a nice cool pitcher of beer. That's where I'd be, believe you me, if I had a farm. What can I do for you?"

"Keeping you pretty busy these days?" said Sidney.

"Oh, yes. One way or another. For mid-summer I can't complain."

"That's good," said Sidney.

"Yes, we've been getting quite a bit of uniform business, quite a few of our young fellows come in with these rush orders, you know. Have to get a uniform."

"That's what I came in for," said Sidney.

"You did? You going in the Army, Mr. Tate? Say, I didn't know anything about that."

"The Navy," said Sidney.

"The Navy? Why I'd of thought they'd have you in the cavalry. I don't have to tell you what a handsome pair of breeches we'd make you. Nice and snug at the knee there, and a nice English-type flare. What made you decide to join the Navy, if that's any my business?"

"Oh, that's all right," said Sidney.

"Not that we don't make a real becoming Navy uniform, too.

It takes a better tailor I guess to make a smart-appearing Navy uniform than an Army. You have to know how to handle your cloth with a Navy uniform. The chest, and the waist, and around the ribs there, has to fit just so or you look like a bell-hop, and then there's those hooks and eyes and the jacket of course is shorter." He considered Sidney's torso. "I think if anything you may've lost a pound or two. You won't be any trouble at all. I don't mind saying I had one or two friends come in and order Navy uniforms and just speaking as a tailor, I wish they'd joined the Army instead. We can do wonders with a man's corporation if all he wants is a suit of clothes or any Army uniform, but these Navy ones show up the excess baggage like I don't know what. I'll have Sam in."

"Well, I don't know, Mr. McSherry," said Sidney. "To tell you the truth, I haven't heard officially yet and I've been wondering, maybe it'd be bad luck to order the uniform before the Navy Department—"

"Now you're not a superstitious man, Mr. Tate. Don't tell me that."

"It isn't exactly superstition, is it? I had my examination, and I'm waiting to hear from them."

"Why you're as good as on a boat, I'd say. Let me call Sam. All right?"

"Well, all right, take my measurements so you'll have them, but don't start cutting the cloth till you hear from me."

"Whatever you say," said McSherry. "Sam! Will you step out here a minute?"

Sam came out, nodded and smiled to Sidney, put out his cigarette in the ash tray and took Sidney's measurements, and returned to the back of the shop without saying a word to Sidney. Doctors and Sam were the only men who ever put a hand on Sidney, but Sam never so much as uttered Sidney's name.

"Would you care to try on a cap?" said McSherry. "I put in a full line of hats and caps for both Army and Navy. Everything's according to Hoyle, too. You don't have to worry about that. I have a booklet that shows what's correct. Now you'll have a cap with a white top on it and that top can be taken off and laundered. And the insignia for the collar. What'll you be?"

"I think I'll be a lieutenant-commander. I'm not sure."

"Lieutenant-commander? On your collar you'll wear—here, I'll show you in the booklet—a leaf. There it is." He handed Sidney the booklet and got out some caps. "You wear about a seven and a quarter? I never sold hats before, but that's the size in your hat."

Sidney put on a cap and looked at himself in the mirror. He grinned. "Makes my head look big, doesn't it?"

"You'll get used to that."

"I hope so—in more ways than one," said Sidney. He held the cap out to McSherry. "Here, take the damn thing. I *am* getting superstitious."

McSherry laughed. He reached for the cap and it dropped to the floor.

"My fault," said Sidney. "I'm sorry."

"*My* fault," said McSherry.

"I thought you had a hold of it and I let go too soon."

"No harm done," said McSherry.

"I'll pay for it, naturally, if I broke the peak or anything," said Sidney.

"Don't you worry about that, Mr. Tate. To tell you the truth, just so it won't worry you, I was going to make you a present of the cap, just a sort of a farewell remembrance."

"Oh, you mustn't do that, Mr. McSherry."

"Sure. I'm not in the hats and caps business. I only handle them for a convenience, and my real good customers, that's only the least I can do. You know, Mr. Tate, I never said anything, but I always appreciated your business. Now we don't take a back seat for anybody, here in this shop, but I always thought it was real nice of you to give us your business when you moved to town."

"Thank you, Mr. McSherry. Of course it worked two ways. I mean I've always been a satisfied customer too, you know."

"That's all right, we saw to that, but you didn't have to come here in the first place, but you did. And a lot of people in this town feel the same way about you. You're a regular fellow. Yes sir. We Fort Penn people, we're harder to get to know than most, I guess. We got strangers in and out every day of the year, the politicians, and people that have to come to the capital for one thing or another, so I guess that makes us more stand-offish than Lancaster or Altoona maybe, or Reading. But I've often heard my friends remark on it, how you were just as hard to get to know, maybe, but one friend of mine, he made the best remark of all. He said there was no putting-on about you."

"Mr. McSherry, that's one of the nicest things I ever heard, and thank you for saying it."

"Well, I just wanted you to know before you went away."

"I'm deeply touched, and very grateful," said Sidney. "And also for the cap, and the thought behind that. I hope I'll be able to tell you to start cutting in a few days."

"Any time. It's a pleasure."

"So long, Mr. McSherry."

"So long, Mr. Tate."

Sidney, on his way back to his car, wanted to recognize someone among the passers-by, but the only persons who stood out were a few soldiers from the new ordnance depot and the usual chin-whiskered Dunkard and their bonneted women. Nevertheless, he had a friendly feeling for one and all and he hummed "Poor Butterfly" on the drive back to the farm.

He was drying himself after a long shower when he heard a knock on his door. "Sir, there's a message for you."

"All right, Anna, what is it?" he said.

"It's a special-delivery letter waiting for you at the post office, in Becksville."

"Why didn't somebody get it?"

"I'm sorry, sir, but I'm all alone here and there was nobody to go. They rang up on the telephone and said they'd leave it at the store, if you'd care to have someone call for it. I'm sorry, sir, but

I didn't hear you come in and I didn't know you were here till I heard the water running."

"All right, Anna. Thanks."

"You're welcome, sir."

He had reached the point of actual dryness during the conversation with Anna, but by the time he had his clothes on again he was sweating. He took the Mercer to Becksville and when he saw that the special delivery was from the Union League in Philadelphia he swore angrily. The bulky letter probably was nothing more important than a request for a loan by his old schoolmate Joe Bartholomew. "I knew he'd want money before we were through," said Sidney. He opened the letter in the car and looked first at the signature. It was signed Douglas G. Williams, and Sidney could think of no one by that name.

Dear Mr. Tate (the letter read):

In writing this letter to you I am following a course of action which could easily lead to my getting into trouble with the Navy and I rely on your discretion to see that the information herein is not divulged to any other party and I strongly urge you to destroy this communication when you have digested its contents. You will observe that I am writing on Union League stationery where I have a guest card in preference to using Navy Department stationery.

When you came for your examination at the Navy Yard I was convinced of your eagerness to serve in the Navy and as I felt you would make a desirable officer I took an interest in your application. I regret to inform you (unofficially) that due to a heart condition of which you must have been unaware you have failed the physical examination. The medical or technical term used to describe your condition is mitral regurgitation. This condition often exists without the knowledge of the individual involved. It also does not always appear in routine physical examinations. Sometimes it goes back to rheumatism in childhood and leaves its mark but does not crop up and passes unnoticed until one day a medical examiner sees the patient at the "right" time and under the "right" circumstances.

That is what happened in your case. You may consult your own physician regarding this and he will confirm the preceding and also very likely prescribe a course of treatment. I hasten to assure you that there is no cause for alarm. However, at your age the Navy will not pass men with that condition for active duty. I assume you wished to go on active duty.

Unfortunately, when a man is rejected for physical reasons in one branch of the service this information is available to other branches. By that I mean that if you are officially rejected by the Navy, the Army can find out that you were so rejected and in some instances they will not bother to give you an examination. That is why I am writing to you. I noticed that you are extremely well connected in and out of the Navy and I therefore suggest to you, in view of the fact that you are eager to serve in the War, that you withdraw your application for a commission in the Navy. This can be done by writing to the Bureau of Navigation. You can tell them that due to circumstances beyond your control you have had to re-consider your application and therefore wish to withdraw it. I then suggest that if you are still anxious to serve in the armed forces you will use your important connections to back up your application for a commission in the Army. I also suggest that you consult your personal physician who may, and probably will, have further suggestions as to taking certain harmless drugs before appearing before Army examiners which may disguise the symptoms of the mitral regurgitation.

In closing, I must again emphasize the importance to me of keeping this letter in strict confidence. I am holding up your papers including the adverse report on the results of your examination. These papers should be on their way to Washington now, but I want to give you time to withdraw your application before I send in the report to the Bureau of Medicine and Surgery. If your letter of withdrawal gets to Washington and is acted upon before my report reaches the Bureau of Medicine and Surgery, the report will no longer have an adverse effect on your Army application. If you follow the course of action as described above I am confident that you are taking the steps most advisable to insure your chances of getting an Army commission. Do not give up hope as under certain circumstances the symp-

*toms may escape notice. In communicating with me please do not address
me at League Island but write to me at the Union League and mark the letter personal. With all good wishes I beg to remain,*

Yours truly,

Douglas G. Williams

Sidney read the letter twice, with anger, disappointment, and
alarm, but when he had read it the second time he said aloud:
"What a hell of a good fellow that is!" He of course would do
everything Williams had recommended but now he wanted to
reward the doctor's kindness. But the way to reward Williams's
kind of man was to appear before him a few weeks hence in an
Army uniform. Sidney drove slowly with one hand and with the
other hand he reached under his shirt and felt his heartbeats.
Nothing unusual, no sign of a disturbance. He felt like the
healthiest sick man on earth and when he got to the farm he put
the car away, put on a bathing suit and swam in the cool dam until
he had worked up an appetite for supper. While he ate he decided not to tell Grace anything about Williams's letter until he
had received the Navy's confirmation of his withdrawal, by
which time he would have had the Governor and the others
using their influence on the Army. A thunderstorm—a real one,
and not the mild kind that they'd had in Lebanon—broke after
supper and notwithstanding the numbers and kinds of things he
had to worry about Sidney slept well. The swimming and diving
had made him wonderfully tired; he had gone through so much
now that he was sure there was nothing bad remaining.

But there was. In the afternoon of the second day after
Williams's letter Anna, the chambermaid, found Sidney lying on
the floor of the den. His mouth was open and his eyes were open,
and she knew he recognized her, but to her "My God, Mr. Tate,
what in God's name is the matter?" he gave no answer, only the
beseeching look in his eyes. The telephone lay on the floor near
him. It was the telephone that had brought her to the den; she

had been trying to make a call on the kitchen telephone but everytime she listened to the receiver she heard a buzz sound which indicated that another extension was in use, and being a well-trained servant she had hung up. Now she called Dr. O'Brien's office and there was no mistaking the urgency in her voice. She reached the doctor at the hospital and he promised to come right away. She could not lift Sidney. She put a pillow under his head and covered him with blankets, as Doctor O'Brien had told her to do. The doctor arrived in his own Packard with a chauffeur and a moment later the ambulance followed, with a driver and a nurse. In a short while the doctor's chauffeur and the ambulance driver carried Sidney out on a stretcher, and Doctor O'Brien lingered to speak to Anna.

"Are you in charge here?"

"Yes, Doctor O'Brien, for one more day."

"Where is Mrs. Tate?"

"In New Jersey, sir. Cape May, New Jersey."

"Do you know where in Cape May? Do you know how she can be reached by telephone?"

"Yes sir, here's the number, I wrote it down for you, and the name of the people she's visiting."

"Fine work, girl. Get the house ready, because they'll be back tonight."

"All of them, sir? The children as well?"

"Very likely. You have a good head on you and don't lose it. Mr. Tate may not get well, and I'll tell you this. If necessary I'm going to tell Mrs. Tate to come back by special train, at least from Cape May. You're going to have your hands full tonight, and we're all counting on you."

"That bad, is it? Could I ask what's the matter with Mr. Tate?"

"Uh—yes. Poliomyelitis, I believe."

"It's all right, Doctor. I know what that is. I know it from the quarantine placards last year."

"Oh, you do?"

"Will I get it from touching him?"

"I don't think so. You're young and healthy."

"So was himself."

"That's true. That's true. But by the same token maybe I'll get it, and the men that carried him, and the nurse. It's a disease we don't know much about, so get out your beads whenever you have a free moment and pray for all of us. Where did he sleep last night, Mr. Tate?"

"In their room."

"Tell Mrs. Tate not to sleep in that room. Air it out and the little room you found him in. Tell her not to use those rooms for a couple of days at least, and don't let anyone use his bathroom. Air that out too."

"What about his clothing, Doctor? His linen?"

"Burn it, especially handkerchieves. And if you know there's any other linen with his handkerchieves or his underwear, burn that too."

"His are all kept separate."

"That's good. Well, I must go now, and I'll be sure and tell Mrs. Tate she's got a good level-headed girl working for her."

"The good level-headed girl is frightened to death, if the truth be told."

"We all are," the doctor said.

There was a small delay in rounding up a crew for the two-coach-and-locomotive train in Cape May. Otherwise the run from the seashore was accomplished expeditiously with the full co-operation of the Pennsylvania Railroad's president, division superintendents, dispatchers, road foreman of engines, conductors, trainmen, and Pullman porters. A Pittsburgh-bound train was held at Philadelphia while a car belonging to one of Grace's cousins followed a motorcycle policeman from the ferry slip to the Broad Street Station. Grace and the children were met at the Fort Penn station by Brock and Connie Schoffstal. Brock took the children to the Caldwell house and Connie drove Grace to the hospital.

"Thank goodness it was you and no one else, Connie," said Grace in Connie's car.

"Yes, I'm glad Brock had sense enough to telephone me."

"Brock's all right," said Grace. "He's for the family."

"Yes, I suppose so. How are you, Grace?"

"I'm all right, I guess. I haven't had time to think," said Grace. "Do you mean how am I about Sidney?"

"Yes."

"He's my husband, Connie. He's me, he's part of me. There's no one else for me."

"Then it's all right," said Connie. "I wouldn't want you to go in that room if you weren't sure. If you didn't feel that. He can't speak, he can hardly breathe. But he can see. He'll be able to tell. And if you went in there and he didn't feel you were pulling for him, he wouldn't have a chance. He hasn't much of a chance as it is."

"Don't say those things to me, Connie. I'll get upset and I might do the wrong thing."

"You won't do the wrong thing if you're pulling for him in your heart. He's dying, Grace, and they know. And this means a lot to you, too, Grace. You have yourself to live with the rest of your life."

"I swear you sound like lines in a play."

"Maybe I do. There's a lot of good wisdom in the lines of some plays."

"All right, let's not argue," said Grace. "Have you been in to see him?"

"Yes."

"You have?" said Grace.

"Yes. I went in the room, I insisted on it. I told Doctor O'Brien I wouldn't talk but I had to give Sidney a message."

"What message?"

"That you were on your way," said Connie.

"Hadn't they told him?"

"Yes, but I knew it'd be closer coming from me."

"What did you do? Write it?"

"No. I pantomimed it. I looked at him and nodded and I put my hand on my breast, meaning you, and then held my hands as if I were holding a telephone and kept nodding, and then I pointed to my wrist watch and made three circles, meaning three hours. That was all, but I could see he knew what I meant."

"I would never have thought of that, putting your hand on your breast to mean me. It's right, though. I can't explain why, but it is. How did you happen to think of it? I've never told you about him and my breasts. Or anything else."

"Because I know things, Grace, that's how."

"I hope he's not in pain. Do you think he is?"

"Pain? He's probably in such high extreme pain that he's living in another world. Grace, you apparently don't realize this and I hate to tell you, but I have to prepare you. Sidney—is strangling. He can scarcely breathe."

"My God. I thought it was in the legs."

"That's one kind. He has another kind."

They were at the hospital. "Wait for me, please, will you Connie?"

"Of course. I'll wait in your room. They have a room for you to sleep in. Three five seven."

"Do I look all right?"

"I don't want you to look too prettied up. I want him to know you came direct from the train."

"Yes, that's best," said Grace.

Sidney's room was at the end of a corridor. A hospital screen had been set up in the center of the corridor and a young nurse was sitting at a desk in front of the screen, doing sentry duty. The nurse looked up from her book and kept her finger on her place. "You're not allowed to pass here, ma'am," said the nurse.

"I'm Mrs. Tate."

"Oh." The nurse rose, put a pencil in her book, closed the book and rested it on the desk. "Will you wait here please?"

"No, I won't wait here. I want to see my husband."

"First I have to speak to Doctor O'Brien."

"Oh, all right, *speak* to Doctor O'Brien."

The girl went to the door of Sidney's room and whispered something and Doctor O'Brien came out.

"Good evening, Grace," he said, as they shook hands. "You

made excellent time. I hope the trip didn't tire you too much."

"No. How is he, Doctor?"

"Well, I don't want to hold out any false hopes. He's still alive, and that's I guess about the most I can say, truthfully."

"He's going to die, isn't he?"

"This is a mysterious disease, we're doing all we can. I've had patients as far gone as Sidney pull through."

"Don't equivocate, Doctor."

"And don't you be impertinent. I make allowances for your being tired but in this hospital I won't have any of that kind of talk from anybody, I don't care who he is or she is. In my opinion Sidney's dying and it's only a matter of hours."

"What are you doing for him?"

"Everything we can. I've just had a consultation with Doctor Wilson from the University of Pennsylvania. I sent for him. He's in there now. Here's Doctor Wilson now. Doctor, this is Mrs. Tate."

Wilson bore a comical resemblance to Donald McSherry, the tailor, and Grace frowned at him. "I've just been chastised for being impertinent, but will you tell me how my husband is please?"

"Madam, your husband's condition is very serious."

"Did you come all the way from Philadelphia to tell me that?"

"No, I came from Philadelphia because Doctor O'Brien wanted another opinion. Doctor O'Brien *has* my opinion and what's more he has my respect and confidence. If you want any more information I'll let him speak for me. Now if you'll excuse me I'm going to have a cup of coffee. Doctor, I'll be in your room."

They watched Wilson walk away in dignified annoyance.

"I'll take you in now, Grace, but first you'll have to put on a mask."

"I'll do no such thing! He doesn't want to see me with a mask on, and I'm not afraid."

"I'm sure of that. Nobody thinks you're afraid—of germs or anything else. But you have three young children and you may pass the germ on to them without contracting the disease your-self."

"Then my children will have to take that chance, because I'm not going to let a dying man think I'm hiding from him."

"He won't think that."

"I want him to see my face, and that's the way I'm going in there."

"Remember, it's on your own responsibility."

"Moxie!" said Grace.

"What did you say?"

"Stop pointing at me, Doctor O'Brien." She started for Sidney's room. The doctor caught up with her and entered the room ahead of her. "Stand here, no closer," he said.

She nodded. The room was in semi-darkness but almost immediately Sidney saw her. She smiled and threw him a kiss and then suddenly she put her hands to her breasts and pressed hard and pointed to him, and made "I love you" with her lips. His gaze fell. O'Brien took her elbow firmly and steered her out of the room.

"God almighty," she said. "The poor thing. So weak. Helpless. I almost wish I hadn't gone in. I don't think he liked me to see him so helpless."

"No, Grace, I think it was a good thing for you to see him and him to see you. I'm glad you refused to wear the mask."

"Where is Room three five seven, Doctor?"

"It's on the third floor at the other end. I'll let you know if there's any change, and every hour or so."

"Thank you," she said.

Connie was sitting on one of the white enameled iron chairs and smoking a cigarette. "They're putting a cot in here for me," said Connie. "I borrowed a couple of nightgowns from the head nurse, Miss Rafferty. She's an old friend of mine. She sent us a brush and comb and toothbrushes and toothpaste."

"Doctor O'Brien's going to keep me posted," said Grace. "He doesn't think Sidney'll last the night. Neither do I."

"Take a warm bath and stretch out for five minutes. Sometimes that's as good as a night's sleep if you can relax."

"All right," said Grace.

Connie looked out the window while Grace undressed. "I copied you," said Grace, when she was completely undressed. "I held my hands to my bosom."

"Take your bath, Grace, and relax." Connie did not turn around, and Grace went in and closed the bathroom door. "I *was* tired," said Grace, getting into the high bed. "Don't let me go to sleep."

"All right," said Connie.

"Could we have some coffee sent up here? It's so long since I've been here—"

"It's coming. I ordered it while you were in the tub."

"Oh, there's a telephone." Grace reached for it.

"That's not resting."

"Yes it is, I only want to call Brock." She called the number. "Brock, this is Grace . . . He's no better . . . They are? That's good. They were terribly tired. That's why I called you. I want you to take them out to the farm tomorrow, right after breakfast. Tell them I'll let them know how Sidney is as soon as they get there, about nine or nine-thirty. I'm going to stay right here. Mrs. Barker can take charge of everything . . . No, don't wake her up. She's had a hard day too. Just tell her I said she was to take charge. Good night."

While Grace was speaking a probationer brought in a pot of coffee, some old toast and a dab of marmalade. Connie gave the girl a dollar and she left. Connie poured two cups of coffee and Grace had a cigarette with hers.

"This is a good time to be Grace Caldwell," said Connie.

"What do you mean by that?"

"Nothing mean or nasty. It's rather complimentary, in fact. If I were in the next room, you know, the way you can hear a person in a hotel talking over the telephone. You can't understand the words, but you get the feeling of the conversation. Anybody in the next room would have thought a minute ago that you were, oh, arranging a luncheon or something like that."

"You mean I'm cold-blooded? Is that what you mean?"

"Not cold-blooded, but not emotional either. Most of the girls I know would be weeping and acting up. Not you, though."

Grace took a slow drag on her cigarette. "Who am I to play the heartbroken wife like one of your actresses? I know what you're thinking. You're wondering if I'm thinking about Bannon, and sorry for misbehaving with him. Of course I am. Sidney's the only person I ever cared for, and enough so that if I could take his place this minute and die instead of him, I'd do it. But I don't think I have any right to cry my eyes out and weep and wail, the way I'm supposed to with my husband dying upstairs. I'd like to. I wish I could, instead of what I'm doing, calling myself every-thing horrible for doing what I did to Sidney. On the train I even blamed myself for his sickness. If I hadn't done that with Bannon, Sidney would have been in Cape May with me and never caught this paralysis. That's a comforting thought to have when you see a man as healthy as Sidney so weak and helpless. And I'll always hate that Bannon, hate him like poison, because he's intruding in our thoughts today, where he has no right to be, the lout. I'm cured of him, you can be sure of that. I'll never remember him any more for the pleasure we had. All I'll think of when I hear his name is how he was between Sidney and me tonight, when I tried to tell Sidney I loved him . . . I thought it was a good idea, putting my hands to my bosom, but I realize it wasn't. It only showed Sidney that you and I'd been talking about him before I went in the room. I wonder what's wrong with me?"

"Selfish."

"Oh, dry up. Everybody's selfish," said Grace. "Except maybe Sidney. I've never known anyone, not another man, woman or child, that had so much real unselfishness, kindness and consid-eration for other people."

Someone knocked on the door.

"I think I know who that is," said Grace.

"Yes?" Connie called.

"It's Doctor O'Brien."

"As I thought," said Grace. She got out of bed and went to the door.

"Sidney just passed away, about six minutes ago. I'm sorry, Grace."

"Come in, Doctor," said Grace. "I guess you've seen people in nightgowns."

"Yes," said the doctor. "Nothing much to tell you. He went into a coma right after you left. He recognized you all right, I'm sure of that, and in fact I wouldn't be surprised if he was fighting to keep alive till you got here. It wouldn't surprise me at all. You see when I was called this afternoon, or yesterday afternoon, to be exact, he was pretty far gone, then. I wouldn't be surprised if he'd had the chills and fever and other signs we go by several days ago, but thought nothing of them. This weather. A little chill, and people think they most likely've been sitting in a draught somewhere. And it's been very hot here in town, hot as it's been all summer. Well, all I can say is a lot of people are going to be shocked and saddened when they hear the news. Sidney Tate may have been a hard man to get to know, but he was well liked by those that knew him. He was a fine man and a real addition to Fort Penn."

"Yes," said Grace. "I wish a few more people had made him see that while he was still alive. He thought people didn't like him."

"Well, you know how Fort Penn is."

"Yes, I ought to," said Grace. "He's dead, is he?"

"Yes," said O'Brien.

"Where is he?"

"He's still in the room upstairs, but you mustn't go there, Grace."

"I don't want to. I saw him tonight and that was bad enough, the poor thing. I wish he didn't have to know I saw him that way. Well, what do we do now?"

"I'll take care of everything at this end, if you like. I'd deem it a privilege, Grace."

"You mean the undertaker and all that," said Grace.

"Yes. You'll have Winebrenner I suppose?"

"I don't know. Is that who we have?"

"He buried your parents," said O'Brien. "He's about the best."

"He's the right one, Grace," said Connie. "I'll call Brock."

"Yes, your brother will most likely want to take charge. Why don't you stay right here tonight and get a good night's sleep and we can make all these arrangements in the morning. Meanwhile I'll talk to your brother."

"I just had a cup of coffee," said Grace.

"Well, I can give you a pill to take. I think that's the best way. You're all ready for bed and there's no use leaving till morning."

"I think that's best, Doctor," said Connie.

"I don't think I'll need a pill, but I guess I'll take one," said Grace. "But I must tell the children myself. I don't want anyone else to tell them. Thank you, Doctor O'Brien. I'm sorry I was rude earlier. Impertinent. Good night."

"I'll send a nurse in with the tablet for her," said O'Brien.

"Very well, Doctor. Good night," said Connie.

Grace sat on the edge of the bed. "I have this guilty feeling about the children," she said. "I feel as if I ought to be out there telling them. I know it's better for them to have their rest, but something tells me I ought to be with them. We ought to be together. But I know I shouldn't wake them up. I just hope to God none of the servants or Brock gives any inkling. I have to be the one to tell them. We'll have to get up early, Connie." She looked at Connie. "Oh, Connie, what a real friend you are! I don't ask you to get up early. I take it for granted you will."

"Of course I will, dear. You leave everything to me. Brock and I, between us, we'll take care of everything. I wish Ham were here, but he can't be, so I'll have to substitute for him. That reminds me, you'll have to have a list made out for people you want to invite to the funeral. If you want me to I'll take care of it."

"I'd just as soon it was private, just family and very few friends."

"That's the way everybody'd like it, I guess, when they have a death in the family. But Sidney was prominent, and a lot of people think of themselves as friends of his. And I think you ought to give Sidney as large a funeral as possible. It'll be nice for his memory. He was always so sure people didn't like him and pretended not to care, and now he doesn't have to care. But religion to one side, Grace, there's a kind of life after death and that's the memory people have of you, and I think you'll be surprised yourself to see how many want to pay their last respects to Sidney. And we owe it to his memory. Do you see what I mean?"

"I think so."

"And when people see how many do turn out, that'll insure his memory. And a good thing for the children when they get older. People will remember their father as a man highly thought of in Fort Penn."

"All right, I'm convinced," said Grace.

"Here's your pill."

"Don't let me oversleep, will you? That's one thing I really count on you for," said Grace.

"I'll wake you up at seven-thirty. That'll give you time to get dressed and drive out to the farm and see the children soon after their breakfast."

"Nowhere of me he didn't kiss, nowhere of him I didn't kiss." She looked down at herself. "And now it's all over." She turned to Connie: "You may be thinking it was over anyway, but it wasn't. He couldn't have lived without me. The worst of it is, I know that now and I wouldn't admit it yesterday. He'd have come around, as soon as he realized I was still his wife. I'm going to tell my daughter, if she wants to misbehave to do it early in her marriage. I never used to believe it, but it's harder to make repairs after you've been married a long time."

"We used to believe marriages never *needed* repairs, that's what we *used* to believe," said Connie.

"Well, I know what Sidney'd call that," said Grace.

———

"They know absolutely nothing," said Brock. "All I told them was that you were on your way out. They asked me how Sidney was and I said they'd find out from you, you were on your way out."

"Thanks," said Grace. She went inside and the children were at the breakfast table. "Good morning, children."

"How is Daddy?" said Anna. The boys let her do the asking.

"Very sick. Finish your breakfasts and then come into the living room. I want to have a talk with you."

"We're finished," said Billy.

Grace peered at their plates and glasses. "Not quite, but all right. Come with me."

They followed her to the living room. "Sit down, everybody. Oh, Alfred, close the doors, please." He did so and took a seat beside the others, facing Grace. "I didn't tell you the truth in the dining room," said Grace. "I didn't want anyone else to hear me, what I have to say. We're all together now, just we four. Alfred, Anna, and Billy and Mummy. Daddy isn't with us any more. He passed away in the night."

"Passed away. Died?" said Billy.

"Yes," said Anna. She put her arm around Billy's shoulders, but he shook it off. Alfred went to his mother and put his arm around her shoulder and Grace held him around the waist. She kissed his cheek and then the others came to her to be kissed, but Billy immediately returned to the davenport and stared at her.

"What did he die of?" said Alfred.

"Sit down, dears, and I'll tell you all I know," said Grace. "Do you remember last year, when they closed the schools and so many people got sick and died?"

"I remember. Infantile paralysis," said Alfred.

"*I* was just *going* to say it," said Anna.

"That's what it was. And remember some older people got sick, not only children," said Grace.

"Yes, some said older people got it from children because it was infantile and children gave it to the older people," said Anna.

"Yes," said Grace. "Only I don't think that's right any more. Anybody can get it, older people or children."

"How did Daddy get it?" said Billy.

"I don't know. Nobody knows. The doctors don't know. Some people get well and some don't," said Grace.

"Johnny Bordener at school had it and he got over it except he can't talk right. He talks as if he had phlegm in his throat," said Alfred.

"What did Daddy do when he died?" said Billy.

"He was asleep, and then he stopped breathing," said Grace.

"Didn't he tell you anything to tell us?" said Billy.

"He sent you all his love, all three of you," said Grace. "He wants you to be good children and not to miss him too much. He wants you to think of him because he'll be thinking of you."

"Where?" said Billy.

"In heaven," said Anna.

"How do *you* know?" said Billy. "You weren't there."

"But that's right, isn't it, Mummy?" said Anna.

"Yes."

"Why didn't he tell us himself?" said Billy.

"It was so late, you were all asleep," said Grace. "It was *after midnight."

"Why couldn't we see him?" said Billy.

"It was too late, Billy. Besides, you couldn't have gone near him."

"Why *not?*" said Billy.

"Because it's contagious," said Alfred. "You can't see people that have contagious disease or you'll get them yourself."

"Then did *you* get it?" said Billy to Grace. "Are you going to die?"

"No, because I didn't get too close to him."

"Didn't you give him a kiss?" said Billy.

"No. I had to think of you. If I *had* kissed him I couldn't kiss you for days and days, for fear you'd get sick."

"Where is Daddy now?" said Billy.

"He's—they're getting him ready for the funeral," said Grace.

"Well, I want to see him," said Billy. "I want to see what he looks like."

"You can't, because they're putting him in the coffin," said Anna.

"Where are they putting him? I don't know what you're saying!" screamed Billy. "I want to see Daddy!"

"Dear Billy, come here and let me explain to you," said Grace.

"I don't want you to explain! I want to see Daddy!"

"You can't because nobody can," said Grace.

"Those people are, they're putting him in the thing. Who? Who are they? I don't know what you're saying, I don't know what you're saying. I hate you all! You, and you, and you." As he spoke he slapped first his sister, then his brother, then his mother.

Alfred took him by the shoulders. "You stop that, how dare you hit Mummy?"

"Let me go!" Billy squirmed, kicking Alfred and throwing himself on the floor.

"Billy darling, please. Please come and sit on my lap. Alfred, let him go, dear. He won't hurt anybody any more. He's sorry and it's only because he misses Daddy just like the rest of us." The older children saw the tears in Grace's eyes and heard the break in her voice and they began to cry. Anna ran to Grace and held her and Grace put out her hand to Alfred. Billy turned his face away from them and put his head in his arms and lay on the floor, weeping in the inconsolable, desperate, eternal way of a child who no longer is a baby but has not yet grown up into anything else. There is nothing to say to him, nothing to do for him, nothing that will stop him, and until he does stop it is the most awful sound we can hear because it is the eternal cry without hope, plea and protest to nobody and nothing. Then the dreadful, terrifying pain of the soul stops and the weeping changes its tone to that of hurt, hurt pride, hurt body, and that hurt can be fought and with the fighting the awfulness has gone.

"Please, Billy," said Anna.

"Sit on Mummy's lap," said Grace.

Then the child got up, still weeping and with his fists to his eyes, and leaned against his mother.

"That's a boy, Billy," said Alfred, patting him on the head. "Good boy."

"Good boy, Billy," said Anna.

"Yes, he's our good boy," said Grace. Anna made room for him at Grace's breast.

"Here's a kiss for you, Billy," said Anna, pressing her lips to his forehead.

"We must all be nice to one another because we all need each other and miss Daddy, and we're all together," said Grace. "And we're not going to let anybody see us cry. Be a lot of people coming here the next few days, and we have to show them we know how to behave and not let them see how we feel inside. Other people have troubles of their own, and we don't want to inflict ours on other people. Not even other children. We won't talk about Daddy first, and when other boys and girls say they're sorry to hear about Daddy we'll say thank-you and tell them they're very kind to offer their sympathy and then talk about something else. And we must try to be a little quieter than usual, but that doesn't mean we have to stay indoors. We can have little games, go for a swim, take the ponies out, and each of you can have one friend come out and spend the day, every day but the day after tomorrow. That day we'll have to go to the funeral, but in the afternoon we'll all come back here after the funeral. And try to make things easier for Mrs. Barker because she'll be doing some of the things I usually do. Now you can all telephone if you like, each one can invite one friend. Alfred, who are you going to invite?"

"Johnny Bordener."

"All right, but not because you want to ask him a lot of questions, I hope."

"Well, it's all right if he tells me, though, isn't it?" said Alfred.

"If he tells you, voluntarily. Anna, what about you?"

"Frannie Wall. I owe her a letter she wrote me to Cape May that I didn't answer."

"Billy, do you want Mrs. Barker to telephone somebody, or do you want to use the telephone yourself?"

"No," said Billy.

"Well, if you change your mind Mrs. Barker'll help you," said Grace. "Now will everybody give me a kiss before I go upstairs?"

"Yes, Mummy," they said.

They went out and Connie came in. "How do you feel?" she said.

"Oh, don't worry about me," said Grace.

"Give yourself a lot to do and it'll keep your mind occupied. I have some things now I have to discuss with you. First, Winebrenner didn't bury your father and mother. It was Schultz & McMullen. But Schultz & McMullen are out of business now and it's only McMullen. The question is, Doctor O'Brien's already spoken to Winebrenner and made arrangements. I don't think you do, but you can change from Winebrenner to McMullen if you have any preference. I don't advise it, but you can."

"Winebrenner," said Grace. "I don't know why one's any different from another, but for goodness' sake let's not have any fuss about *that*."

"Well, except McMullen telephoned Brock and I have to telephone Brock to give him your final decision and pass it on to McMullen."

"Winebrenner by all means, if McMullen telephoned. You mean to say he telephoned Brock and asked him to—do the work?"

"Well, that's their business, you know. It sounds ghoulish to us maybe, but what else is an undertaker's business? I mean, nobody, or very few select their undertaker before they need him. I'm sure Sidney, he was so methodical, he may have something in his will about it—"

"No, he hasn't. I know what's in his will."

"Then if you have you know he can't be buried here on the farm. Brock said Sidney has something in his will about being buried here on the farm, but it can't be done legally. It's against the law."

"He did want to be buried here, but I'm not so sure he still wanted to. The last few months. If I thought he did still want to I wouldn't care anything about the law."

"According to a new law he has to be buried in an approved cemetery or else cremated."

"Well, he's not going to be cremated and that's that."

"Anyway, Grace, it's better to bury him in the regular cemetery. It's closer to Trinity Church and you can go right to the cemetery after the services. Personally I couldn't stand having someone I loved buried on our farm. I know I'd never go near the grave, and I do go to the cemetery to see that the family plot's kept up nicely. Well, I'll check that off. The next thing in importance, just tell me where you keep your invitation lists and I'll handle all that. You and Brock will have to work out the pall-bearers and Brock will get in touch with them. But one important detail you're the only one can supply: What about Sidney's family?"

"He has practically none. On his father's side he has no relations in this country. They all live in England and I can write to them later. On his mother's side he has an elderly aunt and uncle that live in a place called Wappingers Falls, New York, on the Hudson. The aunt is his mother's sister. We'll have to send them a telegram, but they won't make the trip. They're both in their seventies at least, and I'm not even sure the uncle's still alive. I'll give you their name. The aunt is Aunt Fredericka. Mrs. Van Vliet or Van Vleck. I'll have to look it up. I only met them once. They didn't come to Fort Penn when Sidney and I were married but they sent us a beautiful punchbowl. You've seen it."

"Yes. The big one?"

"Yes, Sidney used to say if you got too drunk to drink out of it you could always swim in it and sober up."

"I'll send them a telegram," said Connie. "The next thing is I have Ruth Holtz waiting in the little reception-room. She brought out some black dresses and hats and shoes. I didn't know your shoe size. At least I couldn't remember the width, so she brought several widths in two sizes, some $7\frac{1}{2}$B's and 8A's and 8-double-A's."

"You remembered perfectly," said Grace.

"What else? Oh, yes, I've been out in the kitchen and there're a great many red eyes out there and some weeping. I think what you ought to do is go out speak to them all at once. In the long run that'll be less of a strain on you than having them one by one. And I wouldn't count too much on Joe. Julia said he threatened to leave as soon as he heard about Sidney and she prevailed upon him to stay, but I wouldn't count on him."

"I *don't* count on him," said Grace. "He's given notice, but I was going to discharge him. I think Joe saw me coming home one time from—" she pointed toward the north. "I wish he *would* leave. All he knows is horses. He won't even see that there's gasoline in the cars. And he wasn't the best man with horses, either. We've had horses go lame that I blame him for. He fooled Sidney, but he never fooled me . . . All right, say it. I didn't fool *him*."

"I wasn't going to say that, Grace."

"I know you weren't, Connie, good, kind Connie. I just hate that man Joe, and I hate him worse because he did know about me. Well, he'll be gone very soon, and if he thinks he's going to have the pleasure of telling me off before he goes, I'm going to deprive him of that pleasure."

"I hope you do," said Connie. "Shall I tell Ruth to come in?"

"Upstairs," said Grace.

———

To the dismay of the Fort Penn police it was a horse-drawn funeral. Fire-fighting apparatus, ambulances, and hearses were converted from the horse to the gasoline engine (often with only a change in the motive power while retaining the same bodies) without waiting for the invention of a reliable self-starter, and without much thought to local climatic conditions or to the hilly characteristics of most Eastern cities. Fort Penn was not a hilly city in 1917; large-scale building had not then begun in the hills to the east and the northeast. Consequently the vehicles of the fire department, the hospitals, and the undertaking profession had been motorized more generally than in most cities, and the police had been spoiled by the neatness and dispatch with which a corpse was taken from the family residence to the house of worship to the hole in the ground. In the winter a horse-drawn funeral was enough to cause a Fort Penn traffic officer who knew about it in advance to report off sick, but in summer it was bad enough. The horses themselves ranged from old to very old, because they were not being replaced by younger horses. Undertakers' teams were a more or less special breed of harness horse and small draft horse, preferably blacks and grays. Since the undertakers were buying automobiles instead of new teams, the existing teams were no longer in their prime, and it was not an uncommon occurrence for one of a team to drop dead in harness, or to catch a shoe in a street railway switch-point and break a leg (which meant that the police officer had to shoot the animal while angry men cursed and infuriated women screamed). Another hazard which was not considered funny by motorcycle patrolmen assigned to horse-drawn funerals was the presence of fresh manure, which caused skidding. The waiting line of horse-drawn funeral coaches outside a church was not much more of a nuisance than a line of limousines, but in motion the carriages had nothing like the precise maneuverability of the automobiles, and what was more, the wheels of the carriages had grown dry and brittle and they sometimes ("always," the police said) split a spoke on the trolley tracks at busy intersections. As Connie had predicted, the funeral was large, one of the largest ever for a member of the upper crust who was not also identified with political life. Winebrenner's promise that all the cops would be taken care of had kept the sick list down to a genuine minimum, but the prospect of a five-dollar tip was not enough to make the patrolmen happy. An out-of-town visitor commented that even the policemen looked sad. Oscar Tillinghast at his traffic semaphore post was truly sorrowful because he had known Grace all her life.

There had been no viewing of the body, no last look at Sidney's face by the affectionate or the curious. The Fort Penn Health Department had ruled in the 1916 epidemic that victims of infantile paralysis were to be sealed up immediately. Sidney's body stayed in Winebrenner's funeral parlors until the afternoon of the obsequies and it was waiting in the middle aisle of Trinity Church when the mourners began to arrive.

Once it had been Sidney's wish to be buried from the little church in Becksville, where he and Grace had been married, but the crowd in Trinity Church showed the wisdom of the decision to hold the funeral in town. There were the numerous family connections (without Sidney's Aunt Fredericka and Uncle William) and the pallbearers and invited friends. There were also the Governor and his wife and the Secretary of the Commonwealth and his wife, the mayor of Fort Penn and the directors of the bank. There were four out-of-town members of Death's Head, Sidney's senior society at Yale, and the Delta Kappa Epsilon chapter at Fort Penn U was represented. Practically the entire resident membership of the Fort Penn Club came, along with the trustees of the Hospital and the governors of the Fair. The Yale Club and the Lawrenceville Club, the overseers of the county orphanage, the Navy League, the Shade Tree Commission, the Playground Committee, the Fort Penn Symphony Orchestra, the governors of the Fort Penn Country Club, the Fort Penn Athletic Club, the Farm Bureau, the Sons of the Revolution, the Becksville Board of Supervisors, the Boat Club, the Y. M. C. A., the councils of the Boy Scouts of America and the Camp Fire Girls, the Young Men's Hebrew Association, the Art Commission, the Fort Penn Free Public Library were represented by one or more persons. The parish band of St. Rose of Lima, a church in the Italian section, had volunteered to play as a token of affection for one of the founders and honorary life members of the band. (The double distinction had been forgotten by Sidney, but his name was carried on the band's letterheads.) Winebrenner assured the bandsmen that if any band were to have been chosen, theirs was it, but in this particular funeral no band would fit. Twelve bandsmen attended the funeral in uniform but without instruments, which was just as well since their best piece was a spirited playing of the Garibaldi March.

Old Trinity was packed to the last pew because there were also a good number of people who came not by invitation nor as representatives of organizations, but because they wanted to be there. Donald McSherry had not been invited, and he was present. Lou Ginther, the head mechanic at the Hughes-Pierce Arrow garage, sat next to G. E. Gaynor, who as conductor had a regular run between Fort Penn and Philadelphia. Ernestine, Connie Schoffstal's maid, attended. Luke Laubach, the Governor's private secretary, came with Ed Studebaker, clerk of the county fair. Mrs. Ursula Doyle, who worked on Sidney's handkerchiefs and shirts, brought her rosary beads. The tobacconist Jock Gordon was seen to offer his tin of Copenhagen snuff to Walter Fry, the watchmaker. Bill Flickinger, who never seemed to do any work but was always leaning against the bar of the Schoffstal House, dozed off in the close atmosphere. Miss Elizabeth Lacey, assistant to Doctor McCaffrey, Sidney's dentist, was the prettiest person in her pew, but the good looks of her abundant health were wasted on Karl Wentz, the cobbler, who always told Sidney, "I can't make a shoe good as that, but fix him I can." Captain Ludwig of the State Constabulary somehow had been overlooked in the inviting, but he was present in civilian clothes, said hello to Henry Breitinger, the proprietor of the Farmers Hotel in Becksville. Abe Harris, the custodian of the Union News stand at the railroad station, sat next to a man whose name he did not know and who never had known Sidney; a man named Edward T (for Tate) George, an orderly at the hospital. Tina Ohrbach, the manicurist, knew as well as anyone could know that Sidney never had a manicure, but she went to Sidney's funeral. There was Harry Jones, one of the few musicians who knew all of the Yale, Harvard, Princeton, and Penn songs, and Robbie Powell, no longer a boy but professionally the pool-boy at the Fort Penn Club. None of the owners of the small farms in Sidney's neighborhood could get away for the afternoon, but a party of four of their wives had done their work early by getting up while it was still dark, and had gone on foot to the trolley line and after the funeral would have to go on foot back to their farms. They sat behind the candy-store woman, Mrs. Althaus, proprietor of Althaus's Home Made Candies, whose famous stuffed dates often sent Sidney to the dentist. Peter Ringwalt, the proprietor of the hotel barber-shop, was accompanied by Herman Miller, and they, with Tina Ohrbach and Carter Birdsong Junior, the bootblack, made up a delegation of four from the shop, although Carter did not go with the delegation, preferring to go with his father, Fairfax, of the Fort Penn Club. The name Jim Crow was unheard of in Fort Penn, but Colored always sat in the rear pews of a white church and in the balconies of the theaters. "Only thing I couldn't get to like about Mr. Tate, Poppa," said Carter. "He always made me take the laces out of his shoes before I polished 'em." To which Fairfax replied: "It's the right way to do and he knowed the right way to do, so shut your mouth, boy, and don't criticize." Also in the leather line was Sidney's friend Victor Smith, the harness-maker, who in attending the funeral violated two principles: he had been against funerals on anti-religious grounds, and with the disappearance of horses and their replacement by the automobile he was against undertakers for economic reasons. Schmidt & Burke and Kemp & Bonniwell (although not the original Kemp and Bonniwell), the jewelry families, were there in person. So was Jake M. Maurer, the R.F.D. man from Becksville post office. Bernie Fitzgerald, one of the Sons of Fitzgerald & Sons, Everything for the Home; E. P. Sullivan, of the Auto & Wagon Works; J. J. Dougherty, of Dougherty's Mule Yards, and Chris Cochrane, owner of the Riverside Pavilion, from whom Sidney had bought several rowboats and a naphtha launch, paid their last respects, sitting together as if for mutual defense in the Protestant church.

The service was brief and the eulogy took no longer. The Reverend Lucius Kinsolving Steegmiller, the senior curate and assistant priest, officiated in the absence of the rector, Doctor Edward St. John Bowdoin, who was in Bar Harbor, and at Brock's insistence Doctor Bowdoin had been kept in ignorance of Sidney's death so that he would not interrupt his much-needed and well-earned vacation. Himself an "adopted son" of Fort Penn, Father Steegmiller touched delicately on the adopted-son theme, and told how Sidney would be sorely missed for his activities for the betterment of the community, not the least of which was his serving as a warden of this very parish. Father Steegmiller reminded those of all faiths and all conditions of life that no man knows the day or the hour at which he might be struck down in the very prime of life and called to render an accounting of his stewardship. The address was in extremely good taste and could be heard plainly in the back of the church. With a slight nod in the direction of the chief mourners Father Steegmiller disappeared from the chancel and Dwight DeWitt, the organist, played a hymn with variations of his own improvising. Mr. DeWitt had sent word to Brock that he wanted to play Sidney's favorite hymn, and the only hymn Grace could think of was "Rock of Ages," which, accordingly, Mr. DeWitt played, while the family and close friends went out a side door to their carriages. Burial, which had been announced as private, was private only in the sense that the entire public had not been invited. Grace, Brock, and the children rode together in the first carriage after the hearse, and in the carriage occurred the only incident of an unconventional nature. Grace and Brock sat together and the children sat facing them, riding backwards. "Mummy, I feel sick," said Billy.

"It's riding backwards," said Grace. "Come sit with me, between Uncle Brock and me."

The child stood up in the swaying carriage, lost his balance, and fell against Brock, who caught him and turned him so that he sat down, but when he sat down he vomited on the floor. The vomit covered the boy's own shoes and socks and splattered Brock's shoes and lower trousers.

"Oh, dear, poor boy," said Grace. "It's the excitement." Handkerchieves were brought out and applied.

"Excitement? I didn't see any excitement," said Alfred.

"You children will have to stay here with Billy when we get to the cemetery," said Grace.

"Mummy, I don't want to stay in the carriage," said Anna. "I want to say good-bye to Daddy."

"So do I," said Alfred.

"So do I," said Billy.

"But it's only a formality," said Grace, "and you don't want to be sick again in front of a lot of people, do you, dear?"

"I won't be sick again," said Billy.

"Well, we'll see how you feel when we get there," said Grace.

"Maybe the air'll do him good, too," said Brock. "I must say these musty carriages—when I die, Grace, you have automobiles for me."

"The windows are open," said Grace. "Do you feel better, Billy?" The boy leaned back and lay against her.

"I guess so," said Billy.

"I'll stay with you, Billy," said Anna.

"I don't want you to," said Billy. "I want to say good-bye to Daddy."

"It's only a formality," said Anna. "Didn't you hear Mummy say?"

"Oh, hush up," said Billy.

"Billy, dear," said Grace, "don't talk that way to your nice sister, who's only trying to be helpful and kind."

"Anna can go, I'll stay with Billy," said Alfred.

"You hush up, too," said Billy.

"Well, maybe it won't be necessary for anyone to stay with him, if he feels better. We'll be there soon," said Grace.

"None *too*," said Brock. "And now don't take that the way I don't mean it, Grace. I don't like to say I told you so, but—" he spoke in French "—I told you not to bring the children to the cemetery."

"I know what you said, Uncle Brock," said Anna.

"So do I," said Alfred.

"All right, you *know*." Brock laughed. "That's one on me, I guess."

"It certainly is," said Grace. "They speak better French than you ever did, or ever will."

"I don't doubt that for a minute," said Brock. He patted Billy's legs. "How do you feel, old boy?"

Billy did not answer, and drew closer to Grace. Brock shrugged his shoulders, then looked out the window. "What a day! Isn't it a corker? Poor old Sidney, he—"

"Brock!"

"What? Did I say something?"

"Haven't you any feeling? Don't you realize these three children are going to—"

"Now hold your horses, Grace. I'm just as aware of the children as you are, and what's more I don't think you ought to speak to me like that in front of them."

"You hush up, do you hear?" said Billy.

"Well, I'll be damned," said Brock. "Do you hear that?"

"I heard it. He expressed my sentiments exactly," said Grace.

"Now look here, Grace—"

"Hush UP!" said Billy. "Hush up or I'll slap you."

"Billy, you mustn't speak like that to your Uncle Brock," said Grace, holding the child closer to her.

"Give him a stick of candy, why don't you? Well, here we are, I guess," said Brock. He got out and helped Grace out of the carriage and she took his arm and held Billy by the hand. The family and friends gathered around the grave, and many commented later on the stoic manner of Grace and her children. Indeed, the only audible sobbing came from a man, and that was Paul Reichelderfer. At the words "In the midst of life we are in death . . ." it was as though he had been taken by surprise.

———

Wednesday afternoon, in the week after Sidney was buried, had been agreed upon as the time for Duncan Partridge to call at the farm with Sidney's will. The firm of O'Connell & Partridge had everything at their fingertips, Grace was assured, because Sidney had been in to get his affairs in order before entering the Navy, and this would take only a few minutes. Duncan arrived at two-thirty in his gray Chandler four-passenger sport car. He was all business in his blue flannel suit and with Mr. Hostetter from the bank and a man named Kelly from the office of O'Connell & Partridge, who were carrying dappled cardboard filing boxes. Duncan had been a pallbearer at Sidney's funeral and he and Grace greeted each other with a nicely perfunctory formality that was exactly right for the occasion and in view of the presence of Hostetter and Kelly.

"We can use the den," said Grace, "unless you gentlemen would rather go on the porch. I have to explain, Mr. Hostetter and Mr. Kelly, the den was one of the rooms the doctor said we mustn't use after my husband had the attack. It had to be aired out for safety's sake, but that's been done. But if you'd still feel safer or more comfortable, we can go out on the porch."

"I'd just as soon use the den," said Mr. Hostetter.

"It's been fumigated, too," said Grace.

"It's all right with me," said Mr. Kelly.

"Let's go in there, then. Have you all had your lunch?"

"Yes, Percy and I had it together," said Kelly.

"Mr. Hostetter and Mr. Kelly've been working together the last couple of days," said Duncan.

"I see," said Grace.

They took chairs in the den and Duncan put out his hand to Kelly. "I think you'll want me to read the will, first, Grace," he said.

"Whatever you say," said Grace.

Kelly handed Partridge the will. "It's short and simple. I helped draw it up myself, and I know you're familiar with it, Grace, but I'll read it again now more or less as a formality. I like a simple will, and as a lawyer I guess I oughtn't to say this because it'd put us out of business, but I sometimes wish everybody'd simply say, 'I leave everything to my wife,' and let it go at that. But there's such a thing as having it too simple and sometimes a simple will won't hold up in court when there's a contest. And of course here in Sidney's will he has the provisions about this farm. Well, I'll read it and if you have any questions, don't hesitate to interrupt."

As he finished he looked at Grace, as did Kelly and Hostetter. She looked at them, and as it seemed to be expected of her, she shook her head. "No, I have no questions," she said.

"Very well," said Partridge. "Now suppose Mr. Hostetter reads off the list of Sidney's holdings. Stocks and bonds, mortgages, and so on."

"Very well," said Grace.

Hostetter's reading was different from Partridge's, although both men seemed to take equal pleasure in their performances. Partridge's delivery was histrionic, while Hostetter's was semi-ecclesiastical. Hostetter would call out the name of a stock, pause, and in a lower tone give the number of shares. Kelly sat with his elbows on the arms of his chair, his hands clasped, his thumbs twirling. Hostetter's chant was interrupted not by Grace, but by a knock on the door.

"Who is it please, I'm busy," said Grace.

"It's I, Mrs. Tate. Mrs. Barker."

"Can you come back in a little while, please, or I'll see you when we're finished in here."

"I'm sorry, Mrs. Tate, but I think it's important."

"Excuse me, gentlemen," said Grace. She went out and closed the door. "Is anything wrong?"

"Billy's very sick. I don't know what it is, but it may be diphtheria, except there aren't any white spots in his throat. I think we ought to have the doctor."

Grace stared at her, and the woman stared back. "Will you tell me the truth? Will you please? Do you really think it's diphtheria, or do you think it's something else?"

Mrs. Barker for the first time in her association with Grace made a physical gesture of friendship. She put her hands on Grace's arms. "You poor woman," she said. "I'll stay, I'm not afraid."

"Oh, God," said Grace, sickening and afraid. It sounded more like *gud* than *god*. "You call the doctor. I don't know what I'll tell these people." She returned to the den.

"What is it, Grace?" said Duncan, going to her.

"You'd better not come near me, Duncan. Have you any children, Mr. Hostetter? Mr. Kelly?"

"Yes," they both said they had.

"Then I don't know what you ought to do," said Grace.

"Jesus Christ," said Kelly.

"I'm sorry, I don't know what's best, but I have to tell you, my nurse thinks my little boy may have infantile paralysis too. I don't know whether to tell you to leave here as quickly as you can, or wait till the doctor comes and ask him."

"I'm getting the hell out," said Kelly.

"Wait a minute, Kelly," said Partridge. "We all have families, and maybe Mrs. Tate's right, maybe we ought to wait for the doctor. That's what I'm going to do."

"I think that's the better idea," said Hostetter.

"Wait my ass, you can stick the job up your ass, Partridge. I'm getting out," said Kelly. "That woman's bad luck anyway."

"Go if you like, go, go, go," said Grace.

"Bet your sweet ass I'm going."

"Go ahead, you little yellow son of a bitch," said Partridge. "But I'm calling the state police. See how far you get. This house may be quarantined, and believe me, if it is you're going to prison if you leave."

The word prison had a staying effect on Kelly. He was a member of the bar, not a brilliant lawyer, but he was acute enough to recall the hysteria of the epidemic of the previous year, and he foresaw that he would have no career if he went to prison for breaking quarantine. And Partridge was thinking along the same lines.

"You'll go back to the pick and shovel, like your father. You'll never practice law as long as you live," said Partridge.

"All right," said Kelly. He sat down. "I'll stay in her God-damn house, her God-damn, unlucky house, full of corruption. And she knows what I mean."

"I'll take care of him, Grace," said Partridge.

"How? *Fire* me? I consider myself fired already, *Mister* Duncan Partridge."

"You're getting out of your weight class, little man. You're going to have to be spanked. Going to have to wash your nasty mouth out with soap."

"Don't do anything to him, Duncan," said Grace.

"Oh, I didn't mean now, here," said Partridge.

"He means fix it so I'll never get a job in the county," said Kelly. "But I'm not worried. I know Roger Bannon too, you know." He covered his face and head with his hands and his arms, but Partridge slapped him on the back of the neck and when he put his hands back Partridge slapped his face. Grace hurried out.

"He deserves it," said Hostetter.

"You ass-kisser," said Kelly. "You Dutch ass-kisser."

Partridge stopped slapping him and when Kelly was sure the slapping had stopped he straightened up in his chair. "You'll be sorry for *that,* Partridge," he said. "Nobody treats me that way, nobody. You too, Hostetter. You don't like these people any more than I do, you said so, but you're yellow."

"Have a cigarette, Hostetter?" said Partridge.

"Yes, thank you," said Hostetter.

"I think I'll have to find out who's on Mr. Kelly's draft board. A real fighting Irishman like Mr. Kelly, I'm surprised he didn't go with the Irish Company, but maybe he can still get to France. We'll see if we can use our influence."

"That kind of talk's the way a person tries to frighten little children," said Kelly. "You don't notice it having any effect on me."

"It wasn't intended to have any effect on you. It wasn't said for the effect," said Partridge.

After that they settled down to wait for the doctor; Partridge and Hostetter making desultory conversation, Kelly watching them with a hatred that had to be cold and everlasting because that was the kind of hatred that the situation called for in view of what had been said and done and what had not been done, which was murder, and would have been the only way to end the hatred. After the beating, everything that was said and done in the room contributed to the hatred Kelly felt and the fear felt by Partridge and the confusion of Hostetter. Partridge could not say a word without being over-conscious that it would be heard and sneered at by Kelly, and that made for unnatural speech, which is not unnatural to a veteran lawyer in professional practice, but was cramping and exhausting and eventually completely discouraging to all conversation in that tiny room. Partridge, as the only one of the three men in the room who could lead a conversation, gave it up and they fell into a silence; three silences.

The silences lasted through the striking of the half hour and the hour of the deep and the high bells in what seemed like a house full of clocks. Then they heard the not unmusical grinding and roaring of Doctor O'Brien's big Packard, dropping down to second speed in the driveway. Then his footsteps up the stairway. Then for a while nothing (they did not know that the sick child was two stories above them). Then another half hour signal by the clocks, and now O'Brien entered the den.

"I don't know what's been going on in this room, and I don't care," said Doctor O'Brien. He was angry at the three of them. He clasped his hands behind his back. "I understand neither of you saw the child so I don't think you've been exposed. Therefore you're free to go home. In fact if I were a younger man I'd *kick* you out. With my boots. You're no credit to yourselves or the families you come from, or anything else. You, Duncan, you're the one should have been in control here, and you weren't. You, Kelly, you seem to have turned into a dirty-mouthed guttersnipe."

"Apparently, Doctor, you do know what's been going on in this room," said Partridge.

"It was unwelcome knowledge, and I'll be rid of it as soon as this house is rid of you and your two equals. Don't try to be high and mighty with me, Duncan. I know too much about you. You could all three learn decency from a little boy upstairs."

"Is it safe for us to go home and see our own children?" said Partridge.

"You're the only one in the room's a patient of mine, and I've told you you can go home. The others can go to their own physicians first, if they so desire. How safe you'll be—you're not as safe as you'd be if you'd spent the afternoon in Philadelphia. But you haven't been exposed. On the other hand, if you're still here in five minutes you're going to be quarantined, and I'll see to it that you sleep in the stable." He took out his watch and they left. Grace was coming downstairs as they went out.

"Shall we talk here, Doctor?"

"Yes, sit down, Grace. I'll have a seat, too." He put his elbow on his knee and his hand to his forehead. "We have to face two facts. We have to face the fact that Billy has this awful disease, and the probability is—he will die. You say he vomited in the funeral carriage. I have to make a note of that, because we know that vomiting is often one of the warnings, and also I'm going to have to find out which carriage and tell them to burn it. He probably vomited since then and you didn't know about it. Was he out of sorts since the funeral?"

"Yes, but naturally I thought that was because Sidney died."

"What about the other children?"

"Not upset the way Billy was, but that was because Billy and Sidney were so much closer to each other."

"They haven't been picking at their food? Unusually tired?"

"No," said Grace.

"That's good," said the doctor. "Grace, another fact *I* have to face is we didn't learn much a year ago in the big epidemic, but we did learn a few things. As far as the other children are concerned, one hopeful thing we discovered was that infantile hardly ever attacks more than one child in a family. Why it attacks one and leaves the others alone, we don't know, and last year we lost a chance to find out. Case histories weren't kept, and the people that died were buried right away. But we do know that about only one child in a family. As a general rule. At the same time be on guard for slight colds, vomiting, and if either of the older children has pains in the back and the neck, or bad headaches. I have a theory that the bug—of course I don't mean an actual insect, but the germ—I have a theory it enters here, the nasal passage, but my theories are unimportant. Can't go around with cotton in our noses all the time. But now some questions. Have you an outside privy?"

"Not any more."

"The farmer's house has inside plumbing?"

"Yes, Sidney had it put in two years ago, maybe three."

"I'll have a talk with the farmer's wife. You sell a lot of your milk, don't you?"

"All of it from the Holsteins. The milk we drink is from the Jerseys."

"Well, naturally, you're not going to be able to sell any more milk. You'll have to dump it in the river or some place, and I suggest as a precaution, and you can afford it, I suggest you buy your milk for the next six weeks or so. I'm not saying the milk is infected, but you can afford every precaution, and that's one of them. Throw away the Jersey milk as well as the Holstein milk."

"I'll slaughter the herd if you suggest it."

"I don't, but on the chance that the milk might be contaminated by the same bug that attacked Sidney and the little boy, don't use any milk from this farm. At the end of six weeks, if nobody on the farm has gotten infantile, you can start using the Jersey milk and selling the Holstein."

"By that time our market'll be gone, but I don't care. I'll get rid of the Holsteins then."

The doctor looked at her. She was sitting straight in her chair. Her lips were set tight. She breathed deeply and regularly as though her body were sleeping. Her hands were folded in her lap. Her eyes were tired, but without the faintest sign that she soon would give in to exhaustion.

"Grace, I brought you into the world and I delivered your children, and in many ways I don't know you very well, but I admire you. I don't admire everything you do, but I admire a young woman that can sit here and talk about cows while her child is terribly ill upstairs."

"There's very little admirable about me, Doctor O'Brien. I'm ashamed of myself. I couldn't help that affair, any more than Sidney could help getting sick, and Billy."

"I know. I've seen women get carried away like that. Usually I see them because of the consequences, in one form or another."

"The consequences. Punishment," said Grace. "Well, I'm being punished."

"I don't know about that," said the doctor. "Punishment is punishment when people take it as punishment, if you see what I mean."

"I don't know what you expect, Doctor," she said. "I lost my husband, my child is dying, and a person like that Kelly can talk to me the way he did in my own house."

"Yes. Which is worse?"

"Neither one. Neither one's worse than the other. I have to live through all of them, and I don't think I'll be any better for living through all of them."

"That's a big punishment in itself," he said.

"It might be, if it weren't for one thing. Maybe I'm not *being* punished. Maybe I didn't do anything to deserve punishment. Why punishment, anyway? Payment, maybe, but not punishment. The law of averages, as much pleasure as you get pain. You're trying to make me think like a Catholic, and I don't even believe in God. I don't see how you can, either."

He rose. "Well, I do, and I don't see that this conversation is getting us anywhere."

"It would if you were a younger man," she said, rising.

"I'm very glad I'm not a younger man."

"You didn't have to make me say I was ashamed of myself."

"Grace, I didn't make you say it, and that's why there's hope for you."

"Wait a minute, Doctor," she said. "I don't want to go upstairs yet." They stood with their right hands on the newel post. In a little while, about ten seconds, she said, "All right, I'm ready."

"Aren't you feeling well?" he said.

"I feel all right. I wanted to stop thinking of myself and think of Billy."

He took a deep breath, with his shoulders back. Apologetically he said: "Climbing stairs takes it out of me nowadays." Then: "Don't worry about thinking too much about yourself. Everybody does it all the time, Grace. Everybody's doin' it . . . All right, I'm ready."

The child was wasting into death before their eyes, and his fight was futile and they all knew it. They had been able to tell that Sidney's body, his chemistry, was putting up its fight with help from a conscious, if inarticulated will to live. Not so with Billy. He looked only confusion and terror, and as he went in and out of consciousness, each time he came back he was weaker until they could almost predict, toward the end, when the end would be; how many more intervals of consciousness before there would be no more. Then he was dead, a little boy with the paled skin over the little bones, gas inside him, sun-bleached hair lying on his head and still growing, and the last image behind his eyes an eternal secret of his own, and the curled up hand on the nightgown caught in the final weakness.

Grace saw him die—that is, she was present when he died, since neither she nor anyone else there could tell the moment when he died. The doctor was there, Doctor O'Brien, not the bone man from Fort Penn, who was on his way out from the hospital. Connie Schoffstal was in the room. Nurse Dillon, who had been with Sidney. That was all.

"He died a saint," said Grace. "That's what Julia would say, and it's right. All his sweetness, and his playing, and love for his Daddy. Good God, oh, God." She went to the wall and put up her arm and put her head on her arm and wept. She stayed like that for five minutes and the doctor and the nurse and the friend stood away from her, with a beautiful instinct to leave her alone with her face to the Mother Goose wallpaper. Then she lifted up her head and Connie gave her a fresh white handkerchief.

"Doctor," said Nurse Dillon.

He looked at her questioningly and she held up her own handkerchief and he nodded.

"Keep that handkerchief, Grace," he said. "You mustn't let anyone else use it after you have." He addressed Connie. "It isn't only social manners. It's precautionary. Everybody in the house must be very careful about handkerchieves. The best thing is to use toilet paper and burn the paper or flush it away. Burn it is best."

His little speech brought them all forward to the immediate present and the entire future, thus taking leave of the little boy on the bed. According to their time, the time of the living, he had been dead ten minutes.

For bodies no longer than Billy's there were only white caskets. He was buried beside his father the day after he died, in semi-secrecy. Grace went in to Fort Penn in the limousine, accompanied by Connie. They stopped and picked up Brock at the house in town, and drove to Winebrenner's undertaking parlor. The white casket was lifted into the motor hearse and the two cars drove to the cemetery, where Father Steegmiller, in street clothes, and with his Panama lying on the ground, read the burial service. Then they rode back to the house and Brock left them and Connie and Grace rode back to the farm. In all, Grace was absent from the farm less than two hours. The children were waiting for her in the living room.

"You were very good children," she said. "I'm sorry I couldn't take you with me, but we have to think of other people. It's not only that we may have germs—that's why I can't kiss you, because I was closer to Daddy and Billy. I'm sorry, because Mummy loves you very much, and is proud of you."

"You can kiss me if you want to, I'm not afraid of germs," said her son.

"I know, but maybe we have them and we'll give them to Mummy," said Anna.

Grace smiled. "That isn't very likely, but it's a possibility. We all have to be extremely careful. We'll be quarantined I don't know how long, and we're going to have to be patient with each other, because we're going to have to see each other all the time and not any outsiders. It isn't only because we may have germs. I think I told you yesterday, Doctor O'Brien says hardly ever two children in the same family get it. So we're not really worried about that part of it. But remember last year, how afraid we were that we'd get it from somebody?"

"Everybody was afraid," said the girl. "They closed school and everything."

"Yes," said Grace. "Well, *now* people are afraid of *us*. There's only one other case of infantile paralysis been reported in the whole county, and that's on a farm miles away in the southern part, and nobody knows about that except Doctor O'Brien happened to tell me. So that's why we have to observe the law. Daddy was so well known that it's on people's minds again, and when they hear about Billy people are going to be afraid of us for a little while. And they may act strangely when school opens, but only for a little while. When they see that we haven't got anything they'll stop being afraid of us. There's something else I ought to tell you, too. You're both old enough. You've both been so grown up and sensible since Daddy got sick. You see, children. Alfred, Anna. We have advantages that a lot of people don't have, including a lot of our friends. When you were younger, I remember, Anna, you asked me why the Walls didn't have a big car, like the Pierce, and at that time I had to tell you that maybe they didn't want one. But since then you've guessed why, without my telling you. The reason, of course—we have more money. Why do we have more money? Well, Grandfather Caldwell bought things and sold them at a profit and made more profit than most other people, and his father did the same thing. And Grandfather Tate, in New York, *he* was in business and *he* made more profits than most other people. And Daddy got Grandfather Tate's money when Grandfather Tate died, and Uncle Brock and I got Grandfather Caldwell's money. Do you see?"

"Sure."

"And I will get Daddy's money, just as he'd have got mine if I'd died first. And some day you two will get mine, when I die . . . Now *don't* be sad, children. Everybody has to die. Everybody. Everybody you know, everybody you ever saw. The biggest crowd at the Fair—every one of those people will die some day. All those people on the sidewalk in Philadelphia. Each and every one of them. It's awful when someone you love dies, and we've had that happen to us with two of the ones we love very, very, very dearly, and always will, so soon together, one right after the other. That's an experience most people don't have to go through, and I hope it makes us better people. Any experience that makes us better people isn't all bad. Do you agree with me?"

"Well, I don't think it's fair to have your father die and then your little brother right after," said the boy.

"It doesn't seem fair, but God has a different way of deciding what's fair and what isn't," said Grace.

"Well . . ."

"I don't think it's fair, either," said the girl. "But I know a lot of things that aren't fair. I don't think it's fair to have some people colored people and other people white people. They're always poor. They never have cars, or—"

"They do too. I saw seven of them in a big Hudson Super-Six last week. They weren't poor, with a Hudson Super-Six," said the boy.

"But Anna's right. Some things aren't fair because at least they don't seem fair to us," said Grace. "But that's what I started to tell you. We—I mean, I'm Mrs. Tate, and you're Alfred Tate, and you're Anna Tate, and in Fort Penn, all around here, the people know we have advantages because of the money."

"Oh, I know that. I heard that long ago, us being called rich people," said the boy. "That's nothing new."

"Well, if you've heard it, then it isn't anything new," said Grace. "But all the same—"

"It *in*tails responsibility," said the boy.

"What?" said Grace.

"It *in*tails responsibility. Daddy told me that. If you have more advantages it *in*tails more responsibility. I asked him to increase my allowance, and he said money *in*tails responsibility and I said but what if you didn't have as big an allowance as some fellows, did that *in*tail not as much responsibility and he said no, but who got a bigger allowance and I told him the fellows in our form that got bigger allowances, and he said, well, he would give me as much allowance as anybody in our form so I wouldn't have smaller responsibility, but he didn't want me to have more money just because *he* had more than some fathers."

"I see," said Grace. "But did he explain what responsibility means?"

"No," said the boy.

"Do you *know* what it means?" said Grace.

"Yes," said the boy.

"Could you explain it to your sister?" said Grace.

"Yes," said the boy, and turned to his sister. "Money *in*tails responsibility. Just because we have money that's no reason why we can break the law. That's why we have to stay home."

"Thank goodness!" said Grace. She put out her hands and half rose. "No—I can't kiss you—but you're a good boy, a good man. I'm *so* proud of you."

"But Daddy's the one," he said. "And Billy was sweet."

"Oh, oh," cried Grace.

Anna got up quickly and stood in front of her mother and put an arm around her neck. "We mustn't make Mummy cry," said the girl.

"You don't," said Grace. "I'm just so glad I *have* both of you."

Someone knocked on the door. "That's Mrs. Barker," said Anna.

"Come in," said Grace.

Mrs. Barker came in. She looked from one to another. "Upstairs, children, and don't tire your mother."

"They've been anything but tiring me now, Mrs. Barker, but it *is* time—*is it* time for baths?"

"Tea, Mrs. Tate," said Mrs. Barker. "We've been having tea together. I thought it'd be nice if we had tea together while we're being quarantined."

"That is nice," said Grace. The children went out and Mrs. Barker lingered.

"The tea's only an excuse, Mrs. Tate," she said. "I like to keep an eye on them, just at present. For instance, Alfred could leave here right after lunch and be gone four or five hours without my seeing him. Out in the fields with a horse, down at the river, dear knows where. I don't like him to be out of my sight that long, in case there's any sign of infantile paralysis. It might show up right after lunch—you know, a running nose or one of the signs—and we'd lose four or five hours sending for the doctor. Not that sending for the doctor's much good, except at least he can diagnose the trouble and we can keep the child—the patient—away from the others on the place. So I'm having them come in around ten in the morning and have a cookie and a glass of lemonade. That way I see them in the middle of the morning, and giving them early tea I see them in the afternoon."

Grace smiled. "Like everything you do, Mrs. Barker. Thorough, and shows thinking behind it, and a nice disposition. You know how grateful I am for your help these last few days. You've been housekeeper in addition to your other work, and I'm going to remember it in your next cheque. But money isn't the only thanks. You have mine, deeply and sincerely, Mrs. Barker."

"Mrs. Tate, there never was a finer man or a better father than Mr. Tate, and as for little Billy—that's one child I'm glad the world didn't touch. Maybe in another year he would have changed, but we don't know that. We only know what we know. No little Lord Fauntleroy, he could be a little scamp. And he could take his own part. He didn't have to have someone else take his part for him. But the world never soiled him. You can always remember that. I will."

"I will, and I'll remember you said it, too," said Grace.

"I come to you with dry eyes, because I've done my weeping. I didn't want you to think me heartless."

"You heartless! Nobody could ever think that of you," said Grace.

"They could and they do, elsewhere in this house, but just because I'm Irish doesn't mean I have to parade my feelings for all to see."

"I didn't even know you *were* Irish," said Grace.

"You think of me as Mrs. Barker, but before that I was Mary Shea, of Boston." She smiled. "I'm a mackerel-snatcher, but not the kind that sees nothing but wrong in the cod, if you know what I mean."

"Mary S. Barker. I've written your name so many times without asking what the S stood for. We can live in the same house for years and years without getting to know one another."

"I prefer it that way, and anyway it's going to be that way in the long run. Man and wife, brother and sister, mother and child. Especially man and wife, Mrs. Tate."

"Why especially man and wife?" said Grace.

Mrs. Barker looked at her straight. "The man, the husband, doesn't often give the woman credit for feelings of her own. I'm not a widow, Mrs. Tate. I'm divorced. My *husband* divorced *me*."

"I see," said Grace. "I see. Thank you. Thank you, Mrs. Barker."

"Nineteen years ago I had to make a whole new start in life, and if I had to do over again I guess it'd be the same, but I wish I'd had somebody to tell me—did you ever read *The Scarlet Letter* by Nathaniel Hawthorne?"

"Yes."

Mrs. Barker shook her head. "They used to sew the letter A on the woman's dress, but even in those days I'm sure there were many going around without A's that should have had them. Only I didn't know that nineteen years ago. The world's still one-sided, in favor of the men, because the women like it that way too. They like the men to fetch and carry and make the money, and it's a small price the women pay, to be taken care of after they lose their prettiness and their teeth and run to fat. It's no price at all, because they're far removed from occasions of sin . . . I'm talking too much after I've said what I wanted to say."

"You didn't say what you wanted to say, but thank you for not saying it—at the same time you—conveyed it," said Grace.

"Thank you," said Mrs. Barker. "About deliveries from the stores, Maurer at the Becksville post office, he has no fear of the infantile and he said we could order things sent to him and he'd deliver twice a day, once when he brings the mail, and a special trip in the afternoon. Some of the stores will be squeamish, especially after they read the *Sentinel*."

"What's in the *Sentinel?*"

"It'll be in this afternoon's paper, about Billy."

"I don't want anything in the paper about Billy," said Grace.

"I knew you didn't and I told them so when they telephoned, but they said they had to print something."

"Who did you talk to?" said Grace.

"Mr. Hollister."

"It couldn't be Mr. Hollister, he isn't with the paper any more. He's retired."

"He must be back, because that's the name," said Mrs. Barker.

"I'll *see* about *that*," said Grace. "Thank you for—for our talk, Mrs. Barker."

"You're welcome," said Mrs. Barker.

Grace went to the telephone in the den and called the *Sentinel*. "I would like to speak to Mr. Hollister," she told the operator. The man's voice said hello. "Mr. Hollister?"

"This is Hollister, yes."

"It doesn't sound like you, Mr. Hollister. This is Grace Tate."

"Oh, well this is John Hollister. I'm Arthur James Hollister's son. You don't remember me."

"No wonder I didn't recognize your voice. You say you're Mr. Hollister's son?"

"The son of Arthur James. I want to tell you how sorry we all are down here, Mrs. Tate, and I want to extend my sincere sympathy, for myself and all of us on the staff."

"Thank you, Mr. Hollister, but in my opinion you could have

shown your sympathy in a practical way. I understand you're planning to publish an article about my little boy's death. I don't want you to."

"I'm sorry, Mrs. Tate, but we're not *planning* to publish it. It's been published. It's on the street right now."

"How dare you do that—go against our wishes? Don't you know who owns the paper?"

"Yes, I do. Indeed I do, but we have an obligation to the public, our readers. And that has its practical aspects, Mrs. Tate. If we don't print the news, we won't have a successful, profitable paper."

"That's our concern, whether it's to be a profitable paper. I've had things kept out before, and if you weren't new there you'd know it."

"Mrs. Tate, will you let me explain this to you and I think you'll take a different view."

"Mr. Hollister, you misunderstand me. I'm not interested in your explanation. I'm telling you, I'm ordering you to take that article out of the paper. I own the paper. My brother, Mr. Brock Caldwell and I, *own* the paper. It's our paper, Mr. Hollister. We own the majority of the stock, and I'm simply giving you an order."

"Yes, I understand that, just the way you'd order the maid to wash the dishes."

"Yes. Although you don't have to use that for a comparison."

"But it amounts to the same thing. You're paying the maid and me, so we have to obey your orders."

"If you put it that way, but I'm not comparing your work to a dishwasher's, Mr. Hollister. All I'm doing is telling you to take that article about my son's death out of the paper."

"Why?"

" *Why?* Isn't it enough to have my husband die, and all of that show, that public display, and articles in the papers, without having the same thing a few days later for a little boy hardly nine years old? Wasn't my husband's funeral enough?"

"I was there, Mrs. Tate," said Hollister. "Not as a representative of the paper, but because I'd met your husband and liked him."

"That's very nice I'm sure," said Grace. "But if that's the case why do I have to explain to you why I don't want articles in the paper about my son?"

"Mrs. Tate, let me read what's in the paper about your son. It's short and I can read it over the phone. Are you listening?"

"Go ahead."

"It's on the obituary page, the page where we print the death news. The headline, in small type, says, 'Tate Child Is Paralysis Victim.' It's a headline in small type because we don't want to alarm people. As far as we know, Mr. Tate, and your little boy, and a farmer down near Flieglerville, down in the southern part of the county are the only cases of infantile paralysis reported, and I didn't want people to get hysterical."

"I know. Go on, please."

"The article reads this way: 'William Caldwell Tate, 9, son of Mr. and Mrs. Sidney Tate, died yesterday at his home near Becksville, as a result of infantile paralysis. The child's father, Sidney Tate, prominent Fort Penn citizen, died last week following an attack of the disease. William is survived by his mother, the former Miss Grace Caldwell, and a brother, Alfred, 13, and a sister, Anna, 11. Burial took place today in the family plot in Trinity Cemetery.' That's all there is, and then underneath it we have what we call a shirt-tail, a little paragraph saying that according to the county board of health the only other case is the one in Flieglerville."

"Well, that isn't very long. You ought to be able to take that out without any trouble."

"I'm sorry, Mrs. Tate, but the paper's on the street. It was sent out on the wagons and by trolley, and newsboys are delivering it."

"I see. You just took it upon yourself, even after you were told by someone in this house that we didn't want anything in the paper."

"Yes, I take the responsibility."

"Then you can take the consequences," said Grace.

"All right, but one more thing. I'm sorry you want to fire me, but I'm leaving the paper next week anyway to go in the service, so I'm not losing much. But I think I'm entitled to say this much, Mrs. Tate: I have two children of my own, a little girl six and a boy four, and as a father I'd rather know the facts, that two people have died of infantile paralysis in the county recently, but that there's only one other case been reported. I'd rather have those facts than get a lot of wild rumors that another epidemic has started. And people as prominent as the Tate family—if it got around that they were hushing it up, there'd be no stopping the crazy talk. *I* know what kind of people you are, and how you're being, uh, conscientious about the quarantine regulations, but among the poor people especially, with large families, there's no telling how hysterical they'd get. They'd stay away from school and the factories where they're making munitions, and all that. They'd be out to your farm. I'm not trying to alarm you, but I've had experience with rumors . . . The article's in the paper against your wishes, but frankly I'd have run it even if I'd spoken to you personally. That's my responsibility, my duty, if you don't mind my using a romantic word. . . . I just want you to feel better about it, Mrs. Tate. You've had a tragic time, and I'd rather do anything than contribute to your sorrow, believe me I would. My father and your father were friends, and even though you don't know me, I've always thought very highly of your whole family. And I don't say that about everybody's family . . . Are you still there?"

"Yes," said Grace. "I may have been wrong, Mr. Hollister. And I guess you're right. I hope you'll come back to the paper after the war. Good luck."

"Thank you, Mrs. Tate, and I wish you the same. You've had more than your share of the bad. Good-bye."

"Good-bye," said Grace. She put up the receiver and sat at the desk a minute or so and then went out to the living room. Connie was sitting there.

"Was that Jack Hollister?"

"Yes," said Grace. "He was very nice, and I wasn't."

"You were at the end," said Connie.

"The second time today I learned something about responsibility."

"Who else has been talking to you?"

"My son," said Grace. They sat in silence for a few minutes. "Connie, would you be afraid to sleep in Sidney's bed?"

"Do you mean would I be? I myself? No, I wouldn't be afraid."

"Will you do it, then? Will you stay out here for a few weeks?"

"Yes, I'll stay, but I'd like to have a room of my own. I'll be here all the time, but—I'm so accustomed to my own room, Grace. I don't sleep well in a room with someone else."

"All right, you can have the guest room, on the same floor. I won't disturb you, but I need somebody that—not Brock, or even the children. It's funny, I still think of them as three children, then I have to cut it down to two."

"I know," said Connie.

On the table beside Grace lay a few magazines, recent copies of the humorous magazine *Life*, and Grace reached for one.

"If we're going to sit here I'll get my knitting. You ought to learn," said Connie, leaving the room. When she came back Grace was sitting there with two copies of the magazine in her lap.

"Will you teach me knitting?" said Grace.

"All right, I'd be glad to. Do you want to start now?"

She looked at Grace, who seemed to have become even less her confident self in just the little time Connie had been out of the room. "You used to know how to knit," said Connie. "It won't be difficult."

"Oh, I know how to knit, Connie. I was just thinking, I won't be able to read magazines if they're like these. Look." She held up the copies of *Life*. "Look at the pictures on the cover."

One issue had a picture of a young infantryman shaking hands with a G. A. R. man. "You can trust me, Dad," the caption read. The other magazine, a week later, had a picture of a frigate in action, and quoted underneath were the words: "Our Navy— as it was, is now, and ever shall be,—victorious."

"I see," said Connie. "Well, I guess give up magazines for a while. But you're not going to be able to avoid the war, Grace. No matter how much it reminds you of Sidney, it's in the air. It affects us every which way. The food we eat, the clothes we wear, our families, our friends. Brock's leaving, tomorrow, isn't it?"

"Poor Brock. He can leave, and he'll never be missed. And he knows it."

"He must have somebody."

"He hasn't now. If he'd been nicer to Sidney he'd have me now, but now he knows I only think of him as someone that hated Sidney, and not as a brother. We'll be brother and sister again, when we get older. But now he's better off going away."

"Well—he'll make a very good officer," said Connie.

"Well, he couldn't be anything else. He couldn't be a private. But I don't know. Sidney used to tell me that the reason why some of our friends weren't very good hostesses was because they weren't very good guests. The dominating hostess, that fusses around and runs things too much, she always makes a terrible guest, and vice versa. There are some women that can never be anything but hostesses, and they aren't successful at it. And I wouldn't be surprised if it's the same way in the Army. A good private will make a good officer, and a good officer has to know how to be a good private."

Connie was now knitting. "That's very interesting," she said. "Go on, tell me some more."

"Some more second-hand thinking? Sidney did most of my thinking for me. With him around I didn't have to think for myself." She stopped, and Connie noticed that she had laid the magazines aside.

"Talk to me about Sidney," said Connie.

"Yes, I can to you," said Grace. "The way he really was."

They sat there, the two women, that afternoon, and set a pattern for many talks like it in the ensuing weeks. Grace did not talk about Sidney every day, nor even every day they knitted in front of the fire. But at that place, in the late afternoons—and not at any other time or place—Grace would suddenly speak freely, without preamble or embarrassment, about Sidney, until one day she said: "I have something I want to tell you today."

Connie knew it was important; Grace, with her directness, hardly ever made introductory remarks. "I'm all ears," said Connie.

"I think you'll be glad to know it," said Grace.

"I hope so."

"It's this: I've buried Sidney." Grace had been smiling throughout the prefatory words, but when she uttered the statement she frowned.

"You've buried Sidney," said Connie.

"Yes," said Grace weakly. "Or I thought I had, till just now. Isn't that what you've been wanting me to do? Isn't that why you've been—encouraging me to talk about him?"

"Yes," said Connie.

"Well, why aren't you taking it differently? You sound as if you weren't sure."

Connie smiled. "I am glad you've buried him. You gave me credit for a deeper motive than I had, that's all. That's why I don't react the way I ought to. All I wanted you to do was to talk for the sake of talking, Grace. So you wouldn't brood. But it's been more effective than that."

"You don't sound convinced, but it has been. I've been wanting to tell you all day. I could hardly wait till we got here to tell you. I wanted to tell you that suddenly I'm able to look at his things, all over the house, and they don't *interrupt* me—you know—with a feeling of sadness. They don't interrupt me. I accept it, the fact that Sidney is dead. I thought you had something to do with it."

"Only as a listener," said Connie.

"I don't believe you! You wanted me to talk about him till I'd talked myself out."

"Now really, Grace. Why should I?"

"I don't know, but I have that feeling," said Grace.

"Well, you're wrong, and I wish you didn't try to make me feel I've done something wrong."

"Oh, I'm sorry, Connie. That isn't what I meant. You misunderstand me. The only thing I was accusing you of was denying that you had anything to do with it, and I wanted you to know that I thought you *had*."

"Straighten that out for me, please," said Connie.

"*I* thought you'd been so nice, listening to me and encouraging me to talk about Sidney, so that, by talking about him, I would get over my sadness."

"Oh," said Connie. "Well, that's about right. But I wasn't trying to make you forget him."

They frowned at each other.

"Don't you believe me?" said Connie.

Grace shook her head. "I wish I could say . . ."

"You can say anything you please."

"Well, you'll get mad."

"Then for God's sake don't hold it back," said Connie.

"Well—forgetting everything else, I honestly think you had something to do with my change in feeling toward Sidney's death, that's all."

"Do you think I, uh, hypnotized you?"

"Oh, no. That's ridiculous."

"Hypnotism isn't ridiculous. But it just so happens I am not a hypnotist, exerting my sinister influence over your childish mind."

"Influence, though. I think you exerted influence, only when I say that you take it as an insult. I didn't intend you to," said Grace.

Connie paused, and then resumed her knitting. She knew that Grace was looking at her. "Get to work," said Connie.

"You're not cross with me?"

"No, but I'm afraid I'm going to be."

"Why?"

"Because I've decided to go home tonight."

"You are cross with me," said Grace.

"No, but I will be if you're going to make a fuss about my going home. I can't live here forever, you know, and it's time for you to—oh—throw away your crutch."

"You're not a crutch, you're my best friend."

"As your best friend—I know I'm your best friend—and the best thing I can do for you now is to let you go on your own. I'm getting rid of myself for you, and I suggest you give Mrs. Barker a long vacation and give yourself so much to do you won't have time to think of yourself. You ought to think about moving in to town and spending the winter there, and signing up for a great deal of war work. Buy some new clothes, go to the hairdresser oftener."

Grace hesitated. "Will you give me your word of honor you're not cross with me?"

"I give you my word of honor."

"All right. But I want to drive you in."

"No. I'll borrow the Mercer and bring it back tomorrow and you can come in town with me and we'll go shopping together."

"Oh, Connie . . . What do you want for Christmas? It's still a long way off, but this year I want to give you something wonderful."

"Grace, has it ever occurred to you that I do things for you because I like to?"

"Yes, but you never let me do anything for you."

"Well, maybe I'm a good hostess but a bad guest. Now I'm leaving. I'm a bad guest, because I'm going to let Julia do all my packing for me. Don't get up, don't say good-bye, or anything. I'll call for you tomorrow at nine-thirty. I'm only going to my own house."

She went to her own house and locked herself in her room and drank whiskey and water until she was unconscious.

BOOK THREE

It was a Fort Penn custom every two years to elect George W. Walthour to the office of mayor. The custom had begun in 1905, when George, a handsome and already prosperous dentist of forty-two, got a kind of historical perspective on himself: he had been brought into the world during the afternoon of July 3, 1863, when George Gordon Meade repulsed George Edward Pickett's assault. The infant Walthour also was named George by his patriotic mother, but she had in mind George Washington because the day of her son's birth was so close to the Fourth of July. "The day I was born," George Walthour often said, "people in Fort Penn could hear the cannons at Gettysburg, all the way from Gettysburg, and I guess I heard them too—although—" he would add with a twinkle in his eye "—I can't tell you what they sounded like. Like cannons, most likely." Fort Penn citizens long since had ceased to entertain any doubt that the guns of Gettysburg could be heard at Fort Penn; if the people of Gibbsville, for instance, which was another fifty miles away from Gettysburg for a total of about eighty-five miles, were able to hear the cannonading, then the morning and afternoon of that third day of July must have been a noisy one in Fort Penn. Brock Caldwell made no friends for himself by declaring that he had once taken the trouble to look it up and according to the best authorities (which he did not name) there were only 140 field pieces on the Confederate side and seventy-seven on the Union side, and that he doubted if 217 Civil War guns fired all at once could be heard in Fort Penn. Brock was probably wrong about that, and privately he admitted it, but in that privacy—the privacy of the Fort Penn Club—he freely admitted that George Walthour bored him and that it was George's repetition of the legend that had made him skeptical and inquisitive.

Bore or no bore, George was the man Brock voted for in the primaries and in November, every two years. As Brock also said, "The Walthours and the wallflowers we have always with us." This was a reference to George's rightful claim to a place among Fort Penn's first families, insofar as antiquity was concerned. George was a member of the Society of the Cincinnati, and had the papers and the badge to prove it. His mother also was a County woman, from down around Flieglerville (where there was no doubting that the artillery fire at Gettysburg was audible). On the celebrated afternoon of George's birth and Lee's defeat George's father was at his desk at the old Farmers Bank of Fort Penn, but there was no shame attached to sending a substitute, and George Walthour always maintained that his father had stood ready to take up arms if the Rebels got any closer, just as George himself would have been in the event of a Spanish invasion in 1898. By the time he was forty-two, in 1905, George had put aside all such romantic notions as hurrying to the defense of Savannah or New York. He was the first Walthour in more than a century to have no money worries, but he had another concern: he knew that Laura, his wife, was not equipped to give him a son who could carry on the name, and he was the last of the line. The Cincinnati badge, which he had hoped to keep in the family, would have to go to the County Historical Society at his death since the Bensingers, Laura's people, had no idea of its significance. At forty-two George could extract the stubbornest canine and was ever ready to play a game with his wife that left her weeping and him less than completely satisfied. The money rolled in as the teeth came out. He was still young and vigorous, his name was on barns and fence-rails and roadside rocks all over a ten-mile radius, and he was greeted respectfully by the most prominent bankers and merchants in Fort Penn. The more he thought of his background, the easier it was to summon up the little quantity of courage that was necessary to urge himself upon the Fort Penn politicians as a surprise candidate for mayor. "This," They said, "will take a lot of money, George. A *hell* of a lot of money. Couple other fellows had their heart set on the job."

"How much money?"

"The job *pays* seven thousand," said They, in this instance Ed Eisenhuth, the district attorney.

"Thirty-five hundred a year," said George, who had made investigations. "You can have the seven thousand."

"Well, in that case I'll be glad to talk to the fellows," said Ed.

"Ed, you know you don't have to talk to any fellows. You can promise it to me."

"Yes, I guess I more or less can, George."

"But one thing more, Ed," said George. "I know I couldn't go in and win without you, but I don't have anything against me. What's more, I don't intend to. I may be very good for the party."

"How do you mean, George?"

"Well, what I said. People will have confidence in me. I think I'll bring in more votes. Everybody knows I'm honest."

"I still want to hear what you, uh, that remark about one thing more, George. What else do you want?"

"I want to be re-elected," said George.

Ed laughed. "Hell, every son of a bitch that ever ran for office wants to be re-elected, George."

"But I'm not a son of a bitch, Ed, so I want you to promise me that I'll be re-elected. I want to be mayor at least twice in succession. The money—the salary's yours. I won't keep a cent of it. That's a trade, and I happen to know it's more than the present incumbent kicks back. But I'm going to spend some of my own money on my campaign, and bring—"

Ed chuckled. "You're damn right you are."

"And bring in votes you don't get. People that don't vote are going to vote for me. I'll see to that. Well, when they vote for me they're going to vote for the rest of the ticket, and you gain by that. So in exchange for those votes and a good administration, I want you to agree right now to put me in for a second term. Otherwise I don't want to run for the first term."

Eisenhuth picked his nose and finally snapped out a hair. "I'm ready to say yes if you tell me what's behind all this. That good-administration remark of yours. If we have a reform mayor in this town the only kind of a reformer we want is somebody like Mr. Penrose. That's the kind of a reform mayor we want."

"Mr. Penrose?" said George.

"Yes, Mr. Penrose. He started out as a reformer and he never got to be mayor of Philadelphia, and that's fine and dandy. Then he saw the light. Then he saw the light. Now he's all right. A great man, Mr. Penrose. All for the party."

"I don't understand what you mean."

"Well, in plain words, let's don't have any dreams about reform. That good-administration stuff sounds like reform talk. If you want to be mayor, I'll see to that, as long as you're a regular party man, George. Either you want the honor or maybe you want to advertise your dental business, I don't know which. All right you can be mayor for two terms, with the understanding that you turn over the salary and finance your own campaigns— and of course naturally we'll be looking to see how many of these new votes you get out. Then what, George?"

"After I've been mayor?"

"Yes, what then?"

George smiled. "Maybe I'll want to run for mayor again."

"I see. It's the honor, eh? Not the advertising."

"That's all I want. In Fort Penn I'm next to the Governor," said George.

"But you don't want to *be* Governor. Or, say, senator."

"No, I only want to be mayor. I won't want to give up my practice."

"That's good, because—well, you're a nice fellow, George, but you're not the right kind of a candidate for senator. Maybe you could be Governor some day, but never senator."

"Mayor of Fort Penn and my dental practice is all I want. And I don't think the advertising of mayor is going to hurt me."

"No," said Eisenhuth. "No, it won't, but what I was thinking when I said that, the job of mayor carries more honor if you're elected two terms than it carries advertising. One term it carries advertising. Two terms it gets to be an honor. Who knows, George. Maybe you'll be mayor three times. That's something to tell your grandchildren."

"If I was going to have any grandchildren I wouldn't be here talking to you."

"Then I don't understand why you want the honor? Oh, maybe Laura wants the honor for you."

"No," said George. "Just leave it that way, you don't understand me, Ed. But we understand each other, is that correct?"

"All right, George," said Eisenhuth, rising. "Say, by the way, my wife's complaining about her plate."

"Send her in, Ed, I'll take care of it for her. She should have come to me in the first place."

"You were too young then," said Eisenhuth. "I'm beginning to think maybe *I* should have come to you, and not to get my teeth fixed either."

For four years Eisenhuth had no cause to wonder if he had done the right thing; George was entirely regular, refused nothing, and by his personal respectability and the very cleanliness of his person he seemed to give the office the brightness and shine and white-jacketed atmosphere of his dental parlors, with no implication of associated pain. Away from the dental parlors he was always spic and span, with particular care placed on his starched cuffs and bosom, and he affected a knitted white four-in-hand, which he tucked in just below the collar, which was not an unusual foppery of the day, but which on George became a sanitary, non-Popish, stole. He had one gold-capped canine, a plain gold shirt-stud and a pair of large plain gold cuff-buttons, and a heavy gold ring with a two-carat diamond on his left little finger. Fort Penn people were proud of him on those occasions that required him to represent the city in the company of the officials of the Commonwealth. He was four inches shorter than Penrose, for instance, who did not break his rule of refusing to shake hands, but at gatherings where the two men were present Fort Penn people did not want Penrose to shake hands with George. George, they believed, would be soiled by the other man's touch.

Toward the end of his second term George sent word to Eisenhuth that he would like to see him. Eisenhuth, who had had a slight stroke that he thought was a big secret, was too much of a political realist to tell George to go to hell. He went to George's house in Fourth Street, only a couple of squares from the Caldwell house. It was in the evening, after supper.

"Care for a cigar, Ed?"

"No, thanks, George. I've just about quit smoking."

"Yes, that's right, I forgot."

"You forgot?"

"Well, I knew you hadn't been up to your old self," said George.

"Oh, you knew that, eh, George?"

"Well, you know how a thing like that gets around, no matter how much a man'd like to keep his business his own, and me being a professional man, naturally I had some training. You know dentists take the same courses as M. D.'s before they, uh, specialize in dentistry."

"I didn't know that," said Eisenhuth. "You learn something new every day."

"That's right, Ed," said George. "But I guess you wouldn't call it new, what I'm going to tell you. You won't be surprised."

"No, but go ahead and tell me, George."

"Well, I've decided to run for mayor again."

"We were hoping you would," said Eisenhuth.

"Yes, I gathered that."

"Oh, you been talking with the other fellows?"

"Talking to the other fellows is more like it, Ed. I like being mayor of Fort Penn, where my family lived so many years, and with Laura and I not blessed with children I guess I'm the last of the line, and that's why I want to be mayor three times. Nobody was ever mayor three times. We had a couple that were two, but none three."

"Uh-huh."

"So I just wanted to tell you I'm running again, Ed."

"All right, suits me. The same, uh, terms, George?"

"No, not exactly," said George. "That's what I wanted to tell you, Ed. You know, I'm forty-six. Yes, sir, I'm forty-six years of age. In four years I'll be fifty. I feel fine and all that, but what I have I made myself. When my father died he left me eight hundred dollars, about enough to buy my equipment but no more. Well, Laura and I've been talking it over, and I can't see my way clear to putting up the spondulix for my own campaign. What's more, I might as well let you have it all at once, the kickback is going to be two thousand, a thousand a year."

"You and Laura must have had some long talks, George."

"Not long, and to tell you the truth, I did the talking," said George. "I simply told her what I decided."

"It's getting to be more and more that way, you doing the talking."

"Yes," said George. He tapped the fingertips of one hand against the fingertips of the other. "If you want to talk, go ahead."

"Can Laura hear me?"

"Out to her whist club. Won't be back before nine."

"All right, I'll talk. If you think you can dictate to me you have another think coming, you overstuffed horse's ass. I'll kick your ass out of that mayor's office so quick you won't know what hit you."

"You and who else?" George continued to tap fingertips.

"The organization."

"Nope," said George. "You can't do it. I expected some trouble from you. I didn't expect you to lose your head. I expected you to argue with me, but this name-calling I don't like. I sent for you out of courtesy, because you originally—you were the man I talked to four years ago. But I don't have to sit here in my own house and listen to that kind of abuse from you. You're a has-been, and if you antagonize me you're through all the way. Do you know that?"

"No, I don't know it, but I'd a damned sight rather be through than take any back-talk from you. You want to know why it'd be easy to lick you? No, you don't, but I'll tell you. We could get the people laughing at you. They almost do so's it is. You're comical, George, that's what you are. You're comical."

George thought a moment, and Ed went on:

"You know what I heard one of the fellows say about you? He said, 'George can't hardly wait to get old. He wants to be a dignified old man.' Why, we could not only laugh you out of politics, but we could make you such a laughing-stock people wouldn't even let you pull their teeth. You and your laughing-gas. George Laughing-Gas, heap big Indian chief." Eisenhuth stood up. "I'll give you forty-eight hours to come to my office, but don't come bothering me unless you're agreeing to the same terms as before. Turn over your salary, and pay your own campaign expenses." He started for the door.

"Before you go, Ed," said George. "It won't work."

"What won't work? You think I'm bluffing? Try me and see."

"The George Laughing-Gas idea won't work. You know why? It would have worked if you'd done it when I was up for the second term, but now the people would be voting against themselves. They'd be telling themselves that they'd been damn fools before, and they won't do that."

"What people are you talking about? You're talking about the voters. I'm talking about the fellows in the organization. The county committee, the leaders in the wards. I'm talking about fellows like the one that said you were trying to be a dignified old man. If they don't want you, you don't get the nomination, and if you don't get the nomination you're out on your ass in a snow-storm." He returned to the living-room. "Georgie, I've been in this game thirty-five years. You been in four. I have an organiza-tion, you don't have one. Who the hell can you lick? Now you have a nice home and a good reputation and a good practice. If we started in on you maybe you'd lose it all, the home, the repu-tation, and the practice. Because if you try to fight us in politics we're not going to stop at politics. We'll have to fix it so you won't ever be dangerous to us. Isn't that common sense, Georgie? We wouldn't want to give you a chance to start building up your own organization. So Georgie, you're a likable fellow, and take my ad-vice and stay that way. Now you sleep on it, and then come to my office tomorrow morning at eleven o'clock and I'll be there with some of the fellows and maybe I won't tell them you made me come to see you. Some of them wouldn't think that was grateful of you. Good night, Georgie."

George was at Eisenhuth's office promptly, and from the cool-ness of the fellows and Ed's triumphant smile he knew a full re-port of his revolt had been made, and he knew how close he had come to the end of his ambition and to destruction by ridicule.

"The fellows tell me you've been talking to them, George," said Eisenhuth, remaining seated. "I mean *with* them. Talking *with* them. Well, I cleared that all up and you can be mayor again. Pardon me, but don't sit down, George. We're in the middle of some important business, but when we want you we'll send for you." George looked at the fellows' blank faces and at smiling Eisenhuth, nodded to them all, and went out. It was his only re-volt, and the only warning he ever needed.

He got his third term, his fourth, fifth, sixth, and seventh. From 1905 to 1919 he aged into the dignified elderly man (at fifty-six) that one of the fellows correctly guessed he wanted to be. Relations between him and the fellows were carried on in a

spirit of mutual distrust, which proved to be every bit as effica-
cious as a spirit of mutual respect. For their part, after George's
premature little revolt the fellows never got over their suspicion
of him as a potential reformer, and that made for caution and discretion in their extra-legal activities. They never took too much
or were too bold about what they did take, because they were secretly afraid of their own created monster. It was possible, they
knew, that if it came to a showdown, George would have a
chance of winning. And whether or not it became a question of
winning or losing, they were afraid that if George were suddenly
to become miraculously courageous and denounced them, he
had the power to cause a great deal of damage.

For George's part, as he grew more experienced in politics he
knew that all politicians keep Dirty Files, in which are recorded
the true and half-true items of a man's conduct, from his credit
rating to his sex life. He knew, for example, that one union leader
hated another because the second man possessed a photograph
of the first man in a sexual position that is a popular pose on
filthy postcards. He knew that the fellows could find out in a few
minutes all entries in a man's banking records. He had had access
to such records himself. He knew that he was being watched for
signs of overt homosexuality and infidelity. One of the fellows,
an outspoken one, had said to him: "What do you do with it all,
George? You don't go to whorehouses, and when our wives ain't
getting any younger . . . How do you use it up? Hey?" This particular fellow was by tacit agreement the Dirty-File expert on
sexual irregularities. "I wish I had your chance when you get the
women under that gas."

"Always have a nurse present under those circumstances,"
George had said. "I have to, for my own protection. Some woman
might be under gas and when she came to she might *think* I'd
taken advantage of her, and where would I be?"

"I never thought of that. They could sue you, hey?"

"Put me out of business."

"Well, there must be a lot of them wouldn't mind a little feel.

Some of these rich ones that aren't gettin' much at home. I bet they wouldn't mind. Or widows, young widows like the Tate lady."

"I don't get their business. Never went after their business. My office we attend to a different class of people, not the high society muckity-mucks that think it's wrong to advertise."

George knew that such seemingly casual inquiry was only part of the scrutiny he came under. But he had nothing to hide. Laura was the only person with whom he indulged his passion, and the fellows were free to snoop into his financial dealings at any time, for all the good it did them. Not only was George legally invulnerable (the kickback was a cash proposition; he would deposit his salary cheques, and since most of his dental practice was on a cash-money basis, he made daily deposits and withdrawals as normal routine); the vigilance of the fellows acted as a challenge and an inspiration. There was the matter of the Washington Street Bridge.

The bridge was George's pet project. It was badly needed by the city and the state, and no one was against it. The plans had been approved prior to the Great War by the mayor, the city council, the state highway department, the Corps of Army Engineers and a citizens' committee which included the City Planning Commission. But the war postponed the work, conveniently for George's purpose. George's purpose was to see that the bridge was called the George W. Walthour Bridge. That required an exercise of tact, modesty, and forthrightness. Specialists in municipal bonds welcomed the opportunity to handle the issue, and as mayor George had the final approval of the financial houses that would appear in the transaction. One of the big Philadelphia houses had a man who visited Fort Penn every week or two, and whose house was well connected in Fort Penn. Jim Lawrence made a point of dropping in at the mayor's office once a month during the war, to make sure that his house got its share of the bonds.

"Mr. Mayor," he said one day after the armistice. "We oughta be about ready to get things going on the bridge pretty soon."

"I suppose so, Jim. Suppose so."

"What's the matter? Any hitch?"

"Not exactly," said George. "Not exactly a hitch. You might call it a *half* hitch, if you know what I mean."

Jim laughed. "Tell me about it."

George got up from his desk and walked to the large map of Fort Penn on the wall of his office. "I want to show you something," he said. He picked up a silver pencil and made an invisible circle on the map. "You see this section here, on the west side of the river. Do you know who owns that land?"

"No."

"I do," said George. "Now down here, right here on the map, here's where the bridge is going to be." He put the pencil back in his pocket and sat down and tapped his finger tips.

Jim Lawrence sat down. "I see," said Lawrence.

"What do you see?"

"Well, just between us two, I can see that you're not getting yours," said Lawrence. "Do you, uh, want me to do something about it? Talk to the right fellows? The bridge might as well be up where your land is. That land'll be worth no telling what it'll be worth if the bridge goes there."

"What would you think it'd be worth, just a guess."

"Well, I don't know how much acreage you have, but by the size of your circle—oh, 'way up in the hundred thousands."

"I thought over a million," said George.

"You're probably right. You know Fort Penn land values."

"Indeed I do, Jim. If the bridge went over to my land it'd be worth a million *profit*. I bought that land cheap, years ago."

"Gosh, I don't see why you didn't steer the boys out that direction when they first started talking about the bridge. But I think I can talk to the right fellows now. I think you're entitled to yours. The other fellows have been getting theirs, but from what I hear, you never got a red cent."

George smiled. "You think I'm entitled to mine."

"Absolutely."

"I'm glad to hear you say that," said George. "Tell you why. I've been mayor of this city for fourteen years, and I never took a red cent, and we never had a scandal. I think I'm entitled to something too."

"You sure are."

"I could make a million dollars, legitimately. *But.* I'm not gonna do no such thing. The bridge starts at Washington Street, the way we always planned it. As far as I'm concerned I don't want to make a penny out of it."

"By God I know a lot of fellows in public life, but I never thought I'd live to see the day when one turned down a million dollars legitimately."

"You're seeing one now. All I want is one thing, and if you go to the right fellows and get it for me, I won't forget you."

"I'll get it if it's humanly possible."

"I want the bridge named after me. It's my monument. The George W. Walthour Bridge."

"The George W. Walthour Bridge," said Lawrence. He slapped his thigh. "By God, George, I'll do it. Why, they couldn't think of turning you down."

"It's all I want," said George. "My monument. But I couldn't tell them that, the Planning Commission. The name is up to them. You know those fellows. They aren't politicians. They're the respectable element. If you put it to them the right way, what I could have had and gave up—if they turn me down . . ." He was saddened.

"They'll never turn you down. I know practically all of those fellows. I'll most likely see some of them over at the Fort Penn Club 'safternoon. Let me have a list of all their names. George, I'll do this for nothing. You restore my faith in human nature."

"Because I love my city," said George.

"I hear a lot of mayors say they do, but you're one that can prove it."

"If they turn me down I'll resign." George was now so sentimental over his love and devotion to Fort Penn that Lawrence was afraid he was going to cry or make a speech, and he quickly got to his feet and took leave of the mayor. When he closed the door George put his head on the desk and wept.

Duncan Partridge, who unknowingly served as George's model of an elegant old man, also served as chairman of the City Planning Commission. The Commission was a voluntary, unpaid group with fairly broad powers under the city charter, and it had been said—and repeated—that membership on the Commission was limited to wardens of Trinity Church, governors of the Fort Penn Club, and directors of the Fort Penn Trust Company. It was a self-perpetuating body with a paid architect-consultant whose chief function was to provide technological support for the amateurs' decisions. Duncan Partridge, who had known Jim Lawrence's father, called a special informal meeting (without the architect) at a private dining room of the Fort Penn Club. The commission members turned their faces toward their chairman, half of them resting their arms on their walking sticks.

"No pencils and paper today, gentlemen," said Partridge. "You'll damn soon see why. I think we all know Jim Lawrence, so Jim, tell your story."

Lawrence had an incredulous, silent audience until he finished and sat down, whereupon the consensus was expressed by Partridge: "Isn't that the damnedest thing you ever heard of? I think the fellow's a lunatic, turning down a million dollars to get a bridge named after him. I'm sure if I were in his position I'd take the million and let the credit go. Take the cash and let the credit go, as they say. Personally, I'm against calling it the Walthour Bridge or anything else. At one time I thought it'd be nice to call it the Caldwell Bridge, after Will Caldwell, but he's got enough memorials here and there about the premises, so I changed my mind and decided Washington Street Bridge was the best name."

"Duncan, I think you want to call it the Partridge Bridge," said one member.

"Well, what's the matter with that? Damn near time I got some kudos around here," said Partridge. "Lifetime of service to my fellow man. Never took a dime."

"Ho ho ho. Never gave a dime is more like it," said another member.

"Is that so? Why, the indigent people I used to defend—you don't hear anything about them," said Partridge.

"Because they're all still in jail, thanks to your defending them," said a member.

"That so? You'd be in jail yourself if it weren't for me, you absconder, embezzler, watered-stock artist," said Partridge. "Seriously, gentlemen, I do hope you'll all give this thing some thought between now and our next regular meeting on the 14th. Certain aspects we have to take into consideration. We can't gratuitously insult the fellow by turning him down, and it *is* a fact, as Jim told us, Walthour did refuse to take advantage of his position and try to have the bridge built out near his land. And in my opinion, he could have done so. The bridge would have been just as desirable out there as on Washington Street, if not more so. Also, we'd all like to do Jim a good turn if we can. And finally, I personally don't care whether we call it the Walthour Bridge or the Washington Street Bridge or whatever. I'm sure I'll never use it myself and the same goes for most of you here. We'll all be six feet under by the time the damn thing's finished. Well, I called this little caucus, so I suppose I'll have to stand treat. Everybody to the bar."

George Walthour's threat to resign was genuine. He was a perspicacious man and it took no major prophet to guess that the return of the boys from the Army was going to mean new faces in old jobs. Already, in the winter of 1918–1919 the fellows were making little lists of the dispensable men in city and county jobs, who would have to make way for those ex-service men who could be counted on to secure the returning soldiers' vote. Already in that winter uniformed men with gold chevrons on the right sleeves and red chevrons on the left—the honorably discharged wounded—were to be seen in increasing numbers on the streets of the city. They were especially popular if they wore the red keystone shoulder patch of the 28th Division. George was in the last months of his seventh term as mayor; he expected to be nominated more or less automatically for his eighth term, but he was not at all confident of being nominated for a ninth term. An ex-service man probably would be nominated in 1921; therefore if the bridge was to be named for him it would have to be right away or during his eighth term. The next mayor was not going to let any bridge be named for his predecessor. George wanted to make sure it was his bridge before construction was started. And if he was going to be turned down by the Planning Commission, he wanted to know it right away. If they turned him down, he would resign immediately; he wouldn't want to be mayor any longer. His name was on bronze tablets at the water works and two police station-houses and three grade-school buildings which had been erected during his tenure of office, but the bridge was going to be the biggest monument in Fort Penn. "You go across the Walthour Bridge . . ." The biggest monument for the best mayor.

What George did not know was that the fellows had just about made up their minds that George was already serving his last term. Besides the little lists that they would hand to George so that he could "let go" municipal job-holders in favor of ex-service men (and thereby disrupt any organization he might have been building up) the fellows had another list which they never showed to George. It was a small roster of names of men whom the fellows were considering for mayor. The list, of course, did not exist on paper, but where it was important, in the minds and the meetings of the fellows, the name most often mentioned was Charlie Jay.

Charlie was practically one of the fellows himself. For a few years in his late twenties he had been away from Fort Penn, living in Ohio, but he had not done well there, and he returned to the old home town, got a job in the office of the City Engineer, married a schoolteacher named Louise Dietrich (a distant cousin of Emlen Deatrick), and gave up his society friends. He made himself useful to the fellows by hiring only politically acceptable day laborers; by steady but inconspicuous payroll-padding; by recommendations for purchase of new road-building equipment; by condemning the equipment and ordering it re-sold; and by being continually alert for new opportunities for graft, without stealing on a large scale in any single instance. He would put a gang of eight mythical men on the city payroll, which was only about $24 a day, $144 a week. But he was shrewd enough to discharge the mythical men before their wages attracted attention, and he accepted what the fellows gave him after they had taken theirs. Likewise, he did not grumble over the size of his share after the resale to another town of a piece of almost-new road-building equipment, which he had rendered useless by removing a couple of cotter pins. Charlie did not participate in the big stuff; the awarding of paving contracts, for example. That was for the fellows themselves and the Chief Engineer always was one of the fellows, although the Chief Engineer was not always the same fellow. There again Charlie made himself useful; he could be depended upon to notice any independent grafting by the Chief Engineer and to report the fact to the other fellows.

Charlie would have reached his goal—$25,000 in cash in the imitation fireplace of his modest home—if he had not heard the call to arms. He was older than most volunteers, but he obtained a first lieutenant's commission in the 103d Engineers and being a man who was accustomed to mud and the outdoors, and being fond of violence, he was bothered only by the noise. He was transferred to the infantry, commissioned a captain, was wounded in the neck and nearly bled to death at Chateau-Thierry. He came home with a Croix de Guerre with bronze star and some new ideas about life and himself. His goal of $25,000 cash had been for the purpose of opening a cigar store and upper-class poolroom to cater to the kind of men who belonged to the Fort Penn Athletic Club and the good scouts in the Fort Penn Club. The spirit of the place would be sporting and political, and only the solvent would be welcome. But Charlie had been charmed by his own authority as a captain. "I could always handle hunkies and wops, but I've been giving orders to white men and they're no more trouble than the dagoes," he told Louise. "I know as many people as anybody in this town, but I've been using it wrong. Getting out votes for an old fart like George Walthour—I'm gonna get into politics, and don't be surprised if I run for council."

"Where we gonna get the money?"

"Don't we have around eighteen thousand?"

"That won't last forever," said Louise. "If you ask me, you better go back to your old job so we'll have something coming in instead of everything going out. What about that poolroom you were always going to open?"

"Oh, that. I'm still thinking about that, but if I went back to my old job they'd think that was doing enough for me and they wouldn't pay any more attention to me. Maybe I could open up the cigar store—not poolroom. *Cigar store.* Maybe I could open it up and run for council, but I couldn't run for council if I was only in the engineer's office. I found that out in the Army."

"*What* did you find out in the Army?"

"About rank. Who you associate with. A major in command of a battalion, he's only a major. But a major on the general's staff, he's with the general. You wouldn't understand it."

"Why wouldn't I understand it? If you associate with rich people, other people think of you as rich. Or important politicians."

"That's what I mean."

"All right, let's start associating with your rich friends," said Louise.

"I'll start associating with the important politicians first. I'll renew acquaintance with the rich later."

"All right, but when we get down to fifteen thousand in the fireplace you get a job. We aren't getting any younger."

"How could you say that?" said Charlie, smiling.

"I don't mean that way—and that won't last forever, either."

Charlie, who was not so diffident as George Walthour, turned up at the next weekly meeting of the fellows, in a private dining room at Fritz Gottlieb's Rathskeller. His uniform was pressed, his boots and Sam Browne belt were polished, he carried gloves and a swagger stick, and he wore his French medal. The fellows were surprised to see him, but they were not displeased. They all stood up and he shook hands all around, although he had seen most of them before. Then he sat down among them and they poured him a beer from the pitcher on the table. For the first time there was a slight awkwardness as he showed by his attitude that he was not going to leave in two or three minutes. He looked back of him. "Wanted to be sure that door's closed."

"What's on your mind, Charlie?" a fellow said.

"A lot of things, but only one I came to talk about today. You gentlemen, you have something to talk about—"

"Nothing special," the fellow said.

"Well, I guess you all know I was nicked, over in France. I got it where the chicken got the axe, you might say. Well, I expect to get some money from the government for that, but with prices the way they are, God damn Democrats and all, I have to think of my future. And my wife and two kids. So I came right to you gentlemen. There's going to be an election for council this year, and I've been talking to some of the other fellows that were in the Army, and I think they're gonna wanta be represented on the council."

"Mm-hmm," said the fellow. "Matter of fact, Charlie, we've had that up for discussion at other meetings. We're gonna do the right thing for the ex-soldiers. Have already."

"Yes, I know," said Charlie. "But constable, and clerk in Accounts and Finances, and field engineer in the Chief Engineer's office—those aren't representation on the City Council."

"Did you have your eye on any special job, Charlie? On the council, that is," said the fellow.

"No," said Charlie. "I didn't even say I wanted a job on the council."

"But you could be persuaded."

"I could be persuaded," said Charlie.

"What would we have to offer?"

"What could *I* offer? Well, I was born here, mother and father born here. Many years' experience in the Chief Engineer's office."

"You wouldn't want a bridge named after you, would you, Charlie?" said a fellow.

"Shut up," said the fellow who had been doing most of the talking.

"But you know and I know and, hell, we all know—what I offer is my war record." He touched his medal. "This little thing here, and I'm up for another one."

"Sure," said the principal fellow. "Well, naturally you didn't expect any answer today. We'd have to give it a lot of thought from all angles. But we'll take care of you, I can promise you that. It may not be council. It may be something else. But you'll be taken care of. Is that satisfactory?"

"Absolutely," said Charlie, taking the hint to leave. "I'll leave it up to you, gentlemen."

Charlie spent the greater part of the next two weeks in trying to find out the significance of the one fellow's faux pas about having a bridge named after him. He was, however, entirely unsuccessful; secrets did not leak out of meetings of the fellows, a fact which Charlie should have learned in his years on the outer edges of the Fort Penn *junto;* and while as boy and young man he had known the gentlemen of the Planning Commission, his meetings with them in many years had been few and formal. Consequently he would have learned nothing from them, even if he had known they were in on the secret.

His next appearance at a Rathskeller meeting was by invitation. Although the invitation was tendered over the telephone it bore a resemblance to a summoning to a grand diplomatic reception: "Be at the Rathskeller twelve-thirty tomorrow, Charlie, and *don't wear your uniform*." That was all. The other party to the conversation did not give his name, but that was not necessary. Charlie dressed himself, as always, neatly and in semi-collegiate style. His suit was a dark gray hard worsted, with three buttons. He put on a soft white collar and subdued striped shirt. His shoes were the high, eight-eyelet, plain-toe cordovans that he had bought at the time he was commissioned, when officers were wearing leather puttees. They took a beautiful shine. His new brown hat was a Crofut-Knapp; the crown was folded over in the center, with the fold held in place by being tucked in at both ends. He carried his gold watch, with the chain stretched between the upper pockets of his vest, and for decoration he got out his old Sigma Nu badge. He was so meticulously civilian that he did not even wear his 28th Division button in his lapel.

The invitation itself was flattering; the hour set was exciting. Louise herself did not know that nobody ever got invited to sit down and eat with the fellows. The fellows had men at their meetings nearly every week, but not as luncheon guests.

The meal was sauerkraut, pork, mashed potatoes, dumplings, and baked apple and coffee. The dirty dishes were removed, and a large pitcher of beer was placed on the table, and toofers—two-for-a-quarter cigars—were passed. There had been no serious talk during the meal; these men were serious eaters. After the glass steins were filled and the cigars lighted the principal fellow closed his eyes for a couple of seconds, opened them again and stared at Charlie.

"How would you like to be mayor?" he said.

Amazement, without consternation, was the Fort Penn reaction to George Walthour's resignation. In the bars and barber shops, the clubs and trolley cars, the hose houses, the whorehouses, the cigar stores—wherever people met and talked politics they seemed to have been taking for granted that the office of mayor was permanently George Walthour's, that that was one thing in the peaceful but still troubled world that they did not have to be bothered about. *A mayor? Yes, we have a mayor. We have George Walthour. We have the Nesquehela River, and George Walthour.*

But when the story that the fellows wanted to get around got around George became overnight a positively disliked man. George's statement said ". . . I have decided to devote myself to my home life and the practice of my profession and will no longer take an active part in political affairs." He had refused to insert the conventional statement of availability to the party and his successor, whereupon the fellows spread the word that George had been intractable about supporting a strong ex-soldier's ticket for council. According to the rumor inspired by the fellows George had said that military service did not qualify a man for public life, and that a man who had been in the Army for two years was *unfit* to occupy councilmanic office. George's denials did not get beyond his own small group of friends, and in May, when most of the units of the 28th Division were mustered out, a small band of men and boys made their water on George's front porch. "Hey, Georgie, we hear you sit down to pea. Are you unfit?" was one of the shouted remarks.

The fellows waited a few days until their rumors were assuredly part of the citizens' credo, and they then announced, through the county committee, that in response to sentiment among ex-soldiers and civilians alike, a hero of the war, an experienced public servant, a lifelong resident of Fort Penn, a family man *with two children,* a true representative of the people—was the regular party organization's choice for mayor. No one else had given thought to the possibility of George's death or resignation, with the result that no one else had coveted the job sufficiently to create a sentiment in favor of himself, and Charlie Jay was nominated without opposition except by the Democrats. The Democrats scarcely counted. The average voter in the city and county blamed the Democrats for getting the country in a war with what was to many Das Vaterland; moreover, Fort Penn was a "railroad town," and the tricky mismanagement of the railroads under government control was offensive to the neat railroading mind, which did not seek out subtler reasons. With all of these factors in his favor, Charlie was as good as sworn in the day the committee made its announcement. Only one thing, in fact, was against Charlie, although it was not enough to defeat him: people did not like him.

He knew an imposing number of people, and in the past he always had been able to obtain promises to vote, and signatures to petitions, and if it became necessary he could get work and sometimes money out of people. But they did not want him around. The fellows began to find it out after they had committed the organization to Charlie. It was no cause for alarm, but no more one for rejoicing. "Have any you fellows noticed," one of them said at a weekly meeting. "I always thought Charlie Jay was a likable fellow, but the truth is, he's a little punk."

"Sorry to say it, but I agree with you," said the principal fellow. "But we're electing a mayor, not running a popularity contest. And don't forget *this:* Charlie could *win* a popularity contest. He'd make people give him their votes, maybe to get rid of him, but he'd get them. However, we do have a problem here, because we want to elect Charlie with enough votes so he'll run ahead of anything George Walthour ever got."

"That's gonna be work."

"And anybody that's afraid of work can get out of politics," said the principal fellow.

"I didn't mean it that way. You know that."

"Well, then don't sound as if we were licked before we start. Now the way I look at it, the *Sentinel* is regular, but we gotta have more than that. I know Brock Caldwell well enough, but I don't want to do it that way. Who knows Jack Hollister the best here?"

"If you want to know who knows Hollister best—Charlie Jay. Charlie's his brother-in-law, for Christ's sake."

"He *is?*" said the principal fellow.

"Charlie's wife is Hollister's wife's sister."

"Uh-huh," said the principal fellow. "I knew Charlie used to be friends with Brock Caldwell, but this is news to me. What will Hollister want?"

"Oh, I don't know. Maybe a receivership. I don't think he makes over fifty at the *Sentinel.*"

"Oftentimes they're the greediest," said the principal fellow.

"Well, maybe game warden, or health inspector."

"Does he own his own home?" said the principal fellow.

"First mortgage," said the fellow who was expected to know such things. "He lives in one of those developments Roger Bannon put up."

"Oh, with a little ground around it," said the principal fellow. "We could fix him up with a lawn and rosebushes. Park Department. Or—does he own an auto?"

"No."

"*That's* what we'll do," said the principal fellow. "Make him a building inspector and give him a city auto to use."

"If he'll take it."

"He'll take it," said the principal fellow. "A young man like him won't say no to an auto. What's the saying? If he can't afford a Ford . . ."

"Arthur James wouldn't have taken an auto."

"And died broke, or just as good as," said the principal fellow. "Be that as it may, it's Jack Hollister, not Arthur James Hollister we're dealing with now, and we want young Jack to get behind this campaign. If he got his orders from the top, the *Sentinel* would—well, they'd put on a nice campaign, and we'd win. But what we want to do is fill this young fellow up with his own importance and get him so he thinks he's practically running the campaign himself. You know what I always say about politics: oftentimes it's worth as much to have a fellow do you a favor as it is for you to do him one. Get him doing you a favor and maybe he'll do you another one so he'll get two back. But just do him one favor and he'll think he deserved it and the hell with you when you come to him for something . . . Well, we'll have a little talk with Charlie and get him to work on his brother-in-law."

They sent for Charlie, who was at lunch downstairs, and explained their tactics. They authorized him to sound out Hollister, and to go as high as the use of a city-owned car in perpetuity, provided Hollister, in one fellow's unfortunate phrase, put it over the top with a *bang*. Charlie listened and nodded and departed, but said to himself: "I can't go to Jack and tell him to put some pep in it. That would look as if we thought he hadn't been doing enough." He decided on another stratagem.

He telephoned Jack.

"Don't go home for supper tonight," he said. "Eat downtown with me. I need your advice."

They met at the Rathskeller and sat in a booth, the next thing in seclusion to a private dining room.

"What the hell kind of advice can *I* give *you?*" said Hollister. "I never heard you ask anybody for advice on anything."

"Quit your kidding, I often get advice. Seriously, Jack. What can I do to get more votes than George Walthour ever got?"

"Buy more," said Hollister. "That's what George would have done."

"You know the arrangement with George. He turned back his salary and in addition to that he paid for his own campaigns. I'm flat on my ass. I'll be all right after I'm in, but now . . ."

"Why do you want to get more votes than George? Why do you care as long as you get elected? In two years you oughta be a rich man."

"Maybe, but I'll be twice that rich if I get re-elected, see?"

"Then why don't you be satisfied with being elected this time and *next* time try to get more votes than George?"

"Because if I get a lot of votes this time the organization'll get behind me more next time. They'll say, 'Charlie Jay pulled a big vote in 1919, so he's our man again,' and they won't be thinking of anybody else, the way they were with George Walthour. All the years George was mayor they were always hoping there'd be somebody else they could put up, but if it wasn't for the war, George would still be the candidate this year. I'm running on my war record."

"Oh, I know that all right," said Hollister.

"Now wait—don't—"

"Don't what? We know damn well they wouldn't have put you up if you hadn't been a hero. Don't start believing the rest of that stuff about your being a devoted public servant and all that, Charlie. You're talking to me, now, not the electorate."

Charlie snickered. "You're right," he said. "Well, how can I make a big showing—besides buying votes? You're a newspaperman, you're supposed to be able to influence public opinion."

"Oh, sure," said Hollister. "Well, I'll give you some advice. The first bit of advice, which I don't expect you to take, is leave well enough alone. Be satisfied with the votes you'll get. But the hell with that. The second, why don't you talk to Brock Caldwell and get him to put up some more money for *you?* Not the rest of the ticket. You. After all, didn't you and Brock used to be great buddies?"

"When we were kids. But what good would that do? I don't think it would do any good. Only make the others sore."

"I guess so," said Hollister. "How about—no."

"How about what?"

"Well, you can't win without the labor vote, but nobody ever got all of the labor vote. There's at least a couple thousand labor votes, or voters, that never go to the polls, because they don't think anybody's any good. Maybe some day they will, if the right fellow comes along, but I don't think you're him."

"No, and I don't want to get tied up with them. The money doesn't come from them, it comes from the Caldwells and people like that."

"Well, I guess I'm not very helpful," said Hollister.

"What would you do if you were running my campaign?"

"If I were running your campaign? I'd apologize to the public."

"Come on, Jack, quit your kidding."

"Well, as far as I can see, you're making the most of all your opportunities and qualifications—except one."

"Which one is that?"

"Just a minute ago you said the money comes from people like the Caldwells. Well, you used to be one of that gang. Why don't they form their own committee and support you? You're the only one I ever knew from that crowd that went into politics, so it shouldn't make the others too sore if the Fort Penn Club bunch put up a little money for an old pal. They'd spend the money on you, but it might help the rest of the ticket. At least you could tell the organization it did."

"That's a hell of a good idea."

"Well, I had to come through with one good idea to pay for my supper."

"Who do you think I ought to talk to?"

"Oh, I don't know. You know as well as I do, the rich men and women in Fort Penn."

"Grace ought to put up some money, Grace Tate," said Charlie.

"She has it."

"Yes, and when we were kids I was as close to her as you can ever get."

"How close?"

"I'll tell you how close. I was sent away to Ohio to keep me away from her," said Charlie.

"You mean about ten years ago?"

"Not that time. No. Before that."

"You mean you were giving her the business? When you were kids?"

"Why do you think they sent me away?"

"I'll be God damned. *I* always wanted to dip my socks in her coffee. She's a little older than I am, a couple of years, but I never had a chance. You know. I went with the high school crowd, and my Dad was always against getting mixed up with your crowd. But then I understand a couple of years ago she got very democratic with Roger Bannon. At least that was the story."

"It was true. Sidney was going to leave her over Bannon."

"Yeah? He knew about it, eh? I liked him. Are you sure he knew about it?"

"Absolutely."

"Because now I think of it, the only time I ever talked to her was when he died. She wanted to keep it out of the paper that their kid died. Remember, they had a kid die a few days after Sidney? Well, I talked to her and I remember thinking she was very sad. That's only natural, a woman loses a husband and then a couple days later one of her kids. But she gave me the impression she was grief-stricken, genuinely. Has she got anybody now?"

"Why? Are you thinking of volunteering?"

"I wouldn't tell *you* if I was," said Hollister. "No, I was just wondering what a woman in her thirties does when she's a widow and, like Grace Tate, still pretty but respectable. What does she do when she has to have it?"

"Well, Grace didn't even wait till she was a widow."

"That's true, and Bannon's back. I guess he's getting it," said Hollister. "Too bad. She's too good for him. He's nothing but a hod-carrier, but maybe he carries what she wants. Well, there's no use getting horny about her. She pays my salary and it's a small town, but I don't see her twice in a year, and the only time I ever spoke to her was over the phone."

"Well, I'll tell you what I'll do," said Charlie. "To show my appreciation for your idea, when I go to her for money I'll tell her about the handsome city editor on the *Sentinel*."

"Don't trouble yourself. You don't want to break up my marriage, do you, brother-in-law?"

"No, but I don't want you to miss anything."

"You son of a bitch, you're no good, Charlie. You belong in politics."

"All right, you help keep me in."

A few days later Charlie asked Grace if he could call on her on political business and she invited him to meet her at the town house. In his new dual identity as war hero and candidate for mayor Charlie was being welcomed, if only out of curiosity, by many of the friends of his early youth who in recent years had continued to speak to him but whose lives otherwise had become remote from his own. The new difference was sensed by Charlie and he quickly had taken on a matching new assurance.

He followed the maid to the library and Grace rose to greet him. He had half-expected her to be in mourning, but her dress was dark brown with a white open collar.

"Hello, Charlie, it's very nice to see you again after all these years. Congratulations."

"Thank you, Grace," he said. "You look the same, or better, rather. You look great."

"So do you. How's Louise? And the children?"

"Oh, they're—just fine. And your children?"

"Well, Alfred's at Lawrenceville, and of course Anna's still at Miss Holbrook's, but she'll be going away soon. Brock won't be here. He's in Philadelphia for the day, but I gathered you wanted to talk to me. Isn't it wonderful about you and getting the nomination? I'm so pleased. Charlie Jay, mayor of Fort Penn."

"Not quite, but I suppose—well, that's what I wanted to talk about, Grace. And it gave me a good excuse to call on you."

"Not that you needed one. After all, Louise and I—I often saw her at the Red Cross during the war."

"You did? I didn't know that."

"Well, not for very long at any one time, but almost every week. I was one of the girls that could drive a car, so they had me driving a little Ford truck, but I'd see Louise *almost* every week. I think she's very nice."

"Thank you, Grace. She doesn't know what to make of this mayor business, and frankly I don't either, but they came to me and asked me if I'd run and when I got used to the idea I decided why not? But I made up my mind if I was going to run I'd do it right. The only trouble is—it takes money."

"I should think so. Bill-posters and things like that."

"Exactly," said Charlie. "Well, ordinarily of course the party organization runs the campaign, collects funds and spends the money, and I have very little to do with that end of it. I go around making speeches, if you could call them that, and writing letters and talking to the individual people, and that's what a campaign is. But I was talking with a friend of mine the other day—my brother-in-law he works on the *Sentinel.* Jack Hollister."

"Oh, Mr. Hollister. I talked to him over the telephone one time. He seemed very nice."

"He's very intelligent, very handsome, too."

"He's your brother-in-law?"

"He and I married sisters."

"I see," said Grace.

"And he came out with a suggestion as to how I could get more votes. A very good suggestion, I think. He said why didn't I make a personal appeal to my old friends that, uh, are better off than most of the people, and that way get them interested in the election and contribute. Contribute funds. Most of them to contribute as a matter of course, but Jack mentioned that I was the only one of our old crowd that ever ran for mayor, and—well, he seemed to think my old friends would rally around, you might say."

"Of course. *I'd* be glad to help out. What, uh—how much do you think I ought to give? Brock always gives and I give the same amount for myself, and of course Sidney was a Republican so I give the same amount as though he were still living. But I'd be glad to help out some more for *your* campaign."

"Well—I'd like to be able to say you gave five hundred."

"I see. Is that what Brock gave you?"

"I haven't seen Brock, but that's the amount I'm going to ask him, and if you gave five hundred, I'm sure *he* would, and a lot of other people. You see, what you give, uh, sets a standard for other people. I guess you've found that out."

"All right," she said. "Shall I give you a cheque now?"

"I'd appreciate it if you would."

"How shall I make it out? To the committee? Or to you personally?"

"I guess me personally, because this is kind of a separate campaign, you might say. I'll keep a separate account and you'll know where the money went."

She got up to go to the desk and the sudden rustling of her skirt, the scratching of the pen, her seated figure made her seem alive again, alive for him, and not the mere decoration of the room that she had been throughout the interview. He remembered that there was nowhere of her that his fingers had not been and he was enjoying the memory when she turned around and asked him the date. She could see his confusion and he knew she read his remembering. He told her the date and she tore up the cheque and faced away from him.

"We had some good times in this house," he said.

"I suppose so," she said. "I never liked this house."

"Why not?"

"I always liked the farm better." She pressed the blotter firmly and got up and handed him the new cheque. She did not sit down, so he remained standing.

"Thank you," he said.

"Not at all," she said. "Heavens, I should have offered you a drink of some kind. Can I get you something? I haven't had a gentleman caller for so long, and it's too early for tea."

"No, thanks, Grace. I'll have to be getting along." He knew he was being dismissed and he knew why, why she had expressed a preference for the farm, why she did not acquiesce in his pleasant memories of this house. "Grace, you ought to get married again," he said.

"Ridiculous," she said. "I'll never marry again, you can be sure of that, Charlie."

"That's a pity, because you're young and beautiful."

"You know how old I am, and I never was beautiful."

"I'm a man, and I said what I said."

She smiled politely. "Oh, Charlie, you haven't changed. Anything in skirts, for you."

"Yes, and lifting the skirts."

"Now I think you'd better run along, before we get too reminiscent. That would be boring."

"It wouldn't bore me."

"But it would me, and the next mayor of Fort Penn mustn't be boring. Good-bye, Charlie, and remember me to Louise."

"All right, I'll do that little thing. And thanks very much for the contribution."

"You're quite welcome," she said.

On the way downtown he enjoyed knowing that she would have given a great deal more than five hundred dollars to buy back the fact of his experience with her, but she could *not* buy it back and he *had* the five hundred. He arranged to have a few minutes with Hollister after the last edition had gone to press. They took the booth in the Rathskeller.

He tossed the cheque on the table. "I might have an idea for a story for you," he said.

"Can always use an idea for a story," said Hollister.

"Why don't you write one of those human-interest stories about old Fort Penn residents forming a Charlie Jay Club?"

"Great," said Hollister. "I see you don't want to be mayor. I guess that's a good thing for the town."

"What are you talking about?" said Charlie. "That's a good story."

"It might be a good story, but all the Italians and farm people and everybody else that wasn't born in Fort Penn would say, 'All right, let the native-born vote for him, but we won't.'"

"Hell, you could do it if you wrote it the right way. Why don't you write it yourself?"

"That's not my job."

"All right, but it would have given you a good excuse to call on Grace Tate."

"Well, I never thought of that. That's more like it," said Hollister. "Is she at the farm?"

"She's in and out."

"I wish I owned a car."

"Hell, you don't have to own a car. If you promise to be more generous with stories about me I'll get you a city car tomorrow, and you can keep it as long as I'm mayor."

"Charlie, old chap, let me shake your hand."

———

Telephone conversation between Jack Hollister and Grace Tate:

HOLLISTER: Is this Mrs. Tate?

GRACE: Yes, I'm sorry to keep you waiting, Mr. Hollister. I was out in the garden . . . My maid said it was some business about the paper.

HOLLISTER: Well, it isn't business-department business, Mrs. Tate. It was on the editorial side.

GRACE: You mean you wanted to read me an editorial? I think you'd better wait till my brother gets back and read it to him. I know you do that sometimes, but I wouldn't like to take the responsibility.

HOLLISTER: No, Mrs. Tate, I don't want to read an editorial. It's something else. You see, I understand some of Mr. Jay's old friends are getting up their own, uh, what you might call secondary organization, to support him, in addition to the regular organization. And I was wondering if I could interview you and several others. I understand you've given your contribution.

GRACE: I have. I've given a contribution, and so has my brother, but I don't think I'd like to be interviewed about it. I don't think it would do the least bit of good.

HOLLISTER: You don't? May I ask why not?

GRACE: Well, Mr. Jay's old friends would vote for him anyway. Naturally I'd vote for him if women had the vote too. But I think the less we appear in it—you know, his old friends—the better for him.

HOLLISTER: Frankly, I'm inclined to agree with you, Mrs. Tate. But the story *could* be handled in such a way that it wouldn't antagonize the ordinary vote, the man in the street.

GRACE: Maybe. Of course I'm not a writer.

HOLLISTER: Then would it be convenient if I came out and interviewed you?

GRACE: Did you say when would it be convenient?

HOLLISTER: No, I said *would* it be. I said "*Then* would it be?"

GRACE: Oh. Well, I'm afraid the answer is it won't be, Mr. Hollister. I'll be perfectly, uh, candid with you. It isn't only because I think it might do Mr. Jay's chances any harm. It isn't only that. I guess the real reason is I don't want to be interviewed. I don't like to see my name in the paper at all, even on the society page.

HOLLISTER: It wouldn't be much of a society page without your name.

GRACE: Oh, it'd get along, I imagine, without my name. But I'm not going to make an issue of that. If I go out to a large dinner party and the names are printed, I suppose my name has to be among them. But while we're on the subject, do you have to put it in the paper every time I go shopping in Philadelphia or take my children there? I think it's very bad for children to have their names in the paper, and now that I have you at the other end of the wire I'm afraid I have to ask you to put a stop to it. Once a month I take my little girl to Philadelphia for the day. To have the bands on her teeth changed, as a matter of fact. It isn't a pleasure trip for her, but every time we go, when we get home that evening the *Sentinel* says, 'Mrs. Sidney Tate and daughter, Miss Anna Tate spent the day in Philadelphia.' I don't know who tells you, but I can tell you I don't like it.

HOLLISTER: I realize that, but it's society news.

GRACE: And I should think the business, advertising people wouldn't like it. What do the people that own the stores think when they read in the paper that my daughter and I go to Philadelphia? They must infer that we do some shopping there, and if I owned a store and advertised in the *Sentinel* I wouldn't like to continually pick up the paper and see where one of the owners was spending her money out of town.

HOLLISTER: That's a good point, Mrs. Tate, and I'll be glad to mention it to the advertising department.

GRACE: Well! I accomplished something!

HOLLISTER: Yes, you did, but I didn't.

GRACE: Oh, I'm sorry, Mr. Hollister. I guess I'm not very co-operative, am I? And I always meant to write you a note after my little boy died, that time we talked on the telephone. But then you went to the war almost right away, didn't you?

HOLLISTER: Yes, I joined the Marines.

GRACE: I know. I saw your name on the Roll of Honor.

HOLLISTER: Here, at the paper?

GRACE: Yes, I've been there, you know.

HOLLISTER: Well, the next time you come down I hope you'll let me know.

GRACE: All right, I will. Is there anything else?

HOLLISTER: No, I think I'd better hang up before you keep some more news out of the paper.

GRACE: Not that bad, Mr. Hollister. I like the paper very much.

HOLLISTER: Thank you very much. Good-bye.

GRACE: Good-bye.

Grace had not seen fit to tell the whole truth about her trips to Philadelphia. They were not always in company with her daughter Anna (who could easily have been taken for her much younger sister), and they were not limited to once a month. The trips were approximately fortnightly, and that average had been maintained for two seasons of the year, beginning with the winter of '18–'19. After the influenza epidemic had done its worst (and during which Grace had done her best as driver of a small truck that now and then served as emergency ambulance) she took the children to Philadelphia for their annual inspection of the items that interested them most at Wanamaker's, Strawbridge's, and Schoenhut's. Alfred was old enough to have his own room and Anna slept in one of the twin beds in Grace's adjoining room. They could be safely left at the Bellevue after an early dinner in the Della Robbia Room while Grace broke bread with the Locust Street cousins. That night she met, for the second time, Oscar Stribling, a friend of Locust Street cousins, whose wife, a cousin of the cousins, had died a few weeks earlier in the 'flu epidemic. It was explained to Grace, who had met Stribling in Cape May, that no mention would be made of Oscar's recent loss; this was his first time out and he had agreed to come only when he heard that Grace was to be there. He had known Sidney slightly.

Oscar called for her in his Pierce limousine and he took her home from the dinner party so early that she walked in on Alfred as he was about to drop a laundry-bag water-bomb on Walnut Street.

Grace did not think enough of her second encounter with Oscar Stribling to mention it to Connie Schoffstal, but he wrote to her in January, saying he had enjoyed being with her and asking her if she would have dinner with him the next time she came to Philadelphia. It was an almost startling invitation in an otherwise stiff little note; it was not like Oscar Stribling to invite a lady to dine with him so soon after his wife's death. She waited a few days and wrote in reply that she would be in Philadelphia with her daughter, if he cared to have lunch with her and her daughter, but that she seldom stayed overnight. He took them to Kugler's for lunch and insisted on their using his car the rest of that day and offered to have it meet them every time they were in town. "It's a shame not to use the car," he said. "Nowadays I use it to go to the office and take me home in the afternoon, and that's about all." Grace took him up on the offer—he also said it was practically in the family—and on the next visit she and Anna spent the night in town, dined with him, and Grace, saying good night at the elevator, consented to come to Philadelphia the next week, to dine with him and go to the theater.

They went to see Al Jolson in *Sinbad* and walked home from the theater and said good night at the elevator, without Oscar's having revealed himself as anything but a gentleman of middle age and considerable means, who slightly resembled Woodrow Wilson and whose resemblance to the President was due as much to their association with widowerhood (which Wilson had corrected) as to the pince-nez spectacles which made Oscar look older.

Grace's Philadelphia trips came every two weeks after that. They were her secret because Connie, the only person in whom she might have confided, decided to live in New York and get something to do in the theater; and Oscar said he saw no reason to tell anyone they knew in Philadelphia that they were seeing each other. In the third month he asked her to marry him some time during the '19–'20 winter, and to take as long as she pleased about giving him her answer.

She took a month, and her answer was that she did not think they could get married: she would not live anywhere but in Fort Penn, and he could not leave his insurance—"assurance"—business. He had a married daughter, whom Grace did not know, who was in favor of his getting married again. Grace said her own children would not be in favor of her getting married again.

"But this doesn't mean we have to stop seeing each other," said Oscar.

"No, not unless you decide you ought to spend your time with somebody that would marry you. It was never a question of love with us."

"I think it was with me, Grace, although I've never mentioned the word."

"Then maybe we ought to stop seeing each other."

"No," he said. They were in a corner at Kugler's, and he looked down at his coffee. He looked up again. "Will you be my mistress?"

"No," she said.

"Don't answer like that," he said. "It doesn't have to be love, Grace. You're young, you're so young that you're probably right in not marrying a man ten years older than yourself. But we've both been married and we don't have to pretend. I want you very much and I'd be very happy just to give you pleasure."

"I don't know what that pleasure's like any more. I try not to think of it."

"But thinking won't control it. You're tense. I've noticed you, watching actors on the stage, and that young couple dancing over there. You've been watching them. If I hadn't noticed that tonight I wouldn't have asked you to have an affair with me."

She was silent a moment, and then she took a deep breath and sighed. "It was the young couple," she said. "They haven't had anything yet, I can tell that." She turned to Oscar. "Have you a place where we can go?"

"Yes, I have." He did not explain how he happened to have a place to go, or how long he had had it, but in half an hour they were in an apartment on Spruce Street.

"Is this yours?" she said.

"Yes, it's mine."

"It could be anybody's, couldn't it?"

"I won't tell you why I have it, but I've had it for a long time. By a long time I mean long, long before I knew you."

"Have you things to drink here? I'm shaking."

"I'm shaking, too." He poured out rye whiskey in two high-ball glasses, and they drank, and she left the room. In a little while she called to him. "All right."

He undressed in the living room and put on a dressing gown and went to the bedroom. She was covered up to the neck and she lay still when he drew the covers down.

"I have to look at you, too," she said. "Now hurry, please, I'm ready."

He was too soon for her but she held him until at last they had peace. "The next time I won't only think of myself," she said. "That time I didn't think at all. Will there be another time tonight?"

"If you spend the night," he said.

"I can't do that, but I can stay quite late, and I can help you. Would you like me to help you? I can be very helpful. I like to be helpful. Oh, and I'm so glad you asked to come here. I've been dead so long. Go to sleep if you want to, and then I'll be helpful when you've had a nap."

For nearly six months they met every fourth week. Grace would register at the hotel, have a bath and leave her things to give the room some semblance of being occupied, and then let herself into the apartment. On the last afternoon she unlocked the door and saw not only Oscar but a woman of her own age and station in life. "Hello, Grace, this is Esme."

"How do you do?" said Grace.

"Explain me, Oscar," said Esme.

"Yes, I wish you would," said Grace. "I don't know her last name, but I'll bet she knows mine."

"Esme Bolden," said Oscar. "I thought you'd like it better without the last names."

Grace remained standing. "Now I know as much as I did before."

"Plus my last name," said Esme.

"For what that's worth," said Grace.

"Have a chair, Grace," said Oscar. "Esme is a painter, and I think a darn good one, and she'd like to paint you."

"Thank you, but I think women that have their portraits painted are silly, and I've always thought so."

"This wouldn't be a portrait, exactly," said Oscar. "Grace, I'm afraid I have a kind of confession to make, and I took too much for granted, but if I was willing I thought you'd be. You see, Esme in her own way is a very serious student of painting. She's an old old friend of mine and she told me this idea she had and asked me what I thought of it, and I thought it was excellent. You know how people's faces are on most paintings—lifeless, uninteresting. But Esme thought that if she could study people . . ."

"She was to study *us,* is that the idea?" said Grace.

"Yes," said Oscar.

"I'm not interested in sex, only in the facial expressions," said Esme.

"I'd say you were very much interested in sex," said Grace.

"Well, I suppose I am," said Esme.

"Wouldn't you be embarrassed, Oscar?"

"No, I think I'd rather like it."

"Well, I wouldn't," said Grace, and left the apartment for the last time. Two weeks later, when she brought Anna to the city for her dentist's appointment, Grace saw Oscar, Esme, and a pretty girl of twenty in Oscar's car, but they did not see her.

"There's Mr. Stribling's car," said Anna.

"Yes, we're not going to have it any more. His family came back from Europe," said Grace.

"No loss," said her daughter. "He gave me the creeps."

Grace laughed so gaily that passers-by on South Broad Street stared at her, and the child repeated her comment. "He did, he gave me the creeps."

"Yes, dear, I know exactly what you mean," said Grace. "And I always like you to say what you think about people, amongst ourselves, but only amongst ourselves. It's more fun when we keep them family jokes. But I do know exactly what you mean about Mr. Stribling."

In a vague way it was known among Grace's friends that she took her daughter to the dentist at regular intervals, and that was an index of the kind of social life she led: with Connie away in New York Grace had allowed herself to become part of a small group of old and new friends, but never to the degree of intimacy that she had allowed Connie. In spite of their disagreements and outright quarrels she and Connie through the years had maintained a friendship so close that each knew what the other spent for her clothes; the degree of friendliness either one could show for an outsider without becoming disloyal to the other; the time of the month each was due; the one's capacity for boredom by the other's anecdotes and opinions. After Connie moved to New York no one took her place as confidante. Grace simply did not make herself available to casual droppers-in, and did not encourage confessions or revelations. She thus was able to be silent or vague regarding her planned or accomplished activities, and her affair with Oscar Stribling was a secret not shared by Fort Penn. She had helped to keep the secret by taking a noon train instead of the morning trains that were more popular among Fort Penn people who had a day's business or shopping to do in Philadelphia, and on the homeward journey she took a Pittsburgh train that left Philadelphia shortly after eleven in the morning and made it possible for her to keep a late luncheon appointment in Fort Penn, without any friends knowing she had been out of town. Her conversation with Jack Hollister had taken place after the Stribling affair had come to its abrupt and esoteric conclusion, and her remark about having her comings and goings recorded covered nothing current.

Her remark about her dinner engagements was unfair in that her name seldom appeared in the society column, for the reason that she seldom appeared in society. During the war she learned to play auction bridge and the evening side of her social life was for the most part built around that game. She resisted all efforts to induce her to become a member of a women's bridge club, but she liked the game and played it well, when men were playing, a fact which implied playing in the evening. Now, in 1919, the people she saw most were Edgar and Betty Martindale, Scotty and Natalie Bordener, George and Mary Wall, and Edmund and Nancy Clarkson. It was a well-balanced, if not entirely fashionable, group. Edgar Martindale was not a Fort Penn native, and neither was Natalie Bordener, who was born Natalie Walker in Gibbsville; Edgar was married to Scotty Bordener's sister. The George Walls were solidly native, but neither Ed Clarkson, president of Fort Penn University, nor his wife was a local product. Betty Martindale had no card sense and was as likely to lead a singleton ace of trump into the dummy as the conventional fourth highest card of her longest and strongest suit. But if she had no card sense Betty had the common sense not to inflict herself on the others, and Grace played in her stead. The group met each week at one of the five houses, and Betty would read a book or fall asleep until it was time to drive her husband home. The dinners were kept simple, partly out of consideration for the Clarksons, who had little more than Ed Clarkson's salary, and partly because all the players had reached an age where a big dinner made them sleepy afterward. No wine was served at dinner; home-made butter creams and caramels were eaten during the card-playing; and after the last hand coffee and cold meat sandwiches were brought in. The stakes were high—a half-cent a point—for poor players, but a balance of a sort was achieved here, in that the Clarksons usually won, and Grace, who had the most money, usually was low, or among the low. Edgar Martindale and Ed Clarkson played the same game, even to their mannerisms: they would ask to review the bidding, and when it came his turn to play the dummy's cards Edgar and Ed would slowly slide a hand across the table, lift the desired card and hold it in the air before laying it on the table with a snap. Scotty Bordener was flashy, frequently brilliant, but more than once had said "The rest are mine," only to have one of the others demand to be shown how he could make the small clubs good in the dummy when the lead was in his own hand. He was given to tapping his fine teeth with a card, and when he made a mistake he was more subject to depression than any of the others. Nancy Clarkson and Mary Wall played entirely by Whitehead and they always either kept the score or kept an eye on the adding and subtracting. George Wall, who played in the big weekly poker game at the Fort Penn Club, ignored the conventions and bluffed himself and partner into large winnings or losses. He talked more than anyone else and ate the most candy. Natalie Bordener never touched the candy because she said it would ruin her complexion, which was worth calling attention to—but she talked almost as much as George Wall, and she was a little bit better in the post-mortems than in the actual playing of the hands.

Grace's game was soundly conventional except for a slight tendency to overbid without help from her partner, and an unshakable habit of doubling all little and grand slam bids. The only consistent sufferer from this latter habit was George Wall, who, whether he won or lost on Grace's doubles, as partner or opponent, invariably would say, "I'd have done exactly, *exactly* the same thing, Grace." But George did not realize that Grace was not so much bluffing as stating her doubt that anyone else held cards that were that much better than hers. The mechanics of the game she had learned quickly, she always asked where she had made her mistakes, and her apologies were perfunctory. That summer she taught the game to Alfred and Anna, and in three-handed games Anna always won, and Alfred never won.

The group were reputed to play "for blood," in the language of the day, the preceding day, and many a day thereafter. Their concentration on the game afforded a minimum of opportunity for flirtatiousness; moreover the individuals who were most likely to flirt were married to each other: Scotty and Natalie Bordener. Natalie, who was the youngest person in the group, three or as much as five years younger than Grace, apparently had decided that the men were not worth bothering about. She had, besides, a small chip on her shoulder for Fort Penn, which had accepted her as Scotty's wife and then, in effect, relegated her to the status of helpmeet and mother at the cessation of her brief reign as belle of the ball. Natalie often returned to Gibbs-ville and after all of these visits she would relate to George Wall the latest escapade of someone called Froggy Ogden, a man who had lost an arm in the war, whom George knew in business. One night Ed Clarkson said: "Gibbsville, that's near Scranton, isn't it?"

"Nowhere near Scranton," said Natalie. "We're nearer Fort Penn than we are Scranton."

"But it *is* in the coal regions?" said Ed.

"Of course it is, it's the headquarters of the Coal & Iron Company," said Natalie.

"I see," said Clarkson, who was accustomed to the respect of doctors of philosophy.

"Sidney visited there—my husband—before we were married."

"Who'd he visit?" said Natalie.

"Oh, I don't remember, that was so long ago."

"Try to remember, I'd love to know who he visited," said Natalie. "Was it—"

"I don't think I'd know the name if you told me."

"Well, shall we cut for deal?" said George Wall.

Again it was the concentration on the game that had protected Grace from acute observation after she began her first relationship with a man in two years. The closest anyone ever came was Betty Martindale, who said: "Grace, you look so well lately, not so intense, if you don't mind me saying so. I'm glad you're going out again and seeing people. I loved Sidney dearly, but he wouldn't have wanted you to become a shut-in. I just wanted to tell you."

Betty became a substitute for Connie, but Betty, with three children of her own, had rather less leisure time and was not so demanding on Grace's as Connie had been. In her middle years Betty had become a moderately discontented woman, but that was an improvement over the whining girl she had been in her teens. She had money of her own, and no small sum; Edgar was corporation counsel for the Fort Penn Street Railways and several lesser companies, with an earned income to match her own. She wore horn-rimmed spectacles and was said by her women friends to care nothing about clothes, but she cared enough about clothes to dress herself according to her type: handsome sturdy suits from Mann & Dilks, camel's hair coats, felt hats, sensible shoes. She always looked as though she had just come from the field trials, while Grace, who owned the same outfits, looked as though she were just starting out; and another difference between the two women was that Betty also looked like a lady gun when she was in an evening gown. Actually she had no interest in dogs and was afraid of firearms; she played good tennis and swam nicely, and in a tennis dress or a bathing suit her figure was one that made women declare that something could be done with it. Something was done with it, all the time, although not precisely what the women meant: Betty and Edgar were not a handsome, a striking, an attractive, or even an interesting couple, but they suited each other, and after three children and fifteen years of marriage they were as much in love as any couple in Fort Penn, or possibly in the United States of America. It always surprised their friends to learn over again how much Edgar and Betty, practicing monogamists and virgins at their wedding, knew about sex, when the simple answer was that they were constantly studying and experimenting together. Their laboratory was their own bedroom. Betty's discontent was not traceable to that kind of dissatisfaction or maladjustment, but rather to envy: envy of her friends who had beautiful children in contrast with her own tall and scrawny three, all of whom had worn spectacles since early childhood. She had no cause to envy another woman's money, but she wished she had the gift to get more fun out of hers. Her house, her car, her gloves, her hair, her standing in Fort Penn society were ordinary, not to be compared fairly with those possessed by women with a quarter her income. She always had a book going, but her sister-in-law, Natalie Bordener, who read not more than four books a year, could hold forth, glib and authoritative, while Betty listened with the rest. But as against the secret envies Betty had rightful claim to her reputation for kindness and generosity, which took many forms. It was not easy, for instance, for Betty to part with money, but she gave it. She visited the sick, she buried the dead, she lent her car, she housed the children of afflicted friends, she wrote complimentary notes when her friends had big and little successes. Her bills for flowers, candy, books, and champagne were large not only because of self-indulgence. She would hold a shop door to keep it from swinging back on the next person following—and find herself holding it open for six persons. And what Grace did not know, and never learned from Betty, was that Betty, more than any other woman, had made it unfashionable to discuss Grace's affair with Roger Bannon. In the Red Cross one afternoon Betty, sitting in a room with twenty other women, raised her voice to declare that she had heard enough: "Some of us here grew up with Grace and we're supposed to be her friends, so why can't we behave like her friends. As far as the others go, those that hardly knew Grace, have never been inside her house—they'll never be welcome in my house, or my club, or my husband's club. If I knew that a child's mother was a gossip, I don't think I'd like my children to be in the same school with that child, so naturally I'd use what influence I have to keep that child out of any school my children are going to. My children go to the same schools Grace's children go to, and I'm on the board of one of those schools. So let's not use the Red Cross as a gossip mill." The gossip did not end, but Betty was not blind to the fact that the Red Cross was being used by Fort Penn social-climbers, who mistrusted each other and would conscientiously report to her any violation of her edict against gossip. Betty's declaration in that form also had been useful as a warning to Grace's friends, who had only to think twice to conjure up a situation in which the Caldwell-Tate-Schoffstal-Bordener-Partridge-et al. alliance could do them harm, socially, financially, politically, or all three. Betty's action had discouraged the gossip at its source, and the timing was right: in a few weeks Sidney and Billy were dead, and there was a superstitious revulsion against cheap chatter, a fear of attracting a punishment as severe as Grace's. Punishment was in the air, and the women wanted none of it. Then in October the Guard regiments were federalized and the women took up rumor-mongering. In 1919 there was no one who knew Grace or knew of her who did not believe she had had an affair with Bannon, but it was an old fact, part of the public knowledge of Grace, actually less remarkable for most people than her misfortune. "They say she used to sleep with Roger Bannon" was not quite so startling two years after the fact as "She lost her husband and her little boy within a few days of each other. Of the infantile." The two items could be connected, but the second seemed to demand a reverence that excluded the gleefulness of the first. And another reason Fort Penn so easily forgave Grace was that she had been spectacular: the Caldwells, and the Tates, drove the finest horses and automobiles, lived in the finest homes, possessed the most money, gave the most money away, had the best manners—and provided the juiciest scandal and died on the grand scale. *Will you ever forget Sidney Tate's funeral?... Those people do things big...* and even Betty Martindale's threat was big in its way: she had announced her determination to thwart the social, financial and educational ambitions of the most ambitious individuals in an important, expanding American city.

Betty was a respectable woman. By all the standards implicit in the designation she was respectable (especially when it is borne in mind that a respectable woman is accorded precisely, and no more than, common-usage respect): she was not pretty, therefore did not inspire lust on the part of others; she was not grotesque and therefore did not require drunkenness for herself. She was always referred to as well-off, and never called rich. Her raiment gave her protection from the elements and satisfied the custom, but it was also clean and limited in variety neither by poverty nor eccentricity. She had a husband, but no one coveted him. She had children, but they were three in number, neither too many nor too few. She was polite, but with no condescension given or taken. She had been and for a long time would be without age; without youth and without decrepitude. Respectable woman that she was, Betty was in balance as a friend to Grace like the balance maintained in the eight-person bridge club. At the same time the two women were not wholly unlike as Grace and Connie had been wholly unlike. They were women of passion who for the moment were containing an undefined discontent; if they had hope it was for the future, and they had no choice but to accept the past. They were self-satisfied and waiting. They were strong enough to continue waiting until the undefined that they were waiting for had been defined and, perhaps, lost. If there existed a mutual respect for the other's stupidity it was not the only reason for the growth of their friendship, of great friendships.

The spring of that first post-war year passed quickly for all, with the theme: Welcome Home. The Guard regiments came home in May, with one final parade, reviewed by the Governor, on a hot Fourth of July. Grace and the children saw the parade from the same windows she had looked through to watch the men go away. Connie again was with her, but neither mentioned the romantic circumstances of the other time, and when Captain Bannon, thinner and tanned, marched past, Alfred said: "The Irish Company."

"How do you know?" said Grace.

"It was in the paper yesterday and I cut it out. Here," he handed her the clipping.

"Thanks," she said.

"Well, if you're not gonna look at it can I have it back, please?" She gave it back.

They were silent when the naval division, led by officers of the Navy and the Marine Corps, came into view. Connie broke the silence: "That's Mr. Hollister, with the little rope around his shoulder. Alfred wanted me to point out Mr. Hollister."

"Which one?" said Grace.

"He has that cord around his shoulder, the third from the left."

"It isn't a rope, it's a fourragere," said Alfred.

"I don't think so," said Grace. "Fourragere means—oh, corn and oats, food for animals."

"I beg your pardon but you're wrong, Mum," said the boy. "If you'd look in the clipping you'd see for yourself. It says here: '. . . and marines of the 2d Division, wearing the fourragere.' It's the same as a medal, for bravery."

"Well, maybe. It probably has two meanings, so I may be wrong. I guess I am, because Mr. Hollister probably wrote it himself."

"Have you met him?" said Connie, without glancing away from the marchers.

"No, Connie, I haven't. I just asked you which one he was."

"So you did, so you did," said Connie.

After the parade they all drove out to the farm. It had been agreed that there would be no Cape May that summer. Grace had brought it up a month before: "Children, I want to know what you think about staying on the farm this summer. It occurred to me, this may be the last summer we'll all be together, all summer. Next summer Alfred will most likely want to visit friends, and you too, Anna, although you're not going away to school. But you'll be invited to friends' summer places. It's hard to believe, isn't it, but before we know it, the only time we three'll be together will be Christmas vacation." It then was unanimously agreed to stay on the farm, with the summer to be broken by a week or ten days together in Atlantic City.

The children, who were joined at the farm by six or seven others of their ages, went to the boathouse for picnic lunch and to set off daytime firecrackers. Connie and Grace ate on the porch.

"I'm very pleased, how the children are growing up," said Connie. "I wouldn't have thought it possible six months could have made them so much older, maturer and with real personalities. You must be pleased."

"I am," said Grace. "With my fingers crossed."

"Why?"

"Well, Alfred cares absolutely nothing about his marks. He's bright—every mother says that about her children, but he really is. But he gets worse marks than any of his friends, and I hate to think of him falling behind at Lawrenceville."

"Oh, I wouldn't worry, at his age," said Connie.

"That's not all. He's girl-crazy. He was sent home from a party last Easter. Mary Wall had a party for her kids, and Alfred took some little girl out in the hall and kissed her, but that wasn't enough and she screamed her damn head off, and Mary came down and handed him his hat and told him he'd have to learn to behave himself or he could never come to her house again. She was right, but I wish it'd been anybody but her. I can imagine what sanctimonious Mary said to George that night. 'Like mother, like son.'"

"Oh, more power to him, and the hell with Mary Wall."

"Yes, but I don't want my son to suffer the consequences for something I did."

"What about Anna? Is she boy-crazy?"

"I don't know. I watch her like a hawk."

"Don't forget, Grace, your mother watched you like a hawk and you went pretty far."

"My mother was strict, but not very bright."

"Which reminds me, how did *Charlie Jay* ever—"

"I know. Isn't it ridiculous?" said Grace. "If Charlie's the best they can put up I'm beginning to agree with you, women ought to be allowed to vote."

"They didn't put him up because he was the best," said Connie. "He was nominated because he was anything *but* the best."

"Well, I've never bothered my head about politics, but Charlie—*Jay!*"

"You give money, don't you? Well, next time they want money don't give it unless you're satisfied with the person they've put up."

"I wouldn't know who was good or who was bad," said Grace. "That's a failing of mine, I guess."

"What about your failing? In other words, tell me about yourself. Any love affairs? Have you thought of getting married again?"

"No," said Grace. "My cousins had a widower in Philadelphia all picked out for me, but he was—very uninteresting."

"Was he?"

"Yes, I suppose we were too self-conscious. You know. It was so obvious that we were being thrown together. But he wasn't the kind of man I'd marry."

"Did you see much of him?"

"To tell you the truth, we saw more of his car than we did of him. He lent us his car every month when we went to Philadelphia to Anna's dentist. She's having her teeth straightened, you know."

"I noticed that. Did he ask you to marry him?"

"Well—yes, but only because it was expected of him."

"Are you going to try to get away without telling me his name?"

"His name was Oscar Stribling, if that means anything to you, which I'm sure it doesn't."

"I've met him," said Connie.

"Oh, you have? Then you know I couldn't have married him."

"Next question," said Connie.

"Well?"

"You know what the next question is."

"You mean did I have an affair with him? No, I certainly did not."

"Well, either you're lying to me or you didn't like the way he went about it."

"I'm not lying, Connie."

"Don't be angry, Grace. I'm glad you didn't have an affair with Oscar."

"Why?"

"And very glad indeed you didn't marry him. He's, uh—I've met him in New York at studio parties. He wouldn't be good for you. He wouldn't be at all good for you."

"Is there something peculiar about him?"

"Very," said Connie.

"Does he take dope or something like that?"

"Oh, you're so naive. No, I didn't mean that he took dope. He has other peculiarities that you don't go in for."

"Anna said he gave her the creeps."

"Trust a child's instincts," said Connie. "Was that the only proposal you had?"

"I had one other. Last winter Paul Reichelderfer came to dinner, just the two of us, and after dinner he proposed, if you could call it a proposal. He was sick for a long time and he's thin as a rail. Not that thin, but thin for Paul. Anyhow, he said he'd always loved me, all his life, but never could say anything because I was still so young when I married Sidney, and all the years I was married to Sidney naturally he never gave any inkling. But if I wanted companionship and someone who loved me, there he was."

"That was sweet."

"Yes. Outside of that, no offers of matrimony. In fact no dishonorable proposals, either. I don't think Paul loved me, he loved Sidney. He said he was very fond of the children and thought they ought to have a father, especially a young boy."

"He's right," said Connie. "How much have you told them?"

"What about?"

"About their bodies."

"Very little. I explained to Anna about menstruating, and that was all. Just enough so she wouldn't be frightened."

"And Alfred?"

"Connie, I can't tell him anything."

"Somebody's got to tell him. Shall I ask Ham to?"

"I think he knows everything," said Grace. "I've watched him sizing people up, women. I don't think for one minute that the Walls' party was the first time he ever manhandled a girl. Not for one minute."

"That may be true, Grace, but things like pregnancy and venereal disease—"

"Oh, rats, Connie. The papers were full of articles during the war. It seemed to me every time you picked up the paper the military police were having a raid, and taking the women to be examined for disease. And Alfred read every bit of it, you may be sure of that. Even the *Sentinel* had those articles, you know that. I learned more myself than I ever knew before."

"Grace, it's hard to believe you're living in the twentieth century. You're living in the Dark Ages."

"Well, maybe I am. I don't see why they *call* it the twentieth century, when it's only 1900-and-something. They explained *that* to me in school, but I don't remember what their explanation was. I know I'm an ignorant person, but I'm myself. I don't go around giving a lot of second-hand Bohemian ideas."

"Practically all ideas are second-hand, if you look at them closely, and those that aren't usually come from people you call Bohemians. Does that put you in your place, Mrs. Tate?"

"No, Miss Schoffstal, it does not. Not what you mean by putting somebody in their place. I was in my place before I was born, and I'll live in it and die in it. This is where I belong, and I don't want to change myself because then I might not belong here."

"And have Charlie Jay for mayor."

"If Fort Penn wants Charlie Jay, Fort Penn should have him."

"Now there you've said something."

"Listen to our New York slang," said Grace.

Connie ignored the slur. She lit a cigarette and put her head back and closed her eyes for a moment. "I love this house," she said.

"I do again, now," said Grace.

They sat in silence for a little while, until Grace looked at Connie and saw she was asleep. Grace, in her gum-soled buckskins, got an afghan from inside the house and placed it over her friend and then went back to her chair while Connie, with her graying hair and troubled face lined beyond her years, had her nap. It was ended suddenly with the explosion of the first giant firecracker at the boathouse. Connie opened her eyes, and when she saw Grace smiling she smiled too.

"Thanks for the cover," said Connie.

"Welcome," said Grace. "Want some coffee to wake you up?"

"Pour some on the ice while I wash my face," said Connie. She went inside to the lavatory off the den. The den still had the same furniture, the same silver trophies in a state of high polish, the Yale souvenirs, and the books that all had been there when Sidney used the room. Missing only were the pipes and pipe-racks and the office-type filing cabinets. "When this room is changed," said Connie to herself, "the changes will tell a lot more than Grace will ever tell."

She returned to the porch and drank the iced coffee.

"What about you and your new life? Do you like these new people? I know you must or you'd have come home."

"No, I might stay in New York rather than admit defeat."

"What kind of defeat?"

"That I wasn't able to fit into the scheme of things. So far I'm not a failure or a success. I think a little more a success than a failure, because I like the people—most of them—and they seem to like me. At least the serious ones do. When I leave here next week I'm going up to Cape Cod and work with them. Provincetown."

"Providencetown? Isn't that Rhode Island? Providence is Rhode Island."

"This is Provincetown, on Cape Cod."

"How far is it from Hyannis? Sidney had a friend named

William Eben in Hyannis. I met him and his wife, and I could write them a note for you. You know how places like that are. You have to go there fifty summers before—"

"It's not very far from Hyannisport, but it might as well be a thousand miles, Grace."

"But these people were very nice, the Ebens."

"They wouldn't be if they ever saw my friends. The people I'm going to be with are as Bohemian as they come."

"Oh. Have you met any you thought of marrying? I suppose marriage is old hat with them, but I know you pretty well, and I somehow don't picture you going in for too much of this free love. Is there much of that among your friends?"

"All you want."

"Well, my advice to you, Connie Schoffstal, is take a look at the calendar and see what year it is. We're not getting any younger, you know, and there's nothing in the world more pathetic than a woman in her thirties acting like a promiscuous kid of twenty."

"Where did you ever know a woman in her thirties that acted like a promiscuous kid of twenty? Think hard."

"Well—I know them when I see them. I don't have to know their names. You can tell them when you see them on a train or on the street."

"Oh."

"What do you mean *oh?*"

"I was afraid you might give yourself as a horrible example."

"Maybe I should," said Grace.

"No, that was a real affair, serious, not casual. It was part of the war. In England they say the divorces since the war have been something frightful."

"Well, frankly I never did think of myself as acting like a kid of twenty. But let's not talk about me. I want to give you some advice about yourself. You mustn't fall for this free love, Connie. Look around till you find a nice man, even if he has to be an artist or a writer, and don't let him get away from you. . . . I'd give you a lot more advice, too, if I didn't have the strangest feeling—it's preposterous, I know—but *are* you secretly married to someone, Connie?"

"Grace, what an idea!"

"I know, I know. Maybe I'll have to admit these people are good for you."

"I'm happy with them."

"Yes, happier than you ever were in Fort Penn, I'm afraid. Oh, dear," said Grace. "Just don't let them spoil you."

"How nice of you to say that!"

"Don't sound like New York. Next time you come home you'll be dropping your r's. Well, would you like to go for a swim? We can put on our suits and sit in the shade near the dam for another half hour."

"All right."

"Come on upstairs and I'll lend you a brand-new suit," said Grace.

They changed, as was their custom, in different rooms, but when Connie went to Grace's room Grace was naked. "I'm slow. I put on the suit I wore yesterday but it was still a little damp."

Connie stood at the door. "God, you really are beautiful."

Grace looked at herself in the long mirror. "Who for? It isn't much good if there's no man to enjoy it."

"Oh, you won't have any trouble."

Grace laughed and whispered behind her hand. "I hope not."

"You're a devil," said Connie.

The "last summer they would be together" was made pleasant by turning the farm into an informal club for the children's friends and friends of their friends. Upon the casual advice of a hospital intern Grace had had the dam emptied, a new breast built and the sides lined with concrete, and the cattle were kept out of the creek upstream, in accordance with the doctor's theory that the cows' droppings had had something to do with Sidney's and Billy's attacks of poliomyelitis. Grace expressed her disbelief of his theory, but took the advice because she took any and all advice in the matter. She bought two Old Towne canoes and a new rowboat with an Evinrude motor for the boathouse on the river, and had the boathouse wired for electricity and a hot-water heater installed. She bought a new Pierce-Arrow phaeton to do bus service for the children's friends. Alfred had his own yellow Saxon, which he drove on the country roads in open violation of the laws of the Commonwealth, and Anna had a Red Bug—a small buckboard with a Smith Motor Wheel—which she drove only on the farm property. Grace had had a new French drain built under the tennis court. Sunday-night buffet was attended never by fewer than ten guests and often as many as thirty. The money for all this, of course, had come from the war boom, directly in the case of some stocks, indirectly in the case of enhanced real-estate values which never, Grace had been informed, would be decreased. She would have spent twice the money she did so that the children would have a summer they would always remember. On the irksome side, for Alfred, Grace retained a senior co-ed from the university, who tutored him five mornings a week in Caesar and plane geometry, and who acted as companion for Anna and assistant chaperon for evening parties at the boathouse, which were too much for Mrs. Barker. The girl had been picked for her scholarship—Phi Beta Kappa in junior year—and for her total lack of resemblance to any great beauty, past or present, a lack which was calculated to keep Alfred's mind on the ablative absolutes and isosceles triangles.

Grace played tennis and bridge, rode and swam every day, and slept like an unharassed farmer every night. Friends—many of them with their first automobiles—were encouraged to drive out from town without telephoning in advance, which was a departure from the custom. The continual open house became a subject for discussion among the governors of the Fort Penn Country Club: was Grace depriving the club of revenue, or was she doing the older members a favor by keeping the kids off the golf course? No decision was arrived at, no hints were dropped. Mishaps on the farm were few (the farm had had its lifetime of bad luck in one week in 1917): one of the canoes overturned with three aboard; Anna was found out as a confirmed cigarette-smoker; during a brief cold snap a copperhead was discovered on the porch by the new maid, who dropped a trayful of the second-best breakfast dishes on the flagstones, and fainted when Grace thoroughly dispatched the snake with a poker; Alfred had to be warned about a certain nasty habit of which he and two other boys were suspected; Alfred's myopic and portly tutor fell on her fat face when tripped by a taut wire stretched across the dark path to the boathouse in revenge for her suspected tattling; Betty Martindale got a black eye from a fast volley; one of the Wall children was beaned by a wild-pitched mule shoe and had to have two stitches taken; Brock Caldwell sat on a sheet of Tanglefoot; a Philadelphia cousin gave a Williamsport cousin a bloody nose. The accidents were no more than could be expected in a large and spirited group.

One morning Grace's mail contained a letter addressed in an unfamiliar hand, and marked *Personal.* She had received several anonymous letters of complaint against Alfred and his little yellow car, and the new letter could easily have gone the way of the others—into the wastebasket. But she opened it:

Dear Grace:

Please excuse delay in writing as I meant to extend my sincere sympathy at the time I received the news of your unfortunate loss. But I was in Camp in Ga. at the time, and therefore did not hear immediateley. Also thought you would not care to hear from me. I was very sorry to hear you lost yr husband and little boy & had every intention of sending flowers but did not know how to do so as you can imagine. I often tho't of you in France and my tho'ts were filled with what we had been to each other in the past. I would of come home if I tho't you wanted me but was not sure. Well, am home again back in Fort Penn and would give a lot to see you again. Missed you but could not write & when I came home I was in hopes that I would see you at one of the affairs for the officers. But you were not there. I looked for you at all of them, but did not inquire. As far as I am concerned we still mean a lot to each other & would welcome the opportunity. If you also feel the same way as I do please answer % Fort Penn Athletic Club will reach me and will look in my box twice a day to see if you answer. How can you forget what we have been to each other. Please ans. I will sign myself with my initials.

As ever,
R. B.

P.S.: *Am moving to new apartment soon but did not care to wait.*

She read the letter, re-read it twice and smiled, and answered it:

Dear Roger:
  Thank you for your note of sympathy. I understand, of course, that you were unable to write before, but I appreciate your writing at this time. All good wishes for your continued success.

Sincerely,
Grace C. Tate
(Mrs. Sidney Tate)

She sealed the envelope and took it herself to the R. F. D. box at the end of the lane, put up the little signal flag, and returned to the house. She was humming all the way.

Back in the house she wrote another note:

Connie dear:
  I have a feeling you would like to know this. In today's mail I had a letter from Roger Bannon, no less, the first time I have heard from the gentleman. As I read between the lines he is rather anxious to resume where we left off! But this is what I have to tell somebody and you are the only one; he does not exist! It's as though he had never lived! I am absolutely free of him! Love.

Hastily,
Grace

The letter went out with the rest of the household mail. Two days later there was a telegram from Connie:

THE BEST NEWS SINCE THE ARMISTICE LOVE

CONNIE

And three or four hours after the first telegram a second one arrived:

BEST NEWS SINCE THE REAL ARMISTICE THAT IS PERIOD JUST REMEMBERED THAT REAL ARMISTICE WAS PRECEDED BY FAKE ONE LOVE

CONNIE

Whereupon Grace drove to the railroad station in Becksville and sent a telegram to Connie:

BUT REMEMBER FAKE ARMISTICE WAS FOLLOWED IMMEDI-ATELY BY REAL ONE AND THIS IS REAL ONE LOVE

GRACE

The station agent, who handled all telegrams to and from the farm, was accustomed to some unusual messages. He read what Grace had written, counted the words, looked up the rate in his book, and said: "Looks like you and Miss Schoffstal have some kind of a bet on, Mrs. Tate. All this about real armistice and fake armistice."

"It *is* some kind of a bet, in a way," said Grace.

"Well, I hope you win," he said. "Tell you how to remember the real one. You just remember the number eleven. Eleventh hour, eleventh day, eleventh month. Then you have to remember the year, 1918, but that was only last year, so you oughtn't to have no trouble. Eleventh—"

"I'll remember, thank you, Mr. Killinger," said Grace.

———

One of the advantages of living on the farm during the summer of 1919 was its quiet as compared with the Second Street house, which was in sound range of the construction activity in the downtown and capitol district. At a few minutes past seven every morning the pneumatic riveting hammers would begin, and as the I-beams and channel-beams went higher a single riveter produced more racket than a traffic jam. The highest two buildings, according to plan, were to be the Schoffstal Building—shops on the first two floors and offices above—and the new Nesquehela Hotel; twenty and fifteen stories high, respectively. They had more than their commanding height and dominating racket in common: if there had been no Schoffstal Building, there would have been no Nesquehela Hotel, at least not on the finally selected site of the hotel and not in 1919.

Fort Penn was behind the times in hotel-building, and it was generally agreed that the hotel situation in Fort Penn was a disgrace, the Schoffstal family dissenting. Their dissent was not on aesthetic or sentimental grounds, nor was it a stand which they could not be persuaded to abandon. Before the United States entered the war Ham Schoffstal, as head of the family, easily had been convinced that Fort Penn needed a new hotel, but Ham well knew that a hotel cost money to build; that the money hotels made, even in state capitals, did not justify his tying up that much Schoffstal money; that modern hotels were being built as "community enterprises"; that another term for community enterprise was "merchants' gift"; that he, since he was not actually a merchant, was not going to make a gift of a new hotel or any part of one, and if the merchants of Fort Penn felt that their city (and their business) would be improved by a new hotel, they could damn well make the gift themselves. And Ham also knew that he and his family already owned a hotel, which was not showing a profit, and that it was for sale if the price was right.

The merchants' committee had made an offer and then another for the Schoffstal House, but neither offer was attractive to Ham, and when he went to the Mexican Border the matter seemed to have been dropped. In the months between Ham's return from the Border and his departure for camp in 1917, a great many conferences were held, with and without Ham. Ham gave the merchants an ultimatum: buy the Schoffstal House at his price, or the Schoffstal House would remain in operation; and he pointed out, needlessly, that so long as the Schoffstal House was in existence no new hotel could hope to show a profit; there simply was not enough business for two big hotels. The merchants were aware of that, but they had been hoping Ham was not. "We have our hotel," said Ham. "All built, the equipment all in, and the customers coming through force of habit. You have no hotel. You have talk. Another thing, gentlemen, our hotel is paid for, and we can operate at a loss. You may figure on operating at a loss, too, but your loss'll be much bigger than ours, because you have to pay for your hotel. Let me say this much, we can operate at a loss for three years, but three years' losses will break your hotel. Then maybe I'll come along and buy it for chicken feed. Now what you better do is buy the Schoffstal House and put us out of business. It'll cost you money, but with no competition you stand a better chance of making some money. With us in business you don't have a chance in the world. Buy the Schoffstal House and we'll sign a paper to stay out of the hotel business forever. In other words, that goes with the good will."

They had no choice; they bought the Schoffstal House and made plans to tear it down and build the Nesquehela Hotel after the war, when labor and materials would be obtainable. But they had committed a grievous error: they had become so accustomed to thinking of the Schoffstal House when they thought of *hotel* that they neglected to observe the trend of construction in Fort Penn. Even those merchants who were planning to build after the war forgot that the trend was northward, away from the railroad stations, factories, wholesale houses and office buildings, and the new state office buildings likewise were being built to the north and east. In a sense the merchants awoke one day to find that they were planning a hotel which would be as inaccessible as possible to their own new stores. It was a mistake like that made in the case of the beautiful Philadelphia theater which upon completion was found to have no dressing-rooms for the performers, so that a next-door house had to be bought and a connecting tunnel dug. The merchants realized they, in effect, were planning to build a hotel to attract visitors away from their stores. They sent a delegation of two of their number to Camp Hancock, in Georgia, to confer with Ham.

"I could have told you that," said Ham, "but you never asked for my advice. You were so busy trying to jew me down—I beg your pardon, Mr. Kleinfeld, that just slipped out."

"That's all right, I'm used to it," said Kleinfeld.

"Well, even so, I don't like to hurt people's feelings about their religion."

"It's okay, Mr. Schoffstal. Forget it, forget it, please. What I'm interested, Mr. Larkin and myself, the other gentlemen told us to visit you and see if maybe we could work out some arrangement satisfactory to all—Mr. Larkin, *you* do the talking."

"Well, all right," said Larkin. "Ham, I knew your father very well, and believe me, there wasn't a finer gentleman in the world. I used to see him in church every Sunday morning. Monday morning, render unto Caesar the things that belong to Caesar. But on the other hand, Ham, strict as he was in a business way, he'd hold you to the letter of a contract and do the same himself, live up to it, but irregardless of that, he had a great fondness in his heart for Fort Penn, Ham, and if he thought for one minute a thing would be harmful to Fort Penn, he was against it tooth and nail. Oh, he admired a businessman, a smart intelligent business-man, and so do I. Nobody admires a smart businessman better than I do, Ham, and your father would of admired you selling us the Schoffstal House."

"Thank you," said Ham.

"But justice tempered with mercy, nobody ever went wrong following that motto, Ham. And for the good of Fort Penn, that was another motto of your own father's, and if he was alive today I wouldn't hesitate to go to him and say, 'Mr. Schoffstal, we made a foolish mistake because we thought it was for the good of Fort Penn, this new hotel,' and I'd tell him how a lot of us are in deeper than we ought to be because we love Fort Penn too, and have our business and fami—"

"You're in this because you wanted to build a hotel, Mr. Larkin, and you made a mistake because you got mixed up in a business you don't know anything about," said Ham.

"Mr. Schoffstal is right," said Kleinfeld.

"Of course he's right, of course he is," said Larkin. "I—"

"Let me talk a minute," said Kleinfeld. "Mr. Schoffstal, I didn't know your father but I heard of him, to be sure. I don't know what he'd say if we came to him like we are, coming to you, and asked him to let us off the deal we made. I think maybe he'd say, 'Get the hell outa my office, you're wasting my time,' and you can say, 'Get the hell outa my tent, you're wasting my time.'"

"Well, if you came here for what I think you did, you're wasting *your* time, too," said Ham.

"You don't want to take the hotel back?" said Kleinfeld.

"No," said Ham.

Kleinfeld nodded. "I expected that. In your position I'd do the same. That's business, and business is business."

"I'm sorry. Anyway, you have the hotel, you have that," said Ham. "If you hold on to it, it'll make a lot of money some day. That section's going to come back again."

"But like you said, real estate's a business we don't know anything about," said Larkin.

"Just a minute, please," said Kleinfeld. "All business is you do something for me, I'll do something for you. One hand washes the other. Mr. Schoffstal, I just got an idea. I wasn't given the power to talk for our committee because I just got the idea this minute, but Larkin can listen if you'll give us two minutes' more of your time. Listen to this, please."

"Go ahead," said Ham.

"Supposing our committee held on to the Schoffstal House till after the war and after the war was over we went to the expense of tearing it down, what would you have there? You'd have a vacant lot. But you know what a fellow could do with that vacant lot? He could put up a new building."

"Yes," said Ham. "He could."

"Supposing that fellow is yourself, Mr. Schoffstal. Would that fellow be willing to let us have a certain piece of property at Fourth and Penn for the assessed valuation?"

"Fourth and Penn?" said Ham.

"Northeast corner, you know the property I mean, because I happen to know you own it," said Kleinfeld.

"What makes you think I own it?"

"I know you do, Mr. Schoffstal. I made it my business to find out."

"All right, I do," said Ham. "But why should I let it go for the assessed valuation if it's a good hotel site."

"It isn't a good hotel site, Mr. Schoffstal, not with so little footage, on Penn Street."

"But with the footage adjoining on Penn Street, I happen to know who owns that, and I think I could buy it. Quite sure I could."

"Don't be so sure, Mr. Schoffstal," said Kleinfeld. "You may know who owns it, but don't be so sure you can buy it. Maybe you can't buy it so easy."

"Go on," said Ham.

"The assessed valuation at Fourth and Penn, that corner, that's very low and we could handle that. You'd have your money for the Schoffstal House, and we'd tear it down after the war for you and you could build there. So you could take a little loss on the Fourth and Penn. Yes?"

"I'm not saying yes or no. What about the property next door? I might buy that and build there."

"You can't for one reason. I took an option to buy on that property. I personally."

"You got an option from the Caldwell Estate?"

"I did. Mr. Brock Caldwell and Mrs. Sidney Tate. I paid five thousand dollars for an option, my own money."

"Very smart," said Ham, "but you fellows'd have to pay through the nose for the Caldwell property next door, if they know what you want it for."

"Yes and no. My option only gives me the first bid. By that I mean they can't sell inside of five years unless they give me a chance to bid against the other bidder, and my option money has to be considered part payment."

"I see."

"Well, here's what I'll do. If you sell us the corner property for the assessment money, *and* get Mr. Brock Caldwell and Mrs. Tate to sell their property for their assessment value, I'll throw in my option money. Five thousand dollars. If it's bought for the new hotel. Mr. Caldwell will do anything you say in a business way, and I guess Mrs. Tate also."

"Yes, I have some influence there. But how is it worth it to you to give up your five thousand?"

"Because I want to be a good citizen of Fort Penn and be respected, so if a man wants to be called a good citizen he has to show people he deserves it. That's worth five thousand to me, Mr. Schoffstal—and five thousand dollars is a lot of money."

"Is this agreeable to you, Mr. Larkin? You haven't been saying much."

"Well, if Kleinfeld's willing to pay five thousand more to be a good citizen, I guess I can't kick."

"Then you can tell the committee the terms are okay with me—if," said Ham.

"If what, Mr. Schoffstal?" said Kleinfeld.

"If you give me your word of honor that you don't own the rest of that block," said Ham.

"I promise you, I don't own a square foot anywhere near there," said Kleinfeld.

"I was joking," said Ham.

"You can be sure, absolutely," said Kleinfeld.

The Schoffstal House showed a war profit; it was demolished; Ham made plans for the office building, persuaded Brock and Grace to sell for the assessment price; the merchants commenced construction on their new hotel, and Ellis Kleinfeld became known as a good citizen. He and Ham Schoffstal were also known as the brains behind the hotel deal, and for Kleinfeld it was another big milestone; his emergence from the anonymity of president of the Outlet, a store which sold ladies' ready-to-wear and nine-ninety-five suits for men. "Where'd you get *that?* The Outlet?" was the most insulting comment one well-to-do person could deliver on another's attire. Overnight, it seemed, Kleinfeld's name became coupled with Ham Schoffstal's and hundreds of persons who would not have known him on the street were at least able to identify him when they saw the names Mr. and Mrs. Ellis Kleinfeld in print, usually in Jewish society items or in community charity committee lists. The appellation "brains behind the hotel deal" carried an unflattering implication for the other members of the hotel committee, but they were willing to let Kleinfeld and Schoffstal take all the credit so long as the public remained incurious about the manner in which Kleinfeld and Schoffstal had come by their title. It was better to have the public hear about two heroes than to lose respect for two dozen goats. The public was allowed to know that practically insurmountable problems of a financial, legal, and real-estate nature had been worked out by Kleinfeld and Schoffstal—and the rest was none of the public's business.

The merchants need not have been alarmed. Long before the grand opening of the Hotel Nesquehela the citizens were building up excitement in themselves, with rumors of the cost, the decor of the ballroom, the salary of the chef, the electrically-operated this and that, the depth of the elevator shaft, the miles of linen, the Presidential Suite, the Governor's Suite, the daily *thé dansant,* the stark naked Indian woman in the main lobby mural, the miles of carpet, the coffee shoppe, the failure to include a bar (taken as the soundest indication that war-time Prohibition was here to stay), the misspelling of Nesquehela on 6,000 (actually 200) china ash trays, the miles of telephone wire (a telephone and a bath in every room), and the view on a clear day. Only a few money-minded businessmen cared how much the merchants had lost; the others, and especially but not predominantly the women, were excited about the city touch that the hotel would give Fort Penn: only one new building it was, but it was going to have the famous and the beautiful and the interesting eating and sleeping there in beautiful, interesting, and one-day famous surroundings, and the fascinating strangers would, for the length of their stay, be part of Fort Penn. The well-to-do women never had made it a custom to lunch at the Schoffstal House; indeed they always had felt it necessary to explain their presence there when they were seen in the lobby on any but great social occasions like the Assembly and the Governor's Ball. The Nesquehela was going to be a place where there would be string music during the luncheon hour; the lobby would be brightened with displays of jewelry and smart accessories. There would have to be some brass spittoons, but not two to every lobby chair, as in the Schoffstal House; moreover, ladies were to be allowed to smoke in the main dining room, or Commonwealth Room, as it would be known. Even before the death of one Jack Martin, 32, a rigger who fell from the twelfth story and thus became the first and only fatality in the building of the hotel, women were trying to book the ballroom for the best dates in the Christmas holiday season. Two experienced social secretaries gave up the job before one was found who was confident she could deal with the cajoling and threats that mothers of debutantes were using in their efforts to engage the ballroom for the Friday night after Christmas.

The Nesquehela was erected at approximately twice the originally estimated labor cost, owing to the high incidence of overtime, which was necessary if the hotel were to open on Election Night 1919, and not some date in 1920. The date had been selected with care; the big election would be for the mayoralty, with no great interest attaching to campaigns elsewhere, since a governor had been elected the year before, and the presidential campaign was to be a year later. Charlie Jay was as good as elected when nominated, so there would be no last-minute hitch but only a sporting concern as to Charlie's voting strength against the best ever shown by Walthour the Wallflower. Later there would be a Governor's Night, a second grand opening for the state senators and assemblymen and lobbyists, but Election Night—with the governors and other politicians gone home to vote—would be Fort Penn's own, and if it was in the minds of a few that Walthour the Wallflower would have made a more imposing figure on the dais, they were reminded that the party was not in honor of Charlie Jay; Charlie Jay was merely a symbol of Election Night in Fort Penn.

Grace and Brock were invited by Charlie to sit on the dais on the big night, but they declined gracefully on the ground that they had arranged a small table of their own—and set about to do so. Grace invited the Martindales, the Bordeners, the Walls, the Clarksons, Duncan Partridge, his law partner's widow Mrs. Desmond O'Connell, the Doctor O'Briens, Paul Reichelderfer, and, for Brock, a young Frenchwoman who had married a Fort Penn man named Carl Doerflinger, who had been killed in the war. Mrs. Doeflinger, a rather disappointed girl when she arrived in Fort Penn and saw that she had married beneath her station, was teaching at Miss Holbrook's in the daytime and cultivating Brock Caldwell at night. She apparently had heard about Grace and Roger Bannon at the moment she stepped off the train, and made several attempts to treat Grace as an equal and a possible crony, but after one luncheon at the Second Street house, during which Renée revealed an interest in the marital and financial status of every gentleman she had met, Grace dropped her, and saw her only at the school. Brock had asked her to invite Renée. "She thinks you don't like her, but—"

"I don't."

"Well, invite her anyway, will you?"

"All right."

"What would you say if I told you I was going to marry her?"

"What could I say? I'd say you were a liar or a damn fool."

"Oh, hell, say something original."

"Listen, Brock, you're too selfish to marry anybody, but if you do want to marry her, go ahead. I don't care. Although I don't see what you'd get out of it—that you're not getting now."

"You think I am?"

"Yes, what's so remarkable about that? She wants to marry a rich man, and if sleeping with him'll do it, she'll sleep with him. Get over thinking that she sleeps with you because she can't resist your charm, your adorable wavy hair."

"Oh, go to hell, Sister, go to hell."

She wrote on notepaper: "Renée. . .Doerflinger. I'll invite her. But try to tell her, will you, that Americans get bored hearing that in Frahnss every husband has a mistress and every wife a lover. She—"

"It *is* a touchy subject."

"*You* go to hell, damn you!"

The tickets—$15 a cover—stated that dinner was to be served at nine o'clock. Grace's guests assembled at the Second Street house for cocktails. The women and Doctor O'Brien took sherry, the men, except for Paul, took martinis. Paul drank nothing. The gathering was too large for general conversation and Paul sat with Grace and Betty Martindale.

"Well, Betty, do you think she's weakening? Grace?"

"How, Paul?"

"Me?" said Grace.

"Yes, you," said Paul. "This is the first time you've invited me to anything for a hell of a while. Do you think she'll marry me, Betty?"

"I would, if I were a widow," said Betty.

"Well, if I'd known that I wouldn't have asked Grace first but now I have to find out how she feels, before I start shooting Edgar."

"I can't marry a man that neglects me, the way you do," said Grace.

"Neglects you? Say—"

"And fickle. After what you just told Betty . . ."

"That proved I'm not fickle. I told her I'd wait till I found out what your attitude was."

"Well, you can't deny you neglected me all fall," said Grace. "I suspect you of having a new light of love."

"Well, you couldn't blame me for all the encouragement I get from you. What do you think of her, Betty? Isn't she stubborn?"

"She sure is."

"Man hasn't had a drink in almost two years, doesn't get cigar smoke around the house—I'd make an ideal husband, for some nice girl. Now who's this French éclair?"

"Oh, see? Fickle," said Grace.

"That's quite a piece of pastry there. Is Brock nibbling on that?"

"Paul!" said Grace.

"Now, now, don't be evil-minded. Only speaking metaphorically," said Paul.

"Well, if that's a metaphor it's awfully close to the real thing," said Betty. "I don't think my husband would like me to listen to such conversations. Excuse me. I'll go to talk to Mrs. O'Connell, she doesn't know any metaphors."

"Don't leave me with this beast," said Grace.

"No, don't go away and leave me with this evil-minded woman," said Paul.

"You ought to be good for each other—I mean that, too," said Betty, leaving.

"That's the widow of Carl Doerflinger. She teaches at Miss Holbrook's. I guess she's out to get Brock."

"Brock isn't so easy to get," said Paul. "Unlike me."

"Paul, we shouldn't joke about getting married. I've thought of it."

"Don't think of it if you're always going to say no," he said.

"Joking's as close as we'll ever come to it, Grace. I know that. I'm glad you asked me over here tonight. I won't see you for a long time. I have to go away, according to my doctor."

"Paul! You mean Colorado or some place like that?"

"No, no place with a high altitude. It's my heart, not my lungs. It isn't exactly serious, but I have to get away and rest. All that weight I carried around for years, and eating and drinking. Well, the weight's gone, but some damage was done and I have to take things easy."

"I'm terribly sorry, Paul. When are you leaving?"

"Right after Thanksgiving. I'm going to try California, a friend of mine has a ranch out there and I'll just sit in the sun, I guess, and read a lot of books I meant to read."

Grace was silent for a little while. "If Anna were grown up or at boarding school I think I'd go with you."

"Well, if you knew what that does to my heart you wouldn't say it, but thank you for saying it, Grace. But I wouldn't ask you to go now. That'd be a nursing job. We can't talk about it any more, jokingly or otherwise. But how about taking in the Penn-Cornell game with me, Thanksgiving Day? We can take Anna along. We could even start early and go to Lawrenceville in the morning and see Alfred, then take the train to Philadelphia in time for the game and have dinner after it."

"Oh, I wish we could, but Anna's having a party at the farm Thanksgiving night. With boys."

"I'm sorry."

"Penn-Cornell. Why are you going to that?"

"I couldn't ask you to go to a Yale game, Grace."

She put her hand on his. "You have delicacy," she said.

"Is everything all right with you?"

"No, but much better than it was." She rose. "The hostess is neglecting her other guests."

"Kind of neglecting herself, too, it seems to me."

She put her hand on his shoulder and then left him.

It was closer to ten than to nine as their cars drew up to the Fourth Street entrance to the Nesquehela. The uninvited public was well represented at the marquee, which also had side curtains to protect the invited from a wind that did not blow. It could have been an occasion for a rude demonstration—there was a great steel strike, a coal strike was threatening, and Labor was under the threat of the power of injunction—but Fort Penn was still a railroad town and the Brotherhoods' anti-strike sentiment prevailed. As Roger Bannon's father once had remarked, "A man that carries a watch to work don't consider himself to be a member of the working classes. He can be a bohunk or a dago or a tad, it makes no difference. Put one of them silver potatoes in his pocket and you've the beginning of a little capitalist." In case they might have been misinformed, the police were taking all precautions, and officers in and out of uniform were at their posts near the Fourth Street and the Penn Street entrances. The guardians of law and order, who could not be expected to know everything about female psychology, had a bad moment when Grace's limousine stopped at the door: the chatter of the onlookers suddenly ceased, and the mystified coppers looked all about them, but instead of a bomb or a revolutionary shout, there was a whisper that quickly grew into an appreciative murmur, with Grace's names distinctly heard. Grace was wearing a sealskin cloak over a simple black taffeta gown, and her only jewelry was a thin diamond necklace, but she was *the one.* She was what the younger women could hope to be, and what the older women, who knew her age, could take pride in.

With her in her car were Paul Reichelderfer, Duncan Partridge, and old Mrs. O'Connell. In the lobby they smiled at Grace, frankly pleased by the notice the crowd had taken of her. But as they walked to the elevator behind the older couple Grace said to Paul: "All of a sudden I'm frightened. I'm frightened, Paul."

"Why? Why should you be?"

"Those people—I didn't expect them to notice me."

"Well, that was quite a reception," said Paul.

"I know, but it could have gone the other way. You know what I mean. Two years ago . . ."

"Well, don't think of that," said Paul. "*They* didn't."

"No, they didn't, did they? They didn't . . . Here are the tickets."

The punctual of all persuasions—the unfashionable, the timid, the hungry—already were well along with their dinner when Grace and her party arrived. A few of the more keenly fashionable had been dawdling, pretending to be fascinated by the decorators' efforts while waiting for Grace to enter the Commonwealth Room. They now followed her in and thus made a small confusion that was large enough to divert the mass attention from Grace. Her guests took their places and, in a manner of speaking, the Nesquehela Hotel was a going concern.

The menu was bound in blue leatherette, with yellow silk cord and tassels, and a Napoleonic N on the cover. At twenty dollars per person the hotel corporation was losing money by providing food, wine, silver cigarette cases for the gentlemen and silver vanity cases for the ladies. Charles, the maitre d'hôtel, had advised the committee: "The guests on the Election Night, it is my opinion that the vast majority of them are not the kind of people who will take the menu home with them. I think you will find a great number of the menus on the floor. There*fore*, why spend money? Later, at the dinner for the state Governor, a handsome souvenir menu, perhaps. Paid for, of course, by the contractors and sub-contractors?"

The menu contained a title page, with the date, and an Indian-head medallion which strongly resembled the aborigine who advertised Samoset chocolates; two seating lists; one arranged by the table numbers and the other in alphabetical order; and the bill of fare.

Grace had placed Duncan Partridge on her right, Paul Reichelderfer on her left. The older man had the garrulity of the semi-retired trial lawyer, supported by the confidence of past success with the arrogance of a man who had been well born many years before, and the assurance that comes with being accustomed to being listened to. When he was not talking he was only waiting to start talking again and using the blank minutes of his listening time to put away every scrap of food on every plate. He said it was a damn outrage that old Professor Schoffstal was not furnishing the music, and supposed the reason was that the Ham Schoffstals were getting a little ashamed of the old man. He said—unconsciously agreeing with the maitre d'hôtel—that the printed menus were a waste of good money because people would throw them away, they took up too much space at the table, and everybody was going to eat what was put in front of them and there was no choice anyway, which was what a menu was for, to let a man decide what he wanted to eat. He said he was damn sick and tired of napery that was stiff as a boiled shirt, and speaking of boiled shirts, who was responsible for admitting these fellows in Tuxedoes? The Tuxedo was as out of place at an occasion of this kind as golf knickerbockers, or damn near. The Tuxedo was supposed to be worn at stag dinners and not when ladies were present. "Over there, second table over, I see four men wearing Tuxedoes. I have a damn good notion to speak to them, but it would only make a fuss." Grace obediently looked, and saw that one of the four men was Roger Bannon, who nodded to her. She nodded back. Paul had witnessed the exchange of nods, and he nodded to Bannon.

"You know that fellow?" said Duncan Partridge.

"*I* do," said Paul.

"Well, if he's a friend of yours, Paul, maybe *you* ought to take him in hand, give him some sartorial advice. Grace, my girl, you spoke to him too. Perhaps the gentle feminine touch—"

"I don't think Grace knows him," said Paul. "He was saying hello to me and she thought he was speaking to her."

"He damn well ought to wait for the lady to speak first," said Partridge. He took off his glasses. "Have to get a better look at him." He stared at Bannon.

"Oh," said Partridge. "Oh." He put his glasses on again and cocked his head to whisper to Grace: "Guess I put my foot in it that time, eh, Grace? Sorry. Forgiven?"

She laughed. "Of course."

He leaned toward her again. "Our secret," he said. "If Paul doesn't know you know him, our secret."

"Thank you," she said.

The old man changed the subject from Tuxedoes and Bannon,

but he went on with his monologues. The dessert was being served when he interrupted himself: "Well, by God, look at that!"

"What?" said Grace.

"That's Charlie Jay coming in, and by God who's that going up to congratulate him but Doc Walthour. By God that deserves some applause." He stood up, and regardless of the fact that he was the only one standing, he clapped his hands until the rest of the assemblage caught on and stood applauding, while the new mayor and the old smiled and bowed.

"Now how could you see them when you had to take off your spectacles to see that other person?" said Grace.

"Got my spectacles off now," he said. "And I suppose one can always see what one wants to see, eh?"

"Mr. Partridge, you're a devil," said Grace.

"I *was*, at one time I was, I won't deny that," he said. "Well, now we can sit down, I guess. Charlie's sat down. Few minutes someone'll get to his feet, talk for five minutes without mentioning Charlie's name, say a lot of splendid things about him as though he were embalmed, and Charlie'll sit there listening as though he *were* embalmed. Then *he'll* get up and talk and talk and talk. Modest. Surprised. And we'll sit here, thinking, saying to ourselves, if he hadn't been elected it would have been the greatest surprise in the history of the United States—or at least since Mr. Hughes lost. And I know I'll be saying to myself, 'If you hadn't been elected, I'd like to have my money back.' How much did Charlie's modesty cost you, Grace, if it's any of my business?"

"Uh, five hundred dollars one time, five hundred another, and two hundred and fifty. Twelve-fifty."

"Mm-hmmm. A little more than I donated to the cause of good government. Ahem," he winked at Grace. "Paul, you're a foreigner, you didn't have to contribute."

"Oh, yes I did. I do a lot of business in Nesquehela County, don't forget, and the city of Fort Penn. I put up a few dollars too."

"Be interesting to know how much Charlie got at this table. Be more interesting to find out whether he beat Walthour's record."

"It'll be in the *Sentinel* tomorrow, won't it?" said Grace.

"Yes, but it just occurred to me, why can't we go there after this is over? I have to take Mrs. O'Connell home in a minute or two. Suppose I come back and by that time the dancing will have started and we can leave any time then. What do you say to that, Grace?"

"Is the *Sentinel* open at this time of night?"

"On Election Night, my dear girl, every paper in the country is open."

"Then of course," said Grace. "I don't want to dance, and Brock can be the host, if the others want to stay."

While Partridge was taking Mrs. O'Connell home in Grace's car, Grace and her guests were favored with a personal visit by Charlie Jay, whose speech had been notable for its expressions of modesty and surprise and the determination to give the city that he loved an administration that would be even more efficient— if such a thing were possible—than those of his good friend and predecessor former Mayor Walthour, who had asked not to be called on for a speech but who (Charlie said) certainly was entitled to a round of applause.

Charlie seated himself next to Grace, and he was genuinely enthusiastic. "I think I beat Walthour's record vote," he said. "That's what they think at the club."

"We're going over to the *Sentinel*," said Grace. "Duncan Partridge seems to think they'll have the results there. Would you like to come with us?"

"I'd like to, but I can't, Grace. I've got my wife and her sister and some other people." Charlie was pleased by her interest in his campaign, and Grace refrained from mentioning that the visit to the *Sentinel* was Duncan Partridge's idea.

The rugs and dinner tables were cleared away to make room for the dancing, and while that was going on there was a smoking interval during which the ladies and gentlemen repaired to their respective lavatories. The old lawyer returned and was met outside the lobby by Grace and Paul. Inside the Commonwealth Room smaller tables had been substituted and the second phase of the evening's activities was being carried on in cabaret style.

"What in God's name is that?" said Partridge.

"Is what?" said Grace.

"That infernal racket! That's this new syncopated jass or jazz, I suppose. And look at the people!"

"That's the one-step," said Grace.

"The one-step, eh? Hmm," said the old man. "If you ask me, they've gone *one step* too far. Shall we one-step, two-step, three-step, five-step over to the *Sentinel?* I kept your car waiting, Grace. They said I couldn't leave it there, and I *told* them we'd be right out, but they said the car'd have to move on. '*Is* that so?' I said. So without another word I reached in and took the key out of the switch and put it in my pocket—embarrassed your chauffeur, but I think he was secretly pleased too. So—your car's waiting, and here's the key!"

Grace laughed. "Mr. Partridge! And you the famous lawyer!"

"Don't know about the famous, my dear, but I know enough law to confuse a common ordinary police officer. There won't be any trouble."

There was no trouble, none, at least, for Grace, Paul, Duncan Partridge and Grace's chauffeur. A police lieutenant opened the limousine door for them and they drove away, unaware that a line of forty automobiles had been awaiting their departure.

The *Sentinel* building was in the district that had been deemed unsuitable for the Nesquehela Hotel—upon the committee's second thought. The wisdom of their reconsidering was shown by the deserted streets; it was Election Night, but no celebrating was taking place in the district. Two railroaders carrying two-day buckets were the only persons to see Grace and her companions stepping down from the car. The street-floor office, with a large oaken counter for the classified advertisement and behind it the desks and equipment of the accounting department, was dark except for a weak hanging lamp in front of the vault. In the hallway off the office the watchman, an old man in a sweater and wearing a celluloid collar but no necktie, sat on a kitchen chair. He got up and looked at the three, implying without uttering the question, What did they want?

"This is Mrs. Tate, I'm Duncan Partridge, and this is Mr. Reichelderfer. We'd like to go to the news department."

"Who do you wanta see?"

"Mrs. Tate is one of the owners of the paper," said Partridge.

"Oh, that Mrs. Tate. All right," said the watchman. "You won't find many up there now, though."

"Well, we're not looking for many. We want to find out about the election," said Partridge, allowing the others to pass into the elevator.

"Jay won for mayor, I guess that don't surprise nobody. Watch out for that brass polish there, Lady. It'll get on your furs. I put her on early and let her dry, that makes a higher polish."

Grace gazed admiringly at the brightwork in the elevator. "Beautiful," she said.

"Looks better when I get her all done. I do half the car before I have me lunch, and the other half after. What you're lookin' at's the after-lunch. That aint done yet. If you're gonna be here a while I'll have it nice for you when you go." They had reached the second story while he was speaking, but he did not open the gate. He would have gone on talking to Grace, but Partridge thanked him snappily.

"You go all the way back to the rear of the room, if you want election returns. That'll be the city desk. Hollister. Jack Hollister's your man. Or you want the A. P., the Associated Press, that's that little cubbyhole over—"

"Thank you," said Partridge.

A dozen tin-shaded hanging lamps provided the light for the rear half of the city room. A man with a very bald head and wearing an eyeshade sat at a U-shaped desk, gently stroking his scalp, as he read the newspaper that lay in front of him. At one of several desks that were fenced off a young man in a herring-bone golf suit, with his hat on, sat typing. He stared expressionlessly at the newcomers. Without seeming to break his coma he took off his hat and put it on one side of the desk and studied the bundle of notes on the other side. A third man sat behind a large desk on which were three telephones, a small pile of books, two inkwells and a pen tray, four wire baskets, two spikes, a round cigar humi-dor containing sharpened pencils, and several piles of galley proofs. The man was leaning back in a swivel chair and reading the Philadelphia *North American*. The only sounds in the room were the young man's typing and a telegraph instrument's patter, and then the footsteps of Grace and her friends. The man in the swivel chair slowly looked away from his paper and then sud-denly rose. He tossed the paper to one side and came to greet the newcomers.

"Good evening," he said, addressing Grace. "My name is Hol-lister, Mrs. Tate. Good evening, Mr. Partridge."

"Good evening, Mr. Hollister," said Grace. "This is Mr. Reichelderfer."

"Glad to know you, Mr. Reichelderfer," said Hollister. He shook hands, and he and Paul smiled.

"Good evening, Mr. Hollister," said Partridge. "We thought we'd come down and see how the election was coming out."

"Local, county, or where? Locally, I guess?" said Hollister. He pulled three chairs from behind desks and grouped them near his own.

"Locally, is our principal interest," said Partridge.

"Well, the official returns are posted at the polling places in the morning. They count them all night, you know, but unoffi-cially, we've had reporters checking up and Jay's a few votes ahead of Walthour's figure two years ago. That may change, but it doesn't look like it. He's a little behind in the poorer sections of town, but he'd been told to expect that."

"Why so?" said Partridge.

"Well, sir," said Hollister, grinning, "Maybe because we sup-ported him so strongly. The *Sentinel*, I mean."

"Because we *supported* him?" said Grace.

"Yes, Mrs. Tate," said Hollister. "When we support a man more than just, uh, what you might call casually, more actively than we usually support the regular party candidates, the laboring man, he gets suspicious. Some of them won't even take your money, if that's not too disillusioning, Mrs. Tate."

She laughed. "I wasn't born yesterday, Mr. Hollister."

"Well, then, to speak frankly, they think they smell a rat, or to put it more accurately, they don't know what they think, but they don't like it. Consequently, they get stubborn and either they don't vote the right way, or they don't vote at all. This time they seem to have voted, but not the right way. However, in 06 the middle-class and upper-class precincts Jay made up for his losses in the poorer sections. At least that's the way it looks now, and I don't think there'll be any change. He has nothing to worry about. He'll beat Walthour by a few, and that's what he wanted to do. That's what you were interested in, isn't it?"

"Yes," said Grace.

"Yes, but I'm rather disappointed," said Partridge. "A lot of money was spent down there, on the South Side."

"Well, you know politics, Mr. Partridge," said Hollister. He turned to Grace. "Notice any changes since the last time you were here, Mrs. Tate?"

"No, I don't think so. Are there any?"

"Rearranged the desks. Over there, where that young fellow's working, that's the sports department now. That's where my father used to have his office. Where the bald-headed man is, that's the copy desk. That used to be here, but I moved the city desk here so I'd have a better view of my staff, and they couldn't shoot me in the back. I wasn't only thinking of myself, of course. First of the year a new city editor takes over."

"Are you *leaving* us, Mr. Hollister?" said Grace.

"No, only changing jobs. Beginning the first of the year I'm going to write a column. Have you ever read Jay E. House?"

"No, I don't think so," said Grace.

"Or Christopher Morley?"

"I've *heard* of *him*," she said.

"Well, they write the kind of column I'm going to write for the *Sentinel.*"

"Is it going to be in the paper every day?" she said.

"Every day."

"I'll look forward to it. Under your name?"

"I haven't made up my mind whether to use my name or my initials, but I hope you do read it and let me know what you think of it."

"Congratulations, Mr. Hollister," said Partridge.

"Yes, I'll look forward to it, too," said Paul.

"You're from Lebanon, aren't you, Mr. Reichelderfer?"

"Lebanon is right," said Paul.

"I'm afraid that's *Eagle* territory," said Hollister.

"Reading *Eagle,* he means," said Paul.

"Paul, I'll have the paper sent to you, when you go away," said Grace.

"Oh! You're leaving this part of the country?" said Hollister.

"Yes," said Paul. He smiled at Hollister.

"Would you like to see some of the voting figures?" said Hollister.

"I don't think so," said Partridge. "Do you, Grace?"

"Well, I guess not. I most likely wouldn't understand them. I don't know one district from another."

"That gives me an idea," said Hollister. "All this talk about woman's suffrage. Women interested in politics. I think I'll run after each designation, I'll run a line telling exactly where the precinct is. We've never done it before, but this would be a good year to start." He scribbled a note on a pad. "Mrs. Tate, if you were working for the paper I'd give you a five-dollar bonus."

"Give it to me anyway," said Grace. "If I earned the money I think I ought to have it. The first money I ever earned."

"All right," said Hollister. He opened a desk drawer. "This is a voucher you can cash tomorrow. Today, that is." He wrote and spoke as he wrote: " 'Grace C. Tate, five and no one hundredths dollars. For: bonus. Parenthesis. Suggestion covering election returns. Close parentheses. Signed. John Hollister.' Here you are. Take it to the cashier in the morning and you'll get your money."

"Couldn't I save it?" said Grace.

"Not and get the cash. Tell you what I'll do, though. After you cash it I'll send down for it and if you like I'll mail it to you, or save it for the next time you visit us."

"How nice of you!" said Grace. She waved the slip of blue paper. "I'm a wage-earner. The next time I'm in the office I'll stop and get my voucher."

"Well, don't you think we ought to stop bothering Mr. Hollister, now that we've got our information and you earned your daily bread?" said Partridge.

"Yes," she said. They all rose. Grace and Hollister shook hands, and Partridge and Hollister shook hands. Paul and Hollister did not shake hands; Paul was busy putting on his coat.

They took Partridge to his house in Monument Square and drove to the Second Street house, where both Grace and Paul were spending the night.

"Are you hungry?" said Grace.

"No," said Paul.

"I know there's some roast chicken and ham in the icebox, if you are. Are you sure?"

"I'll eat something if you're hungry," said Paul.

"I'm not, but I thought you'd be," she said. "What's the matter, Paul?"

"Nothing. I'm tired, that's all," he said. Then: "No it isn't all, Grace. Lord knows when I'll ever see you again, so I have to speak the truth. I love you, Grace. In a few minutes you'll go to bed, in a few minutes I'll go to bed. Under the same roof. On the same floor. If it were the same room that's the way I'd like it to be the rest of my life."

"I know."

"I'll never ask you again. It's no, isn't it?"

"Yes, it's no, Paul. You were a brother to Sidney, and you've always been more of a real brother to me than Brock ever was, but if I married you—well, I can't marry you, so there's no use our talking about it."

"What were you going to say? If you married me."

"If I married you, in a year I'd—you'd be unhappy because I wasn't right for you."

"No, I wouldn't be unhappy. And I'd be right for you. Grace, I'll write something on a piece of paper, and you keep it and don't look at it for a year. Then see if I'm right."

"Don't write anything on a piece of paper. Tell me what it is."

"All right, I'll tell you. I was only going to write a name. The name of the next man in your life. Do I have to tell you?"

"I'm sure you don't know any more than I do," she said.

"We both do," said Paul.

"He's married and has children. He's happily married. If I want that kind of thing I can have it with Roger Bannon. He wants me back."

"Yes, but you don't like Roger Bannon. I saw that tonight," said Paul.

"Paul, we're almost quarreling about something that—we mustn't quarrel. I'm not going to have anything to do with him. This is a small town and I've learned my lesson." She stood up. "I'm tired, too, dear. Don't bother about the lights, if you're going to stay up a while. Brock'll be late."

He stood up and went to her and put his arms around her. She put up her cheek to be kissed. "Good night, dear," she said. He kissed her cheek but did not let her go. He kissed her mouth and her neck and held her with one hand and put his other hand over her breast.

"Stop it, Paul," she said. "You're getting yourself excited and I can't help you. Let me go, please."

"No."

"I won't do anything for you, Paul. No matter how excited you get, do you hear? I'm *not going to help you*. You're doing this to yourself, do you hear? I'm not helping you. I'm not going to help you."

"Please, Grace."

"No, nothing," she said. "No, no."

"Grace."

"No. No."

"I love you."

"No."

"Oh, God. God."

"No," she said. Then he held her less tightly, but did not take his arm away. They stood there, he with his head on her shoulder and she with her face turned away. "Are you all through?" she said.

"Yes."

"Then let me go, please."

"All right," he said.

"I'll never be able to wear *this* dress again."

"I'm sorry, Grace."

"I'm sorry, too. It has to be love with me, Paul. Or the other so much that I don't know where it comes from, and can't help it. Good night."

"I'll leave first thing in the morning."

"All right."

She left the room and went upstairs. In a little while he went up the stairs. A few steps beyond her room he heard the key turning in the lock of her door. "That wasn't necessary," he said. He said it aloud but so indistinctly that she probably thought he was muttering to himself.

Grace was not habitually a late sleeper, nor was she later than usual the next morning, but at eight-fifteen, when she came down for breakfast, Paul had gone. "Mr. Reichelderfer had to leave early, ma'am," said the maid. "He said to tell you he had to see about his car. And he left this note for you."

"So I see," said Grace. The sealed envelope was propped against the salt and pepper shakers at Grace's place. "Two soft-boiled eggs, please."

"Yes ma'am," said the maid. "Uh—Cook and I both hope the gentleman, Mr. Reichelderfer, uh, all he took for breakfast was a cup of coffee and I told him we'd have a regular breakfast for him, but he didn't understand me. He went out of the house so fast, and I wouldn't want anyone thinking it was our fault for not having his breakfast ready."

"Oh, he probably had something on his mind. His car."

"Maybe, ma'am, only he didn't come by car. He come by train, remember?"

"So he did, but—maybe he meant his car's being fixed in Lebanon, where he lives."

"Mm. Only he said he was walking to the garage to see about his car."

"Well, I don't know what was on his mind. Men have business problems. I'd like my eggs, please, Mary."

The maid went out and in due course took away the cereal dish and served the eggs. She stood behind Grace's chair while Grace was opening the eggs. "Are they done the way you want them, ma'am?"

"Just right. By the way, Mary, who does my room now?"

"I do, ma'am."

"Well, I ruined the dress I wore last night. You'll find it in the closet, on the floor. Just throw it away."

"Such a pretty dress," said Mary. "They phoned from the farm. Do you want your mail brought in today or will they leave it there?"

"Leave it there."

"That reminds me, it's too early for the mail yet, but a letter come for you by hand," said the maid. "It's in the kitchen, I'll bring it. I thought it was a bill or an ad of some sort."

"Well, get it, please."

Mary got the letter from the kitchen. "I'm the guilty party, ma'am. I opened it."

"Since when did Mr. Brock or I give you permission to open anything?"

"It isn't anything, ma'am. Only a page from a newspaper."

"But it was addressed to me, and you opened it. You have a lot to learn, and if you want to keep this position I'd suggest you start learning quickly, and stop chattering at breakfast and opening other people's mail. It happens this *is* important. We own the paper, my brother and I. You may go."

"You didn't open Mr. Reichelderfer's letter, ma'am."

"I said you may go—or were you thinking of opening it yourself?"

"I'm giving notice, ma'am," said Mary.

"Speak to Cook, but now will you stop bothering me? You can't give notice to me. I didn't hire you in the first place."

"No, that's the trouble. Nobody knows who's boss around this house."

"Get out!"

The woman left and immediately Grace took her letter from Paul and the larger envelope to the library. She examined the newspaper page first. It was a proof of the Election Extra front page, and a ring had been drawn in blue crayon around a one-column box: "At the suggestion of a woman reader who desires to remain unidentified, the *Sentinel* publishes today the street locations of the Fort Penn and near-by voting precincts. This is done in order to assist readers who heretofore have been unable to recognize the various sections of the city and suburbs by the precinct numbers. In appreciation of the suggestion a $5 bonus has been paid to the reader. The *Sentinel* will continue to pay for worthy suggestions, news 'tips' and exclusive photographs published in this newspaper."

She smiled, and then stopped smiling and opened Paul's letter:

Dear Grace:

I am writing this at four A.M. *in your library. I was not able to sleep. Brock has come home and gone to bed. I tried to read, but the words did not mean anything, so I got up and came down here to write to you.*

There is not much for me to say, but I shall express my thoughts as they come to me. I have to admit at the outset that I have been wrong in my analysis and judgment of you. Curiously enough, I am not displeased to have to make this admission, for if I had been correct, the unpleasant incident would have been pleasant by virtue of your co-operation, but since you did not co-operate to make it pleasant I realize that you were stating the truth in saying that "it has to be love" or if not love, passion that is mysterious in origin and something beyond your control. If you had cooperated with me, I fear I might have gone away under the impression that you would co-operate under the same circumstances with other men. I misjudged you, but I am glad to correct my judgment. In the cold light of dawn, I begin to see that I also underestimated your ability to have a friendship with a man which went beyond the confines of friendship. Therefore, I wish to withdraw my accusation that you were about to embark upon a serious relationship with the gentleman whom we met after the party at the hotel. Reconsidering the facts in the light of my new knowledge of your emotional stability, I am confident that you will be able to master the situation if one should arise. I could not help but notice that he is younger than yourself, nevertheless with you in command, the situation need not develop to the degree that it developed in the case of you and me.

I have dabbled in psychological studies so much that I could offer an explanation of my behavior on psychological grounds. Unfortunately, however, I fear that lacking the psychological information, you would not be inclined to accept my explanation. I therefore express my regret over the incident in conventional terms. I admire you more than any woman I have ever known. Today (now 5:40 A.M.) I admire you more than ever. I hope you will write to me. I shall send you my address.

As ever,
Paul

P.S.: Please thank Brock for his hospitality. I enclose $5 for the cook and $2 for the maid.

P. R.

She went to the kitchen and gave the five-dollar bill to the cook. "Did Mary give notice?" said Grace.

"Yes. I'm just as glad. She wouldn't do here. She got worse by the day. A nosey-parker and a gabby one at that. Clean, but she has to be more than that to get along here. And the clean ones often have the dirtiest minds."

"What makes you say that? Did she have a dirty mind?"

"Did she? She made the remark to me, she said, 'I can always tell when there was two in a bed.' She said, 'They can straighten it out as much as they want to, but I can tell.' "

"What made her say that?"

The cook smiled. "Well, working for a bachelor aint the same thing as working for a husband and wife, Miss Grace."

"Oh. I see," said Grace.

She went to her room, where Mary was airing the bed. "This is yours," said Grace, holding out the two dollars. "Mr. Reichelderfer left it for you." Mary hesitated. "Oh, take it," said Grace. "I'm not giving it to you. It's from Mr. Reichelderfer."

"Why should he tip me? He was only here the one night."

"Because he's generous and always does it. He gave Cook five dollars because he always does."

"Thank him," said Mary, putting the money in her apron pocket.

Grace did not reply. She took the receiver off the house telephone on the wall and pressed the garage button. "This is Mrs. Tate," she said. "Bring my car around please. We're going to the farm." She hung up. "You can finish this room later, Mary, after I've gone."

Mary muttered something.

"What did you say?" said Grace.

"I said, 'Yes, ma'am.' "

"It sounded like something else. What was it?"

"I said—all right. I said: 'How can you expect a person to finish their work?' There's too much work for one maid so's it is."

"On the contrary, most of the time there's hardly enough to

keep a maid busy. Even one that's busy examining beds to see
how many people slept in them. I want you to pack your things
and leave this house today."

"Oh, Cook's been tattling, is that it?"

"Cook doesn't tattle. Cook and I have talks."

"Huh. I'll bet she could tell some stories."

"Now get out." Grace walked to the bathroom and closed the
door behind her. When she came out Mary had gone.

———

The girl behind the classified-advertising counter had a milk-
maid's complexion and perfect-bite teeth which she flashed
when Grace entered the office. It was apparent that she recognized Grace and was not surprised to see her.

"Good afternoon, Mrs. Tate," said the girl.

"Good afternoon. Were you expecting me?" said Grace.

"More or less. The cashier is." The girl laughed. "We hope
you'll come in often. I'll take you back to the cashier's cage."

The cashier smiled and nodded with friendly politeness, and
put out his hand for the voucher. "Care to have cash or a cheque,
Mrs. Tate? Understand this is something you wanted to keep a
memento of, so I suggest you take the cash, five-dollar bill, and
then I'll have a photo made in the photo-engraving department.
Make it as big as you like. That way, you'll have your memento,
and we can hold onto the original voucher. If you kept the
voucher or a cheque—oh, my. Raise the dickens with our book-
keeping. We couldn't close our books if we didn't have that
voucher or that cheque."

"Oh, I don't want to make a nuisance of myself."

"Notta tall. Easy to do if you let me have the photograph
made. It'll make a real nice memento. Get it this big, or this big—
not too big, though, or the writing won't show up as well. Say
about three times the size of this voucher."

"That'd be fine," said Grace. "You know, now that I'm earning
money on the paper, I think we ought to get better acquainted,
and I'm sorry but I don't know either of your names."

"Well, I can remedy that. My name is Arthur Bull. Just think of a bull in a cage and that'll make it easy to remember. I've been with the paper thirty-one years. I was head bookkeeper when your father died, and now I'm assistant treasurer and cashier all in one. Had a great admiration for William P. Caldwell, and so did everybody came in contact. This young lady, this is our little Mary sunshine, always a smile for everybody and a good word."

"Oh, Mr. Bull, you exaggerate all the time. My name is Mary Kemper."

"Not the only Kemper with the paper, either. I could show you payroll accounts going back—well, her Dad came before me. That's Tom Kemper, in the composing room. I guess you don't know him either, Mizz Tate, but he's a real old-timer." Bull gazed away in reminiscence. "Yes, indeed, old Tom Kemper, years ago, he used to set the letters your brother Brock used to send in, caused such a commotion years ago. Oh, we got quite a number of what you might call *Sentinel* families. Jack Hollister, city editor, of course. Son of Arthur James Hollister. Guess you knew Arthur James, he and William P. Caldwell were pretty close friends. Then there's Frank McCoy, in the sports department. He's a son of J. J. McCoy that covered legislature for years. Only died a year ago, J. J. did. And if you wanta take into consideration the carriers."

"I was a carrier," said Mary Kemper.

"You were?" said Grace.

"Oh, sure. A lot of girls used to have routes," said Mary Kemper.

"I didn't know that."

"Oh, sure. I had both sides of Nesquehela. Nesquehela *Street*, not the Nesquehela Drive. I had Nesquehela Street, both sides, from Ninth to Fifteenth till we moved away from there."

"In the winter, too?"

"Oh, yes. After school, winter and summer. If you didn't carry in winter they wouldn't let you have a good route in summer. The ones that only carried summers, we called them sissies. That's how I paid for my music lessons."

"You did? Do you still play? What instrument do you play?"

"I started violin because we didn't have a piano then, but then I took piano till I was in junior year high."

"I'd like to hear you play some time. Why did you stop?" said Grace.

"She got inarrested in boys, I think," said Bull.

"Oh, Mr. Bull, I did not. I quit because I wanted to finish high and I had to take a job after school, that's why."

"Do you still play?"

"Only ragtime. Popular music."

"Now that she has a daytime job she goes to dances every night," said Bull.

"I do not. Once a week."

"Well, dances are fun, aren't they, Mary?"

"Hey, Mary, you have a customer," said Bull.

"Excuse me," said Mary.

"Then is that all right, have a photo made, Mrs. Tate?"

"Oh, of course."

"Fine girl, Mary Kemper. I like to tease her, but I don't mean anything by it. Straight as a die, good hard worker. No monkey business about Mary. And she brightens up this office, I can tell you. You know. Sometimes the paper's bound to make mistakes and the readers come in here with murder in their eye, but if Mary can get hold of them first she calms them down and pacifies them and half the time they forget what they came for."

"How much does she make?"

"Mary makes seventy-five. She's worth it. And in another year she'll be making twenty a week. Pretty good for a girl twenty years of age, but she's worth it, she's worth it. Here from eight to six. Runs that classified counter, takes dictation for me when I need a stenographer, and she can read and proof too."

"A very nice girl. I like her very much."

"I'll tell her you said that. It'll please her."

"I wish you would. And tell Mr. Hollister that you're taking care of it for me, the voucher."

"Oh, my. Oh, no, I got so busy talking—I'm supposed to tell

him when you came in. Oh, my. He wouldn't give me a minute's peace if I let you get outa the building without telling him. Can you spare another minute or two?"

"All right."

He picked up the telephone. "Let me talk to Jack Hollister, Ruth . . . Jack, a certain party's down here with a vou—he hung up. That means he's on his way down," said Bull. "You don't mind waiting another minute or two, Mrs. Tate?"

"No, I don't mind," said Grace. "I should wait anyway, because I have to thank Mr. Hollister for helping me earn my first pay."

"Here he is," said Bull. "Guess he slid down the banister."

"No, I didn't, Arthur," said Hollister. "We have a brass pole like the fire companies. Only use it on special occasions. How do you do, Mrs. Tate?"

"Very well, thank you. I hope you—I didn't take you away from your work, did I?"

Hollister laughed, and looked up at the Western Union clock on the office wall. "Ten of four," he said. "If you don't think you took me away from my work—city editor of an afternoon paper—ten of four—Mrs. Tate, you've a lot to learn about the newspaper business."

Bull appeared tentatively disturbed at Hollister's impertinence.

"But I left word with Arthur if you came in, no matter when it was he was to let me know."

"I *am* taking you away from your work," said Grace.

Bull now looked at Grace to try to read her reaction. It was not legible.

"I hope so. I was hoping we'd go to Yaissle's and you'd treat, this being your first earned money. And five dollars. Not everybody starts with five."

Bull now frowned at Hollister's familiarity.

"Seriously, if I *am* taking you away, or disturbing your work, I'll leave this minute."

"Seriously, Mrs. Tate, I left a good man in charge. The next edition will come out without my help. Remember I told you last night we're getting a new city editor? Well, he's taken over in my absence."

"Well, in that case I'll be glad to stand treat. We'll all go to Yaissle's. Mr. Bull, will you come with us? And Mary Kemper? Can I take her away from her counter?"

"Oh, I couldn't go, Mrs. Tate, thanking you very much I'm sure, but I can't leave here for another hour and a half. And Mary has to stay till six."

"No," said Grace. "What's the use of being one of the owners if I haven't got any say around here. Mr. Bull, I'll buy you a banana split. No banana split for Mary, not with her complexion—"

"Do you mean it?" said Bull.

"I never meant anything more in my life."

"All right, all right," said Bull. He tapped a bell several times and Mary Kemper came back to the cage. "Put on your hat and coat, Mary. Mrs. Tate's treating us at Yaissle's."

"Oh, I—" said Mary.

"Hat and coat, Mary. It's too long to walk, but I have my car outside," said Grace.

"The one with the top down?" said Mary.

"Yes, but I'll drive slowly. We won't blow away."

"Oh, I want the top down, so everybody'll see me," said Mary, leaving for the women's locker-room.

"Five squares too far to walk?" said Hollister. "Most of the people in Mr. Bull's china-shop walk at least twenty squares twice a day, don't they, Arthur?"

"Yes, and if the people in your department walked a little more they'd look healthier and live longer," said Bull, putting on his overcoat.

"No coat for you, Mr. Hollister?" said Grace.

"Not in this weather. In my department we're all fresh-air fiends," said Hollister.

"They won't spend their money on overcoats, Mrs. Tate. They spend it on *other things*—and not at Yaissle's, either."

Yaissle's was the best soda fountain in a town where it was almost impossible not to get good ice cream, and in recent years it also had become the fashionable place for lunch. Karl Yaissle professed to be unconcerned over the threatening competition from the Nesquehela Hotel. "When I don't have no more people calling up to reserve a table the night before, maybe then I'll worry," said Yaissle. "Anyhow, who is the hotel buying their ice cream off of? Yaissle's. You know what? I can lose money on my soda fountain and lunch business. I don't, but I could afford it. I sell ice cream as far as Johnstown, and I own this little building. Only four stories and a cellar, but this corner I could sell any day and retire."

"I hope you never retire, Mr. Yaissle," said Grace.

"Once I wanted to, now I ain't so sure yet," said Yaissle. "Wanted to pay a visit to the old country, but not now no more, not since the war was."

He was a friendly but not a jovial man who, to people of Grace's age and a few years older, had seemed since their childhood to be some relative of Santa Claus's. He was without guilt. "How come you folks having a soda together? Mrs. Tate? Arthur? Jack? And this pretty young lady I don't know the name of? . . . Oh, the paper. That explains it. The paper." The counterman served the orders: chocolate ice-cream sodas, all dark, for the ladies, and double cokes for the men. They raised their glasses in a gesture of toasting Grace.

"Here's to many more bonuses," said Hollister.

"Here's to my colleagues," said Grace. She paid the bill—eleven cents each for the cokes, twenty-two cents for the sodas—and they returned to the *Sentinel*. Hollister sat in front with Grace.

"Would you like to come in and have a look around the shop?" he said.

"I won't have time today," she said. "Have to stop at school for my daughter."

"Well, I hope you can soon. Bring your daughter some time. We have a regular tour for schoolchildren, you know."

"I'll do that," said Grace. "It was nice to see you all—Mary, Mr. Bull, Mr. Hollister." They said good-bye and she drove off.

"Isn't she wonderful?" said Mary.

"Well, she's prettier than her brother," said Hollister. "I'll say that for her."

"Oh, Brock Caldwell has funny ways about him, but he's no fool," said Bull.

"You'd be in a hell of a fix if I asked you to prove that," said Hollister.

"I would not," said Bull.

"Oh, my proofs. I'll be here all night," said Mary.

"Well, you had your soda from the great lady," said Hollister. "Now we can all go back to work."

Mary left the men and Bull said to Hollister, "What's the matter? There for a minute I thought you were taking a shine to Mrs. Tate, but now I got the idea you don't think much of her."

"I don't know, Arthur," said Hollister. "She means well, I guess. But a soda at Yaissle's—you can't expect me to be as impressed by that as Mary Kemper."

"Impress you? I don't think that's what it was done for, to impress you or I *or* Mary. She doesn't strike me as the kind of a woman that tries to impress people, and if she did, with the amount of money she can put her hands on she wouldn't take us to Yaissle's."

"Probably not."

"Don't be so suspicious of everybody, Jack, and you'll get along better in this world. Well, we both have work to do. See you tomorrow."

"Right," said Hollister. He walked up the stairs rather than wait for the elevator, and settled down at his desk. He was at his tasks for more than an hour—helping on the re-plate, giving night and overnight assignments, and looking at proofs of the next day's early-press stuff—and was almost ready to go home when Harold Jaffe, utility assistant-city-editor-head-copyboy-rewrite-man-basketball-reporter, called to him, "On Five, Jack, for you."

"Who is it?"

"A woman. Personal."

Hollister picked up the telephone on which was painted the numeral 5. "Hello," he said.

"Mr. Hollister? This is Grace Tate."

"Oh!"

"I was hoping you'd still be there," she said. "I'll tell you why I called. I just got home. I'm at the farm, and on the way out I began thinking about myself, and walking into the office as though I owned the place—"

"You do, don't you?"

"What?"

"Own the place," said Hollister.

"Yes, and that's what I'm embarrassed about, why I called. I had no right to march in like that and all but order you and Mr. Bull and Mary Kemper to go to Yaissle's with me. Driving out I realized what I probably did, take you all away from your work so you'd have to work past the regular hours. I already asked for Mr. Bull and Mary, but they've gone home."

"But everybody enjoyed it, Mrs. Tate. It was very nice of you."

"You don't sound as though you meant that, and I don't blame you. That's why I called. To apologize. I want you to know I don't like that sort of thing, and I never did like Lady Bountiful, but I'm afraid that's who I seemed like this afternoon . . . Well, that's all I have to say. I'll speak to Mr. Bull and Mary tomorrow."

"Don't do it, at least don't to Mary. She's in seventh heaven and if you apologize you'll take some of the fun away. Bull—you can mention it to him the next time you see him, but don't make a big issue of it."

"I see," said Grace.

"Hello, hello."

"I'm still here. I was just thinking. Then you're the only one I really have to apologize to."

"You don't have to apologize to me. I had a pleasant time!"

"Mr. Hollister, I don't *have* to apologize to *anybody*. This is a free-will apology, you know."

"All right. If you insist on apologizing, I accept it." He laughed.

"What's funny? Why do you laugh?"

"I was just thinking, if you don't mind my saying so, I was thinking a while ago, I don't like Lady Bountifuls either. Am I fired?"

"Did you say 'fired'?"

"Yes. Discharged. Given the sack."

"Mr. Hollister, you have an entirely erroneous impression of me and I wish you'd correct it. I'd never fire you, especially not for any subtle dig at me. It isn't my job to fire you. As far as I know your work is very satisfactory, so I wouldn't think of firing you or even suggesting that you be fired. I *did* fire *one* person today, though. But that was a maid. And it *is* my job to see that my brother and I don't keep unsatisfactory maids."

"I better look out," said Hollister. "If you begin to take a more active interest in the paper—"

"No, even if I took a more active interest in the paper I'd never fire you for a personal matter."

"But I'll bet you wouldn't take me to Yaissle's for a soda."

"I realize that was a mistake, Mr. Hollister. It won't happen again, and I'm very sorry if I made you work late today."

"Wait a minute, Mrs. Tate, before you hang up."

"Yes?"

"It's my turn to apologize," said Hollister.

"What for?"

"Not for the Lady Bountiful remark," he said. "It's for something deeper than that. I apologize for being suspicious and having bad manners, and because I didn't have the decency to take what you did this afternoon in the spirit it was intended. That's a big mouthful, but I mean it sincerely. And I apologize for misjudging you. I should have known better, because you've never tried to use your authority when you wanted something kept out of the paper, and you *could have.*"

"Thank you, Mr. Hollister," said Grace.

"I try to be independent, but independence is one thing and rudeness is another."

"Yes," said Grace. "Well, now we're friends?"

"I hope so."

"I hope so, too," said Grace. "There's one thing more, and I hope you'll—have you a bad temper?"

"Pretty bad, but not as bad as it used to be."

"Then maybe I'd better not tell you what I was going to."

"I'll lose my temper if you don't," said Hollister.

"Yes, and we just agreed to be friends, and as a friend I have to tell you this. You just said you try to be independent?"

"All my life I've tried to be."

"Then be independent and give back that car," said Grace.

"Car?"

"You've been using a city car, haven't you?"

"Yes, I have. I see what you're driving at."

"I don't know anything about it, never seen the car, but other people have and there's been some talk. Give it back, Mr. Hollister. If you have to have a car the paper can lend you the money to buy one and you can pay it back out of your salary. But don't keep the car you have. It's bad for you, and it's bad for the paper."

"You're right. Thanks for the tip."

"You can easily guess how I heard about it."

"Through your brother?"

"Yes, it was. He doesn't like it and neither does your boss. In fact, Mr. Campion intends to drop you a strong hint. If I were you I'd get rid of the car before he does that."

"I will. I promise you. You *are* a friend."

"When I am I am. Good-bye, Mr. Hollister."

"Good-bye, Mrs. Tate."

In a little while Hollister left the office, got into the car and drove to the municipal garage. The head mechanic came over as Hollister was carefully closing the door. "What is it, the starter again, Jack?"

"No, the starter's okay. I'm not using the car any more, turning it in."

"What's the matter? Have some trouble? I thought you were in solid at city hall, especially now."

"Oh, I'm all right there. I just got religion."

The mechanic laughed. "Well, it won't lie idle, I can tell you that."

Hollister went home by trolley.

———

The Northend Park development, of which the Hollisters' house was a unit, had a nice standing in Fort Penn. It was the first of its kind in or around Fort Penn and it attracted young couples, precisely for whom it had been intended. It had three clay tennis courts, with a small clubhouse, Colonial type, in which there was a locker room without lockers, a shower which never gave forth hot water, and a larger room which had been designed for community dances and meetings. The larger room sometimes was used for meetings of Northend Park colonists, but as of 1919 no dances for the young fathers and mothers had been held, although the idea came up once or twice a season. The young parents still were too busy making a living and making a home to give much time to community social life, and anyone with the necessary time on his or her hands was automatically suspect: one servant, who was referred to as a maid, but in other parts of Fort Penn was called the hired girl, was the limit to a house. The maid did her half of everything that the young wife did: the cooking, the household chores, and that part of the laundry which was not sent to the laundress, elsewhere called the washerwoman. The maid was supposed to live out, and to be through for the evening at eight-thirty. Every house-plan in Northend Park had included a maid's room, but nearly all of the maid's rooms were being taken over by Junior or Joan. But notwithstanding the close quarters and the inconveniences, Northend Park had a nice standing. When a young woman gave her address as Washington, Adams, Jefferson, or Garfield Terrace, or Massachusetts, Ohio, or Florida Drive, the person waiting on her in a Fort Penn department store would look up and smile and say, "That's Northend Park, isn't it?" and whether the clerk said so or not the young colonist would know that the clerk was hoping some day to live there. It was a synonym and a symbol of young, white-collar, Gentile, at least second-generation Fort Penn, most of whom could be sure of small legacies in the not too remote future, and the young colonist would not have to wait while her charge account was being verified. The earlier houses were modified California bungalows, the second batch were Cape Cod cottages, modified to allow for the porch. All Northend Park houses had large porches.

Jack Hollister's half-soled officer's shoes announced his arrival, and the door was opened for him by his eight-year-old son, Arthur James Hollister 2d, who was joined in greeting by Joan Hollister, six years old. His wife called: "Jack? I didn't hear the car."

"Came out by trolley," said Hollister.

"Supper'll be ready in a jiff," said his wife.

"In two shakes of a lamb's tail," said Arthur James 2d. He and his sister kissed their father.

"Ram's tail," said Hollister. He hung his trench coat and suit coat on the clothes-tree and rolled up his sleeves. "Are your hands clean?"

His son held them out, his daughter held hers up.

"Good work. Now it's my turn." He went upstairs and washed his hands and face and came down for the evening meal, which was known as supper in Northend Park, in some measure due to the repeated discovery that maids did not mind cooking or helping with supper, but the word dinner made them afraid they would be kept later.

Hollister and the children stood behind their chairs until their wife and mother had kissed Hollister and seated herself. She was followed closely by Nancy, the maid.

"Good evening, Nancy," said Hollister.

"Evening," said Nancy. She put down the mashed potatoes and the creamed carrots, came in again with the calves' liver and bacon, and again with a large pitcher of milk, after which she went back to the kitchen, not to return until summoned by the tiny silver bell. There was a rule of silence at table until Nancy had put the things on the table.

"Pass the bread, please," said Hollister.

"Buddy, pass Daddy the bread," said Joan.

"Buddy's off in a coma," said Hollister.

"I was thinking," said the boy.

"No wonder he's tired," said his mother. "Came in for his sugar-bread and milk after school and that was the last we saw of him till supper-time. *Past* supper-time."

"Where were you?" said Hollister.

"I bet I know where he was," said Joan.

"You do not! You think you know it all, but you don't. You think you know everything, but you don't know anything."

"Well, where were you?" said Hollister.

"Out," said the boy.

"We know that. Your mother just told us that. Out where?"

"Thirtieth Street," said the boy.

"What were you doing all afternoon on Thirtieth Street, and who gave you permission to go there?"

"I just went. I wasn't told I *couldn't* go," said the boy.

"Do your mother and I have to tell you the names of all the places you're not to go to? That's large order. Do you think you could remember all the streets in the city directory?"

"No."

"No, I don't either. But it's easy to remember where you *are allowed* to go, isn't it?"

"Yes."

"Yes? Then see if you do remember," said Hollister. "Tell us where you're allowed to go."

"Northend Park," said the boy.

"Correct," said Hollister. "Is Thirtieth in Northend Park?"

"Not quite," said the boy.

"*Not quite!* Haw!" said his sister. "Not quite! It's a mile away."

"A mile! It is not," said the boy.

"It might as well be a mile," said Hollister.

"Joan, eat your carrots before they get cold. Here, I'll mash them for you, although creamed carrots, they aren't hard," said the mother.

"Once you set foot out of Northend Park it doesn't make any difference whether it's a mile or two inches. You've disobeyed."

"I'm sorry. I didn't mean to disobey. I just went with the rest."

"To Thirtieth Street. What for? What was going on at Thirtieth Street that attracted so much attention. I didn't hear anything at the office. Was there a story there for the paper?"

"Dynamiting," said the boy.

"Jesus Christ!" said Hollister.

"Jack! Please!" said his wife.

"I beg your pardon, everybody. You see what you made me do, Buddy? You made me do something I'm sorry for. Now who was dynamiting what?"

"Trees. Where that big house was that has the ghosts in it that walk around at midnight and everybody in town said it was a hunted house—"

"Haunted. Haun-ted," said Hollister. "Not hunted. Haun-ted. You mean the old Rothermel house?"

"Uh-huh. They tore it down and took all the wood away and chopped down the trees and the brick fence they took that away too."

"Oh, I see. They were dynamiting the tree-stumps, is that it?" said Hollister.

"Uh-huh."

"Yes, Daddy, not uh-huh," said Hollister.

"Yes, Daddy. The man'd push a stick in a box and *bang! BANG! BANG!* Up it'd go, smashed to smithereens, all over the dirt out of the ground and up in the sky and the dust got all over everywhere and the man had to hold his ears. All the men. They had to hold their ears. I didn't hold my ears the first time but oh boy, I couldn't hear anything except dinggggggg, dinggggggggggg."

"You mean to say you got that close?"

"Well, I didn't know where they were going to dynamite. We were all hiding behind a pile of those bricks that they took down off the wall because yesterday they chased us away and wouldn't let us stay and watch. We weren't doing anything but they just said go away. They had a mule and a horse and pulling the tree stumps yesterday but the mule and the horse couldn't pull the tree stump but oh boy, the dynamite did."

"Stop talking now and finish your supper," said the mother. "Nancy has prayer meeting and wants to go home early."

"Well, you see why your mother and I don't want you to leave Northend Park. There wouldn't be much left of you if you were sitting on a tree stump and they set off a charge of dynamite under it."

"Aw, Daddy, I wouldn't sit on any tree stump they were going to put dynamite under."

"If they didn't know you were behind the pile of bricks they might set off the dynamite without informing you beforehand. Up you'd go and you'd never know what happened to you, and neither would we. Hereafter—Northend Park is big enough for an eight-year-old boy. You can get into enough trouble close to home, without being dynamited or run over by a coal truck. There's hardly a day passes without some boy your age getting hit by a car or a truck."

"What's the matter with our car, Daddy?" said the boy.

"It wasn't our car. It was only loaned to us," said Hollister, looking at his wife. "It's gone back to the owner."

"Aren't we going to have a car any more?" said Joan.

"Not that car," said Hollister. "We won't talk about it any more now."

"There's no dessert because Nancy wants to go to prayer meeting. Everybody finished their supper?"

"Yes," said Hollister.

"All right, children. Upstairs. Buddy, you can take the funnies with you. Say good night to Daddy." She tinkled the bell for Nancy, tore the half page of comic strips out of the *Sentinel* and the full page from the Philadelphia *Bulletin*, and when the children had given Hollister a good-night kiss they went upstairs with their mother. She was down in half an hour.

"What happened about the car?" she said.

"It *almost* got me into trouble," said Hollister. "Jesus, sometimes I wish I'd studied medicine or been a cop or something. Newspaper business you never know where you are."

"Well, you're in it."

"Yes, but that doesn't say... Came back from the war and they gave me my job back and a small raise. Then when I told them about my wanting to write a column, they're all for it. Agree to take me off the desk, another little raise, and a pretty decent expense account. But that son of a bitch Campion—at this very minute do you know what's going on in his mind? He's thinking of firing me. Now don't get excited. I beat him to it by giving the car back."

"How'd you find this out? Or *what* did you find out?"

"Campion and Brock Caldwell are sore because I took the loan of that damn car, but they wouldn't say anything to *me*. They let me go on thinking everything was hunky-dory, but this afternoon I happened to have a talk with Caldwell's sister—"

"Grace Tate?"

"That's the only sister he's got, isn't it? Please don't interrupt till I tell you the story. She came in the office and took Arthur Bull and Mary Kemper and me for a soda. Now shut up till I've finished. When we got back to the paper she told me, right out of the blue, she said take a friendly tip and give the car back to the city or I'd get in trouble. So after work I drove to the city garage and told them to keep the car, I was through with it. Now Campion and Caldwell are in for a surprise when they say something about the car. I'll be way ahead of them, without getting any hint from them."

"Since when has Grace Tate been playing Lady Bountiful and taking the employees for a soda? Yaissle's, I'll bet."

"It was Yaissle's," said Hollister.

"The only place where she'd ever have a soda. Does she do this every day?"

"No, she doesn't do this every day. She was in the office late last night with a fellow from Lebanon and old man Partridge, and she had an idea, so as a joke I told her I'd give her a bonus . . ."

"That was cute of you, I must say. You giving Grace Caldwell bonuses. So she came in to collect her bonus and spent it on sodas for you and Arthur and Mary Kemper."

"Exactly."

"That was sweet of her, I'm sure."

"Well, what's wrong with that? If she hadn't come in to collect the bonus—it was the first money she ever earned, and if she hadn't collected it I know I'd have thought she was too high and mighty to bother about five measly dollars. But she came in, and the people that happened to be there—she took them for a soda. I happened to be one of the people."

"You happened to be? How long did you happen to be?"

"Listen, she gave me the tip about returning the car. That's the important thing about this conversation. Not anything I told you about the sodas, or your sarcastic interruptions. That was a hell of a big favor, and when somebody does me a favor I'll be God damned if I think I ought to hate the person, or tell him to go screw."

"Why should *she* do *you* a favor? That's what arouses my curiosity. I guess she started out by doing favors for Roger Bannon. Well, Roger Bannon wasn't a married man with two children. From what I heard she did him a lot of favors, too."

"We didn't have a soda. I was in bed with her all afternoon," said Hollister.

"No, you weren't. I know that, all right. But the whole town knows what she was with Roger Bannon, and you keep away from her. You don't see her doing me any favors, or the children."

"She told me her brother and Campion didn't like the idea of driving a city car, it gave the paper a bad name, and me a bad name."

"Well, all I hope is she's always careful about you getting a bad name."

"Jesus, you're jealous."

"Not the way you think. It's protecting my husband and children. Roger she could go to bed with, and when she was tired of him she could give him the gate. Or he could give her the gate. With you it's different."

"Of course it's different."

"Of course it's different, of course it's different. You bet it is. If I as much as look at another man you want to go over and beat him up. I didn't even dance with anybody all the time you were away. Well, you do the same. Don't you go having sodas at Yaissle's with Mrs. Sidney Tate. What do you call her? Grace?"

"No. We call each other lovey-dovey."

Nancy called from the dining-room: "Goin', ma'am."

"All right, good night, Nancy."

Hollister called softly, not loud enough for Nancy to hear, but loud enough for his wife: "Pray for me, Nancy. Ah sho am a sinful man."

"Oh, you," said his wife, getting up. She started to pass near him and he reached out and pulled her to his lap. "Cut it out."

"Cut what out? I wouldn't want to cut one of these out."

"Take your hands out of my dress."

"What do you call these?"

"People can see in. Let me go, Jack. Jack. Take your hand out, please. My camisole's too tight."

"All right. What's this? What do you call this?"

"What if somebody came up on the porch and saw us like this?"

"They'd go away, if they were polite."

"The kids aren't asleep yet. I didn't hear Nancy close the kitchen door. There! There is somebody. I heard them out front!" As she spoke there were footsteps on the porch, and without further warning the front door was opened. The visitors were Charlie Jay and his wife Louise.

"Sitting on your husband's lap," said Charlie. "You know that's a crime in Massachusetts?"

"Only on Sunday," said Hollister, standing up. "Hello, Louise."

"Hellow, Amy," said Charlie.

"Hello, Charlie. This is the first chance I had to congratulate you, the new mayor."

"Thanks, Amy. We interrupting anything?"

"By the look of Amy's dress we were," said Louise. "Look at her blushing."

"Maybe we better go," said Charlie. "How soon do you want us back?"

"Charlie!" said Amy.

"Take off your things and sit down," said Hollister. "What can I get you? We have some beer in the ice-box."

"No we don't," said Amy, "but would you like a cup of coffee or something?"

"We just ate dinner," said Charlie. "Don't bother."

"I'm thirsty. We had ham, and ham always makes me thirsty," said Louise. "What I'd like is a good drink of water. I'll get it."

"No, I'll get it. You'll just get everything all mixed up in the ice-box. Does anybody else want a drink of water?"

"How about you, Charlie? I'll have one," said Hollister.

"We all will. I'll go with you," said Louise. The two sisters left the living-room and Charlie and Hollister sat down.

"Well, I guess you did it," said Hollister.

"It looks that way. Just so I got one more vote than Walthour. I didn't care how many more. Just so I'd be able to say I got *more.* Those son of a bitches down around the South Side knifed me, but wait till they want new streets, a new sewer."

"I don't know, Charlie," said Hollister.

"What don't you know? You know they didn't vote, and if those that said they were gonna vote for me would have, I'd have licked Walthour's biggest tally without a minute's worry. They knifed me. They double-crossed me."

"They didn't vote against you," said Hollister.

"They might as well have. What gives me the pain in the ass, I know those bastards, and I used to be the one that'd get all those votes for Walthour down there. I used to get more votes for him than I got for myself! An actual fact!"

"Well, you have to look at it this way: those are working people, and this steel strike and now the coal strike—if it hadn't been that the *Sentinel* was so strong for you, the South Side might have made a better showing."

"That's what two or three of the boys say."

"Well, then, for once I agree with the boys."

"Now, now, Jack. You shouldn't talk like that. With me mayor I can do a lot of things for you and a lot of things for the paper that you'll get the credit for."

"In a pig's ass. I heard today I almost got my walking papers for using that city car."

"From the paper?"

"Sure," said Hollister.

"Well whoever told you that's crazy. Why Brock Caldwell—"

"Yeah. Brock Caldwell. A friend of yours. Sure. But I happen to know he was going to fire me, he and Campion, because it gave the paper a bad name to have me driving a city car. He didn't happen to tell you that, did he?"

"Where'd you get that information?"

"A very good source."

"If that's so why did the *Sentinel* support me? No, Jack. Your very good source is no good at all."

"That's where you're wrong. The person that told me is in Brock's confidence."

"Nobody's in Brock's confidence. I know that much. I used to be, but nobody since then."

"Well, take my word for it. But this is something you don't understand and you ought to put it away for future reference: the *Sentinel* supported you because you were the regular candidate, and the regular candidate always gets the *Sentinel's* support. But the other way of looking at it is, they can support you without taking any responsibility for you. Or anybody. If you get in a mess they'll forget they ever knew you. They're not going to have you or anybody else as their responsibility. And that's why they didn't like it when I had the city car. I work on the paper, and people might think the paper was mixed up in a little private graft. See what I mean?"

"Well, maybe."

"They never yet backed up a man that got into trouble. My father told me that years ago. In fact it was his policy originally. Never defend anybody. And never get in a position where you have to defend somebody in order to defend yourself. I should have known that, or rather I knew it all right, but I never thought of it as applying to me and the car. So tonight after work I took the car to the city garage and told the mechanic I wouldn't be using it again."

"Well, there's other ways of getting a car."

"Uh-huh. Buy one."

"Well, of course that's always the best way if you have the money," said Charlie. "You don't feel like telling me who gave you the information? If I knew who Brock confides in it'd come in handy some time. Somebody at the Fort Penn Club, is it?"

"No."

"That Frenchwoman he's jazzing?"

"No. I don't know about any Frenchwoman, but don't keep asking me, Charlie. I have to have some private sources, you know."

"All right. Maybe Brock and I'll get to be buddies again, now that I'm mayor. Brock's changed. A little more serious now. But that's all right, so am I. But we used to have some good times together when we were younger, Brock and I. And he isn't the only member of that family I had some good times with. I—"

"Pipe down."

"What?" said Charlie. The sisters were coming back from the kitchen. "Oh."

"Here's your water," said Louise. "Telling Jack a dirty joke, I guess. Is that why you shut up all of a sudden? Amy, a person might think you were a little innocent, the way Charlie won't tell a joke in front of you. Maybe he's afraid of you."

"No, it's Jack I'm afraid of. If I told a dirty joke in front of Amy, Jack'd order me out of the house."

"No, I wouldn't. But Amy doesn't like them."

"I don't either, but this one comes home every night with a new one. He had a raw one tonight. It was so bad it'd make Jack blush," said Louise.

"Didn't make you blush," said Charlie.

"Let's play some cards," said Amy.

"What'll we play—500?" said Louise. "I'm learning to play bridge. Let's play that."

"Let's not and say we did," said Charlie. "Or you know that Frenchwoman that Brock Caldwell's going around with? She catches on to American slang. I was sitting with Brock's party last night and I happened to say, 'Let's not and say we did,' but the Frenchie said, *'Let's*—and say we *didn't.'* "

"Oh, at the hotel banquet," said Amy. "What did Grace Tate wear?"

"A black taffeta—" said Louise.

"Cut so low you could see everything she had," said Charlie.

"Like hell you could," said Hollister.

"You weren't there, how do *you* know?" said Charlie.

"He saw her, though," said Amy. "She went over to the paper late."

"Oh," said Charlie. He looked at Hollister.

"Well, are we going to play cards or aren't we?" said Hollister.

"Say, is that twenty-five after eight?" said Charlie.

"What did you think it was? Twenty of five?" said Louise.

"No, but I thought it was earlier. I didn't know it was that late. We better vamoose if we're gonna see everybody we have to see, before they all go to bed."

"A person might think you were mayor already," said Louise. "All right. I'll get my coat on."

Everyone rose. "Say, Jack, if you're gonna be in your office to-morrow morning around ten-thirty I'll call you up and something I wanted to ask you."

"I'll be there," said Jack.

The Jays left and Amy put her arms around her husband's

waist. "I didn't pay any attention to half of what they were saying," she said. "All I could think of was I wanted to be with you.
You put the lights out and I'll go up. Do you love me?"

"Nobody else," he said.

———

It was not strange that Grace and Jack Hollister did not become
friends until they were in their thirties. Their fathers, it is true,
had been friends, but Arthur James Hollister in his own way was
as prideful a man as an English butler or an American railroad
conductor. The kind of friendship he enjoyed with William
Caldwell was not at all exceptional: they had gone to the same
college and during their separate times at Lafayette they had
joined the same fraternity, Zeta Psi, but the bonds of a common
college and a common fraternity made some, but not the greatest, difference when Caldwell was choosing a man to run the *Sentinel.* After Hollister had been hired the fraternity and the college
occasionally provided a topic of conversation, a nice field of
agreement, rather than the whole, the sole reason for their continuing acquaintanceship. Arthur James, a Southerner, had gone
to Easton because his father had been a Presbyterian preacher.
William Caldwell had been sent to Lafayette because it was in
Pennsylvania, it was a good college, and it was not in Philadelphia. They could have gone to separate colleges and been on just
as good terms; in fact, Arthur James would have preferred it that
way. In his dealings with Caldwell he gave advice, offered suggestions, made his comments, and contradicted Caldwell, and he
put out a good newspaper, for the time, because he was honest,
intelligent, had good taste, was cautious, and knew that Caldwell
would back him up even when Caldwell was not in agreement
with him. He was progressive only in mechanical matters. He regarded himself as a self-respecting citizen who was running a
newspaper that was owned by a rich man. His ambition was to
provide comfort and security for his wife and son, and to die a
self-respecting citizen. He held to his ambitions and principles,
with the result that long before he died he was conscious of the

fact that it was not only self-respect that he had maintained, but the respect of the community that he had achieved. And the consciousness of that fact did not cause him to sacrifice or compromise his principles in order to retain his position in the public's good opinion.

The wives of the two men had been introduced to each other, and, in due course, might have become friends had it not been for Hollister's refusal to encourage any such relationship between the two families. The Hollisters dined once, and only once, at the Caldwells'. "Everyone else came in carriages," said Hollister. "It was nice of them to invite us, but we won't go again until we can afford our own carriage!" He joined the Fort Penn Club for business reasons, at the urging of Caldwell, and Mrs. Hollister had her son and her church work.

When Jack was old enough to go to college he was offered a football scholarship at Fort Penn University. As a high school end he had been good enough for that, without being good enough to be offered the same kind of prize at Lafayette, and in his studies he had not been good enough to get that kind of scholarship at either school. "What shall you do? Well, what do you want to do? I'd like to see you go to Lafayette, of course, but Lafayette has this reputation as a rich man's college and you're not a rich man's son. Fort Penn isn't as good, but it's getting better, and you have to take into consideration the money involved. If you can go to Fort Penn for nothing, after you get your degree you'll have the money I've put aside for your college expenses. You might want to travel. You might even get a Rhodes Scholarship at Fort Penn, although I don't hold out much hope of that. It's your decision, son." Young Hollister's decision had been to go to Fort Penn University, where he failed to become football captain only because he was a Phi Gamma Delta (there was no Zeta Psi chapter at Fort Penn) in a year that the Phi Kappa Psis dominated athletics. At Fort Penn he became acquainted with young men from other towns in Nesquehela County and elsewhere in the Commonwealth; one Chinese boy, one Japanese, two

Cubans, four Ohioans, four New Yorkers, four Marylanders, and one boy who had attended Phillips Academy, Andover, for two and a half years; five boys who had gone to Mercersburg, two boys who had gone to Franklin & Marshall Academy, three boys from Kiskiminetas Springs School, one boy from Bellefonte Academy, and in senior year, a newcomer to Fort Penn who had two withered legs and had to attend classes in a wheel chair. With those exceptions Jack was continuing his high-school friend-ships, as to individuals and as to types. He was graduated in the lower half of his class and within two years of commencement he used the money that had been saved for his education to marry Amy Clarke.

For a year his father and mother had known what was coming. Jack had gone to work as a reporter on the *Sentinel* after gradua-tion. It was the only business or profession that had attracted him; in college he had been editor of the Fort Penn *Lookout,* the humorous magazine; he had been a messenger boy between the *Sentinel* and the state capitol; he had covered high-school activi-ties for the *Sentinel* for four years; his hero was Richard Harding Davis. As a full-fledged $12-a-week reporter, with a nickel-plated police badge and passes to the burlesque shows, he had the advantages of a local reputation as an athlete, his friendliness, and his good looks. The good looks, the friendliness, and his charm got him into no trouble, because from the moment he first had laid eyes on Amy Clarke he wanted no one else and wanted no one else to have her.

He was introduced to her at the Senior Prom, the university's annual dance for sophomores, juniors, and seniors. He was at-tending the Prom alone; the girl he had invited was at home with scarlatina (she never quite got over the effects of the malady or the effects of Jack's introduction to Amy). He got his name on her dance card for three waltzes.

She was a jolly girl in company but after two or three dates alone with Jack—sitting on her porch until nine o'clock in the Spring evenings—they would talk about the world, this life, the future. Then one night nine o'clock came too soon and he said to her: "Amy, I don't want to go home from you. I want to marry you."

"I want to marry you, too, but I can't for a while yet."

"You love me, though, don't you?"

"Yes, I love you, Jack."

"Will you let me kiss you?"

"Yes, but we have to stand out of the light. They can see us from inside." She got up from her chair and he got up from the porch step and they kissed freely. She opened her mouth for him and they kissed for minutes until she whispered to him: "They'll hear we're not talking. And there's nine striking."

"I know." He kept his voice low in pitch, so that it could be heard but without the words being distinct. "Will you wear this?" He took the diamond-shaped pin from his vest and held it out to her.

"All right," she said. "If you want me to. But I have to finish Normal. That's two years and I didn't even start yet."

"I want you to wear it, though. Are you sure you have to go to Normal?"

"They wouldn't let me get married. They like you, Jack, but—"

"I have over three thousand dollars we can get married on. We can tell your father that."

"That's not it," she said. "Poppa isn't the one that's making me go to Normal. It's Momma. She says if I graduate from Normal I'll always have that to fall back on, teaching school."

"Two years, though."

"I know, but we'll be together every minute we can. I'll see you every minute I can, and I'll write to you every day from Normal," she said. "And in two years you'll be making enough so we won't have to touch the other money. We can't live on twelve a week."

"You're right, I guess. I wonder how much my father gets. Do you know how much yours gets?"

"No. Why?"

"I was wondering how much it'd cost to have a nice house and live like your family, or my family."

"Don't forget your family live better than we do. Your father's a salaried man, and mine only gets paid when he works. Carpenters get paid by the hour. You find out so we can plan ahead," she said.

"Amy! It struck nine," her mother called.

"All right, Momma."

"Ask her if I can't stay till ten after this."

"I'll ask her, but I know what she'll answer. And Jack . . ."

"What, Amy?"

"We have to be careful—about kissing."

"They couldn't see us."

"I didn't mean that. I meant when we go for a walk, when people can't see us. We don't want to get so we can't stop. You know what I mean, Jack. It was my fault tonight."

"No it wasn't, Amy."

"Yes, it was, and the girl's the one that's supposed to be careful."

"Not only the girl. If the fellow's a gentleman."

"We can kiss here, but not where we don't have to worry about people seeing us. Kiss me now and I'll go to my room and think about you."

"Amy! I don't want to have to call you again."

"All right, Momma."

The Hollisters, father and son, often walked home together when their days' work permitted. Jack stopped in his father's office late in the afternoon following the date with Amy. The father was looking at the paper, not reading it but studying the make-up professionally before reading the news. "Hello, son," he said.

"Will you tell Mother I'm eating downtown? I have a night assignment."

"All right. What's the assignment?"

"Last meeting of the committee that's running the Six-County Firemen's Convention."

"Well, that's a pretty good assignment. Front page. You have anything on the front page in this paper?"

"Not today." The son sat down.

The father looked over his spectacles. "Have you lost anything?"

"Lost anything? Not that I know of. Did you find something?"

"Didn't find anything, but I noticed something, and maybe made a discovery thereby."

"What's that?"

"Well, if *you* won't tell *me* I guess *I'll* have to tell *you*," said the father. "I observe that you're not proclaiming your membership in the brotherhood of Phi Gamma Delta."

"Oh," said the son.

"Well?"

Jack grinned. "I didn't lose it. I gave it."

"Amy Clarke?"

"Yes."

"What are the terms of the, uh, understanding?"

"Well, she's going to Normal in September, and that takes two years."

"Then what?"

"Then we'll get married."

"Have you discussed it with her father? Her mother?"

"Not yet. There's plenty of time."

"Yes, there's plenty of time for that, and for getting married too."

"But you're in favor of it, I hope, Father."

"Yes, congratulations." The father reached out his hand and when the son took it they both had tears in their eyes. The son sat down again. "She's a lovely thing," said the father. "Pretty, vivacious, healthy."

"She's all of those things and more."

"Naturally I expected you to look for more in the girl you wanted to marry. And the most important thing *isn't* that she must love you, Jack."

"Isn't?"

"Is not," said the father. "The most important thing about her—any girl you think of marrying—is, can you picture her when beauty's gone, and youth's gone—can you imagine yourselves happy together? Has this girl—now I'm not talking about Amy, but any girl—has this young woman got the character and the characteristics that *I'll* want to live with when I'm sixty-five? Notice I say *I'll* want, meaning you, Jack Hollister, not me, Arthur Hollister. I'll be deep, deep down in the ground by the time *you're* sixty-five, and I wouldn't want you to be influenced too much by my disapproval *or* my approval. You're too independent for that anyway, and by and large I respect your judgment."

"I'm glad to hear that," said the son. "I was a little afraid you and Mother might want me to marry somebody—a girl with more money and social position."

"There you did us an injustice. If you had picked a rich girl, one of the old families, we'd have been reassured regarding your financial security, but I think we might have worried about your happiness. Amy's father's a carpenter. Well, that calls for a high degree of skill, to be a good carpenter. A carpenter has problems that you or I couldn't solve, and at the same time he's working with his hands. I think carpentry's one of the best trades there is. In our business, now I think of it, we don't get many police-court stories about carpenters. Tell you the truth, I can't recall any."

"That never occurred to me."

"As to Amy's mother, I've never met her and I don't know the first thing about her, but they seem to have a nice home, from what little you've told me, and that means she does her job well."

"Yes, she's the one that's making Amy go to Normal."

"The other sister married Charlie Jay," said the father. "Well, I don't know anything about her, either, except that she's kept Charlie out of jail. I always thought Charlie Jay'd—well, no matter. I never had any use for him, and I never will. What are your plans?"

"Work and try to save money."

"You know you have over three thousand dollars coming to you? I daresay you took that into consideration."

"I did."

"Did you tell Amy you had that much money?"

"Yes, she knows it."

"Ahhhhhhhh, *that's* the girl to marry, Jack. Damn it all, let's stroll over to McBride's and have a drink of whiskey."

The engaged couple had only two serious quarrels in two years. The first was during Amy's first year at Normal. Jack had seen her off at the station after Thanksgiving. The two-coach train for the short trip to Normal was pulling out and Jack was standing on the platform when a young man, obviously a fellow-student of Amy's, boarded the train, entered Amy's coach, and took the seat beside her. She turned to look at the newcomer, and by the time she had spoken to him the train was on its way and out of sight.

In the letter she wrote that night she made no mention of the man who had been her seat-mate, and in the letter Jack wrote to her there was mention of very little else. Who was the fellow? Who did he think he was? What right did he have to sit next to her without asking for permission? It took more than a week for Jack to approximate a mood of acceptance of Amy's explanation, and the acceptance never was complete and genuine. The second quarrel occurred in the second year of their understanding, and was a more serious threat to their love. It was during the Christmas vacation, two days before Christmas. Jack, walking on State Street, literally bumped into Amy coming out of one of the department stores. The flash of pleasure at the chance meeting was gone immediately when Jack saw that Amy was with her brother-in-law, Charlie Jay.

"Hello, Jack," said Charlie.

"Hello," said Jack, coldly.

"Well, don't I get a hello?" said Amy.

"Hello."

"Well, thanks very much, Amy. I guess we'll see you tomorrow night, Jack?"

"Think so?"

"Why, yes, aren't you and Amy coming to help trim the tree?"

"No," said Jack.

"Yes we are," said Amy.

"Well, I thought you were. So long," said Charlie. He left them standing in front of the store.

"What's the matter with you?" said Amy.

"I have no use for that fellow," said Jack.

"Well, I can't help that. He's married to my sister, don't forget."

"Did you buy him something nice? Something pretty?"

"I didn't buy him anything. We don't exchange presents. I was—"

" 'Thank you very much, Amy.' "

She laughed. "Oh, you're crazy as a loon. I was helping him buy a bathrobe for Louise."

"I don't believe it."

They glared at each other for a moment and then Amy unbuttoned her coat, undid the safety clasp and handed Jack his fraternity pin. "All right," she said. "Don't believe it." She darted away from him, but she need not have hurried. He walked off in the opposite direction to cover his assignment. He went to McBride's after work and was drunk before eight o'clock. He picked a fight with a police sergeant, who laid him out with two punches to the stomach and the chin, and it took ten of McBride's dollars to keep the sergeant from running him in. McBride and a couple of pressmen carried him to McBride's living quarters over the saloon, and when he had come to and was sick he went to the Exchange Hotel for the night. He quit work early the next day, went home to change his clothes and get Amy's present, and bought gifts for Louise's children. He presented himself at Louise's door at half-past eight, clean, sober, shaky, and penitent.

"Hello, Jack," said Louise. "Stay here a minute. I'll get Amy."

Amy came out to the hall and when she saw him she ran to him and he took her in his arms with the parcels still in his hands. All she said was "Oh, Jack, Jack." There were no recriminations between them, and Charlie Jay—coached by Louise, who had been told the whole story—pretended nothing had happened. Charlie and Louise went to bed early and left them in the parlor. They turned down the lamp until the room was quite dark and they made love beyond anything they had done before. She did not stop his hand under her skirt and she touched him from the outside of his clothing, the first time for them together.

They were married according to their schedule, in late June of 1910. The ceremony took place in the Lutheran church, a few doors from Amy's home. The best man was Andrew McClintock, a classmate, teammate, and fraternity brother of Jack's, and the matron of honor was Louise Jay. Amy's father—in whom Arthur James Hollister discerned certain amusing resemblances to himself—was opposed to putting on a show, with the result that the wedding and the party that followed were small and unpretentious. The happy couple's honeymoon, as the *Sentinel* noted, combined business with pleasure, as the groom had accepted a position on the editorial staff of the Philadelphia *North American*.

They lived in Philadelphia for three years. Amy had her children there. Jack was paid $25 a week, but it cost more to live in Philadelphia, and they had had to dip into the old education fund and the thousand-dollar wedding present from Arthur James. The *North American* wanted Jack to stay, but he had learned the workings of a big paper and was ready to go back to Fort Penn and the *Sentinel*. Amy held the infant Arthur while Jack, facing them in the railway coach, held Joan. As the train began to move Jack grinned. "I feel as if the Governor'd just given me a pardon," he said.

"It's like recess," said Amy. "I don't care if I never go there again. Not even Wanamakers."

BOOK FOUR

BOOK FOUR

In conformity with her decision to "go out more" Grace, early in December, informed Charles, the maitre d'hôtel of the Nesquehela, that after the first of the year she would like to engage the corner table for luncheon every Friday. There were four corners in the Commonwealth Room, but there was no question in Charles's mind as to which corner Mrs. Tate was referring to, no more than there was any long-lived doubt that the table would be hers, in spite of the fact that several senators, lobbyists, and women in Fort Penn society asked for that table whenever they lunched at the hotel. Charles knew his business; he knew how to seat a room. The two-dollar tip from the politicians or the bright smile from the Fort Penn lady was nice enough to have, but Charles was a forward-looking man, who was planning to work in Fort Penn for five years, save his money, and open a small, exclusive, expensive restaurant of his own in competition with the Commonwealth Room. He would make the Commonwealth Room fashionable by seeing to it that Mrs. Tate was comfortable there, so comfortable that he could count on her to dress the room at least twice a week, and not only the once a week she had spoken for. It was the only opportunity most Fort Penn women had to study Grace, her manners and her clothes; that made certain a sizable patronage by Fort Penn women who could afford to spend a dollar and a quarter for the prix-fixe lunch. Charles also had had experience with politicians, who like to eat where there are pretty women, and Grace was the handsomest woman in Fort Penn. Not a girl any longer, but surely an interesting woman with fascinating possibilities once one had one's own restaurant—five years? Well, she would be past forty then but interesting times could be had with women past forty—and meanwhile it would be a pleasure to bring the smile to her passionate mouth—Madam, when you move your lips like that you make me think of other things... On the Tuesday, then, which was the last day of the old year, Grace received the following note:

> *Dear Madam:*
>
> *In accord with your instructions it gives me great pleasure to inform you that the corner table in the Commonwealth Room has been reserved for you for Friday next, 2 January, and each Friday thereafter. I look forward to the opportunity to serve you. Believe me, Madam, I am*
>
>

Yours respectfully,
Charles
(Maitre d'hôtel)

Grace smiled and immediately telephoned Betty Martindale, because she was her friend; Natalie Bordener, because she was pretty; and Mary Wall, because she dressed well. And then she telephoned Connie Schoffstal, who was in town for the holidays. "I engaged a table at the hotel and then forgot all about it," she told the women. "Will you come to lunch Friday?" To Connie she added the information that she had engaged the table for every Friday, but was hoping not to have the same women every week. "I see them all at bridge club every week, and that's enough for a steady diet," she said.

It was a mild, sunny day; bastard spring, Connie called it. The women in Grace's party were dressed for New York, except

Connie, who, living in New York, now was always dressed for the country. She was a stranger to Charles, but he put her down as an Englishwoman whom Mrs. Tate had met in her travels.

The room was surprisingly well filled, for the most part with mothers, and mothers-and-fathers having lunch with their boys and girls on boarding-school vacation. "If anybody ever tells me Fort Penn's a hick town—they won't be able to tell me that again. This is practically the Waldorf-Astoria," said Connie.

"Isn't it exciting?" said Grace.

"The Schoffstal House was never like this," said Connie.

"Oh, but we had good times at the Schoffstal House," said Grace. "I'll always love it."

"I went down and had a look at it yesterday," said Connie. "I hadn't had a good look at it since they put up the office building. My, my."

"You left at the wrong time," said Mary Wall. "Just when we're getting to be a real city."

"Yes, have you heard about the subway?" said Betty.

"Subway? In Fort Penn?" said Connie.

"Absolutely," said Betty. The women kept silent and Connie looked from one to the other.

"I don't believe it. What do they need a subway for?" said Connie. "I think it's a damn outrage to put a subway in Fort Penn."

"Don't worry, Connie," said Grace. "Your traction company stock is safe. The subway's a new joke for you out-of-towners. That's what they're calling the—"

"They're building a viaduct near the station and underneath'll be a tunnel. That's our Fort Penn subway. It's a half a square long," said Betty.

"That's long enough," said Connie. "I'll bet neither one of you's ever been in the New York subway."

"I've been in the Philadelphia one," said Mary Wall.

"Just you take a ride in the New York one during rush hour," said Connie. "A very good friend of mine came home in tears last week just shaking, shaking. But I'd rather not talk about it."

"But what happened?" said Betty.

"A man," said Connie.

"But what?" said Betty.

"Insulted her," said Connie.

"What did he say?" said Betty.

"Did, not said, Betty. You always want to know all the details," said Connie.

"Naturally, and the way you're stringing it out he might as well have I don't know what," said Betty.

"He practically did I-don't-know-what, all the way from Times Square to Sheridan Square."

"Is that far? Come on, now, Connie. What was he doing? We're all married except you, and you're the one that knows the story. *I* may want to ride in the New York subway some time and I'd like to know what to expect."

"I don't think you'd find it very funny, Betty Martindale," said Connie.

"Just think of being insulted all the way from Times Square to wherever it was," said Betty.

"Maybe you'd like it, I don't know," said Connie.

"Well—maybe I would—who can tell?" said Betty.

"Well, why don't you come to New York and find out," said Connie.

"What really happened, Connie?" said Grace. "That is, if you can tell it."

"In spite of Betty, it was frightful," said Connie. "The girl, this friend of mine, is a very sensitive, beautiful person. Just divorced from her husband less than a year ago, and very unhappy and sensitive. Well, she got on the subway during the rush hour and suddenly she felt this fat little man getting closer and closer to her and when she realized he was doing it deliberately, not just an accident she tried to move away, but she was hemmed in. She didn't want to make a scene and she had to stay right where she was till Fourteenth Street."

"What happened at Fourteenth Street?" said Betty.

"She got off and took the local."

"And he followed her?" said Betty.

"No, when I said Sheridan Square I meant Fourteenth Street, that's the express stop after Penn Station."

"Penn Station? Where does that come in? That's just a few squares from Times Square, isn't it?" said Betty.

"Yes," said Connie.

"Then why didn't she get off at Penn Station?" said Betty.

"Because she was hemmed in," said Connie. "Really—"

"But she got off at *Fourteenth* Street, and she was hemmed in there," said Betty. "I don't see why she didn't get off the first chance she got, Penn Station, instead of letting him, uh, insult her all the way to wherever it was. Fourteenth Street."

"I'll never try to tell you anything again, believe me," said Connie. "You have to have a Baedeker and a moving picture."

"No, I don't," said Betty, "but I like to get a story straight in my mind."

"A man did that to me once," said Natalie. "But it was on a train coming back from Princeton."

"Well, that made it all right," said Betty.

"You don't have to be sarcastic," said Natalie.

"Sorry," said Betty. "The trouble is I don't think it's always the man's fault."

"I beg your pardon?" said Natalie.

"Oh, now, don't you be sensitive, too, Natalie. You're too sensible. You wouldn't let a man bother you all the way from Times Square to wherever."

"I certainly would not. I turned around and slapped this man's face."

"What about the man you were with? What did he do?"

"It *was* the man I was with. That was the last game I ever went to with him," said Natalie.

"I imagine it would be," said Betty.

"I've ordered dessert, but if anybody wants to change the order?" said Grace.

"I don't want to change the order, but I'd just as soon change the subject," said Mary Wall.

"So would I," said Grace, laughing.

"To what?" said Betty.

"Something cheerful," said Grace.

"The Pillbox," said Mary Wall. "That's cheerful. I think it's a very good idea. Who is J. H., Grace?"

"I'm sure I haven't the faintest idea what you're talking about," said Grace.

"Don't you still own the *Sentinel,* you and Brock?" said Mary.

"We have a lot of stock in it, but the *Sentinel* isn't The Pillbox, or whatever you said," said Grace.

"Then don't you read your own paper?" said Mary. "The Pillbox is a column in the *Sentinel,* signed J. H. It started yesterday."

"Oh, Lord. I didn't read it. I didn't read the paper at all yesterday, I was so busy with the children," said Grace.

"Who is J. H.?" said Mary. "Is it anyone we know?"

"Jack Hollister," said Grace. "He's the son of Arthur James Hollister, you remember?"

"Well, I think he's a very entertaining writer," said Mary. "Did you read it, Betty?"

"Yes, I think he's very amusing, at least the article yesterday was," said Betty. "You mean about New Year's Resolutions?"

"Yes," said Mary. "He said he picked New Year's to start his column because that gave him a subject to write about right away. But he said he ransacked his brain—wasn't that it, Betty?"

"Mm-hmmm."

"Ransacked his brain for something original to say about New Year's resolutions and the only thing he could think of was to resolve never to start another column on New Year's Day. It wasn't what he said but the way he said it. Get the paper and read it, Grace. You know. I get so tired of reading the editorials, always know so much and so impersonal. This man's a welcome relief. Casual, and friendly, and doesn't pretend he knows it all."

"He has a nice light touch," said Betty. "He reminded me a little of somebody else but I can't think who. *Not* his *father*. He was a wonderful man, Arthur James Hollister, but very reserved and aloof. At least that's the way he struck me."

"Scotty knows Jack Hollister. He's very good-looking. Has a moustache and very well built. He used to play football for Fort Penn and Scotty and some of the others tried to get him to coach the Academy team. That's how I met him," said Natalie. "I didn't know he wrote, too. I never read anything but the society page, but if he's good I'll start today. Where is his article? What page?"

"The editorial page," said Mary.

They finished their lunch and Mary, Betty and Natalie had things to do. "Can I take you anywhere, Connie?" said Grace.

"You can take me with you," said Connie. "Where are you going?"

"Well—I'll be honest with you," said Grace.

"The *Sentinel*," said Connie.

"Yes, but not to see him. To get yesterday's paper."

"Let me do that for you," said Connie.

"It's all right, Connie. Please don't start worrying about me. I appreciate what you're trying to do, but honestly there's absolutely nothing to worry about."

"Grace, I saw your face when you realized you hadn't read the paper yesterday. You promised you would, I guess, and then you forgot."

"I told him last fall I'd look forward to it," said Grace. "But that ought to prove there's nothing to get concerned about."

"It proves you haven't been seeing him, but the look on your face proves something else."

"What, for heaven's sake?"

"You thought you'd hurt him, and you wouldn't do that for the world. You hurt somebody you cared about."

"All right, that's what I was thinking."

"Oh, God," said Connie. "Grace, can't you keep out of trouble? Am I going to have to come back to Fort Penn and keep an eye on you?"

"You were here in 1917 and nothing kept me out of trouble then—nothing. But this time I'm going to keep out of it myself."

"I hope so, I hope to God."

"But it's true. I haven't even seen him since the day after this hotel opened. Don't you think I could have seen him if I'd wanted to?"

"Yes, but—"

"Come on, come with me," said Grace. "We can't keep standing here in a hotel lobby."

The Fourth Street car-call flashed the number of Grace's Pierce and they got in.

"Where to, ma'am?"

"The *Sentinel* office, first," said Grace. She hung up the speaking tube. "You can get the paper for me, I'll wait in the car. Then I'll take you wherever you want to go."

"After you've prepared yourself by reading his article, what then?"

"Would you like to go for a ride? I'll bet you haven't been on a horse since last summer."

"Do you mean it? It's a wonderful day for it."

"Sure I mean it. Brock bought a horse for hacking around, principally to lose weight. I just hope the poor horse won't be foundered when we get there. Brock rode him for two weeks and after that if I didn't ride him he got no exercise."

"I don't trust you, Grace."

"Oh, well."

"We can ride tomorrow. I'll get the paper and you can read it so you'll be prepared."

"I'm not going to see him."

"I think you'd better. I'm against it, but I'm *your* friend, not his."

"Yes," said Grace, eagerly. "You can get the paper and I'll read it and I can see him for a minute. If I see him now, it's a busy time at the paper, and I can only see him for just a minute or two. There's no harm in that, seeing him the same way I see hundreds of people. 'Hello, how are you, it was a nice article, good luck, good-bye.' I do need to see him, and then I won't for a long while. But just now I do, it's been so long."

"Yes," said Connie.

"I really hate that Natalie Bordener," said Grace.

"Yes," said Connie. "Now how're we going to do this? I'll go in and buy a paper and bring it out for you to read. Then are you going in and congratulate him on what a wonderful writer he is?"

"Then you'd have to sit and wait in the car," said Grace. "No, you buy the paper and I'll take you wherever you're going and then I'll come back and congratulate him."

"I'd rather wait in the car."

"So you can be here when I come out," said Grace. "So you can read the expression on my face again?"

"Yes, frankly," said Connie.

"Well, if you're going to do me a favor I guess I have to do one in return, if you call that a favor, looking at a girl's face to see what's going on inside her."

"I'm interested in what goes on inside my friends," said Connie.

They stopped at the *Sentinel* building and Grace sat in the car while Connie was buying the paper. Grace was speaking to the chauffeur through the tube: "We'll go from here to Miss Schoffstal's, I think. Then you can take me to the Boston Store and leave me there, and go back to Second Street and wait. Miss Anna's at a party and I'll need you again at five. I'll take a taxi home."

"I'm afraid you'll have a hard time getting a taxi today, ma'am."

"Then I'll walk."

The chauffeur was listening to her with his head far back and cocked so that he was facing to the right; Grace, with the tube in her hand, was looking in his direction, forward and to the left.

"There's a gentleman wants to speak to you, ma'am," said the chauffeur.

Grace turned her head, and it was Hollister, standing beside the car and smiling. He had no hat or overcoat. She smiled and opened the door. "Hello, Mr. Hollister, get in or you'll catch cold."

"I recognized your car," he said, getting in and sitting beside her. "Is there anything I can get for you?"

"Uh, no thanks. Miss Schoffstal went in to buy a paper. Yesterday's paper."

"Most important issue the *Sentinel* ever put out," said Hollister.

"Indeed it was, indeed it was. I hope they're not all sold out."

"Oh, they ran fifty thousand extra for people that admire good writing," he said. "Are we talking about the same thing?"

"I think we are."

"How did you like it, the first one?" he said. "I guess you haven't seen today's."

"No, I haven't seen today's," she said. She looked away from him and then back. "The paper she's getting is for me."

"Oh. Well."

"I missed it yesterday, Mr. Hollister. I didn't read the paper at all. I blame my children and their holiday, but—what's the use? I forgot."

"Oh, that's all right," he said.

"Not when I'd been looking forward to it. I knew there was something special about New Year's Day this year."

"Did you really come down to get the paper—for that reason?"

"Yes. I sent Miss Schoffstal in to get it because I wanted to read the column before I saw you. In five more minutes I'd have read it. But that would have been cheating. I'd have pretended I read it yesterday and you'd have believed me. In a way I'm glad I was found out. Here's Miss Schoffstal." She spoke quickly. "Will-you-be-here-fifteen-minutes-from-now-I'll-call-you-please-be-here."

"All right," he said. He got out and held the door for Connie, who was carrying the paper.

"Miss Schoffstal, Mr. Hollister."

They muttered and Connie got in the car. They said good-bye to Hollister and the car began to move.

"Where are we going?" said Connie. "I didn't hear you give any directions."

"To your house, I thought. Don't you want to go home?"

"Really, Grace, *I* saw him getting in the car and I gave you a couple of minutes alone with him."

"What does my face show?" said Grace.

"Enthusiasm. Exhilaration. You're in love with that man."

"Well, you knew that before. Is he in love with me—you're so good at reading faces?"

"Let's go skating, Grace."

"There's no ice on the river," said Grace.

"There was no finality about the way he left. When are you going to see him again? Today?"

"I'm going to call him in fifteen minutes, as soon as I take you home and get to a pay station."

"Have you a place to go to bed with him? Grace, you're out of your mind! If you see him the way you are now, the two of you, even if you don't go to bed with him—everybody that sees you'll know you're in love."

"Well, what if we are!"

"What if you are? How can you ask that? How can you *ask* that?"

"If he wants me he can have me."

"If he wants you! *How,* wants you?" Connie suddenly grabbed Grace's arms and shook her. "Stop this, do you hear?"

Grace laughed.

"Stop this! Stop!" said Connie. "Get some sense into yourself, Grace. You have children, he has children and a wife. His new job. A future. You heard people say they like his writing, maybe he's good. He might be a playwright, or write a novel. But you won't help him."

"How do you know I won't? She hasn't, his wife. Maybe I would help him," said Grace, still laughing, and then abruptly becoming serious. "Connie, you spend so much time with your theatrical people you're getting like them. Everything's a play."

"Am I? Well, everything is a play."

"Oh, it is not," said Grace. "I told him to take us to your house. Is that where you want to go?"

"If you insist."

"I'm sorry, but I do insist. You've taken all the pleasure out of the afternoon."

"That's what I meant to do."

"Is that so? But I'm still going to call him," said Grace. "You and your Greenwich Village. Bohemians. I hate that side of you."

"You hate the sight of me?"

"I hate that *side* of you. It's cheap, and nasty. I *am* in love with Hollister, but all that means to you is sex."

"That's what it means to you, too. You were a *spec*tacle when I got in this car. Like an animal. You talk about cheap and nasty? There's a side to you I hate, too, you know. Roger Bannon, Oscar Stribling—"

"*Os*car *Strib*ling?"

"Yes, Oscar Stribling. I know about him and I know what he is."

"*What* is he?"

"He's one of the most degenerate men I've ever met."

"And you meet a lot of them."

"Exactly, and I meet a lot of them," said Connie.

"How do you know him?" said Grace. "And how well do you know him?"

"He's been to my apartment. And when he found out where I was from and knew you . . ."

"What?"

"He thinks you're naive."

"I am, when it comes to his kind of thing."

"Oh, his kind of thing," said Connie. "I thought you didn't know what kind of man he was."

"I found out," said Grace.

"Who was the other girl?"

"*You* find out. It shouldn't be any trouble if he told you about me right off the bat."

"It wasn't right off the bat, but even if it had been I wouldn't have been surprised. I just hope you weren't seen with him too much by certain people in Philadelphia."

"Why?" said Grace. "What certain people?"

"What you might call Greenwich Village people. *They* wouldn't believe you were naive if they saw you often with Oscar."

"They can believe what they like. *Two* people know I'm not like *them:* Oscar and that other woman," said Grace.

The car was stopped in front of the Schoffstal house. "Come on in, Grace. You can make your telephone call from here and I won't listen."

"Did you ever—how shall I put it?—participate with Oscar and one of his friends?"

"Grace!"

"Don't fly off the handle. I wouldn't be shocked. If that's what some people like, that's what they like. I may be naive, but I'm not a saint. *Or* a hypocrite."

"Well, rest assured I didn't, and I don't know why you have the crust to ask me such a question."

"No?"

"No."

"Well, it was because you've been going on all day about studying the expressions on people's faces. That was what Oscar's friend said she wanted to do."

"Well, not me," said Connie.

"All right, *clam* yourself, *clam* yourself, as Alfred says."

Connie shook her head slowly. "To think of us sitting here in front of my house in Fort Penn, P-A, and talking like this."

"Well, before we drop the subject permanently, why would Oscar Stribling tell a total stranger he'd had an affair with me?"

"He didn't say it in so many words, but of course I knew, as soon as he said you were naive. But he wasn't a total stranger. People like that aren't total strangers to one another."

"Are you like that, Connie?"

"Of course I'm not, you don't have to insult me, but he came to my apartment and some of the people were like that, that kind of people and I guess he took for granted I was one of the fraternity. They have a kind of a fraternity. Boston. Chicago. Cleveland. They all know each other or know about each other."

"I don't see how you can stand living with them."

"You can't? It's because I'm homely and they're nice to me, that's why I live with them and spend my time with them. And I'm rich. I know that has something to do with it, their liking me. But it isn't the only reason. They respect me and they let me work with them and feel useful, instead of rotting here in this town as an old maid."

"I'd rather rot here."

"Would you? All right, rot here. One thing about us—my friends in New York and myself—we're not hurting anybody but ourselves, if we are hurting anybody. We don't involve innocent children and wives, not to mention young men with a future."

"I'm not coming in, Connie, and you can get out any time you feel like it."

"Thank you for the lunch and thank you for the lift, Mrs. Tate," said Connie. She got up and the chauffeur, who was standing on the curb, opened the car door for her.

Loud enough for Connie to hear, Grace said to the chauffeur: "Lower that window, will you please? Need some fresh air in here."

The chauffeur got back on the box. "Now the Boston Store, ma'am?"

"Yes, please," said Grace.

There was a single telephone pay-station booth just inside the Boston Store, and it almost never was occupied because customers who wished to use the telephone made for the battery of six booths near the center of the store. Grace saw that the single booth was occupied, but since no one was waiting she became the next user. The door of the booth opened and a girl stepped out. "Hello, Mrs. Tate," she said.

"Hello. Oh, hello, Katty Grenville, how are you? You're so grown-up."

The girl laughed unpleasantly. "I guess you knew I was grown up before most people did," she said.

"I've forgotten all about that, Katty, and I hope you do too."

"I was just talking to a friend of yours," said the girl.

"Oh, were you? Who?"

"That'd be telling," said the girl.

"So it would," said Grace. "Are you finished with the booth now?"

"Initials R. B."

"What?"

"Initials—R. B.," the girl repeated.

"Richard Barthelmess," said Grace.

"Since when are you a friend of Richard Barthelmess's?" said the girl.

"I've never met the gentleman, but that's who I thought of with those initials. Excuse me now, Katty."

"Is that the only one you thought of with initials R. B.?"

"Now, Katty, if you want to be grown up *act* like a grown-up, not like a nasty little girl. I'm not interested in whoever you were talking to, but I'm sure your mother would be. Go tell *her* what R. B. stands for."

"I wouldn't have to tell her it was a friend of yours, Mrs. Tate. She knows that already."

"I'm so glad I kept *your* secret, Katty. You're such a grateful little thing. You remember when you had appendicitis?"

The girl walked away and Grace finally picked the receiver off the hook and called Hollister.

"Congratulations," she said. "I *have* read it *this* time, and I think it's a very excellent, amusing article."

"Well, thank you very much," he said. "But I can hardly hear you."

"It isn't the fault of the telephone this time, it's my fault. I'm rather—"

"Is there something wrong?"

"No, no. A couple of little things that happened to me this afternoon, since I saw you earlier. I shouldn't have called you now, but I said I would in fifteen minutes and I was afraid you might be waiting."

"I *was* waiting, twenty-four minutes."

"I'm sorry," she said.

"No, no, I was glad to wait as long as I knew you'd call."

"Thank you," she said. "Well, I wanted to tell you I enjoyed yesterday's article, and I'm looking forward to today's."

"Will you do me a favor? Don't read them while you're upset. They're supposed to be light, and cheerful, but I don't believe reading cheers you up. It never did me."

"No, it doesn't me, either, but I could see that you're a talented writer even if it didn't have the effect of cheering me up."

"Could I cheer you up? Or could I take your mind off your troubles?"

"Oh, could you not!" she said.

"Well, what do—"

"No, not today," she said.

"Well, when?"

"When?" said Grace. "When—and where? We'd have to think of where, too. Yaissle's is a little too public for a man with a wife and two children and a widow with two children."

"Yes, but it's a good-sized city, at least we like to think so."

"It's still too small for us to be seen together, Jack."

"Thank you for Jack."

"And thank you for Grace, even if you haven't said it yet. Why did I suddenly call you by your first name?"

"Because you're upset about something and you need a friend to talk to."

"I guess you're right, but if I'm a friend I'll leave you alone."

"That wouldn't be a friendly act, not when I've wanted to talk to you."

"What about?"

"I'll tell you when I see you."

"That had better be a long time from now," said Grace.

"Don't you ever go for a ride in your Mercer in this nice weather?"

"Not in the Mercer, but I have a Ford coupé I drive."

"You have? When'd you get that? It's even better."

"I bought it last fall. It's handy for shopping and going back and forth from the farm in nasty weather. Why is it better than the Mercer?"

"Inconspicuous."

"Yes, that's true. I could be a doctor, or a visiting nurse, couldn't I?"

"Take a ride down toward Emeryville tomorrow and just before you get to Emeryville you know where the main road makes a right-angle turn?"

"Yes."

"Well, keep going straight instead of making the turn. I'll be up that road about a half a mile. It's in pretty good condition."

"How do you know it so well?"

"I was over it this morning, looking at an old stone house that Washington was supposed to have slept in. I wrote a column about it."

"But then there'll be hundreds of people looking at it."

"The article won't appear till Monday."

"What time shall I be there?" said Grace.

"Three o'clock? Is that convenient for you?"

"Yes," she said. "But if you change your mind, I'll understand."

"I'll understand if you do, too."

"I'll be there, but I almost wish you won't be."

"If you're there you'll see me," he said.

———

It was the next day, Saturday.

He got out of his car as she stopped at the side of the road. He was smiling as he came toward her. "It isn't so damn inconspicuous," he said.

"My Ford?" she said, smiling.

"It's a Ford, but it doesn't look like any visiting nurse's car I ever saw. It's painted like a Pierce-Arrow, and wire wheels."

"Well, at least it isn't a Mercer," she said. "I had it painted and varnished at Mr. Sullivan's. Do you think it's too conspicuous? Do you think I ought to muddy it up?"

"It'd be a shame. It doesn't even look as if it'd ever been rained on."

"Of course not. It's washed after every rain."

"What color do you call this?"

"Victoria blue," she said. "What color do you call your car?"

"Your car," he said.

"No, your car," she said.

"That's yours, too," he said. "That belongs to the *Sentinel*."

"It does? How nice! When did you get it?"

"I didn't get it, but I can use it whenever I can get my hands on it."

"Then you got rid of the city car?" she said.

"I got rid of it the same night you told me to. I drove it straight to the city garage."

"I'm so glad you did that. I was so worried you wouldn't that I never asked about it."

"Will you have a cigarette?"

"Yes, thanks," she said.

They lit their cigarettes, and while they were so doing a farmer with a manure spreader and a team of mules went by at a walk. "Hyuh," said the farmer, and Hollister replied the same. The farmer kept going.

"I guess he saw *your* cigarette, so he knows I'm not just helping a lady in distress."

"But he didn't see *my* cigarette, and you are helping a lady in distress."

"Two automobiles together here is the same as a traffic tie-up in town," said Hollister. "Are you still in distress? How do you feel today?"

"Are you worried about that farmer?"

"I don't like what he's probably thinking."

"Don't forget I'm a farmer, and I know what farmers think, too," she said.

"Then you know what he's thinking."

"Yes, but I know he's wrong. So will anyone else be that ever thinks that about us."

"Will they?" he said.

"Yes," she said.

"They'll always be wrong?"

"Yes, always," she said. "That's how it'll have to be, so you can always go home and face your wife and children with a clear conscience."

"I didn't think that was the way it was going to be, Grace," he said.

"No, and yesterday it wouldn't have been. That's why I didn't want to see you yesterday."

"What happened yesterday?"

"I'll tell you some time. It had nothing to do with you. What happened and what I just said are two separate things."

"They don't seem to be."

"No, not the way I tell it, but the way I felt about *you* yesterday, that was because I had seen you after so long *without* seeing you. The things that happened that upset me, they were just—I quarreled with two women. And I did need a friend, you were right. I was sunk."

"Are you in love with me?" he said.

She did not answer.

"Are you, Grace?"

She still did not answer.

"No?" he said.

She did not speak.

"Yes?" he said.

"I've only said that to two men in my life, and I've only meant it once."

"Which time did you mean it?"

"My husband," she said.

"Not Roger Bannon," he said.

"No, I didn't love him," she said. "Don't ask me if I love you. Maybe what I feel is only what I felt for Roger Bannon."

"I wish you felt for me the way you did for Bannon," he said.

"Maybe I do, I don't know yet," she said. "If that's all it is I'll go away with you some time and it'll be all over in a week."

"In a *week?*"

"That's all it was with Roger. We had one week together of being together as much as we wanted to, and after that it was finished."

"That's not what I understood."

"I don't really care *what* you understood. Any other time I saw him before that week didn't matter."

"It mattered enough to make you want that week," he said.

"Yes, I admit that, but it was that week that was important. Don't you see that? If a week was enough?"

"Was it enough?"

"More than enough. Don't you think I could be seeing him now? He tried to see me after he came back from the war. People don't know that, but Roger Bannon knows it."

"Would you go away with me for a week?"

"Yes."

"Shall we do it?"

"If that's all you want," she said.

"What if we went away for a week and I found out that *wasn't* all I wanted?"

"It would have to be all," she said. "I'd never see you again."

"But what if you were in love with me?"

"I'd leave Fort Penn," she said. "My son's away at school now, and my daughter's ready to go away. I could leave." She looked up at him. "But *you* couldn't."

"No, I guess not," he said.

"You see, Jack? That's why—what that farmer was thinking has to be wrong."

He smiled at her. "And what I was thinking, too," he said. "Will you kiss me, Grace?"

"I want to kiss you," she said.

"But as if it were going to be more than a kiss?"

"Yes," she said.

He kissed her and she him and she did not resist when his hand went inside her blouse and then under her skirt and inside her bloomers.

"Enough," she said suddenly.

He took his hand away from her, his other arm from behind her. "Yes," he said. He looked at her and she was chewing her lip and staring at the steering wheel. She reached for his hand and kissed it and held it to her cheek.

"All my good resolutions," she said. "I'd go anywhere with you now. It's my fault."

"What?" he said, waiting.

"There's more room in your car," she said. She took his hand again. "Come." They got out of the coupé. "Daylight. Farmers. It isn't your fault. Don't blame yourself," she said. They got into the back of the *Sentinel* car and she took off her bloomers and lay back.

It was over, and they were back in the coupé. "Have you another cigarette, please?" she said.

"Yes."

"I'm not sorry, Jack. Don't you be. You will be, but it was my doing."

"Where was I? I was there," he said.

"The time to stop wasn't this afternoon. I thought I had stopped when I stayed away from the paper, but I was wrong. But I'll go away next week. I think I'll go to California. A man out there wants me to marry him, and that would be a good thing. I told him I wouldn't, but if I appeared there he'd know I'd changed my mind."

"But I love you."

"Not like this. You couldn't help this. I'll go away next week and then when you want me again I simply won't be here, and that way—well, that's the way it'll be, and after a while you'll remember this as a strange afternoon. Nothing more. But above all, don't tell your wife, ever. That's why I'm going away, to save you from trouble, but if you think you have to tell her you're wrong."

"You're talking too much, but I guess you're right," he said.

"I know I'm right. I usually do know what's right, if I only followed it," she said. "A quiet kiss now? A peaceful good-bye?"

He kissed her lips.

"I love you," she said. "And I'm happy. Good-bye, Jack."

"Good-bye, Grace," he said. He got out of the coupé and watched her drive up the road to a lane, turn around, and blow him a kiss as she passed him. "Well, that's that," he said, but as he stepped on the starter he remembered having said "that's that" at other times in his life, when his wanting a sense of finality had caused him to welcome it before it was there; when he had got aboard a ship that did not sail for two days; when the doctor told him his leg was broken and he had settled down to a pleasant convalescence before the long, dull pain had begun; when he had accepted philosophically the loss of the football captaincy before he had had a chance to feel the disappointment; when his idol, his father, had died, and he had been so concerned with funeral details that he had not been allowed the time to contemplate a world without Arthur James. "That's that" never had worked for him as a signal to summon finality, and now he wished the words had not come so easily.

It was Saturday afternoon and the Emeryville–Fort Penn road was busy with farmers' cars, and he thought of something for his column in the news that 3,000,000 cars would be manufactured in 1920. He worked and played with the statistic joke until it sounded right—but he wished he had not said "That's that."

He made a stop at the paper on his way home, but no one— meaning Amy—had telephoned. Nothing in Amy's greeting, no conversation at supper, no incident or question in the course of the Saturday night at home confirmed his suspicion that there

had been or would be an accident to the story he had cooked up
for his afternoon. "Did you work late?" Amy had said.

"Not what you'd call work," he had replied. "I took the car and
drove down to Emeryville again. You know, the George Washington stuff, for Monday. It was a good excuse to go for a ride."

"Think up a good excuse so we can all go for a ride some Sunday."

"All right. I could probably get the car any Sunday I ask for it,
but I don't want to ask for too many favors till my column makes
an impression."

"And then don't ask for favors, ask for a raise," she had said.

"In June, if the readers like the column."

In November he had formed the habit of bringing home the
exchanges—papers from New York and Philadelphia, Pittsburgh and Chicago, St. Louis, Kansas City, and Baltimore—to
assist him in the preparation of dummy columns. The comic sections, in spite of some duplications through syndication, added
to the children's popularity in the neighborhood, and Amy could
read the women's pages. Hollister clipped the papers for odd
items and typographical breaks, and the reading of so many papers kept him busy night after night. He was glad to have the papers this night.

He put them on the bridge table in the front room, with his
pastepot, large scissors, copy paper and pencils. The children
had been kissed good night, and Amy, in her chair in the light of
the piano lamp, was reading the day's supply of household hints
and endless serial stories from the exchanges. Nothing was
wrong. All was peace and contentment. In a little while she
would go upstairs to see how the children were, and then she
would come downstairs again and study the ads in the out-of-
town papers he had finished. Then it would be time to go to bed
and because it was Saturday night and they still had the sense of
no school tomorrow, he would go to her or she would go to him
and they would make love, in a routine but mutually satisfactory
fashion. And sometimes on the alternate Sundays that Nancy

came to work they would make love again in the morning before they arose. Saturday was not their only night for intercourse, but the only Saturdays they missed had been during Amy's pregnancies, Hollister's absence in the war, and Amy's menstrual periods.

"Take a look at the kids," said Amy.

The remark did not call for a reply, and he made none. And then he broke out in a sweat: what if he went to bed with her and minutes passed, and a half-hour, and an hour, and he had no erection? In the first few days after he came home from the war he had been no good for her, incapable of waiting for her or being ready for her. "It'll be all right, honey, Louise said it happened to Charlie too," she had told him. And she was right; in a week it was better than ever. But now, whether he was capable or not, he did not want her. He did not actively want her, he actively did not want her. She would come downstairs and make some remark about the children, sit under the piano lamp again, fold her paper and drop it in her chair, walk behind him and run her hand across his shoulders as she passed. She would go upstairs and take off her clothes and lie there until he joined her. And tonight he had no excuse: they had not made love for a week. . . . Yes they had. Of course they had, on New Year's Eve, but that was Wednesday night and this was Saturday.

He heard her careful light steps and he turned to face her. "Do you know what I feel like?" he said.

"What?"

"A drink."

"A *drink?*" she said.

"Yes, I was just reading about this damned Prohibition and it made me want to have a drink."

"All right, I'll have one too," she said.

She got a bottle of Old Overholt out of the sideboard and set it on the bridge table with two shot glasses and two tumblers of water. "Down with Prohibition," he said.

"Here goes," she said.

They drank from the shot glasses, and then he toasted Con-

necticut and Rhode Island, which had not joined in the ratifica-
tion. Amy contented herself with one drink. "Now don't get the
idea you have to finish the whole bottle," she said.

"Why not? In two weeks it'll be against the law," he said.

"Well, you're not used to it, that's why. You'll get drunk. You
got pretty drunk Wednesday night, and you know how you felt
Thursday."

"What the hell, tomorrow's Sunday."

"Yes, and don't forget Sunday the kids come in and jump all
over you Sunday morning," she said. "Don't drink them so fast."

"I believe in personal liberty. My father did, too."

"I'll bet you never saw him drunk, though."

"No, but he had a drink of whiskey every day of his life, and
he'd be against this Prohibition."

"Well, I've had mine. I hope you don't intend to sit up till you
finish that bottle," she said. She stood up. "Sometimes I think
you're a little crazy." She ran her hand across his shoulders and
went upstairs. He had, all told, six drinks, and when he went to
join her he was ardent and a bit rough but Amy enjoyed herself.

The next day he remembered everything. He had got through
that night, but he could not count on getting slightly drunk every
time Amy expected him to make love to her. And then he remembered something else: Mrs. Tate, Grace, was leaving town,
and that fact, when it became a fact—it might make him need
Amy and want her—but it also might make him want Grace, and
hate Amy. He did not know. He did not know at all.

He was at the *Sentinel* office early Monday morning and stayed
late, but Grace did not telephone. She probably was busy arranging for her trip. Again she did not telephone on Tuesday, and
Wednesday afternoon, when she had not called him up he believed that she was going to leave town without telephoning. It
gave him a sense of relief. Now he could say that's that, and there
was a lady. Thursday came and went, and then on Friday he was
sure, he was positive that she had gone, and on Saturday he was
back with Amy and his marriage and his home and his job. He

had even convinced himself that with his agony on the previous Saturday night he had paid for his unfaithfulness of that same Saturday afternoon. He wondered if Grace would write to him.

Upon thinking it over, his admiration for Grace increased until she was easily his ideal woman. She possessed more than anyone else the quality he most admired in man or woman, independence. She had displayed courage of her own, and independence, in her affair with Roger Bannon, when she said to hell with family, home, and what people thought. Another quality that she had was kindness; she could act on an impulse, a small thing like taking people to Yaissle's, and then when she realized that her kind impulse also had an element of the inconsiderate—by taking people away from their work when they could hardly refuse, and thus making them work after hours—she was big enough to apologize. And going back a few years, she did not use her authority at the paper to order people about. Then again, going back only a week, her behavior at Emeryville was courageous, and kind, in that she wanted him, made him want her, and did not leave herself or him in a mess of unfilled passion. He believed furthermore that her concern for his marriage was sincere. She had behaved well, she was rich, she was handsome, and she was his friend. He believed that there would be no time in the future that he could not count on her, and after such a satisfactory conclusion to his brief episode with her he hoped that when she came East again he could stay with her. A large bed in a large, luxurious room, with the things she had said to him at Emeryville coming true—that was his pipe dream for her and for him. And no one who saw him at his desk would ever know that he was not all this time writing a column about ice-boating on the Nesquehela River. But when his reverie was finished he wrote the column and handed it in to Campion, his boss.

"You were up in the clouds writing this one," said Campion. "You might as well have been a thousand miles from here."

"Three thousand," said Hollister. He took the chair beside Campion's, who read the piece through.

"Say, I like this. Go off in more trances if this is what comes of them," said Campion.

"Thanks, Boss," said Hollister. "No questions?"

"No questions, except what kind of tobacco do you smoke? Maybe I could get the others on this paper to smoke the same kind and get the same results."

"Blue Boar," said Hollister.

"Like Lincoln said when some generals—"

"Find out the brand of his whiskey?" said Hollister.

"Oh, you know the story."

"My father told it to me," said Hollister.

He disliked even praise from Campion, who had been the brilliant, drunken managing editor of a New York paper and now was working his way back from the gutter, doing it ruthlessly, with efficiency-expert methods. Hollister disliked him because he suspected that Campion's approval of his transfer to the column job was motivated by an eagerness to put one of his own men in as city editor, Hollister's old job. Crowley, the new city editor, was doing Campion's dirty work while Campion antagonized no one but took credit for the good results. Hollister had no illusion that Campion had given him professional recognition. But he was sure Campion claimed him as his discovery, now that the column had caught on, practically overnight. And Brock Caldwell would believe Campion.

Back at his own desk Hollister read the noon edition, page by page in numerical order. When he came to Page 7 he read the society chit-chat, conducted by Penelope Penn, who was also known as Charlotte Buchwalter, a niece of Walter B. Buchwalter. Penelope had this to say: "Despite the return to college of the many local students, social activity in Fort Penn continues. Pre-Lenten gaiety is in full swing, centering about the Nesquehela Hotel, where I glimpsed several interesting tables over the week-end. On Friday, officiating as hostess at her usual corner table, was Mrs. Sidney Tate, whose guests that day were Mrs. Edgar Martindale and Mrs. Winfield Scott Bordener. Mrs. Tate divulged en passant that she had entertained on Thursday at the first of a series of small dinner parties she is planning. They will all take place at the Second Street residence of her brother, Mr. Brock Caldwell. I also learned that Mrs. Tate is busily engaged in supervising extensive alterations to her country home at Riverside Farm, near Becksville, which she anticipates will be completed ere the first harbingers of Spring . . ."

"God damn her," said Hollister. So she had not gone away, and was not planning to. Was, in fact, planning to be very much at home. He recognized her change of plan as a display of independence, but he refused to see any irony or inconsistency in cursing her for a quality that only minutes before he had been admiring. And dimly—because reluctantly—he realized that this was a stronger, much more independent woman than the rather mild person of his rather patronizing reverie. The trouble was—and he knew it well—that he had been thinking of her as he remembered her in passion, in violent need of him and what he could do for her. And he began to admit that at that moment she had been least independent. He was not quite ready to admit that independence was the quality in her that he admired only in the abstract, and feared the most.

But after the first shock of what he regarded as her deception, and the annoying confusion that accompanied his adjusted evaluation of her, he derived great comfort from the historic fact that once in her life he had owned her body and made her call out to the world that he was what she needed. "It's a good thing we had a car that day; horses would have run away," he thought.

"What's the joke, Mr. Hollister?"

Mary Kemper was standing beside his desk.

"The joke? Oh, about automobiles," he said.

"Here's a lot of mail for you," she said. "Fifteen letters. These days you get more mail than anybody else on the paper."

"That's because they don't know we have *you*, Mary," he said. A pretty girl, Mary Kemper.

"Tell that to the Marines," she said, but pleased.

"A Marine's telling it to you," he said. "You gettin' much, Mary?"

"Now don't *you* start talking like that, Mr. Hollister. The others are bad enough, without you."

"But *are* you?" he said.

"Wouldn't you like to know?" she said.

———

On the Sunday after her Emeryville experience Grace wrote a long letter to Paul Reichelderfer. She went to bed early. At one o'clock she got out of bed, removed the letter from the locked drawer on her desk and burned it in the fireplace.

On the Monday after that Sunday she had dinner with Brock and Anna. Anna went upstairs immediately after the dessert. School had reopened that day, Alfred was back at Lawrenceville, and for the first time in two weeks the little library was without a Christmas tree, the first-floor windows of the house without their holly wreaths.

Brock stretched out in his chair. "Say, Grace, let's have a few small dinner parties."

" 'Grace, let's have a few small dinner parties,' " she repeated.

He smiled, recalling their father's method of trying to break Brock of the habit of beginning questions with the word "say." "God, remember that?"

"It didn't do much good," she said. "Why a few small dinner parties? To introduce Madame Doerflinger?"

"Partly, partly."

"Why do you say 'partly'? You'd want to have her at all of them, wouldn't you?"

"Yes, I suppose I would, but what if she is? A new face is always welcome."

"And figure," said Grace.

"And figure. All right, and figure. I won't try to put anything over on you. But it isn't only me. It's time you began blossoming out a little more, get a little fun out of life."

"By giving small dinner parties for your mistress?"

"Well, she wouldn't have to be here every time."

"I'll bet she'd be at every one you were here for. If she wasn't invited she wouldn't let you come."

"Hmm. If she *knew* about it," he said. "You seem to have the idea that this is an entirely one-sided relationship. You know, Grace, your little old brother isn't altogether the sap you take me to be. Just allow me to remind you, old girl, I've known the lady for a year, and I'm still a bachelor. Put that in your pipe and smoke it."

"Mm-hmmm," Grace nodded.

"Mm-hmm indeed," said Brock.

"Mm-hmmm."

"Exactly," said Brock.

"But I don't quite understand why you want to have these parties. Forget about any nonsense about me blossoming out. Why do you want to go to all the trouble?"

"No trouble for me, you'd be giving the parties, on my money," he said. "I'll be frank with you. What I said a minute ago's true, of course. I'm still a bachelor. But she's a good-looking woman and we hit it off very well together, and I'm getting to the age now where I'm going to have to settle down pretty soon. Now just shut up a minute, Grace, and don't interrupt me, please. So, she's the only person around I'm at all interested in and I've given the matter a great deal of thought. Weighed the pros and cons, so to speak. Well, if I did marry her, I don't think I'd have a hard time persuading *her* to give dinner parties, all right. But I wouldn't want them to turn out to be one fiasco after another, and that of course leads me to my plan."

"Your plan being to have me give a series of dinners."

"Precisely. The advantages? Numerous. If she liked my friends and my friends liked her, I'd be sure of a nice, pleasant life if I married her. If, on the other hand, she hated my friends—the respectable ones, now, I'm talking about—then I'd never in the world marry her, because I plan to live in this house the rest of my life, and friends become more important the older you get.

No possibility of her getting me to leave Fort Penn, either. But she's a very wise woman, very clever. And if she saw she was never going to get along with the people you and I know, she's young, and she'd be satisfied to go along for a few more years, uh, under the present arrangement. No marriage. I'd go on helping her out financially. Place to live. Some money for clothes. Little present now and then. You get my point?"

"I do, but you know I'm not overly fond of her, to say the least. All I'd have to do to prevent a marriage would be to give the worst parties that ever were."

"Well, I don't think you would. I think you're too honest to do that, and besides, if you said you *would* give the parties I hardly think you'd inflict that much boredom on yourself. Not you."

"Probably not," said Grace. "Well, if I do give the parties, how do you hope it'll turn out? Would you rather have her as your mistress or your wife?"

"At this very minute? As my mistress. But I repeat, if the dinners are successful, and they all get along like bugs in a rug, I'd be glad to marry her. She's young and healthy. Might have a kid or two, and the French are wonderful with children, you know."

"Now what do you know about how the French are with children?"

"It's what I've always heard, and *you* certainly don't know otherwise. You've never been anywhere in your life, and I've at least been to France twice. First time, of course, I didn't make the trip to study the God-damn little brats. At least, those under seventeen. But in the Army I remember they were always nice to their kids. Living in a place like Tours, you know, you get to see the family life—"

"Yes, of course," said Grace. "How many of these *intime* little parties did M'sieur have in mind."

"Well, what's today? Today's the 13th of January. Say we had one at the end of the month, then every two weeks till May. Or we could start sooner than that. Thursday, this coming Thursday let's have some people in."

"Let me do some mental arithmetic. February, March, April, three months times two is six, plus one or two this month? How many people at each party?"

"Oh, keep it small."

"How small? We'd be having the same people very soon."

"Eight or ten at a time, and we wouldn't have to have the same people all the time. In fact we wouldn't have to have the same people twice. I've made a list."

"You've thought of everything," said Grace. "All right. I'll do it."

"Good girl, Grace. Here's a present for you." He took an oblong box out of his pocket.

"Were you so sure that you bought a present in advance? Why, Brock Caldwell!"

"Open it up," he said.

It was a slender hammered silver cigarette case. "So soon after Christmas, too!" she said.

"Well, God damn it, Grace, we're flesh and blood, the same flesh and blood, I mean. It's time we got along better."

"Why, this is really handsome, Brock."

"Glad you like it, and I'll tell you this much. If you'd refused to give these parties I was going to give the case to Mrs. Doerflinger, and I'd have told you about it, too."

Grace laughed.

"And don't think you have to get anything for me. I have everything I need," said Brock. "Including a woman, one way or the other."

She was still laughing a minute later when the new maid entered. "There's a gentleman on the telephone, ma'am."

"All right," said Grace. She looked at Brock.

"Okay, I'll be in the sitting-room," he said.

"I'll answer it in here, Norma." She picked up the receiver and waited a moment and then said, "All right, Norma, you can hang up." The telephone clicked, and Grace said hello.

The man's voice said, "Grace?"

"Yes, who's this?"

"Is the maid still on the line?"

"No, she hung up, but who's this?" said Grace.

"You'll know in a minute. I understand you're threatening Katty. You know who I mean."

"Oh, it's you," said Grace. "Did she say I threatened her?"

"To go to her mother."

"What did Katty tell you about my threatening her?"

"All she told me was you were threatening her, and—"

"Look, here," said Grace, and gave an accurate version of her encounter with Katty Grenville. "And if that's threatening her, I did. Now what are you calling me for? To threaten *me?* With what?"

"I'm in love with that kid," said Bannon. "You keep your nose out of it."

"What did you call me for? To tell me that?"

"I told you why I called you, to tell you to keep your nose out of my business."

"Your business? I'll be glad to keep my nose out of your *business.* I hear it has a very nasty smell. And if you ever have the gall to telephone me again you're going to wish you hadn't." She hung up, and opened the library door.

"All right," she called to Brock.

"What's the matter?" he said. "Is something wrong?"

"That was Roger Bannon," she said, and repeated the conversation and the incident at the booth.

"That son of a bitch has to be taught a lesson," said Brock.

"Wait and see if he calls me again," said Grace. "Besides, what would you do?"

"I don't know yet," said Brock. "I can find out who holds his paper, of course. I could do that quickly enough."

"His paper?" said Grace.

"Bank loans, things like that. A man in the building business has to keep on the good side of the banks," said Brock. "But that isn't enough for him. I know another way to cause him a lot of trouble. Charlie Jay."

"What could he do?"

"Oh, there are all kinds of city ordinances that a contractor breaks all the time. They don't usually enforce them because if they did no new buildings'd ever get finished. But they're on the books, just in case the contractors become forgetful during political campaigns."

"What kind of ordinances?"

"Oh, technical things, and blocking traffic, and providing places for pedestrians. Fire laws. But that's not good enough, either. I'd like to drive him out of town. I'll think of something, and don't you worry, kid." He put his hand on her shoulder. "Same flesh and blood, you know."

"I'm sorry, Brock," she said.

"We all make mistakes, and I've made a lot that you never knew about," he said. "It's up to me now to find out what mistakes Mr. Bannon made, and I'm sure he's made quite a few. The quickest way is to find out through his enemies, but the *surest* way is to find out through his *friends*. Who are his friends?"

"Miles Brinkerhoff," said Grace. "I happen to know that, only too well."

"Miles Brinkerhoff. Big fat Miles Brinkerhoff. I saw him just the other day, and at the Club, of all places. Having lunch with somebody. Now who? I'll look in the guest book tomorrow."

"But don't do anything till he calls me again."

"I won't, but preparedness is the watchword. Boy Scout. Be Prepared. That's me," said Brock. "Do you want me to stay in tonight? In case Mr. Bannon might take a notion to honor us with a visit?"

Grace smiled. "I'd shoot him like a dog."

Brock did not smile. "Well, would you know where to find my revolver?"

"He'd never come out here."

"There's a .32 in this drawer, right here in the desk, and my .45 is upstairs hanging in the closet in my bedroom. Do you want me to show you how to fire a .45?"

"Sidney taught me."

"Good. They're both loaded, and the safety's on the .45, but not on the .32."

"And I have a little .25, so I'm well protected," she said. "We certainly have enough weapons in this house."

"I recommend the .45 for that son of a bitch," he said. "I'll be home early. Good night, Grace." He kissed her cheek.

"Good night, Brock," she said.

The night, and the week, passed without her receiving another telephone call from Roger Bannon. On Tuesday she went to the Bordeners' for their turn as hosts of the bridge club; on Thursday she had her first small dinner party for Brock (he thought it went off very well, and told her she had earned her cigarette case already); on Friday she lunched at the hotel. On Friday afternoon she had a conversation with Anna.

In spite of the middy blouse which was the school uniform the emphasis in the girl's figure was noticeably moving from her belly to her chest. She was taking her proper shape, and the short pleated skirt over her legs made her look from the shoulders down like a mature woman at a fancy dress party, or a member of a vaudeville team. Grace was in the library, casting household accounts. Anna came in from school, dropped her books on a chair, kissed Grace's cheek, and leaned against the break-front.

"What are you doing, Mummy?"

"Paying bills," said Grace.

There was a pause. The girl whistled notes without a melody. Grace looked up and smiled. "You remind me of your father," she said.

"Do I? Most people say I look like you."

"I wasn't thinking of your looks," said Grace. "The way you whistle."

"I was doing it unconsciously," said Anna. "I wasn't a bit conscious that I was whistling."

"Don't stop, though. I rather like it. It's the way Daddy used to whistle when he was working, with his hands, that is. Polishing silver, boning his boots."

"He was lovely," said Anna.

"He was indeed, all of that," said Grace. "I'm glad you remember how lovely he was, and Billy too."

"Oh, I'll always remember," said Anna. "I couldn't forget a tragic experience like that."

"What?"

"It was a tragic experience, everybody says it was," said the girl.

"It was, Anna, but that's such an older peoples' expression for a girl your age," said Grace. "A girl not quite fourteen shouldn't think of herself as, you might say, the victim of a tragic experience."

"But if it was, it was."

"I'm not denying that, but I just don't want you to think of yourself as Anna Tate, the girl who underwent a tragic experience. It sounds too much like—theatrical, stage people. In other words, artificial and posey. The nicest people are natural people. Be natural with yourself and other people will recognize that, and be your friends. The ones you'd like to have your friends. The others don't matter."

"Uh-huh. That reminds me of something."

"It reminds me of something, too. Excuse me for holding the floor, but I've been wanting to say something about this. I wish you'd wear your hair another way."

"What's wrong with this?"

"It's too old for you," said Grace. "Now you have nice hair and a nicely shaped head, but why do you prefer to part your hair in the middle and down tight like that? I haven't noticed any of the other girls doing that."

"Some are," said Anna.

"Then it must be very recently, since Christmas."

"I've only been doing it since Christmas, too," said the girl.

"Why? Some movie actress you saw in a picture?"

"No. Miss Tuckerman. She started wearing it this way just before school closed."

"Miss Tuckerman, the teacher? Well, it's all right for her, if she wants to wear her hair that way, but she's a good deal over fourteen. And don't you think it must embarrass her when a crowd of silly girls come into class all wearing their hair like hers?"

"She does not feel embarrassed! At least not with me."

"Did she tell you so?" said Grace.

"I know she doesn't, because I'm her favorite pupil. She practically told me that," said Anna.

"Well, that's good, I suppose," said Grace. "What else did she practically tell you?"

"That I ought to go to boarding school and get out of Fort Penn. She said I'd stagnate if I stayed here all my life."

"I thought she just taught English."

"She does, but she's my adviser, too. Since last September we all have advisers. You know that."

"Yes, but I didn't know the advising took in other matters besides studies. Did she say what school she'd picked out for you?"

"Not Farmington, not Westover, not Shipley, not Foxcroft, not St. Timothy's, not Rosemary, not—not *any* of *those* schools."

"Well I have a rough idea what she's *against*. What is she *for?*" said Grace. "What school did she go to herself?"

"She went to high school in Chicago."

"I'm afraid a Chicago high school is out of the question for you."

"But a Philadelphia one isn't. We have relations in Philadelphia."

"All of whom send their children to schools like Shipley and Miss Irwin's," said Grace.

"But I wouldn't have to go to the same schools. I could live with our cousins and go—"

"Well, that's out of the question, too. But tell me, why does Miss Tuckerman think you ought to get out of Fort Penn?"

"Because I'll stagnate here."

"Did she explain that?" said Grace.

"She said I'd just grow up to be a big frog in a little pond."

"In a stagnant little pond, I suppose," said Grace. "Is that all she said?"

"No."

"Well, what else did she say?" said Grace.

"She said I ought to get a job."

"A job? I'd have thought she'd be against child labor, judging by the rest of—"

"Not now, but when I'm older. Eighteen or nineteen."

"And take a job away from some girl that needed the money?" said Grace.

"No, she said there were other things a girl could do. The same kind of work that the Junior League's supposed to do, only *do* it."

"But in the meantime she wants you to go to high school in Philadelphia."

"She didn't say exactly that, Mummy. She said that would be ideal, high school in a big city."

"I see," said Grace. "Did you ever stop to think that if Miss Tuckerman's family could have sent her to a nice private school, she'd have gone?"

"No."

"Or that if she could have been a big frog in a little pond she'd have been one? Instead she was a little, tiny frog in a very very big pond. And right here in Fort Penn, a little pond, she's still a little frog. She must have gone to college. Where did she go, do you know?"

"University of Wisconsin."

"Well, I suppose I've heard of it. I've heard of Wisconsin, and all those places have universities. But I never knew anyone that went there."

"She thinks I ought to go there."

"Oh, I'm sure of that," said Grace. "It's my own fault. If I took more of an interest in the school affairs her kind wouldn't be hired."

"She's the most popular teacher on the whole faculty."

"Why shouldn't she be? Making you all believe you're too good for your birthplace and your families. What she is really doing is making you all too big for your britches," said Grace.

"Before you get any more of Miss Tuckerman's ideas—let's see—where did I put—I guess they're at the farm. Anyway, what I wanted to show you, Anna, was three letters, from Foxcroft, Westover, and Shipley. Answers to my application for you to enter, the year after next. You have your choice of those three. Most girls have no choice at all, but go where they're sent, and if I hear any more of Miss Tuckerman's nonsense I'll make the choice without consulting you. Kindly bear that in mind. I don't want to be cross with you, but I don't think it was very nice of you to listen to an outsider talking that way about Fort Penn. Don't forget your family helped to build it, and were one of the founders of it, when George Washington was alive."

"Daddy didn't like Fort Penn."

"There you're wrong. Daddy died before he realized that Fort Penn liked him, that was the trouble," said Grace. "Now go on, take your bath."

Grace waited a minute or two and then telephoned Betty Martindale. "Betty, you're still on the board at school, aren't you?"

"Yes."

"Let's have lunch again tomorrow. I want to talk to you about this Miss Tuckerman."

"I've been expecting that," said Betty.

Grace laughed. "Well, I hope I didn't keep you waiting too long. I'll see you at the hotel, one o'clock?"

At the Commonwealth Room the next day Charles was desolated that he had given the corner table to Mrs. Bauer and party. He seemed to be on the verge of cutting his throat until Grace was able to tell him that she actually, honestly, positively *preferred* a table for two when she was lunching with one other lady. Then an excellent window table for Mrs. Tate and Mrs. Martindale? Fine. And he very ostentatiously held up the back of the menu and crossed out a name, the name of the wife of the Governor.

"The trouble with him is," said Betty, "he thinks we're impressed by the Governor."

"Well, if *he's* impressed, what he did impresses me," said Grace. "It's a good way to start this conversation. I'm very angry with all outsiders today, or at least the ones that make their living here and try to tear it down." She related the conversation with Anna.

"Well, I'm not as upset as you are, but I'm in sympathy with you, for the most part. The difficulty is it's hard to get good teachers at the salaries we pay. We have a private school with a good reputation, but we don't pay as much as a lot of the public schools. Of course it's true that in the public schools a big percentage of those large salaries goes back to the school board. That's certainly true in the coal regions, and I suppose it's true right here in Fort Penn. Fort Penn politicians aren't holy angels."

"Then why can't our school pay better salaries?"

"If we raised the tuition as little as ten dollars a year a lot of nice girls would have to drop out. Don't forget we have girls from families that have to watch every dollar. It's too bad we can't just take the tuition from girls like Katty Grenville over there and use the money for the ones that would appreciate."

"Where is Katty Grenville?"

"She's sitting over on the other side of the room. She's with Roger Bannon, Grace, so don't look around."

"Not look around? I certainly will," said Grace. She turned and stared until they both had seen her staring.

"Why did you do that?" said Betty. "Now they're talking and he's calling the waiter. He's arguing with the waiter. Now they're getting up. He's leaving some money on the table, not waiting for his change. Now they're going out, and they're both looking over here. He's in a rage, Grace."

"*He* is!" said Grace.

"Has he been bothering you?" said Betty.

"Have a cigarette. I don't as a rule smoke here, but—" she held out her case and Betty took one. "Isn't it a handsome case? Brock gave it to me."

"I don't like to smoke here, either, but I'd be afraid to refuse, the temper you're in. Settle down, Grace."

"I will in just a minute."

They lit up and inhaled deeply, to the fascination of an assemblyman from Schuylkill County and his wife and two daughters at the next table. Grace saw them and inhaled again.

"I have every reason to trust you, Betty, so here goes." She told Betty about the encounter with Katty Grenville, the telephone call, and, in part, her conversation with Brock. ". . . And, judging by Mr. Bannon's behavior, Brock must have done something without telling me."

"It must have been pretty serious, whatever he did. As soon as he saw you he acted like a crazy man. Snapping at the waiter, making poor little Katty leave without finishing her lunch."

"*Poor* little Katty."

"Well, I pity any girl that's mixed up with a man like that."

"I was. You know that."

"Of course I knew it, and I pitied you."

"You did? Do you know, that's the first time in my whole life I wanted pity. I needed it then. I wish you'd said something."

"I say it now."

"Yes, but if I'd known there was one person in the world to turn to then—oh, hell, I guess it would have been the same mess."

"Well, I don't think you want to talk any more about it. Shall we go back to Miss Tuckerman?"

"No, to hell with Miss Tuckerman, too," said Grace. "Just so you discharge her in June. Let's talk about clothes, shall we?"

"All right."

"And let's buy some, this very afternoon. We'll go over to Ruth Holz and make her show us all her new things, before anyone else sees them."

"Grace, you're as changeable as the weather."

"No, but I don't want to talk about Miss Tuckerman, and I don't want to bore you any more with Mr. Bannon. Not to mention *poor* little Katty."

Thus had Grace spent the week in which Hollister had been leading up to his reverie of the following Monday.

He watched Mary Kemper's progress through the office, from desk to desk with the noon mail, from bawdy greeting to bawdy greeting. The moment she took her pretty self out of the office he lost interest in his surroundings. He was rolling down his sleeves when he heard Crowley say, "Jesus!" and knew that something was up. He went over to Crowley's desk and Crowley handed him a bulletin from the Associated Press Morse wire. It read:

> Hagerstown, Md., Jan. 13 (A.P.)—The bodies of a man and woman killed in an automobile accident here last night have been identified as Roger Bannon, 34, and Katherine Grenville, 18, both of Fort Penn. More TK

"More to come! I'll say," said Hollister. "Everything we can get. Bob, you—I'm sorry, Crowley."

"That's all right," said Crowley. "Do you want to write it?"

"I'll write it, but somebody better call Brock Caldwell to see how he wants this one handled. Just a tip, Crowley. He'll be at the Fort Penn Club, most likely. If not there, try his home, North Second Street. Nothing goes without his say-so, even if we don't make the two-o'clock."

"I didn't think these people were *that* important. I recognized their names, but—"

"You haven't been here long enough," said Hollister, rolling down his sleeves. "Earl, get me a Blue Book and a Boyd's Directory, and see if we have anything on Grenville, g, r, e, n, ville. Crowley, you get after Caldwell."

"Now, listen, Hollister."

"Oh, quit delaying the game and get on the story. I'll argue with you later," said Hollister. He picked up the phone. "Pauline? This is Jack Hollister. I want you to stick with me. Just watch my calls and let the other girls double up. First, get me the chief of police in Hagerstown, Maryland, and while you're getting him, ask the Hagerstown operator to connect you with the coroner's office. She'll know. Then I want to talk to a fellow named Bill Irving on the Hagerstown *Mail.* He knows me. Tell him I'm calling. He'll probably be expecting me. You got all that? Now give me a local chief operator . . .

"Chief operator? This is Mr. Hollister, city editor of the *Sentinel.* I have a very important story and I want an operator to stick with me. Thank you . . . Operator? First ring three-three-four-six . . . Keep ringing, please . . . Hello, is this the Grenville residence?"

"There's nobody at home," said a woman's voice.

"When do you expect Mrs. Grenville back, may I ask?"

"I don't know. She didn't say when. I don't know nothing."

"Well, this is Mr. Brock Caldwell," said Hollister.

"I don't know," said the woman.

"Brock Caldwell. Cald-well?"

"Oh, what is it, Mr. Caldwell?" said the woman.

"I was terribly upset to hear the bad news. Very upset. When did Mrs. Grenville hear about it? This morning?"

"No, yesterday afternoon three o'clock."

"Oh, yesterday afternoon at three o'clock. Then the accident happened Saturday evening?"

"Some time. Saturday night. Early Sunday morning."

"I see. Were they in Mr. Bannon's car?"

"Must be. Miss Katty don't have no car and Mrs. took the Cadillac with the chauffeur."

"And drove to Hagerstown yesterday afternoon around three."

"Yes, sir."

"And I hope they didn't have any pain. They were killed instantly, weren't they?"

"And burnt up," said the woman.

"Yes, of course. The car caught fire and they were pinned inside. Well, we all hope they were killed outright. To burn to death is so shocking. Lying there in a ditch."

"No ditch. A barn. Right beside the road it was. They bumped into the barn. They skitted into it and bumped."

"Just outside of Hagerstown."

"Uh-huh. Near."

"And had they been married before the accident? We heard they were."

"Can't say, Mr. Caldwell. Mrs. thought so, so did I, but who knows."

"Yes, who knows? Well, thank you very much. It's a sad thing, a sad ending. Good-bye."

"Good-bye, Mr. Caldwell," said the maid.

Crowley, holding his hand over the mouthpiece of his phone, spoke to Hollister: "Caldwell. Wants to talk to *you*."

"Hello, Mr. Caldwell, this is Hollister."

"Have you any more information on this thing?" said Brock.

"Well, not much. I've placed several calls."

"Well, tell me what you have."

"Well, just that they were killed, and that's about all. I confirmed that."

"How did you confirm it?" said Brock.

"Uh, through the Associated Press," said Hollister. "Did you want to speak to me about something special, Mr. Caldwell?"

"Yes, of course. I wanted to tell you how to handle this story. Naturally it'll have to be on the front page, but we don't want any lurid details. I assume they were eloping, and I guess you might as well say that. At least it covers up, uh, gives a kind of aura of respectability. But we don't want a lot of speculation about whether they spent the night together. Oh, now, Hollister, you know what the *Sentinel* wants and doesn't want. Arthur James was your father, and I don't have to tell you. And Mrs. Grenville's a very nice woman and a friend of mine and my sister's. You understand, Hollister?"

"Yes, sir."

"I think you do. I don't think I have to say any more, do I?"

"Well—in other words, be discreet?"

"Exactly, and now I don't want to exchange innuendoes or subtleties. You know this story has a certain distant connection with a member of my family, and we're both men of the world, Hollister, and I think your new column is first rate. Meant to tell you that before. First rate."

"Thank you, sir. Good-bye."

"Good-bye," said Brock.

"Did you get anything?" said Crowley.

"Christ, I got everything but one detail. I have to find out whether they got married or not. And by the way, the A. P. is wrong. They were killed Saturday night, not last night . . . Hello, this Bill Irving? Hello, you son of a bitch, how are you? Do you like Hagerstown better than Philly? . . . Sure I do . . . Listen, Bill, I suppose you know what I'm calling you for. It's a pretty big story here. He was a well-known contractor, an Irish prick on his way up. She was a local society kid, on her way down, from what little I know about her. I don't move in those circles, but you hear things. Give me what you have."

"Well, I guess I have it all," said Irving. "This Bannon must have been a real bad actor. I talked to a Pennsylvania state cop and he told me Bannon had got into a fight in some roadhouse over the Pennsylvania state line. Owner of the roadhouse sent for the cops, but Bannon was gone by the time they got there. That was around eleven o'clock Saturday night. Bannon and the kid were there from some time late in the afternoon and the cop as much as told me the two of them, Bannon and the girl, went up-stairs for a jump and anyway the proprietor got a little worried about her age and that was how the fight started. Bannon broke the proprietor's nose and knocked out a couple teeth. Then I guess they beat it over the state line into Maryland and nobody knows what they did till about one-forty-five A.M. Sunday. This farmer—do you want his name?"

"All right."

"James E. Buchanan."

"A grandson of the President, maybe," said Hollister.

"That would make him a second-generation bastard. Buchanan was a bachelor."

"I know, I know. Go on."

"Well, he thought there was an earthquake, the world coming to an end. His barn runs right along the edge of the highway and it isn't the first time it was hit by a car, but this was the loudest ever. And when he looked out his window the car was on fire."

"The barn catch fire?"

"A little, but not very much. It's stone construction on the ground floor. But I'll tell you this. Two cows had calves before they were due. He told me that."

"How did they identify Bannon and the kid?"

"Well, it was easy to identify him. First through the license tags and then his brother came down here and said yes, that was Roger."

"What about the girl?"

"That's your end. The girl's mother came down too, but no-body here knew who she was, the girl I mean. And the cops say they didn't phone the mother. My guess is Bannon's brother knew who the girl was, phoned the mother, and the mother came down on his say-so."

"The license tags weren't destroyed?"

"The front one was, not the back one. It was a Kissel Kar. Wish I had one myself, but not that one."

"No chance of their being married?"

"Not a chance. It isn't as easy as that to get married in this state, not even in Elkton. And here, Saturday night you can't even get a license. Nice safe way to get a piece of tail, Jack. Take the woman to Maryland on a Saturday night, tell her you'll marry her Monday."

"It doesn't sound so easy to me, and anyway, I'm married."

"I know. How's Amy?"

"Fine, thanks. You still single?"

"Yes, sir. I got out of Philly to stay single. Get out of here, too, if my little schoolteacher starts hinting. It turned out well for you, Jack, but you have to admit you're the exception."

"Well, if you ever come up this way, I'll be here."

"Say, are you J. H.?"

"Uh-huh."

"Well, congratulations. I didn't know you had it in you. I read you every day. Good luck, Jack."

"Same to you," said Hollister. He clicked the receiver arm. "Cancel the other Hagerstown calls, Pauline. But I'll be back in a minute or two."

Crowley said, "Got everything?"

"All we can use," said Hollister. "Give you about a half a column for a top head, Number 5, for the two o'clock. Then I'll give you more later for the three o'clock, and you can jump it to Page Three."

"Thanks, Boss," said Crowley.

"Well, what the hell, Crowley. You could have farted around all afternoon," he grinned. "I'm the best Fort Penn newspaper man in Fort Penn, and that's *all I* want to be. Earl! Books, please. Books!"

He rolled the first book of copy paper, carbons, and flimsies into the typewriter and went to work.

At the Fort Penn Club Brock had given up the thought of lunch. He telephoned the house, but Grace was not there. He telephoned the farm; she was somewhere around but they didn't know where. Was she riding? No, just strolling about. Well, ask her to wait at the house, he would be right out. Important.

Brock, who owned a slicked-up Ford coupé like Grace's, drove to the farm, where Grace was sitting on the doorsteps, smoking a cigarette and hunched up in a raccoon coat. Brock opened the door of his car and told her to get in. "Are you frozen? Why didn't you wait in the farmhouse?"

"There's no heat in our house, but there's too much in the farmhouse. Besides, you told me to meet you here. What's on your mind?"

"Well, I'm not the bearer of good tidings or bad tidings. A little of both," he said.

"Is somebody dead?"

"Yes. Have you heard?" he asked.

"No, but your manner—who is it?"

"Roger Bannon and Katty Grenville were killed in an automobile accident."

"Today?"

"No. Late Saturday night. In Maryland. Hagerstown. Their car skidded into a barn and they were killed. They may have been burned to death, or, they may have been killed instantly."

"Roger Bannon, killed in an automobile accident. I saw him Saturday at lunch."

"You weren't *with* him?"

"Anything but. We exchanged looks of hate, across the dining-room at the hotel."

"You didn't talk to him or anything?"

"No, Brock," she said. "He was on one side of the room, and I was with Betty Martindale on the other. He was with Katty. I suppose I had something to do with it."

"Nonsense. How?"

"I just think it. I wanted to make sure he saw me and I stared him down and he got so angry he couldn't finish lunch. Betty saw that part of it, I didn't. She said he made a scene with the waiter, didn't wait for his change. Then I suppose he went somewhere and got drunk."

"I don't know," said Brock. "But don't blame yourself."

"I'm not exactly blaming myself, but it was the same as if I'd told him I hated him in letters as big as a house. And I did. Just seeing me was enough to set him off, I guess."

"Yes, *that's* true," said Brock.

"Why do you say it that way?"

"The sight of you or me, either one of us, would have set him off on Saturday."

"Why?"

"Friday afternoon his roof fell in. He found out who was boss around here."

"What did you do?" she said.

"Well, he dealt with the Commercial, Chester Buchwalter's

bank, and Chester owes us a couple of favors. Pretty big favors, as far as Chester's concerned. The Commercial isn't any too good a bank, you know."

"No, I don't know. What did you do?"

"Merely told Chester I'd been hearing funny things about Bannon's corporation and he'd better have a talk with Bannon."

"What kind of a talk?" said Grace.

"Merely a stern, business-like talk. Be more punctual with payments, stop asking for extensions. Nothing immediate, you understand. Chester has to do just about what we say because we came to his rescue last year. Of course what Chester doesn't know is that we would have come to his rescue in any case, because bank failures are bad for all banks."

"Then?"

"Then after Chester'd had his talk with Bannon *I* had *my* talk with Bannon. I telephoned him at his office and said, 'Bannon, you just had a meeting with Chester Buchwalter. You're going to have meetings like that every week from now on. I don't like your face,' I said, 'and I don't like people that threaten women.' "

"Did he know who it was?"

"Certainly he knew who it was. I told him."

"What did he say?"

"I didn't give him a chance to say anything. I was doing the talking. I said, 'The next meeting you have to go to won't be with Chester. It'll be with somebody else, Monday,' and I said, 'After that you'll have still another meeting, I'm not telling you when.' "

"What were all these meetings going to be?" said Grace.

"Well, the city health department, to discuss the sewers he put in out at Northend, during Walthour's administration. That pleased Charlie Jay. And the other I was going to keep as a last resort. He beat up a prostitute a couple of years ago. I remembered hearing something about it at the time."

"And he didn't say anything while you were talking to him?"

"Not till I was finished. Then he said, 'What do you want me to do?' And I said, 'Leave town, and don't come back.' "

"What did he say?"

"He hung up," said Brock.

"Well—you're thorough. I told you not to do anything till he called me up again."

"I know you did, but I know how to deal with scum like that. Like one of your horses. You have to be the boss from the beginning, the very first time he acts up. That fellow might have killed you."

"Yes, he might have. But we killed him."

"Oh, no. Oh, no. He killed himself. We're all living in the jungle, Grace. He was just a—a kind of a hyena that went after a lion, and that's the same as killing yourself."

"Do you think of us as lions?"

"Oh, hell, not as noble animals, but by God when you're attacked you damn well fight back with all you've got."

"All of Fort Penn's going to know you—we—showed him who was boss."

"What if they do? Actually they're not, because Chester Buchwalter and Charlie Jay will keep their mouths shut. But what if all Fort Penn did know? They'd only be learning what they should know anyway by this time."

"Well, it's done," said Grace. "He's dead."

"Come on, girl, you ought to be relieved about it. I don't like to see a man killed, but I'd rather see him dead than you."

"I know, I know. If I were honest I suppose I'd say I am relieved. It's just that I'll take a while to think of him as dead."

"Well, I suppose that's natural under the circumstances, if you don't mind my saying so," said Brock. "Uh, you're not planning to leave town or anything like that, are you?"

"No."

"Good. Just be your normal self, see your friends, go shopping, as though nothing had happened."

She smiled. "My normal self? I wish I knew what that was."

"Now, now, now," he said. "Now, now."

Harold, one of the farmer's children, came to the car and spoke to Grace: "Mrs. Martindale wants you on the telephone."

Brock sat in the car while Grace followed the boy to the farm-house and spoke to Betty.

"She hear the news?" said Brock, upon Grace's return.

Grace nodded. "I'm going to start leading my normal life," she said. "She wants me to go to her house. Thank you for coming out."

"Oh, that's all right," said Brock, attempting to be casual. "It's pretty nice out here today. But I'm no country fellow, I'm a town man, every time. See you later."

She followed him into Fort Penn and parked her car in the driveway of the Bordener house on Front Street,* which Betty Martindale owned, and rang the bell for the side door.

Betty opened the door herself, and they went upstairs to her sitting-room. Grace stood at the bay-window. "You could skate on the river today, all right."

"Well, like Eliza crossing the ice," said Betty, "Jumping from one cake to another. Why, have you been wanting to skate?"

"When Connie was here I thought of it," said Grace. She made herself comfortable on a sofa.

"I asked you to come here because that's what Connie would have done, your best friend."

"I appreciate it," said Grace. "I don't know whether Connie would or wouldn't have. I guess she would. We had another of our spats just before she went back to New York. This one may take longer to heal. I said things I shouldn't have, and wouldn't have, until a year or two ago. But Connie's changed, and I guess I have, too. So—I said them."

---

* At the time the Caldwell house was built, Second Street actually was the river-front street. The larger houses on Front Street came later, shutting off the Second Streeters' view of the river, but providing the growing city with substantial new revenues from the re-assessed properties, as well as more imposing residences than the large but undeniably staid homes on Second Street. Curiously enough, Second Street land values increased rather than decreased, because, it was said, old families like the Caldwells and the Schoffstals stubbornly refused to move to Front Street, and Second Street thus held its prestige.

"Yes, she's changed, no question about that. More sure of herself, and at the same time—one thing Connie never had was humility, even when she seemed to be waiting on you hand and foot. But now she has something on the order of humility. Maybe she's finding out in her work that she doesn't know everything, and maybe it's just being with strangers."

"Oh, but they're not strangers. They're her friends."

"Friends like those can become strangers like *that!*" Betty snapped her finger. "All they have to do is mention a person they know, or a part of their lives that Connie doesn't know, and they become strangers. You know what I mean?"

"Shut her out."

"Yes. The opposite of you and I. You and I were good friends even when we weren't apparently friends at all. That's because we've known each other all our lives. Those New York friendships can be good, I'm sure, but they suffer by comparison with the friendships you've had all your life."

"Lordy, where did you learn so much about New York friendships?"

"Watching my adorable sister-in-law Natalie. Natalie came here from Gibbsville and was a success over night, you might say. Was taken up by our crowd and Scotty's crowd. But all one of us has to do is mention a picnic or a sail down the river, something that happened before she came here, and Natalie acts as though we'd put up a spite-fence."

"Maybe that was Sidney's trouble. It was, to some extent."

"Yes," said Betty. She waited, but Grace was also waiting, and they both remained silent.

"I'm having bridge club tomorrow night. You're coming, of course?"

"Yes. Do you think people are going to expect me to go into some kind of mourning? If they do, they have another think coming, as Alfred says."

"With some people whatever you do will be right, and with some others, whatever you do'll be wrong."

"That's what I've known without being able to put it in words," said Grace. "You saw both of us Saturday, so you know there was no love lost between him and me."

"Yes, I wouldn't have liked it if you'd tried to put on a long face," said Betty.

"You wouldn't have liked *me.*"

"That's the truth of it. I wouldn't have liked you."

"Well, no fear of my doing anything like that. I'll try to go on with my normal life," said Grace. She smiled. "That's what Brock told me to do. I don't know what's come over Brock lately. We've been such great friends as we've never been in all our lives. He's so brotherly, and he never was before."

"He never could be as long as Sidney was alive, the way they felt about each other. He was jealous of Sidney, of course."

"He had no reason to be. Sidney was all for leading separate lives."

"Grace, for a woman of the world—you're a woman of the world, so don't deny that—but there are a lot of things you don't know about, or don't like to face. The relationship between brother and sister isn't the pure sweet thing it's supposed to be."

"I've known about that," said Grace. "What's new about that? Both of us know—well, we don't have to mention any names. But I hope you don't think at this late date that Brock ever *attacked* me. He'd die if he knew you even thought that, Betty."

"Oh, sure he would, and I don't think it. But the instinct is there, in millions of cases."

"Not Brock, not me."

"Not you, but Brock. He didn't know it, but there it was. I'm sure of it. Just because it doesn't come out in the open doesn't mean it isn't there, Grace. That's the whole trouble, in a lot of cases."

"Are you trying to say that Brock was in love with me?"

"Yes, sure. I know Scotty was in love with me. I didn't know it at the time, but all the symptoms were there till he got very much taken with other girls. Don't look horrified."

"Betty, you know a lot about these things, I'll admit, but this time no. Incense. What's the word? It isn't incense, but almost that."

"Incest."

"Incest! You could tell me a lot of things I'd believe about Brock, but not that. You think he hated Sidney because Sidney was my husband?"

"Sleeping with you."

"Having sexual intercourse with me, if you want to be plain-spoken," said Grace, smiling. "That's as far as I'll go. If you want to trump me, go ahead."

"I'll trump you tomorrow night, dear, if I have to play bridge. But seriously, if you know about these things in human nature you understand people better. You become a little more tolerant of human failings, little by little, the more you get to know."

"For instance, are you more understanding of Roger Bannon than most people are?"

"I think so," said Betty.

"Did you like him?"

"No, but I think I understood him, I was more tolerant of him."

"Why? How?"

"Because I don't think he liked women at all. I think—"

"Oh, *well,* Betty. Now all your theories can go *right out the window* and right down on the ice, down to Chesapeake Bay. That's enough for me, because I know you're wrong about that. And if you can be wrong about that, you can be wrong about everything else you think you understand."

"All right," said Betty. "I won't try to convince you, but I think he was homosexual."

"What *does* that mean? I thought *homo* meant *man,* but I don't know where I saw something, it said something about two women that were homosexual. Then I thought that must mean they like men for certain things, in certain ways. But then later on it said something that unmistakably meant they didn't like men at all, or any part of them . . . I just accidentally made a risqué joke."

"I thought the same as you did, *homo* means *man*. But that is the Latin. In Greek it means *the same*. So when it happens between two men it's homosexual, and when it happens between two women it's homosexual too."

"Well, whatever else he was, he wasn't that. Why, you *know* that, Betty. How can you sit here and say that to me, of all people in the world? I'm the living evidence."

"And Katty Grenville's the dead evidence," said Betty.

They fell silent.

"I don't know," said Grace, after a while. "But the only person I feel sadly about is Katty's mother. That poor, stupid, misled woman. Do you think you or I would ever be so blinded?"

"I don't think I will be. You might be."

"Because I don't subscribe to your theories?"

"They aren't my theories, Grace. Famous European professors have been working for years—"

"In Europe when a man wants to go to the bathroom for Number 1 he does it right on the street."

"I've seen it happen in Fort Penn, too."

"Well, down on the South Side, but over there it's the common practice, the accepted thing. They have no qualms about it, or about a lot of other things. Why, in Europe I'd have been the rule rather than the exception. French women have lovers one right after the other, and not the poorer classes I'm not speaking of. And the men have mistresses, the husbands."

"Maybe—well, never mind."

"Maybe I should have lived in Europe? That's what you were going to say. But you're wrong. I made a great mistake, Betty, and I had to take the consequences." She stood up and went to another chair. "What were the consequences? The consequences were that my husband, the only man I ever loved, died hating me. The last time I saw life in his eyes there was no love for me, Betty. That's the consequences. I know what else you're thinking, too.

I'm grateful for your asking me here, but maybe you're sorry I came."

"No, never, Grace. I could never be sorry to see you."

"Thank you, but I know what's been going on in your mind. You can't help it. You think, 'This woman's lover has been killed in an accident, and she's as cold about it as though it'd been a fly that was killed.' Well, I am cold about it. Do you know why? Do you notice who we've talked about? Not Roger Bannon. *Sidney*. Roger Bannon was part of something that made my husband die hating me." She got up again and returned to the sofa. "I'll come to your house tomorrow night and people will be just a tiny bit nervous about how I'll act, and then when I don't act any way at all, they'll think how strong I am. How—self-controlled. But they'll be wrong. There isn't any self-control to it, because I don't feel anything. Not about Roger Bannon. I used to hope he'd be killed in the war, so he wouldn't come back to be a reminder. But he was around for almost a year, as a reminder. Well, now he's dead, and I didn't have to shoot him, not even in self-defense."

"I knew most of that," said Betty, quietly.

"Did you? I hope you did," said Grace. "I have hardly anyone to talk to. Usually I don't need anyone, but sometimes I do." She leaned forward and crossed her legs.

"Betty," she said, "will you please get me a small glass of whiskey?"

"Of course." She went across the hall to a tiny room that was designated as Edgar's study, and came back with a highball glass containing three inches of whiskey. "That's Mount Vernon. If you'd like some bourbon, we have some downstairs."

"This'll be fine, thanks," said Grace. "I have slight cramps anyway, and then like a damn fool I sat out in the cold for a half an hour waiting for Brock."

"Oh, dear," said Betty. "That on top of everything else."

"It's not bad, and I guess pretty soon it won't be at all," said Grace, taking a sip of the whiskey. "Me, with the change of life!"

"Grace, it'll be years," said Betty. "You don't want to think of it now, maybe, but I expect you to get married and have at least one more child."

"This proves I'm not going..." She stopped herself but not in time. Betty looked at her worriedly, pityingly, solicitously. She sat beside Grace and put her arm around her.

"What is it, Grace?"

"It's love," she said. "Not Bannon. All I said about him was true. Nobody you know, nobody you ever see, nobody you can help me with. God himself wouldn't help me with this. It's hopeless."

"Almost nothing is hopeless, Grace."

"This is."

"Maybe not. Do you want to tell me about it?"

"Oh, Betty—I guess not. When a woman tells another woman about a hopeless love, she's thinking all the time—maybe her wishes'll come true. This—it's so hopeless it isn't worth talking about."

"But you thought you might be pregnant. That means you have that much."

"That was once. One time. The worst mistake of all—or maybe not. It's better to know I love him, I guess. But I'm not sure of that, either," she said. "Betty, could I lie down for a few minutes? Just stretch out here and put something over me?"

"Why don't you get undressed and get into my bed, Grace? Take a nap. I'll wake you up in time for dinner."

"I think I *will* do that, thanks."

"Or better yet, spend the night. In my old room you won't be disturbed. You won't be able to hear the kids, and you have your own bathroom."

"I'd have to write Anna a note, wouldn't I?" said Grace. "Now I'm not planning to camp here, Betty. But I do feel chilly and if I could spend the night?"

Betty helped her undress and put her to bed, with a hot-water bottle and aspirin.

"Don't tell anybody my secret, Betty?"

"No, of course not."

"Not even Edgar."

"Not even Edgar."

"At least for a long time. You can tell Edgar next year," said Grace.

"Next year, maybe, if he's good."

"It's only my little secret," said Grace, falling asleep.

Betty reached down and felt her hot forehead, took her pulse, and sent for Doctor O'Brien.

———

"Pneumonia," said the doctor, when he came out of the sick-room. "That's what it looks like to me."

"Doctor, she can have everything here she can have at the hospital. Will you let her stay here?"

"It's going to clutter up your household, Betty," he said. "Day nurse and night nurse, you know. Oxygen equipment."

"The nurses can use the room next to hers, and there's plenty of room for everything else. And don't forget I worked with you in the flu epidemic."

"I'm not forgetting for one minute. That's why I say yes. I'll call the registry and arrange for the nurses. Have your man take these to the drug store and get them filled right away. I'll be back again at ten o'clock."

"Good."

"Isn't her boy away at boarding-school?"

"Shall I send for him?"

"Well, not yet," said the doctor. "It isn't very far away, is it? Pottstown?"

"Lawrenceville."

"Well—I'll let you know," he said. "How old is Grace? I ought to know that, I suppose."

"She'll be thirty-seven in April."

"Mm-hmmm. Well, I have to go now, Betty. I'll be back at ten."

"Very well, Doctor O'Brien."

She followed him downstairs and helped him on with his coat.

He had his hat in hand. "Now you're sure you want to keep her here, Betty?"

"If she has pneumonia I want her here."

"Why, I wonder?"

"Doctor, you know Grace," said Betty. "She goes her own way, and doesn't like to be bothered by people. But when you're sick you need somebody besides a head nurse, and Grace has nobody. No mother, no sister, and no husband either."

"Ah, that's very true, Betty. They're all like children when they get sick—except maybe children."

He left for a few hours and returned shortly after ten o'clock. He went into the sickroom and talked with the nurse and when he came out Betty was sitting with Edgar and Brock in the room Edgar called his study.

"She's a very sick woman, and I see no reason to change what I said before. It looks to me like pneumonia. What we call lobar pneumonia." He sat down. "If you want a second opinion, I'm more than willing, but I'd suggest you wait a day or two. If I'm right, she'll get worse, a lot worse, before she gets better, so be prepared for that."

"Do you think I ought to send for her son?"

"Not yet. However, if you want to get in touch with the head of his school and let him know ahead of time, that might be a good idea. Without telling the boy, of course. Everything indicates pneumonia. The onset. The chills. The breathing. I listened to her breathing, and it's laborious, getting painful. I gave her a sixth of a grain of morphia, a small dose, but in pneumonia we can't give much more."

"Grace has never been sick a day in her life before," said Brock.

"They're the kind of people that get pneumonia, and I want to repeat this because I'm talking to sensible people. She's going to be worse before she's better. This is a disease that attacks the strong and healthy, as though Nature had one special weapon against them. A reminder that Nature always wins in the end, anyway—if you want to think of Nature as opposed to the human body. If you want to look at it another way, the human body defeats Nature from birth and even before, and in pneumonia the human body often defeats Nature."

"Can we see her?" said Brock.

"It won't do you any good to see her, Brock. She's asleep. I just told you we gave her a sixth of a grain of morphia. Now I want to be agreed on this: Betty has kindly volunteered to have Grace stay here, so hereafter I'll discuss the case with Betty as though she were Grace's mother. I'll answer your questions, Brock, and you'll have to make the decisions such as calling another physician for consultation. But to all intents and purposes, Betty's the one I'll deal with. Is that agreed? Brock? You, too, Edgar?"

They agreed.

"And Betty's taken orders before, so she knows not to interfere with the nurses. They're the best in town, and we're lucky to have them, because the kind of care they give a patient is what's most important in this kind of case. I just want all these things understood, because you know me. I can be sharp. Well, that'll be all for tonight. Don't come to the door, please. I can open it myself. Good night."

He left them. Brock was the first to speak. "I wouldn't let anyone else talk to me that way, I'll tell you."

"Not many people *would* talk to you that way, Brock. It does you good, and he's a wonderful doctor."

"He's getting on, though."

"A doctor isn't supposed to be any good till he's seventy," said Edgar.

"And by that time they're usually dead," said Brock.

"I'd rather have him than the kind that make you think everything's just sunshine and roses," said Betty.

"Oh, so would I, any day in the week. I just don't like to be made feel that I'm being addressed by a hard-boiled elderly colonel, like one I had at Fort Riley," said Brock.

"Brock, you go home and go to bed, unless you want to spend the night here," said Betty.

Brock smiled. "Now don't you start talking like Doctor O'Brien. I don't have to put up with it from you."

"Oh, yes, you do. Didn't you hear what he said?"

Brock rose. "You're all right, Betty." He put his hand on her shoulder and kissed her cheek. "Good night, you two."

Betty and Edgar were alone. They looked at each other. "This is all right with you, isn't it?" she asked.

"Sure it is," said Edgar.

"She has no friends. I'm her only friend. She may die in this house, you know."

"I know," said Edgar.

"She has an awful life, Edgar."

"Yes, I suppose."

"In some ways—no, I won't say that," said Betty.

"It wouldn't be true. If she died there'd be no chance of its getting better. Is she having another love affair?"

Betty nodded. "Hopeless, too."

"Who is it?"

"So hopeless she wouldn't tell me. I'm just as glad I don't know."

"Why?" said Edgar. "We might want to send for him."

"No. I don't think he could come, whoever he is. But I don't want to know who he is because of the maids' talk two years ago. Remember? When Sidney and then Billy died, and how she was unlucky? Now there's Roger Bannon. And if I knew who the man is, the present one, I'd be like the maids, waiting to see if he was unlucky too."

"Now, now, Betty. Luck. Superstition."

"Yes, but that's only what the maids call it. Luck. It could be more than that. That she affected Roger Bannon so seriously that he got into an automobile drunk and got killed. That doesn't have to be luck."

"Sidney and Billy died of infantile paralysis."

"Sidney might not have caught it if he'd been in Cape May with Grace, so that doesn't have to be luck either. Billy didn't get it till after he came back here."

"Grace didn't get it, the other two children didn't get it," said Edgar.

"Oh, I'm not trying to prove all this. In fact I don't want to talk about it any more, but if I knew who the man is, I would have that in the back of my mind. I wouldn't be able to help myself. And it'd be on your mind, too."

"I suppose."

"We're going to have to have Anna stay here, too," said Betty.

"Naturally."

"Edgar, dear, you wish I hadn't made Grace stay, don't you?"

"No, not a bit. I think you had to do it, as a friend."

"You wish I hadn't, though," she said.

"Well, I can't pretend that I don't like my comfort and a normal household. Suddenly we have a sick person, two strange women in white uniforms, a little girl, a brother, and at least one doctor in our house. Isn't it all right if I say I'd rather have just my own family?"

"Of course it is."

"All right. Well, I've said it, and now I feel better about it. I won't say any more, and I think you did the only thing possible. It was a good impulse, and I like you better for acting on it. Shall we retire to our chambers and conduct all further conversation in somewhat cozier surroundings? On the morrow I shall have to don my coif and wax incisive and eloquent in the matter of Schoffstal v. the Pennsylvania Railroad, a little dispute involving a property line. I shall make the rafters ring as my stentorian tones fill the halls of justice with talk of surveyors and such."

"Not so loud, Edgar. I'll go down to the kitchen first and see if everything's all right there, then I'll be right up."

"Make haste, woman. I am not to be put off with your chatter of the doings in the scullery."

"I'll be right up."

"Shall I leave this light on?"

"Yes. It lights the hall, in case the night nurse has to go downstairs."

The Martindales and Brock decided not to call in another doctor; O'Brien on the third day, Wednesday, told them it was unmistakably pneumonia. Grace had a high temperature, she was weak and delirious, coughing rusty sputum, and taking oxygen by nasal catheter. It was a house of quiet; of careful footsteps; of subdued censure when the Martindales' gardener struck his horseshoe-nail ring on the oxygen tank; of new sounds quickly becoming familiar sounds, such as the click of the glass vials in Doctor O'Brien's black bag, and cardboard-muffled bells in the kitchen, and florists' delivery men with their unvarying "Flowers for Tate, sign here," who in the same week had been saying "Flowers for Grenville, sign here" and "Flowers for Bannon, sign here." And the sound that went all through the house at night; Grace's cough, starting with a single cough, high in pitch, and then lower and repeated fast until it was stopped.

The visits—by Betty, Anna and Brock—were cut shorter daily as the nurse noticed Grace's increasing difficulty in holding up her hand in greeting. On Friday the visits were suspended by Miss Carmody's suggestion and Doctor O'Brien's order.

"Miss Carmody," said Betty that day, "does she ever seem to ask for anyone in particular?"

"I haven't noticed that, Mrs. Martindale. You mean in delirium?"

"Yes."

"No," said the nurse. "But if she *did* I wouldn't pay much attention to it. They often ask for things they don't want at all, and names they mention can be like for instance names they read in the paper, nobody they know."

"I see."

"When the little boy, Jack, gets here, we'll let her see him. He's coming this afternoon, the way I understand. He can go in for a minute. But answering your question, you very seldom get any sense out of what they say."

"Thank you, Miss Carmody," said Betty.

"Notta tall, I'm sure," said Miss Carmody.

None of the Jacks that Betty knew could possibly have been the man in Grace's secret. She went through her address book, the Fort Penn Club and the country-club membership rosters, and all she got out of that was the superfluous reassurance that the man was not Edgar Martindale, and the discovery that there was a disturbingly large number of men named John whom she could momentarily suspect of adultery, but each of whom for one reason or another she discarded as likely to be the individual in Grace's delirium. The name Jack was a piece of information so utterly useless that she did not even give it to Edgar, who, since his single declaration of sentiments, had been genuinely solicitous and concerned for Grace's welfare.

The crisis occurred some time during the Sunday afternoon. Miss Carmody, who was on duty, told Betty to telephone Doctor O'Brien while the Martindales, the Tate children and Brock were at noon dinner. The doctor arrived, stayed for an hour, went away for two hours, came back and stayed another hour, went out again, and came back again. An oxygen tank was being carried up the stairs while the doctor was having a cup of tea in Edgar's study. Brock entered the room, but the doctor did not speak. Brock sat down, put his elbows on his knees and rested his chin on his folded hands.

"This is the crucial time, isn't it, Doctor?"

"Mm-hmm." The doctor was chewing a ham sandwich and washing it down with the tea. "To be literal, it's the critical time. The adjective for crisis, Brock."

"Doctor, I know you don't think much of me, but I hope you save Grace."

"I have nothing against you, Brock. You're an idler, but you can afford it. You may be doing the world a favor by being an idler, and in any case it's none of my business." He poured himself another cup of tea.

"What are her chances?"

"I don't know."

"Well, we're doing the best we can for her."

"Is that a question?" said the doctor.

"It may have sounded like one. But haven't I a right to ask a question?"

"You have a right to ask a question, but you have no right to question what we're doing for Grace." He wiped his mouth with the serviette. "I don't expect you to question what we're doing any more than the husband of a Negress I saw this afternoon. Do you know what a janiceps is?"

"I never heard the word before. How do you spell it?"

"J, a, n, i, c, e, p, s."

"It sounds like some kind of an instrument."

"It isn't. It's a monster, a baby with two faces and one head. That's what the black woman had this afternoon. That's why I was in and out of here. I'd never seen one before. We're trying to save the mother, and I can tell you about her chances, if you'd like to know. They're not very good."

"What the hell do I care about some nigger woman with a two-headed baby?"

"I don't care about her, either, and I do about Grace, but I care what happens to them, enough to give them the benefit of whatever I know."

"God damn it, Doctor, you can't—"

"Don't be angry with me. I'm an old man and I have to hoard my strength. You're not a boy any more, either, Brock. Now I must get back to my patient. Pour yourself a cup of tea."

The two families ate soup and a cold supper at six-thirty, then the Martindale children, as hosts, tried to entertain the Tates with spit-in-the-ocean in the library, while Betty and Edgar and Brock read the Philadelphia papers. At about eight-fifteen Doctor O'Brien joined the adults in the sitting-room. His age and his weariness were upon him, but he smiled. "She'll get well," he said, "she'll get well."

He sat down on the edge of a straight-backed chair. "She passed the crisis about four hours ago and her temperature's been going down," he said. "Steadily. No complications, none expected." He stood up and blew his breath. "Rest, rest. The best of care, lots of rest, that's the important thing now. She's sleeping, and you can't see her tonight, but tomorrow you can go in for a minute, one at a time. Rest, rest, let's all get some rest. God bless all here."

Grace remained at the Martindales' until the doctor told her she was well enough to begin going for short drives in the closed car (he had a prejudice against the word limousine). She told him that the first short ride she wanted to take was to Second Street, so that the Martindales could resume their family life. The house on the farm was undergoing the extensive repairs reported by Charlotte Buchwalter-Penelope Penn, but O'Brien told Grace that he preferred to have her in town anyway, so that he could drop in to observe at varying hours of the day the effect of the change from an almost straight-liquid diet to solid foods. She was thin and weak, and liable to "try to do too much all of a sudden," in the words of Miss Carmody, who stayed on after the departure from the Martindales'. The dietary regimen was meat and potatoes and milk, green vegetables and fruit; no rich foods or sauces, a minimum of seasoning; no cigarettes or alcohol. A hairdresser and a manicurist came once a week, and Ruth Holz gave Grace a private showing of the spring clothes she had not bought a few days before her collapse but which she now bought with—for Grace—abandon. She ordered shoes from the Philadelphia catalogues, and gave most of them to Miss Carmody when she discovered that the loss of weight had been from head to toe; her usual shoe size no longer was right for her.

To put in the time she wrote thank-you notes to the friends who had sent flowers. Betty not only had saved the cards, but had written down the names of the flowers, an evidence of efficiency as well as confidence in Grace's ultimate recovery. Grace thus was able to mention jonquils to senders of jonquils weeks after the senders had forgotten what they had sent. Grace would write three or four notes at a sitting, and that much would tire her in the beginning of her convalescence. She therefore put off answering Mary Kemper's note, which read:

Dear Mrs. Tate:—

 *Mr. Hollister and Mr. Bull selected me to pick out the flowers as I am a
girl, men knowing little or nothing about flowers. All hope they will help to
brighten your room and wish you a speedy recovery.*

Very sincerely yours,
Mary Kemper

It was not known to Grace that Brock and Hollister had had a
policy conference over the *Sentinel's* mention of her illness. Hollister, upon hearing the news from Charlie Jay, had telephoned
Brock. Brock said he wanted to talk about that and would Hollister meet him at the Fort Penn Club that afternoon?

"Thank you for coming over," said Brock. "By the way, you
ought to be a member here. Your father was. There's a little waiting list, but I think I could get them to jump your name over
some of these out-of-towners."

"I'm on another waiting-list, Mr. Caldwell," said Hollister.

"Another club?"

"No, I belong to the A. C.," said Hollister. "But I'm on the
breadline. I just bought a car. I borrowed the money from the
paper to pay cash, and I'm paying it back out of my salary."

"I know," said Brock. "We're going to make an adjustment
about that. We haven't decided exactly what, but somewhere
around half. You need a car and we think the paper ought to—
well, we'll talk about that some other time. Right now, about my
sister, Mrs. Tate. She has pneumonia. It's hard to get anything
out of Doctor O'Brien one way or the other, but she's on the critical list. She may not pull through."

"Good God, I didn't know that."

"Well, you know it now," said Brock. "A great many son of a
bitches in this town probably think she pulled a fake because of,
well—we understand each other, Hollister. We've skirted
around this subject before, on Monday, I think it was."

"You don't have to say any more," said Hollister.

"Good," said Brock. "Well, I don't want anything in the paper about her being ill, not till next week anyway, after some of this accident stuff's died down a bit. Bastards can whisper what they please. Maybe when they find out my sister's at death's door they'll have the decency to reconsider, although I doubt that. But according to Doctor O'Brien the crisis usually comes in a week to ten days. Either way I'll call you Monday and you can tell Crowley to run a paragraph on the society page, that she's critically ill with pneumonia at the home of Mrs. Edgar Martindale, where she was stricken last week. Something to that effect. Put in Doctor O'Brien's name, two nurses in attendance. Anything with Doctor O'Brien's name on it the gossips will know it's a fact. If she gets well you can put something in once a week, report of her condition."

"How is she today?—Not for publication."

"Well, I see her for two or three minutes at a time. You'd think you couldn't tell much that way, but you've seen my sister, you know what a picture of health she's always been. Not now. Delirious. Weak. She can't raise her hand, for Christ's sake. They have to give her oxygen so she can breathe. That's the new thing nowadays, an oxygen tank in the sickroom. To me it makes her look more helpless than ever, that iron tank, and the rubber hose. I look at the God-damn thing and I say to myself, 'My sister's life is in there, in that big iron bottle.' My sister's life."

"Could we send her some flowers?"

Brock smiled sardonically. "I think it'd be very nice, but later on, when she can appreciate them. I don't even think she even recognized me, today."

"Well, anything we can do for her at the paper," said Hollister.

"I'm very touched by that, Hollister. I mean your sincerity. I can always tell when a man's sincere. Well, you can tell the people at the *Sentinel* just what I told you. And thanks for coming over."

When she was ready Grace replied to Mary:

Dear Mary:

I was especially pleased to be remembered by you and Mr. Hollister and Mr. Bull, my fellow-employees of the Sentinel. *The lovely chrysanthe-*

*mums brightened my room and cheered me up more than you will ever
know. Now that I seem to be on the way to recovery I hope to see you very
soon. Next week I am to be allowed a few visitors a day. If you are in the
neighborhood, won't you stop in? Please thank Mr. Bull and Mr. Hollister
for me. Again, my thanks to you.*

> *Sincerely,*
> *Grace C. Tate*

Mary responded as though the note had been a summons. "A
Miss Kemper to see you," said Miss Carmody. "Is she the-
Kemper-that-worked-on-the-*Sentinel's* daughter?"

"Yes," said Grace.

"I nursed him for a gall-stone operation when I started out
private calls, that's how I recognized the name. Now, only ten
minutes, Mrs. Tate. They tire you, and I don't want you getting
tired before bedtime."

Grace received the girl in the upstairs sitting-room. "Hello,
Mary," she said, reaching out her hand.

"How do you do, Mrs. Tate," said Mary. "These are from me.
I didn't tell Mr. Hollister—Mr. Bull when I was coming." She
shook hands with Grace and laid a bunch of hot-house roses on
her lap. "Shall I put them in a vase for you?"

"They're beautiful, Mary. I'd just like to hold them, but I want
to keep them fresh as long as possible. I guess those lilies on the
table are about ready to go. Will you do it for me? I'm not supposed to walk any more today."

The girl changed the flowers and joined Grace.

"How *are* Mr. Bull and Mr. Hollister?"

"About the same. Well, no. Mr. Hollister's easier to get along
with. Not that he wasn't before, but he had that other job that he
was busy every minute and half the time their mind is so occupied, you know. A city editor. But the Pillbox, everybody that I
spoke to likes it very much, only those that can hardly read or
write, they don't catch on to some of the jokes. But it's a big success. What we needed."

"Yes, I like it too, now that I'm allowed to read the papers again. Mr. Bull, how is he?"

"He's always the same. Well, of course he was out two days with a cold last—week *before* last, it was. Nothing serious. Mr. Hollister bought a new car."

"That's nice. Have you seen it?"

"Oh, I had several rides in it. It's a Chevrolet touring. I had several rides home in it."

"That's convenient."

"Convenient if it's convenient, if you know what I mean. You can't count on it, one trouble. See, if I go down and get on the trolley at the turn-out I can always get a seat, but that way Mr. Hollister doesn't see me waiting at the corner, and then sometimes when I do wait at the corner he doesn't come and I have to take the trolley and don't get a seat all the way home."

"You ought to make an arrangement with him."

"Oh, you can't arrange with Jack Hollister. Not him. I never saw anybody so independent in my life. Even if you arranged it with him he'd change his mind at the last minute. He's as changeable as the weather. He has his column on his mind day and night, Mrs. Tate. A wonderful sense of humor, but one of the hardest workers around." The girl shifted in her chair. "How long before you can be up and around again?"

"Oh, two weeks, maybe a month. They want me to gain weight but slowly."

"Milk, I guess they make you drink a—" she stopped with the slow, significant entrance of Miss Carmody.

"It's over ten minutes, Mrs. Tate," said Miss Carmody.

"It can't be," said Grace.

"But it is."

The girl said good-bye and promised to come soon again and went down the stairs and out of the house and over to Front Street, where Jack Hollister was waiting in his car.

"How was she?" he said.

"Pale, but just as nice as ever. Even nicer." Simply and naturally she held up her arms and moved into a close embrace and a long kiss. They both knew exactly how far she would let him go and let herself go. It had become a ceremony with them, with no satisfactory completion for him, but he was unable to deny himself her kisses and the few minutes' play with her breasts. It had begun in the office, in the dusty room in which the back files and reference books were kept, and to which both had legitimate and frequent access. He followed her there one afternoon, came up behind her without any attempt at surprise, turned her around and she kissed him immediately and freely, held on to him so long as he kept it at kissing.

It was a new experience for him, the long process of seduction, without offering love, giving love, expecting love, and without being expected to love. There was love in her voice only when she spoke of the members of her family, and one other person—Grace Tate. He believed that Mary prayed for Grace Tate to get well; he had heard her say that no movie actress compared with Grace, and she had offered the information that Grace's thank-you note was locked in her chiffonier drawer, in a handkerchief box that was just the right size for Grace's envelope. He reluctantly inferred that Mary never had noticed him much in the three years they had been working in the same building, and that she had made herself attractive to him principally because Mrs. Tate had seemed to like him. Mary conveyed these thoughts in words that were intended to keep his pride intact, but about the thoughts themselves there was no doubt. He considered, very briefly, the effect on Mary if he were to tell her that Grace had given what Mary denied. The effect, of course, would be that Mary would call him a liar.

In Mary's eyes the best was not enough for Grace; it had to be the right best. Grace was the best-dressed woman in Fort Penn—*but without trying*. She was the handsomest—*but without caring*. She was the kindest—*but expected nothing*. She did everything the right way—*but without stopping to think about it*. To find in his own life a comparable admiration of one human being for another Hollister had to go back to his appraisal of his father—and he was not willing to concede that in his case the judgment was not more justifiable. Indeed, he was not willing to make the comparison at all; what he knew about his father was fact; what Mary felt about Grace was childlike, rather charming, and a bit cheap. Sometimes, during one of Mary's panegyrics, Hollister wanted to shut her up with details of his own intimate knowledge of Grace, and the consequences be damned. But he had his own self-control, originating in his now daily need to touch this girl, to excite her, and, eventually, to ruin her. He did not believe that the ultimate seduction of a virgin was automatically ruinous; he was too sophisticated for that. But this girl believed in her morality, her strength of character, and her self-control, and they would automatically die when her virginity was ended. He excused himself in advance by his unexpressed advance reminder to her that she should have known where it would end, all this playing. The only times he hesitated were when he would become aware of his father in his conscience, his conscience which was the memory of his father. But those times did not obtain when Mary was in plain sight. Her incredible skin and coloring, the resistance in her young breasts, her stride, her cleanliness as to her person and the things she wore, and her cheerfully acknowledged need of him (and the *growing* need of which she kept herself unaware) were all on the one side, and when he was looking at her there was no other side. In his secondary thinking, underneath his willing thinking, he was conscious of a curious possibility: he never had considered giving up Amy and the children for Grace, whom in his fashion he loved; but he could imagine himself so desperate for Mary that nothing else would count. It was a possibility, all right.

For her part, Amy could see that something was going on, but she thought it was only Jack getting a swelled-head. Now when she went shopping downtown the clerks would say, "Mrs. John Hollister? Is your husband 'J. H.'?" He had told her of the man-to-man talks with Brock Caldwell, the invitation to join the Fort

Penn Club, the absorption of the cost of their car. She was pleased with the discovery that fraternal organizations, church groups, high schools and other get-togethers were willing to go as high as $25 to have Jack speak. Organizations that had not been interested in a football reputation now were glad to present the editor of the Pillbox, the new column in the *Sentinel* that everybody was talking about. On the window-cards he was J. H. (Jack Hollister), author of the Pillbox column, star football player, ex-hero of the 5th Marines, witty after-dinner speaker with a message for all. He had a self-effacing manner that was becoming to a young man who looked the part of football star and war hero, he was a safely married man with two children, he was a Fort Penn boy who had had several paragraphs quoted in *The Literary Digest,* and the witty after-dinner message was not so forbiddingly witty and message-laden that he was not being asked to come back the next year. He had several set speeches; the high-school basketball-team banquet speech, the mixed-audience church-supper speech, the men's club church-supper speech (which included a hell and a damn after the expressed hope that the Reverend would forgive him), and the all-ladies speech ("If my wife could only see me now!"). The message for the basketball banquets was play-the-game, and was constantly freshened up by lifting Grantland Rice's poems from the New York *Tribune;* the mixed-audience church-supper message was homey and humorous but with a serious undertone in favor of the married state that had some of them nodding in agreement and some of them even furtively holding hands; the all-men double-barreled church-supper message substituted the business word co-operation for the high-school word teamwork, and acknowledged the presence of God on the battlefields of France and the reliance on Him by the bravest of men, who were not ashamed to pray. He found that he lost nothing by giving credit where credit was due, to Mark Twain, Elbert Hubbard, Shakespeare, Walt Mason, and Arthur James Hollister, whose son he was proud to be. In a subtle way it showed he was generous and well read, and not merely the well-built athletic young fellow that they saw before them. A good speaker, a man's man, a real gentleman but not stuck-up—thus his hearers of high and low degree.

A speech brought him back into Grace's life.

On an evening late in March he came home with news for Amy. "Well, guess who wants me to give a talk now?"

"Search me," said Amy.

"There's twenty-five dollars in it, but I don't know whether to take it or not."

"Well, if it's a worthy charity—but charity begins at home, don't forget."

"I wasn't thinking of whether to take the money or not. What I was thinking was whether I want to take the engagement."

"Who is it?"

"They want me to speak at the Spring Day lunch at Miss Holbrook's School."

"Don't tell me you're thinking of turning it down! You crazy? I want to send Joan there next year. Jack it's the chance of a lifetime."

"Amy, my father was always against—"

"So was my father too. Well, these are *our* children, not our fathers', and I want them to have the best. If we can send Buddy to college I want him to go to Harvard, see? Not just Lafayette. Harvard! And Joan'll go to Vassar, if I have to scrub floors."

"Well, stay off your knees."

"Well, then don't you talk about turning down $25 at Holbrook's. And it isn't only the money. If you make a good impression I happen to know they have scholarships for bright girls, and Joan's bright. Turn it down nothing. I guess I can't go but I wish I could. What is it? Just for the parents?"

"Uh-huh. Mrs. Edgar Martindale's the one that asked me. She's on the trustees."

"Well, you do whatever she wants. Does she want you to speak on any particular subject? I'll look up stuff if you need help."

"Fort Penn. They want to raise money and she thinks I ought

to say what a wonderful place Fort Penn is and how lucky to have a good school here, like Miss Holbrook's."

"Well, don't be so swell-headed. It's a good school—"

"If you don't stop calling me swell-headed I'm gonna clout you."

"If you ever dared to clout me, Jack Hollister, you know what'd happen."

"What would happen?"

"I'd walk out of that door and take the children and never come back, and you know it."

He raised his hand to arm's length.

"Don't joke about it," she said. "A woman that'd live with a man that hit her has no self-respect."

"Self-respect. Self-control. You women."

"I didn't say anything about self-control. You're the one has to have that, and I'll keep my self-respect. Now go wash. Nancy has a meeting."

"Funny Nancy's friends don't ask me to speak."

"Maybe Nancy knows your speeches by heart. Maybe she gives them down in Darktown." Amy laughed.

"I notice you don't laugh when I hand over the checks."

She patted his behind. "Go get some soap and water on your face-and-hands." She watched him with affection and gratitude.

———

The first of May was on a Saturday that year, and unofficially only those Holbrook fathers who were engaged in retail trade were excused from attendance at Spring Day. Doctors, lawyers, dentists, bankers and all others who could possibly get Saturday off were sternly invited to be present at the parents' luncheon in the auditorium, but the doctors and dentists insisted upon their office hours, and consequently the guest speaker faced a critical assemblage of lawyers and bankers, with their less critical wives. The barristers, schooled in forensics, were prepared to examine his address from the technical point of view, sitting as judges and as Shakespearean actors witnessing the special, inferior performance of a vaudeville trouper. The bankers, mindful of the coming drive for funds, gazed at him with the patronizing smile of the money-lender listening to a wretch who wants gold for an old rubber boot.

Mary Wall, toastmaster, introduced Hollister. "I don't think anyone, at least in my life-long residence in Fort Penn, has ever taken our city by storm so completely, and yet with our whole-hearted consent, as the gentleman I am about to introduce. We have all known, of course, of his enviable position in his chosen field of journalism and that of his father before him. Likewise, we have all heard of his earlier prowess on the football gridiron while a student at our own Fort Penn University. And as an officer in the United States Marines Corps he brought honor and glory to our city and country . . ."

("Isn't she awful?" said Betty Martindale.)

("She gets worse every year," said Grace.)

". . . But what we're not aware of, at least not until the first of January last, was still another hidden talent that our guest was secreting under a bushel-basket and I refer to a literary ability which I can safely say is second to none in the whole field of journalism. I wonder how many of us know that the name of the Fort Penn *Sentinel* is carried to the far reaches of wherever the English language is spoken, by virtue of quotations from the column known as the Pillbox in the *Sentinel*. And yet that is true. Magazines and newspapers galore seize upon his trenchant comments, at once rapier-like in their sharpness, but softened by a kindly wisdom rare in one so young in years. Fort Penn may well be proud of the manner in which we are represented in every state in the Union and abroad. Canada and other English-speaking countries. And it is all due to the extraordinary talent of a man who was born and brought up and educated here in our own old home town. Therefore it gives me great pleasure to introduce Mr. Jack Hollister, the illustrious J. H., of the Fort Penn *Sentinel!*"

("If I were George," said Betty, "I'd take her right home and beat her.")

("Imagine calling him Jack. Does she know him as Jack? His name is John," said Grace.)

Suddenly and slowly Betty knew something she had not known before, and had wanted not to know, and had trained herself not to be curious about. Even now she tried hard to disbelieve, but it was no use. If Grace had spoken the name Jack once and no more, it would have gone unnoticed, but she had said the name twice, in such quick succession that Betty's mind went back to the conversation with Miss Carmody and the nurse's assumption that Jack was the name of Grace's son. The repetition of the name sounded exactly as Betty thought Grace would have uttered it in her delirium, although she never had heard her say it. She was glad now of one thing: Grace had no idea that she ever had spoken the name. She could watch Grace without her becoming suspicious.

Hollister stood up, and now there was no doubt. Betty had only to shift in her chair and glance at the face of the unsuspecting Grace. He was the man. Grace was not smiling, but her face—her mouth, her eyes, her slightly bowed head—was in placid contemplation of a man she loved. She clapped her hands impersonally, as though that gesture had been directed by another brain—as indeed it was; the brain of Mary Wall, who was leading the applause. Betty did not hear much of the talk, but Grace seemed to follow it closely, applauding in the same impersonal way, but on cue with the other men and women in the room. After twenty minutes Hollister sat down and Mary got up again to introduce Ham Schoffstal, who almost immediately got to the point: pledge cards were being passed around, and he wanted to know who would be the first to pledge five thousand dollars. Senior girls were moving up and down the aisles to accept the pledges. Well, if no one else would start the ball rolling, Ham guessed it was up to him. Grace wrote on her pledge, folded it, and signaled to one of the girls. "Betty, you give yours at the same time," said Grace.

"We're giving a thousand," said Betty.

She handed the girl her pledge.

"Let's go," said Grace.

They were stepping over the threshold when they heard Ham's voice: "Mrs.—Sidney—Tate—five—thousand—dollars." He paused and called out: "Grace, are you here?"

"She just left," came the chorus.

"I shouldn't stay too long," said Grace. "Anna doesn't expect me to. I'll just say hello to your girls. There they are."

They spoke to Anna and the Martindale girls and then Betty said, "Do you want me to ride home with you?"

"But you have to stay here, Betty."

"I suppose so. Not because mine are getting any prizes. In fact, just the opposite. Because they're not. I have to stay a little while so the mothers of the bright ones won't think I left because of sour grapes."

"Didn't one of yours win something this morning?"

"Betsy got second in high jump. Nice lady-like sport."

"Well, Anna got runner-up in the doubles. Come on, go for a ride with me," said Grace.

"Do you really want me to?"

"I really do," said Grace.

"Oh, hell, why not? I've been here every day this week. They'd rather have Edgar than me anyway. I don't think I'll be missed. Where's your car?"

"I have the Pierce, but Charles can take us home and we can get the Ford, if you'll drive."

"Yes, let's do that," said Betty.

They made the transfer to the coupé and Betty said, "Any particular place or direction?"

"Let's just drive anywhere the spirit moves you."

"North, south, east, or west?"

"South, I guess. I haven't been that direction for dear knows how long. But let's not stay on the main road."

"I don't know, Grace. Some of those side roads, in the Spring, some of the ruts." They turned southward.

"Well, we'll see," said Grace. "If we get stuck in the mud we'll let them think we're nurses from the King's Daughters."

"Who'd believe that?"

"Anybody, you look so healthy, you'd be the nurse, and I still look like an invalid."

"Oh, you do not."

"Yes, I do," said Grace. "A lot of the people at the lunch, they hadn't seen me since I had pneumonia, and I frightened some of them. I'm trying to get the weight back, but it's taking longer than I thought. And I'm still not as strong as I always used to be. Goodness, when I think of what I used to do! Up at seven every morning, three children to get ready for school, ride in the morning with Sidney. Lunch at home, drive in town and do some shopping, drive out again. Play with the children, help them with their lessons. Dinner out, spend the evening at a friend's house, get to bed at one or two in the morning, and up again at seven."

"But you didn't do all that every day, Grace, now you know you didn't."

"No, of course not, but once or twice a week, and sometimes oftener. But I wouldn't last out the day if I tried it now."

"Naturally. You've been sick, at death's door."

"Death's door. I was not. I was uncomfortable, in pain part of the time, disgusted with myself, hot and cold and angry. I never gave any thought to heaven or hell or death's door. I was a little afraid I might die, but that was only because I didn't want to miss anything, not fear of hell or the wrath of God. I'm not a better woman in any way whatsoever, Betty. If anything, I'm worse. If I was at death's door it might have been better for all concerned if I'd pushed a little harder and gone in."

"You very nearly did. That Saturday night and Sunday Doctor O'Brien didn't think you were going to live. He didn't hold out any hope whatsoever."

"When are you going to make up your mind what you want for

being so nice to me? If you don't make it up soon I'm coming over some day and examine the house and buy things that you won't want."

"Don't change the subject, Grace. I want to know why you're so bitter about getting well."

"Don't you change the subject, either. I want to know what you want for your house."

"A Victrola, one of the big ones."

"It's not enough, and you can buy that yourself and get the kind you want. I want to do something that when you see it you'll think of me as the one that gave it to you, not the woman that asked you for a drink of whiskey and settled down with her whole family and two nurses and a doctor and God knows what else. Edgar won't take a penny and you won't take a present. You don't keep friends by having them obligated to you as much as I am. Not that I can ever repay you, but I can at least make myself believe I tried to."

"I think you must be getting well. You're so cantankerous."

"If you want to know the truth, I don't much care whether I get well or not."

"The day you got sick you told me about—"

"I know I did," said Grace. "Did I ever say anything when I was delirious? I've been fighting off asking you. Did I?"

"Oh—"

"Did I? I did, didn't I? What did I say? Does that Carmody woman know?"

"I don't know what she knows."

"Do *you* know?" Grace leaned forward and stared sideways at her friend.

"I'll tell you the only thing I know." She related Miss Carmody's confusion over the name of Grace's son.

"I see. Is that all you know?" said Grace. "You never heard me yourself?"

"No, but I know who the man is."

"Oh, God no! You don't, Betty! Please say you don't know. You can't. I don't want anyone to know, not anyone in the world. How do you know? What makes you think you do? I've been so careful—I don't believe you. What are his initials?"

"Right now he's as well known by his initials as he is by his full name."

Grace nodded. "Yes, that's who it is," she said, quietly. "How did you guess it? It wasn't anything I did or said."

"Both, in a way," said Betty. She gave her reasons for knowing the man was Hollister.

"Well," said Grace, "you see how hopeless it is."

"Yes."

"You agree with me that it *is* hopeless?"

"Yes, I do," said Betty. "You don't want me to agree with you, but I do."

Grace smiled. "You have to admit you were awfully ready to agree on the hopelessness of it."

"I was indeed. Grace, why don't you get married?"

"That's a fine question, the minute you know I'm in love with somebody and find out who it is. You're not suggesting I marry him."

"Most certainly not. You ought to marry a man like Brock. When I say like Brock I mean a man who's a few years older, sophisticated, rich. Somebody that might want to step out, as they say."

"Step out with another woman, you mean?"

"Yes."

"I'd never in the world marry a man under those conditions. I suppose this man would expect me to step out, too?"

"If he had any sense he would."

"Well, thank you, no. Betty. You must think I'm the worst tart you've ever known."

"No I don't at all, but if you were married—"

"I was married," said Grace.

"And in all those years, one mistake."

"Have you ever made that kind of a mistake?"

"No, but I'm not beautiful. It's the last thing most men think of in connection with me."

"Have you ever been *tempted?*"

"Wanted to, you mean?"

"Yes."

"I have," said Betty. "I love Edgar, but—shall I tell you something?"

"What?"

"If Sidney had ever wanted me I'd have gone with him. I always liked Sidney."

"But never anything between you?"

"Never. I was always awkward and shy with him, probably because of that very reason. And Roger Bannon, I didn't like him at all, but just as an animal—I could easily understand how that happened, Grace."

"And this other one?" said Grace.

"No. Too young, too—well, just young. That's where you and I differ on him."

"Well, that's good, although I don't know why it's good or bad."

"It's good."

"Go straight at Emeryville. Don't stay on the main road," said Grace.

They left the Pike and drove along the same road where Grace and Hollister had had their rendezvous. "This is an awful road," said Betty.

"You can turn around up there past those sycamores."

"I see you know this road."

"Oh, yes. You see that man on the cultivator? In that plowed field?"

"Yes."

"He owns a Deering manure spreader."

"Who is he?"

"I have no idea, but he owns a Deering manure spreader. Yes, I know this road," said Grace.

"Why did you want to come here?"

"Now?" said Grace. "Today?"

"Yes."

"To see if I could find out anything about myself."

"Have you?"

"Nothing I didn't know before," said Grace.

"Well, that's not very good."

"Why?"

"It means you haven't changed."

"I haven't changed a bit. I told you that a few minutes ago," said Grace. "I'm as bad as you think I am. But I'll say this much for myself. I think you're bad, too. Not for liking Sidney and Mr. Bannon. But for suggesting one of those marriages. I could have married Paul Reichelderfer under those conditions, and I didn't. At least I didn't do that, Mrs. Martindale."

"Oh, I never said I wasn't bad," said Betty. She took her eyes off the road and smiled at Grace, who smiled back. "If I had your looks, God help Fort Penn!"

"If *I* had my looks, God help Fort Penn!" said Grace. They laughed together. But after the laughter they were quiet and sober all the way to Betty's house. They had agreed that Grace was strong enough to drive the short distance from Betty's to Second Street. Betty got out and Grace slid over to the place behind the steering wheel.

"Thank you, thank you for everything," said Grace.

"You're welcome, Grace. Now stop worrying about everything. It's hopeless, all right, but I believe you'll be the better for it."

"Develop a noble character?"

"No, I hope not that, but a fairly happy woman. And one advantage you have over other women in the same circumstances."

"What's that?" said Grace.

"You know where your fellow's been all week, who he's been seeing."

"How do I know that? . . . Oh, you mean in his column."

"Yes, every Saturday," said Betty.

"I know who he's been seeing that he writes about, if he tells the whole truth."

"He certainly tells all about himself. I like it, but I must say he doesn't give himself much privacy."

"Hmm. Well, thanks again, Betty. See you Tuesday, if not before," said Grace.

(Hollister's Saturday column was based on a formula that neither originated nor ended with the Pillbox: he told what he had done throughout the week, and mentioned as many names as possible. It was the second most popular column of his week. The readers' favorite column appeared on Friday; that was his Home Life column. The column he liked least was the most popular with the public; the column he liked best—his Monday column—was the least popular, but it was the one that got him quoted in *The Literary Digest* and in other newspapers.

On Mondays he printed a column of paragraphs, comments on important and freak news items.

On Tuesdays he usually reported his own impressions of sports events.

On Wednesdays he wrote what he called a County column, for which he obtained information by driving to towns and villages in Nesquehela County, chatting with postmasters and storekeepers and farmers. It was often a dreary task, but the circulation department loved it.

On Thursdays he held forth on the movies, the stock company, road shows of Broadway plays, or books. He was good-humored.

On Friday he would write about his car, his weight, his likes and dislikes in food, repairs to his house, his antipathy to gardening, his moustache, his wife and children, and sometimes his job. He kept himself extremely average-American; willing, but not very handy, with tools and light-fuses; devoted to his car, which he called Gaston, after Gaston Chevrolet; and normally vain, but only when his vanity could be deflated at the end of the column. He called Amy The Duchess, and he referred to the children as Miss J and Master B, and in a remarkably short time Amy was being called The Duchess by her friends. She liked it, but prevailed upon him to keep mentions of the children to a minimum.)

———

"I know a politician that has an apartment, and he lives in Allentown," said Hollister to Mary. "The apartment's here, but he's only in it part of the time."

"But he'd know it was you."

"Are you sure you want to?"

"Yes, it isn't only because you want to. I have to be honest with myself."

"I'll ask the politician. He isn't a bad fellow, and it's his job to do favors. He's a lobbyist. He used to have a house but now he has an apartment."

"What's his name?"

"Ed Wachtel."

"Yes, I've heard of him. He's the one that used to give the wild parties."

"Yes."

"I wish it didn't have to be him. Make him believe it's for somebody else, not you. Can you?"

"Wachtel doesn't believe anybody's any good, so he won't be surprised."

"Maybe nobody is. I thought I was."

———

"Ed, I have a little favor to ask you," said Hollister to Wachtel in the Fort Penn A. C. lounge.

"It's yours if I can grant it or see the party that can. Fire away."

"Well, it isn't political," said Hollister.

Wachtel squinted and grinned. "Aha. If it's liquor, I can get you the best pre-war and if it isn't too large a quantity it'll cost you nothing. Bonded goods. But you're too young to care about liquor, so I have a hunch it's appertaining to the fair sex."

"Right," said Hollister.

"Something you have your eye on, that I should know about, Jack?"

"Not quite. It's something I have my eye on, but you shouldn't know about it. Neither should anybody else, if you get what I mean."

"I'm with you. You wish to dally with the fair maiden in my little flat? Am I right this time?"

"You are indeed," said Hollister.

"This evening?"

"No, not this evening, but the sooner the better."

"Always the sooner the better in such cases. And the oftener the better, at your age. Well, I'm going to Washington tomorrow morning and I'm due back Monday the seventeenth day of this month. That oughta give you some leeway, a week. And after the first of June, you can have the damn place all summer, if you like. I was going to close it for the summer, but the key is yours."

"But you come to Fort Penn in the summer."

"I do, but now that we have the first decent hotel the fair city's ever known, I'll stay there. Won't go near the apartment. No chance of my catching you *in flagrante*. I'm afraid the linen will be your problem, but otherwise my bed, my liquor, and my books are yours to enjoy with all good wishes. I'm sure you'll spend many happy hours with the books."

"I'm sure."

"I *have* some books there that have done the trick when all my wiles and persuasion failed. You'll find them on the shelf *behind* Ridpath's History of the World. Where shall I leave the key? I know, in your mailbox here in the club. You can keep that key, and I'll be in touch with you before I leave for the summer, just to make sure. I only wish I were in your shoes, but I guess I've got out of my own often enough for the same purpose. The world doesn't owe me anything, not a damn thing. I was just thinking about that before you came. Well, I'm leaving for Washington on the early morning train and my blackamoor will most likely scurry out of the apartment the minute I leave. Good luck, and enjoy yourself. The key'll be in your box tomorrow morning. I'll put it in an envelope and send it over by William after breakfast.

It's the second floor, you know. Upholstery shop on the street floor, I'm on the second, and the third is occupied by the lady friend of one of our Pittsburgh legislators. We all mind our own business. If we all did that we'd all be happier, but there wouldn't be any lobbyists."

"And I wouldn't have a place to go. Thanks very much, Ed. I guess you know how I appreciate this."

"Oh, sure. I've played Cupid before, and I've also had his help. So long, Jack."

———

Amy was in the front room in her bathrobe and mules with her darning basket.

"Did you call me?" he said. "At the office?"

"When?" she said.

"I don't know, about an hour or so ago. I went to the can and on my way back I heard my phone ringing, but by the time I got to my desk there was nobody there. I thought it was probably you."

"You did?"

"Uh-huh. It wasn't you?"

"Not an hour or so ago," she said.

"Oh, earlier."

"Where did you eat?"

"At the Greek's."

"You write your column?"

"Sure. I got a hold of an old *Collier's* from before the war." He was speaking the truth; he had written the column early in the afternoon. "The old ads and so forth."

"Who did you eat with?"

"Nobody. I ate at the counter. What time did you call me?"

"I called you at six-thirty, and seven, seven-thirty, eight-thirty, and nine-thirty. Then I gave up."

"Well, I was in and out. What did you want?"

"When I first called you I wanted you to bring home a jar of mucilage. We're out of it and I couldn't leave here. But after the first couple of calls I wanted to see if you were *ever* going to answer. And you never did. You were out."

"I told you I was in and out. Your Honor, I object to the manner of this questioning. It presumes—"

"And so was Grace Tate out."

"What?"

"You weren't in the office all night, because Crowley was and he answered the phone three times when I called. And Grace Tate was out too."

"Are you out of your head?"

"If I am it's no wonder."

"What are you talking about—Grace Tate."

"I phoned her house and found out she wasn't home."

"You must be crazy. They'll think—what did you *do?* Do you mean to say you telephoned her house?"

"That's what I said. I called her house and asked if she was home, and they said she was out for the evening, so I hung up."

"Well, at least they didn't know it was a crazy woman that called. I'm going to bed."

"Where were you tonight?"

"I'll be a son of a bitch if I'll tell you where I was. Tonight or any other night."

"I see through you. You think now you'll use this fight for an excuse, you big hypocrite. Pretending to be the husband and father. Well, you're only making a fool of yourself, but you're not going to make one of me. Or those children. Fancy boy to a rich whore, that's what you are. Don't come near me!"

"Ah, put away your scissors, you crazy bitch. Calling Mrs. Tate's house. What if she'd answered the phone?"

"Then I'd have known she was there. But she wasn't there, see? Of course she was out for the evening."

"Call her now, for Christ's sake. It's still early."

"Out with the football star. War hero. Popular stuck-up."

———

The anger between Amy and Hollister became a coldness that they successfully hid from the children, but it reduced their own conversations to discussions of ways and means. Amy progressed from her angry conviction to angry suspicion to uncertain suspicion to genuine doubt for lack of proof. As the real summer came she was full of the doubt and eager to be shown her error, but Hollister ignored her conciliatory smiles.

———

It was Natalie Bordener's turn to have the bridge club. They finished play a little earlier than usual and Natalie took a poll: "What are you doing over the Fourth?" The Clarksons were going to Maine in June, George and Mary Wall would be in Edgartown over the holiday. The Martindales? They were going to spend July at Grace's farm. Why? Well, Natalie wanted to get up a party to go to the Gibbsville Assembly, the Summer Assembly. The Fourth was on a Sunday this year, so the Assembly would be on the 2nd. The Lantenengo Country Club had a rule that Saturday-night dances had to stop at one A.M., but the rule was being suspended for the Assembly. Why didn't Betty and Edgar and Grace drive up to Gibbsville with Natalie and Scotty and go to the dance and spend the night at her house, and still be back the next day in time to spend most of the Fourth on the farm with the Martindale and Tate children?

The Martindales and Grace automatically declined, but it was a fact that they had no real reason for declining, and Grace and Betty and Edgar left Natalie's house as her guests-to-be for the Gibbsville Assembly. "When my sister-in-law makes up her mind it's hard to stop her," said Betty, in the car.

"She's a real organizer, all right," said Edgar.

"Why did I say I'd go?" said Grace. "I don't know anybody in Gibbsville."

"In all fairness, though, we've had some good times there, Grace," said Edgar. "They are hospitable. The first time we went was to Natalie and Scotty's wedding."

"Hospitable people—well, I'm not one, so I'm not a fair judge. I'm not speaking of your kind of hospitality, Martindales. I had in mind the wholesale kind, everybody so hearty and hail-fellow.

I like to choose my own friends. That's probably why I have so few. I'm a fool to say I'd go to Gibbsville."

"If we go you have to go, Grace, and I don't see any way out of it for us. In fact, if you want to know what *I* think, I think the whole idea is to get you to visit Natalie's family, so you'll see what nice people she comes from."

"Me? Why me? I'm sure she comes from a respectable family. I never made any issue of that, did I?"

"No, but Natalie thinks you look down on her."

"Oh, Lord. I have to leave my comfortable, cool, charming, newly done-over house because Natalie—why didn't Scotty marry a Fort Penn girl?"

The three friends made the trip in Edgar's Peerless. They arrived in Gibbsville in time for a large tea party, at which there were at least fifty men and women past thirty, neither more nor less friendly than any similar gathering of similar people on the Eastern seaboard. A man told Grace he had gone to Yale with Sidney, but before she got his name Natalie took her away to meet some other people. The same thing occurred with a man who said he knew Brock. A Doctor Somebody told Grace that she would be better off in Gibbsville, with its altitude, than in low-lying Fort Penn, after a bout of pneumonia—and she had had pneumonia, lately, hadn't she? She admitted she had had pneumonia, but expressed the hope that it was not so obvious to everyone else. He reassured her: only a doctor would know. Then Betty took her away from him and at ten minutes of seven the guests began to leave, and at ten minutes past seven they all had gone. Grace had a nap, and was downstairs, dressed for the evening, at nine. Dinner guests had been asked for nine o'clock, but they did not begin to turn up until nine-thirty. Some of the tea-party people returned for dinner. The men wore white flannels and blue serge coats and four-in-hands; there was no deviation from the costume, except in the selection of neckties, which were figured or striped. The man who was to be Grace's gentleman for the evening wore a red-and-blue stripe, not for the University of Pennsylvania, but for the New York Racquet & Tennis

Club, a fact which was made known to Grace several times in the course of the evening; Ned Minor was the only man in Gibbsville who belonged to that club. Ned was a cousin of Natalie's mother, a fifty-ish bachelor who lived in clubs wherever he went; in Gibbsville, at the Gibbsville Club; in Philadelphia, at the Racquet Club; in New York at the Racquet & Tennis Club; in Boston, at the Tennis & Racquet Club. He kept a saddle horse and he drove a dark red Pierce-Arrow roadster. He played bridge every day of his life, was acquainted with Whitehead personally, and was always called upon to settle local bridge disputes. He had been county singles champion and had taken up golf, and he had had dancing lessons from Irene and Vernon Castle. All of these facts came out before, during, and after dinner. An additional fact he vouchsafed to Grace in the red roadster: he had not known Sidney, but he too had belonged to Death's Head at Yale and on his rare visits to Fort Penn (where he stayed at the Fort Penn Club) he had been tempted to introduce himself to Sidney, who, he had heard from Paul Reichelderfer, was a fine, fine gentleman.

The dancing was under way when Natalie and her guests gathered at the country club. Grace had a minute with Betty, who asked her how she was getting along with Ned Minor.

"Effortless, effortless," said Grace. "But why does he live in Gibbsville? I should think he'd be misunderstood here."

"Because he's a fairy?" said Betty.

"Well—yes."

"The funny thing is, he isn't. Or not entirely. You may find that out before the night's over. He'll spend the first part of the evening describing himself as a perfect little gentleman, and the second part trying to get you off in a corner. That's what he did with me, so you look out."

There was a roll of the snare-drum and a cymbal crash. "Ladies, and gentlemen!" said the orchestra leader. "I wish to announce that all encores will be cut-ins. All encores—will be cut-ins. I thank you."

"Yoooooooooooou're *welcome!*" shouted a young man who was

standing behind Grace. He moved around and faced Grace, bowed, and said to her: "This is our encore, I believe."

"I don't think so," she said.

"No, I don't either," said the young man, who was about twenty, tall and thin, dressed in blue four-button jacket and white flannels. "See why?" She turned and Ned Minor was waiting. The young man said: "Good evening, Ned."

"Good *evening*," said Minor.

The boy next addressed Betty: "This is our encore, I believe."

"I'm sorry, but I'm waiting for my husband."

"How long have you been waiting?"

"A few minutes."

"But I've been waiting for you all my life. Come on, come on, come on, come on, come on."

"I'm sorry, but here he is," said Betty.

Grace and Minor danced away but they had gone only once around the room before the young man tapped Minor on the shoulder, and said: "Sorry, Ned."

"Sorry my eye, run along," said Minor.

"Sorry, Ned. All encores are cut-ins," said the young man. "Go to your room."

"You haven't met this lady, and what's more you're—"

"It's all right. I don't mind," said Grace.

"Good-bye, Ned," said the boy. He danced Grace away. "Thank you for interceding and welcome to our fair city. I heard there was a ball of fire coming to town, but you're stuff, Mrs. Tate, you're stuff."

"Am I?" she said. "You know my name."

"Oh. *Oh.* And you fulfill the—you don't say fulfill the bill. No. You live up to all my expectations. Why, you're the keenest, most attractive. That's no line, either. I'm as sincere as God made little apples, Mrs. Tate. Say, would you like to have a drink of whiskey with me?"

"I don't think so, thanks. I like to dance with a good dancer."

"So do I, and I am dancing with one, but most of all I want to get you off this floor and declare my admiration for you."

"Well, thank you, but you're declaring it very nicely here."

"This piece is going to end in—good! Now nobody can cut in on me. That's what I was worried about. Now I have a bottle of rye whiskey, my father's, so it's good, hidden behind a pillar, and if you'd care to join me I would like to declare my admiration for you."

"I'd rather have a cigarette."

"Yes ma'am." He led her to the end of the porch and gave her a cigarette.

"Have a drink if you like," she said.

"No, let's sit down and talk." He got two chairs and they sat down.

"How did you know my name?"

"Impossible not to know your name, Mrs. Tate. My girl is a cousin of Natalie Walker's. Mrs. Bordener. That also makes her a cousin of Ned Minor's, but Natalie's more impressed with that than I am. Ned doesn't approve of me, and I don't approve of Ned. No, that's wrong. You can't disapprove of Ned."

"Where is your girl tonight? What's her name?"

"Carolyn Walker. She's flitting about. She's not really my girl. I just say that—oh, at strange times in my life. I don't even know who she's with tonight."

"Are you away at college?"

"I am a student in questionable standing at Lafayette College, Easton, Pennsylvania, founded 1826."

"My father went there," said Grace.

"He did? How nice. Well, my father went there too. But how nice that *your* father went there. What fraternity was he?"

"Zeta Psi."

"Well, now that makes me wish I'd been a Zeta Psi, but after all Zeta Psi and Deke aren't too far apart. They get a lot of fellows we want and we get some they want."

"Yes, I've heard my father say he liked the Dekes. Was your father a Deke?"

"No, my father was Phi Delta Theta. Have you met my father and mother?"

"You haven't told me your name, you know."

"My name is Julian English. My father is Doctor English. He and Mother were at your older-set tea-fight this afternoon. I'm twenty, but that's not old enough to do a lot of things. I wasn't in the damn war . . ."

"Oh, please, Julian!"

"What? What did I say? Please, I wouldn't hurt you for the world."

"You didn't." She put her hand on his arm. "It's just that my husband wanted to get in the war, and he died before he could."

"Oh, hell, I *am* sorry."

"It's all right," she said.

He flicked his cigarette out on the lawn. "I love sitting here talking with you." He turned and smiled. "That's more than I can say about anyone else in the world at this moment."

"I love sitting with you, Julian. I'm having a better time than I expected to have," she said. "Are you only twenty?"

"That's all. How old are you?"

"Thirty-seven."

He smiled again. "Well, you could have been my mother, but I'm awfully glad you're not."

"I am too," she said, returning his smile. "I think now you'd better dance with me or take me back to my friends."

He laughed. "I think we'd better get out of *here*. Don't you?"

She laughed. "Yes, I do." She took his arm and they marched in step back to the dance floor.

"Ned Minor isn't supposed to cut in on me, but he will. You're not supposed to cut back, but if old Ned had his way there wouldn't be any cut-ins at all. Wonderful schottische dancer, Ned."

"What have you got against him?" said Grace.

"Mrs. Tate, I wish I didn't have anything against him, then I could just razz him on principle. But I have something. He told my father he thought I was too young to drive a car."

"But you're old enough to drive a car."

"I wasn't then. That was when I was twelve, and that was how my father found out I'd swiped the car when he was away."

"Julian, I'm beginning to think you're wild," said Grace.

"Not any wilder than a lot of fellows, but the trouble is I'm there when the police come."

"Maybe you shouldn't have been there in the first place."

"I don't think you mean that," the boy said.

"Why not?"

"Oh, you're too nice to take that tone. Have you any boys?"

"I have a son at Lawrenceville."

"Well, he's lucky. I don't think you'd ever lecture him just because you happen to be his mother."

"I'm stricter than you think."

"But I'll bet I'm right, no matter how strict you are, I'll bet anything you don't get your son on the carpet just to hear yourself talk like a preacher. 'O, God, in my infinite wisdom,' and so forth."

"No, but I imagine you're a handful and always have been."

"You're a nice armful and I hope you always will be," he said.

"That's getting a little fresh, isn't it?" said Grace.

"Yes, but if you keep pretending you're on *their* side I might as well be fresh."

"Julian, I don't think I've ever met anyone like you."

"I've never met anyone like you, either, so don't spoil it by—uh oh—here's a spoiler. Hello, Ned, you know you're not supposed to cut back. That's the rule."

"If Mrs. Tate hadn't wanted me to cut in she wouldn't have signaled me. Go on, now, Julian."

The three were standing near one of the open French windows. The boy looked at Grace for confirmation or denial, and when she indicated neither he smiled unpleasantly, bowed to her, and said: "Oh, hell, in *that* case . . ." and left the room.

"I wish you hadn't said that," said Grace.

"But you did nod to me," said Minor.

"But I didn't want to hurt his feelings. He's just had a little too much to drink."

"I live in Gibbsville, and we Gibbsville people don't have to be so careful of his feelings. He's riding to a fall. Wild, fresh—I don't see how his father and mother put up with him."

"Especially when he steals his father's car," said Grace.

"Oh, I suppose he made me out a tattler. Hmm. That's one side of it. But do we have to talk any more about a fresh kid? Don't forget, he was a tattler to tell you that story."

"Not the same kind of tattler, and never would be," said Grace.

"If you'd rather not dance we can sit out on the verandah. I'm very sorry I've been put in a bad light by young Mr. English." They stopped dancing and went out and sat on the porch, where Natalie had established claim on a large table. Minor addressed the Martindales, the Bordeners, and a Gibbsville couple, who were drinking highballs: "Mrs. Tate will excuse me, I'm sure." He left no doubt that he had had some sort of tiff with Grace. He nodded and was gone.

"What's eating *him?*" said Scotty.

Natalie, with her confused loyalties, said, "Nothing. I didn't notice anything."

"I didn't ask *you*," said Scotty.

"You asking me, Scotty?" said Grace.

"Well, you're the one to ask," said Scotty, laughing.

"If there was anything it's probably none of your darn business, Scotty," said Natalie.

"All right," said Scotty. "Grace, how about a highball?"

"I'll be back in a minute, if you'll excuse me," said Grace. She walked slowly all the way around three sides of the clubhouse until she could hear and see a group of men and women which included young Julian English. They were having a crap game in the driveway, in the light from the kitchen windows. "Fifty open," someone was saying. "Half a buck open."

"You're faded," said Julian. He tossed a dollar bill on the ground and picked up a fifty-cent piece. Grace moved to his side.

"Julian," she said.

He turned to look at her. "Oh, do you want to get in this?" he said. "Not *you*, Mrs. Tate."

"I'd like to talk to you," she said.

"I'm sorry, I'm busy," he said.

"I'll only keep you a minute," she said.

"Five's my point," said the man with the dice. He rolled them again. "Oh, nuts!"

"Whose dice? Yours, Julian," said someone.

Julian moved forward and picked up the dice. "I'll shoot a dollar. A buck open, who's got it?" Someone threw a dollar on the ground, and Julian rolled the dice. "Ten!"

"Four-to-one no ten," said someone, recklessly.

"For a dollar," said Julian, covering the bet. He rolled the dice again. "Ten!" he shouted. "Ten right! Stick around, Mrs. Tate, you bring me luck. Shoot, uh, what's in there? Shoot seven dollars. Seven dollars open." He kept shaking the dice near his ear until the money was covered. He ignored Grace, and she returned to Natalie's table.

"Well, I just brought somebody luck," she said.

"Who?" said Betty.

"You don't have to say it so incredulously. A boy shooting crap. He said I brought him luck," said Grace.

"Don't you think it's about time you danced with your host?" said Scotty. "I'm your host, you know."

They left before lunch the next day, making a homeward journey by way of Lykens and Millersburg. Grace sat with Betty in the back seat, and Edgar concentrated on his driving.

"You came home with Natalie, didn't you?" said Betty.

"Mr. Minor and I didn't hit it off. He was too perfect for my tastes."

"I think Natalie had him all picked out as a husband for you."

"She has to do better than that. Did you have a nice time?"

"Well, of course I know more Gibbsville people than you do."

"Yes, and I guess I didn't make a very favorable impression. At least I didn't on the two people I liked the most and the least." Grace told Betty the story of her experience with the English boy.

"Too bad," said Betty. "A thing like that can make you disappointed in the whole week-end. But at least you brought him luck, and that ought to heal his wounds. A twenty-year-old boy likes money in his pocket. I'm sure you're all forgiven."

"I'm not. I'm almost tempted to write to him."

"Well, don't do that," said Betty.

"Why not?"

"Why *not?* Are you serious? Writing to a twenty-year-old boy? Would you like to have your letter posted on the fraternity-house bulletin board?"

"I'm not at *all* sure I won't write to him," said Grace.

"Grace, sometimes I think you're coo-coo. I used to think Brock was, but now I'm beginning to think you are."

"Well, you seem determined to always have some Caldwell coo-coo. I'm sure the Bordeners are always just as sane as can be—I don't *think!* Would a man in his right mind marry Natalie?"

"She's so pretty maybe he *wasn't* in his right mind."

"Do you girls want to stop at the Delaneys'?" Edgar called back to them.

"Who are they?" said Grace.

"Mr. Delaney has something to do with the Lykens bank and he's a client of Edgar's," said Betty. "Do you want to go to the bathroom?"

"No," said Grace.

"No, we don't want to stop," Betty called to Edgar.

"Your wife thinks I'm coo-coo, Edgar, so you'd better get me home."

"She's a fine one to talk," said Edgar. "Well, be sure and wave if the Delaneys are on the porch. They know this car, and they're a nice family."

"You can tell them you couldn't stop because you had a crazy woman with you," said Grace.

———

One afternoon, while the Martindales were staying at the farm, Edgar came out from town early because of the heat. He appeared on the porch, carrying the coat of his Palm Beach suit and fanning himself with his stiff straw hat. Grace was there alone.

"Hello, Grace," he said. "You holding the fort by yourself? Where is everybody?"

"Where I'd be if I could get up enough energy. They're down at the boathouse. It *is* cooler there, under the trees and along the river. But I think I'm better off here. I think I'm much smarter than they are. They'll get cool, but then they have to trudge back up the hill, and you watch—they'll all come back and make a bee-line for the shower baths."

"Most likely. I think I'll profit by your example. I'll have a cigarette with you and then take a shower and change my clothes." He stretched out on one of the swings, lit a cigarette, wiped off his spectacles and laid them on the table beside the swing. "Lord, I'm glad you asked us out here. It was a hundred and one at Yaissle's thermometer. Oscar Tillinghast, you know—"

"The policeman," said Grace.

"Yes. He keeled over during the lunch hour."

"Sunstroke?" said Grace.

"I guess that's all. I hope so. Oscar isn't as young as he used to be."

"Who is?" said Grace.

"You are."

"Oh, no I'm not. Thanks for the compliment, but I know better."

"Oh, the pneumonia, of course."

"But I've taken so long to get well again. A year ago I would have been suggesting some mixed doubles."

"Thank the Lord you're not suggesting it today. You could count me out. As the British say, I'd stand down. But getting well's just a matter of getting enough sleep and the right things to eat. And I notice you've started smoking again, and cocktails."

"This is my first cigarette today. No, second. I had one after breakfast. And cocktails! Edgar, how many cocktails have you seen me drink since you've been here?"

"Every night before dinner you have one."

"One, and I don't always finish that," she said. "Do you and Betty worry about me, Edgar?"

"Yep," he said.

"Not only about my health, I'll bet."

"Nope," he said.

"I never get to talk with you. Betty gives me lectures, and a lot of good advice, very little of which I take. But what do *you* think I ought to do? What do *you* say about me when you and Betty talk?"

"Well, I don't know," he said. "I'm usually supposed to represent the entire male sex, Grace, and that's a large order. Betty will say something and what I say is supposed to be the masculine point of view."

"I'd like to hear what that is."

"Well, I can't tell you unless I have a specific situation where there might be two points of view, the masculine and the feminine. A lot of situations could come up where there wouldn't be any cleavage between the male and the female attitudes. They'd be the same."

"Well, as a man, do you think I'm too masculine in my behavior?"

"I think you ought to re-state that, re-phrase it."

"Well, all right. Now if a man sees a woman and is attracted to her, it's the usual masculine thing for him to go after her, isn't it?"

"In theory, yes."

"Well, I saw one one time."

"Yes," said Edgar.

"That's all."

"Oh, you want to know if I thought you were too masculine in your behavior with Roger Bannon?"

"That's one thing I'd like to know, yes."

"The answer is—my answer is—you were entirely feminine. This is 1920, and people are a little more enlightened than they were in our mother's day. All enlightened means is not superior knowledge, but just a little more honest about the motives behind our actions. What's perfume? Perfume is merely the woman's way of behaving like a man. What's a low-necked dress? The same thing. The only masculine aspect is where the woman does go after the man the way the man is expected to. In 1920 that means calling him on the telephone, pursuing him that way."

"I did that. I called him on the telephone."

"Then I suppose that has to be called masculine, Grace. That's, if you'll pardon the word, forward technique, masculine technique, as distinguished from feminine, or low-necked-dress technique. I don't suppose in our lifetime and in our civilization the woman will be able to be aggressive without being called by that old word forward. Maybe never. That takes us right down to elementals. The stallion smells the mare a mile away, and by God he goes after her. But, if you'll again pardon my frankness— whose perfume was it? The mare's, of course. I guess what people don't like, our civilization doesn't like, is that people don't think it's right for a woman to have that perfume and *also* go after the stallion. All mares are supposed to take the chance that their particular perfume will be wafted toward a near-by stallion. And when one of the mares, uh, goes all the way to the fence to make sure her perfume is carried to the stallion, the other mares get very angry and are likely to kick her to pieces."

"In a real fight horses bite, not kick. They try to break each other's legs by biting, but otherwise I think you're right," said Grace. She lit her third cigarette of the day. "I suppose you were trying to convey a warning?"

"How so?"

"Warning me that the other mares are likely to kick me to pieces."

"Well, I don't know. Maybe I was," he said.

"To stay away from Jack Hollister, that was the warning."

"Hollister?" he said.

"Edgar, you and Betty have no secrets from each other. She tells you everything, so don't pretend."

He nodded. "Yes, that's what I was trying to tell you. You mustn't start anything with Hollister."

"No, Edgar. Let's be honest."

"All right, you mustn't *continue* with Hollister, or start *again*. Hollister is private property. What's more, Grace, he's getting to be a kind of a small idol, a minor deity, or maybe a minor deity is too strong, unless you emphasize the minor. But people talk about him all the time. Everybody reads him, quotes him, misquotes him. I was talking to the Governor yesterday and I'll be damned if he didn't start telling us a story that was in the Pillbox. I didn't think the Governor read anything, including the bills he signs. Anyway, if you get mixed up with Hollister it'll be a nasty scandal, Grace, because he's a people's god. And they'll take it out on you."

"They'll kick me to pieces?"

"Yes. And not only the mares, Grace. The other stallions that can't have you."

"This metaphor, we're overworking it, considering that I never thought of myself as in pasture. But what if the gentleman wants to jump the fence, without any encouragement on my part?"

"Grace, Grace, Grace."

She laughed. "Well, at least I know where I stand with you, Edgar."

"Ma'am, I sho nuf got my woman and I aint no triflin' man. I don't believe any man that says he doesn't want you—"

"Do many say that, pray?"

"It was probably said about Cleopatra, so don't let it disturb you. But I can easily understand why a man would want to convince himself that he was impervious to your charms. Frankly, I've done it myself. I just go along in my easy-going way, thinking of you as a friend of Betty's. And I know you've never looked upon me with lust in your eye, or we wouldn't have reached this July day 1920 in our present innocent state. And may it continue that way."

"Why, you insulting son of a bitch," she said.

He laughed. "Not at all, I'm afraid of you. I'm so afraid I'm going upstairs and take a cold shower." He stood up and stretched, and hooked his forefinger in the collar of his coat and hung the coat over his shoulder.

"I have no use for a coward," she said.

He put his hand on the top of her head. "Grace, you save us for friends, Betty and me."

She reached up and patted his wrist. "Is that a warning, too? Do you think I'll need them?"

"Well, if you do, you have us."

"You think I'm going to need friends?" She held on to his wrist. "Sit down a minute, Edgar. I don't know what made me think of this." He sat on the wicker foot-rest at her feet. "One time, oh, it must have been five years ago. Before we got in the war, before I got in any trouble, when Sidney and I were just a nice married couple. One day, during the fall. October. The children were at school and I'd gone into town. It was raining that day, and I guess Sidney didn't hear the car when I got back, and I came back to that room right there, the little den. Well, I looked out that window and Sidney was sitting here on the porch and he had about a dozen pairs of shoes, his and mine and the children's, and rags and brushes and shoe-polish. That was one of the things he did on rainy days, see that the shoes got a good cleaning. Well, he was rubbing polish on a shoe and humming away, quietly. And then he stopped. He just stopped and looked out at the rain and stayed that way for two or three minutes, and I could just barely see his face, and oh, God, Edgar, how lonely he was! It was so awful to be there and see him like that. I wanted to come out and *comfort* him, and *tell* him I loved him and we all loved him. But I knew that would be wrong. I knew nobody could ever penetrate that loneliness." She began to weep, but she went on. "And all I could do was leave him there, without letting him know I'd seen him that way. That was the only thing I could do. That's all."

Edgar nodded and his eyes were full of tears. Grace had her handkerchief to her eyes.

"I don't know why I'm telling you now. Maybe what you said about needing friends. But what good did they do Sidney? We all loved him but nobody could help him. I wonder if anybody's ever seen me that way? Don't ever look at anyone you love when they think they're all alone. Don't ever let anyone see you."

"I know. I've watched faces in courtrooms, the spectators, when they were concentrating on what was going on, listening to the judge or counsel. That's what Sidney was doing, I guess. Watching a trial, but maybe it was for his own life." He stood up. "I'll go now, and I won't look through that window."

She smiled. "You wouldn't see anything. Not since that day. I don't think I've ever given anyone the chance to see me that way."

"In five years?"

"In five years."

"Nobody's ever caught you with your guard down?"

"Nobody. Except when I was delirious, and that isn't the same thing."

"No, that wasn't you. That was you and someone else. It isn't the same."

He took a shower and lay on the bed with a sheet over him and had almost dozed off when Betty came in.

"What are you smiling about, my lord and master?"

"You almost caught me with my guard down. The very thing I've been trying to avoid."

She was undressing rapidly. "What's this guard down? Oh, a shower'll feel good. It was quite nice down at the boathouse—"

"But you had to trudge back up the hill, and got hot again. Grace is right about a lot of things. I'll tell you when you've had your shower."

Betty was not entirely engrossed in the conversation. She stood naked before going into the bathroom. "I wonder if there is anything to that, that showers are bad for your breasts."

"I hope not. As I often say, you're pretty good for an old hag with three children."

She straightened up and put out her chest. "I think I am, too. Well, here goes."

He was dressed, except for his coat, when she came out of the shower, and he told her Grace's story about Sidney and some of his earlier conversation. "You fool," said Betty. "Why did you admit I blabbed everything to you?"

"You must have admitted it yourself, she was so sure."

"Maybe I did, inadvertently. She's sharp. She studies people, our Grace. Will you remind me to or will you buy me a new bathing cap tomorrow?"

He lit a cigarette and went to the window. "Brody," he said, using a private nickname.

"What?"

"We have to get Grace married, or at least get her a prospect."

"Goodness knows I've tried."

"We have to try harder."

"Why?" said Betty.

"I may be wrong, but I think she's headed for bad trouble. I didn't tell her this, but there's been some talk about her and Hollister."

"Well, it isn't true! She's told me the truth, and I'll stake my life on it."

"Nevertheless, there's been talk, and there *is* talk," he said.

"Who told you?"

"Well, I saw Charlie Jay today at the club."

"At the Fort Penn Club? Did he get in?"

"He got in. He took his chances, and there was a great deal of murmuring and grousing, but he had Brock behind him and Brock said Charlie was a damned sight better than some that were in. Well, he was there at lunch and he said he wanted to see me, so I waited for him. First crack out of the box he said, 'You tell Grace I have to have a talk with her the next time she's in town,' and I asked if he meant she was to go to City Hall and he said yes, and I laughed in his face. I told him, 'Charlie, you haven't been crowned king, you've only been elected mayor and you're not even in your second term yet.' 'I'll have my second term, don't you worry about that,' he said, and I said, 'Maybe I *will* worry about it,' and that brought him down to earth, the least little bit."

"Don't let him have it. It's bad enough to have a crook for

mayor, but an arrogant pup-crook is too much. And what about Grace?"

"Well, he said he knew we were staying out here and had more chance to talk to Grace than anyone else, so forth and so on."

"Yes?" said Betty.

"Grace is headed for a peck of trouble, he said. He said his sister-in-law, Jack Hollister's wife, was convinced that Jack was having an affair with somebody, and that that somebody was Grace."

"Oh, for goodness' sake," said Betty.

"Now wait a minute. Uh, Amy, that's Mrs. Hollister, Amy began to suspect them a couple of months ago, and one night she checked up on them. Hollister said he was going to be at the office and she found out he never went near the office, and she called Brock's house—Grace was staying there at the time—and Grace was out for the evening. Apparently Hollister must have convinced her that he hadn't been out with Grace, and she began to believe him. But then Hollister began ignoring Amy and hardly spoke to her for weeks, and she began to suspect him again, and he went away the week-end of the Fourth and never told her anything about where he was going or anything else. Well, of course I told Charlie where Grace was over the Fourth. With us. But Charlie said, rightly or wrongly, Amy suspects Grace now, and what he wanted me to do was to tell Grace that if she was mixed up in this, to stop it before there was trouble. 'What kind of trouble?' I said, and he said, 'The worst kind of trouble, the worst.' I said did he mean Amy was carrying a gun or something like that? He said not to joke about it, Grace couldn't afford another scandal. 'How afford it?' I said, and he said—and he's right, the pup—if she's the cause of the trouble between Hollister and his wife, the people in Fort Penn will rub Grace's nose in it. He said he'd known Grace all his life and been a friend of hers all his life, but now he had to remember she was ruining his wife's sister's marriage."

"And what did you say to that?"

"I told him he was a cheap busybody with an inflated ego, and if he had anything to say to Grace, say it himself, or say it to Brock. I said I wouldn't talk to Grace about it, or even mention it. Well, then he got lordly again. 'Edgar,' he said, 'you're making up your mind this minute that you're going to fight my nomination the next time, but let me tell you, if it comes to a show-down,' he said, 'with Grace on the one side, and Amy and the common people on the other, I can win without a nickel or a vote from you people.' And I'm afraid he's right. What he was implying was he'd even make that a kind of a mud-slinging issue."

"He would, too. He's capable of it."

"Then I said, 'Why not have a talk with Hollister, if you're so sure?' And I also said, if I did go to Grace, or Brock, they'd fire Hollister—"

"Not too fast, there," said Betty. "Don't forget they did actually have that one affair."

"Oh, hell, that's right," said Edgar. "Well, I said they'd fire Hollister in a minute, but Charlie said they could fire him, but that wouldn't do his votes any harm. That would *prove* that Grace was Hollister's mistress."

"And that's how mayors get elected?"

"That's one way," said Edgar.

They were busy thinking for a minute.

Edgar spoke first: "It's an interesting thing. You know a woman is always better off with a man to protect her. She can be somebody's mistress, and everybody can know about it, but if her husband stays married to her, it is protection. Once she loses her husband, in the mind of the public she's a whore. It's morality in the mass, and hypocritical and inconsistent, but it's a fact. And the Lord knows Brock's no protection. He's never been taken seriously since his father died. *He* had to have the protection of a man."

"That's why we have to get Grace married."

"There's another reason, too, Bordy."

"What's that?"

"A selfish one. If Charlie Jay *should* win an election, with what he calls the common people versus the aristocracy, this town will go to hell so fast that we won't know what happened to us. The people aren't going to win anything. They'll lose. It's people like Brock and Mr. Partridge, and me in my small way, that keep the fear of God in those thieves, the organization. I don't say the respectable element are respectable out of lofty principle, but at least we don't countenance the kind of looting that'll go on if Charlie's elected in spite of us. Charlie's a cheap crook. He wouldn't know how to go about the big stuff. But those boys that hang around the Rathskeller, if they think they can win against us they'll bankrupt the city in two years. Our bonds won't be worth anything, real estate will go to hell, so will the schools, the water, public health. Suddenly I can't believe we're living in the twentieth century."

"Well, it's slipping away by the minute, and we're going to be late for dinner."

"I hope Grace has some other guests."

"Brock and his French pastry, they're coming."

"I think I'll have three Martini cocktails, one right after the other."

"Then *you'll* slip away by the minute," said Betty.

"Would I be missed?" said Edgar.

"The first second."

———

Hollister came home one evening and he thought he noticed something strange about the house, even before he got out of his car. It was something about the lighting of the house. It was August, a few minutes past seven o'clock, and the kitchen lights should have been on, and were not; the upstairs lights should have been on, and were not. The light was on in the front room, and someone, a man, was sitting in his chair. "Someone's sitting in *my* chair," he said, in the tone that he often had used for the story of the bears and Goldilocks.

The someone was Amy's father, who did not rise when Hollister entered.

"Hello, Mr. Clarke. Here for supper?"

"No," said Clarke. "I guess there won't be any supper here this evening, unless you care to get it yourself."

"How come? Where's Amy?"

The visitor emptied his pipe in the ash tray. "Amy's gone home."

"To *your* home. *This* is *her* home."

"Sit down, John," said Clarke. There was a notable hesitation before he spoke Hollister's first name. He put the pipe back in a side pocket of his dark gray suit, crossed his legs, and stuck a thumb between his white cotton sock and high black kid shoe. "Young fellow, we have to have a talk, us two. Maybe we should of before this, but I'm against butting in between two married people. What are you doing to Amy?"

"Doing to Amy? Nothing. But before you say any more, maybe you *are* butting in."

"I know that now. I know I'm butting in. On purpose. When Amy comes home like today, I have to think of her as my daughter. So I'll butt in. I'd like to see anybody try to stop me from butting in."

"Well, what do you want to know, Mr. Clarke?"

"I want to know what makes my daughter so miserable she comes back to my house, with her two children. What's going on here that this house don't mean home to her?"

"Well, now, you said a minute ago you thought you should have butted in before, so you must know something. You weren't surprised."

"I knew there was trouble, but the family that don't have some troubles I've yet to meet them. So I stayed out of it. But I can't stay out of it when it comes to where my daughter has to leave her own home and come to mine."

"I don't know what you expect me to say."

"I expect you to be a man. Is that a man, that's such a poor husband that his wife up and leaves him? Is that all you think of Amy and the youngsters? What's the matter with you, anyway? Don't you have no decency?"

"I want to know what Amy had to tell you."

"You could find that out quick enough by going to my house. But *I* want to find out whether I'll let you *in*. Amy'd let you in, but the way things are now I'd as lief slam the door in your face. Amy's a woman, your wife, and loves you, but I don't love you, God knows. The way you're treating her, I'd as soon shoot you as sit here in your own house and look at you, a stuck-up woman chaser."

"Did you bring a gun?" said Hollister.

Clarke sat perfectly still for a few seconds. "Yes, I'm ashamed to say I did. And with the intention of using it. But the trolley-ride out give me the chance to think things over. You dead, and me going to the electric chair is no help or solution for Amy. If *you* want to live like an animal is no reason why the rest of us have to . . . I'll go now."

"Wait a minute," said Hollister. "What did you come out here for?"

Clarke was standing, leaning over to pick up his hat. "I left my house to kill you, then I thought it over and decided I wouldn't, but the longer I stay here with the gun in my pocket the closer I get to my original intentions."

"You'd better give me the gun then."

Clarke nodded. "Yes, I better. I might come back." He took a .32 Smith & Wesson out of his hip pocket and tossed it into the chair where he had been sitting.

Hollister picked it up and broke it and extracted the five cartridges, which he held in his hand. "Sit down a minute, Mr. Clarke."

"What good'll that do?"

"Well, more good than shooting me."

"I have my doubts," said Clarke.

"You're a religious man, and I'm not."

"I was a religious man till this evening. Now I'm just like anybody that never heard of God."

"That makes it easier to talk to you," said Hollister.

"All right," said Clarke.

"Put the revolver back in your pocket. I'll keep the cartridges for the time being," said Hollister. Clarke sat down and Hollister did likewise. "Mr. Clarke, this is man-to-man. I'm not saying Amy did or didn't have any right to leave this house the way she did. By that I mean, I'm not admitting or denying that I treated her in such a way as to cause her to leave. That's between Amy and me, and always will be. But all question of guilt or innocence to one side, do you honestly think, as a religious man, do you honestly believe a woman has the *right* to leave her husband, no matter how good or bad he was? Do you believe that? Don't you believe the wife, when she marries her husband, doesn't she make a contract to stay with him, no matter what happens? For richer, for poorer? In sickness and in health? Does that only mean financially, the kind of sickness the doctor has to treat? I'm not a religious man, but I've listened to religious people talk, and they often say it doesn't only mean that kind of sickness. That it means whatever happens. Even if the man and wife aren't getting along together, they're supposed to stay married. That's what I was brought up to believe, and that's what you taught Amy and Louise. Isn't that right?"

"That's what they were taught."

"Well, if you taught them that you must have believed it and made them believe it. But as man to man I ask you, what good is it? Is it just so much talk? Now wait before you say anything. I want to ask you a question. What good are those beliefs if the wife leaves the husband the first time they're put to any test? It's all right to go on saying you believe those things, those principles, as long as everything's going smoothly, but what about when a man and wife run into difficulties? What happens to the principles then? Do you stand by them, or do you admit that they're just so much talk—all right for them when all is peaceful and serene, but no good when they're put to the test. In other words, Mr. Clarke, do you think Amy abided by her principles?"

"If you look at it that way, no."

"I'm not saying how I look at it. I'm asking you how you look at it."

"That's what I meant," said Clarke. "But—"

"No, Mr. Clarke. Not but. You were going to say Amy may have had reason to leave this house. I won't argue that. I won't argue it, because I won't discuss it. We agreed, you and I agreed, that we were talking about the principles, not about whether I gave her cause to leave. You agreed with me that that was between Amy and me, and always will be. That's between husband and wife. All I want you to go away remembering is whether the wife had the right to leave her husband."

"A person can only stand so much," said Clarke.

"I don't agree with you. There's no limit to what he or she has to stand if the principles are involved. Rather than break up a home the wife or the husband has to stand unlimited sorrow and trouble."

"Would you stand unlimited trouble?" said Clarke.

"Mr. Clarke, I keep telling you, we're not *talking* about me. We're talking about the principles, the religious beliefs. The right of the wife to leave the husband. If we start talking about me, and whether I'm a good husband or a bad husband, we'll have to go back over every day since Amy and I were married—*the good things as well as the bad,* Mr. Clarke. The richer *and* the poorer. I don't go to church often, but I have principles and I've lived by them. All you know is that Amy got sore at me and left this house and took the children. But where's the principle there? I came home expecting to find Amy and the children here as usual, so that ought to prove I had nothing on my conscience. I came home for supper, expecting to find my wife and children, but instead of that I find my father-in-law here with a gun. Where are the principles there? I had nothing to fear, or I wouldn't have come home. I had nothing to fear from your gun, or I wouldn't have asked you to give it up. I didn't fight to take it away from you. I *asked* you to hand it to me. Here, here are your cartridges ... You tell Amy everything we've talked about. I'm going to cook myself something to eat, and if she wants to come home tonight, nothing'll be said, at least by me. And if she wants to sleep at your house, I'll get my own breakfast. You just tell Amy *this* is *my* home, not where my mother lives, or my father used to live."

Clarke reinserted the cartridges in the revolver, saying, "I'll tell her all you said, John, about the principles."

"And anything else you care to."

"Only about the principles. That'll be enough for her." The aging carpenter studied the revolver a moment, then put it back in his pocket. "I'll only be able to make her believe what I believe myself."

"That's all I want you to do."

"Oh, I'm not doing it because you want me to." He lifted his hat half way to his head, hesitated, smiled contemptuously, and finished putting the hat on.

Hollister was still asleep when Amy came in their room on the following morning. She made no extra effort to be quiet, and he got awake. She was changing to her gingham wrap-around. "Are you getting up?" she said.

"What did you think I was doing?"

"Search me," she said.

"What would I find if I searched you?"

"I guess nothing you don't find on some other woman."

"A gun, maybe," he said. "Where are the children?"

"I left them at their Grandma Clarke's."

"If I hadn't married you I could make a joke about Grandfather Clarke's," he said. "In my column."

"You make it around here often enough. You're feeling very good this morning."

"Christ, why shouldn't I? I'm lucky to be alive. Old men coming around with guns in their pockets."

"The children don't know why I took them to their grandparents'."

"That's nothing. I don't either."

"No, I guess not. Any more than you understand why I came

back." She paused in the tying of her shoe. "My poor father, trying to make me believe in principles, and doubting them himself."

"What the hell made you fly the coop yesterday, if I may be so
bold as to inquire?"

"Oh, nothing, only this." She opened the drawer of the
chiffonier, where lay a box of contraceptive apparatus. "Sooner
or later you'd leave one around. I stopped looking for them long
ago. I thought maybe she was getting too old to have children,
but I guess not. Will you take these out of this house?"

"Some day maybe you'll know how wrong you are."

"Oh, cut it out," she said. "What wonders me is why you got Pop
to make me come back. For the sake of appearances? Is that why?"

"Yes."

"Why do you care anything about appearances? You could
marry your lady friend and have all the appearances you want.
Big automobiles, and a farm with a swimming pool and all that."

"Listen, get Grace Tate out of your crazy mind, will you?"

"You get her out for me. Will you swear on your father's honor
that you never did it with her? Your father's honor's just about the
only thing you have respect for. Go ahead, swear it, and get her
out of my crazy mind."

"I wouldn't take that kind of an oath."

"You *can't*, that's why, and you know it and I know it just by looking at you. So I'll keep her in my crazy mind. Tell her I'll divorce
you when my father dies, not before. But he's hale and hearty and
maybe by that time she'll want another younger fellow."

He met Mary Kemper that evening and showed her a note he
had received in the afternoon mail. It was from Ed Wachtel.

Dear Jack:
   *Much as I dislike intruding my senile presence in the garden of love, I
am compelled to advise you that I shall be returning to Fort Penn during
the first or second week in September. As my return will be of a permanent
nature I regret to inform you that it will necessitate the termination of our*

present arrangement, if you know what I mean. Pending my return I trust
that you will continue to enjoy the remaining hours.

Cordially yours,
Ed.

P.S. If what a small bird has whispered to me is true, I should think that
the other party to the arrangement would have no more difficulty in re-
establishing yourselves than the mere stroke of a pen. I am proud of you
for aiming so high and for hitting the bull's eye, if I may be indelicate. Fur-
thermore, it gives me great vicarious pleasure to have been of assistance.

E. W.

"What does he mean by all that bushwa?" said Mary.
"Well, at least we have two or three more weeks here."
"No, but the postscript," said Mary. "He doesn't mean me."
"I guess he means Grace Tate."
"Grace Tate? Why do they connect you up with her? I'll begin
to believe it myself pretty soon."
"You'd never believe it," he said.

In the days of the autumn Hollister frequently thought of himself as an onlooker, watching the slow destruction of his marriage to Amy and the improvement in his work and the maturing
of his love for Mary. It was possible for him to see that week by
week it was Mary who was becoming his woman and that in a few
months he had experienced with Mary the best, or at least the
pleasantest, stages of his life with Amy; from the early excitement to the deliberate passion and the mutual trust and acceptance of one another. They now met for love-making in the
home of a man named Nick Lucci, a neighborhood grocer in the
Italian section of Fort Penn, who conducted a wine and grappa
business in a back room, behind the grocery store, and, for high-
class men like Hollister, would provide a clean bedroom on the
second floor of the house. Lucci had no personal curiosity about
Mary, and in some ways the arrangement was superior to that

with Ed Wachtel; Mary would wait in the car until Hollister cased the back room, and when the coast was clear he would tell Mary. Wachtel's flat was in a neighborhood where there was always a chance of encountering friends. The only interruption they ever had at Nick's was caused by one of the Lucci children who knocked on the door and asked them to give him his speller and arithmetic books.

As for Amy, she had settled into a grim impersonal relationship with Hollister, in which she avoided calling him by name and kept to an absolute minimum even the essential exchanges. She would say, at the supper table, "We'll have to ask your father for ten dollars extra this week to buy some shoes for you two, and stockings," or, "There's a sale on at the Boston Store, if your father wants to buy himself some new shirts." Their daughter Joan was in Miss Holbrook's School (she had been accepted without delay or question; Betty Martindale had seen to that), their son was at Northend public school, and Amy had taken up bridge. There was only one flare-up. "I have something I want to tell you," said Amy one night when they were in the twin beds that they now occupied.

"What?"

"I don't care what people say about you behind your back, or what you do. But just remember this: don't you and your friend be seen in public. I don't have to stand for that."

"What brought *that* on?"

"You were talking to her at the hotel yesterday."

"Who?"

"You know who. The Tate woman."

"Mrs. Tate was at the hotel yesterday, with five other women. I said hello to all but one and I was introduced to her. A nice old lady from New York."

"Yes, you and your nice old ladies. Well, just remember, Joan's in that school and I don't want the other children making remarks."

"Ah, pipe down," he said.

In that spirit and temper they came to the twenty-fifth of November, Thanksgiving of 1920; a cloudy day from the Alleghenies to the Atlantic, and in Worcester, Massachusetts, a day so miserable with snow that Holy Cross called off its football game with Fordham, but there was no snow in central and southern Nesquehela County, and the game between Fort Penn University and Bucknell took place as scheduled.

The Martindales were passing Thanksgiving Eve at home. "Which do you want to do tomorrow, go to the football game, or Grace's?" said Betty.

"Grace is expecting us, isn't she?"

"She's invited a lot of people, so it won't make any difference if we don't show up," said Betty.

"I don't think it'll be a very good game. Bucknell ought to beat Fort Penn without any trouble. I'd rather go to Grace's. I haven't been to a turkey shoot since Sidney died."

"There hasn't been one."

"That's what I mean. I think everybody ought to go. It's nice of Grace, I think. Those parties were always fun, even for Sidney. He did most of the work, but he enjoyed it, it gave him pleasure."

"*Even* for Sidney? *Especially* for Sidney," said Betty. "Only— didn't he used to have them on Election Day?"

"Election Day?" said Edgar. "You're right, he certainly did. He had them on Election Day. Now isn't that strange? Do you 'spose Grace thinks they were on Thanksgiving Day? She couldn't make a mistake like that."

"Not a woman that runs her house as well as Grace does," said Betty. "No, I think she probably remembered it on Election Day this year, and decided Thanksgiving would be as good a time. And I must say I agree with her."

"Why?"

"Well, isn't it nice to have something to do Thanksgiving afternoon, instead of lying around stuffed with turkey, or going to a Fort Penn football game? Most of us have dinner at one o'clock and nothing to do all afternoon after that. This way we'll at least get some fresh air."

The Martindales, children included, sat down to their Thanksgiving dinner at twelve-thirty and in spite of the parents' precept and example in the matter of masticating the food and not eating so fast, the mince pie and plum pudding were on the table at ten minutes past one, at which point Edgar was notified that he was wanted on the telephone by Mr. Brock Caldwell.

"Edgar, this is Brock, I hope you weren't just this minute sitting down to dinner."

"We're just about getting up. What's on your mind?"

"Well, I'm sorry I took you away from your mince pie, but could you do me a favor?"

"Sure, I could do you lots of favors, Brock. What one do you want today?"

"Well, I'll tell you. I went over to the *Sentinel* office this morning, you know, to get the score sheets for this afternoon, and I ran into Jack Hollister. You know Jack. And I invited him and his wife to come out to the farm this afternoon."

"Oh, *you did?*"

"Now don't sound so Christ-almighty judiciary, will you? That's exactly the reason why I invited them."

"What's exactly the reason?"

"Oh, to put a stop to this talk about him and Grace. I know damn well there's nothing to it and so do you, and I think if people saw Jack and his wife together, with Grace there, everybody'd know in a minute how silly the talk is."

"I'll bet four hundred thousand dollars you haven't discussed this with Grace," said Edgar.

"Well, you're right. It'll look more natural—it'll *be* more natural, if they just appear at the farm. And you know Grace. Good hostess and very charming when she wants to be."

"I think you're nutty, but what has Mrs. Hollister said about this?"

"Well, we haven't been able to get her on the telephone. Hollister thinks she's on her way to her mother's house, so I thought if you could give Hollister a lift out to the farm, *I'd* stop and pick up Mrs. Hollister, and that'd make everything hunky-dory. There'd be Grace's brother, don't you know, playing the host to Mrs. Hollister, and so forth and so on. I might say, by the way, Hollister is all for the idea. Naturally we didn't discuss the gossip, but he could read between the lines, he knew what I was aiming at. The fellow has an absolutely clear conscience, and I'm no fool about such things, Edgar."

"Oh, no. Of course not," said Edgar. "I never thought Hollister was a fool, either—till now. Now, listen, Brock, what you call my judiciary mind makes me ask this question: why isn't Hollister having Thanksgiving dinner with his wife and family?"

"He was working. That's how I happened to see him. He was at the office, working."

"That isn't a very satisfactory answer. Why doesn't he finish his work and go to his mother-in-law's?"

"Now listen, Edgar, I'm his boss, aren't I? Well, his boss told him he could take the afternoon off. It's as simple as that."

"It's too simple for me, but I guess it's gone too far to do anything about it now," said Edgar.

"Edgar, you may be a very good lawyer and all that, but I know more about other kinds of intrigue than you'll ever know. Now be a good fellow and you and Betty drive that cheap, broken-down car of yours over to the *Sentinel* and Hollister'll be waiting for you."

Betty's amazement was profound and angry. "Brock and his damned meddling. Grace was all right. I know it. I talked to her only last week and she told me Hollister's out of her life. She *told* me, Edgar. God *damn* that Brock Caldwell! She said she supposed if Hollister came and played the mandolin under her balcony she might raise the window a little higher, but she said she wasn't going to pursue him. She *joked* about it. Well, the only thing I can do is call her and warn her."

"Do you think that's a good idea?" said Edgar.

"Are you crazy too?" She went to the telephone and the maid got Grace. Betty told Grace, who listened without interruption until Betty was finished.

"Well," said Grace. "There isn't much to say or do, is there? I can't very well call the Hollisters one by one and disinvite them. Tell Edgar he may have to defend a woman for accidentally-on-purpose shooting her brother."

"I wouldn't blame you a bit. I'm not going to so much as touch a gun or I'd shoot Brock myself."

"Poor Brock," said Grace. "He wants everything to be so nice and neat."

"Grace, what if we just whizz by the *Sentinel* office and pretend we couldn't find Hollister?"

"Yes, but Brock isn't going to whizz by and not pick up Mrs. Hollister. You know Brock. He has a manner. He'll go to Mrs. Hollister's mother's house, and be so polite and nice and she won't be able to refuse him. And after that it'll be up to me. All I can say is thank God we're expecting a lot of people. At least forty coming. It's going to be like the Battle of the Marne here this afternoon. Who won the Battle of the Marne? Did we win it?"

"Grace, I love you," said Betty. "I never liked you as much as I do this minute."

"Thanks, Betty, and thanks for forewarning me," said Grace. "I'll brazen this out."

"Good girl," said Betty.

It would have been impossible to whizz by and pretend not to find Hollister; the Martindales could see him a block away, standing in front of the *Sentinel* office. He was wearing a trench coat—in point of fact not the one he had worn on active service; it was a more recent purchase, for military funerals and parades—and smoking a cigarette without taking his hands out of his pockets. They drew alongside the curb and he got in. Betty, in the divided front seat on the right, sat with her arm on the back of the seat in an attitude of courtesy to Hollister in the rear of the tonneau.

"This is very kind of you, to give me a ride," said Hollister.

"Not at all," said Edgar. "Glad to. Do you like to shoot?"

"Well, I'm not very good with a shotgun. That's what this is, isn't it?" said Hollister.

"Yes, you've seen these turkey shoots, haven't you?"

"Yes, but they're all different," said Hollister.

"They are?" said Betty, not very politely.

"Yes, some are with rifle," said Edgar.

"With a rifle?" said Betty.

"Yes," said Hollister. "They put the turkey in a box, behind thick planking, with just his head showing, and the first one to shoot the head off wins. It's against the law, but it's still done, at private shoots."

"Well, this is a private shoot, of course, but Mr. Caldwell and Mrs. Tate would never go in for that kind of thing. *That* is *horrible,* I think."

"It is, but it's the only chance I'd have. That's one thing about the Marine Corps. They teach you to shoot with a rifle."

"Not at turkeys' heads, I hope," said Betty.

"No," said Hollister. He knew he was being snubbed, but he refused to take offense.

"What *did* you shoot at?" said Betty.

"If you mean at Parris Island, we shot at target and at figures the size of a man."

"Oh, and then did you shoot at men over there?" said Betty.

"Yes, ma'am," said Hollister.

"Germans?" said Betty.

"For the most part."

"How do you mean for the most part?"

"Well, we tried to shoot more Germans than Americans."

"Mr. Hollister, I think you're kidding me," said Betty.

"And succeeding very well," said Edgar. "Don't forget, Mr. Hollister's a humorist."

"Oh, *I* know *that,*" said Betty. "But now tell me more, Mr. Hollister. Did you ever kill a German?"

"Yes, ma'am."

"Oh, you *did?*"

"Yes, ma'am."

"With a rifle?" said Betty.

"Yes, with a rifle."

"You say that as though you'd killed them with something else, too. What else?"

"Pistol."

"Oh, you carried a pistol too?"

"We all did. Officers carried pistols, .45 caliber automatics, and other personnel carried rifle and pistol, or machine gun and pistol. Everybody was issued a pistol."

"I hate to sound so bloodthirsty, but didn't you just tell me you killed a German with a rifle? I thought you were an officer. Didn't I read that you were an officer? On one of those billboards with your picture?"

"I was, but you see, ma'am, in battle there isn't anybody going around taking notes on officers that carry a rifle. In other words, Mrs. Martindale, in battle you do what you think best, for your own protection. Sometimes you didn't *have* to use a rifle, or you didn't think it was best for your own protection. You can imagine a situation where a pistol would be enough, I'm sure. For instance, if it wasn't a question of life or death I only carried my pistol. And also, sometimes when I had my pistol *and* my rifle I didn't use them. I waited till I was ready to use them. You see what I mean?"

"Oh, of course, Mr. Hollister. I see exactly what you mean. You make it very clear. If you thought your enemy could be, uh, disposed of with just the pistol you didn't bother with the rifle."

"Right."

"But of course you have to admit you were quite lucky, weren't you?"

"Well, I suppose so. It depends on how you look at it. I wasn't shot by an individual German. I was wounded by shrapnel. But I *was wounded.*"

"Shrapnel," said Betty. "They had to use a cannon to shoot you, didn't they?"

"Speaking of shrapnel," said Edgar, "if I may interrupt this very warlike conversation, I'll tell you the rules for this afternoon, Mr. Hollister."

"Good."

"We use 12-gauge shotguns, and we take a wad, about the size of a nickel, and glue it to a board at twenty paces. A wad for each contestant, or as many wads as you want to buy chances. Clear so far?"

"Yes sir."

"You fire your gun and whoever has the wad with the most shot, he wins. You count the perforations and that decides the winner. The money, by the way, goes to the Becksville Sunday School. Mrs. Tate and Mr. Caldwell don't make anything on it." Edgar's attempt to be funny was too soon after the clash between Betty and Hollister to be successful.

"And is there betting on the high gun?" said Hollister.

"Oh, yes, quite a good deal."

"Then I'll bet on Mrs. Martindale."

"Why would you bet on me, Mr. Hollister? For all you know I've never held a shotgun in my hand in my whole life."

"Just a hunch that you'd be a very good shot."

"Really? Well, unfortunately I'm not shooting this afternoon, so you'll have to back someone else." She slowly lowered her arm, discontinuing the attitude of courtesy, and Hollister settled back in his seat. The few remaining miles were traveled in silence.

They stayed in the car until Edgar parked it with others in the barnyard. "Contest doesn't start till three o'clock," said Edgar. "But drinks are being served, if you'd care to join us in violating the law."

"That suits me," said Hollister.

"I see Grace," said Betty. "She's with those people at the spring-house."

There were about thirty persons at or near the spring-house, representing the higher sporting life of Nesquehela County. Betty Martindale and three other women carried shooting-sticks; several women were in riding breeches, as were most of the men, whose breeches belonged to their officers' uniforms. Some of the men likewise wore field boots from the war, others wore high-laced hunting boots and some wore knickerbockers and plaid stockings and thick-soled shoes with fringed tongues. Hollister was in the minority by wearing a trench coat; the others, men and women, wore camel's hair coats or tweed. Dr. O'Brien, in fact, wore a long tweed greatcoat with a short attached cape. The men's and women's stockings and the women's coats and scarves provided welcome spots of bright color in the scene; the day was overcast and cold, with a continuing threat of snow, and the life had gone out of the greens and browns of the trees and hedges and pasture land. Some of the guests already were gathered about a good-sized bonfire and most of the others were staying close to the spring-house, where there was a stand with a two-gallon coffee pot kept warm by a kerosene stove, piles of sandwiches wrapped in waxed paper, tin coffee cups, and bottles of whiskey and brandy, and shot-glasses. The stand—planks on horses—was set up on the concrete flooring near the door of the spring-house, two steps below the ground level. Grace, with a cigarette in her mouth and her head at an angle to keep the smoke out of her eyes, was sitting behind the refreshment stand, checking off the names of the guests who had entered the shoot. Sitting beside her, smoking a rough-bowl pipe, was Ham Schoffstal. He was peering over her shoulder at the list. He put his finger on the list, and Grace nodded and called out: "George Wall hasn't paid. Come here George Wall, and pay up. Joe Cunningham, you too—come and pay up. All those who haven't paid might as well do so now. Worthy charity, everybody." The others took up the call to pay up. "Ah, there's George," said Grace. "Did you think you were going to get away with something?"

"Well, I tried my best. What is it, two dollars?"

"One dollar for each shot," said Grace.

"Oh, aren't you clever? And most of us have double-barrelled guns, so you take two dollars, hey?" said George.

"Unless you have a pump gun. Ham had to pay five dollars, so there," said Grace.

"Where's the turkey?" said Joe Cunningham. "I don't think I'll pay up till I see the turkey."

"I have a notion to charge you extra for that remark," said Grace. "The turkey is alive and crated and eating my food, *my corn.*"

"I wish he'd eat my corn," said Cunningham, holding up his foot in a field boot. "I think my feet must have gotten smaller since the Army."

"What a terrible joke," said Grace. "Two dollars, thank you. Two from you, Joe? Thank you. Anyone else on our list?"

"Emlen Deatrick," said Ham.

"Emlen Deatrick!" Grace called. "Em-len Dea-trick."

The others were repeating Deatrick's name and suddenly they stopped, with the arrival near the spring-house of the Martindales and Hollister. Over the silence was the echoing of Deatrick's name, and only those few men and women in complete control of their manners restrained themselves from staring as Grace greeted the newcomers.

"Hello, Bet, Edgar—hello, Jack." Grace had her list in one hand and her cigarette in the other. She spoke Hollister's first name distinctly, and said, "Ham, you two know each other."

"Oh, sure. How are you, Hollister?" said Schoffstal.

"How do you do?" said Hollister, simultaneously. They did not shake hands.

"Your wife isn't here yet," said Grace. "I guess Brock had to stop for something or other."

"They were starting later," said Hollister.

"Well, Edgar, did you bring a gun?" said Grace.

"No, you said I could borrow one."

"Of course I did. But you have to pay. Two dollars, please. Jack, would you like to borrow a gun?"

"I—guess I'd better not, thanks."

"Betty?" said Grace.

"No gun, thanks," said Betty. "But I'll give you a dollar for a drink of whiskey. I'm cold."

"Already?" said Edgar.

"The difference between you and me is I admit I'm cold. You men have to pretend you don't mind this weather. It's eggy."

"I'll admit it," said Hollister. "I'll give a dollar for a drink. I'll even buy you one, Mrs. Martindale."

Partly because of the actual words that reached the other guests, and partly because of the apparently casual manner of Grace and the persons surrounding her, the attitude of the others began to relax, ever so slightly at first, but increasingly so as Grace poured drinks. But the little groups held to themselves, did not open a place for Hollister. Betty moved away and joined one of the groups; Edgar, with more sense of social responsibility, remained with Hollister, who leaned against the spring-house with a glass in his hand. Grace was kept moderately busy for the next ten minutes with her list of competitors and her position as hostess. Edgar filled in the ten minutes with a repetition of the rules, and a visit to the shooting grounds with Hollister. They returned to the spring-house just as Brock and his French woman arrived.

"Jack, I'm awfully sorry, but your wife said she couldn't come. We tried our best to persuade her, but she felt she couldn't leave."

"That's too bad," said Grace. "Then I guess we'll have to start. It's past three, isn't it?"

"Yes," said Brock. He took the list and began calling out the names in the order of their listing. He finished the reading and said, "Now we all know who's to shoot when. Ham will start off and next after him is, uh, George. George Wall. All right, Ham. Good luck."

The guests took positions to watch the beginning of the shooting, and Brock unobtrusively made his way to Hollister's side. He pretended to be watching Schoffstal and to be explaining, with gestures, what Ham was aiming at and trying to do, but in a low tone he said, "I'm sorry it didn't work out the way I wanted it to."

"So am I," said Hollister.

"Uh—it isn't only that she wouldn't come," said Brock.

"No? What else?" said Hollister.

"Well—she made quite a scene," said Brock. "I was wondering if it wouldn't be a good idea for you to call her up."

"What did she say?"

"A lot of things she didn't mean. She went off the handle. It was my fault, Jack, and I'm terribly sorry."

"No it wasn't your fault," said Hollister. "It was a damn decent thing for you to do, all around. What did she say?" Brock, so precise and neat in his polo coat and a hat with a feather in the band, was obviously distressed by what must have been a uniquely disorderly encounter with Amy.

"Oh—do I have to tell you? You're a writer. You can imagine the sort of thing. She implied that I was trying to bribe her—with I don't know what. Talk about social position, you know."

"Where was all this?"

"On the porch at your father-in-law's house."

"Charlie Jay and his wife there?" said Hollister.

"Yes, I saw Charlie in the front room. He didn't come out, but I saw him. Do you want to come up to the house and call her up? I really think you'd better, Jack."

"What could I say to her?"

"Well—explain that this is just an innocent gathering. Not the kind of wild party she made it out to be. I don't think she believes that, but it's what she said."

"All right."

The two men went up to the house and Hollister followed Brock into the den and gave the Clarkes' number. Louise answered.

"Louise, this is Jack. Let me talk to Amy."

"She isn't here."

"Where is she? Did she go home?"

"She went home to get her things, but she won't be there long. Who do you think you are, trying to parade your wife before that woman and those friends of hers? Your father never fell for them, but you—you fell for them and you even want to make a fool out of your own wife, in front of them. Wait a minute, Charlie wants to talk to you."

"Hello," said Hollister.

"Jack, this is Charlie. I'm warning you, you went too far this time. Amy doesn't have to stand for that. You take my advice and get out of there and get the hell home or you're going to have a lot of trouble on your hands. You don't seem to realize—"

"I realize you and your wife have been making Amy think—"

"Now listen to me, I don't have to take any crap from you. You better watch what you're saying. If it wasn't for me, Amy—"

"Oh, balls," said Hollister. He hung up the receiver.

"Not very satisfactory, eh?" said Brock.

"He may be right, though. He said I ought to go to my house. That's where my wife is now. Is there a car I could borrow, Mr. Caldwell?"

"Oh, sure. By all means. My little Ford's right outside in the driveway. Take *it*. You explain to her, will you? I thought she'd welcome the chance to—well, you know what I'm driving at."

"I'll go and say good-bye to Mrs. Tate," said Hollister. "Uh—is that whiskey in that decanter? I'm half way between God-damn mad at Charlie and his wife, and my own wife, and going out there in front of all your friends—"

"A drink'll do us both good."

He took the stopper out of the decanter and they drank a couple of ounces apiece. "The old-timers used to say when women were gone, we'd still have our whiskey, but now they're trying to take that away. By God, I'll have my little nip or else move out of the country. Well, shall we go?"

They heard a car in the driveway but Brock said he would greet the latecomers at the range. Brock took Grace by the arm and drew her away from the group of spectators, who had just cheered Scotty Bordener derisively for some bad marksmanship. Brock and Grace came to Hollister, near the spring-house.

"I'm sorry you have to go, Jack," said Grace. She put out her hand.

"Well, it's better for me to go now, I guess. Mr. Caldwell will give you the de—" Hollister was looking at Grace, who now abruptly stopped smiling and frowned, her attention focusing on something over Hollister's shoulder.

"Look out!" she said, and pushed Hollister to one side, as a shot, sharper and higher in pitch than the reports of the guns, went off.

Hollister and Brock turned around and saw Amy with a .45 wobbling in her hand. The weapon, three pounds in weight, almost jumped out of her hand at the second and third reports. She was standing about twenty yards away from the threesome and Hollister got to her in two seconds and knocked her wrist with his fist, the pistol falling to the ground. He picked it up and put it in his pocket.

Amy laughed. "I saw you, you whore. You pushed him out of the way," she said.

The invited guests at the firing-line had turned at the first pistol shot and were watching the incident in fascinated confusion. Grace went to Amy, who was being pulled away by Hollister. "Wait a minute," said Grace. "What's the matter with you, you crazy-woman? Of course I pushed him out of the way. Give her her gun."

"No," said Hollister.

"No, no," said Brock. "She'd kill you."

"No, she wouldn't. *She* wouldn't. She wasn't going to kill anybody, and she knows I know it. She lost her nerve. Didn't you, Amy?"

"Thanks, Grace," said Hollister.

"Let me have the gun again, if you're so sure," said Amy.

"You'd better take her away, Hollister," said Brock.

Amy faced the spectators. "*Look* at you! *Look* at you!"

"Oh, take her away, will you please?" said Grace. She looked at Brock and turned her head to indicate the spectators. He nodded, and she walked alone to the house. Hollister got a firm grip on Amy's arm and led her, muttering but unresisting, to their car. Brock waited until they were out of sight behind the big house and then moved a few steps closer to the spectators. "Ladies and gentlemen," he began. He held out his hands, shrugged his shoulders, and let his hands drop. Edgar Martindale came forward to Brock, while Betty went to the house.

Edgar faced the group. "Ladies and gentlemen, we all know what Brock wants to say. We're all friends of Grace's and Brock's. Guests of theirs. With the duties and responsibilities of guests toward people who've been kind and gracious through many years. Brock, I know I speak for everyone here, every single one of us—we'll leave you now, because there are too many of us—but we'll honor our responsibility as guests. Keep this to ourselves. And all here will give thanks that no worse consequences happened from this—this rash act of a foolish woman. Ladies and gentlemen, let's go home quietly now—and let's remember that ladies and gentlemen do observe certain rules regarding what happens when they're guests in a friend's house."

"Hear, hear!" said Ham Schoffstal. He clapped his hands, and since the gesture was at least an action and seemed to express approval, it was repeated by the others. The French woman, who had joined Brock during the departure of Hollister and Amy, linked her arm with his and walked with him to the house.

It was almost half an hour before the last car drove out of the barnyard and down the lane to the pike, and not until then did Grace come downstairs. Brock and his lady friend, Edgar and Betty were in the den.

"Oh, Betty, Edgar, I didn't know you stayed," said Grace. "Brock, will you give me a highball, please?"

"I'll get it," said Edgar. "Scotch and soda?"

"Please," said Grace. "What do you think I ought to do? Leave Fort Penn?"

"Heavens, no," said Betty.

"I'm talking about it from Anna's point of view. Do you think they'll be cruel to her? I haven't even made up my mind what to tell her when she gets home tonight. She's at Mary Wall's, so she'll be getting some story just about this minute. What do you tell a girl in her teens if a crazy-woman shoots a pistol at her mother? And the crazy-woman's husband is standing right there."

"You say just that. A crazy-woman," said Betty.

"That won't be enough for Anna. Not for her mind. She knows so much, and so little."

"God, I'm sorry, Grace," said Brock.

"Oh, Brock, you couldn't help it. If it'd worked the way you wanted it to, think how brilliant we'd have said you were," said Grace. "Don't accuse yourself."

"Maybe the best thing would be to tell Anna the truth," said Edgar.

"I'm inclined to think so, too," said Betty.

"The whole truth?" said Grace.

"Well, what happened this afternoon," said Edgar. "Give her a straight story."

"But not quite the whole truth—as you know it," said Grace.

"Well, I don't know exactly what you mean by that, Grace," said Edgar.

"Just that there was gossip about Jack Hollister and me, and his wife heard it," said Grace. "Renée, you surely heard it, so this doesn't embarrass you."

"Yes, I did hear. I am not embarrassed, Grace," said Renée.

"I think that's what you ought to tell her," said Betty.

"So do I," said Edgar.

"Well, all right," said Grace. "That's what I'll tell her." She sipped her drink for the first time. "It's funny, I hear everything you say and I say, but yet I have this deaf feeling. The noise in my head."

"That *should* be reassuring," said Edgar, with gentle humor.

"Why so?" said Grace.

"It proves you weren't killed," said Edgar.

"By the way, Edgar," said Brock. "There won't be any legal, uh, mumbo-jumbo about this, will there?"

"Well—no, I guess not," said Edgar. "There could be, a lot.

Against Mrs. Hollister, of course. I believe she could be arrested on a felonious assault charge."

"Well, she won't be, of course," said Brock.

"No, but let's not disregard the possibility, *as* a possibility," said Edgar. "Let's keep it in mind for a day or two, anyway. Hollister probably knows criminal law better than I do. Some newspaper men do. And a felonious assault charge is something that you just don't treat lightly. Then there's carrying a concealed deadly weapon, another charge of attempt to kill. As I say, I'm not an authority on criminal law, but I'll bet there are five or six charges she could be brought up on. And of course we'd have forty witnesses and she'd have none."

"Hollister," said Betty.

"Oh, her lawyer wouldn't have him testify, even if Hollister wanted to, which I doubt," said Edgar. "If he wanted to prosecute there'd be forty people to testify that Grace pushed Hollister out of the way—"

"And that would sound nice in court," said Grace. "I'm not up on the law—in fact, I've never been in a courtroom—but in books and plays wouldn't the lawyer for the defense make all sorts of implications about *why* I pushed him out of the way?"

"Very true," said Edgar, nodding.

"I don't think we have to go to court for that, either," said Brock. "Forty people have already drawn a certain inference from that." He laughed humbly. "I don't like to be one of those forty people, but I can't help remembering that instinctively you pushed *Hollister* out of the way, not *me*, your *brother.*"

"She wasn't going to shoot you, I knew that," said Grace.

"Anybody that has as bad aim as she has could have shot anybody," said Brock. "Bad Amy, we'll call her."

All but Renée smiled at the little joke.

"Grace personified," said Betty. "That's what you were, too, Grace. Bad Amy, and Grace personified. That's exactly what it was. You did the right thing instinctively—nothing against you, Brock, but it was the right thing. And you showed great courage."

"Jack was the one that showed courage. He went up to her while she still had the gun in her hand," said Grace.

"I repeat what I said about her bad aim," said Brock. "The closer you were to that woman, the safer you were. I don't give him anything for courage."

"Well, I do," said Grace. "Full marks."

"So do I," said Edgar.

"Then you don't believe she was bluffing?" said Brock. "You told her she wouldn't shoot, you said she'd lost her nerve."

"Then I was the one that was bluffing," said Grace.

"You mean to say you didn't really think she'd lost her nerve, when you went up and spoke to her?" said Brock.

"I don't know. I think she had lost her nerve. The thought flashed through my head that she hadn't really tried to kill anybody," said Grace. "I was the only one that could see her, you know. I was facing you two, Brock and Jack, and I looked over Jack's shoulder and there she was with the pistol, raising it, and she fired and I pushed Jack to one side—"

"You pushed him first, then she fired," said Brock.

"I don't think so. I don't think I had time," said Grace.

"This is getting to be an example of how lawyers earn their living," said Edgar. "Conflicting stories or rather conflicting versions of the same story so they might as well be different stories. That's the way to attack the credibility of a witness."

"Please, Edgar, I would like to hear Grace," said Renée.

The others looked at her involuntarily, but they nodded in agreement.

"Sorry," said Edgar.

"Well, then after the first shot I thought I could see her expression change, or at least something in her expression that made me believe she wasn't going to kill anybody." As she spoke Grace was straightening up in her chair, lost to the others, lost in her recollections. "The noise was like a big, enormous hoop. It came from where Amy was standing and got bigger and bigger as it came toward us. And then it surrounded us, the three of us. But not a hoop really, or not a cowboy's lasso either. It was like a small circle, the mouth of the pistol, getting larger and larger. Invisible, but you knew it was there. It got bigger and bigger until we were all in it. Not only the three of us, but Amy too. And that was the world. From the mouth of the pistol, that little round hole, to this enormous round thing of sound. I remember now that I didn't know whether I was hit or not. I knew the others weren't, because they didn't fall, but I was so terrified that I didn't quite know what I was doing, and I remember now thinking I might be dead. The only thing that made any sense to me was that look in Amy's eyes. That was real, and ordinary, and something I could understand. It was weakness. She was weak and afraid. She hadn't wanted to make all that noise, that's what I thought. I know it's hard to believe that you can have so many thoughts in such a short time, but honestly I do recall all these thoughts." She sat back in her chair. "I recall them too well, that's the trouble. Reach me a cigarette, will you, please, Edgar?"

Edgar produced a cigarette, handed it to Grace, waited while she put it in her mouth, held a match to it, shook the match, tossed it in the fireplace, and sat down. They all watched the operation with an intense curiosity that was commoner in the day of Sir Walter Raleigh. They were glad to be relieved, if only for that brief minute, of the obligation to comment on Grace's recital.

"I have often wondered how one felt when one is in war," said Renée.

"Well, it isn't like that, I can tell you," said Brock.

"How did you feel, Brock?" said Betty.

"This afternoon? Christ, by the time I turned around it was all over," said Brock. "And not all over but the shooting, either. The shooting was all over."

"No, it wasn't, dear," said Renée. "You were facing this Amy when the second and third shots exploded. I saw you."

"Well, maybe I was. I guess I wasn't focusing right," said Brock. "I guess I turned around and saw the God-damn woman and didn't expect the shots to come from her."

"Renée, you were the only one to leave the crowd. That took courage. More than I had," said Betty.

Renée flicked her hand in a tiny gesture. "You stayed with your husband, I went to Brock. Naturally. Grace pushed Hollister. It was natural. Hollister? Hollister did not desert Grace. I do not imply that. Hollister is a fighter, and he went into battle. Do you see, Betty? Everyone acted naturally."

Edgar nodded. "That's extremely—an extremely excellent analysis, Renée. Gallic. We're supposed to have more common sense than any other people, but I think the French have."

"Thank you, Edgar," said Renée. She smiled. "I am also part Italian, but of course I was raised in France."

"I'm glad you don't seem to mind this conversation," said Grace. "But you're practically a member of the family."

"Just about," said Brock.

Renée smiled rather formally. "Brock and I have had so many things to tell one another, but this we both know."

"Nonsense, Girl," said Brock. "You'll have to tell me all about it some day. But not today, if you don't mind. Are we all staying for supper, Grace?"

"Of course," said Grace.

"Yes, and let's stay all night, too," said Brock. "God damn it, we're all here together, and that's the way I want it to be. Edgar and Betty, you're just about our best friends, and Renée's going to be a member of the family after the first of the year, so I can't think of anybody else we'd want, can you Grace?"

"No."

"Well, then, let's all have another drink and forget about it. We'll hear enough about it the rest of our lives, so let's have an evening without it."

"No, Brock," said Renée. "We have to help Grace. She asked us a question but we never answered it."

"What question?" said Brock.

"Shall she leave Fort Penn?" said Renée.

"I answered it, I said no," said Betty.

"Betty, that was a reply, but not an answer," said Renée.

"I'm sorry, but I consider it an answer," said Betty.

"Please, Betty, I do not criticize you. Far from it. I say it was a *loyal* reply, with affection and loyalty, but it is not the answer to Grace's question. Grace would like to know what is best for her to do not for herself alone, but for Anna and Alfred. If we are real friends of Grace we must think with our heads and not only feel with our hearts. Do you agree?"

"I agree with the latter part," said Betty.

"Then let us face the facts and try to think with our heads. Think of the bad things. First, will this Amy again attempt to shoot Grace?"

"Well, that's ridiculous. Of course not," said Betty.

"Most likely not," said Edgar. "Nevertheless a possibility."

"I must say I never gave that a thought, but it is a possibility," said Brock.

"I think not," said Grace. "I'm sure not."

"So am I, Grace," said Renée. "But it is a possibility. Perhaps minute, but a possibility. Secondly, will Grace be made unhappy by her enemies and friends? Will her enemies and friends, little by little, day by day, small thing by small thing, like the water falling on the stone to wear it away—"

"Little snubs, and gossip—I know what you mean, Renée," said Grace. "But I think I can stand it."

"Can you, Grace? Can anyone?" said Renée. She looked for a second at each person in the room, then went on. "May I speak quite frankly?"

They nodded.

"Then I shall. Grace was successful in ignoring gossip one other time, but that was an affair of the heart. This is an affair of the gun. There is something so terrible about an affair of the gun, the use of a firearm." She made the gesture of firing a pistol. "I wish I had more English."

"Say it in French," said Grace.

"Not for me," said Brock.

"Me either," said Edgar.

"I think you're doing well in English," said Betty.

"Very well," said Renée. "Grace, this time it is not gay gossip, sly, laughing. 'Oho! Grace is sleeping with that man.' I know how that gossip is. This is different. It is mean, angry. A gun is not funny to laugh at and wink. It is ugly. Iron. Steel. The bullet makes a little hole in front, a big hole in back where it comes out. Ugh. It creates fear. It frightens with the sound, the noise. It is a big, ugly, noisy fact. It is not love, it is ugly hate."

"But what's this got to do with Grace?" said Brock.

"Please, Brock, be quiet. Can't you see? They will say horrible things because they think that if they say horrible things they push Grace away from them and push the horrible gun away from them."

"What kind of things, Renée?" said Grace.

Renée studied Grace before replying: "That you must have deserved the shooting, that Amy was in desperation, that any woman would have done the same thing as Amy did."

"Well, there you're wrong," said Betty. "The people that would say that weren't Grace's friends to begin with."

"I didn't say it would be friends. I have been saying friends and enemies. But gossip is conducted by both, Betty. Gossip would die if it depended only on enemies."

"I know I wouldn't gossip about Grace," said Betty. "And you surely wouldn't, so close to being a member of the family."

"And hardly the one to gossip about anyone, since I have been so much gossipped about," said Renée.

Edgar cleared his throat. "Well, then you think Grace ought to leave Fort Penn for a while?"

"I didn't say that either, Edgar," said Renée. "On the contrary, I think—tomorrow is Friday, Grace always has lunch at the hotel Friday. I think she ought to go there as always, with Betty and me, and others. I think Grace ought to do her Christmas shopping, see friends. But after Christmas I think she will want to go away. I hope I am wrong, but I think not. In the month to come the little things will happen. Nasty little smiles, little looks, shopgirls.

I had it as Brock's mistress. They would whisper 'ooh-la-la' but loud enough for me to hear."

"And what about Anna?" said Grace.

"They will be cruel to her," said Renée.

"I don't think they were before," said Grace. "I know they weren't."

"No, but why?" said Renée. "Why? Because you have a good friend here, Betty. A *strong* good friend, who silenced their mothers. I thought of something else. That Amy, you know, she has a daughter at school. I have her in one of my classes. They will be cruel to her, too."

"Too bad her mother didn't think of that," said Brock.

"What else did her mother think of?" Renée turned on Brock in hot anger. "She was a crazy-woman because her home was in danger."

"Grace wasn't endangering her home," said Betty.

"I know that, I know that," said Renée. "But Amy didn't know that."

"Are you defending her?" said Brock.

"Yes! And so would Grace!" said Renée. "Ask Grace!"

They looked at Grace.

"She's right," said Grace. "Renée's right."

They were quiet a moment.

Brock shook his glass, whirling the whiskey and water. "Well, you seem to have been doing a lot of Gallic analysis. Maybe you can tell me what to do about Hollister. On the paper, that is."

"Of course I can," said Renée.

"Fire him?" said Brock.

"You are a crazy man, Brock. You are so simple it is insane," said Renée. "Fire Hollister? Never! By keeping him with the paper it is the best answer to the gossip. You pretend it does not exist. It is the same thing as Grace shopping in the stores and seeing her friends."

"I concur," said Edgar.

"I do too," said Betty.

"So do I," said Grace.

"Well, if you do, Grace, that settles it. It looks as though you'll be the one to bear the brunt of the whole thing," said Brock.

"What is this brunt?" said Renée.

"To bear the brunt," said Brock. "It's an expression, like uh, carrying the load. At least that's what I think it means."

"A brunt is a load? A brunt of coal, for instance?" said Renée.

Brock stood up. "God damn it, this is the way I'm learning to speak English. I say something I've been saying all my life, and she wants to know what it means and I have to look it up in the dictionary. Edgar, do you know what a brunt is? How many tons in a brunt? How many cubic yards in a brunt of sand?" He put down his glass and swung open the dictionary. While he was busy they all stole glances at Grace, and because she was smiling placidly they smiled too. Thus with disproportionate responses to little jokes and simple acts they tried to compel the return of normal social intercourse, and in that artificial atmosphere they sat down to supper. They had a great choice of foods; ten others also had been asked to stay after the shoot, with the result that those who actually remained—the Martindales, Brock, and Renée—were offered a feast, but compromised with a snack.

The men and women stayed together after the meal. As usually happened in that house, the den was the room to which they returned.

"If anybody'd like to go upstairs?" said Grace. The other women declined. "More coffee, anyone?" All declined the coffee.

Two guns were standing in corners of the room. Brock picked each up and broke it and held the barrel to the light. "Well, these guns won't have to be cleaned. Neither one was fired," he said.

"They should be cleaned, though," said Grace. "I'll do it."

"Why should they be cleaned?" said Brock.

"Because they were out in the air, and the air's damp."

"Well, I'll do it," said Brock. "We're all staying overnight, aren't we?"

"I have to go home," said Renée. "I have to mark papers."

"Nonsense, Girl."

"Not nonsense," said Renée. "I am still a schoolteacher and Betty is one of my bosses."

"I won't report you," said Betty.

"Thank you, but I think I must go home in a little while. I can drive myself in your little Ford."

"No sir," said Brock. "And not because I'm polite, either. Far from it. Because I don't want anything to happen to that car, and believe me it would if you were at the wheel. Don't forget I'm the one's been trying to teach you."

"I make no apologies for my driving, and when we are married you may buy me a little Peugeot and I shall prove I am a good driver."

"When we're married you'll have a chauffeur. A man of sixty or more. A German. And married to a hausfrau twice his size," said Brock.

Renée saw that her part and Brock's as entertainers had been played out, and she looked to Grace and Betty to start another conversation.

"Is it just me," said Grace, "or does anyone else have the same feeling, that we're waiting for some news, or something like that? That thing this afternoon, it's all over I know, but I have this strange feeling that we're waiting for something else."

"It's all over, all right," said Brock. "All over Fort Penn by this time."

"Brock!" snapped Renée.

"I suppose so," said Grace. "Maybe that's what I'm waiting for, since nobody else seems to have the same feeling."

"I have it, too," said Betty. "Only I think it's very easily explained. I think you're waiting for Anna to come home."

"That's very true. I am. That's what it is, I guess," said Grace. "Do you think I ought to call the Walls'?"

"I don't think so," said Edgar. "Knowing Mary, I'd make a guess that she and George cooked up some story to tell Anna, and if you called there you might bollix it up."

"Probably," said Grace. "Nevertheless, I think I'll call them." She gave the Walls' number and asked to speak to Mrs. Wall.

"Mary? Grace . . . Oh, fine. Just sitting here. Edgar and Betty, and Renée and Brock . . . You were? Why? . . . No, I never thought of that. At least not that way. We did discuss it as a possibility, but I don't think she will . . . No. No, Mary. Thank you very much, but I'll send the car for her . . . No, don't you. No, please . . . Well, all right. Thank you ever so much, Mary." She hung up the receiver. "Mary hadn't cooked up any story, and hasn't told Anna anything. But she was afraid Amy might come back and so she planned to keep Anna there overnight, but I think Anna ought to be here, so George and Mary are bringing her home."

"You see, Edgar," said Renée. "It was a possibility that occurred to a non-Gallic mind such as Mary Wall's."

"Yes, but only a possibility, Renée," said Grace. "A possibility like the possibility that I might take one of those guns and pay a call on Amy. A possibility, but extremely unlikely."

"To be sure," said Renée. "Well, Brock, I am ready to go home."

"All right," said Brock.

They all rose and Grace shook hands with Renée. "I'm very glad you're having lunch with me tomorrow, Renée."

"Oh, yes, and thank you for letting me invite myself, but I think it is a good idea. Since I am marrying Brock so soon, don't you agree?"

"Of course I do," said Grace.

"And Grace, I had an appointment with Natalie to have lunch at her house. Shall I break it, or will you invite Natalie too?"

"Why, I'd be glad to have her," said Grace.

"Natalie is my closest friend in Fort Penn," said Renée.

"I know. Of course. Will you ask her, please? I'd rather not telephone anyone tonight," said Grace.

"Naturally. Good night, Grace. Try to have a good rest." Renée touched her cheek to Grace's.

"Thank you. Good night, Renée. Good night, Brock."

"Got a kiss for your brother, that you wouldn't even push out of the way?" said Brock.

She kissed him and patted his cheek, and they left.

Edgar and Betty and Grace did not speak until they heard Brock's car departing.

"The new Mrs. Caldwell," said Grace.

"Had you known about it?" said Betty.

"I knew it was coming, I didn't know it was so definite," said Grace.

"It wouldn't surprise me to learn that Brock hadn't known it was so definite, either," said Betty.

"Oh, yes. It was on-again, off-again," said Grace. "Well, she was all right. She behaved very well."

"Out on the field she did, not in here," said Betty.

"She didn't bother me, and she did make sense in a lot of things she said," said Grace.

"She will bother you, though," said Betty.

"I'm afraid so, too," said Edgar.

"Why? How?" said Grace.

"I don't know if Edgar's thinking of the same thing I am, but she isn't only the new Mrs. Caldwell. She's the whole Caldwell family. The grande dame."

"That's what I was thinking," said Edgar.

"She started to take over the reins right in this room, this afternoon. Such assurance!"

"Really?" said Grace. "She was more self-confident, but I put that down to—I don't know. As though she felt someone had to do the talking, and this was her first chance."

"It's her first chance, all right," said Edgar. "And she's snatching it up. I don't think I go quite so far as Betty, but I do think the minute she's married to Brock she's going to make her presence felt."

"In Fort Penn?" said Grace, skeptically.

"In Fort Penn," said Edgar. "She'll be the first Mrs. Caldwell since your mother died."

"There are dozens of them in Darktown," said Grace.

"Now, Grace," said Edgar. "Be consistent."

"Yes, you can't doubt Renée's new position one minute and then in the next breath pretend the Caldwells don't mean anything," said Betty.

"We'll see how much they mean in the next month, if Renée's right," said Grace.

"On that score I'm afraid she's right," said Betty.

"Yes, I guess that's why I have that feeling of something yet to happen. Probably thinking of lunch tomorrow."

"I wish you didn't have to do that, but you do," said Betty.

"Oh, by all means," said Edgar.

Their conversation was concluded by the arrival of the Walls and Anna. The Walls said they had to go right back, and did so, and the Martindales excused themselves gracefully, to leave Anna with Grace.

"I have to tell you an unpleasant story, dear," said Grace, when they were alone.

"Can't it wait, Mummy? Till tomorrow? I had such a nice time today."

"Unfortunately, this won't keep till morning. It may affect the rest of our lives," said Grace.

"Are we poor?" said the girl.

"No, and we can be very glad we're not," said Grace.

"All right, tell me."

"Well, you're fourteen, going on fifteen, and I guess you've heard or read about jealous wives. Wives that were jealous because they thought their husbands were falling in love with someone else."

"Oh, yes," said the girl.

"Well, this afternoon a jealous wife tried to shoot me."

"Mummy! Are you in earnest?"

Grace laughed. "I'm very much in earnest, and I must say I didn't expect you to take it that way."

"Well—she didn't, though. You're all right—aren't you?"

Grace laughed again. "I don't know why I'm laughing. It's a terribly serious matter, dear. This afternoon a woman came to this farm and pointed a pistol at me and fired three shots. I think it was three."

"Who?"

"It was Mrs. Hollister, the wife of Mr. Hollister on the *Sentinel.*"

"Is he supposed to be in love with you?" said the girl.

"She thought so."

"But you're not, are you?"

"No, of course not. He's never been here before."

"Oh, he was here too?" said Anna. "Did she shoot him?"

"No, nobody was shot. She was stopped. Now let me tell you about it, because I want you to know the truth so that when other girls ask you—well, just listen to me for a moment. Your uncle had heard that there was some talk, nasty gossip, about Mr. Hollister and me, so naturally, not believing it, knowing better, he invited Mr. and Mrs. Hollister to come out for the turkey shoot. So Mr. Hollister came out with Mr. and Mrs. Martindale and we expected Mrs. Hollister to come with Uncle Brock, but she refused to come with him, and then around four o'clock she came out alone, in her car. And I was standing near the spring-house with Mr. Hollister and Uncle Brock, and suddenly I saw her near us, with a pistol in her hand. And she raised it and fired it."

"She meant to kill *you?*"

"I don't really think she did. I think she wanted to make a nuisance of herself, and *that* she certainly *did*. But she could have killed one of us. So Mr. Hollister took the pistol away from her and took her home, and then I think Mr. Martindale or Uncle Brock asked our other guests to—under the circumstances—to go home."

"How far away was she when she shot the pistol?"

"Oh, perhaps from here to the front door. A little less."

"Heavens," said the girl. She had been sitting on the sofa with Grace, but now she moved closer to her, and took her mother's hand. "Did they arrest her?"

Grace put her hand on the girl's head, and stroked her hair. "There isn't going to be anything like that. She was obviously hysterical from gossip she heard. Nothing's going to be done about it. Mr. Hollister will still be with the paper, and we're going to act as though nothing happened. After Christmas we may go away for a while, but for the time being—as though nothing had happened."

"Like when Daddy and Billy died."

"Yes," said Grace. "And you were very good then, too."

"Are you going to write a letter to Alfred?"

"Yes," said Grace. "Tonight."

"That's good, before anyone else—this will cause more gossip, won't it?"

"I'm afraid so, and yet it's the kind of thing that ought to stop it, when gossip goes so far that one person nearly kills another."

"Where will we go after Christmas?"

"Where would you like to go?"

"I wish I could go to boarding-school."

"Maybe you can. I would like to see you in boarding-school. I never went, remember, and I think a girl probably misses a lot by not going."

"Will you sell the farm?"

"No, why do you ask that?"

"Well—if we go away, we won't come back. Will we?"

"Why, I only thought of going away for a little while," said Grace.

The girl looked at her feet. "But maybe we won't come back, though."

"Why do you say that, sweet?"

"Because I think it, Mummy. But I won't care."

"Wouldn't you? If we stayed—if we tried it for a year?"

"Just let's stay here till Christmas is over and then go?"

"All right, dear. That's what we'll do," said Grace. "And I wasn't going to tell you this, but you own the farm, you and Alfred. At least it's in trust for you children till you're twenty-one. Daddy left it to you in his will."

"That was nice of him to do that," said the girl.

"Yes, he particularly wanted you and Alfred to have it if you wanted it," said Grace. "Now I think it's time for you to kiss me good night."

The girl kissed her and went out of the room, but in a minute or less than two she came back.

"What is it, dear?" said Grace.

"Mummy, don't stay here alone, just looking out the window."

"Was I looking out the window? I can't see anything, it's so dark."

"Mummy, why don't you come upstairs, too?"

"In a little while, dear. Give me another kiss, and then off to bed."

The girl put her arms around Grace's neck. She drew Grace's head to her young body, and then kissed her and went upstairs.

The house was quiet, the distantly soft footsteps and the tub and toilet sounds had died down, before Grace seated herself at Sidney's desk and laid a sheet of the large farm stationery on the blotter and took up the silver-bound Conklin pen that someone had given Sidney. She studied the pen and its ornate mounting, and two facts occurred to her: she had no idea who had given Sidney the pen; that was one fact; and the other fact was that in all the years the pen had been on that desk, in constant use, she herself never had filled it. It never had been empty, but she never had filled it. Suddenly she began to write, and once she had begun she wrote steadily.

Dearest Alfred:

I thought this was going to be the most difficult letter I have ever composed but now I know it is going to be easy and I only hope that it will be as easy to read and digest. First, let me prepare you by saying that it will contain some unpleasant news but having had to impart the news to Anna, and being so proud of her acceptance of it, I am even more confident that you, being older and more mature, will make me just as proud of you. I have no doubt that this is true, because otherwise I should not suddenly feel that it will only be necessary for me to state all of the facts and you will understand.

About a year ago I became friendly with Mr. Hollister, who writes the humorous column on the Sentinel, but you must believe me when I say that our casual friendship did not and never could have amounted to more than that, as he is married, with, I believe, two children, and several years younger than I. However, unbeknownst to me there was some nasty gossip which reached the ears of Mrs. Hollister, his wife. I wish to emphasize that there was nothing between Mr. Hollister and myself, which you have only to recall the past summer to realize that it was to say the least extremely unlikely that I could have seen him when I spent the summer on the farm. Nevertheless the nasty rumors must have become so exaggerated by the time they reached Mrs. Hollister that the poor woman was driven half out of her mind. The gossip also reached your Uncle Brock, who, with the best intentions in the world, decided that to end the idle chatter he would invite Mr. and Mrs. Hollister to come out to the farm for the turkey shoot, which I wrote you we were having today or yesterday, as it is now past midnight. Mr. Hollister came out with the Martindales in their car but Mrs. Hollister was unwilling to accompany Uncle Brock. But much to our amazement, she did come out later, but when she arrived she was alone and was carrying a pistol. She approached Mr. Hollister, Uncle Brock and me, and drawing the pistol, fired several shots, none of which took effect, I hasten to reassure you. Mr. Hollister then ran to her and disarmed her, leading her away. Naturally the spirit of the occasion was shattered by her action and our guests, more than forty in number, went home. Anna's first question was whether there would be an arrest made, but I need not tell you that we do not contemplate any such drastic action. However I have given the matter long and serious thought and discussed it with your sister and I have decided that it will be best for all concerned if we close this house and leave Fort Penn for at least a year. I shall be frank with you and tell you further that it is in my mind to consider making our home elsewhere. At any rate we are going to try it for a year and if you and Anna find that you can be *happy in another city (or in the country, but not here) I think it will be better.*

Before going into the reasons for this decision I will answer your logical question: yes, we are going to be here for Christmas. I do not wish to interfere with any plans you may have made for the holidays. In fact, I would not think of leaving before the first of the year even if we could conveniently do so. It may or may not surprise you to hear me say that I care too much for "appearances" to leave now. Tomorrow, for instance, I am going to have lunch as usual every Friday at the hotel which is one way of showing that I have nothing but contempt for gossip but at the same time do care for "appearances." I am confident that there will be nothing to mar or spoil your holidays growing out of the regrettable incident yesterday, but not to take that risk would be unworthy of us and of your father, who always admired courage both physical and moral. As I told Anna (or as she told me) we shall behave in much the same manner we did three years ago when we lost our sweet brother and son and loving father and husband. I realized then so well how you fulfilled our highest expectations of you and Anna. I have always been proud of you both but never more so than during that period of sorrow and anguish, in which you conducted yourselves with dignity far beyond your years. Now three years have passed and the circumstances are different, but they require in some respects more dignity than then. I am so confident of you both that I am not going to make a single suggestion for any particular situation which may arise, but will rely on your own judgment.

If it may at first appear that we are leaving while under fire, so to speak, I can only say that again we must risk that criticism. But we are not behaving in cowardly fashion if we know that the decision to leave is our own, arrived at independently, without even a whisper by an outsider. What is more important to remember is that we are leaving Fort Penn, Fort Penn is not leaving us. It may at first be difficult to understand that, but the difference is important. We are who we are and what we are and by the very act of leaving we are making a protest against the things that have been happening to Fort Penn in recent years. We still have our good friends, whom we have always known, but our town has been changing so rapidly that in ten more years it won't be the same place we used to know and love and the time to leave is now. This farm belongs to you and Anna, under the terms of your father's will, and will remain so at least until Anna is 21. You will always have it to return to, especially in the summer vacations. However Anna is going to boarding-school after the holidays and you both have told me that you expect to spend more and more time away, so there is not much to hold us here. You have already made many friendships at school and more and more your friends will be the young people you meet at Yale or Princeton. I would also like to see you go into business in New York, although that is still too far ahead to think of now. Anna also wants to go to college, which will keep her away from here and create friendships elsewhere. As to myself, I plan to spend most of the winter in New York until I find a house and next summer we can all go abroad together. After all it is time I also was seeing something of the world besides Pennsylvania and I hope we can do a lot of traveling, making New York our headquarters.

For the present I am not going to say anything about this except to our relations and closest friends and I must ask you not to reveal our plans until after the holidays. I am taking you into my full confidence now because you are the man of the family. You have always been a splendid son and brother and Anna and I will continue to count on you. I could go on at greater length but you will have, I should think, many questions to ask me by letter before the holidays. I shall answer them as frankly as I know how, with the knowledge that they come from my loving son to

His loving Mother

She re-read the letter and put it in the envelope, sealed and stamped it. Then she placed it on the newel-post in the hall, but reconsidering, took a tweed coat from the closet, and with the letter and a small nickel-plated flashlight in her pockets, she walked slowly down the lane to the mailbox, stuck the letter in the box and raised the metal flag. She stood there for a little while, looking up at the sky. The night was cold and the moon was hidden and she turned up the collar of her coat and put her hands deep in her pockets and was starting up the lane again when a light was flashed in her face.

"Oh, it's you, Ma'am," said a man's voice.

"It's me, but who are you? I can't see you with that light in—"

"State Trooper Duffy, Ma'am." He flashed the light on his own face. He was wearing his uniform greatcoat with holster belt strapped around it. "I was sent out to keep an eye on things. Do you have a flashlight?"

"Right here in my pocket," said Grace. "But of course I know every foot of the way."

"Are you armed?"

"No."

"Then I'll walk back with you."

"All right, thank you. Can I make you some coffee? And a sandwich?" They started to walk.

He laughed. "You're not supposed to know I'm here."

"Where's your horse?"

"I'm using an automobile. It's behind your barn," he said. "I'm not supposed to let you know the place is being guarded."

"Well, that being the case I'll pretend I don't know you're here. I'll put some coffee in a thermos and some sandwiches on the kitchen table, and if they're gone in the morning—*I* won't know who took them. Not if I don't see someone take them."

"That's correct," said Duffy.

"And if I leave the kitchen door unlocked, and the light on, that could be just forgetfulness on my part."

"I heard of that happening."

"Well, here we are. Thank you for guarding us, Duffy, and good night."

"Good night, Ma'am."

He stood among the trees, watching the light go on in the kitchen, then the other downstairs lights going off, then some upstairs lights going on and then they went off. A little while later he went around to the kitchen and let himself in. The thermos

and a cup and saucer and cream pitcher and sugar bowl and napkin were on the table. He lifted a second napkin and saw a dozen
sandwiches, wrapped in waxed paper, lying on a large plate.
"Christ, a full meal," he said. "These bastards know how to live."

———

He took off his hat, unbuckled his holster belt, removed his
greatcoat, and commenced to feed himself. And the big house
was quiet, as in a deep sleep.

POSTLUDE

On Sunday, the twenty-first of December 1947, Grace had a few people in for cocktails. The reason for the party was to help cheer up Edgar Martindale, who was passing through New York on his way to the Fahy Clinic in Boston. Edgar and Betty were stopping overnight at Grace's hotel and they had been firm in their refusal to go to the theater, but out of Edgar's hearing Betty agreed that a small party might help to take his mind off the multiple hemorrhagic sarcoma that had been giving him trouble. It was made easier for Grace by the fact that the Brock Caldwells also were in New York for Renée's Christmas shopping, and Grace made it difficult for Edgar to stay away by announcing that Alfred and his wife and Anna and her husband usually dropped in of a Sunday afternoon.

The party serves a useful purpose for this narrative because it provides the reader with a fair picture of an afternoon in Grace's life nearly thirty years after she left Fort Penn. It is easy enough to end a story when the story has been told, and the story of Grace and Fort Penn has been told in the preceding pages. But the reader has at least an arguable right to ask what happened to Grace, and a condensed report of this 1947 party gives part of the answer.

Most, but not all, of the people Grace invited have been introduced earlier in these pages. They will be brought up to date or introduced as necessary, and after each introduction or reintroduction there will be a snatch of dialogue to illustrate, if possible, the relationship between each person and Grace.

ALFRED

Alfred, now in early middle age, in recent years had achieved the ambition that had been denied his father; during the war he had been a lieutenant commander. He had put in for sea duty on several occasions, but his wish was not granted and as an instructor in OSS he shuttled between "Q" Building in Washington and one of the secret camps in the Virginia hills. He qualified for an ETO ribbon by similar work (code instruction) in England, but he did not see active service. After the war he returned to his legal work with Murphy & Oglethorpe, lawyers, of 46 Wall Street. He lived at 999 Park Avenue and he had a summer home in Southampton.

GRACE: What can I get you?

ALFRED: Nothing, thanks.

GRACE: Is this something new?

ALFRED: New, and temporary.

GRACE: I'm sorry about the temporary.

ALFRED: Talk like that will make it even more temporary, Ma. I'm not a drunk.

GRACE: I was only thinking of your figure.

ALFRED: Oh, sure.

ALFRED'S WIFE

The former Monica Fitzpatrick was born into the Irish Catholic society of Southampton. She was a product of the Sacred Heart, New York; the Sacre Coeur in Paris; Spence, and Manhattanville College. She was almost uncompromisingly devout, humorless, handsome, taut, and a snob. Her older sister was married to an

Italian, a Papal count and notorious homosexual whose political activities under Mussolini nearly had kept Alfred out of OSS. But at least Capelli made Monica's own marriage seem to her to be, by comparison, unlimited bliss, and she willingly lied to herself to deny the evidence that Alfred went after other women. She had three daughters: Ann, Rose, and Brenda, at Miss Hewitt's Classes, and a boy, Sidney (Patrick John) Tate II, at the Portsmouth Priory. She tried to understand Alfred, and, failing that, she loved the good manners that kept him from flaunting his misbehavior to the degree where she would want a divorce that she never could consent to.

GRACE: Sidney looks well, doesn't he?

MONICA: Very.

GRACE: I was hoping your mother'd drop in. I guess she was at church when I called this morning, so I left word.

MONICA: I think she was going to Mrs. Iselin's after Mass, so she may not have gotten your message.

GRACE: I haven't bought Alfred's Christmas present yet. Can you give me any ideas?

MONICA: Not offhand. I'm giving him a billiard table for Water Mill. It's the only thing I've heard him mention that he wanted. Maybe if you gave him something for golf he'll start playing again.

GRACE: Oh, no. Not me. Not golf.

ANNA

Anna was present with Charles Francis Mills, her second husband, by whom she had a daughter, Ann Mills, a Foxcroft student. The girl also was present, but not present was her half-brother, Arthur Silberman Junior, of Deerfield Academy, who was Anna's son by her first marriage. Anna alone, and neither good manners nor legal action, could control Charlie Mills' ferocity when he talked about Jews. His monologues were filled with references to Jew York, Franklin D. Rosenfeld, and the close resemblance between the German and the American people— "our kind of people"—who should not have fought a war against each other, but together against the Russians and Great Britain. According to the terms of the divorce, the boy was to divide his time equally between Anna and his father, who was a heart specialist, but as he grew older the boy grew to look more like his father, and Charlie would leave the room when Arthur entered. The boy was not quite thirteen years old when he overheard Charlie shouting to Anna that Arthur's presence in the house with Ann created a dangerous situation, one that Charlie would not be responsible for. That day Arthur joined his father and never again spent a night under Charlie's roof. When Senator Truman asked pointed questions about Charlie's airplane plants the senator immediately jumped from obscurity to a high priority on Charlie's hate list, alongside Franklin D. Roosevelt and Dr. Arthur Silberman.

GRACE: When does Arthur get home?

ANNA: He got home yesterday.

GRACE: I hope he's coming to see me.

ANNA: He's getting older, Mother.

GRACE: Of course he is. What do you mean by that?

ANNA: Well, he can understand me, my divorcing his father and falling in love with another man, but when I talked to him on the phone he said he didn't know whether he was going to call on you or not, he said he didn't like the back-door treatment.

GRACE: I've never given him the back-door treatment. He's my grandson and he's always welcome here. I'm not overly fond of Jews either, but I'd rather have Arthur—well, let's not talk about it.

ANNA: Say it, I don't care. You'd rather have Arthur than Charlie.

GRACE: Well, why shouldn't I? Arthur's my own flesh and

blood, at least half. And Charlie, when he gets on the subject he talks like a fool.

BROCK

Brock was the only man at the party in a short black coat and striped trousers. The effort of dressing was a major one in Brock's daily routines, but it was one he made. After attiring himself in the manner of a career diplomat or champagne salesman he did little more than sit in his clothes, his snakewood cane with him always, his hand resting on the crook like a motorman's grip on the air brake. He had had a prostatectomy in 1940 and he preferred the company of a few friends because of the unpredictability of his bladder. Renée had had a mammectomy in 1936 but it had not immediately caused her to reduce her social and philanthropic activities. But after Natalie Bordener, her best friend, died of cerebral hemorrhage in 1938, Renée curtailed her luncheon schedules and was now a little old lady, trying to help her husband, who did all he could to help her.

GRACE: Are you getting tired?

BROCK: Why should I get tired? I've done nothing but sit on my bony ass and watch the passing show. Anna's daughter is what we used to call a looker.

GRACE: She's pretty, but I wish she didn't say 'Hi' whenever she meets somebody.

BROCK: Oh, well, when Anna was her age you were trying to make her stop saying hello to people.

GRACE: No, that was Mother, trying to teach *me* not to say hello.

BROCK: Well. Like to continue this conversation, but I've got to make my water.

GRACE: Can I help you?

BROCK: How? Thanks, Grace, but this is one thing a man has to do for himself. Go chat with Renée.

CONNIE

Connie Schoffstal arrived at the party after the Alfred Tates and the Charlie Millses had gone. Connie was accompanied by her full-time companion, a sculptress of dogs who called herself Nel Flagg, although she bore the full name of Eleanor d'Autremont Flagg. The two women did not dress alike as twins dress alike, but they had short haircuts (blue, in Nel's case) and lumpy, wrinkled cashmere coats and skirts, Hollywood-director scarves, thick rubber-soled oxfords. In Grace's sitting-room, in this company, their clothes looked too young for them, but in their own set the get-up was practically a uniform, with no exclusive claim by the young. Connie took a cigarette from her silver case, and Nel flicked her lighter aflame before the cigarette was in Connie's mouth. Nel did not bother to converse with anyone, but followed Connie (whom she called Con) around the room like an aide, or a sub-deacon. They drank weak highballs, five parts water to one part Scotch.

GRACE: Can you stay and have some supper? Betty and Edgar, Brock and Renée, and I'm expecting Ned Minor and Doctor Crocker.

CONNIE: Ho ho. That cooks it. Ned Minor.

GRACE: Why? Don't you like Ned? I thought he was a friend of yours.

CONNIE: Hardly that. Hardly. Rang him up a bit ago because Nel here fancied she'd like to do a Dandie Dinmont a friend of Ned's owns. Champion, wasn't it, Nel?

NEL: Yes it was, Con. Champion Bewitched Border Boy.

CONNIE: Never a jingle out of our Ned. We've dropped *that* one, you may be sure. Tiresome individual at best, that one.

GRACE: I'm sorry to hear that. It must have been an oversight. They're coming for supper.

CONNIE: Crocker the Croaker coming? Not a bad sort.

GRACE: I hope not. He's my doctor.

CONNIE: He's all right for you, Grace-girl. You're the health-iest. But why don't you give women doctors a break? We know a swell person, and by Jove next time you need a doc we're going to make you give 'er a try.

GRACE: No thanks. I'm satisfied with Doctor Crocker.

NED

Ned Minor, now a permanent resident of New York, did not ap-pear at the party. Grace's maid said Mr. Minor wished to speak to her, and Grace said she would take the call in her bedroom.

GRACE: You're late, you two.

NED: I know, I'm sorry. Here's somebody wants to speak to you.

GRACE: Hello.

PETER COOPER CROCKER: Hello, my dear.

GRACE: Happy birthday, my dear.

CROCKER: Thank you, Grace. I'm sorry I can't come.

GRACE: So am I, Peter. But we've had other birthdays.

CROCKER: Lovely ones, thanks to you.

GRACE: And you.

CROCKER: I'd hoped to drop in, just for a minute, but we're still at the hospital. Ned came along to watch me operate.

GRACE: Will you come to see me tomorrow?

CROCKER: About five-thirty?

GRACE: I'll have your present ready for you.

CROCKER: My girl.

GRACE: Get some rest, dear. Don't work so hard.

CROCKER: I won't. I have to go now. Do you want to talk to Ned again?

GRACE: Yes, please.

NED: Hello, Grace.

GRACE: Has he gone?

NED: Uh—yes, now he has.

GRACE: How is he? Is he tired?

NED: Very. He was operating for over four hours.

GRACE: Make him get some rest, Ned. How is *she?*

NED: About the same, I guess. I hardly ever see her. Her usual yelling and screaming at him, I guess.

GRACE: Oh, I wish she'd die.

NED: She never will, Grace.

GRACE: No. No. Well, try to make him rest, Ned.

NED: I'll try.

GRACE: Good night, Ned.

NED: Good night, Grace.

A Note on the Type

The principal text of this Modern Library edition
was set in a digitized version of Janson, a typeface that
dates from about 1690 and was cut by Nicholas Kis,
a Hungarian working in Amsterdam. The original matrices have
survived and are held by the Stempel foundry in Germany.
Hermann Zapf redesigned some of the weights and sizes for
Stempel, basing his revisions on the original design.